[CONTACTS]

94th edition published
by The Spotlight, 7 Leicester Place, London WC2H 7RJ

t: 020 7437 7631   f: 020 7437 5881
e-mail: info@spotlight.com   www.spotlight.com

Editor: Kate Poynton
Production: Kathy Norrish

Welcome to the new-look 2005 edition of Contacts: the essential handbook for anyone working in the UK entertainment industry.

This year's edition contains over 5000 listings for companies, services and individuals across all branches of Television, Stage, Film and Radio. All entries have been updated and many new ones added, to bring you the most accurate information available.

Contacts is published annually. If you would like to appear in the next edition please contact:

e: advertising@spotlight.com   t: 020 7440 5025 for advertising
e: info@spotlight.com   t: 020 7437 7631 for free, text-only entries

To purchase additional copies of Contacts please e-mail sales@spotlight.com or call 020 7440 5032.

Contents

Index To Advertisers
See page 345

A

Agents

Advertising	*4*
Agents & Personal Managers	*10*
Children's & Teenagers'	*86*
Extras & Walk-ons	*100*
Literary & Play	*107*
Presenters	*110*
Voice-Over	*114*

Animals	122
Arts Centres	125
Arts Councils	130

C

Casting Directors	131
Concert & Exhibition Halls	144
Concert Promoters & Agents	145
Consultants	146
Costumes, Wigs & Make-up	153
Critics	160

D

Dance Companies & Organisations	161
Dance Training & Professional Classes	163
Drama Schools (Conference of)	165
Drama Training, Schools & Coaches	167

E

European Trades' & Actor's Unions	196

[CONTACTS2005]

F

Festivals	198
Film & Television Distributors	200
Film Preview Theatres	200
Film & Video Facilities	201
Film, Radio, Television & Video Production Companies	205
Film & Television Schools	218
Film & Television Studios	220

G

Good Digs Guide	221

H

Health & Wellbeing	227

O

Opera Companies	233
Organisations	234

P

Photographers (Advertisers only)	242
Press Cutting Agencies	245
Properties & Trades	246
Publications	260
Publicity & Press Representatives	264

R

Radio	
BBC Radio (London)	266
BBC Local Radio Stations	268
Independent Local Radio	269
Recording Studios	272
Rehearsal Rooms & Casting Suites	274
Role Play Companies/Theatre Skills in Business	286
Routes to Film & Television Studios	287

S

Set Construction, Lighting, Sound & Scenery	288

T

Television	
BBC Television (London)	291
BBC Television & Sound (Regional)	293
Independent	296
Theatre Producers	301
Theatre	
Alternative & Community	312
Children's, Young People's & TIE	317
English Speaking in Europe	320
London	321
Outer London, Fringe & Venues	324
Provincial/Touring	331
Puppet Theatre Companies	338
Repertory (Regional)	339

V

Vehicles & Transport	343

A

Agents
*Advertising
Agents & Personal Managers*

Key to areas of specialization:
C Cabaret F Films G General M Musicals
Md Models PM Personal Managers
S Singing TV Television V Variety

For information regarding membership of the
Personal Managers' Association please contact:
Personal Managers' Association Limited
1 Summer Road, East Molesley, Surrey KT8 9LX
t: 020 8398 9796 e-mail: info@thepma.com
✱ Denotes PMA Membership

For information regarding membership of the
Co-operative Personal Management Association
please contact: Secretary
CPMA, c/o 1 Mellor Road, Leicester LE3 6HN
t: 07981 902525 e-mail: cpmauk@yahoo.co.uk
● Denotes CPMA Membership

*Children's & Teenagers'
Extras & Walk-ons*

For information regarding membership of National
Association of Supporting Artistes Agents (NASAA)
See website: www.nasaa.org.uk
e-mail: extrasagencies@hotmail.com
■ Denotes NASAA Membership

Literary & Play

For information regarding membership of the
Personal Managers' Association please contact:
Personal Managers' Association Limited
1 Summer Road, East Molesley, Surrey KT8 9LX
t: 020 8398 9796 e-mail: info@thepma.com
✱ Denotes PMA Membership

*Presenters
Voice-Over*

**Animals
Arts Centres
Arts Councils**

[CONTACTS 2005]

ABBOT MEAD VICKERS BBDO Ltd
151 Marylebone Road, London NW1 5QE
Fax: 020-7616 3580   Tel: 020-7616 3500

AKA
1st Floor
115 Shaftesbury Avenue, London WC2H 8AF
Website: www.akauk.com
e-mail: aka@akauk.com
Fax: 020-7836 8787   Tel: 020-7836 4747

BANKS HOGGINS O'SHEA FCB
55 Newman Street, London W1T 3EB
Fax: 020-7947 8001   Tel: 020-7947 8000

BARTLE BOGLE HEGARTY
60 Kingly Street, London W1B 5DS
Fax: 020-7437 3666   Tel: 020-7734 1677

BATES TAVNER RESOURCES INTERNATIONAL Ltd
International House
1 St Katharine's Way, London E1W 1UN
Fax: 020-7702 2271   Tel: 020-7481 2000

BDH/TBWA
St Paul's, 781 Wilmslow Road
Didsbury Village
Manchester M20 2RW
Website: www.bdhtbwa.co.uk
e-mail: info@bdhtbwa.co.uk
Fax: 0161-908 8601   Tel: 0161-908 8600

BURNETT Leo Ltd
Warwick Building, Kensington Village
Avonmore Road, London W14 8HQ
Fax: 020-7348 3855   Tel: 020-7751 1800

ALSO KNOWN AS

ADVERTISING

BOX OFFICE & SALES

CORPORATE SERVICES

DESIGN

MARKETING

MERCHANDISE

NEW MEDIA

PROMOTIONS

FOR THE

ENTERTAINMENT

INDUSTRY

115 Shaftesbury Avenue
Cambridge Circus London WC2H 8AF
Telephone +44 (0)20 7836 4747
Facsimile +44 (0)20 7836 8787
www.akauk.com

CDP TRAVIS SULLY
9 Lower John Street, London W1F 9DZ
Fax: 020-7437 5445   Tel: 020-7437 4224

COGENT ELLIOT
Heath Farm, Hampton Lane
Meriden, West Midlands CV7 7LL
Fax: 0121-627 5038   Tel: 0121-627 5040

DDB LONDON
12 Bishops Bridge Road
London W2 6AA
Fax: 020-7402 4871   Tel: 020-7258 3979

DEWYNTERS Plc
48 Leicester Square, London WC2H 7QD
Fax: 020-7321 0104   Tel: 020-7321 0488

DONER CARDWELL HAWKINS
26-34 Emerald Street, London WC1N 3QA
Fax: 020-7437 3961   Tel: 020-7734 0511

EURO RSCG LONDON
Cupola House, 15 Alfred Place, London WC1E 7EB
Fax: 020-7467 9210   Tel: 020-7240 4111

GOLLEY SLATER & PARTNERS (LONDON) Ltd
St George's House, 3 St George's Place, Church Street
Twickenham TW1 3NE
Fax: 020-8892 4451   Tel: 020-8744 2630

GREY WORLDWIDE
215-227 Great Portland Street
London W1W 5PN
Fax: 020-7637 7473   Tel: 020-7636 3399

HERESY
102 Sydney Street, London SW3 6NJ
Fax: 020-7349 6801   Tel: 020-7349 6800

HOLMAN ADVERTISING Ltd
Holman House, 30 Maple Street, London W1T 6HA
e-mail: holman.house@lineone.net
Fax: 020-7631 5283   Tel: 020-7637 3533

LEAGAS DELANEY LONDON Ltd
1 Alfred Place, London WC1E 7EB
Website: www.leagusdelaney.com
Fax: 020-7758 1760   Tel: 020-7758 1758

LEITH AGENCY The
37 The Shore, Edinburgh EH6 6QU
Fax: 0131-561 8601   Tel: 0131-561 8600

LEVY McCALLUM ADVERTISING AGENCY The
203 St Vincent Street, Glasgow G2 5NH
Website: www.levymccallum.co.uk
e-mail: ads@levymccallum.co.uk
Fax: 0141-221 5803   Tel: 0141-248 7977

LOWE & PARTNERS
Bowater House
68-114 Knightsbridge, London SW1X 7LT
Website: www.loweworldwide.com
Fax: 020-7584 9557   Tel: 020-7584 5033

McCANN-ERICKSON ADVERTISING Ltd
7-11 Herbrand Street
London WC1N 1EX
Fax: 020-7837 3773   Tel: 020-7837 3737

MEDIACOM
180 North Gower Street, London NW1 2NB
Fax: 020-7874 5999   Tel: 020-7874 5500

MEDIAJUNCTION
40A Old Compton Street, Soho, London W1D 4TU
Website: www.mediajunction.co.uk
e-mail: mailbox@mediajunction.co.uk
Fax: 020-7439 0794   Tel: 020-7434 9919

MUSTOES
2-4 Bucknall Street, London WC2H 8LA
Fax: 020-7379 8487   Tel: 020-7379 9999

OGILVY & MATHER Ltd
10 Cabot Square, Canary Wharf, London E14 4QB
Fax: 020-7345 9000   Tel: 020-7345 3000

PARTNERS BDDH
Cupola House
15 Alfred Place, London WC1E 7EB
Fax: 020-7467 9210   Tel: 020-7467 9200

PUBLICIS Ltd
82 Baker Street, London W1U 6AE
Fax: 020-7487 5351   Tel: 020-7935 4426

RAINEY KELLY CAMPBELL ROALFE Y & R
Greater London House
Hampstead Road, London NW1 7QP
Fax: 020-7611 6011   Tel: 020-7404 2700

RICHMOND TOWERS Ltd
26 Fitzroy Square, London W1T 6BT
Fax: 020-7388 7761   Tel: 020-7388 7421

MILIND SHIRKÉ
PHOTOGRAPHY
www.milindshirke.com
07930 462 589

RPM 3
William Blake House
8 Marshall Street, London W1V 2AJ
Fax: 020-7439 8884   Tel: 020-7434 4343

SAATCHI & SAATCHI
80 Charlotte Street, London W1A 1AQ
Fax: 020-7637 8489   Tel: 020-7636 5060

SMEE'S ADVERTISING Ltd
3-5 Duke Street, London W1U 3BA
Fax: 020-7935 8588   Tel: 020-7486 6644

SWK COMMUNICATIONS Ltd
27-29 Fitzroy Street, London W1T 6DS
e-mail: firstname.surname@swk.co.uk
Fax: 020-7637 6801   Tel: 020-7637 6800

TBWA LONDON
76-80 Whitfield Street
London W1T 4EZ
Fax: 020-7573 6667   Tel: 020-7573 6666

TBWA/GGT
82 Dean Street, London W1D 6HA
Fax: 020-7434 2925   Tel: 020-7439 4282

THOMPSON J Walter CO Ltd
1 Knightsbridge Green
London SW1X 7NW
Website: www.jwt.co.uk
e-mail: firstname.lastname@jwt.com
Fax: 020-7656 7010   Tel: 020-7656 7000

TMP WORLDWIDE
Chancery House
53-64 Chancery Lane
London WC2A 1QS   Tel: 020-7406 5000

TV MANAGEMENTS
Brink House, Avon Castle
Ringwood
Hants BH24 2BL   Tel: 01425 475544

WCRS
5 Golden Square, London W1F 9BS
Fax: 020-7806 5099   Tel: 020-7806 5000

YOUNG & RUBICAM Ltd
Greater London House
Hampstead Road
London NW1 7QP
Fax: 020-7611 6570   Tel: 020-7387 9366

SCOTT MICHAEL CARROLL
PHOTOGRAPHY
PORTRAIT & DRAMA
STUDIO & LOCATION
0161 273 7277 / 07802 918238

PR Photography
Penny Rowling
SURREY
01483-755837
Studio/Location
Relaxed atmosphere
Student Rates

Philippe Duterloo

www.pr-photography.com
penny@pr-photography.com

Marene Van-Holk

1984 PERSONAL MANAGEMENT Ltd•
PM Co-operative
Suite 508, Davina House
137 Goswell Road, London EC1V 7ET
e-mail: info@1984pm.com
Fax: 020-7250 3031   Tel: 020-7251 8046

21ST CENTURY ACTORS MANAGEMENT
Co-operative
E10 Panther House, 38 Mount Pleasant, London WC1X 0AN
e-mail: twentyfirstcenturyactors@yahoo.co.uk
Fax: 020-7833 1158   Tel: 020-7278 3438

2MA
(Sports & Stunts)
Spring Vale, Tutland Road
North Baddesley, Hants SO52 9FL
Website: www.2ma.co.uk
e-mail: mo@2ma.co.uk
Fax: 023-8074 1355   Tel: 023-8074 1354

41 MANAGEMENT*
74 Rose Street North Lane, Edinburgh EH2 3DX
e-mail: mhunwick@41man.co.uk
Fax: 0131-225 4535   Tel: 0131-225 3585

A & B PERSONAL MANAGEMENT Ltd*
PM Write
Suite 330, Linen Hall
162-168 Regent Street, London W1B 5TD
e-mail: billellis@aandb.co.uk
Fax: 020-7038 3699   Tel: 020-7434 4262

A & J MANAGEMENT
242A The Ridgeway
Botany Bay, Enfield EN2 8AP
Website: www.ajmanagement.co.uk
e-mail: ajmanagement@bigfoot.com
Fax: 020-8342 0842   Tel: 020-8342 0542

A LIST MODELS & ENTERTAINERS AGENCY
Unit 3, The Business Competitiveness Centre
Kimpton Road, Luton, Beds LU2 0SX
Fax: 01582 522432   Tel: 01582 522436

A-LIST LOOKALIKES & ENTERTAINMENTS Ltd
1 Hodson Fold, Bradford, West Yorkshire BD2 4EB
Website: www.alistlookalikes.co.uk
e-mail: info@alistlookalikes.co.uk
Mobile: 07866 583106   Tel: 01274 634634

A PLUS
(16-26 year olds)
54 Grove Park, London SE5 8LG
Website: www.kidsplus.co.uk
e-mail: janekidsplus@aol.com
Mobile: 07759 944215   Tel/Fax: 020-7737 3901

ABBOTT June ASSOCIATES
The Courtyard
10 York Way, King's Cross, London N1 9AA
Website: www.thecourtyard.org.uk
e-mail: jaa@thecourtyard.org.uk
Fax: 020-7833 0870   Tel: 020-7837 7826

Sharron Ashcroft Management Ltd

NORTHERN | SOUTHERN ACTORS   NORTHERN | SOUTHERN BASED

DEAN CLOUGH
HALIFAX
WEST YORKSHIRE
HX3 5AX

t | 01422 343949
f | 01422 343417
e | info@sharronashcroft.com
w | www.sharronashcroft.com

ABSOLUTE MODELS & ACTORS Ltd
(Character & Fashion Models)
Newleigh House
Hillbrow Road
Esher, Surrey KT10 9UD
Website: www.absolutemodels.co.uk
e-mail: enquiries@absolutemodels.co.uk
Fax: 01372 479798   Tel: 01372 479797

ACCESS ASSOCIATES
PO Box 39925
London EC1V 0WN
Website: www.access-associates.co.uk
e-mail: mail@access-associates.co.uk   Tel: 020-8505 1094

ACROBAT PRODUCTIONS
(Artists & Advisors)
The Circus Space
Coronet Street
London N1 6HD
Website: www.acrobatproductions.co.uk
e-mail: info@acrobatproductions.co.uk   Tel: 020-7613 5259

ACT ONE AGENCY
31 Dobbin Hill
Sheffield S11 7JA
e-mail: info@actonedrama.co.uk
Fax: 07971 112153   Tel: 0114-266 7209

ACT OUT AGENCY
22 Greek Street
Stockport
Cheshire SK3 8AB
e-mail: ab22actout@aol.com   Tel/Fax: 0161-429 7413

ACTING ASSOCIATES
PM
71 Hartham Road
London N7 9JJ
Website: www.actingassociates.co.uk
e-mail: fiona@actingassociates.co.uk
Tel/Fax: 020-7607 3562

ACTIVATE DRAMA SCHOOL
Priestman Cottage
Sea View Road, Sunderland SR2 7UP
e-mail: activate_agcy@hotmail.com
Fax: 0191-551 2051   Tel: 0191-565 2345

ACTORS AGENCY
1 Glen Street
Tollcross, Edinburgh EH3 9JD
Website: www.stivenchristie.co.uk
e-mail: info@stivenchristie.co.uk
Fax: 0131-228 4645   Tel: 0131-228 4040

ACTORS ALLIANCE•
Co-operative
Disney Place House
14 Marshalsea Road, London SE1 1HL
e-mail: actors@actorsalliance.fsnet.co.uk
Tel/Fax: 020-7407 6028

ACTORS' CREATIVE TEAM•
Co-operative
Albany House, 82-84 South End, Croydon CR0 1DQ
Website: www.actorscreativeteam.co.uk
e-mail: office@actorscreativeteam.co.uk
Fax: 020-8239 8818   Tel: 020-8239 8892

ACTORS DIRECT Ltd
Gainsborough House, 109 Portland Street
Manchester M1 6DN   Tel/Fax: 0161-237 1904

ACTORS FILE The•
PM Co-operative
Spitfire Studios, 63-71 Collier Street, London N1 9BE
Website: www.theactorsfile.co.uk
e-mail: mail@theactorsfile.co.uk
Fax: 020-7278 0364   Tel: 020-7278 0087

ACTORS' GROUP The (TAG)•
PM Co-operative
21-31 Oldham Street, Manchester M1 1JG
e-mail: agent@tagactors.co.uk
Fax: 0161-834 5588   Tel: 0161-834 4466

ACTORS IN SCANDINAVIA
Vuorimiehenkatu 20D, 00150 Helsinki, Finland
Website: www.actors.fi
e-mail: lauram@actors.fi
Fax: 00 358 9 68 404 422   Tel: 00 358 9 68 40440

ACTORS INTERNATIONAL Ltd
Conway Hall, 25 Red Lion Square, London WC1R 4RL
e-mail: mail@actorsinternational.co.uk
Fax: 020-7831 8319   Tel: 020-7242 9300

ACTORS IRELAND
Crescent Arts Centre
2-4 University Road
Belfast BT7 1NH
e-mail: geraldine@actorsireland.com   Tel: 028-9024 8861

ACTORUM Ltd
PM Co-operative
3rd Floor
21 Foley Street, London W1W 6DR
Website: www.actorum.com
e-mail: actorum2@ukonline.co.uk
Fax: 020-7636 6975   Tel: 020-7636 6978

ACTUAL MANAGEMENT Ltd
7 Great Russell Street
London WC1B 3NH
Website: www.actualmanagement.co.uk
e-mail: agents@actualmanagement.co.uk
Fax: 0870 8741199   Tel: 020-7631 4422

ADAMS Juliet MODELS & TALENT CASTINGS
19 Gwynne House
Challice Way, London SW2 3RB
Website: www.julietadams.co.uk
e-mail: info@julietadams.co.uk
Fax: 020-8671 9314   Tel: 020-8671 7673

ADF MANAGEMENT & MODEL CASTING AGENCY
South Manchester TV Studios
Battersea Road
Heaton Mersey, Stockport SK4 3EA
Website: www.adfmanagement.co.uk
e-mail: info@adfmanagement.co.uk
Fax: 0161-442 2677   Tel: 0870 7771360

Gaby Roslin 2004

Terry Stone 2004

Photography by
PETER SIMPKIN

020 8883 2727
e-mail: petersimpkin@aol.com
website: www.petersimpkin.co.uk

AFFINITY MANAGEMENT
Jessops Farm, Tonbridge Road, Bough Beech, Kent TN8 7AU
e-mail: cathy.bird1@btopenworld.com   Tel: 01892 870067

AGENCY AT BODYWORK COMPANY The
25-29 Glisson Road, Cambridge CB1 2HA
Website: www.bodyworkdanceuk.com
e-mail: agency@bodyworkdanceuk.com
Fax: 01223 568231   Tel: 01223 309990

AGENCY The Ltd
(Teri Hayden)
47 Adelaide Road, Dublin 2, Eire
Website: www.the-agency.ie
e-mail: info@tagency.ie
Fax: 00 353 1 6760052   Tel: 00 353 1 6618535

AHA
(See HOWARD Amanda ASSOCIATES Ltd)

AIM (ASSOCIATED INTERNATIONAL MANAGEMENT)*
Nederlander House
7 Great Russell Street, London WC1B 3NH
Website: www.aimagents.com
e-mail: info@aimagents.com
Fax: 020-7637 8666   Tel: 020-7637 1700

ALANDER AGENCY
TV F S V
135 Merrion Avenue
Stanmore, Middlesex HA7 4RZ   Tel: 020-8954 7685

ALEXANDER PERSONAL MANAGEMENT Ltd
PO Box 834, Hemel Hempstead, Herts HP3 9ZP
Website: www.apmassociates.net
e-mail: apm@apmassociates.net
Fax: 01442 241099   Tel: 01442 252907

ALEXANDER Suzanne MANAGEMENT
170 Town Lane, Higher Bebington
Wirral CH63 8LG
e-mail: suzyalex@hotmail.com   Tel/Fax: 0151-608 9655

ALL STAR SPEAKERS
(After Dinner Speakers)
23 Tynemouth Street, Fulham, London SW6 2QS
e-mail: laura@allstarspeakers.co.uk
Fax: 020-7371 7466   Tel: 020-7371 7512

ALLGOOD ASSOCIATES
24 South Road
Bisley, Surrey GU24 9ES   Tel: 01483 487831

ALLSORTS
114 Avenue Road, Beckenham, Kent BR3 4SA
Website: www.childsplaymodels.co.uk
e-mail: info@childsplaymodels.co.uk
Fax: 020-8778 2672   Tel: 020-8659 9860

ALLSORTS DRAMA FOR CHILDREN
(In Association with Sasha Leslie Management)
34 Pember Road, London NW10 5LS
e-mail: sasha@allsortsdrama.com
Fax: 020-8969 3196   Tel: 020-8969 3249

ALPHA PERSONAL MANAGEMENT Ltd•
PM Co-operative
Studio B4, 3 Bradbury Street, London N16 8JN
Website: www.alphaactors.com
e-mail: alpha@alphaactors.com
Fax: 020-7241 2410   Tel: 020-7241 0077

ALRAUN Anita REPRESENTATION*
Write, no e-mails
5th Floor, 28 Charing Cross Road, London WC2H 0DB
e-mail: anita@cjagency.demon.co.uk
Fax: 020-7379 6865   Tel: 020-7379 6840

ALTARAS Jonathan ASSOCIATES Ltd*
11 Garrick Street, Covent Garden, London WC2E 9AR
e-mail: helen@jaa.ndirect.co.uk
Fax: 020-7836 6066   Tel: 020-7836 8722

ALVAREZ MANAGEMENT
86 Muswell Road, London N10 2BE
e-mail: sga@alvarezmanagement.fsnet.co.uk
Fax: 020-8444 2646   Tel: 020-8883 2206

ALW ASSOCIATES
1 Grafton Chambers, Grafton Place, London NW1 1LN
e-mail: alweurope@onetel.com
Fax: 020-7813 1398   Tel: 020-7388 7018

AMBER PERSONAL MANAGEMENT Ltd
PM
189 Wardour Street, London W1F 8ZD
Website: www.amberltd.co.uk
e-mail: info@amberltd.co.uk
Fax: 020-7734 9883   Tel: 020-7734 7887

28 St Margaret's Chambers
5 Newton Street, Manchester M1 1HL
Fax: 0161-228 0235   Tel: 0161-228 0236

Anne-Marie Duff

Paul Bettany

Superb casting photographs

ROBERT WORKMAN

Tel: 020 7385 5442   www.robertworkman.demon.co.uk

Yvonne Kaziro

Steve McFadden

Tiffany Chapman

Claire Grogan
P h o t o g r a p h y

020 7272 1845
mobile 07932 635381
www.clairegrogan.co.uk
student rates

AMERICAN AGENCY The
14 Bonny Street, London NW1 9PG
e-mail: americanagency@btconnect.com
Fax: 020-7482 4666   Tel: 020-7485 8883

ANA (Actors Network Agency)•
PM Co-operative
55 Lambeth Walk, London SE11 6DX
Website: www.ana-actors.co.uk
e-mail: info@ana-actors.co.uk
Fax: 020-7735 8177   Tel: 020-7735 0999

ANDREW'S MANAGEMENT
203 Links Road, London SW17 9EP
e-mail: atj@andrewsman.fsnet.co.uk
Fax: 020-8677 8973   Tel: 020-8769 7416

ANDREWS Amanda AGENCY
30 Caverswall Road, Blythe Bridge
Stoke-on-Trent, Staffordshire ST11 9BG
e-mail: amanda.andrews.agency@tesco.net
    Tel/Fax: 01782 393889

ANDREWS HAMILTON Ltd*
First Floor, 69 Charlotte Street, London W1T 4PJ
e-mail: info@andrewshamilton.com
Fax: 020-7462 0070   Tel: 020-7436 5080

ANGEL FACES MANAGEMENT
Studio 223, 186 St Albans Road, Watford WD25 4AS
Website: www.angelfacesmanagement.co.uk
e-mail: enquiries@angelfacesmanagement.co.uk
    Tel/Fax: 020-8428 9625

ANGEL Susan & FRANCIS Kevin Ltd*
Write, no e-mails
1st Floor, 12 D'Arblay Street, London W1F 8DU
e-mail: angelpair@freeuk.com
Fax: 020-7437 1712   Tel: 020-7439 3086

ANOTHER FACE
10-11 D'Arblay Street, London W1F 8DS
Website: www.anothergroup.com
e-mail: mia@anotherface.com
Fax: 020-7494 7080   Tel: 020-7494 7001

A.P.M. ASSOCIATES (Linda French)
(See ALEXANDER PERSONAL MANAGEMENT Ltd)

ARAENA/COLLECTIVE
10 Bramshaw Gardens, South Oxhey, Herts WD1 6XP
e-mail: patricia@araena.watford.net
    Tel/Fax: 020-8428 0037

ARC ENTERTAINMENTS
10 Church Lane
Redmarshall
Stockton on Tees, Cleveland TS21 1EP
Website: www.arcentertainments.co.uk
e-mail: arcents@aol.com   Tel: 0870 7418789

ARCADIA ASSOCIATES
18B Vicarage Gate, London W8 4AA
e-mail: info.arcadia@btopenworld.com
    Tel/Fax: 020-7937 0264

ARENA ENTERTAINMENT CONSULTANTS
(Corporate Entertainment)
Regent's Court, 39 Harrogate Road, Leeds LS7 3PD
Website: www.arenaentertainments.co.uk
e-mail: stars@arenaentertainments.co.uk
Fax: 0113-239 2016   Tel: 0113-239 2222

harrispearson

Melanie Harris and Paul Pearson

Personal Representation	64 - 66 Millman St
Film	Bloomsbury
Television	London WC1N 3EF
Theatre	T: +44 (0)207 430 9890
Commercials	F: +44 (0)207 430 9229
	E: agent@harrispearson.co.uk
Members of the P M A	www.harrispearson.co.uk

Jessica Harris

Charles Shirvell

DANIEL HARWOOD-STAMPER
photographer

Tel: 020-7930 1372

dan_stamper@hotmail.com

ARENA PERSONAL MANAGEMENT Ltd
Co-operative
Room 11, East Block, Panther House, 38 Mount Pleasant
London WC1X 0AP
Website: www.arenapmltd.co.uk
e-mail: arenapmltd@aol.com   Tel/Fax: 020-7278 1661

A R G (ARTISTS RIGHTS GROUP Ltd)
4 Great Portland Street, London W1W 8PA
e-mail: argall@argtalent.com
Fax: 020-7436 6700   Tel: 020-7436 6400

ARGYLE ASSOCIATES
PM (Richard Argyle) (SAE for Unsolicited Mail)
St John's Buildings, 43 Clerkenwell Road, London EC1M 5RS
e-mail: argyle.associates@virgin.net
Fax: 020-7608 1642   Tel: 020-7608 2095

ARTISTS INDEPENDENT MANAGEMENT
32 Tavistock Street, London WC2E 7PB
Fax: 020-7240 9029   Tel: 020-7257 8725

ARTS MANAGEMENT
First Floor
10 Goddard Place, Maidenbower, West Sussex RH10 7HR
Website: www.artsmanagement.co.uk
e-mail: artsmanagementltd@hotmail.com
Tel: 01293 885746

ARTSWORLD INTERNATIONAL MANAGEMENT Ltd
1 Farrow Road, Whaplode Drove, Nr Spalding PE12 0TS
e-mail: bob@artsworld.freeserve.co.uk
Fax: 01406 331147   Tel: 01406 330099

ASH PERSONAL MANAGEMENT
3 Spencer Road, Mitcham Common, Surrey CR4 1SG
e-mail: ash_personal_mgmt@yahoo.co.uk
Tel/Fax: 020-8646 0050

ASHCROFT ACADEMY OF DRAMATIC ART & AGENCY
Malcolm Primary School
Malcolm Road, Penge, London SE20 8RH
e-mail: geri.ashcroftacademy@tiscali.co.uk
Mobile: 07799 791586   Tel/Fax: 020-8693 8088

ASHCROFT Sharron MANAGEMENT Ltd
Dean Clough, Halifax
West Yorkshire HX3 5AX
Website: www.sharronashcroft.com
e-mail: info@sharronashcroft.com
Fax: 01422 343417   Tel: 01422 343949

ASIAN TALENT AGENCY Ltd The
(Specialist in Bollywood UK & India Casting, Artist
Management, Events & PR, Research)
7 The Monastery
Carmelite Drive, Reading, Berkshire RG30 2SA
Website: www.ata-uk.com
e-mail: enquiries@ata-uk.com   Tel: 0118-958 8315

ASQUITH & HORNER
PM Write with SAE
The Studio, 14 College Road, Bromley, Kent BR1 3NS
Fax: 020-8313 0443   Tel: 020-8466 5580

ASSOCIATED ARTS
(Directors, Designers, Lighting Designers)
8 Shrewsbury Lane, London SE18 3JF
Website: www.associated-arts.co.uk
e-mail: karen@associated-arts.co.uk
Fax: 020-8856 8189   Tel: 020-8856 4958

tanya moodie

katie vandyck
digital photographer
07941•940259
www.iphotou.co.uk

HUGO SPEER

CATHERINE SHAKESPEARE LANE
PHOTOGRAPHER
020 7226 7694

ASSOCIATED SPEAKERS
(Lecturers & Celebrity Speakers)
24A Park Road, Hayes
Middlesex UB4 8JN   Tel: 020-8848 9048

ASTRAL ACTORS MANAGEMENT
7 Greenway Close, London NW9 5AZ
Website: www.astralactors.com
e-mail: info@astralactors.com
Fax: 020-8200 3694   Tel: 020-8728 2782

AVALON MANAGEMENT GROUP Ltd
4A Exmoor Street
London W10 6BD
Fax: 020-7598 7300   Tel: 020-7598 8000

AVENUE ARTISTES Ltd
C G TV
8 Winn Road
Southampton SO17 1EN
Website: www.avenueartistes.com
e-mail: info@avenueartistes.com
Fax: 023-8090 5703   Tel: 023-8055 1000

AWA - ANDREA WILDER AGENCY
23 Cambrian Drive
Colwyn Bay, Conwy LL28 4SL
Website: www.awagency.co.uk
e-mail: casting@awagency.co.uk
Fax: 07092 249314   Tel: 01492 547542

www.jgpm.co.uk   **jgpm**

Jo Gurnett Personal Management Ltd
No. 2 New King's Road
London SW6 4SA
Tel   020 7736 7828
Fax   020 7736 5455
Email   info@jgpm.co.uk

Presenters Television Radio Performers Specialists Corporate Voice-Overs

RICHARD WILSON FOR 'SHELTER'

JULIETTE CHEVELEY

DAVID CONVILLE

LUKE KELLY PHOTOGRAPHY

310a Upper Richmond Road West
(Entrance 310a Elm Road)
East Sheen
London SW14 7JM

TEL: 020-8878 2823

AWARD COMMUNICATIONS Ltd
PO Box 650, St Albans AL2 3WZ
Website: www.award.co.uk
e-mail: agency@award.co.uk
Fax: 01923 662473   Tel: 01923 662472

AXM*
Actors' Exchange Management
PM Co-operative
206 Great Guildford Business Square
30 Great Guildford Street, London SE1 0HS
Website: www.axmgt.com
e-mail: info@axmgt.com
Fax: 020-7261 0408   Tel: 020-7261 0400

THE AGENCY AT BODYWORK COMPANY

DANCERS
SINGERS
ACTORS
CHOREOGRAPHERS
CABARET
CORPORATE ENTERTAINMENT

www.bodyworkdanceuk.com
Tel: 01223 309990
Fax: 01223 358923
Email: agency@bodyworkdanceuk.com

25/29 Glisson Road, Cambridge CB1 2HA

AZA ARTISTES
(Existing Clients only)
652 Finchley Road
London NW11 7NT   Tel: 020-8458 7288

BaK MANAGEMENT
Linton House, 39-51 Highgate Road, London NW5 1RS
e-mail: bkmanagement@aol.com   Tel: 020-7428 7707

BALLROOM, LONDON THEATRE OF
(Ballroom/Social Dancers for Film/TV/Theatre)
24 Ovett Close, Upper Norwood, London SE19 3RX
e-mail: paulharrisdance@hotmail.com
Mobile: 07958 784462   Tel: 020-8771 4274

B A M ASSOCIATES
41 Bloomfield Road, Bristol BS4 3QA
Website: www.ebam.tv
e-mail: casting@ebam.tv   Tel/Fax: 0117-971 0636

BARKER Gavin ASSOCIATES Ltd*
(Gavin Barker, Michelle Burke)
2D Wimpole Street, London W1G 0EB
Website: www.gavinbarkerassociates.co.uk
e-mail: rachel@gavinbarkerassociates.co.uk
Fax: 020-7499 3777   Tel: 020-7499 4777

B.A.S.I.C./JD AGENCY
C V S
3 Rushden House, Tatlow Road
Glenfield, Leicester LE3 8ND   Tel/Fax: 0116-287 9594

BECKER Paul Ltd*
223A Portobello Road, London W11 1LU
Fax: 020-7221 5030   Tel: 020-7221 3050

BELCANTO LONDON ACADEMY MANAGEMENT
(Children & Young Adults)
Performance House
20 Passey Place, Eltham, London SE9 5DQ
Fax: 020-8850 9944   Tel: 020-8850 9888

BELFRAGE Julian ASSOCIATES
46 Albemarle Street, London W1S 4DF
Fax: 020-7493 5460   Tel: 020-7491 4400

BELL Olivia Ltd
189 Wardour Street, London W1F 8ZD
e-mail: info@olivia-bell.co.uk
Fax: 020-7439 3485   Tel: 020-7439 3270

BENJAMIN Audrey AGENCY
278A Elgin Avenue, Maida Vale, London W9 1JR
e-mail: aud@elginavenue.fsbusiness.co.uk
Fax: 020-7266 5480   Tel: 020-7289 7180

SHEILA BURNETT
PHOTOGRAPHY

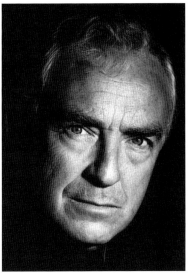

Paul Freeman

Imelda Staunton

Patsy Palmer

Ewan McGregor

020 7289 3058
www.sheilaburnett-photography.com

Student Rates

BETTS Jorg ASSOCIATES*
Gainsborough House, 81 Oxford Street, London W1D 2EU
e-mail: jorgbetts@aol.com
Fax: 020-7903 5301   Tel: 020-7903 5300

BIG MANAGEMENT (UK) Ltd
4th Floor, 5 Dean Street, London W1D 3RQ
Website: www.bigmanagementuk.com
e-mail: camilla@bigmanagementuk.com
Fax: 020-7287 9934   Tel: 020-7287 9949

BILLBOARD PERSONAL MANAGEMENT
(Full-time Agent with Co-operative Assistants)
Unit 5, 11 Mowll Street, London SW9 6BG
Website: www.billboardpm.com
e-mail: billboardpm@btconnect.com
Fax: 020-7793 0426   Tel: 020-7735 9956

BILLY MARSH DRAMA Ltd
(Actors & Actresses)
See MARSH Billy DRAMA Ltd

BIRD AGENCY
(Personal Performance Management)
Birkbeck Centre, Birkbeck Road, Sidcup, Kent DA14 4DE
Fax: 020-8308 1370   Tel: 020-8300 6004

BISHOP BURNETT AGENCY & MANAGEMENT
47 Dean Street, London W1D 5BE
e-mail: keithbishop@themcsagency.com
Fax: 020-7734 9996   Tel: 020-7734 9995

BIZ MANAGEMENT
(In Association with Kidz in The Biz Theatre Academy)
5 Brittendon Parade, Green Street Green, Kent BR6 6DD
e-mail: thebizmanagement@aol.com
Mobile: 07763 958096   Tel/Fax: 01689 882850

BLACKBURN SACHS ASSOCIATES
2-4 Noel Street, London W1F 8GB
Website: www.blackburnsachsassociates.com
e-mail: actors@blackburnsachsassociates.com
Fax: 020-7292 7576   Tel: 020-7292 7555

BLOND Rebecca ASSOCIATES
69A Kings Road, London SW3 4NX
e-mail: info@rebeccablondassociates.com
Fax: 020-7351 4600   Tel: 020-7351 4100

BLUE WAND PRODUCTIONS Ltd
PM TV F G
2nd Floor, 12 Weltje Road, London W6 9TG
e-mail: lino@bluewand.co.uk
Mobile: 07885 528743   Tel/Fax: 020-8741 2038

BMA MODELS
(Models)
The Stables, 5 Norcott Hall Barns, Norcott Hill
Berkhamsted, Herts HP4 1RB
Website: www.bmamodels.com
e-mail: info@bmamodels.com
Fax: 01442 879879   Tel: 01442 878878

BODENS AGENCY
PM
99 East Barnet Road
New Barnet, Herts EN4 8RF
Website: www.bodensagency.com
e-mail: bodens2692@aol.com
Fax: 020-8449 5212   Tel: 020-8447 0909

BOOKERS UK
7 Green Avenue, Mill Hill
London NW7 4PX   Tel/Fax: 020-8201 1400

Hugh Bonneville

Sarah Ozeke

Tom Burke

SOPHIE BAKER
Photography

0 2 0 - 8 3 4 0   3 8 5 0   *Special rates for students*

BOSS MODEL MANAGEMENT
Half Moon Chambers
Chapel Walks, Manchester M2 1HN
Website: www.bossmodelmanagement.co.uk
e-mail: vicky@bossmodels.co.uk
Fax: 0161-832 5219   Tel: 0161-834 3403

BOYCE Sandra MANAGEMENT*
1 Kingsway House, Albion Road, London N16 0TA
e-mail: info@sandraboyce.com
Fax: 020-7241 2313   Tel: 020-7923 0606

BRAIDMAN Michelle ASSOCIATES*
3rd Floor Suite, 10-11 Lower John Street, London W1F 9EB
e-mail: info@braidman.com
Fax: 020-7439 3600   Tel: 020-7437 0817

BRAITHWAITE'S THEATRICAL AGENCY
8 Brookshill Avenue, Harrow Weald
Middlesex HA3 6RZ   Tel: 020-8954 5638

BREAK A LEG MANAGEMENT Ltd
Units 2/3 The Precinct, Packington Square, London N1 7UP
Website: www.breakalegman.com
e-mail: agency@breakalegman.com
Fax: 020-7359 3660   Tel: 020-7359 3594

BROADCASTING AGENCY
Unit 23, Canalot Studios
222 Kensal Road, London W10 5BN
e-mail: info@broadcastingcompany.tv
Fax: 020-7460 5223   Tel: 020-7460 5222

John Virgo

Lisa Maxwell

Simon Russell Beale

JONATHAN
DOCKAR-DRYSDALE

Tel: 020 8560 1077
Mobile: 07711 006191

E-mail: j.d-d@lineone.net

Student Discount
Studio/Outdoors

DIRECT LINE

LONDON
St. John's House
16 St. John's Vale
London SE8 4EN
Tel/fax 020 8694 1788

Personal Management
Personal Manager: Daphne Franks

e-mail: daphne.franks@dline.org.uk
website: www.dline.org.uk

LEEDS
Park House
62 Lidgett Lane
Leeds LS8 1PL
Tel/fax 0113 266 4036

HARVEY BERGER FCA
CHARTERED ACCOUNTANT

For over 25 years, I have been looking after the tax affairs of actors, writers, designers, theatre & tv technicians, etc.

If you need help with your Accounts, Self-Assessment Tax Returns, VAT, National Insurance or any other aspects of your tax affairs, please contact me on:- Telephone/fax: (020) 8449 9328 or E-mail: harvey.berger@tesco.net

First meeting free

BROOD MANAGEMENT
3 Queen's Garth, Taymount Rise, London SE23 3UF
Website: www.broodmanagement.com
e-mail: broodmanagement@aol.com
Mobile: 07932 022635   Tel: 020-8699 1071

BROOK Dolly AGENCY
PO Box 5436, Dunmow CM6 1WW
Fax: 01371 875996   Tel: 01371 875767

BROOK Valerie AGENCY
10 Sandringham Road, Cheadle Hulme, Cheshire SK8 5NH
e-mail: colinbrook@freenetname.co.uk
Fax: 0161-488 4206   Tel: 0161-486 1631

BROOKS Claude ENTERTAINMENTS
1 Burlington Avenue, Slough, Berks SL1 2JY
Fax: 01753 520424   Tel: 01753 520717

BROOKS Neil MANAGEMENT
153 Rathgar Road, Rathgar, Dublin 6, Eire
Website: www.neilbrooksmanagement.com
e-mail: nbm2@eircom.net   Tel/Fax: 00 353 1 496 6470

BROWN & SIMCOCKS*
(Barry Brown & Carrie Simcocks) PM Write
1 Bridgehouse Court, 109 Blackfriars Road, London SE1 8HW
e-mail: mail@brownandsimcocks.co.uk
Fax: 020-7928 1909   Tel: 020-7928 1229

BROWNING Malcolm
Room 103
Merchant House, 89 Southwark Street, London SE1 0HX
e-mail: info@malcolmbrowning.com
Fax: 0870 4581766   Tel: 020-7960 4669

BRUNSKILL MANAGEMENT Ltd*
PM M S TV Write
Suite 8A, 169 Queen's Gate, London SW7 5HE
e-mail: contact@brunskill.com
Fax: 020-7589 9460   Tel: 020-7581 3388

The Courtyard, Edenhall, Penrith, Cumbria CA11 8ST
Website: www.brunskill.com
e-mail: contact@brunskill.fsbusiness.co.uk
Fax: 01768 881850   Tel: 01768 881430

BSA Ltd
(See HARRISON Penny BSA Ltd)

BUCHANAN Bronia ASSOCIATES Ltd*
Nederlander House
7 Great Russell Sreet
London WC1B 3NH
Website: www.buchanan-associates.co.uk
e-mail: info@buchanan-associates.co.uk
Fax: 020-7631 2034   Tel: 020-7631 2004

BUMPS & BABIES
53 Westover Road, London SW18 2RF
Website: www.bumps-n-babies.co.uk
e-mail: judi@bumps-n-babies.co.uk
Fax: 020-8874 4484   Tel: 020-8870 1762

BURNETT GRANGER ASSOCIATES Ltd*
(Barry Burnett, Lindsay Granger)
3 Clifford Street, London W1S 2LF
e-mail: associates@burnettgranger.co.uk
Fax: 020-7287 3239   Tel: 020-7437 8008

DOUBLE ACT
CELEBRITY LOOK ALIKES
London based look alike agency

PO Box 25574, London NW7 3GB

Tel: 020 8381 0151 Fax: 020 8201 1795

Email: info@double-act.co.uk   Website: www.double-act.co.uk

Contact: Lydia Wolfson.   Member of The Agents Association (GB).

BYRON'S MANAGEMENT
(Children & Adults)
North London Performing Arts Centre
76 St James Lane
Muswell Hill, London N10 3DF
Website: www.byronscasting.co.uk
e-mail: byronscasting@aol.com
Fax: 020-8444 4040   Tel: 020-8444 4445

C.A. ARTISTES MANAGEMENT
Md Featured Commercials
26-28 Hammersmith Grove, London W6 7BA
Website: www.caartistes.com
e-mail: casting@caartistes.com
Fax: 020-8834 1144   Tel: 020-8834 1615

CADS MANAGEMENT
(BIRMINGHAM)
209 Abbey Road, Bearwood, Birmingham B67 5NG
Website: www.cadsgroup.com
e-mail: birmingham@cadsgroup.com
Fax: 0121-434 4909   Tel: 0121-420 1996
(LONDON)
114 The Dormers, Highworth, Wiltshire SN6 7PF
e-mail: london@cadsgroup.com

CAM*
PM Write
19 Denmark Street, London WC2H 8NA
Website: www.cam.co.uk   e-mail: info@cam.co.uk
Fax: 020-7240 7384   Tel: 020-7497 0448

Jonathan Race   Sarah Briggs   Steven James Tyler

Steve Lawton

PHOTOGRAPHY

LONDON

07973 307487

www.stevelawton.com

Student rates

Natalie Anderson   Damien Thomas   Natalie Cox

Siri Svegler

Owen Evans
Photography
07940 700294

London

Special rates for students

Ben de Sausmarez

CAMBELL JEFFREY MANAGEMENT
(Set, Costume, Lighting Designers)
11A Greystone Court, South Street, Eastbourne BN21 4LP
e-mail: cambell@theatricaldesigners.co.uk
Fax: 01323 411373   Tel: 01323 411444

CAMPBELL Alison MODEL & PROMOTION AGENCY
381 Beersbridge Road, Belfast BT5 5DT
Website: www.alisoncampbellmodels.com
e-mail: info@alisoncampbellmodels.com
Fax: 028-9080 9808   Tel: 028-9080 9809

CAMPBELL ASSOCIATES
Campbell Park, Fernhurst Road
Milland, Nr Liphook, Hants GU30 7LU
Fax: 01428 741648

2 Chelsea Cloisters, Sloane Avenue
Chelsea, London SW3 3DW
e-mail: info@campbellassociates.org.uk
Fax: 020-7584 8799   Tel: 020-7584 5586

CAPITAL ARTS THEATRICAL AGENCY
Wyllyotts Centre, Darkes Lane, Potters Bar, Herts EN6 2HN
e-mail: capitalartstheatre@o2.co.uk
Mobile: 07885 232414   Tel/Fax: 020-8449 2342

CAPITAL VOICES
(Anne Skates) Session Singers, Studio, Stage, TV & Film
Brook House, 8 Rythe Road, Claygate, Surrey KT10 9DF
Website: www.capitalvoices.com
e-mail: capvox@aol.com
Fax: 01372 466229   Tel: 01372 466228

CARDIFF CASTING•
Co-operative Actors Management
Chapter Arts Centre
Market Road, Cardiff CF5 1QE
Website: www.cardiffcasting.co.uk
e-mail: admin@cardiffcasting.co.uk
Fax: 029-2023 3380   Tel: 029-2023 3321

CAREY Roger ASSOCIATES*
PM
Garden Level, 32 Charlwood Street
London SW1V 2DY
e-mail: rogercarey@freeuk.com
Fax: 020-7630 0029   Tel: 020-7630 6301

CARNEY Jessica ASSOCIATES*
PM Write
4th Floor, 23 Golden Square, London W1F 9JP
e-mail: info@jcarneyassociates.co.uk
Fax: 020-7434 4173   Tel: 020-7434 4143

CAROUSEL ENTERTAINMENT & EVENT MANAGEMENT
(Entertainment for Corporate & Private Events)
18 Westbury Lodge Close, Pinner, Middlesex HA5 3FG
Website: www.carouselentertainments.co.uk
e-mail: info@carouselentertainments.co.uk
Fax: 0870 7518668   Tel: 0870 7518688

CARTEURS
170A Church Road, Hove, East Sussex BN3 2DJ
Website: www.stonelandsschool.co.uk
Fax: 01273 770444   Tel: 01273 770445

john|clark
photo|digital

The finest digital photography for the industry

020 8854 4069 - 07702 627237

For information about sessions, the casting shot, fees and portfolio

www.johnclarkphotography.com
info@johnclarkphotography.com

georgina mellor

adam rickitt

michael pollard
photographer
manchester

tel : 0161 456 7470
email : info@michaelpollard.co.uk
website : www.michaelpollard.co.uk

studio/location/student rates

CASAROTTO MARSH Ltd
(Film Technicians)
National House, 60-66 Wardour Street, London W1V 4ND
Website: www.casarotto.uk.com
e-mail: casarottomarsh@casarotto.uk.com
Fax: 020-7287 5644　　　　　　Tel: 020-7287 4450

CASTAWAY ACTORS AGENCY
30-31 Wicklow Street, Dublin 2, Eire
Website: www.irish-actors.com
e-mail: castaway@clubi.ie
Fax: 00 353 1 6719133　　　　　Tel: 00 353 1 6719264

CASTCALL & CASTFAX
(Casting & Consultancy Service)
106 Wilsden Avenue, Luton LU1 5HR
Website: www.castcall.co.uk
e-mail: casting@castcall.co.uk
Fax: 01582 480736　　　　　　Tel: 01582 456213

CASTING COUCH PRODUCTIONS Ltd
(Moira Townsend)
97 Riffel Road, London NW2 4PG
e-mail: moiratownsend@yahoo.co.uk
Fax: 020-8208 2373　　　　　　Tel: 020-8438 9679

CASTING DEPARTMENT The
Elysium Gate
Unit 15, 126-128 New Kings Road, London SW6 4LZ
e-mail: jillscastingdpt@aol.com
Fax: 020-7736 2221　　　　　　Tel: 020-7384 0388

CASTING FACES UK
Park House, 17 Sugar House Lane, London E15 2QS
Website: www.castingfaces.com
e-mail: office@castingfaces.com
Fax: 0871 4337304　　　　　　Tel: 020-8555 6339

CASTING UK
88-90 Gray's Inn Road, London WC1X 8AA
Website: www.castinguk.com
e-mail: info@castinguk.com
Fax: 020-7430 1155　　　　　　Tel: 020-7430 1122

C B A INTERNATIONAL
(Cindy Brace)
31 rue Milton, 75009 Paris, France
e-mail: c_b_a@club-internet.fr
Fax: 33 148 74 51 42　　　　　Tel: 33 145 26 33 42

166 Waverley Avenue, Twickenham TW2 6DL

C C A MANAGEMENT*
PM Write (Actors and Technicians)
Garden Level, 32 Charlwood Street, London SW1V 2DY
e-mail: cca@ccamanagement.co.uk
Fax: 020-7630 7376　　　　　　Tel: 020-7630 6303

CCM•
Co-operative
Panther House, 38 Mount Pleasant, London WC1X 0AP
Website: www.ccmactors.com
e-mail: casting@ccmactors.com
Fax: 020-7813 3103　　　　　　Tel: 020-7278 0507

CDA
(See DAWSON Caroline ASSOCIATES)

CELEBRITY MANAGEMENT Ltd
12 Nottingham Place, London W1U 5NE
Website: www.celebrity.co.uk
e-mail: info@celebrity.co.uk
Fax: 020-7224 6060　　　　　　Tel: 020-7224 5050

Michael Garrett Associates
Personal Management

Director   **Michael Garrett**

Television and Film   **Niki Winterson**

Musical Theatre   **Simon Bashford**

                                               Chris Sheils

Michael Garrett Associates
23 Haymarket
London, SW1Y 4DG

Tel: 020 7839 4888
Fax: 020 7839 4555

E-mail: enquiries@michaelgarrett.co.uk
www.michaelgarrett.co.uk
www.theatricalagent.co.uk

Members of the Personal Managers' Association

PLA

PAT LOVETT ASSOCIATES

Pat Lovett, Dolina Logan

43 Chandos Place, London, WC2N 4HS Tel: 020 7379 8111 Fax: 020 7379 9111

5 Union Street, Edinburgh, EH1 3LT Tel: 0131 478 7878 Fax: 0131 478 7070 www.pla.uk.com

CENTRAL LINE•
PM Co-operative
11 East Circus Street
Nottingham NG1 5AF
Website: www.the-central-line.co.uk
e-mail: mailact@the-central-line.co.uk Tel: 0115-941 2937

CENTRE STAGE AGENCY*
7 Rutledge Terrace
South Circular Road, Dublin 8, Eire
e-mail: geraldinecenterstage@eircom.net
Tel/Fax: 00 353 1 4533599

CHANCE David A. ASSOCIATES
(See CINEL GABRAN MANAGEMENT)

CHAPMAN AGENCY
The Link Building
Paradise Place, Birmingham B3 3HJ
e-mail: agency@bssd.ac.uk
Fax: 0121-262 6801   Tel: 0121-262 6807

CHARACTERS MANAGEMENT Ltd
28 Fletching Road, London E5 9QP
e-mail: cmltd1@btconnect.com
Fax: 020-8533 5554   Tel: 020-8533 5500

CHARLESWORTH Peter & ASSOCIATES
68 Old Brompton Road, London SW7 3LQ
e-mail: petercharlesworth@tiscali.co.uk
Fax: 020-7589 2922   Tel: 020-7581 2478

CHATTO & LINNIT Ltd
123A Kings Road, London SW3 4PL
Fax: 020-7352 3450   Tel: 020-7352 7722

CHURCHILL Hetty PERSONAL MANAGEMENT
Thorne, Merrion, Pembrokeshire SA71 5EA
e-mail: actors@hettychurchill.com   Tel: 01646 661240

CINEL GABRAN MANAGEMENT*
Tŷ Cefn
14-16 Rectory Road
Canton, Cardiff, South Wales CF5 1QL
Website: www.cinelgabran.co.uk
e-mail: info@cinelgabran.co.uk
Fax: 029-2066 6601   Tel: 029-2066 6600

CIRCUIT PERSONAL MANAGEMENT Ltd•
Suite 71 S.E.C.
Bedford Street, Shelton, Stoke-on-Trent, Staffs ST1 4PZ
Website: www.circuitpm.co.uk
e-mail: mail@circuitpm.co.uk
Fax: 01782 206821   Tel: 01782 285388

CIRCUS MANIACS AGENCY
(Physical Artistes & Corporate Events)
Office 8A, The Kingswood Foundation, Britannia Road
Kingswood, Bristol BS15 8DB
e-mail: agency@circusmaniacs.com
Mobile: 07977 247287   Tel/Fax: 0117-947 7042

CITY ACTORS' MANAGEMENT Ltd•
PM Co-operative
Oval House
52-54 Kennington Oval, London SE11 5SW
Website: www.city-actors.freeserve.co.uk
e-mail: info@city-actors.freeserve.co.uk
Fax: 020-7793 8282   Tel: 020-7793 9888

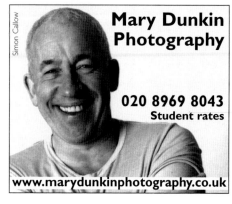

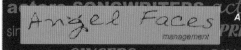

C.K.K. ENTERTAINMENT
PO Box 24550, London E17 9FG
e-mail: ckk.entertainment@virgin.net
Fax: 020-8923 0983   Tel: 020-8923 0977

CLARKE AND JONES Ltd
4B Ainsworth Way, St John's Wood, London NW8 0SR
e-mail: mail@clarkeandjones.plus.com
Fax: 0870 1313391   Tel: 020-7372 3421

CLARKE Jean & BROOK Jeremy MANAGEMENT
International House, 223 Regent Street, London W1R 7DB
Fax: 020-7495 7742   Tel: 020-7495 2424

CLAYPOLE MANAGEMENT
PO Box 123 DL3 7WA
e-mail: claypole_1@hotmail.com
Fax: 0870 1334784   Tel: 0845 6501777

CLOUD NINE AGENCY
96 Tiber Gardens, Treaty Street, London N1 0XE
e-mail: cloudnineagency@blueyonder.co.uk
                    Tel/Fax: 020-7278 0029

CMA (COULTER MANAGEMENT AGENCY)
(Anne Coulter)
333 Woodlands Road
Glasgow G3 6NG
e-mail: cmaglasgow@btconnect.com
Fax: 0141-357 6676   Tel: 0141-357 6666

CMP MANAGEMENT
Tandy House, 30-40 Dalling Road, London W6 0JB
e-mail: info@ravenscourt.net
Fax: 020-8741 1786   Tel: 020-8741 3400

COCHRANE Elspeth PERSONAL MANAGEMENT*
14/2 2nd Floor, South Bank Commercial Centre
140 Battersea Park Road, London SW11 4NB
e-mail: info@elspethcochrane.co.uk
Fax: 020-7622 5815   Tel: 020-7622 0314

COHEN MAYER Charlie
(UK and USA Talent) (Incorporating Jimmy D.
Literary/Screenplay Agency)
PM, 121 Brecknock Road
London N19 5AE   Mobile: 07979 856199

COLLINS Shane ASSOCIATES*
39-41 New Oxford Street, Bloomsbury, London WC1A 1BN
Website: www.shanecollins.co.uk
e-mail: info@shanecollins.co.uk
Fax: 020-7836 9388   Tel: 020-7836 9377

COLLIS MANAGEMENT
182 Trevelyan Road, London SW17 9LW
e-mail: marilyn@collismanagement.co.uk
Fax: 020-8682 0973   Tel: 020-8767 0196

COMEDY CLUB Ltd The
2nd Floor, 28-31 Moulsham St, Chelmsford, Essex CM2 0HX
Website: www.hahaheehee.com
e-mail: info@hahaheehee.com
Fax: 01245 255507   Tel: 08700 425656

COMIC VOICE MANAGEMENT
2nd Floor, 28-31 Moulsham Street
Chelmsford, Essex CM2 0HX
Website: www.comicvoice.com
e-mail: info@comicvoice.com
Fax: 01245 255507   Tel: 08700 425656

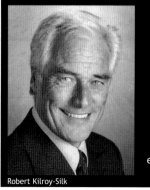

Gabrielle Bradshaw

ROSIE STILL
(PHOTOGRAPHER)

Chris Jarvis

Robert Gray

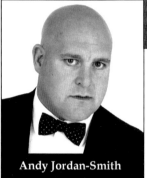

Andy Jordan-Smith

Debra Stephenson

Bella Emberg

Bonnie Bridgman

Henry McGee

Michael Barber

Christopher
Parker

Own South London Studio
Top quality results
Affordable prices
Relaxed atmosphere

Rebecca Loudonsack

020 8857 6920   www.rosiestillphotography.com   **07957 318919**

COMMERCIAL AGENCY Ltd The
(See TCA)

CONTI Italia AGENCY Ltd
S M TV F Write or Phone
23 Goswell Road, London EC1M 7AJ
e-mail: agency@italiaconti.co.uk
Fax: 020-7253 1430   Tel: 020-7608 7500

CONWAY Clive CELEBRITY PRODUCTIONS Ltd
32 Grove Street
Oxford OX2 7JT
Website: www.celebrityproductions.info
e-mail: clive.conway@ntlworld.com
Fax: 01865 514409   Tel: 01865 514830

CONWAY VAN GELDER Ltd*
PM
3rd Floor, 18-21 Jermyn Street
London SW1Y 6HP
Fax: 020-7287 1940   Tel: 020-7287 0077

COOKE Howard ASSOCIATES*
19 Coulson Street, Chelsea, London SW3 3NA
Fax: 020-7591 0155   Tel: 020-7591 0144

CORNER Clive ASSOCIATES
73 Gloucester Road, Hampton, Middlesex TW12 2UQ
e-mail: cornerassociates@aol.com
Fax: 020-8979 4983   Tel: 020-8287 2726

the actor's
one-stop
shop

showreels
photographs
CVs

t: 020 8888 7006

www.actorsone-stopshop.com

Caroline Summers

Session includes make up artist

020-7223 7669

Short notice possible

CORNISH Caroline MANAGEMENT Ltd*
(Technicians Only)
12 Shinfield Street, London W12 0HN
Website: www.carolinecornish.co.uk
e-mail: carolinecornish@btconnect.com
Fax: 020-8743 7887   Tel: 020-8743 7337

COULSON Lou ASSOCIATES Ltd*
1st Floor, 37 Berwick Street, London W1F 8RS
Fax: 020-7439 7569   Tel: 020-7734 9633

COVENT GARDEN MANAGEMENT
(See SPLATS Agency)

CRAWFORDS
PO Box 44394, London SW20 0YP
Website: www.crawfords.tv
e-mail: cr@wfords.com
Fax: 020-8879 1437   Tel: 020-8947 9999

CREATIVE MEDIA
PM Write
22 Kingsbury Avenue
Dunstable, Bedfordshire LU5 4PU   Tel/Fax: 01582 510869

CREATIVE MEDIA MANAGEMENT*
(Film, TV & Theatre Technical Personnel only)
3B Walpole Court
Ealing Studios, Ealing Green, London W5 5ED
e-mail: enquiries@creativemediamanagement.com
Fax: 020-8566 5554   Tel: 020-8584 5363

CREDITS ACTORS AGENCY Ltd
29 Lorn Road, London SW9 0AB
e-mail: credits@actors29.freeserve.co.uk
                           Tel: 020-7737 0735

CRESCENT MANAGEMENT•
PM Co-operative
10 Barley Mow Passage, Chiswick, London W4 4PH
e-mail: mail@crescentmanagement.co.uk
Fax: 020-8987 0207   Tel: 020-8987 0191

CROUCH Sara MANAGEMENT
59 Nassau Road, Barnes, London SW13 9QG
e-mail: sara.crouch@btinternet.com
Fax: 020-8563 8558   Tel: 020-8563 8111

CROWD PULLERS
(Street Performers)
14 Somerset Gardens, London SE13 7SY
e-mail: jhole@crowdpullers.co.uk
Fax: 020-8469 2147   Tel: 020-8469 3900

CRUICKSHANK CAZENOVE Ltd*
(Directors, Designers, Choreographers)
97 Old South Lambeth Road, London SW8 1XU
Fax: 020-7820 1081   Tel: 020-7735 2933

CS MANAGEMENT
The Croft, 7 Cannon Road, Southgate, London N14 7HE
Website: www.csmanagementuk.com
e-mail: carole@csmanagementuk.com
Fax: 020-8886 7555   Tel: 020-8886 4264

C.S.A.
(Christina Shepherd Advertising)
13 Radnor Walk, London SW3 4BP
e-mail: csa@shepherdmanagement.co.uk
Fax: 020-7352 2277   Tel: 020-7352 2255

CSM (ARTISTS)
PM
Honeysuckle Cottage, 93 Telford Way, Yeading
Middlesex UB4 9TH
e-mail: csmartists@aol.com   Tel/Fax: 020-8839 8747

CURTIS BROWN GROUP Ltd*
(Actors, Producers, Directors)
Haymarket House, 28-29 Haymarket, London SW1Y 4SP
e-mail: cb@curtisbrown.co.uk
Fax: 020-7393 4404   Tel: 020-7393 4400

CYBER-ARTISTS
In The Can Ltd
The Studio, Kingsway Court
Queen's Gardens, Hove BN3 2LP
Website: www.cyberartists.co.uk
e-mail: cyber.1@btconnect.com
Fax: 01273 739984   Tel: 01273 821821

D Lisa MANAGEMENT Ltd
Unit 5, Gun Wharf, 241 Old Ford Road, London E3 5QB
e-mail: casting@lisad.co.uk
Fax: 020-8980 2211   Tel: 020-8980 0117

DALY David ASSOCIATES
586A King's Road, London SW6 2DX
e-mail: agents@daviddaly.co.uk
Fax: 020-7610 9512   Tel: 020-7384 1036

DALY David ASSOCIATES (MANCHESTER)
(Clare Marshall)
16 King Street, Knutsford WA16 6DL
e-mail: clare@daviddaly.co.uk
Fax: 01565 755334   Tel: 01565 631999

DALZELL & BERESFORD Ltd
26 Astwood Mews, London SW7 4DE
Fax: 020-7341 9412   Tel: 020-7341 9411

DANCERS
1 Charlotte Street, London W1T 1RD
e-mail: info@dancersagency.com
Fax: 020-7636 1657   Tel: 020-7636 1473

Benedict Cumberbatch   Elizabeth Marmur   Ryan Romain

ric bacon

07970 970799

www.ricbacon.co.uk

Justin Salinger   Tamsin Pike   Elize Du Toit   Rupert Hill

MAGNUS HASTINGS   t: 020 7033 9757   m: 07905 304 705   www.magnushastings.co.uk

DARRELL Emma MANAGEMENT
(Producers, Directors & Existing Writers only)
North Vale, Shire Lane, Chorleywood, Herts WD3 5NH
e-mail: emma.mc@virgin.net
Fax: 01923 284064   Tel: 01923 284061

DAVID ARTISTES MANAGEMENT AGENCY Ltd The
F TV Md Write or Phone
26-28 Hammersmith Grove, London W6 7BA
Website: www.davidagency.net
e-mail: casting@davidagency.net
Fax: 020-8834 1144   Tel: 020-8834 1615

DAVIS Dabber PRODUCTIONS
(Write or Phone)
24A Park Road, Hayes
Middlesex UB4 8JN   Tel: 020-8848 9048

DAVIS Lena, JOHN BISHOP ASSOCIATES
Cotton's Farmhouse
Whiston Road, Cogenhoe, Northants NN7 1NL
Fax: 01604 890405   Tel: 01604 891487

DAWSON Caroline ASSOCIATES*
125 Gloucester Road, London SW7 4TE
e-mail: cda@cdalondon.com
Fax: 020-7373 1110   Tel: 020-7373 3323

DEALERS AGENCY BELFAST
23 Queen's Square, Belfast BT1 3FF
Website: www.dealersagency.co.uk
e-mail: patrickduncan609@msn.com
Fax: 028-9023 4072   Tel: 028-9024 2726

DEBUT MODELS Ltd
1 Thrice Fold, Thackley, Bradford, West Yorkshire BD10 8WW
Website: www.debutmodels.co.uk
Fax: 01274 532353   Tel: 01274 532347

DENMAN CASTING AGENCY
Burgess House, Main Street
Farnsfield, Notts NG22 8EF   Tel/Fax: 01623 882272

DENMARK STREET MANAGEMENT•
PM Co-operative Write SAE
Packington Bridge Workspace
Unit 11, 1B Packington Square, London N1 7UA
e-mail: mail@denmarkstreet.net
Fax: 020-7354 8558   Tel: 020-7354 8555

DEREK'S HANDS AGENCY
26-28 Hammersmith Grove, London W6 7BA
Website: www.derekshands.com
e-mail: casting@derekshands.com
Fax: 020-8834 1144   Tel: 020-8834 1609

de WOLFE Felix*
PM Write
Kingsway House, 103 Kingsway
London WC2B 6QX
e-mail: info@felixdewolfe.com
Fax: 020-7242 8119   Tel: 020-7242 5066

DIAMOND MANAGEMENT*
31 Percy Street, London W1T 2DD
e-mail: agents@diman.co.uk
Fax: 020-7631 0500   Tel: 020-7631 0400

DIESTENFELD Lily
(Personal Manager for 45+ Playing Ages)
(No unsolicited Mail)
28B Alexandra Grove
London N12 8HG   Tel: 020-8446 5379

DIMPLES MODEL & CASTING ACADEMY
Suite 2, 2nd Floor
Magnum House
33 Lord Street, Leigh, Lancs WN7 1BY
e-mail: dimples_m_c_a@btinternet.com
Fax: 01942 262232   Tel: 01942 262012

DIRECT LINE•
PM (Personal Manager: Daphne Franks)
St John's House
16 St John's Vale, London SE8 4EN
Website: www.dline.org.uk
e-mail: daphne.franks@dline.org.uk   Tel/Fax: 020-8694 1788

Park House, 62 Lidgett Lane
Leeds LS8 1PL   Tel/Fax: 0113-266 4036

DOUBLE ACT CELEBRITY LOOK ALIKES
PO Box 25574
London NW7 3GB
Website: www.double-act.co.uk
e-mail: info@double-act.co.uk
Fax: 020-8201 1795   Tel: 020-8381 0151

DOWNES PRESENTERS AGENCY
96 Broadway, Bexleyheath, Kent DA6 7DE
e-mail: downes@presentersagency.com
Fax: 020-8301 5591   Tel: 020-8304 0541

DQ MANAGEMENT
1st Floor, 115 Church Road, Hove, East Sussex BN3 2AF
e-mail: info@dqmanagement.com
Fax: 01273 277255   Tel: 01273 721221

DREW Bryan Ltd
PM Write
Mezzanine
Quadrant House, 80-82 Regent Street, London W1B 5AU
e-mail: bryan@bryandrewltd.com
Fax: 020-7437 0561   Tel: 020-7437 2293

DUDDRIDGE Paul MANAGEMENT
26 Rathbone Place, London W1T 1JD
Website: www.paulduddridge.com
e-mail: mail@paulduddridge.com
Fax: 020-7580 3480   Tel: 020-7580 3580

EARLE Kenneth PERSONAL MANAGEMENT
214 Brixton Road, London SW9 6AP
Website: www.entertainment-kennethearle.co.uk
e-mail: kennethearle@agents-uk.com
Fax: 020-7274 9529   Tel: 020-7274 1219

EARNSHAW Susi MANAGEMENT
PM
5 Brook Place, Barnet, Herts EN5 2DL
Website: www.susiearnshaw.co.uk
e-mail: casting@susiearnshaw.co.uk
Fax: 020-8364 9618   Tel: 020-8441 5010

EDWARDS REPRESENTATION Joyce
PM Write
4 Turner Close, London SW9 6UQ
e-mail: joyce.edwards@virgin.net
Fax: 020-7820 1845   Tel: 020-7735 5736

E.K.A. MODEL & ACTOR MANAGEMENT
The Warehouse Studios, Glaziers Lane, Culcheth
Warrington WA3 4AQ
Website: www.eka-agency.com
e-mail: kate@eka-agency.com
Fax: 01925 767563   Tel: 0871 7501575

ELLIOTT AGENCY The
PO Box 2772, Lewes, Sussex BN8 4DW
Website: www.elliottagency.co.uk
e-mail: info@elliottagency.co.uk
Fax: 01273 400814   Tel: 01273 401264

ELLIS Bill Ltd
(See A & B PERSONAL MANAGEMENT Ltd)

EMPTAGE HALLETT*
24 Poland Street, London W1F 8QL
e-mail: mail@emptagehallett.co.uk
Fax: 020-7287 4411   Tel: 020-7287 5511

2nd Floor, 3-5 The Balcony, Castle Arcade, Cardiff CF10 1BU
e-mail: gwenp@emphal.entadsl.com
Fax: 029-2034 4206   Tel: 029-2034 4205

ENGLISH Doreen '95
Write or Phone
4 Selsey Avenue
Aldwick, Bognor Regis
West Sussex PO21 2QZ   Tel/Fax: 01243 825968

PROFILE PRINTS

Black & White and Colour Repros

From negatives, photographs, disks or emails
Stored negative service for telephone re-orders
Enlargements and Stickybacked Photos in various sizes
Photos may be sub-titled

By-return Mail-Order service at unbeatable prices

For an order form and samples, please call **01736 365222**
or email: **people@courtwood.co.uk**

PROFILE PRINTS
Courtwood Film Service Ltd (Est 1956)
FREEPOST TO55, Penzance, TR18 2BF.
Fax: **01736 350203** - **www.courtwood.co.uk**

Photo of Rupert Friend (ICM) by Peter Simpkin   Photo of Donna Dandridge (CMP Management) by John Clark

01736 365222

EPSTEIN June ASSOCIATES
Write
Flat 1, 62 Compayne Gardens, London NW6 3RY
e-mail: june@june-epstein-associates.co.uk
Fax: 020-7328 0684   Tel: 020-7328 0864

ESSANAY*
PM Write
PO Box 44394, London SW20 0YP
e-mail: info@essanay.co.uk
Fax: 020-8879 1437   Tel: 020-8879 7076

ETHNICS ARTISTE AGENCY
86 Elphinstone Road, Walthamstow, London E17 5EX
Fax: 020-8523 4523   Tel: 020-8523 4242

ETTINGER BROS GROUP
(Representation & Management)
Gladstone House, 2 Church Road, Liverpool L15 9EG
e-mail: philipettinger@blueyonder.co.uk
Fax: 0151-733 2468   Tel: 0151-734 2240

ET-NIK-A PMC Ltd
Prime Management & Castings
Ground Floor, 30 Great Portland Street, London W1W 7QU
Website: www.et-nik-a.com
e-mail: agents@et-nik-a.com
Fax: 020-7299 3558   Tel: 020-7299 3555

**EUROKIDS & ADULTS INTERNATIONAL CASTING &
MODEL AGENCY**
The Warehouse Studios
Glaziers Lane
Culcheth, Warrington WA3 4AQ
Website: www.eka-agency.com
e-mail: becky@eka-agency.com
Fax: 01925 767563   Tel: 0871 7501575

EVANS & REISS*
100 Fawe Park Road, London SW15 2EA
e-mail: marcia@evansandreiss.co.uk
Fax: 020-8877 0307   Tel: 020-8877 3755

EVANS Jacque MANAGEMENT Ltd
Top Floor Suite, 14 Holmesley Road, London SE23 1PJ
Website: www.jacqueevansltd.com
Fax: 020-8699 5192   Tel: 020-8699 1202

EVOLUTION TALENT MANAGEMENT
The Truman Brewery Building
Studio 21, 91 Brick Lane
London E1 6QB
Website: www.evolutionmngt.com
e-mail: info@evolutionmngt.com
Fax: 020-7375 2752   Tel: 020-7053 2128

Nick Gregan
PHOTOGRAPHY

The easiest and the best headshot you'll ever have -
By one of London's premier theatrical photographers.

Film or Digital | Studio or Location | Retouching
Student Rates | Central London | Same or next day delivery

For contemporary, natural headshots for the acting profession, contact Nick on
Tel: 020 75381249 | Mobile: 07774 421878 | www.nickgregan.com

FACE FACTORY
3 Nottingham Court, Covent Garden, London WC2H 9AY
Website: www.facefactoryuk.com
e-mail: facefactory@btconnect.com
Fax: 020-7240 0565 — Tel: 020-7240 2322

FARNES Norma MANAGEMENT
9 Orme Court, London W2 4RL
Fax: 020-7792 2110 — Tel: 020-7727 1544

FASTCAST UK
239 Old Street, London EC1V 9EY
Website: www.fastcastuk.co.uk
e-mail: mrblack@fastcastuk.co.uk
Mobile: 07961 911027 — Tel: 020-8839 9354

FAWKES Irene MANAGEMENT
2nd Floor, 91A Rivington Street, London EC2A 3AY
e-mail: irenefawkes@fsbdial.co.uk
Fax: 020-7613 0769 — Tel: 020-7729 8559

FBI AGENCY Ltd The
PO Box 250, Leeds LS1 2AZ
Website: www.fbi-agency.ltd.uk
e-mail: casting@fbi-agency.ltd.uk
Fax: 0113-279 7270 — Tel: 07050 222747

FBI Ltd
4th Floor, 20-24 Kirby Street, London EC1N 8TS
Website: www.fullybooked-inc.com
Fax: 020-7242 8125 — Tel: 020-7242 5542

FEAST Sadie MANAGEMENT*
10 Primrose Hill Studios, Fitzroy Road, London NW1 8TR
e-mail: office@feastmanagement.co.uk
Fax: 020-7586 9817 — Tel: 020-7586 5502

FEATURES
1 Charlotte Street, London W1T 1RD
e-mail: info@features.co.uk
Fax: 020-7636 1657 — Tel: 020-7637 1487

FIELD Alan ASSOCIATES
3 The Spinney, Bakers Hill
Hadley Common, Herts EN5 5QJ
e-mail: alanfielduk@aol.com
Fax: 020-8447 0657 — Tel: 020-8441 1137

FILM RIGHTS Ltd
PM Write
Mezzanine, Quadrant House
80-82 Regent Street, London W1B 5AU
Fax: 020-7734 0044 — Tel: 020-7734 9911

FIRST ACT PERSONAL MANAGEMENT
2 Saint Michaels, New Arley, Coventry CV7 8PY
e-mail: firstactpm@aol.com — Tel: 01676 540285

FITZGERALD Sheridan MANAGEMENT
(Write only with SAE)
87 Western Road
Upton Park, London E13 9JE — Tel: 020-8471 9814

FLETCHER ASSOCIATES
(Broadcast & Media)
25 Parkway, London N20 0XN
Fax: 020-8361 8866 — Tel: 020-8361 8061

FLETCHER JACOB
(Artist Management)
9 Oman Court, Oman Avenue
London NW2 6AY
e-mail: info@fletcherjacob.co.uk — Tel/Fax: 020-8452 3853

Finty Williams

Portrait & Production
Photography by

Robin Watson

Studio or location
Special rates for students

020 7833 1982
07956 416 943

Ben Harris

robin@robinwatson.biz – www.robinwatson.biz

FOX Clare ASSOCIATES
(Designers & Lighting Designers)
9 Plympton Road, London NW6 7EH
e-mail: cimfox@yahoo.co.uk
Fax: 020-7372 2301   Tel: 01483 535818

FRENCH Linda
(See ALEXANDER PERSONAL MANAGEMENT Ltd)

FRESH MANAGEMENT
Level 3, 3 Stevenson Square, Manchester M1 1DN
e-mail: freshmanagement@btconnect.com
Fax: 0161-237 9938   Tel: 0161-237 9925

FRESH PARTNERS Ltd
15 Westland Place, London N1 7LP
Website: www.fresh-partners.com
e-mail: hello@fresh-partners.com
Fax: 020-7702 5088   Tel: 020-7566 1770

FRONTLINE ACTORS' AGENCY DUBLIN
Bayview House, 49 North Stand Road, Dublin 3
Website: www.frontlineactors.org
e-mail: frontlineactors@eircom.net
Fax: 00 353 1 8365252   Tel: 00 353 1 8364777

FRONTLINE MANAGEMENT•
PM Co-operative
Colombo Centre
34-68 Colombo Street, London SE1 8DP
e-mail: frontlineactor@freeuk.com   Tel/Fax: 020-7261 9466

FUNKY BEETROOT CELEBRITY MANAGEMENT Ltd
(Actors, TV Celebrities, Casting & Personal Management)
PO Box 143, Faversham, Kent ME13 9LP
Website: www.funky-beetroot.com
e-mail: info@funky-beetroot.com
Fax: 01227 752300   Tel: 01227 751549

Rachel Weisz

CAROLE LATIMER
P H O T O G R A P H Y
113 Ledbury Road W11
Tel: 020 7727 9371 Fax: 020 7229 9306

Alistair McGowan

adam farr   matt ryan   sarah croft   lois tucker

david price photography

contact:
07950-542-494
www.davidpricephotography.co.uk

FUSHION
27 Old Gloucester Street, London WC1N 3XX
Website: www.fushion-uk.com
e-mail: info@fushion-uk.com
Fax: 08700 111020   Tel: 08700 111100

GAGAN Hilary ASSOCIATES*
PM
187 Drury Lane, London WC2B 5QD
e-mail: hilary@hgassoc.freeserve.co.uk
Fax: 020-7430 1869   Tel: 020-7404 8794

GALLIARDS MANAGEMENT
P O Box 9331, Colintraive PA22 3YE
Website: www.galliards.net
e-mail: daisy@galliards.net
Mobile: 07909 970781   Tel: 01369 820116

GALLOWAYS ONE
15 Lexham Mews, London W8 6JW
e-mail: hugh@gallowaysone.com
Fax: 020-7376 2416   Tel: 020-7376 2288

GARDNER HERRITY Ltd*
Douglas House, 16-18 Douglas Street, London SW1P 4PB
e-mail: info@gardnerherrity.co.uk
Fax: 020-7828 7758   Tel: 020-7828 7748

GARRETT Michael ASSOCIATES*
23 Haymarket, London SW1Y 4DG
Website: www.michaelgarrett.co.uk
e-mail: enquiries@michaelgarrett.co.uk
Fax: 020-7839 4555   Tel: 020-7839 4888

GARRICKS*
5 The Old School House
The Lanterns, Bridge Lane, London SW11 3AD
e-mail: megan@garricks.net
Fax: 020-7738 1881   Tel: 020-7738 1600

GAY Noel ARTISTS
19 Denmark Street, London WC2H 8NA
Website: www.noelgay.com
Fax: 020-7287 1816   Tel: 020-7836 3941

GILBERT & PAYNE
Room 236, 2nd Floor
Linen Hall, 162-168 Regent Street, London W1B 5TB
e-mail: ee@gilbertandpayne.com
Fax: 020-7494 3787   Tel: 020-7734 7505

GJS MANAGEMENT
173 Wellfield Road, London SW16 2BY
Website: www.gjsmanagement.co.uk
e-mail: info@gjsmanagement.co.uk
                                     Tel/Fax: 020-8769 6788

Northern Lights Management

Personal representation of Actors from the North and in the North

Agents: Maureen Magee and Angie Forrest

Dean Clough Mills, Halifax, West Yorkshire HX3 5AX

Tel: 01422 382203
Fax: 01422 330101

email: info@NLManagement.co.uk

GLASS Eric Ltd
25 Ladbroke Crescent, Notting Hill, London W11 1PS
e-mail: eglassltd@aol.com
Fax: 020-7229 6220   Tel: 020-7229 9500

GLYN MANAGEMENT
The Old School House, Brettenham, Ipswich IP7 7QP
e-mail: glyn.management@tesco.net
Fax: 01449 736117   Tel: 01449 737695

GO ENTERTAINMENTS Ltd
(Circus Artistes, Chinese State Circus, Cirque Surreal,
Bolshoi Circus "Spirit of The Horse")
The Arts Exchange, Congleton, Cheshire CW12 1JG
Website: www.arts-exchange.com
e-mail: phillipgandey@netcentral.co.uk
Fax: 01260 270777   Tel: 01260 276627

GOLDMAN KING
16 St Albans Road
Kingston, Surrey KT2 5HQ
Website: www.goldmanking.com
e-mail: contacts@goldmanking.com   Tel: 020-8287 1199

GORDON & FRENCH*
Write
12-13 Poland Street, London W1F 8QB
e-mail: mail@gordonandfrench.net
Fax: 020-7734 4832   Tel: 020-7734 4818

GOSS Gerald Ltd
19 Gloucester Street, London SW1V 2DB
Fax: 020-7592 9301   Tel: 020-7592 9202

G.O.T. PERSONAL MANAGEMENT
1 Balliol Chambers, Hollow Lane
Hitchin, Herts SG4 9SB
Website: www.guild-of-thieves.com
e-mail: cast@guild-of-thieves.com   Tel: 01462 420400

GRANTHAM-HAZELDINE
5 Blenheim Street, London W1S 1LD
Fax: 020-7495 3370   Tel: 020-7499 4011

GRAY Darren MANAGEMENT
(Specializing in representing/promoting Australian Artists)
2 Marston Lane, Portsmouth, Hampshire PO3 5TW
Website: www.darrengraymanagement.co.uk
e-mail: darren.gray1@virgin.net
Fax: 023-9267 7227   Tel: 023-9269 9973

GRAY Joan PERSONAL MANAGEMENT
PM F TV
29 Sunbury Court Island
Sunbury-on-Thames
Middlesex TW16 5PP   Tel/Fax: 01932 783544

GRAYS MANAGEMENT & ASSOCIATES
PM
Panther House, 38 Mount Pleasant, London WC1X 0AP
Website: www.graysman.com
e-mail: e-mail@graysmanagement.idps.co.uk
Fax: 020-7278 1091   Tel: 020-7278 1054

GREEN & UNDERWOOD
PM Write
PO Box 44394, London SW20 0YP
e-mail: info@greenandunderwood.com
Fax: 020-8879 1437   Tel: 020-8879 1775

GREIG Miranda ASSOCIATES Ltd
92 Englewood Road, London SW12 9NY
e-mail: mail@mirandagreigassoc.co.uk
Fax: 020-7228 1400   Tel: 020-7228 1200

Kim Medcalf

Todd Carty

chris baker

photographer

020 8441 3851

e: chrisbaker@photos2000.demon.co.uk

studio/location
digital output available

GRESHAM Carl GROUP
PO Box 3, Bradford, West Yorkshire BD1 4QN
Website: www.carlgresham.co.uk
e-mail: carl@carlgresham.co.uk
Fax: 01274 827161 Tel: 01274 735880

GRIFFIN Sandra MANAGEMENT
6 Ryde Place, Richmond Road
East Twickenham, Middlesex TW1 2EH
e-mail: office@sandragriffin.com
Fax: 020-8744 1812 Tel: 020-8891 5676

GROUP 3 ASSOCIATES
PM (Henry Davies)
35D Newton Road, London W2 5JR Tel: 020-7221 4989

GURNETT J. PERSONAL MANAGEMENT Ltd
2 New King's Road, London SW6 4SA
Website: www.jgpm.co.uk
e-mail: mail@jgpm.co.uk
Fax: 020-7736 5455 Tel: 020-7736 7828

HALLY WILLIAMS AGENCY The
121 Grange Road
Rathfarnham, Dublin 14, Eire
e-mail: hallywilliams@eircom.net
Fax: 00 353 1 4933076 Tel: 00 353 1 4933685

HAMILTON HODELL Ltd*
24 Hanway Street, London W1T 1UH
e-mail: info@hamiltonhodell.co.uk
Fax: 020-7636 1226 Tel: 020-7636 1221

HARGREAVES Alison MANAGEMEMT
(Designers & Lighting Designers)
89 Temple Road, London NW2 6PN
e-mail: alisonhargreaves@hotmail.com
Fax: 020-8208 1094 Tel: 020-8438 0112

HARRIS AGENCY Ltd The
52 Forty Avenue, Wembley Park, Middlesex HA9 8LQ
e-mail: sharrisltd@aol.com
Fax: 020-8908 4455 Tel: 020-8908 4451

HARRISON Penny BSA Ltd
Trinity Lodge
25 Trinity Crescent, London SW17 7AG
e-mail: harrisonbsa@aol.com
Fax: 020-8672 8971 Tel: 020-8672 0136

HARRISPEARSON MANAGEMENT Ltd*
64-66 Millman Street
Bloomsbury, London WC1N 3EF
Website: www.harrispearson.co.uk
e-mail: agent@harrispearson.co.uk
Fax: 020-7430 9229 Tel: 020-7430 9890

HATSTAND CIRCUS
(Special Skills Perfomers)
39 Old Church Road, Stepney, London E1 0QB
Website: www.hatstandcircus.com
e-mail: helenahatstand@btopenworld.com
Tel/Fax: 020-7791 2541

HATTON McEWAN
PM Write (Stephen Hatton, Aileen McEwan)
PO Box 37385, London N1 7XF
Website: www.thetalent.biz
e-mail: info@thetalent.biz
Fax: 020-7251 9081 Tel: 020-7253 4770

HAZEMEAD Ltd
(Entertainment Consultants)
Camellia House, 38 Orchard Road
Sundridge Park, Bromley, Kent BR1 2PS
Fax: 020-8460 5830 Tel/Fax: 0870 2402082

H C A
(See COOKE Howard ASSOCIATES)

HEATHCOTE George MANAGEMENT
38 Great Queen Street, London WC2B 5AA
e-mail: gheathcote@freeuk.com
Fax: 020-7404 8681   Tel: 020-7404 8680

HEAVY PENCIL MANAGEMENT
(with Elinor Hilton Associates) PM
BAC, Lavender Hill, London SW11 5TF
e-mail: heavypencil@btconnect.com
Fax: 020-7924 4636   Tel: 020-7738 9574

**HENRIETTA RABBIT CHILDREN'S ENTERTAINMENTS
AGENCY**
(Magiciennes, Punch & Judy, Balloonologists,
Face Painters, Jugglers etc)
The Warren, 12 Eden Close, York YO24 2RD
e-mail: info@henriettarabbit.co.uk   Tel: 01904 345404

HENRY'S AGENCY
53 Westbury, Rochford, Essex SS4 1UL
Website: www.henrysagency.co.uk
e-mail: info@henrysagency.co.uk
Fax: 01702 543654   Tel: 01702 541413

HICKS Jeremy ASSOCIATES
11-12 Tottenham Mews, London W1T 4AG
Website: www.jeremyhicks.com
e-mail: info@jeremyhicks.com
Fax: 020-7636 8880   Tel: 020-7636 8008

HILL Edward MANAGEMENT
Teddington Film & Television Studios, Broom Road
Teddington TW11 9NT
e-mail: info@edagent.com
Fax: 020-8614 2694   Tel: 020-8614 2678

HILLMAN THRELFALL
33 Brookfield, Highgate West Hill, London N6 6AT
e-mail: emma@hillmanthrelfall.net
Fax: 020-8340 9309   Tel: 020-8341 2207

HILTON Elinor ASSOCIATES
PO Box 946
High Wycombe, Bucks HP10 8ZN
Website: www.elinorhilton.co.uk
e-mail: agent@elinorhilton.co.uk   Tel/Fax: 01494 817444

HINDIN Dee ASSOCIATES
9B Brunswick Mews
Great Cumberland Place, London W1H 7FB
Fax: 020-7723 3706   Tel: 020-7258 0651

HIRED HANDS
12 Cressy Road, London NW3 2LY
e-mail: models@hiredhands.freeserve.co.uk
Fax: 020-7267 1030   Tel: 020-7267 9212

HOBBS Liz GROUP Ltd
(Artiste Management)
First Floor, 65 London Road, Newark, Notts NG24 1RZ
Website: www.lizhobbsgroup.com
e-mail: casting@lizhobbsgroup.com
Fax: 0870 3337009   Tel: 08700 702702

HOBSON'S ACTORS
62 Chiswick High Road, Chiswick, London W4 1SY
Website: www.hobsons-international.com
e-mail: actors@hobsons-international.com
Fax: 020-8996 5350   Tel: 020-8995 3628

HOLLOWOOD Jane ASSOCIATES Ltd
50 Copperas Street, Manchester M4 1HS
e-mail: janehollowood@ukonline.co.uk
Fax: 0161-834 8333   Tel: 0161-834 8334

HIGH QUALITY, LOW COST, PUBLICITY SPECIALISTS:

TM Photography

www.tmphotography.co.uk

Sessions from:

£70

Approx. 30 shots
contact sheets,
2 10"x8" prints
free retouching
of blemishes

* View your photos immediately.
* Walk away with your prints.
* All prints b&w or colour.
* Contact sheets.
* Free retouching.
* Portfolio CDs available.

Repro Service

CVs

Websites

Model Cards

Portfolios

Weekend Shoots

Friendly
Atmosphere

020 8924 4694

mob: 07931 755252 e.mail: tm.photography@ntlworld.com

All major credit/debit cards accepted

HOLLY Dave ARTS MEDIA SERVICES
The Annexe
23 Eastwood Gardens
Felling, Tyne & Wear NE10 0AH
Fax: 0191-438 2722   Tel: 0191-438 2711

HOPE Sally ASSOCIATES*
108 Leonard Street, London EC2A 4XS
e-mail: casting@sallyhope.biz
Fax: 020-7613 4848   Tel: 020-7613 5353

HOWARD Amanda ASSOCIATES Ltd*
21 Berwick Street, London W1F 0PZ
Website: www.amandahowardassociates.co.uk
e-mail: mail@amandahowardassociates.co.uk
Fax: 020-7287 7785   Tel: 020-7287 9277

HOWE Janet
Studio 1, Whitebridge Estate
Whitebridge Lane, Stone, Staffs ST15 8LQ
e-mail: janet@jhowecasting.fsbusiness.co.uk
Tel/Fax: 01785 818480   Tel/Fax: 01785 816888

40 Princess Street, Manchester M1 6DE
Mobile: 07801 942178   Tel/Fax: 0161-234 0142

HOWELL Philippa
(See PHPM)

HUDSON & WARNER Ltd
(Nancy Hudson & Charlotte Warner)
3rd Floor, 50 South Molton Street, London W1K 5SB
Website: www.hudsonandwarner.co.uk
e-mail: agents@hudsonandwarner.co.uk
Fax: 020-7499 0884   Tel: 020-7499 5548

HUNTER Bernard ASSOCIATES
13 Spencer Gardens, London SW14 7AH
Fax: 020-8392 9334   Tel: 020-8878 6308

IAM Ltd
First Floor
55 Shelbourne Road, Ballsbridge, Dublin 4, Ireland
Fax: 00 353 1 6676474   Tel: 00 353 1 6676455

I C M (International Creative Management)*
Oxford House, 76 Oxford Street, London W1D 1BS
Fax: 020-7323 0101   Tel: 020-7636 6565

ICON ACTORS MANAGEMENT
Tanzaro House, Ardwick Green North, Manchester M12 6FZ
Website: www.iconactors.net
e-mail: info@iconactors.net
Fax: 0161-273 4567   Tel: 0161-273 3344

Vincent Ebrahim

Susan Kyd

Rupert Frazer

PHOTOGRAPHY

RICHENDA CAREY

LBIPP, LMPA, LRPS

07980 393 866

I.M.L.•
PM Co-operative
Oval House, 52-54 Kennington Oval, London SE11 5SW
Website: www.iml.org.uk
e-mail: iml.london@btconnect.com   Tel/Fax: 020-7587 1080

IMPACT INTERNATIONAL MANAGEMENT
2nd Floor, 16-18 Balderton Street, London W1K 6TN
e-mail: colin@impactinternationalgroup.com
Fax: 020-7495 6515   Tel: 020-7495 6655

I-MAGE CASTINGS
Regent House Business Centre
Suite 22, 24-25, Nutford Pl, Marble Arch, London W1H 5YN
Website: www.i-mage.uk.com
e-mail: jane@i-mage.uk.com
Fax: 020-7725 7004   Tel: 020-7725 7003

INDEPENDENT THEATRE WORKSHOP The
2 Mornington Road, Ranelagh, Dublin 6, Eire
Website: www.independent-theatre-workshop.com
e-mail: itw@esatclear.ie   Tel/Fax: 00 353 1 4968808

INFANT PHENOMENA
85B Highbury Hill, London N5 1SX
Website: www.infantphenomena.co.uk
e-mail: info@infantphenomena.co.uk
Fax: 0871 8729181   Tel: 020-7288 2441

INSPIRATION MANAGEMENT
PM Co-operative
Room 227, The Aberdeen Centre
22-24 Highbury Grove, London N5 2EA
Website: www.inspirationmanagement.org.uk
e-mail: mail@inspirationmanagement.org.uk
Fax: 020-7704 8497   Tel: 020-7704 0440

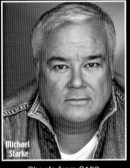

Michael Starke

NORTHERN BASED

Shoots from £100
Digital and Film   Colour & B&W
CD AVAILABLE!

Liz Robertson

NORTHERN BASED

STEPHANIE DE LENG
www.stephaniedeleng.co.uk

Stephen Fletcher

Tel 0151 476 1563
Mobile 07740 927 765
deleng@blueyonder.co.uk

Tamira Henry

Nick Bonner

Suzanne Collins

BILLY MARSH DRAMA LIMITED
(LINDA KREMER & ASSOCIATES)
Personal Management / Representation
Film   Television   Theatre   Commercials

11 Henrietta Street, Covent Garden, London WC2E 8PY
Tel: 020 7379 4800   Fax: 020 7379 7272   E-mail: info@billymarshdrama.co.uk

INTERNATIONAL ARTISTES Ltd*
4th Floor
Holborn Hall, 193-197 High Holborn, London WC1V 7BD
Website: www.intart.co.uk
e-mail: reception@intart.co.uk
Fax: 020-7404 9865   Tel: 020-7025 0600

INTERNATIONAL ARTISTES MIDLANDS OFFICE
Lapley Hall, Lapley, Staffs ST19 9JR
Fax: 01785 841992   Tel: 01785 841991

INTERNATIONAL THEATRE & MUSIC Ltd
(Piers Chater Robinson)
Shakespeare House
Theatre Street, London SW11 5ND
Website: www.internationaltheatreandmusic.com
e-mail: inttheatre@aol.com
Fax: 020-7801 6317   Tel: 020-7801 6316

INTER-CITY CASTING
PM
Portland Tower, Portland Street, Manchester M1 3LF
Website: www.iccast.co.uk
e-mail: mail@iccast.co.uk   Tel/Fax: 0161-238 4950

IRISH ARTS NETWORK
Victor House, Marlborough Gardens, London N20 0SH
e-mail: rosemaryifbco@aol.com   Tel/Fax: 020-8361 0678

JAA
(See ALTARAS Jonathan ASSOCIATES Ltd)

JAMES Susan
(See SJ MANAGEMENT Ltd)

JAMESON Joy Ltd
PM
2.19 The Plaza, 535 Kings Road, London SW10 0SZ
Fax: 020-7352 1744   Tel: 020-7351 3971

JAY Alex PERSONAL MANAGEMENT
8 Higher Newmarket Road
Newmarket, Gloucestershire GL6 0RP
e-mail: alex@alex-jay-pm.freeserve.co.uk
                                Tel/Fax: 01453 834783

JB ASSOCIATES*
First Floor, 3 Stevenson Square, Manchester M1 1DN
Website: www.j-b-a.net
e-mail: info@j-b-a.net
Fax: 0161-237 1809   Tel: 0161-237 1808

JEFFREY & WHITE MANAGEMENT*
PM
9-15 Neal Street, London WC2H 9PW
Fax: 020-7240 0007   Tel: 020-7240 7000

J.G.M.
15 Lexham Mews, London W8 6JW
Website: www.jgmtalent.com
e-mail: mail@jgmtalent.com
Fax: 020-7376 2416   Tel: 020-7376 2414

JLM PERSONAL MANAGEMENT*
(Janet Lynn Malone, Sharon Henry)
259 Acton Lane, London W4 5DG
e-mail: jlm.pm@btconnect.com
Fax: 020-8747 8286   Tel: 020-8747 8223

JOHNSON WHITELEY Ltd
12 Argyll Mansions, Hammersmith Road, London W14 8QG
e-mail: jwltd@freeuk.com
Fax: 020-7348 0164   Tel: 020-7348 0163

JOHNSTON & MATHERS ASSOCIATES Ltd
PO Box 3167, Barnet EN5 2WA
Website: www.johnstonandmathers.com
e-mail: johnstonmathers@aol.com
Fax: 020-8449 2386   Tel: 020-8449 4698

Lindsay Duncan

Alan Rickman

FATIMAH NAMDAR

Photography

TEL 020 8341 1332

www.fatimahnamdar.com

JPA MANAGEMENT
30 Daws Hill Lane, High Wycombe, Bucks HP11 1PW
Website: www.jackiepalmer.co.uk
e-mail: jackie.palmer@btinternet.com
Fax: 01494 510479   Tel: 01494 520978

K ENTERTAINMENTS Ltd
140-142 St John Street, London EC1V 4UA
Website: www.k-entertainments.com
e-mail: info@k-entertainments.com
Fax: 07092 809947   Tel: 020-7253 9637

KAL MANAGEMENT
Write
95 Gloucester Road, Hampton, Middlesex TW12 2UW
Website: www.kaplan-kaye.co.uk
e-mail: kaplan222@aol.com
Fax: 020-8979 6487   Tel: 020-8783 0039

KANAL Roberta AGENCY
82 Constance Road, Twickenham, Middlesex TW2 7JA
e-mail: roberta@kanal.fsnet.co.uk
Tel/Fax: 020-8894 7952   Tel: 020-8894 2277

KARUSHI MANAGEMENT
5th Floor, 97-99 Dean Street, London W1D 3TE
Website: www.karushi.com
e-mail: lisa@karushi.com
Fax: 020-7484 5151   Tel: 020-7484 5040

KASTKIDZ
40 Sunnybank Road, Unsworth, Bury BL9 8HF
Website: www.kastkidz.com
e-mail: kastkidz@ntlworld.com
Mobile: 07905 646832   Tel/Fax: 0161-796 7073

KEARNEY Dee MANAGEMENT
Rolekall Casting
1 Dunwood Bridge, Bridge Street, Shaw OL2 8BG
e-mail: dee@rolekall.fsnet.co.uk   Tel/Fax: 01706 882442

KEDDIE STOTT ASSOCIATES
45 Maynards Quay
Garnet Street, Wapping, London E1W 3RY
Website: www.ks-ass.co.uk
e-mail: fiona@ks-ass.co.uk   Mobile: 07786 070543

KELLY'S KIND
(Dance Agency & Production Company)
Third Floor, 17-18 Margaret Street, London W1W 8RP
e-mail: office@kellyskind.co.uk   Tel: 0870 8701299

KENIS Steve & Co*
Royalty House
72-74 Dean Street, London W1D 3SG
e-mail: sk@sknco.com
Fax: 020-7287 6328   Tel: 020-7434 9055

Markham & Marsden
Personal Management for Actors & Directors
in the fields of Film, Television, Theatre, Radio & Voice Work

405 Strand London WC2R 0NE
t: 020 7836 4111   f: 020 7836 4222
e: info@markham-marsden.com w: markham-marsden.com

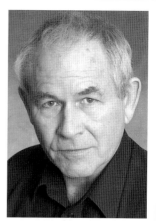

Emma   Somi Guha   Don McCorkindale

ANTHONY STRAEGER
PHOTOGRAPHER

MOBILE : 07963 838 633

E-MAIL: straeger@hotmail.com   WEBSITE : www.straegerphoto.co.uk

KENT Tim ASSOCIATES
(Formerly Moviestyle Artist Management)
Pinewood Studios
Room 131, Pinewood Road
Iver Heath, Bucks SLO 0NH
Website: www.tkassociates.co.uk
e-mail: mail@tkassociates.co.uk
Fax: 01753 785163   Tel: 01753 785162

KING Adrian ASSOCIATES
33 Marlborough Mansions
Cannon Hill
London NW6 1JS
e-mail: akassocs@aol.com
Fax: 020-7435 4100   Tel: 020-7435 4600

K M C AGENCIES Ltd
PO Box 122, 48 Great Ancoats Street
Manchester M4 5AB
e-mail: casting@kmcagencies.co.uk
Fax: 0161-237 9812   Tel: 0161-237 3009

11-15 Betterton Street, London WC2H 9BP
e-mail: london@kmcagencies.co.uk
Fax: 0870 4421780   Tel: 0870 4604868

KNIGHT AYTON MANAGEMENT
114 St Martin's Lane
London WC2N 4BE
Website: www.knightayton.co.uk
e-mail: info@knightayton.co.uk
Fax: 020-7836 8333   Tel: 020-7836 5333

THEATRICAL AGENTS

ACTORS

DANCERS

SINGERS

MODELS

PRESENTERS

CHOREOGRAPHERS

Success

www.successagency.co.uk

ROOM 236, LINEN HALL

162-168 REGENT STREET

LONDON W1B 5TB

TEL: 020 7734 3356

FAX: 020 7494 3787

e-mail: ee@successagency.co.uk

KNIGHT Ray CASTING
21A Lambolle Place, London NW3 4PG
Website: www.rayknight.co.uk
e-mail: casting@rayknight.co.uk
Fax: 020-7722 2322   Tel: 020-7722 1551

KREATE PRODUCTIONS
Unit 210, 30 Great Guildford Street, London SE1 0HS
e-mail: kreate@btconnect.com
Fax: 020-7401 3003   Tel: 020-7401 9007

KREMER ASSOCIATES
(See MARSH Billy DRAMA Ltd)

LAINE MANAGEMENT Ltd
131 Victoria Road, Salford M6 8LF
e-mail: info@lainemanagement.co.uk
Fax: 0161-787 7572   Tel: 0161-789 7775

LAINE Betty MANAGEMENT
The Studios, East Street, Epsom, Surrey KT17 1HH
e-mail: enquiries@betty-laine-management.co.uk
      Tel/Fax: 01372 721815

LAMONT CASTING AGENCY
94 Harington Road, Formby, Liverpool L37 1PZ
Website: www.lamontcasting.co.uk
e-mail: diane@lamontcasting.co.uk
Fax: 01704 872422   Tel: 01704 877024

LANGFORD ASSOCIATES Ltd
17 Westfields Avenue, Barnes, London SW13 0AT
e-mail: barry.langford@btconnect.com
Fax: 020-8878 7078   Tel: 020-8878 7148

L'BROOKE PERSONAL MANAGEMENT
The Bake House, 5C Blackheath Village, London SE3 9LA
e-mail: lbrooke@btopenworld.com   Tel: 020-8852 6994

LE BARS Tessa MANAGEMENT*
(Existing Clients Only)
54 Birchwood Road, Petts Wood, Kent BR5 1NZ
e-mail: tessa.lebars@ntlworld.com
Mobile: 07860 287255   Tel/Fax: 01689 837084

LEE Wendy MANAGEMENT
4th Floor Suite, 40 Langham Street, London W1W 7AS
e-mail: wendylee@wendyleemanagement.fsworld.co.uk
Fax: 020-7580 8700   Tel: 020-7580 4800

LEE'S PEOPLE
16 Manette Street, London W1D 4AR
Website: www.lees-people.co.uk
e-mail: lee@lees-people.co.uk
Fax: 020-7734 3033   Tel: 020-7734 5775

LEHRER Jane ASSOCIATES*
100A Chalk Farm Road, London NW1 8EH
Website: www.janelehrer.com
e-mail: janelehrer@aol.com
Fax: 020-7482 4899   Tel: 020-7482 4898

LEIGH MANAGEMENT
14 St David's Drive, Edgware, Middlesex HA8 6JH
e-mail: leighmanagement@aol.com   Tel/Fax: 020-8951 4449

LESLIE Sasha MANAGEMENT
(In Association with Allsorts Drama for Children)
34 Pember Road, London NW10 5LS
e-mail: sasha@allsortsdrama.com
Fax: 020-8969 3196   Tel: 020-8969 3249

LIFE IMAGE
4 Blenheim House, Victoria Docks, London E16 7TZ
Website: www.lifeimage.org
e-mail: actors@lifeimage.org   Mobile: 07950 733993

LIME ACTORS AGENCY & MANAGEMENT Ltd
1st Floor, Alexandra Buildings, 28 Queen Street
Lincoln Square, Manchester M2 5LF
e-mail: debbie.pine@limemanagement.co.uk
Fax: 0161-835 2550   Tel: 0161-835 3550

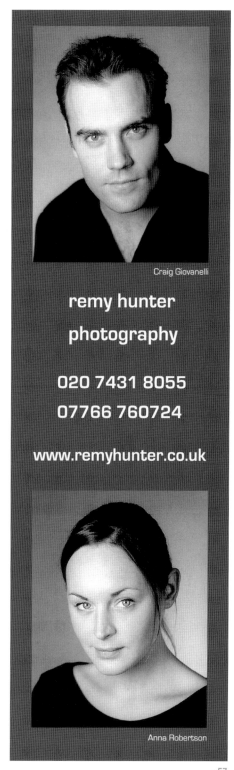

Acknowledgments: Sir Richard Branson, Miss Pinto and Rat, Mr Andy Hamilton, Diana Dors, Richard Burton (Time Square)
Sylvia Kristel ('Emmanuelle' by Just Jaeckin), Natalie Palys (Child star in The Madness of King George)

See opposite page for contact details -->
Will C has worked as principal stills photographer on over 30 major film productions.

Tokyo • New York • Amsterdam • Paris • London

THEATRICAL PHOTOGRAPHY
ACTOR/ACTRESS PORTRAITS
for all your publicity and Spotlight needs

on location or in our fully equipped studio in Kilburn 10 minutes from Marble Arch

with special thanks to
the following:

Richard Burton
Brigitte Bardot
Sophia Loren
Kojak
Peter Sellers
Judi Dench
Derek Jacobi
John Lennon
Virginia McKenna
Don Johnson
Grace Jones
Roger Moore
Bruce Willis
Demi Moore
Patrick Swayze
Sir Richard Branson
Diana Dors
David Bellamy
Michael Bolton
Eric Morcambe
Frank Muir
(Dancer) Miyako Yoshida
Soo Soo
Richard O'Sullivan
Marie Helvin
Sam Fox
and all the rest
too many to mention...

To photograph advanced and established actors and artists	**To photograph young actors, actresses and beginners**
	Special beginners pack
30 black and white prints 7x5	30 black and white prints OR
30 colour prints 7x5	colour photographs your choice
2 high quality 300 DPI *	30 prints of the above 7x5
- CD of all of the above	1 high quality 300 DPI * - CD
	containing all the photographs
£130	**£110**

*We can supply a top hair & make-up artist on request. We can also produce one or more high quality hand printed 10x8 prints of any of the above for £15 each suitable for taking to any repro house

Portraits and Personalities

Tel/Fax: 020 8438 0202   www.london-photographer.com

Messages: 020 8438 0303   www.theukphotographerexhibition.co.uk

Mobile: 07712 669 953   www.theukphotographer.com

Email: billy_snapper@hotmail.com   www.billysnapper.com

**photographer
to the stars**

Regency Agency

Principal : BEVERLEY COLES

0113-255 8980 25 CARR ROAD, CALVERLEY, LEEDS, LS28 5NE

Licensed under the Employment Agencies Act, 1973

ACTORS AND ACTRESSES
AVAILABLE FOR TELEVISION, FILMS, THEATRE, COMMERCIALS

LINKS MANAGEMENT
34-68 Colombo Street, London SE1 8DP
Website: www.links-management.co.uk
e-mail: agent@links-management.co.uk
Tel/Fax: 020-7928 0806

LINKSIDE AGENCY
21 Poplar Road, Leatherhead, Surrey KT22 8SF
e-mail: linkside_agency@yahoo.co.uk
Fax: 01372 801972   Tel: 01372 802374

LINTON MANAGEMENT
3 The Rock, Bury BL9 0JP
Fax: 0161-761 1999   Tel: 0161-761 2020

LITTLE ACORNS MODELLING AGENCY
London Hse, 271-273 King St, Hammersmith, London W6 9LZ
Fax: 020-8390 4935   Tel: 020-8563 0773

LONDON MUSICIANS Ltd
(Orchestral Contracting)
Cedar House, Vine Lane, Hillingdon, Middlesex UB10 0BX
e-mail: mail@londonmusicians.co.uk
Fax: 01895 252556   Tel: 01895 252555

LONGTIME MANAGEMENT
(Existing Clients only)
36 Lord Street, Radcliffe, Manchester M26 3BA
e-mail: longtime_mgt@btopenworld.com
Tel/Fax: 0161-724 6625

LOOKALIKES (Susan Scott)
26 College Crescent, London NW3 5LH
Website: www.lookalikes.info
e-mail: susan@lookalikes.info
Fax: 020-7722 8261   Tel: 020-7387 9245

LOOKS
12A Manor Court, Aylmer Road, London N2 0PJ
e-mail: lookslondonltd@btconnect.com
Fax: 020-8442 9190   Tel: 020-8341 4477

LOVETT Pat ASSOCIATES
(See P.L.A.)

LSW PROMOTIONS
181A Faunce House
Doddington Grove, Kennington, London SE17 3TB
Website: www.londonshakespeare.org.uk/promos
e-mail: lswpromos@hotmail.com   Tel/Fax: 020-7793 9755

LYNE Dennis AGENCY*
108 Leonard Street, London EC2A 4RH
e-mail: dennis@dennislyne.com
Fax: 020-7739 4101   Tel: 020-7739 6200

MACFARLANE CHARD ASSOCIATES Ltd*
33 Percy Street, London W1T 2DF
Website: www.macfarlane-chard.co.uk
e-mail: derick@macfarlane-chard.co.uk
Fax: 020-7636 7751   Tel: 020-7636 7750

MACNAUGHTON LORD 2000 Ltd
(Writers, Designers, Directors, Composers/Lyricists/Musical Directors)
19 Margravine Gardens, London W6 8RL
Website: www.ml2000.org.uk
e-mail: info@ml2000.org.uk
Fax: 020-8741 7443   Tel: 020-8741 0606

MAC-10 MANAGEMENT
Office 69, 2 Hellidon Close, Ardwick, Manchester M12 4AH
Website: www.mac-10.co.uk
e-mail: info@mac-10.co.uk
Fax: 0161-275 9610   Tel: 0161-275 9510

MADELEY Paul PUBLICITY
17 Valley Road, Arden Park
Bredbury, Stockport, Cheshire SK6 2EA
e-mail: madeleypublicity@talk21.com
Tel/Fax: 0161-430 5380

MAGNET MANAGEMENT
310 Greenhouse, The Custard Factory
Gibb Street, Digbeth, Birmingham B9 4AA
Website: www.magnetmanagement.co.uk
e-mail: enquiries@magnetmanagement.co.uk
Fax: 0121-224 7677   Tel: 0121-224 7676

MAGNOLIA MANAGEMENT*
136 Hicks Avenue, Greenford, Middlesex UB6 8HB
e-mail: jaffreymag@aol.com
Fax: 020-8575 0369   Tel: 020-8578 2899

MAIDA VALE SINGERS
(Singers for Recordings, Theatre, Film, Radio & TV)
7B Lanhill Road
Maida Vale, London W9 2BP
Website: www.maidavalesingers.co.uk
e-mail: maidavalesingers@cdtenor.freeserve.co.uk
Mobile: 07889 153145   Tel/Fax: 020-7266 1358

MAITLAND MANAGEMENT
PM (Anne Skates)
Brook House, 8 Rythe Road
Claygate, Surrey KT10 9DF
Website: www.maitlandmusic.com
e-mail: maitmus@aol.com
Fax: 01372 466229   Tel: 01372 466228

Eva Pope

Lee Williams

Paris Jefferson
P H O T O G R A P H E R

020 7252 0328
07876 586601

studio/location

MANAGEMENT 2000
23 Alexandra Road, Mold, Flintshire CH7 1HJ
Website: www.management-2000.co.uk
e-mail: jackey@management-2000.co.uk
Tel/Fax: 01352 771231

MANIC MANAGEMENT
112 Skyline Plaza, 80 Commercial Road, London E1 1NZ
Website: www.themanicgroup.com
e-mail: info@themanicgroup.com
Fax: 020-7481 1898   Tel: 020-7059 0498

MANS Johnny PRODUCTIONS Ltd
PO Box 196, Hoddesdon, Herts EN10 7WG
e-mail: real@legend.co.uk
Fax: 01992 470516   Tel: 01992 470907

MANSON Andrew PERSONAL MANAGEMENT Ltd*
288 Munster Road, London SW6 6BQ
Website: www.andrewmanson.com
e-mail: post@andrewmanson.com
Fax: 020-7381 8874   Tel: 020-7386 9158

MARCUS & McCRIMMON MANAGEMENT
3 Crouch Hall Road, London N8 8HT
Website: www.marcusandmccrimmon.com
e-mail: info@marcusandmccrimmon.com
Fax: 020-8347 0006   Tel: 020-8347 0007

MARKHAM & FROGGATT Ltd*
PM Write
4 Windmill Street, London W1T 2HZ
e-mail: admin@markhamfroggatt.co.uk
Fax: 020-7637 5233   Tel: 020-7636 4412

MARKHAM & MARSDEN*
(John Markham, David Marsden)
405 Strand, London WC2R 0NE
e-mail: info@markham-marsden.com
Fax: 020-7836 4222   Tel: 020-7836 4111

MARSH Billy ASSOCIATES Ltd*
76A Grove End Road, St Johns Wood, London NW8 9ND
e-mail: talent@billymarsh.co.uk
Fax: 020-7449 6933   Tel: 020-7449 6930

MARSH Billy DRAMA Ltd*
(Actors & Actresses)
11 Henrietta Street, Covent Garden, London WC2E 8PY
e-mail: info@billymarshdrama.co.uk
Fax: 020-7379 7272   Tel: 020-7379 4800

MARSH Sandra MANAGEMENT
(Film Technicians)
c/o Casarotto Marsh Ltd
National House, 60-66 Wardour Street, London W1V 4ND
e-mail: casarottomarsh@casarotto.uk.com
Fax: 020-7287 5644   Tel: 020-7287 4450

MARSHALL Ronnie AGENCY
S F M PM TV Write or Phone
66 Ollerton Road
London N11 2LA   Tel/Fax: 020-8368 4958

MARSHALL Scott PARTNERS Ltd*
Suite 9, 54 Poland Street, London W1F 7NJ
e-mail: smpm@scottmarshall.co.uk
Fax: 020-7432 7241   Tel: 020-7432 7240

MARTIN Carol PERSONAL MANAGEMENT
19 Highgate West Hill, London N6 6NP
Fax: 020-8340 4868   Tel: 020-8348 0847

MAY John
Garden Flat, 6 Westbourne Park Villas, London W2 5EA
e-mail: john@johnmayagent.freeserve.co.uk
Fax: 020-7229 9828   Tel: 020-7221 7917

GEORGE PASSMORE

PHOTOGRAPHY

■ student rates available ■ fulham based studio ■ instant service

m: 07775 658 515

E-mail: georgepassmore@mac.com

MAYER Cassie Ltd*
5 Old Garden House, The Lanterns
Bridge Lane, London SW11 3AD
e-mail: info@cassiemayerltd.co.uk
Fax: 020-7350 0890   Tel: 020-7350 0880

MBA (Formerly John Mahoney Management)
Concorde House
18 Margaret Street, Brighton BN2 1TS
Website: www.mbagency.fsnet.co.uk
e-mail: mba.concorde@virgin.net
Fax: 01273 685971   Tel: 01273 685970

McCORQUODALE Anna PERSONAL MANAGEMENT
43 St Maur Road, London SW6 4DR
e-mail: anna@amcmanagement.co.uk
Fax: 020-7371 9048   Tel: 020-7731 1721

McKINNEY MACARTNEY MANAGEMENT Ltd
(Technicians)
The Barley Mow Centre
10 Barley Mow Passage, London W4 4PH
Website: www.mckinneymacartney.com
e-mail: mail@mckinneymacartney.com
Fax: 020-8995 2414   Tel: 020-8995 4747

McLEAN Bill PERSONAL MANAGEMENT Ltd
PM Write
23B Deodar Road
London SW15 2NP   Tel: 020-8789 8191

McLEAN-WILLIAMS MANAGEMENT
212 Piccadilly, London W1J 9HG
e-mail: alex@mclean-williams.com
Fax: 020-7917 2805   Tel: 020-7917 2806

aaron ashton

simon holland roberts

simon watts

R a f e   A l l e n
PHOTOGRAPHER
07980 840 757

McLEOD HOLDEN ENTERPRISES Ltd
Priory House
1133 Hessle High Road, Hull HU4 6SB
Website: www.mcleod-holden.com
e-mail: peter.mcleod@mcleod-holden.com
Fax: 01482 353635   Tel: 01482 565444

McREDDIE Ken Ltd*
PM
21 Barrett Street, London W1U 1BD
Fax: 020-7408 0886   Tel: 020-7499 7448

MEDIA LEGAL
PM F TV Voice-overs (Existing Clients only)
West End House, 83 Clarendon Road
Sevenoaks, Kent TN13 1ET   Tel: 01732 460592

MEDIA MODELLING & CASTING AGENCY
53 Astley Avenue
Dover, Kent CT16 2PP
Website: www.mediamc.co.uk
e-mail: info@mediamc.co.uk
Mobile: 07812 245512   Tel: 01304 204715

MILNER David MANAGEMENT
22 Violet Road, London E17 8HZ
e-mail: milner.agent@btopenworld.com
Tel/Fax: 020-8503 2808   Tel/Fax: 020-8923 8118

MIME THE GAP
(Mime & Physical Theatre Specialists)
2A Redcross Way
London SE1 9HR
Website: www.mimethegap.com   Mobile: 07970 685982

MINT MANAGEMENT
8A Barry Road
London SE22 0HU
e-mail: lisi@mintman.co.uk
Fax: 020-8693 2976   Tel: 020-8637 0351

MIRTH CONTROL MANAGEMENT Ltd
62 Station Road
Petersfield, Hants GU32 3ES
Website: www.mirthcontrol.org.uk
e-mail: chaz@mirthcontrol.org.uk   Mobile: 07766 692322

M.K.A.
11 Russell Kerr Close, Chiswick, London W4 3HF
e-mail: mkaforactors@tiscali.co.uk
Fax: 020-8994 2992   Tel: 020-8994 1619

ML 2000 Ltd
(See MACNAUGHTON LORD 2000 Ltd)

MONDI ASSOCIATES Ltd
30 Cooper House
2 Michael Road, London SW6 2AD
e-mail: mondi.sw@virgin.net
Fax: 020-7351 7628   Mobile: 07817 133349

MONTAGU ASSOCIATES
Ground Floor, 13 Hanley Road, London N4 3DU
Fax: 020-7263 3993   Tel: 020-7263 3883

MOORE Jakki
23 Willowside Park
Haverigg, Cumbria LA18 4PT
e-mail: jakki@jakkimoore.com
Mobile: 07967 612784   Tel/Fax: 01229 776389

MORGAN & GOODMAN
Mezzanine
Quadrant House
80-82 Regent Street, London W1B 5RP
e-mail: mg1@btinternet.com
Fax: 020-7494 3446   Tel: 020-7437 1383

MORRIS Andrew MANAGEMENT
Penthouse Offices, 60 Reachview Close
Camden Town, London NW1 0TY
e-mail: morrisagent@yahoo.co.uk
Fax: 020-7482 0451   Tel: 020-7485 9748

MOSS Jae ENTERPRISES
Riverside House, Feltham Avenue
Hampton Court, Surrey KT8 9BJ
Website: www.jaemossenterprises.co.uk
e-mail: enquiries@jaemossenterprises.co.uk
Fax: 020-8979 9631   Tel: 020-8979 3459

MOUNTVIEW MANAGEMENT
Ralph Richardson Memorial Studios
Kingfisher Place, Clarendon Road, London N22 6XF
e-mail: theagency@mountview.ac.uk
Fax: 020-8829 1050   Tel: 020-8889 8231

MPC ENTERTAINMENT
Write or Phone
MPC House 15-16 Maple Mews
Maida Vale, London NW6 5UZ
Website: www.mpce.com
e-mail: mpc@mpce.com
Fax: 020-7624 4220   Tel: 020-7624 1184

MR.MANAGEMENT
29 Belton Road
Brighton, East Sussex BN2 3RE
e-mail: mr.management@ntlworld.com
Fax: 020-8579 6360   Tel: 01273 232381

Lucy Smith ~ photographer

Debra Teng

Craig Urbani

Paula Tappenden

Mac Elsey

Emma Tugman

Telephone
020 8521 1347

www.thatlucy.co.uk

MUGSHOTS AGENCY
50 Frith Street, London W1D 4SQ
Fax: 020-7437 0308   Tel: 020-7292 0555

MURPHY Elaine ASSOCIATES
Suite 1, 50 High Street
London E11 2RJ
e-mail: emurphy@freeuk.com
Fax: 020-8989 1400   Tel: 020-8989 4122

MUSIC INTERNATIONAL
M
13 Ardilaun Road, London N5 2QR
e-mail: music@musicint.co.uk
Fax: 020-7226 9792   Tel: 020-7359 5183

MW MANAGEMENT
11 Old School Court
Drapers Road, London N17 6PZ
e-mail: the@gents.co.uk
Fax: 020-8376 2789   Tel: 020-8376 2025

MYERS MANAGEMENT
63 Fairfields Crescent
London NW9 0PR   Tel/Fax: 020-8204 8941

NARROW ROAD COMPANY The*
22 Poland Street, London W1F 8QH
e-mail: agents@narrowroad.co.uk
Fax: 020-7439 1237   Tel: 020-7434 0406

182 Brighton Road, Coulsdon, Surrey CR5 2NF
e-mail: coulsdon@narrowroad.co.uk
Fax: 020-8763 2558   Tel: 020-8763 9895

4th Floor, Grampian House
144 Deansgate, Manchester M3 3EE
e-mail: manchester@narrowroad.co.uk
Tel/Fax: 0161-833 1605

NCI MANAGEMENT Ltd
51 Queen Anne Street, London W1G 9HS
Fax: 020-7487 4258   Tel: 020-7224 3960

NCM ASSOCIATES (Nicola Clarkson Associates)
12 Kings Gate, London SW9 6JX
e-mail: nikki.clarkson1@btopenworld.com
Fax: 020-7793 7053   Tel: 020-7582 7343

NCM MANAGEMENT
Unit 4, 121 Long Acre, Covent Garden, London, WC2E 9PA
e-mail: clairencmmanagement@postmaster.co.uk
Fax: 020-7836 3347   Mobile: 07980 807062

NEVS AGENCY
Regal House, 198 King's Road, London SW3 5XP
Website: www.nevs.co.uk
e-mail: getamodel@nevs.co.uk
Fax: 020-7352 6068   Tel: 020-7352 4886

NEW CASEY AGENCY
The Annexe, 129 Northwood Way
Middlesex HA6 1RF   Tel: 01923 823182

NEW FACES Ltd
2nd Floor, The Linen Hall
162-168 Regent Street, London W1B 5TB
Website: www.newfacestalent.co.uk
e-mail: val@newfacestalent.co.uk
Fax: 020-7287 5481   Tel: 020-7439 6900

NICHOLSON Jackie ASSOCIATES
PM
Suite 44, 2nd Floor
Morley House, 320 Regent Street, London W1
Fax: 020-7580 4489   Tel: 020-7580 4422

N M MANAGEMENT
16 St Alfege Passage, Greenwich, London SE10 9JS
e-mail: nmmanagement@hotmail.com
Tel: 020-7581 0947   Tel: 020-8853 4337

NOEL CASTING
(Specializing in Character Actors & Ethnic & Asian Actors)
Suite 501, International House
223 Regent Street, London W1B 2QD
e-mail: noelcasting@yahoo.com
Fax: 020-7544 1090   Tel: 020-7544 1010

NORTH OF WATFORD ACTORS AGENCY
Co-operative
Bridge Mill, Hebden Bridge, West Yorks HX7 8EX
Website: www.northofwatford.com
e-mail: info@northofwatford.com
Fax: 01422 846503   Tel: 01422 845361

NORTH ONE MANAGEMENT•
HG08 Aberdeen Studios
Highbury Grove, London N5 2EA
Website: www.northone.co.uk
e-mail: actors@northone.co.uk
Fax: 020-7359 9449   Tel: 020-7359 9666

NORTHERN FILM & DRAMA
21 Low Street, South Milford, North Yorkshire LS25 5AR
Website: www.northernfilmanddrama.com
e-mail: alyson@connew.com   Tel/Fax: 01977 681949

NORTHERN LIGHTS MANAGEMENT Ltd
PM
Dean Clough Mills, Halifax, West Yorks HX3 5AX
e-mail: info@nlmanagement.co.uk
Fax: 01422 330101   Tel: 01422 382203

NORTHERN PROFESSIONALS
(Casting, Technicians, Action Safety, Boat & Diving
Equipment Hire)
21 Cresswell Avenue, North Shields, Tyne & Wear NE29 9BQ
e-mail: bill.gerard@northpro83.freeserve.co.uk
Fax: 0191-296 3243   Tel: 0191-257 8635

NSM
(Natasha Stevenson Management)
85 Shorrolds Road, Fulham, London SW6 7TU
e-mail: nsm@netcomuk.co.uk
Fax: 020-7385 3014   Tel: 020-7386 5333

NUMBER ONE CASTING & MODEL MANAGEMENT Ltd
408F The Big Peg, 120 Vyse Street
The Jewellery Quarter, Birmingham B18 6NF
Website: www.numberonemodelagency.co.uk
e-mail: info@numberonemodelagency.co.uk
Tel: 0121-233 2433

NUTOPIA-CHANG PERSONAL MANAGEMENT
Number 8, 132 Charing Cross Road, London WC2H 0LA
Website: www.nutopia.co.uk
Fax: 029-2070 9440 Mobile: 07801 493133

NYLAND MANAGEMENT Ltd
20 School Lane, Heaton Chapel, Stockport SK4 5DG
e-mail: nylandmgmt@freenet.co.uk
Fax: 0161-432 5406 Tel: 0161-442 2224

OFF THE KERB PRODUCTIONS
22 Thornhill Crescent, London N1 1BJ
Website: www.offthekerb.co.uk
e-mail: info@offthekerb.co.uk
Fax: 020-7700 4646 Tel: 020-7700 4477

3rd Floor, Hammer House
113-117 Wardour Street, London W1F 0UN
e-mail: offthekerb@aol.com
Fax: 020-7437 0647 Tel: 020-7437 0607

ONE MAKE UP/ONE PHOTOGRAPHIC Ltd
4th Floor, Poland Street, London W1F 7ND
Website: www.onemakeup.com
Fax: 020-7287 2313 Tel: 020-7287 2311

OPEN DOORS MANAGEMENT Ltd
Les Palmes
No 6, 2 Rathmore Road
Torquay, Devon TQ2 6NY
e-mail: barrygout@tiscali.co.uk
Mobile: 07899 965420 Tel: 01803 200558

OPERA & CONCERT ARTISTS
M Opera
75 Aberdare Gardens
London NW6 3AN
Fax: 020-7372 3537 Tel: 020-7328 3097

ORDINARY PEOPLE Ltd
(Actors and Wardrobe/Stylists/Make-up Artists)
8 Camden Road, London NW1 9DP
Website: www.ordinarypeople.co.uk
e-mail: info@ordinarypeople.co.uk
Fax: 020-7267 5677 Tel: 020-7267 7007

ORIENTAL CASTING AGENCY Ltd (Peggy Sirr)
Afro/Asian Artists Write or Phone
1 Wyatt Park Road
Streatham Hill, London SW2 3TN
Website: www.orientalcasting.com
e-mail: peggy.sirr@btconnect.com
Fax: 020-8674 9303 Tel: 020-8671 8538

OTTO PERSONAL MANAGEMENT Ltd•
PM Co-operative
The Printer's Loft
111 Arundel Lane, Sheffield S1 4RF
Website: www.ottopm.freeuk.com
e-mail: admin@ottopm.co.uk
Fax: 0114-275 0550 Tel: 0114-275 2592

PAN ARTISTS AGENCY Ltd
Cornerways
34 Woodhouse Lane
Sale, Cheshire M33 4JX
e-mail: bookings@panartists.freeserve.co.uk
Fax: 0161-962 6571 Tel: 0161-969 7419

PANTO PEOPLE
3 Rushden House, Tatlow Road
Glenfield, Leicester LE3 8ND Tel/Fax: 0116-287 9594

PARAMOUNT INTERNATIONAL MANAGEMENT
Talbot House, 204-226 Imperial Drive
Harrow, Middlesex HA2 7HH
Website: www.ukcomedy.com
e-mail: mail@ukcomedy.com
Fax: 020-8868 6475 Tel: 020-8429 3179

PARK PERSONAL MANAGEMENT Ltd•
PM Co-operative
Unit C3, 62 Beechwood Road, London E8 3DY
e-mail: actors@park-management.co.uk Tel: 020-7923 1498

PARK STREET CASTING
2nd Floor, 46 Park Street, Bristol BS1 5JG
Website: www.parkstreetcasting.co.uk
e-mail: parkcasting@yahoo.co.uk Tel/Fax: 0117-929 2900

PARR & BOND
The Tom Thumb Theatre
Eastern Esplanade
Cliftonville, Kent CT9 2LB Tel: 01843 221791

PAUL Yvonne MANAGEMENT
Elysium Gate, Unit 15
126-128 New Kings Road
London SW6 4LZ
e-mail: yvonne@yvonnepaul.co.uk
Fax: 020-7736 2221 Tel: 020-7384 0300

P B J MANAGEMENT Ltd*
(Comedy)
7 Soho Street
London W1D 3DQ
Website: www.pbjmgt.co.uk
e-mail: general@pbjmgt.co.uk
Fax: 020-7287 1191   Tel: 020-7287 1112

PC THEATRICAL & MODEL AGENCY
(Large Database of Twins)
10 Strathmore Gardens
Edgware, Middlesex HA8 5HJ
Website: www.twinagency.com
e-mail: twinagy@aol.com
Fax: 020-8933 3418   Tel: 020-8381 2229

PELHAM ASSOCIATES*
PM (Peter Cleall)
The Media Centre, 9-12 Middle Street, Brighton BN1 1AL
Website: www.pelhamassociates.co.uk
e-mail: petercleall@pelhamassociates.co.uk
Fax: 01273 202492   Tel: 01273 323010

PEMBERTON ASSOCIATES Ltd*
193 Wardour Street, London W1F 8ZF
e-mail: general@pembertonassociates.com
Fax: 020-7734 2522   Tel: 020-7734 4144

Suite 35-36 Barton Arcade
Deansgate, Manchester M3 2BH
Fax: 0161-835 3319   Tel: 0161-832 1661

PEPPERPOT PROMOTIONS
(Bands)
Suite 20B, 20-22 Orde Hall Street, London WC1N 3JW
e-mail: chris@pepperpot.co.uk
Fax: 01255 473107　　　　　　　Tel: 020-7405 9108

PERFECT MANAGEMENT
2nd Floor, Berkeley Square House
Berkeley Square
London W1J 6BD
Website: www.perfectmanagement.co.uk
e-mail: info@perfectmanagement.co.uk
Fax: 020-7887 1941　　　　　　　Tel: 020-7887 1940

PERFORMANCE ACTORS AGENCY•
PM Co-operative
137 Goswell Road, London EC1V 7ET
Website: www.p-a-a.co.uk
e-mail: performance@p-a-a.co.uk
Fax: 020-7251 3974　　　　　　　Tel: 020-7251 5716

PERFORMERS DIRECTORY
(Actors, Dancers, Models and Extras)
PO Box 29942, London SW6 1FL
Website: www.performersdirectory.co.uk
e-mail: admin@performersdirectory.com
　　　　　　　　　　　　　　　Tel: 020-7610 6699

PERFORMING ARTS*
(Directors/Designers/Choreographers/Lighting Designers)
6 Windmill Street
London W1T 2JB
Website: www.performing-arts.co.uk
e-mail: info@performing-arts.co.uk
Fax: 020-7631 4631　　　　　　　Tel: 020-7255 1362

PERRY George
(See PROFILE MANAGEMENT)

PERSONAL APPEARANCES
20 North Mount, 1147-1161 High Road, Whetstone N20 0PH
e-mail: pers.appearances@talk21.com
　　　　　　　　　　　　Tel/Fax: 020-8343 7748

PFD*
PM
Drury House, 34-43 Russell Street, London WC2B 5HA
Website: www.pfd.co.uk
e-mail: postmaster@pfd.co.uk
Fax: 020-7836 9544　　　　　　　Tel: 020-7344 1010

PHD ARTISTS
24 Ovett Close
Upper Norwood, London SE19 3RX
Website: www.phdartists.com
e-mail: office@phdartists.com　　Tel/Fax: 020-8771 4274

PHILLIPS Frances*
Millennium Studios, Elstree Way
Borehamwood
Herts WD6 1SF
e-mail: derekphillips@talk21.com
Fax: 020-8236 1367　　　　　　　Tel: 020-8236 1366

PHPM
(Philippa Howell Personal Management)
184 Bradway Road
Sheffield S17 4QX
e-mail: philippa@phpm.co.uk　　Tel/Fax: 0114-235 3663

PHYSICALITY Ltd*
(Physical Skills Specialists)
Unit 8, Hatherley Mews, Walthamstow, London E17 4QP
Website: www.physicality.co.uk
e-mail: info@physicality.co.uk
Fax: 020-8521 3744　　　　　　　Tel: 020-8521 5522

PHYSICK Hilda
PM Write
78 Temple Sheen Road
London SW14 7RR
Fax: 020-8876 5561　　　　　　　Tel: 020-8876 0073

PICCADILLY MANAGEMENT
PM
23 New Mount Street
Manchester M4 4DE
e-mail: piccadilly.management@virgin.net
Fax: 0161-953 4001　　　　　　　Tel: 0161-953 4057

PICOT Nic ENTERTAINMENT
25 Highfield
Carpenders Park WD19 5DY
Website: www.nicpicot.co.uk
e-mail: nic@nicpicot.co.uk
Fax: 020-8421 2700　　　　　　　Tel: 020-8421 2500

PINEAPPLE AGENCY
159-161 Balls Pond Road
London N1 4BG
Fax: 020-7241 3006　　　　　　　Tel: 020-7241 6601

P.L.A.*
(LOVETT Pat ASSOCIATES)
5 Union Street, Edinburgh EH1 3LT
e-mail: edinburgh@pla-uk.com
Fax: 0131-478 7070　　　　　　　Tel: 0131-478 7878

43 Chandos Place, London WC2N 4HS
Website: www.pla-uk.com
e-mail: london@pla-uk.com
Fax: 020-7379 9111　　　　　　　Tel: 020-7379 8111

Icon Actors Management
Tel: 0161 273 3344 Fax: 0161 273 4567
Tanzaro House, Ardwick Green North, Manchester. M12 6FZ.
info@iconactors.net www.iconactors.net

PLATER Janet MANAGEMENT Ltd
D Floor
Milburn House
Dean Street
Newcastle upon Tyne NE1 1LF
e-mail: magpie@tynebridge.demon.co.uk
Fax: 0191-221 2491   Tel: 0191-221 2490

PLUNKET GREENE ASSOCIATES
(In conjunction with James Sharkey Assocs Ltd)
(Existing Clients Only)
PO Box 8365
London W14 0GL
Fax: 020-7603 2221   Tel: 020-7603 2227

POLLYANNA MANAGEMENT Ltd
PO Box 30661
London E1W 3GG
Website: www.eada.demon.co.uk/pollyanna
e-mail: pollyanna-mgmt@btinternet.com
Fax: 020-7480 6761   Tel: 020-7702 1937

POOLE Gordon AGENCY Ltd
The Limes
Brockley
Bristol BS48 3BB
Website: www.gordonpoole.com
e-mail: agents@gordonpoole.com
Fax: 01275 462252   Tel: 01275 463222

POPLAR MANAGEMENT
22 Knightswood
Woking
Surrey GU21 3PY
e-mail: karenfoley@fsmail.net   Tel/Fax: 01483 828056

POWER MODEL MANAGEMENT CASTING AGENCY
Capitol House
2-4 Heigham Street
Norwich NR2 4TE
Website: www.powermodelmanagement.co.uk
e-mail: powermodelmanagement@btinternet.com
Fax: 01603 621101   Tel: 01603 621100

DUDLEY SUTTON

CORAL BEED

Natasha Greenberg

020 7642 5468
07932 618111

THE TOMMY TUCKER AGENCY
THE BEST DANCERS & CHOREOGRAPHERS
Telephone 020 7370 3911 Fax 020 7370 4784 e-mail: tommytuckeragency@yahoo.co.uk

POWER PROMOTIONS
PO Box 61
Liverpool L13 0EF
Website: www.powerpromotions.co.uk
e-mail: tom@powerpromotions.co.uk
Fax: 0870 7060202   Tel: 0151-230 0070

PPM ARTISTS MANAGEMENT
73 Leonard Street
Shoreditch, London EC2A 4QS
Website: www.ppmlondon.com
e-mail: mail@ppmlondon.com   Tel/Fax: 020-7739 7552

PREGNANT PAUSE AGENCY
(Pregnant Models, Dancers, Actresses)
11 Matham Road
East Molesey KT8 0SX
Website: www.pregnantpause.co.uk
e-mail: sandy@pregnantpause.co.uk
Fax: 020-8783 0337   Tel: 020-8979 8874

PRICE GARDNER MANAGEMENT
85 Shorrolds Road
London SW6 7TU
e-mail: info@pricegardner.com
Fax: 020-7381 3288   Tel: 020-7610 2111

PRICHARD Peter at INTERNATIONAL ARTISTES Ltd
4th Floor, Holborn Hall
193-197 High Holborn
London WC1V 7BD
Website: www.intart.co.uk
e-mail: (name)@intart.co.uk
Fax: 020-7404 9865   Tel: 020-7025 0600

PRINCIPAL ARTISTES
PM Write
4 Paddington Street
Marylebone
London W1U 5QE
Fax: 020-7486 4668   Tel: 020-7224 3414

PRODUCTIONS & PROMOTIONS Ltd
2 Sharpcroft
Hemel Hempstead
Herts HP2 5YY
Website: www.prodmotions.com
e-mail: stuartw@prodmotions.com   Tel/Fax: 01442 236821

PROFILE MANAGEMENT
(George Perry)
The Old Chapel
9 West End, Ashwell
Herts SG7 5PH
e-mail: georgeperryprofile@hotmail.com
Fax: 01462 742967   Tel: 01462 743843

PROSPECTS
The Post Office Theatre, The Malvern
Bevington Road, London W10 5TN
e-mail: hprospects@aol.com   Tel/Fax: 020-8861 5779

PROTOCOL
2/7 Harbour Yard
Chelsea Harbour, London SW10 0XD
e-mail: stars@protocoltalent.com
Fax: 020-7349 1533   Tel: 020-7349 8877

PVA MANAGEMENT Ltd
Hallow Park, Worcestershire WR2 6PG
e-mail: clients@pva.co.uk
Fax: 01905 641842   Tel: 01905 640663

QUICK Nina ASSOCIATES
(See TAYLOR Brian ASSOCIATES)

RAGE MODELS
(Young Adults Fashion)
Tigris House, 256 Edgware Road, London W2 1DS
Website: www.ugly.org
e-mail: info@ugly.org
Fax: 020-7402 0507   Tel: 020-7262 0515

RAINBOW REPRESENTATION
45 Nightingale Lane, Crouch End, London N8 7RA
e-mail: rainbowrp@onetel.net.uk   Tel/Fax: 020-8341 6241

RAMA MANAGEMENT
Huntingdon House
278-290 Huntingdon Street, Nottingham NG1 3LY
Website: www.rama-mgt.com
e-mail: admin@rama-mgt.com
Fax: 0115-948 3696   Tel: 0115-952 4333

RANDALL RICHARDSON
PO Box 35197, London SE5 7YB
Website: www.randallrichardson.co.uk
e-mail: mail@randallrichardson.co.uk
Fax: 020-7701 3872   Tel: 020-7701 3914

RATTLEBAG ACTORS AGENCY Ltd●
Co-operative PM
Everyman Theatre Annexe
13-15 Hope Street, Liverpool L1 9BH
Website: www.rattlebag.co.uk
e-mail: actors@rattlebag.co.uk
Fax: 0151-709 0773   Tel: 0151-708 7273

RAVENSCOURT MANAGEMENT
Tandy House
30-40 Dalling Road, London W6 0JB
e-mail: info@ravenscourt.net
Fax: 020-8741 1786   Tel: 020-8741 0707

RAWHIDE COMEDY
Central Hall, Roscoe Gardens
28 Mount Pleasant, Liverpool L3 5SA
Website: www.rawhidecomedy.com
e-mail: info@rawhidecomedy.com
Fax: 0870 7871241   Tel: 0870 7871240

RAZZAMATAZZ MANAGEMENT
Mulberry Cottage, Park Farm
Haxted Road, Lingfield RH7 6DE
e-mail: jillmcgrogan@btconnect.com Tel/Fax: 01342 835359

RBM
PM (Comedy)
3rd Floor
18 Broadwick Street
London W1F 8HS
Website: www.rbmcomedy.com
e-mail: info@rbmcomedy.com
Fax: 020-7287 5020   Tel: 020-7287 5010

RDF MANAGEMENT
The Gloucester Building
Kensington Village
Avonmore Road, London W14 8RF
e-mail: debi.allen@rdfmanagement.com
Fax: 020-7013 4101   Tel: 020-7013 4103

REACTORS AGENCY
Co-operative
1 Eden Quay, Dublin 1, Eire
Website: www.reactors.ie
e-mail: reactors@eircom.net
Fax: 00 353 1 8783182   Tel: 00 353 1 8786833

RE.ANIMATOR MANAGEMENT
Mulberry House
583 Fulham Road
London SW6 5UA
Website: www.reanimator.co.uk
e-mail: management@reanimator.co.uk
Fax: 020-7471 1840   Tel: 020-7471 1740

REDDIN Joan
PM Write
Hazel Cottage
Frogg's Island, Wheeler End Common
Bucks HP14 3NL   Tel: 01494 882729

REDROOFS ASSOCIATES
Room 160/161
The Admin Building
Iver Heath, Bucks SLO 0NH
e-mail: agency@redroofs.co.uk
Fax: 01753 785443   Tel: 01753 785444

REDWAY John ASSOCIATES (in association with AIM)
Nederlander House, 7 Great Russell Sreet
London WC1B 3NH
Website: www.aimagents.com
e-mail: info@aimagents.com
Fax: 020-7637 8666   Tel: 020-7637 1700

REGAN RIMMER MANAGEMENT
(Leigh-Ann Regan, Debbie Rimmer)
36-38 Glasshouse Street
London W1B 5DL
e-mail: thegirls@regan-rimmer.co.uk
Fax: 020-7287 9006   Tel: 020-7287 9005

Empire House, 1st Floor
Mount Stuart Square
Cardiff Bay, Cardiff CF10 6QZ
e-mail: reganrimmer@hotmail.com
Fax: 029-2046 2266   Tel: 029-2047 0077

REGENCY AGENCY
F TV
25 Carr Road, Calverley
Leeds LS28 5NE   Tel: 0113-255 8980

REPRESENTATION JOYCE EDWARDS
(See EDWARDS REPRESENTATION Joyce)

REYNOLDS Sandra MODEL & CASTING AGENTS
Md F TV
62 Bell Street, London NW1 6SP
Website: www.sandrareynolds.co.uk
e-mail: tessa@sandrareynolds.co.uk
Fax: 020-7387 5848   Tel: 020-7387 5858

35 St Georges Street
Norwich NR3 1DA
e-mail: info@sandrareynolds.co.uk
Fax: 01603 219825   Tel: 01603 623842

RHINO MANAGEMENT
Oak Porch House
5 Western Road, Nazeing, Essex EN9 2QN
Website: www.rhino-management.co.uk
e-mail: info@rhino-management.co.uk
Mobile: 07941 453043   Tel/Fax: 01992 893259

RICHARDS Lisa
46 Upper Baggot Street, Dublin 4, Eire
e-mail: info@lisarichards.ie
Fax: 00 353 1 6603545   Tel: 00 353 1 6603534

RICHARDS Stella MANAGEMENT
(Existing Clients only)
42 Hazlebury Road, London SW6 2ND
Fax: 020-7731 5082   Tel: 020-7736 7786

RIDGEWAY MANAGEMENT
Fairley House
Andrews Lane, Cheshunt, Herts EN7 6LB
e-mail: info@ridgewaystudios.co.uk
Fax: 01992 633844   Tel: 01992 633775

ROGUE ARTISTES MANAGEMENT Ltd
196 Broadhurst Gardens
West Hampstead, London NW6 3AY
Website: www.rogueuk.com
e-mail: actors@roguemgt.com
Mobile: 07909 695492   Tel: 020-8451 3314

ROGUES & VAGABONDS MANAGEMENT Ltd•
PM Co-operative
The Print House, 18 Ashwin Street
London E8 3DL
e-mail: rogues@vagabondsmanagement.com
Fax: 020-7249 8564   Tel: 020-7254 8130

ROLE MODELS
12 Cressy Road, London NW3 2LY
Website: www.hiredhandsmodels.com
e-mail: models@hiredhands.freeserve.co.uk
Fax: 020-7267 1030   Tel: 020-7284 4337

ROSEBERY MANAGEMENT Ltd•
PM
Diorama Arts Centre, 34 Osnaburgh Street
London NW1 3ND
e-mail: roseberymgt@aol.com
Fax: 020-7692 3065   Tel: 020-7813 1026

ROSEMAN ORGANISATION The
51 Queen Anne Street, London W1G 9HS
Website: www.theromanorganisation.co.uk
e-mail: info@theromanorganisation.co.uk
Fax: 020-7486 4600   Tel: 020-7486 4500

ROSS BROWN ASSOCIATES
PM
Rosedale House, Rosedale Road
Richmond, Surrey TW9 2SZ
e-mail: rossbrownassoc@freeuk.com
Fax: 020-8398 3925   Tel: 020-8398 3984

ROSS Frances - CFA MANAGEMENT
22 Church Street, Briston
Melton Constable, Norfolk NR24 2LE
e-mail: frances@cfamanagement.fsnet.co.uk
                                  Tel/Fax: 01263 860650

DarkSide

A company offering high quality work with personal attention at very competitive prices.

FREE COPY NEG & CAPTION FOR 50 PRINTS OR MORE

GENUINE PHOTOGRAPHIC REPROS

PRINTS FROM NEGATIVES, ORIGINALS AND DIGITAL MEDIA

GLOSS OR MATT FINISH IN A RANGE OF SIZES

RE-ORDERS BY TELEPHONE

POSTAL AND COURIER SERVICES AVAILABLE

ALL MAJOR CREDIT CARDS ACCEPTED

DISCOUNTS FOR SCHOOLS & COLLEGES

020 7250 1200

DarkSide Photographic Ltd.
4 Helmet Row, London EC1V 3QJ
email: info@darksidephoto.co.uk
www.darksidephoto.co.uk

Nyland management

20 School Lane, Heaton Chapel,
Stockport SK4 5DG
Tel: 0161 442 2224
Fax: 0161 432 5406
e-mail: nylandmgmt@freenet.co.uk

ROSSMORE PERSONAL MANAGEMENT
70-76 Bell Street
London NW1 6SP
e-mail: agents@rossmoremanagement.com
Fax: 020-7258 0124   Tel: 020-7258 1953

ROWE ASSOCIATES
33 Percy Street, London W1T 1DE
Website: www.growe.co.uk
e-mail: agents@growe.co.uk   Tel/Fax: 01992 308519

ROYCE MANAGEMENT
34A Sinclair Road, London W14 0NH
Fax: 020-7371 4985   Tel: 020-7602 4992

RSM - RICHARD STARNOWSKI MANAGEMENT
(FBI) 4th Floor
20-24 Kirby Street, London EC1N 8TS
Website: www.fullybooked-inc.com
e-mail: info@rsm.uk.net
Fax: 020-7242 8125   Tel: 020-7242 5542

RUBICON MANAGEMENT
27 Inderwick Road, Crouch End, London N8 9LB
e-mail: jack@rubiconmgt.fsnet.co.uk
                                     Tel/Fax: 020-8374 1836

RUDEYE AGENCY
PO Box 38743, London E10 5WN
Website: www.rudeye.com
e-mail: info@rudeye.com   Tel/Fax: 020-8556 7139

RWM MANAGEMENT
The Aberdeen Centre
22-24 Highbury Grove
London N5 2EA
e-mail: rwm.mario-kate@virgin.net
Fax: 020-7226 3371   Tel: 020-7226 3311

SANDERS Loesje*
(Designers, Directors, Choreographers, Lighting Designers)
Pound Square
1 North Hill, Woodbridge, Suffolk IP12 1HH
Website: www.loesjesanders.com
e-mail: loesje@loesjesanders.org.uk
Fax: 01394 388734   Tel: 01394 385260

SARABAND ASSOCIATES
(Sara Randall, Bryn Newton)
265 Liverpool Road, London N1 1LX
e-mail: brynnewton@btconnect.com
Fax: 020-7609 2370   Tel: 020-7609 5313

SBS Ltd (The Casting Information Service)
Suite 1, 16 Sidmouth Road
London NW2 5JX
e-mail: casting@sbsltd.demon.co.uk
Fax: 020-8459 7442   Tel: 020-8459 2781

SCA MANAGEMENT
TV F S M Write
77 Oxford Street, London W1D 2ES
e-mail: agency@sca-management.co.uk
Fax: 020-7659 2116   Tel: 020-7659 2027

SCHER Anna THEATRE The
PM
AST Management
70-72 Barnsbury Road, London N1 0ES
e-mail: agent@astm.co.uk
Fax: 020-7833 9467   Tel: 020-7278 2101

SCHNABL Peter
The Barn House, Cutwell, Tetbury
Gloucestershire GL8 8EB
Fax: 01666 502998   Tel: 01666 502133

SCOTT Tim
284 Gray's Inn Road, London WC1X 8EB
e-mail: timscott@btinternet.com
Fax: 020-7278 9175   Tel: 020-7833 5733

SCOTT-PAUL YOUNG ENTERTAINMENTS Ltd
S.P.Y. Promotions & Productions
Northern Lights House, 110 Blandford Road North
Langley, Nr Windsor, Berks SL3 7TA
e-mail: sp.young@blueyonder.co.uk   Tel/Fax: 01753 693250

SCREENLITE AGENCY
Shepperton Film Studios
Shepperton, Middlesex TW17 0QD
e-mail: screenlite@dial.pipex.com
Fax: 01932 592507   Tel: 01932 562611 Ext 2272

SCRIMGEOUR Donald ARTISTS AGENT
(Dance)
49 Springcroft Avenue, London N2 9JH
e-mail: vwest@dircon.co.uk
Fax: 020-8883 9751   Tel: 020-8444 6248

SEARS MANAGEMENT Ltd
2 Gumping Road, Orpington, Kent BR5 1RX
e-mail: lindasears@btconnect.com
Fax: 01689 862120   Tel: 01689 861859

SECOND SKIN AGENCY
50 Elmwood Road, Chiswick, London W4 3DZ
e-mail: jenny@secondskinagency.com
                          Tel/Fax: 020-8994 9864

SEDGWICK Dawn MANAGEMENT
3 Goodwins Court
Covent Garden, London WC2N 4LL
Fax: 020-7240 0415   Tel: 020-7240 0404

S.F.X.
(Sports Management Company)
35-36 Grosvenor Street, London W1K 4QX
Website: www.sfxsports.co.uk
Fax: 020-7529 4347   Tel: 020-7529 4300

SHALIT GLOBAL MANAGEMENT
7 Moor Street, Soho, London W1D 5NB
e-mail: info@shalitglobal.com
Fax: 020-7851 9156   Tel: 020-7851 9155

SHAPER Susan MANAGEMENT
Queens House
1 Leicester Place
London WC2H 7BP
e-mail: shapermg@dircon.co.uk
Fax: 020-7534 3317   Tel: 020-7534 3316

SHAW Vincent ASSOCIATES Ltd
51 Byron Road
London E17 4SN
Website: www.vincentshaw.com
e-mail: info@vincentshaw.com
Fax: 020-8521 1588   Tel: 020-8509 2211

SHEDDEN Malcolm MANAGEMENT
1 Charlotte Street
London W1T 1RD
Fax: 020-7636 1657   Tel: 020-7636 1876

SHEPHERD MANAGEMENT Ltd*
13 Radnor Walk
London SW3 4BP
e-mail: info@shepherdmanagement.co.uk
Fax: 020-7352 2277   Tel: 020-7352 2200

SHOW TEAM PRODUCTIONS The
(Dancers & Choreographers)
18 Windmill Street, Brighton, Sussex BN2 0GN
Website: www.theshowteam.co.uk
e-mail: info@theshowteam.co.uk   Tel: 01273 671010

SHOWBUSINESS ENTERTAINMENT &
TELEVISION CASTING AGENCY
304 College Street
Long Eaton, Nottingham NG10 4GT
Fax: 0115-946 1831   Tel: 0115-973 5445

SHOWSTOPPERS!
(Celebrity Booking Services, Promotions & Entertainments)
42 Foxglove Close, Witham, Essex CM8 2XW
Website: www.showstoppers-group.com
e-mail: mail@showstoppers-group.com
Fax: 01376 510340   Tel: 01376 518486

SILVESTER MANAGEMENT
24 Lake View, Edgware HA8 7RU
e-mail: silvestermgmt@freeuk.com
Fax: 020-8958 7711   Tel: 020-8958 5555

SIMONES INTERNATIONALE
(Artistes Management)
PO Box 15154, London W5 3FW   Tel/Fax: 020-8861 3900

SIMPSON FOX ASSOCIATES Ltd*
(Set, Costume and Lighting Designers, Directors,
Choreographers)
52 Shaftesbury Avenue, London W1D 6LP
e-mail: info@simpson-fox.com
Fax: 020-7494 2887   Tel: 020-7434 9167

SINGER Sandra ASSOCIATES
21 Cotswold Road
Westcliff-on-Sea, Essex SS0 8AA
Website: www.sandrasinger.com
e-mail: sandrasingeruk@aol.com
Fax: 01702 339393   Tel: 01702 331616

SINGERS INC/DANCERS INC Ltd
MWB Business Exchange
2 Gayton Road, Harrow, Middlesex HA5 2XU
Website: www.singersinc.co.uk
e-mail: enquiries@singersinc.co.uk
Fax: 020-8901 4001   Tel: 020-8901 4010

SIRR Peggy
(See ORIENTAL CASTING AGENCY Ltd)

SJ MANAGEMENT Ltd
5 Denmark Street, London WC2H 8LP
e-mail: sj@susanjames.demon.co.uk
Fax: 020-7836 5724   Tel: 020-7836 5723

Actors for work in films, television, theatre & commercials.

1st Floor
Alexandra Buildings
Lincoln Square
Manchester M2 5LF
t: 0161 834 0990 f: 0161 834 0014
e: liz@nmsmanagement.co.uk

SMILE TALENT
Hope Cottage
London Road, Newport, Essex CB11 3PN
e-mail: talent.smile@stepc.fsnet.co.uk
Fax: 01799 541658　　　　　　　　　Tel: 01799 541113

SONGTIME/CHANDLER'S MANAGEMENT
Shepperton Studios
Studio 64
Shepperton
Middlesex TW17 0QD
Website: www.songtimetheatrearts.co.uk
e-mail: info@songtime.co.uk
Fax: 01932 593335　　　　　　　　　Tel: 01932 593336

SOPHIE'S PEOPLE
(Dancers & Choreographers)
26 Reporton Road
London SW6 7JR
Website: www.sophiespeople.com
e-mail: sophies.people@btinternet.com
Fax: 0870 7876447　　　　　　　　　Tel: 0870 7876446

SOUL MANAGEMENT
88-90 Gray's Inn Road, London WC1X 8AA
Website: www.soulmanagement.co.uk
e-mail: info@soulmanagement.co.uk
Fax: 020-7404 0498　　　　　　　　　Tel: 020-7404 0499

SOUTH WEST MANAGEMENT & CASTING CO Ltd
The Courtyard, Whitchurch
Ross-on-Wye HR9 6DA
Website: www.southwestcasting.co.uk
e-mail: agent@southwestcasting.co.uk
Fax: 01600 891099　　　　　　　　　Tel: 01600 892005

SPARE PARTS
(Body Parts Specialists)
26-28 Hammersmith Grove, London W6 7BA
Fax: 020-8834 1144　　　　　　　　　Tel: 020-8834 1609

SPEAK Ltd
(No Unsolicited Mail)
59 Lionel Road North, Brentford, Middlesex TW8 9QZ
Website: www.speak-voices.com
e-mail: info@speak.ltd.uk
Fax: 020-8578 0333　　　　　　　　　Tel: 020-8578 0666

SPEAKERS CORNER
(Speakers, Presenters, Facilitation and
Cabaret for the Corporate Market)
Tigana House, Catlins Lane, Pinner
Middlesex HA5 2HG
Website: www.speakerscorner-uk.com
e-mail: info@speakerscorner-uk.com
Fax: 020-8868 4409　　　　　　　　　Tel: 020-8866 8967

SPIRE CASTING
PO Box 372, Chesterfield S41 0XW
e-mail: mail@spirecasting.com　　　　Tel: 01246 224798

SPLATS AGENCY
(Now called COVENT GARDEN MANAGEMENT)
5 Denmark Street, London WC2H 8LP
e-mail: agents@coventgardenmanagement.com
Fax: 020-7240 8409　　　　　　　　　Tel: 020-7240 8400

SPLITTING IMAGES LOOKALIKES AGENCY
25 Clissold Court, Greenway Close, London N4 2EZ
Website: www.splitting-images.com
e-mail: info@splitting-images.com
Fax: 020-8809 6103　　　　　　　　　Tel: 020-8809 2327

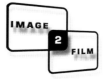

david **fernandes**
photographer

Studio in London & Brighton
T 01273 549967 M 07958 272 333
www.image2film.com
Actors • Models • Presenters • Showreels

SPORTABILITY Ltd
(Sporting Personalities)
Unit 2, 23 Green Lane, Dronfield, Derbyshire S18 2LL
Fax: 01246 290520   Tel: 01246 292010

SPORTS WORKSHOP PROMOTIONS Ltd
(Sports Models)
PO Box 878, Crystal Palace
National Sports Centre, London SE19 2BH
e-mail: info@sportspromotions.co.uk
Fax: 020-8776 7772   Tel: 020-8659 4561

SPORTSMODELS.COM
1A Calton Avenue, Dulwich Village, London SE21 7DE
Website: www.sportsmodels.com
e-mail: info@sportsmodels.com
Fax: 020-8299 8600   Tel: 020-8299 8800

SPYKER Paul MANAGEMENT
7 Garrick Street, Covent Garden, London WC2E 9AR
e-mail: info@pspy.com
Fax: 020-7379 8282   Tel: 020-7379 8181

ST. JAMES'S MANAGEMENT
PM Write SAE
19 Lodge Close, Stoke D'Abernon, Cobham, Surrey KT11 2SG
Fax: 01932 860444   Tel: 01932 860666

STACEY Barrie PROMOTIONS
Apartment 8, 132 Charing Cross Road, London WC2H 0LA
Website: www.barriestacey.com
e-mail: hopkinstacey@aol.com
Fax: 020-7836 2949   Tel: 020-7836 4128

STAFFORD Helen MANAGEMENT
14 Park Avenue, Bush Hill Park, Enfield, Middlesex EN1 2HP
e-mail: helen.stafford@blueyonder.co.uk
Fax: 020-8482 0371   Tel: 020-8360 6329

STAGE CENTRE MANAGEMENT Ltd•
PM Co-operative
41 North Road, London N7 9DP
e-mail: stagecentre@aol.com
Fax: 020-7609 0213   Tel: 020-7607 0872

STARLINGS THEATRICAL AGENCY
45 Viola Close, South Ockendon, Essex RM15 6JF
Website: www.webspawner.com/users/starlings
e-mail: julieecarter@blueyonder.co.uk
                          Mobile: 07941 653463

STEVENSON Natasha MANAGEMENT
(See NSM)

STIVEN CHRISTIE MANAGEMENT
(Incorporating The Actors Agency of Edinburgh)
1 Glen Street, Tollcross, Edinburgh EH3 9JD
Fax: 0131-228 4645   Tel: 0131-228 4040

STONE Annette ASSOCIATES*
(See ALTARAS Jonathan ASSOCIATES Ltd/JAA)

STONE Ian ASSOCIATES
4 Masons Avenue, Croydon, Surrey CR0 9XS
Fax: 020-8680 9912   Tel: 020-8667 1677

STONE Richard PARTNERSHIP The*
2 Henrietta Street, London WC2E 8PS
e-mail: all@richstonepart.co.uk
Fax: 020-7497 0869   Tel: 020-7497 0849

STORM ARTISTS MANAGEMENT
1st Floor, 5 Jubilee Place, London SW3 3TD
Website: www.stormartists.com
e-mail: info@stormartists.co.uk
Fax: 020-7376 5145   Tel: 020-7437 4313

STRALLEN MANAGEMENT
14 Hemstal Road, West Hampstead, London NW6 2AN
e-mail: casting@thecastingoffice.co.uk
Fax: 020-7328 9805   Tel: 020-7692 3154

STREETJAM
(Dancers, Choreographers, Singers, Stylists,
Make-up Artists)
95 Blenheim Gardens
London SW2 5DA
Website: www.streetjamagency.com
e-mail: stjamltd@aol.com   Tel: 020-8671 4618

SUCCESS
Room 236, 2nd Floor
Linen Hall, 162-168 Regent Street, London W1B 5TB
Website: www.successagency.co.uk
e-mail: ee@successagency.co.uk
Fax: 020-7494 3787   Tel: 020-7734 3356

SUMMERS Mark MANAGEMENT
9 Hansard Mews, Kensington, London W14 8BJ
Website: www.marksummers.com
e-mail: mark@marksummers.com
Fax: 0870 4435623   Tel: 0870 4435621

SUMMERTON Michael MANAGEMENT Ltd
PM M C
Mimosa House, Mimosa Street, London SW6 4DS
Fax: 020-7731 0103   Tel: 020-7731 6969

T.A. MANAGEMENT
18 Kingsdale Gardens, Notting Hill, London W11 4TZ
e-mail: tamanagement@hotmail.com
                          Tel/Fax: 020-7603 3471

TAKE FLIGHT MANAGEMENT
e-mail: morwenna@takeflightmanagement.co.uk
                          Tel/Fax: 020-8835 8147

jamie hughes photography

Michael Douglas

Thora Birch

Martin Scorsese

Dennis Quaid

Alicia Silverstone

Vin Diesel

Sean Bean

Fearne Cotton

Lemar

Spike Lee

Stella Rimmington

Mikey Green

07850-122977

singers - dancers - session vocalists
corporate entertainment
choreographers - directors
make-up artists - stylists
bespoke shows
radio broadway - m the songbook of motown

singers inc.   **+44 (0) 20 8901 4010**   **dancers inc.**
www.singersinc.co.uk   enquiries@singersinc.co.uk   www.dancersinc.co.uk

TALENT ARTISTS Ltd*
59 Sydner Road, London N16 7UF
e-mail: talent.artists@btconnect.com
Fax: 020-7923 2009   Tel: 020-7923 1119

TALENT PARTNERSHIP Ltd The*
Riverside Studios, Crisp Rd, Hammersmith, London W6 9RL
e-mail: info@thetalentpartnership.co.uk
Fax: 020-8237 1041   Tel: 020-8237 1040

TALKBACK MANAGEMENT*
20-21 Newman Street, London W1T 1PG
Fax: 020-7861 8061   Tel: 020-7861 8060

TAYLOR Brian ASSOCIATES*
50 Pembroke Road, Kensington, London W8 6NX
e-mail: briantaylor@nqassoc.freeserve.co.uk
Fax: 020-7602 6301   Tel: 020-7602 6141

TCA
(The Commercial Agency)
7 Cornwall Crescent, London W11 1PH
e-mail: mail@thecommercialagency.co.uk
Fax: 020-7792 9802   Tel: 020-7243 9844

TCG ARTIST MANAGEMENT
(Rachel Cranmer-Gordon, Kristin Tarry)
Fourth Floor, 6 Langley Street, London WC2H 9JA
Website: www.spotlightagent.info/tcgam
e-mail: info@tcgam.co.uk
Fax: 020-7240 3606   Tel: 020-7240 3600

TELFORD Paul MANAGEMENT
PM Write
3 Greek Street, London W1D 4DA
e-mail: paul@telford-mgt.com
Fax: 020-7434 1200   Tel: 020-7434 1100

T.G.R. DIRECT
88 Recreation Road, Poole, Dorset BH12 2AL
e-mail: tatianaroc.tgrdirect@virgin.net
Fax: 01202 721802   Tel: 01202 721222

THEATRE EXPRESS PERFORMING ARTS AGENCY
Write
Spindle Cottage, Allens Farm, Digby Fen
Billnghay, Lincoln LN4 4DT

THOMAS & BENDA ASSOCIATES Ltd
Top Floor, 15-16 Ivor Place
London NW1 6HS   Tel/Fax: 020-7723 5509

THOMPSON Jim
Herricks, School Lane
Arundel, West Sussex BN18 9DR
e-mail: jim@jthompson42.freeserve.co.uk
Fax: 01903 885887   Tel: 01903 885757

THOMPSON Peggy OFFICE The
PM
1st & 2nd Floor Offices
296 Sandycombe Road
Kew, Richmond, Surrey TW9 3NG
Fax: 020-8332 1127   Tel: 020-8332 1003

THORNTON AGENCY
(Specialist Agency for Small People)
72 Purley Downs Road, Croydon CR2 0RB
Website: www.dwarfs4hire.com
e-mail: thorntons.leslie@tinyworld.co.uk
Fax: 020-7371 7466   Tel/Fax: 020-8660 5588

THRESH Melody MANAGEMENT ASSOCIATES Ltd (MTM)
27 Ardwick Green North
Ardwick, Manchester M12 6FZ
e-mail: melodythreshmtm@aol.com
Fax: 0161-273 5455   Tel: 0161-273 5445

TILDSLEY Janice ASSOCIATES
8 Addison Road, London E17 9LT
e-mail: info@janicetildsleyassociates.co.uk
Fax: 020-8521 1174   Tel: 020-8521 1888

TIMID ASSOCIATES
44 Summerlee Avenue
Finchley, London N2 9QP
Website: www.timidassociates.com
e-mail: info@timidassociates.com Tel/Fax: 020-8883 1277

TINKER Victoria MANAGEMENT
(Technical, Non-Acting)
Birchenbridge House
Brighton Road, Mannings Heath
Horsham, West Sussex RH13 6HY   Tel/Fax: 01403 210653

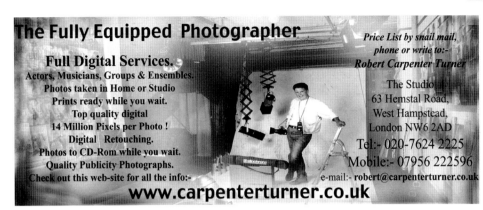
TONER CASTING Ltd
Unit E6 Brunswick Business Centre
Brunswick Dock
Brunswick Way, Liverpool L3 4BD
Website: www.tonercasting.com
e-mail: tonercastings@btconnect.com
Fax: 0151-707 8414   Tel: 0151-708 6400

TOP LOOK ALIKES/REEL TO REAL PRODUCTIONS
Website: www.toplookalikes.co.uk
e-mail: toplookalikes@hotmail.com Tel: 020-8362 1484

TOP MODELS Ltd
57 Holland Park, London W11 3RS
Fax: 020-7243 6046   Tel: 020-7243 6042

TOTS-TWENTIES
Suite 3, Ground Floor, Clements Court
Clements Lane, Ilford, Essex IG1 2QY
Website: www.tots-twenties.co.uk
e-mail: sara@tots-twenties.co.uk
Fax: 020-8553 1880   Tel: 020-8478 1848

TRAIN HOUSE The
27 Prospect Road
Long Ditton, Surrey KT6 5PY
e-mail: agents@trainhouse.demon.co.uk
Fax: 020-8873 2782   Tel: 020-8873 7932

TRENDS AGENCY & MANAGEMENT Ltd
54 Lisson Street
London NW1 5DF
Website: www.trendsgroup.co.uk
e-mail: info@trendsgroup.co.uk
Fax: 020-7258 3591   Tel: 020-7723 8001

TROLAN Gary MANAGEMENT
PM Write
30 Burrard Road, London NW6 1DB
e-mail: garytrolanmgmt@aol.com
Tel/Fax: 020-7794 4429   Tel: 020-7431 4367

TUCKER Tommy AGENCY
Suite 66, 235 Earl's Court Road, London SW5 9FE
e-mail: TTTommytucker@aol.com
Fax: 020-7370 4784   Tel: 020-7370 3911

TV MANAGEMENTS
Brink House, Avon Castle, Ringwood, Hants BH24 2BL
Fax: 01425 480123   Tel: 01425 475544

TWINS
(See PC THEATRICAL & MODEL AGENCY)

TWINS & TRIPLETS
(Identical Babies, Children, Teenagers & Adults for
Film/Television)
15 Holmhurst Road, Upper Belvedere DA17 6HW
e-mail: twinsontv@aol.com
Fax: 01322 447250   Tel: 01322 440184

TWIST & FLIC SPORTS AGENCY
(Sports Model Agent)
1A Calton Avenue, Dulwich Village, London SE21 7ED
Website: www.sportsmodels.com
e-mail: info@sportsmodels.com
Fax: 020-8299 8600   Tel: 020-8299 8800

TWO'S COMPANY
244 Upland Road, London SE22 0DN
e-mail: 2scompany@britishlibrary.net
Fax: 020-8299 3714   Tel: 020-8299 4593

UGLY MODELS
Tigris House, 256 Edgware Road, London W2 1DS
Website: www.ugly.org
e-mail: info@ugly.org
Fax: 020-7402 0507   Tel: 020-7402 5564

UNIQUE MANAGEMENT GROUP
Beaumont House
Kensington Village, Avonmore Road, London W14 8TS
Website: www.unique-management.co.uk
e-mail: celebrities@uniquegroup.co.uk
Fax: 020-7605 1101   Tel: 020-7605 1100

UNITED COLOURS OF LONDON Ltd
4th Floor (FBI), 20-24 Kirby Street, London EC1N 8TS
Fax: 020-7242 8125   Tel: 020-7242 5542

UNITED PRODUCTIONS
(Choreographers, Dancers, Musicians, Stylists)
6 Shaftsbury Mews, Clapham, London SW4 9BP
Website: www.united-productions.co.uk
e-mail: info@united-productions.co.uk
                          Tel/Fax: 020-7720 9624

UPBEAT MANAGEMENT
(Theatre Touring & Events - No Actors)
PO Box 63, Wallington, Surrey SM6 9YP
Website: www.upbeat.co.uk
e-mail: info@upbeat.co.uk
Fax: 020-8669 6752   Tel: 020-8773 1223

URBAN TALENT
1st Floor, Alexandra Buildings
Lincoln Square, Manchester M2 5LF
e-mail: liz@nmsmanagement.co.uk
Fax: 0161-834 0014   Tel: 0161-834 0990

VACCA Roxane MANAGEMENT*
73 Beak Street, London W1F 9SR
Fax: 020-7734 8086   Tel: 020-7734 8085

VALLÉ ACADEMY THEATRICAL AGENCY The
The Valle Academy Studios
Wilton House, Delamare Road, Cheshunt, Herts EN8 9SG
Website: www.valleacademy.co.uk
e-mail: agency@valleacademy.co.uk
Fax: 01992 622868   Tel: 01992 622861

VAMP ARTISTS & MUSICIANS
Ealing House, 33 Hanger Lane, London W5 3HJ
e-mail: info@vampevents.com   Tel: 020-8997 3355

VIBES UK Ltd
(Choreographers, Dancers, Models & Creative Directors)
68A Rochester Place, London NW1 9JX
Website: www.vibesuk.com
e-mail: info@vibesuk.com
Fax: 020-7485 2225   Tel: 020-7485 2221

VICIOUS MANAGEMENT
79 Wardour Street, Soho, London W1D 6QB
Website: www.viciousmanagement.com
e-mail: info@viciousmanagement.com
                          Mobile: 07967 102769

VIDAL-HALL Clare*
(Directors, Designers, Choreographers, Lighting Designers,
Composers)
28 Perrers Road, London W6 0EZ
e-mail: clarevidalhall@email.com
Fax: 020-8741 9459   Tel: 020-8741 7647

VINE Michael ASSOCIATES
(Light Entertainment)
29 Mount View Road, London N4 4SS
e-mail: mpvine@aol.com
Fax: 020-8348 3277   Tel: 020-8348 5899

VISABLE PEOPLE
(Artists with Disabilities only)
PO Box 80, Droitwich WR9 0ZE
Website: www.visablepeople.com
e-mail: louise@visablepeople.com   Tel/Fax: 01905 776631

W6 AGENCY The
Riverside Studios
Crisp Road
Hammersmith, London W6 9RL
e-mail: info@thew6agency.co.uk
Fax: 020-8237 1041   Tel: 020-8237 1046

WALMSLEY Peter ASSOCIATES
(Freelance Locum. No Representation, Do Not Write)
37A Crimsworth Road, London SW8 4RJ
e-mail: associates@peterwalmsley.net
Mobile: 07778 347312   Tel: 020-7787 6419

WARING & McKENNA*
22 Grafton Street, London W1S 4EX
e-mail: dj@waringandmckenna.com
Fax: 020-7409 7932   Tel: 020-7491 2666

WAVE ENTERTAINMENT
The Thatched House, Cheselbourne, Dorchester DT2 7NT
Website: www.wave-entertainment.co.uk
e-mail: paul@wave-entertainment.co.uk   Tel: 0870 7606263

WEBSTER MANAGEMENT
75 Hewison Street, London E3 2HZ
e-mail: danniwebster@onetel.net
Mobile: 07708 154250   Tel/Fax: 020-8980 5299

WEEKS Kimberley MANAGEMENT
116 Earlham Grove, Forest Gate
London E7 9AS   Tel: 020-8519 4473

WELCH Janet PERSONAL MANAGEMENT
11 Sunbury Court Island, Lower Hampton Road
Sunbury-on-Thames, Middlesex TW16 5PP
e-mail: info@janetwelchpm.co.uk
Fax: 01932 766191   Tel: 01932 766190

WESSON Penny*
(Directors)
26 King Henry's Road, London NW3 3RP
e-mail: penny@pennywesson.demon.co.uk
Fax: 020-7483 2890   Tel: 020-7722 6607

WEST CENTRAL MANAGEMENT
Co-operative
Room 4, East Block, Panther House
38 Mount Pleasant, London WC1X 0AN
Website: www.westcentralmanagement.co.uk
e-mail: mail@westcentralmanagement.co.uk
                    Tel/Fax: 020-7833 8134

WEST END MANAGEMENT
(Maureen Cairns)
188 St Vincent Street, Glasgow G2 5SP
Website: www.west-endmgt.com
e-mail: info@west-endmgt.com
Fax: 0141-226 8983   Tel: 0141-226 8941

WHATEVER ARTISTS MANAGEMENT Ltd
1 York Street, London W1U 6PA
Website: www.wamshow.biz
e-mail: wam@agents-uk.com
Fax: 020-7487 3311   Tel: 020-7487 3111

WHITEHALL ARTISTS
10 Lower Common South, London SW15 1BP
e-mail: mwhitehall@msn.com
Fax: 020-8788 2340   Tel: 020-8785 3737

WILD THEATRICAL MANAGEMENT
PO Box 222, Rainham, Essex RM13 7WQ
e-mail: wildtm@lineone.net   Tel: 01708 505543

WILDE Vivien Ltd*
2A, 59-61 Brewer Street, London W1F 9UN
e-mail: info@vwilde.co.uk
Fax: 020-7439 1941   Tel: 020-7439 1940

WILKINSON David ASSOCIATES*
(Existing Clients Only)
115 Hazlebury Road, London SW6 2LX
Fax: 020-7371 5161   Tel: 020-7371 5188

WILLOW PERSONAL MANAGEMENT
(Specialist Agency for Short Actors)
151 Main Street, Yaxley, Peterborough, Cambs PE7 3LD
e-mail: email@willowmanagement.co.uk
                    Tel/Fax: 01733 240392

WILLS Newton MANAGEMENT
The Studio
29 Springvale Avenue, Brentford, Middlesex TW8 9QT
e-mail: newtoncttg@aol.com
Fax: 00 33 241 823108   Tel: 07989 398381

WILSON-GOUGH MANAGEMENT
2nd Floor, 22 Great Windmill Street, London W1D 7LD
e-mail: info@wilson-gough.com
Fax: 020-7439 4173   Tel: 020-7439 4171

WINSLETT Dave ASSOCIATES
6 Kenwood Ridge, Kenley, Surrey CR8 5JW
Website: www.davewinslett.com
e-mail: info@davewinslett.com
Fax: 020-8668 9216   Tel: 020-8668 0531

WIS CELTIC MANAGEMENT
(Welsh, Irish, Scottish)
86 Elphinstone Road, Walthamstow
London E17 5EX   Tel: 020-8523 4234

WISE BUDDAH TALENT
74 Great Titchfield Street, London W1W 7QP
Website: www.wisebuddah.com
Fax: 020-7307 1602   Tel: 020-7307 1617

WYMAN Edward AGENCY
F TV (English & Welsh Language)
67 Llanon Road, Llanishen, Cardiff CF14 5AH
Website: www.wymancasting.fsnet.co.uk
e-mail: edward@wymancasting.fsnet.co.uk
Fax: 029-2075 2444   Tel: 029-2075 2351

X-FACTOR MANAGEMENT
6 Fulham Park Studios
Fulham Park Road, London SW6 4LW
e-mail: info@xfactorltd.com
Fax: 0870 2519560   Tel: 0870 2519540

XL MANAGEMENT
Edmund House
Rugby Road, Leamington Spa, Warwickshire CV32 6EL
Website: www.xlmanagement.co.uk
e-mail: office@xlmanagement.co.uk
Fax: 01926 811420   Tel: 01926 810449

YELLOW BALLOON PRODUCTIONS Ltd
Freshwater House, Outdowns, Effingham, Surrey KT24 5QR
e-mail: yellowbal@aol.com
Fax: 01483 281502   Tel: 01483 281500

ZWICKLER Marlene & ASSOCIATES
2 Belgrave Place
Edinburgh EH4 3AN
Website: www.mza-artists.com   Tel/Fax: 0131-343 3030

A & J MANAGEMENT
242A The Ridgeway, Botany Bay, Enfield EN2 8AP
Website: www.ajmanagement.co.uk
e-mail: ajmanagement@bigfoot.com
Fax: 020-8342 0842   Tel: 020-8342 0542

ABACUS AGENCY
The Studio
4 Bailey Road, Westcott, Dorking, Surrey RH4 3QS
Website: www.abacusagency.co.uk
e-mail: admin@abacusagency.co.uk
Fax: 01306 877813   Tel: 01306 877144

ACADEMY MANAGEMENT
123 East Park Farm Drive
Charvil, Reading, Berks RG10 9UQ   Tel: 0118-934 9940

ACT ONE AGENCY
31 Dobbin Hill, Sheffield S11 7JA
Website: www.actonedrama.co.uk
e-mail: casting@actonedrama.co.uk
Fax: 07971 112153   Tel: 0114-266 7209

ACT OUT AGENCY
22 Greek Street, Stockport, Cheshire SK3 8AB
e-mail: ab22actout@aol.com   Tel/Fax: 0161-429 7413

ACTIVATE DRAMA SCHOOL
(Drama School & Agency)
Priestman Cottage
Sea View Road, Sunderland SR2 7UP
e-mail: activate_agcy@hotmail.com
Fax: 0191-551 2051   Tel: 0191-565 2345

ADAMS Juliet CHILD MODEL & TALENT AGENCY
19 Gwynne House, Challice Way, London SW2 3RB
Website: www.julietadams.co.uk
e-mail: models@julietadams.co.uk
Fax: 020-8671 9314   Tel: 020-8671 7673

AGENCY K-BIS
Clermont Hall
Cumberland Road, Brighton BN1 6SL
e-mail: k-bis@zoom.co.uk   Tel/Fax: 01273 564366

ALEXANDER Suzanne MANAGEMENT
170 Town Lane
Higher Bebington, Wirral CH63 8LG
e-mail: suzyalex@hotmail.com   Tel/Fax: 0151-608 9655

ALLSORTS DRAMA FOR CHILDREN
(In Association with Sasha Leslie Management)
34 Pember Road, London NW10 5LS
e-mail: sasha@allsortsdrama.com
Fax: 020-8969 3196   Tel: 020-8969 3249

ALPHABET KIDZ
189 Southampton Way
London SE5 7EJ
Website: www.alphabetkidz.co.uk
e-mail: lisa@alphabetkidz.co.uk   Tel/Fax: 020-7252 4343

ANGEL FACES AGENCY Ltd
Studio 223, 186 St Albans Road, Watford WD25 4AS
Website: www.angelfacesagency.co.uk
e-mail: contactus.angelfaces@virgin.net
    Tel: 020-8428 9625

ANNA'S MANAGEMENT
(Formerly of ALADDIN'S CAVE)
25 Tintagel Drive, Stanmore, Middlesex HA7 4SR
e-mail: annasmanage@aol.com
Fax: 020-8238 2899   Tel: 020-8958 7636

ARAENA/COLLECTIVE
10 Bramshaw Gardens
South Oxhey, Herts WD1 6XP   Tel/Fax: 020-8428 0037

ARTS ACADEMY The (T.A.A.)
15 Lexham Mews, London W8 6JW
Fax: 020-7376 2416   Tel: 020-7376 0267

ASHCROFT ACADEMY OF DRAMATIC ART
Malcolm Primary School
Malcolm Road, Penge, London SE20 8RH
Website: www.ashcroftacademy.co.uk
e-mail: geri.ashcroftacademy@tiscali.co.uk
Mobile: 07799 791586   Tel: 020-8693 8088

AWA - ANDREA WILDER AGENCY
23 Cambrian Drive, Colwyn Bay, Conwy LL28 4SL
Website: www.awagency.co.uk
e-mail: casting@awagency.co.uk
Fax: 07092 249314   Tel: 01492 547542

BARDSLEY'S Pamela UNIQUE AGENCY
c/o 6 Loxley Road, Southport, Merseyside PR8 6NR
e-mail: pamela_bardsley@hotmail.com
Mobile: 07802 411446   Tel: 01772 815395

BELCANTO LONDON ACADEMY Ltd
(Stage School & Agency)
Performance House, 20 Passey Place, London SE9 5DQ
e-mail: enquiries@theatretraining.com
Fax: 020-8850 9944   Tel: 020-8850 9888

BIZ MANAGEMENT
(In Association with Kidz in the Biz Theatre Academy)
5 Brittendon Parade, Green Street Green, Kent BR6 6DD
Website: www.kidzinthebiz.co.uk
e-mail: thebizmanagement@aol.com
Mobile: 07763 958096   Tel/Fax: 01689 882850

James Pallister Ant & Dec's Saturday Night Take Away

YOUR IMAGINATION
Drama School and Agency

Actors, Extras, Models, Licensed Chaperones and Tutors with all round training for Theatre, T.V., Film and Commercial work

Contact: Lesley McDonough BA (Hons)

Priestman Cottage, Sea View Road, Sunderland SR2 7UP

Tel: 0191 565 2345   Mob: 07989 365737
Fax: 0191 551 2051

http://www.lineone.net/~lesley.mcdonough
e-mail: activate_agcy@hotmail.com

JACKIE PALMER AGENCY
30 Daws Hill Lane
High Wycombe, Bucks
Office 01494 520978
Fax 01494 510479
E-mail jackie.palmer@btinternet.com
Website: www.jackiepalmer.co.uk

Well behaved, natural children, teenagers and young adults. All nationalities, many bi-lingual. Acrobatics are a speciality. Pupils regularly appear in West End Theatre, including RSC, National Theatre and in Film and Television.

We are just off the M40 within easy reach of London, Oxford, Birmingham and the South West. Licensed tutors and chaperones

BIZZYKIDZ
Studio 7, Leigh House
7 Station Approach, Bexleyheath, Kent DA7 4QP
Website: www.bizzykidz.com
e-mail: bookings@bizzykidz.com   Tel/Fax: 020-8303 2627

BODENS AGENCY
99 East Barnet Road, New Barnet, Herts EN4 8RF
Website: www.bodensagency.com
e-mail: bodens2692@aol.com
Fax: 020-8449 5212   Tel: 020-8447 0909

BOURNE Michelle ACADEMY & AGENCY
Studio 1, 22 Dorman Walk, Garden Way, London NW10 0PF
Website: www.michellebourneacademy.co.uk
e-mail: info@michellebourneacademy.co.uk
Mobile: 07956 853564   Tel: 020-8451 3261

BOURNEMOUTH YOUTH THEATRE The (BYT)
14 Cooper Dean Drive, Bournemouth BH8 9LN
Website: www.thebyt.com
e-mail: klair@thebyt.com
Fax: 01202 393290   Tel: 01202 854116

BRUCE & BROWN
203 Canalot Studios, 222 Kensal Road, London W10 5BN
Website: www.bruceandbrown.com
e-mail: info@bruceandbrown.com
Fax: 020-8964 0457   Tel: 020-8968 5585

BUBBLEGUM
Ardreigh, Beaconsfield Road
Farnham Royal, Bucks SL2 3BP
e-mail: kids@bubblegummodels.com
Fax: 01753 669255   Tel: 01753 646348

BYRON'S MANAGEMENT
(Babies, Children & Adults)
North London Performing Arts Centre
76 St James Lane, Muswell Hill, London N10 3DF
Website: www.byronscasting.co.uk
e-mail: byronscasting@aol.com
Fax: 020-8444 4040   Tel: 020-8444 4445

CAMPBELL ASSOCIATES
2 Chelsea Cloisters
Sloane Avenue, Chelsea, London SW3 3DW
e-mail: info@campbellassociates.org.uk
Fax: 020-7584 8799   Tel: 020-7584 5586

CAPITAL ARTS
Wyllyotts Centre, Darkes Lane, Potters Bar, Herts EN6 2HN
e-mail: capitalartstheatre@o2.co.uk
Mobile: 07885 232414   Tel/Fax: 020-8449 2342

CARR Norrie MODEL AGENCY
(Babies, Children & Adults)
Holborn Studios, 49-50 Eagle Wharf Road, London N1 7ED
Website: www.norriecarr.com
e-mail: info@norriecarr.com
Fax: 020-7253 1772   Tel: 020-7253 1771

CARTEURS THEATRICAL AGENCY
170A Church Road, Hove, East Sussex BN3 2DJ
Website: www.stonelandsschool.co.uk
e-mail: dianacarteur@stonelandsschool.co.uk
Fax: 01273 770444   Tel: 01273 770445

CHARACTERS MANAGEMENT Ltd
28 Fletching Road, London E5 9QP
e-mail: cmltd1@btconnect.com
Fax: 020-8533 5554   Tel: 020-8533 5500

CHILDREN OF LONDON ACTING & MODEL AGENCY
The Playhouse
273 Malden Road, Surrey KT3 6AH
e-mail: childrenoflondon@aol.com
Fax: 020-8949 0522   Tel: 020-8949 0450

CHILDSPLAY MODELS LLP
114 Avenue Road, Beckenham, Kent BR3 4SA
Website: www.childsplaymodels.co.uk
e-mail: info@childsplaymodels.co.uk
Fax: 020-8778 2672   Tel: 020-8659 9860

CHRYSTEL ARTS AGENCY
6 Eunice Grove
Chesham, Bucks HP5 1RL
e-mail: chrystelarts@beeb.net   Tel: 01494 773336

CIRCUS MANIACS AGENCY
(Circus, Theatre, Dance, Extreme Sports)
Office 8A
The Kingswood Foundation
Britannia Road
Kingswood
Bristol BS15 8DB
e-mail: agency@circusmaniacs.com
Mobile: 07977 247287   Tel/Fax: 0117-947 7042

CITY LITES
PO Box 29673
London E8 3FH
e-mail: gulcan@freeuk.com
Mobile: 07773 353645   Tel/Fax: 020-7683 9016

COLIN'S PERFORMING ARTS AGENCY & MANAGEMENT
(Colin's Performing Arts Ltd)
The Studios, 219B North Street, Romford, Essex RM1 4QA
Website: www.colinsperformingarts.co.uk
e-mail: agency@colinsperformingarts.co.uk
Fax: 01708 766077   Tel: 01708 766444

COLLINS STUDENT MANAGEMENT
93 Telford Way
Yeading UB4 9TH
e-mail: collinsstudents@aol.com   Tel: 020-8839 8747

CONTI Italia AGENCY Ltd
23 Goswell Road, London EC1M 7AJ
e-mail: agency@italiaconti.co.uk
Fax: 020-7253 1430   Tel: 020-7608 7500

CS MANAGEMENT
(Children & Young Adults)
The Croft, 7 Cannon Road, Southgate, London N14 7HE
Website: www.csmanagementuk.com
e-mail: carole@csmanagementuk.com
Fax: 020-8886 7555   Tel: 020-8886 4264

CYBER-KIDS
(Principal Hilary Wiltshire)
25 Southdown Road
Shoreham-by-Sea, West Sussex BN43 5AL
e-mail: hilliwiltshire@aol.com
Fax: 01273 739984   Tel: 01273 462999

The Studio, Kingsway Court
Queen's Gardens, Hove BN3 2LP
Website: www.cyberartists.co.uk
e-mail: cyber.1@btconnect.com
Fax: 01273 739984   Tel: 01273 821821

D & B MANAGEMENT & THEATRE SCHOOL
470 Bromley Road, Bromley, Kent BR1 4PN
Website: www.dandbperformingarts.co.uk
e-mail: bonnie@dandbperformingarts.co.uk
Fax: 020-8697 8100   Tel: 020-8698 8880

DIMPLES MODEL & CASTING ACADEMY
(Children, Teenagers & Adults)
Suite 2, 2nd Floor, Magnum House
33 Lord Street, Leigh, Lancs WN7 1BY
e-mail: dimples_m_c_a@btinternet.com
Fax: 01942 262232   Tel: 01942 262012

DMS AGENCY
30 Lakedale Road, Plumstead, London SE18 1PP
Mobile: 07740 288869   Tel/Fax: 020-8317 6622

DOE John ASSOCIATES
19 Stanley Crescent, Notting Hill, London W11 2NA
Website: www.johndoeassociates.com
e-mail: info@johndoeassociates.com
Mobile: 07979 558594 Tel: 020-7229 4300

DRAGON DRAMA
(Drama for Children)
1B Station Road, Hampton Wick, Kingston KT1 4HG
Website: www.dragondrama.co.uk
e-mail: info@dragondrama.co.uk   Tel/Fax: 020-8943 1504

DRAMA STUDIO EDINBURGH The
(Previously Juno Casting Agency)
19 Belmont Road, Edinburgh EH14 5DZ
Website: www.thedramastudio.co.uk
e-mail: thedra@thedramastudio.co.uk
Fax: 0131-453 3108   Tel: 0131-453 3284

EARNSHAW Susi MANAGEMENT
5 Brook Place, Barnet, Herts EN5 2DL
Website: www.susiearnshaw.co.uk
e-mail: casting@susiearnshaw.co.uk
Fax: 020-8364 9618   Tel: 020-8441 5010

ENGLISH Doreen '95
(Gerry Kinner)
4 Selsey Avenue, Aldwick, Bognor Regis
West Sussex PO21 2QZ   Tel: 01243 825968

EUROKIDS & ADULTS INTERNATIONAL CASTING & MODEL AGENCY
The Warehouse Studios, Glaziers Lane, Culcheth
Warrington, Cheshire WA3 4AQ
Website: www.eka-agency.com
e-mail: info@eka-agency.com
Fax: 01925 767563   Tel: 0871 7501575

EXPRESSIONS CASTING AGENCY
3 Newgate Lane, Mansfield, Nottingham NG18 2LB
e-mail: expressions-uk@btconnect.com
Fax: 01623 647337   Tel: 01623 424334

EXTRAS UNLIMITED
9 Hansard Mews, Kensington, London W14 8BJ
Fax: 0870 4435621   Tel: 0870 4435622

FBI AGENCY Ltd The
PO Box 250, Leeds LS1 2AZ
e-mail: casting@fbi-agency.ltd.uk   Tel/Fax: 07050 222747

FIORENTINI Anna THEATRE & FILM SCHOOL & AGENCY
25 Daubeney Road, Hackney, London E5 0EE
Website: www.annafiorentini.co.uk
e-mail: info@annafiorentini.co.uk   Tel/Fax: 020-7682 1403

FOOTSTEPS THEATRE SCHOOL CASTING
55 Pullan Avenue, Eccleshill, Bradford BD2 3RP
e-mail: helen@footsteps.fslife.co.uk
Tel/Fax: 01274 637429   Tel: 01274 636036

FOX Betty AGENCY
The Friends Institute
220 Moseley Road, Birmingham B12 0DG
e-mail: bettyfox.school@virgin.net   Tel/Fax: 0121-440 1635

GLYNNE Frances MANAGEMENT
12 Stoneleigh Close, Leeds LS17 8FH
e-mail: franandmo@yahoo.co.uk
Fax: 0113-237 1038   Tel: 0113-266 4286

GO FOR IT CHILDREN'S AGENCY
(Children & Teenagers)
47 North Lane, Teddington, Middlesex TW11 0HU
Website: www.goforitts.com
e-mail: info@goforitts.com
Fax: 020-8287 9405   Tel: 020-8943 1120

GOBSTOPPERS MANAGEMENT
50 Bencroft Road, Hemel Hempstead, Herts HP2 5UY
e-mail: chrisgobstoppers@btopenworld.com
Mobile: 07961 372319   Tel: 01442 269543

GOLDMAN'S Shana THEATRICAL SCHOOL & AGENCY
74 Braemore Road, Hove, East Sussex BN3 4HB
Website: www.shana-goldmans.co.uk
e-mail: casting@shana-goldmans.co.uk
   Tel/Fax: 01273 329916

G. P. ASSOCIATES
4 Gallus Close, Winchmore Hill, London N21 1JR
e-mail: clients@gpassociates.co.uk
Fax: 020-8882 9189   Tel: 020-8886 2263

GRAYSTONS
843-845 Green Lanes, Winchmore Hill, London N21 2RX
e-mail: graystons@btinternet.com
Fax: 020-8364 2009   Tel: 020-8360 5700

GREVILLE Jeannine THEATRICAL AGENCY
Melody House
Gillotts Corner
Henley-on-Thames, Oxon RG9 1QU
Fax: 01491 411533   Tel: 01491 572000

HARLEQUIN STUDIOS AGENCY FOR CHILDREN
223 Southcoast Road
Peacehaven, East Sussex BN10 8LB   Tel: 01273 581742

HARRIS AGENCY Ltd The
52 Forty Avenue, Wembley Park, Middlesex HA9 8LQ
e-mail: sharrisltd@aol.com
Fax: 020-8908 4455   Tel: 020-8908 4451

HEWITT PERFORMING ARTS
160 London Road, Romford, Essex RM7 9QL
Website: www.hewittperformingarts.com
e-mail: hewittstudios@aol.com   Tel: 01708 727784

HOBSON'S KIDS
62 Chiswick High Road
London W4 1SY
Website: www.hobsons-international.com
e-mail: kids@hobsons-international.com
Fax: 020-8996 5350   Tel: 020-8995 3628

HORNIMANS MANAGEMENT
31 Stafford Street, Gillingham, Kent ME7 5EN
Mobile: 07866 689865   Tel/Fax: 01634 576191

STAGECOACH AGENCY

in association with
Stagecoach Theatre Schools, represents
Children and Teenagers who are available
for television, films, stage, commercials
and corporate work

The Courthouse, Elm Grove, Walton-on-Thames, Surrey KT12 1LZ
T: 01932 254 333   F: 01932 222 894   www.stagecoach.co.uk

HOWE Janet CHILDREN'S CASTING &
MODELLING AGENCY
Studio 1
Whitebridge Estate
Whitebridge Lane, Stone, Staffs ST15 8LQ
e-mail: janet@jhowecasting.fsbusiness.co.uk
Tel/Fax: 01785 816888   Tel/Fax: 01785 850698

40 Princess Street
Manchester M1 6DE   Mobile: 07801 942178

INTER-CITY KIDS
Portland Tower
Portland Street
Manchester M1 3LF
Website: www.iccast.co.uk
e-mail: mail@iccast.co.uk   Tel/Fax: 0161-238 4950

ITV JUNIOR WORKSHOP
(Birmingham Group)
Central Court
Gas Street
Birmingham B1 2JT
e-mail: colin.edwards@carltontv.co.uk
Fax: 0121-633 9906   Tel: 0121-633 9916

ITV JUNIOR WORKSHOP
(Nottingham Group)
Central Court
Gas Street
Birmingham B1 2JT
e-mail: ian.smith@carltontv.co.uk
Fax: 0115-964 5552   Tel: 0115-964 5614

Connor Doyle TVC for Comet

Tuesdays Child

Television & Model Agency
(Est. 1976)

Children and Adults from all parts of the UK
Casting Suite available - 40 mins from
Manchester. Direct rail links -
Euston: Birmingham: Macclesfield

Tel: 01625 501765 and 612244

bookings@tuesdayschildagency.co.uk
www.tuesdayschildagency.co.uk

Début Models Ltd

YORKSHIRE'S PREMIER CHILD MODEL AGENCY
REPRESENTING CHILDREN FROM 0 TO 18 YEARS
for
*Photographic * Catwalk * Catalogue*
*TV Commercials * Advertising & Promotions*

WHY CHOOSE A "DÉBUT" MODEL?
• You need the right look?
- *Our Kidz are!*
• Your models need to be "quick" on the uptake?
- *Our Kidz can!*

• You want models who have some acting
experience, to get the right expression?
- *Our Kidz do!*

Whatever you are looking for,
Début Models have the answer

Tel: 01274 532347

for more details or visit our website
www.debutmodels.co.uk
WHY CHOOSE ANYONE ELSE?

www.scallywags.co.uk

scallywags agency

tel 020 8553 9999

JABBERWOCKY AGENCY
(Children & Teenagers 6 Months-18 Years)
Hop Farm Country Park, Beltring
Paddock Wood, Kent TN12 6PY
Website: www.jabberwockyagency.com
e-mail: donna@jabberwockyagency.com
Mobile: 07771 722480   Tel: 01622 873273

JB ASSOCIATES
(Children & Teenagers 6 Months-18 Years)
3 Stevenson Square, Manchester M1 1DN
Website: www.j-b-a.net   e-mail: info@j-b-a.net
Fax: 0161-237 1809   Tel: 0161-237 1808

High Fashion & Character Models

julietadams
Model & Talent Castings Agency

19 GWYNNE HOUSE, CHALLICE WAY, LONDON SW2 3RB

TEL: (020) 8671 7673

Agents Also For: **TOP UK Look-A-Likes &**

Child & Adult

Film & TV Extras & Support Artists

E-mail: **models@julietadams.co.uk**

Web site: http://**www.julietadams.co.uk**

Agents for Artists from London & Across the UK

JIGSAW ARTS MANAGEMENT
(Representing Children & Young People from Jigsaw
Performing Arts Schools)
64-66 High Street, Barnet, Herts EN5 5SJ
Website: www.jigsaw-arts.co.uk/agency Tel: 020-8447 4530

JOHNSTON & MATHERS ASSOCIATES Ltd
PO Box 3167, Barnet, Herts EN5 2WA
Website: www.johnstonandmathers.com
e-mail: johnstonmathers@aol.com
Fax: 020-8449 2386   Tel: 020-8449 4968

KASTKIDZ
40 Sunnybank Road, Unsworth, Bury BL9 8HF
e-mail: kastkidz@ntlworld.com
Mobile: 07905 646832   Tel/Fax: 0161-796 7073

KENT YOUTH THEATRE & AGENCY
Pinks Hill House, Briton Road, Faversham, Kent ME13 8QH
Website: www.kentyouththeatre.co.uk
e-mail: info@kent.org.ukTel/Fax: 01795 534395

KIDDIEWINKS
(Child Modelling & Photographic Agency)
40-42 Neville Road, Dagenham, Essex RM8 3QS
Website: www.kiddiewinks.biz
e-mail: info@kiddiewinks.biz
Fax: 020-8983 8737   Tel: 020-8595 5955

KIDS LONDON
67 Dulwich Road, London SE24 0NJ
Website: www.kidslondonltd.com
e-mail: kidslondon@btconnect.com Tel/Fax: 020-7924 9595

KIDS PLUS
54 Grove Park, London SE5 8LG
Website: www.kidsplus.co.uk
e-mail: janekidsplus@aol.com
Mobile: 07759 944215   Tel/Fax: 020-7737 3901

KIDZ NATIONAL MODEL & CASTING AGENCY
21 Bolton Road, Manchester M28 3AX
Website: www.kidzltd.com
e-mail: info@kidzltd.com
Tel/Fax: 0870 2416260   Tel: 0870 2414418

K M C AGENCIES AND THEATRE SCHOOL
PO Box 122, 48 Great Ancoats Street, Manchester M4 5AB
e-mail: kids@kmcagencies.co.uk
Fax: 0161-237 9812   Tel: 0161-237 3009

KRACKERS KIDS THEATRICAL AGENCY
6/7 Electric Parade, Seven Kings Road, Ilford, Essex IG3 8BY
Website: www.krackerskids.co.uk
e-mail: krackerskids@hotmail.com Tel/Fax: 01708 502046

GRAYSTONS
Agency

**Children, Teenagers, Young Adults
with all-round training for
Theatre, TV, Films and Commercials**
845 Green Lanes, Winchmore Hill, London N21 2RX
Tel: 020 8360 5700   Fax: 020 8364 2009
mobile 07710 403002 e-mail: graystons@btinternet.com

LAMONT CASTING AGENCY
94 Harington Road, Formby, Liverpool L37 1PZ
Website: www.lamontcasting.co.uk
e-mail: diane@lamontcasting.co.uk
Fax: 01704 872422   Tel: 01704 877024

LESLIE Sasha MANAGEMENT
(In Association with Allsorts Drama for Children)
34 Pember Road, London NW10 5LS
e-mail: sasha@allsortsdrama.com
Fax: 020-8969 3196   Tel: 020-8969 3249

LINTON MANAGEMENT
3 The Rock, Bury BL9 0JP
e-mail: carol@lintonmanagement.freeserve.co.uk
Fax: 0161-761 1999   Tel: 0161-761 2020

LITTLE ACORNS
London House, 271-273 King Street, London W6 9LZ
e-mail: acorns@dircon.co.uk
Fax: 020-8390 4935   Tel: 020-8563 0773

LITTLE ADULTS ACADEMY & MODELLING AGENCY Ltd
Studio 11, Suite 13, Essex House, 375-377 High Street
Stratford, London E15 4QZ
Website: www.littleadults.co.uk
e-mail: donna@littleadults.demon.co.uk
Fax: 020-8519 9797   Tel: 020-8519 9755

LITTLE GEMS
11 Thorn Road, Farnham, Surrey GU10 4TU
e-mail: littlegems30@hotmail.com
Mobile: 07960 978439   Tel/Fax: 01252 792078

LIVE & LOUD
The S.P.A.C.E., 188 St Vincents St, 2nd Floor, Glasgow G2 5SP
e-mail: info@west-endmgt.com
Fax: 0141-226 8983   Tel: 0141-222 2942

MILLENNIUM KIDZ
73 Hatfield Road
Dagenham, Essex RM9 6JS
e-mail: millkidz1@aol.com   Tel/Fax: 020-8220 5111

MONDI ASSOCIATES Ltd
30 Cooper House, 2 Michael Road, London SW6 2AD
e-mail: mondi.sw@virgin.net
Fax: 020-7351 7628   Mobile: 07817 133349

MOVIEMITES AGENCY
12 Gladding Road
Cheshunt, Herts EN7 6XB
Website: www.moviemitesagency.com
e-mail: kids@moviemitesagency.com   Tel/Fax: 01992 301319

MRS WORTHINGTON'S
(6-15 Years)
16 Ouseley Road, London SW12 8EF   Tel/Fax: 020-8767 6944

NOEL CASTING
(Specializing in Character Actors & Ethnic & Asian Actors)
Suite 501, International House
223 Regent Street, London W1B 2QD
e-mail: noelcasting@yahoo.com
Fax: 020-7544 1090   Tel: 020-7544 1010

NORTHERN FILM & DRAMA
21 Low Street
South Milford, North Yorkshire LS25 5AR
Website: www.northernfilmanddrama.com
e-mail: alyson@connew.com   Tel/Fax: 01977 681949

NUTOPIA-CHANG PERSONAL MANAGEMENT
Number 8, 132 Charing Cross Road, London WC2H 0LA
Website: www.nutopia.co.uk
Fax: 029-2070 9440   Mobile: 07801 493133

O'FARRELL STAGE & THEATRE SCHOOL
(Babies, Children, Teenagers & Young Adults)
36 Shirley Street, Canning Town, London E16 1HU
Mobile: 07946 545656   Tel: 020-7511 9444

ORR MANAGEMENT AGENCY
(Children, Teenagers & Adults)
1st Floor, 147-149 Market Street, Farnworth BL4 8EX
Website: www.orrmanagement.co.uk
e-mail: barbara@orrmanagement.co.uk
    Tel/Fax: 01204 579842

PALMER Jackie AGENCY
30 Daws Hill Lane, High Wycombe, Bucks HP11 1PW
Website: www.jackiepalmer.co.uk
e-mail: jackie.palmer@btinternet.com
Fax: 01494 510479   Tel: 01494 520978

PATMORE Sandra SCHOOL AND AGENCY
(Dancing, Drama & Acrobatic)
173 Uxbridge Road
Rickmansworth, Herts WD3 2DW   Tel/Fax: 01923 772542

PC THEATRICAL & MODEL AGENCY
10 Strathmore Gardens, Edgware, Middlesex HA8 5HJ
Website: www.twinagency.com
e-mail: twinagy@aol.com
Fax: 020-8933 3418   Tel: 020-8381 2229

PEAK MANAGEMENT
45 Highfield Drive, Matlock, Derby DE4 3FZ
e-mail: ljh@entertainmentservices.freeserve.co.uk
    Tel/Fax: 01629 581745

PHA YOUTH
Tanzaro House, Ardwick Green North, Manchester M12 6FZ
Website: www.pha-agency.co.uk
e-mail: youth@pha-agency.co.uk
Fax: 0161-273 4567   Tel: 0161-273 4444

POLLYANNA MANAGEMENT Ltd
PO Box 30661, London E1W 3GG
Website: www.eada.demon.co.uk/pollyanna
e-mail: pollyanna-mgmt@btinternet.com
Fax: 020-7480 6761   Tel: 020-7702 1937

POWER MODEL MANAGEMENT CASTING AGENCY
Capitol House, 2-4 Heigham Street, Norwich NR2 4TE
Website: www.powerchildmodels.co.uk
e-mail: powermodelmanagement@btinternet.com
Fax: 01603 621101   Tel: 01603 621100

RASCALS MODEL AGENCY
13 Jubilee Parade, Snakes Lane East
Woodford Green, Essex IG8 7QG
Website: www.rascals.co.uk
e-mail: kids@rascals.co.uk
Fax: 020-8559 1035   Tel: 020-8504 1111

RAVENSCOURT MANAGEMENT
Tandy House, 30-40 Dalling Road, London W6 0JB
e-mail: info@ravenscourt.net
Fax: 020-8741 1786   Tel: 020-8741 0707

REBEL SCHOOL OF THEATRE ARTS
46 North Park Avenue, Roundhay, Leeds LS8 1EJ
e-mail: rebeltheatre@aol.com
Mobile: 07808 803637   Tel: 0113-305 3796

REDROOFS THEATRE SCHOOL AGENCY
Room 160-161, The Admin Building
Pinewood Studios, Iver, Bucks SL0 0NH
e-mail: agency@redroofs.co.uk
Fax: 01753 785443   Tel: 01753 785444

REFLECTIONS AGENCY
9 Weavers Terrace
Fulham, London SW6 1QE   Tel/Fax: 020-7385 1537

RIDGEWAY STUDIOS SCHOOL OF PERFORMING ARTS
Fairley House, Andrews Lane, Cheshunt, Herts EN7 6LB
Website: www.ridgewaystudios.co.uk
e-mail: info@ridgewaystudios.co.uk
Fax: 01992 633844   Tel: 01992 633775

ROI-BELL CASTING CO.
7B Wakefield Road
London N15 4NN
e-mail: roibellcasting@hotmail.com   Tel/Fax: 020-8808 1500

S.A.M. YOUTH AGENCY
London Road Business Centre
Suite 3:2, 106 London Road
Liverpool L3 5JY   Tel/Fax: 0151-608 9655

SBZ AGENCY
PO Box 350, Ashford, Kent TN24 9ZE
e-mail: sbzagency@aol.com   Tel/Fax: 01233 650045

SCALLYWAGS AGENCY Ltd
90-92 Ley Street, Ilford, Essex IG1 4BX
Website: www.scallywags.co.uk
e-mail: kids@scallywags.co.uk
Fax: 020-8553 4849   Tel: 020-8553 9999

SCHER Anna THEATRE The
Anna Scher Theatre
70-72 Barnsbury Road, London N1 0ES
e-mail: agent@astm.co.uk
Fax: 020-7833 9467   Tel: 020-7278 2101

SCREAM MANAGEMENT
32 Clifton Street, Blackpool, Lancs FY1 1JP
Website: www.screammanagement.com
e-mail: info@screammanagement.com
Fax: 01253 750829   Tel: 01253 750820

SEQUINS THEATRICAL AGENCY
Winsome, 8 Summerhill Grove
Enfield EN1 2HY   Tel: 020-8360 4015

SHARONA STAGE SCHOOL AGENCY & MANAGEMENT
82 Grennell Road, Sutton, Surrey SM1 3DN
Fax: 020-8642 2364   Tel: 020-8642 9396

SINGER Sandra ASSOCIATES
21 Cotswold Road, Westcliff-on-Sea, Essex SS0 8AA
Website: www.sandrasinger.com
e-mail: sandrasingeruk@aol.com
Fax: 01702 339393   Tel: 01702 331616

SMITH Elisabeth Ltd
81 Headstone Road, Harrow, Middlesex HA1 1PQ
Website: www.elisabethsmith.com
e-mail: models@elisabethsmith.com
Fax: 020-8861 1880   Tel: 020-8863 2331

SOUTH WEST CASTINGS Ltd
The Courtyard, Whitchurch, Ross-on-Wye HR9 6DA
Website: www.southwestcasting.co.uk
e-mail: agent@southwestcasting.co.uk
Fax: 01600 891099   Tel: 01600 891160

SPEAKE Barbara AGENCY
East Acton Lane, London W3 7EG
e-mail: speakekids2@aol.com
Fax: 020-8740 6542   Tel: 020-8743 6096

S.R.A. AGENCY
Suite 94, The London Fruit and Wool Exchange
Brushfield Street, London E1 6EP
e-mail: agency@susanrobertsacademy.co.uk
     Tel: 020-7655 4477

STAGE 01 THEATRE SCHOOL & AGENCY
32 Westbury Lane
Buckhurst Hill, Essex IG9 5PL
Website: www.stage01.com
e-mail: stage01@lineone.net
Mobile: 07939 121154   Tel/Fax: 020-8506 0949

STAGE 84 YORKSHIRE SCHOOL OF PERFORMING ARTS
Old Bell Chapel, Town Lane, Bradford, West Yorks BD10 8PR
e-mail: valeriejackson@stage84.com
Mobile: 07785 244984   Tel: 01274 569197

STAGE DOOR AGENCY
The Stage Door Centre, 27 Howard Business Park
Waltham Abbey, Essex EN9 1XE
Website: www.stagedoorschool.co.uk
e-mail: stagedoorschool@aol.com
Fax: 01992 652171   Tel: 01992 717994

STAGE KIDS DRAMA SCHOOL & AGENCY
1 Greenfield, Welwyn Garden City, Herts AL8 7HW
Website: www.stagekids.co.uk   Tel: 01707 328359

STAGECOACH AGENCY
The Courthouse
Elm Grove, Walton-on-Thames, Surrey KT12 1LZ
Website: www.stagecoach.co.uk
e-mail: abrookes@stagecoach.co.uk
Fax: 01932 222894   Tel: 01932 254333

STARLINGS THEATRICAL AGENCY
45 Viola Close, South Ockendon, Essex RM15 6JF
Website: www.webspawner.com/users/starlings
e-mail: julieecarter@blueyonder.co.uk
     Mobile: 07941 653463

Roi-Bell Casting Co.
London-Paris
London's Leading Agency
In Association With Schools Of Dance & Drama
Representing Professional Children & Young Adults
Specializing In
* TV * FILM * THEATRE *
* COMMERCIAL * MUSIC * VIDEO * MODELLING
TEL/FAX: 020 8808 1500
Email: roibellcasting@hotmail.com
7B Wakefield Road, London, N15 4NN

STONELANDS SCHOOL OF BALLET & THEATRE ARTS
170A Church Road, Hove, East Sussex BN3 2DJ
Website: www.stonelandsschool.co.uk
e-mail: www@stonelandsschool.co.uk
Fax: 01273 770444   Tel: 01273 770445

SUMMERS Mark MANAGEMENT & AGENCY
9 Hansard Mews, Kensington, London W14 8BJ
Website: www.marksummers.com
e-mail: mark@marksummers.com
Fax: 0870 4435623   Tel: 0870 4435621

SUPERARTS AGENCY
26-28 Ambergate Street
London SE17 3RX   Tel/Fax: 020-7735 4975

T.A.A.
(See ARTS ACADEMY The)

TANWOOD
46 Bath Road, Swindon, Wilts SN1 4AY
Website: www.tanwood.co.uk
e-mail: tanwood@tiscali.co.uk
Tel: 01793 643219   Tel: 01793 523895

THAMES VALLEY THEATRICAL AGENCY
PO Box 233, Wallingford, Oxfordshire OX10 9ZN
Website: www.thamesvalleytheatricalagency.co.uk
e-mail: donna@thamesvalleytheatricalagency.co.uk
                                   Tel/Fax: 01491 659009

THEATRE ARTS (WEST LONDON)
18 Kingsdale Gardens, Notting Hill, London W11 4TZ
e-mail: theatreartswestlondon@hotmail.com
                                   Tel/Fax: 020-7603 3471

THEATRE EXPRESS
Spindle Cottage, Allens Farm, Digbey Fen
Billinghay, Lincoln LN4 4DT   Tel: 01526 860360

THOMPSON Jim CHILDREN'S SECTION
(Jenny Donnison)
Herricks, School Lane, Arundel, West Sussex BN18 9DR
Fax: 01903 885887   Tel: 01903 885757

TOTS 2 TEENS Ltd
6 Fulham Park Studios, Fulham Park Road
London SW6 4LW
Fax: 0870 2519560   Tel: 0870 2519530

TOTS-TWENTIES AGENCY
Suite 3 Ground Floor, Clements Court
Clements Lane, Ilford, Essex IG1 2QY
Website: www.tots-twenties.co.uk
e-mail: sara@tots-twenties.co.uk
Fax: 020-8553 1880   Tel: 020-8478 1848

TRULY SCRUMPTIOUS Ltd
66 Bidwell Gardens, London N11 2AU
Website: www.trulyscrumptious.co.uk
e-mail: bookings@trulyscrumptious.co.uk
Fax: 020-7251 5767   Tel: 020-7608 3806

TUESDAYS CHILD
(Children, Teenagers & Adults)
Oakfield House, Springwood Way, Macclesfield SK10 2XA
Website: www.tuesdayschildagency.co.uk
e-mail: bookings@tuesdayschildagency.co.uk
Tel/Fax: 01625 501765   Tel: 01625 612244

TWINS
(See PC THEATRICAL & MODEL AGENCY)

TWINS & TRIPLETS
(Identical Babies, Children, Teenagers & Adults for
Film/Television)
15 Holmhurst Road, Upper Belvedere DA17 6HW
e-mail: twinsontv@aol.com
Fax: 01322 447250   Tel: 01322 440184

URBAN ANGEL MODELLING AGENCY
Unit 506, The Chandlery
50 Westminster Bridge Road, London SE1 7QY
e-mail: info@urbanangelsagency.com
Fax: 0870 8710046   Tel: 0870 8710045

VALLÉ ACADEMY THEATRICAL AGENCY The
The Valle Academy Studios, Wilton House
Delamare Road, Cheshunt, Herts EN8 9SG
Website: www.valleacademy.co.uk
e-mail: agency@valleacademy.co.uk
Fax: 01992 622868   Tel: 01992 622861

WHITEHALL PERFORMING ARTS CENTRE
Rayleigh Road, Leigh-on-Sea
Essex SS9 5UU   Tel/Fax: 01702 529290

WHIZZ KIDS STAGE & SCREEN AGENCY
3 Marshall Road, Cambridge CB1 7TY
Website: www.whizzkidsdrama.co.uk
e-mail: goforit@whizzkidsdrama.co.uk
Fax: 01223 512431   Tel: 01223 416474

WINGS AGENCY
(Affiliated to Angels Theatre School)
Pound Corner, 2 Farncombe Hill
Godalming, Surrey GU7 2AY
Website: www.angelstheatreschool.co.uk
e-mail: wingsagency@hotmail.com
Fax: 01483 429966   Tel: 01483 428844

WYSE AGENCY
1 Hill Farm Road
Whittlesford, Cambs CB2 4NB
e-mail: frances.wyse@btinternet.com
Fax: 01223 839414   Tel: 01223 832288

YOUNG ACTORS FILE The
65 Stafford Street
Old Town, Swindon SN1 3PF
e-mail: young.actorsfile@virgin.net   Tel/Fax: 01793 423688

YOUNG 'UNS AGENCY
Sylvia Young Theatre School
Rossmore Road
Marylebone
London NW1 6NJ
e-mail: enquiries@youngunsagency.co.uk
Fax: 020-7723 1040   Tel: 020-7723 0037

YOUNGBLOOD
The Talent Partnership
Riverside Studios
Crisp Road
Hammersmith, London W6 9RL
e-mail: info@thetalentpartnership.co.uk
Fax: 020-8237 1041   Tel: 020-8237 1040

YOUNGSTAR AGENCY
Youngstar Drama School
5 Union Castle House
Canute Road, Southampton SO14 3FJ
Website: www.youngstaragency.com
e-mail: louisayoungstar@aol.com
Fax: 023-8045 5816   Tel: 023-8033 9322

10 TWENTY TWO CASTING ■
PO Box 1022
Liverpool L69 5WZ
Website: www.10twentytwo.com
e-mail: contact@10twentytwo.com
Fax: 0151-207 4230
Tel: 0151-298 1022

2 CASTING AGENCY & MANAGEMENT
Tiptoes House
2 Collingwood Place
Layton
Blackpool FY3 8HU
e-mail: tiptoes2casting@hotmail.com
Fax: 01253 302610
Tel: 01253 302614

2020 CASTING Ltd
2020 Hopgood Street
London W12 7JU
Website: www.2020casting.com
e-mail: info@2020casting.com
Fax: 020-8735 2727
Tel: 020-8746 2020

A LITTLE EXTRA!
67 Stafford Street
Old Town, Swindon, Wiltshire SN1 3PF
Website: www.a-little-extra.co.uk
e-mail: extrasfile@aol.com
Mobile: 07950 776462
Tel: 01793 610936

ALLSORTS THEATRICAL AGENCY
Three Mills Film Studios
Unit 1, Sugar House Business Centre
24 Sugar House Lane, London E15 2QS
Website: www.allsortsagency.com
e-mail: bookings@allsortsagency.com
Fax: 020-8555 0909
Tel: 020-8555 0099

ARENA CASTING
PO Box 81, Liverpool L10 9WY
e-mail: sue@arena-casting.fsnet.co.uk
Tel/Fax: 0151-523 9910

AVENUE ARTISTES Ltd
8 Winn Road, Southampton SO17 1EN
Website: www.avenueartistes.com
e-mail: info@avenueartistes.com
Fax: 023-8090 5703
Tel: 023-8055 1000

AWA - ANDREA WILDER AGENCY
23 Cambrian Drive
Colwyn Bay, Conwy LL28 4SL
Website: www.awagency.co.uk
e-mail: casting@awagency.co.uk
Fax: 07092 249314
Tel: 01492 547542

BALDIES CASTING AGENCY
(The only agency purely for bald people)
6 Marlott Road
Poole, Dorset BH15 3DX
Mobile: 07860 290437
Tel: 01202 666001

BRISTOL EXTRA SERVICE TEAM (B.E.S.T.)
(Ernest Jones) (Film & TV Actors, Extras, Speciality Artists)
21 Ellesmere, Thornbury, Near Bristol BS35 2ER
e-mail: ernestjones.best@virgin.net
Mobile: 07951 955759
Tel/Fax: 01454 411628

John Doe Associates

John Doe Artistes / ARTISTS & CASTING

19 Stanley Cresent, Notting Hill, London W11 2NA

t 020 7229 4300   m 07979 558594
e info@johndoeassociates.com
w www.johndoeassociates.com

TONER CASTING LTD
Experienced TV & Film actors and background artists
Unit e6 Brunswick Business Centre, Brunswick Dock, Liverpool, L3 4BD Tel: 0151 708 6400 Fax: 0151 707 8414
www.tonercasting.com   email: tonercasting@btconnect.com

BROADCASTING AGENCY
Unit 23 Canalot Studios
222 Kensal Road, London W10 5BN
e-mail: info@broadcastingcompany.tv
Fax: 020-7460 5223   Tel: 020-7460 5222

BROMLEY CASTING
(Film & TV Extras)
77 Widmore Road
Bromley, Kent BR1 3AA
Website: www.bromleycasting.tv
e-mail: admin@bromleycasting.tv   Tel/Fax: 020-8466 8239

BROOK Dolly CASTING AGENCY
PO Box 5436
Dunmow CM6 1WW
Fax: 01371 875996   Tel: 01371 875767

CAIRNS AGENCY The
(Maureen Cairns)
188 St Vincent Street
Glasgow G2 5SP
Website: www.west-endmgt.com
Fax: 0141-226 8983   Tel: 0141-226 8941

CAMCAST ■
Laragain
Upper Banavie, Fort William
Inverness-shire PH33 7PB
Website: www.camcast.co.uk
e-mail: anne@camcast.co.uk
Fax: 01397 772456   Tel: 01397 772523

CARTEL 1
Studio 103
Westbourne Studios
242 Acklam Road, London W10 5JJ
Website: www.cartel1casting.com
e-mail: info@cartel1casting.com
Mobile: 07760 366496   Tel: 020-8964 5798

CASTING COLLECTIVE Ltd The ■
Olympic House
317-321 Latimer Road
London W10 6RA
Website: www.castingcollective.co.uk
e-mail: enquiries@castingcollective.co.uk
Fax: 020-8962 0333   Tel: 020-8962 0099

CASTING FACES UK
Park House
17 Sugar House Lane
London E15 2QS
Website: www.castingfaces.com
e-mail: office@castingfaces.com
Fax: 0871 4337304   Tel: 020-8555 6339

CASTING NETWORK Ltd The ■
2nd Floor
10 Claremont Road
Surbiton, Surrey KT6 4QU
Website: www.thecastingnetwork.co.uk
e-mail: casting-network@talk21.com
Fax: 020-8390 0605   Tel: 020-8339 9090

Northern Professionals Casting Co.

Licence No. L1299.....

Casting - Supporting/Principal Artistes

Action Safety Consultant

Diving support teams - Boat Hire - Diving Equipment Hire

Office: 0191 2578635 Mob: 07860 186978 Fax: 0191 2963243
21 Cresswell Avenue, North Shields, Near Tyne & Wear NE29 9BQ
www.northernprofessionalscastingco.com

Bill Gerard

CELEX CASTING Ltd ■
(Children available)
11 Glencroft Drive
Stenson Fields, Derby DE24 3LS
Website: www.celex.co.uk
e-mail: anne@celex.co.uk
Fax: 01332 232115   Tel: 01332 232445

CENTRAL CASTING Ltd ■
(See also KNIGHT Ray CASTING)
21A Lambolle Place, Belsize Park, London NW3 4PG
Website: www.rayknight.co.uk
e-mail: casting@rayknight.co.uk
Fax: 020-7722 2322   Tel: 020-7722 4111

COAST 2 COAST PERSONALITIES
6 Fulham Park Studios
Fulham Park Road, London SW6 4LW
Website: www.coast2coastpersonalities.com
e-mail: info@c2cp.co.uk
Fax: 0870 2519560   Tel: 0870 2519550

CORNWALL FILM AGENCY
22 Church Street, Briston
Melton Constable, Norfolk NR24 2LE
Website: www.cornwallfilmagency.co.uk
e-mail: frances@cornwall-film-agency.fsnet.co.uk
    Tel/Fax: 01263 860650

CYBER-ARTISTS
In The Can Ltd
The Studio, Kingsway Court
Queen's Gardens, Hove BN3 2LP
Website: www.cyberartists.co.uk
e-mail: cyber.1@btconnect.com
Fax: 01273 739984   Tel: 01273 821821

DAVID AGENCY The ■
26-28 Hammersmith Grove, London W6 7BA
Website: www.davidagency.net
e-mail: casting@davidagency.net
Fax: 020-8834 1144   Tel: 020-8834 1615

DOE John ASSOCIATES
19 Stanley Crescent
Notting Hill, London W11 2NA
Website: www.johndoeassociates.com
e-mail: info@johndoeassociates.com
Mobile: 07979 558594   Tel: 020-7229 4300

DRAG QUEEN AGENCY The
(David Gordon)
58 Newland Road
Worthing, West Sussex BN11 1JX
e-mail: lavendersub@hotmail.com   Tel: 01903 202895

ELLIOTT AGENCY The ■
PO Box 2772
Lewes, Sussex BN8 4DW
Website: www.elliottagency.co.uk
e-mail: info@elliottagency.co.uk
Fax: 01273 400814   Tel: 01273 401264

EUROKIDS & ADULTS INTERNATIONAL CASTING & MODEL AGENCY
The Warehouse Studios
Glaziers Lane, Culcheth
Warrington, Cheshire WA3 4AQ
Website: www.eka-agency.com
e-mail: info@eka-agency.com
Fax: 01925 767563   Tel: 0871 7501575

EXTRAS UNLIMITED.COM
9 Hansard Mews
Kensington, London W14 8BJ
Website: www.extrasunlimited.com
e-mail: info@extrasunlimited.com
Fax: 0870 4435621   Tel: 0870 4435622

EXTRASPECIAL Ltd
38 Commercial Street
London E1 6LP
Website: www.extraspecial2000.com
e-mail: info@skybluecasting.com
Fax: 020-7375 1466   Tel: 020-7375 1400

NEMESIS

www.nemesisagency.co.uk

Extras, Walk-Ons, Crowd Artistes, Fashion and Photographic Models
Largest selection of professional equity and non equity supporting artistes in North West

Manchester Head Office tel. 0161 834 9988
Leeds tel. 0113 244 4644 **Birmingham** tel. 0121 554 7878
Premier city centre casting studios in all three locations

F2F MARKETING Ltd
527 Fulham Road, London SW6 1HD
Website: www.f2fmarketing.co.uk
e-mail: info@f2fmarketing.co.uk
Fax: 020-7836 6780   Tel: 020-7386 6789

FACE FACTORY
3 Nottingham Court
Covent Garden, London WC2H 9AY
Website: www.facefactoryuk.com
e-mail: facefactory@btconnect.com
Fax: 020-7240 0565   Tel: 020-7240 2322

FACES CASTING AGENCY ■
95 Ditchling Road, Brighton, East Sussex BN1 4ST
Fax: 01273 719165   Tel: 01273 329436

FACT PRESENTATIONS
9 The Shrubberies
George Lane, South Woodford
London E18 1BD
e-mail: enquiries@factpresentations.com
Fax: 020-8532 2228   Tel: 020-8532 2229

FBI AGENCY Ltd The ■
PO Box 250, Leeds LS1 2AZ
e-mail: casting@fbi-agency.ltd.uk
Fax: 0113-279 7270   Tel: 07050 222747

FBI Ltd
4th Floor, 20-24 Kirby Street, London EC1N 8TS
Website: www.fullybooked-inc.com
Fax: 020-7242 8125   Tel: 020-7242 5542

FLOSS EXTRAS
14 Ritz Buildings, Church Rd, Tunbridge Wells, Kent TN1 1HP
Website: www.newmangroup.co.uk
e-mail: floss.extras@newmangroup.co.uk
Fax: 01892 514173   Tel: 01892 524122

FRESH AGENTS
Whitepoint Studios, Unit 2, Hove Business Centre
Fonthill Road, Hove, East Sussex BN3 6HA
Website: www.freshagents.com
e-mail: info@freshagents.com
Fax: 01273 711778   Tel: 01273 711777

FTS CASTING
55 Pullan Avenue, Eccleshill, Bradford BD2 3RP
e-mail: helen@footsteps.fslife.co.uk
Fax: 01274 637429   Tel: 01274 636036

G2 ■
15 Lexham Mews, London W8 6JW
Website: www.g2casting.com
e-mail: g2@galloways.ltd.uk
Fax: 020-7376 2416   Tel: 020-7376 2133

GUYS & DOLLS CASTING ■
Trafalgar House, Grenville Place, Mill Hill, London NW7 3SA
Fax: 020-8381 0080   Tel: 020-8906 4144

HOWE Janet CASTING AGENCY
Underwood Farm, Sturbridge, Eccleshall, Staffs ST21 6LZ
e-mail: janet@jhowecasting.fsbusiness.co.uk
                           Tel/Fax: 01785 850697
40 Princess Street, Manchester M1 6DE
Mobile: 07801 942178   Tel/Fax: 0161-234 0142

nidges
casting agency

arguably the north of england's most established casting agency
we have a comprehensive selection of experienced, quality Equity & non-Equity
supporting artistes available for work in any sphere of the theatre,
television, film, video & advertising industries

Half Moon Chambers Chapel Walks Manchester M2 1HN
Tel: 0161 832 8259 Fax: 0161 832 5219 www.nidgescasting.co.uk

Background & supporting artistes for the film and television industry

Online Brochure at www.10twentytwo.com

T 0151 298 1022 | F 0151 207 4230
email: contact@10twentytwo.com
PO Box 1022 Liverpool L69 5WZ
24 hours, 7 days a week

Member of the National Association of
Supporting Artistes Agents (NASAA)

JACLYN 2000 ■
52 Bessemer Road, Norwich, Norfok NR4 6DQ
Website: www.jaclyn2000.co.uk
Fax: 01603 612532   Tel: 01603 622027

JB AGENCY ONLINE Ltd ■
7 Stonehills Mansions
8 Streatham High Road, London SW16 1DD
Website: www.jb-agency.com
e-mail: christian@jb-agency.com
Fax: 020-8769 9567   Tel: 020-8769 0123

KNIGHT Ray CASTING ■
(See also CENTRAL CASTING Ltd)
21A Lambolle Place, Belsize Park, London NW3 4PG
Website: www.rayknight.co.uk
e-mail: casting@rayknight.co.uk
Fax: 020-7722 2322   Tel: 020-7722 4111

KREATE PRODUCTIONS
Unit 210, 30 Great Guildford Street, London SE1 0HS
e-mail: kreate@btconnect.com
Fax: 020-7401 3003   Tel: 020-7401 9007

LEE'S PEOPLE
16 Manette Street, London W1D 4AR
Website: www.lees-people.co.uk
e-mail: lee@lees-people.co.uk
Fax: 020-7734 3033   Tel: 020-7734 5775

LEMON CASTING
23 Lucas Road, Farnworth, Bolton BL4 9RP
e-mail: andreaking.tv@ntlworld.com
Mobile: 07752 455510   Tel/Fax: 01204 456253

LINTON MANAGEMENT
3 The Rock, Bury BL9 0JP
Fax: 0161-761 1999   Tel: 0161-761 2020

MAC-10 MANAGEMENT
Office 69, 2 Hellidon Close
Ardwick, Manchester M12 4AH
Website: www.mac-10.co.uk
e-mail: info@mac-10.co.uk
Fax: 0161-275 9610   Tel: 0161-275 9510

MAD DOG CASTING Ltd ■
Top Floor, 10 Warwick Street, London W1B 5LZ
e-mail: production@maddogcasting.com
Fax: 020-7287 5983   Tel: 020-7434 1211

M.E.P. MANAGEMENT
1 Malvern Avenue
Highams Park, London E4 9NP
Website: www.global-theatre-company.net
e-mail: mep@btclick.com   Tel/Fax: 020-8523 3540

NEMESIS AGENCY
1st Floor, Alexandra Buildings
28 Queen Street, Manchester M2 5LF
Website: www.nemesisagency.co.uk
e-mail: sheila@nmsmanagement.co.uk
Fax: 0161-834 0014   Tel: 0161-834 9988

NIDGES CASTING AGENCY
Half Moon Chambers, Chapel Walks, Manchester M2 1HN
e-mail: moneypenny@nidgescasting.co.uk
Fax: 0161-832 5219   Tel: 0161-832 8259

NORTHERN PROFESSIONALS CASTING COMPANY
21 Cresswell Avenue, North Shields, Tyne & Wear NE29 9BQ
e-mail: bill.gerard@northpro83.freeserve.co.uk
Fax: 0191-296 3243   Tel: 0191-257 8635

OI OI AGENCY
Pinewood Film Studios, Room 131
Pinewood Road, Iver Heath, Bucks SL0 0NH
Website: www.oioi.org.uk
e-mail: info@oioi.org.uk
Fax: 01753 875163   Tel: 01753 655514

ORIENTAL AFRO ASIAN ARTISTS
(FBI Ltd) 4th Floor, 20-24 Kirby Street, London EC1N 8TS
Website: fullybooked-inc.com
e-mail: fbi@dircon.co.uk
Fax: 020-7242 8125   Tel: 020-7242 5542

ORIENTAL CASTING AGENCY Ltd (Peggy Sirr) ■
(Afro/Asian Artists)
1 Wyatt Park Road, Streatham Hill, London SW2 3TN
Website: www.orientalcasting.com
e-mail: peggy.sirr@btconnect.com
Fax: 020-8674 9303   Tel: 020-8671 8538

PAN ARTISTS AGENCY Ltd
Cornerways, 34 Woodhouse Lane, Sale, Cheshire M33 4JX
e-mail: bookings@panartists.freeserve.co.uk
Fax: 0161-962 6571   Tel: 0161-969 7419

PC THEATRICAL & MODEL AGENCY
10 Strathmore Gardens, Edgware, Middlesex HA8 5HJ
Website: www.twinagency.com
e-mail: twinagy@aol.com
Fax: 020-8933 3418   Tel: 020-8381 2229

PEAK MANAGEMENT
45 Highfield Drive, Matlock, Derby DE4 3FZ
e-mail: ljh@entertainmentservices.freeserve.co.uk
                          Tel/Fax: 01629 581745

PHA CASTING
Tanzaro House, Ardwick Green North, Manchester M12 6FZ
Website: www.pha-agency.co.uk
e-mail: info@pha-agency.co.uk
Fax: 0161-273 4567   Tel: 0161-273 4444

PHOENIX AGENCY
PO Box 387, Bristol BS99 3JZ
Fax: 0117-973 4160   Tel: 0117-973 1100

POWER MODEL MANAGEMENT CASTING AGENCY
Capitol House, 2-4 Heigham Street, Norwich NR2 4TE
Website: www.powermodelmanagement.co.uk
e-mail: powermodelmanagement@btinternet.com
Fax: 01603 621101   Tel: 01603 621100

PRAETORIAN ASSOCIATES
(Specialist Action Extras)
Pierce Lodge, 61 Spruce Hills, London E17 4LB
Website: www.praetorianasc.com
e-mail: info@praetorianasc.com
Fax: 020-8923 7177   Tel: 020-8923 9075

PRIDE ARTIST MANAGEMENT
The Burnside Centre
Burnside Crescent, Middleton, Manchester M24 5NN
Website: www.pride-artist-management.co.uk
e-mail: extras@pride-artist-management.co.uk
                          Tel/Fax: 0161-643 6266

faces
casting agency

Manager ~ **Nicholas Groush**
95 Ditchling Road, Brighton BN1 4ST
Tel: 01273 329436
Fax: 01273 719165   Mobile: 07876 074606

RAY'S NORTHERN CASTING AGENCY
7 Wince Close
Alkrington
Middleton, Manchester M24 1UJ   Tel/Fax: 0161-643 6745

REYNOLDS Sandra MODEL & CASTING AGENTS
62 Bell Street, London NW1 6SP
Website: www.sandrareynolds.co.uk
e-mail: tessa@sandrareynolds.co.uk
Fax: 020-7387 5848   Tel: 020-7387 5858

35 St Georges Street, Norwich NR3 1DA
Fax: 01603 219825   Tel: 01603 623842

SCREAM MANAGEMENT
32 Clifton Street
Blackpool, Lancs FY1 1JP
Website: www.screammanagement.com
e-mail: info@screammanagement.com
Fax: 01253 750829   Tel: 01253 750820

SKYBLUE CASTING Ltd
38 Commercial Street
London E1 6LP
e-mail: info@skyblue-extraspecial.com
Fax: 020-7375 1466   Tel: 020-7375 1400

SOLOMON ARTISTES
30 Clarence Street
Southend-on-Sea, Essex SS1 1BD
Website: www.solomon-artistes.co.uk
e-mail: info@solomon-artistes.co.uk
Fax: 01702 392385   Tel: 01702 392370

SÉVA DHALIVAAL

Mobile:
07956 553879

SOUTH WEST CASTING Ltd
The Courtyard, Whitchurch, Ross-on-Wye HR9 6DA
Website: www.southwestcasting.co.uk
e-mail: agent@southwestcasting.co.uk
Fax: 01600 891099   Tel: 01600 891160

SOUTH WEST FILM AGENCY
39 Vicarage Road, St Agnes, Cornwall TR5 0TF
Website: www.swfilmagency.co.uk
e-mail: steve@swfilmagency.co.uk
Mobile: 07813 007565   Tel: 01872 552741

STAV'S CASTING AGENCY
82 Station Crescent
Tottenham, London N15 5BD
Website: www.stavscasting.co.uk
e-mail: stavroslouca@btinternet.com
Mobile: 07816 336158   Tel: 020-8802 6341

TONER CASTING Ltd
Unit E6, Brunswick Small Business Centre
Brunswick Dock, Liverpool L3 4BD
Website: www.tonercasting.com
e-mail: tonercastings@btconnect.com
Fax: 0151-707 8414   Tel: 0151-708 6400

TUESDAYS CHILD Ltd
(Children & Adults)
Oakfield House, Springwood Way, Macclesfield SK10 2XA
Website: www.tuesdayschildagency.co.uk
e-mail: bookings@tuesdayschildagency.co.uk
Tel/Fax: 01625 501765

UGLY ENTERPRISES Ltd
Tigris House, 256 Edgware Road, London W2 1DS
Website: www.ugly.org
e-mail: info@ugly.org
Fax: 020-7402 0507   Tel: 020-7402 5564

UNITED COLOURS OF LONDON Ltd
(FBI) 4th Floor, 20-24 Kirby Street, London EC1N 8TS
Website: www.fullybooked-inc.com
e-mail: fbi@dircon.co.uk
Fax: 020-7242 8125   Tel: 020-7242 5542

ZEN DIRECTORIES
Suite 21, 571 Finchley Road, Hampstead, London NW3 7BN
Website: www.zendirectories.co.uk
e-mail: zendirectories@btconnect.com
Fax: 020-8458 9718   Tel: 020-8458 9671

SAMUEL FRENCH LTD

Publishers of Plays • Agents for the Collection of Royalties
Specialist Booksellers
52 Fitzroy Street London W1T 5JR
Tel 020 7255 4300 (Bookshop) 020 7387 9373 (Enquiries)
Fax 020 7387 2161 www.samuelfrench-london.co.uk
e-mail: theatre@samuelfrench-london.co.uk

A & B PERSONAL MANAGEMENT Ltd*
Suite 330, Linen Hall
162-168 Regent Street, London W1B 5TD
e-mail: billellis@aandb.co.uk
Fax: 020-7038 3699   Tel: 020-7434 4262

A J ASSOCIATES LITERARY AGENTS
Higher Healey House
Higher House Lane
White Coppice, Chorley PR6 9BT
e-mail: info@ajassociates.net
Tel/Fax: 01257 273148

A M HEATH & Co Ltd
(Fiction & Non-Fiction only)
79 St Martin's Lane, London WC2N 4RE
Fax: 020-7497 2561   Tel: 020-7836 4271

ABNER STEIN
10 Roland Gardens, London SW7 3PH
e-mail: abner@abnerstein.co.uk
Fax: 020-7370 6316   Tel: 020-7373 0456

ACTAC
7 Isles Court, Ramsbury, Wiltshire SN8 2QW
Fax: 01672 520166   Tel: 01672 520274

AGENCY (LONDON) Ltd The*
24 Pottery Lane
Holland Park, London W11 4LZ
Website: www.theagency.co.uk
e-mail: info@theagency.co.uk
Fax: 020-7727 9037   Tel: 020-7727 1346

ASPER Pauline*
Jacobs Cottage
Reservoir Lane, Sedlescombe
East Sussex TN33 0PJ
e-mail: pauline.asper@virgin.net
Tel/Fax: 01424 870412

BERLIN ASSOCIATES*
14 Floral Street, London WC2E 9DH
Fax: 020-7632 5280   Tel: 020-7836 1112

BLAKE FRIEDMANN
(Novels, Non-Fiction & TV/Film Scripts)
122 Arlington Road, London NW1 7HP
Website: www.blakefriedmann.co.uk
e-mail: julian@blakefriedmann.co.uk
Fax: 020-7284 0442   Tel: 020-7284 0408

BRITTEN Nigel MANAGEMENT*
Riverbank House
1 Putney Bridge Approach, London SW6 3JD
e-mail: nbm.office@virgin.net
Fax: 020-7384 3862   Tel: 020-7384 3842

BRODIE Alan REPRESENTATION Ltd*
(Incorporating Michael Imison Playwrights)
211 Piccadilly, London W1J 9HF
Website: www.alanbrodie.com
e-mail: info@alanbrodie.com
Fax: 020-7917 2872   Tel: 020-7917 2871

BRYANT Peter (WRITERS)
3 Jasper Road, London SE19 1SJ
Fax: 020-8670 7310   Tel: 020-8670 7820

BURKEMAN Brie*
14 Neville Court
Abbey Road, London NW8 9DD
e-mail: brie.burkeman@mail.com
Fax: 0709 2239111   Tel: 0709 2239113

CANN Alexandra REPRESENTATION*
12 Abingdon Road, London W8 6AF
e-mail: enquiries@alexandracann.com
Fax: 020-7938 4228   Tel: 020-7938 4002

CASAROTTO RAMSAY & ASSOCIATES Ltd*
National House, 60-66 Wardour Street, London W1V 4ND
Website: www.casarotto.uk.com
e-mail: agents@casarotto.uk.com
Fax: 020-7287 9128   Tel: 020-7287 4450

CLOWES Jonathan Ltd*
10 Iron Bridge House, Bridge Approach, London NW1 8BD
Fax: 020-7722 7677   Tel: 020-7722 7674

COCHRANE Elspeth PERSONAL MANAGEMENT*
14/2 2nd Floor
South Bank Commerical Centre, 140 Battersea Park Road
London SW11 4NB
e-mail: info@elspethcochrane.co.uk
Fax: 020-7622 5815   Tel: 020-7622 0314

CREATIVE MEDIA CONSULTANCY
(No unsolicited scripts, first instance sypnopsis only)
22 Kingsbury Avenue
Dunstable
Bedfordshire LU5 4PU   Tel/Fax: 01582 510869

CURTIS BROWN GROUP Ltd*
5th Floor
Haymarket House, 28-29 Haymarket
London SW1Y 4SP
e-mail: cb@curtisbrown.co.uk
Fax: 020-7393 4401   Tel: 020-7396 6600

DAISH Judy ASSOCIATES Ltd*
2 St Charles Place, London W10 6EG
Fax: 020-8964 8966   Tel: 020-8964 8811

de WOLFE Felix*
Kingsway House
103 Kingsway, London WC2B 6QX
e-mail: info@felixdewolfe.com
Fax: 020-7242 8119   Tel: 020-7242 5066

DENCH ARNOLD AGENCY The*
10 Newburgh Street, London W1F 7RN
e-mail: contact@dencharnold.com
Fax: 020-7439 1355   Tel: 020-7437 4551

DREW Bryan Ltd
Mezzanine, Quadrant House
80-82 Regent Street, London W1B 5AU
e-mail: bryan@bryandrewltd.com
Fax: 020-7437 0561   Tel: 020-7437 2293

FARNES Norma MANAGEMENT
9 Orme Court, London W2 4RL
Fax: 020-7792 2110   Tel: 020-7727 1544

FILLINGHAM Janet ASSOCIATES
52 Lowther Road, London SW13 9NU
e-mail: office@jfillassoc.co.uk
Fax: 020-8748 7374   Tel: 020-8748 5594

FILM RIGHTS Ltd
Mezzanine, Quadrant House
80-82 Regent Street, London W1B 5AU
Website: www.filmrights.ltd.uk
e-mail: information@filmrights.ltd.uk
Fax: 020-7734 0044   Tel: 020-7734 9911

FITCH Laurence Ltd
Mezzanine, Quadrant House
80-82 Regent Street, London W1B 5AU
Fax: 020-7734 0044   Tel: 020-7734 9911

FOSTER Jill Ltd*
9 Barb Mews, London W6 7PA
Fax: 020-7602 9336   Tel: 020-7602 1263

FRENCH Samuel Ltd*
52 Fitzroy Street, Fitzrovia, London W1T 5JR
Website: www.samuelfrench-london.co.uk
e-mail: theatre@samuelfrench-london.co.uk
Fax: 020-7387 2161   Tel: 020-7387 9373

FUTERMAN, ROSE & ASSOCIATES
(TV/Film/Stage Play Scripts, Showbiz & Music Biographies)
Heston Court Business Park
Camp Road, Wimbledon, London SW19 4UW
Website: www.futermanrose.co.uk
e-mail: guy@futermanrose.co.uk
Fax: 020-8605 2162   Tel: 020-8947 0188

GILLIS Pamela MANAGEMENT
46 Sheldon Avenue, London N6 4JR
Fax: 020-8341 5564   Tel: 020-8340 7868

GLASS Eric Ltd
25 Ladbroke Crescent, Notting Hill, London W11 1PS
e-mail: eglassltd@aol.com
Fax: 020-7229 6220   Tel: 020-7229 9500

HALL Rod AGENCY Ltd The*
3 Charlotte Mews, London W1T 4DZ
Website: www.rodhallagency.com
e-mail: office@rodhallagency.com
Fax: 020-7637 0807   Tel: 020-7637 0706

HANCOCK Roger Ltd*
4 Water Lane
London NW1 8NZ
e-mail: info@rogerhancock.com
Fax: 020-7267 0705   Tel: 020-7267 4418

HIGHAM David ASSOCIATES Ltd*
5-8 Lower John Street, Golden Square, London W1F 9HA
e-mail: dha@davidhigham.co.uk
Fax: 020-7437 1072   Tel: 020-7434 5900

HOLLOWOOD Jane ASSOCIATES Ltd
9A Niederwald Road, London SE26 4AD
e-mail: theresaharrild@aol.com   Tel: 020-8291 5545

HOSKINS Valerie ASSOCIATES Ltd
20 Charlotte Street, London W1T 2NA
e-mail: vha@vhassociates.co.uk
Fax: 020-7637 4493   Tel: 020-7637 4490

HOWARD Amanda ASSOCIATES Ltd*
21 Berwick Street, London W1F 0PZ
Fax: 020-7287 7785   Tel: 020-7287 9277

HURLEY LOWE MANAGEMENT*
3 Cromwell Place, London SW7 2JE
Fax: 020-7589 9405   Tel: 020-7581 1515

I C M (International Creative Management)*
Oxford House, 76 Oxford Street, London W1D 1BS
Fax: 020-7323 0101   Tel: 020-7636 6565

IMISON Michael PLAYWRIGHTS Ltd
(See BRODIE Alan REPRESENTATION Ltd)

KASS Michelle ASSOCIATES*
36-38 Glasshouse Street, London W1B 5DL
Fax: 020-7734 3394   Tel: 020-7439 1624

KENIS Steve & Co*
Royalty House, 72-74 Dean Street, London W1D 3SG
e-mail: sk@sknco.com
Fax: 020-7287 6328   Tel: 020-7434 9055

LONDON MANAGEMENT
14 Floral Street, London WC2E 9DH
Fax: 020-7632 5280   Tel: 020-72836 1112

LOWE Ian
26 Clive Street
Hereford HR1 2SB
e-mail: ian-lowe@btconnect.com   Tel/Fax: 01432 351900

MACFARLANE CHARD ASSOCIATES Ltd*
33 Percy Street, London W1T 2DF
Website: www.macfarlane-chard.co.uk
e-mail: louise@macfarlane-chard.co.uk
Fax: 020-7636 7751   Tel: 020-7636 7751

MACNAUGHTON LORD 2000 Ltd
19 Margravine Gardens, London W6 8RL
Website: www.ml2000.org.uk
e-mail: info@ml2000.org.uk
Fax: 020-8741 7443   Tel: 020-8741 0606

MANN Andrew Ltd*
1 Old Compton Street, London W1D 5JA
e-mail: manscript@onetel.net.uk
Fax: 020-7287 9264   Tel: 020-7734 4751

MANS Johnny PRODUCTIONS Ltd
PO Box 196, Hoddesdon, Herts EN10 7WQ
Fax: 01992 470516   Tel: 01992 470907

MARJACQ SCRIPTS Ltd
34 Devonshire Place, London W1G 6JW
Website: www.marjacq.com
e-mail: enquiries@marjacq.com
Fax: 020-7935 9115   Tel: 020-7935 9499

MARVIN Blanche*
21A St Johns Wood High Street, London NW8 7NG
e-mail: blanchemarvin17@hotmail.com
                          Tel/Fax: 020-7722 2313

M.B.A. LITERARY AGENTS Ltd*
62 Grafton Way, London W1T 5DW
e-mail: agent@mbalit.co.uk
Fax: 020-7387 2042   Tel: 020-7387 2076

McLEAN Bill PERSONAL MANAGEMENT Ltd
23B Deodar Road
London SW15 2NP   Tel: 020-8789 8191

ML 2000 Ltd
(See MACNAUGHTON LORD 2000 Ltd)

MORRIS William AGENCY (UK) Ltd*
52-53 Poland Street, London W1F 7LX
Fax: 020-7534 6900   Tel: 020-7534 6800

NARROW ROAD COMPANY The*
182 Brighton Road, Coulsdon, Surrey CR5 2NF
e-mail: richardireson@narrowroad.co.uk
Fax: 020-8763 2558   Tel: 020-8763 9895

P F D*
Drury House, 34-43 Russell Street, London WC2B 5HA
Fax: 020-7836 9539   Tel: 020-7344 1000

PLAYS AND MUSICALS GROUP The
Lantern House, 84 Littlehaven Lane
Horsham, West Sussex RH12 4JB
Website: www.playsandmusicals.co.uk
e-mail: sales@playsandmusicals.co.uk
Fax: 0700 5938843   Tel: 0700 5938842

POLLINGER Ltd
9 Staple Inn, Holborn, London WC1V 7QH
Website: www.pollingerltd.com
e-mail: info@pollingerltd.com
Fax: 020-7242 5737   Tel: 020-7404 0342

ROSICA COLIN Ltd
1 Clareville Grove Mews, London SW7 5AH
Fax: 020-7244 6441   Tel: 020-7370 1080

RUPERT CREW Ltd
(No Plays, Films or TV scripts)
1A King's Mews, London WC1N 2JA
e-mail: rupertcrew@compuserve.com
Fax: 020-7831 7914   Tel: 020-7242 8586

SAYLE SCREEN Ltd*
(Writers, Screenwriters & Directors for Film & TV)
11 Jubilee Place, London SW3 3TD
Fax: 020-7823 3363   Tel: 020-7823 3883

SEIFERT Linda MANAGEMENT*
91 Berwick Street, London W1F 0NE
e-mail: contact@lindaseifert.com
Fax: 020-7292 7391   Tel: 020-7292 7390

SHARLAND ORGANISATION Ltd
The Manor House
Manor Street, Raunds, Northants NN9 6JW
e-mail: tsoshar@aol.com
Fax: 01933 624860   Tel: 01933 626600

SHEIL LAND ASSOCIATES Ltd*
(Literary, Theatre & Film)
43 Doughty Street, London WC1N 2LH
e-mail: info@sheilland.co.uk
Fax: 020-7831 2127   Tel: 020-7405 9351

STEEL Elaine*
(Writers' Agent)
110 Gloucester Avenue, London NW1 8HX
e-mail: ecmsteel@aol.com
Fax: 020-8341 9807   Tel: 020-8348 0918

STEINBERG Micheline ASSOCIATES*
4th Floor
104 Great Portland Street, London W1W 6PE
e-mail: info@steinplays.com
Fax: 020-7631 1146   Tel: 020-7631 1310

STEVENS Rochelle & Co*
2 Terretts Place, Upper Street, London N1 1QZ
Fax: 020-7354 5729   Tel: 020-7359 3900

TENNYSON AGENCY The
10 Cleveland Avenue
Merton Park, London SW20 9EW
e-mail: mail@tenagy.co.uk   Tel/Fax: 020-8543 5939

THEATRE OF LITERATURE
(c/o Calder Publications)
51 The Cut, London SE1 8LF
e-mail: info@calderpublications.com
Fax: 020-7928 5930   Tel: 020-7633 0599

THURLEY J M MANAGEMENT
Archery House
33 Archery Square, Walmer, Deal CT14 7AY
e-mail: jmthurley@aol.com
Fax: 01304 371416   Tel: 01304 371721

WARE Cecily LITERARY AGENTS*
19C John Spencer Square, London N1 2LZ
e-mail: info@cecilyware.com
Fax: 020-7226 9828   Tel: 020-7359 3787

WEINBERGER Josef Ltd*
12-14 Mortimer Street, London W1T 3JJ
Website: www.josef-weinberger.com
e-mail: general.info@jwmail.co.uk
Fax: 020-7436 9616   Tel: 020-7580 2827

ALEXANDER PERSONAL MANAGEMENT Ltd
PO Box 834, Hemel Hempstead, Herts HP3 9ZP
Website: www.apmassociates.net
e-mail: apm@apmassociates.net
Fax: 01442 241099   Tel: 01442 252907

A.P.M. (Linda French)
(See ALEXANDER PERSONAL MANAGEMENT Ltd)

ARLINGTON ENTERPRISES Ltd
1-3 Charlotte Street
London W1T 1RD
Website: www.arlingtonenterprises.co.uk
e-mail: info@arlington-enterprises.co.uk
Fax: 020-7580 4994   Tel: 020-7580 0702

BLACKBURN SACHS ASSOCIATES
2-4 Noel Street
London W1F 8GB
Website: www.blackburnsachsassociates.com
e-mail: presenters@blackburnsachsassociates.com
Fax: 020-7292 7576   Tel: 020-7292 7555

BURNETT GRANGER ASSOCIATES Ltd
3 Clifford Street
London W1S 2LF
Fax: 020-7287 3239   Tel: 020-7437 8008

CAMERON Sara MANAGEMENT
(See TAKE THREE MANAGEMENT)

CANTOR WISE REPRESENTATION
(See TAKE THREE MANAGEMENT)

CHASE PERSONAL MANAGEMENT
Celebrity Division of Modelplan
4th Floor, 4 Golden Square, London W1F 9HT
e-mail: sue@sammon.fsnet.co.uk
Mobile: 00 33 6 11 09 01 40   Tel: 020-7287 8444

CRAWFORDS
PO Box 44394
London SW20 0YP
Website: www.crawfords.tv
e-mail: cr@wfords.com
Fax: 020-8879 1437   Tel: 020-8947 9999

CURTIS BROWN GROUP Ltd
Haymarket House, 28-29 Haymarket, London SW1Y 4SP
e-mail: cb@curtisbrown.co.uk
Fax: 020-7393 4401   Tel: 020-7393 4400

CYBER-ARTISTS
In The Can Ltd, The Studio
Kingsway Court, Queen's Gardens, Hove BN3 2LP
Website: www.cyberartists.co.uk
e-mail: cyber.1@btconnect.com
Fax: 01273 739984   Tel: 01273 821821

DAVID ANTHONY PROMOTIONS
PO Box 286, Warrington, Cheshire WA2 8GA
Website: www.davewarwick.co.uk
e-mail: dave@davewarwick.co.uk
Fax: 01925 416589   Tel: 01925 632496

DOWNES PRESENTERS AGENCY
96 Broadway, Bexleyheath, Kent DA6 7DE
e-mail: downes@presentersagency.com
Fax: 020-8301 5591   Tel: 020-8304 0541

EVANS Jacque MANAGEMENT Ltd
Top Floor Suite, 14 Holmesley Road, London SE23 1PJ
e-mail: jacque@jemltd.demon.co.uk
Fax: 020-8699 5192   Tel: 020-8699 1202

EXCELLENT TALENT COMPANY The
19-21 Tavistock Street, London WC2E 5PA
Website: www.excellentvoice.co.uk
e-mail: ruth@excellentvoice.co.uk   Tel: 020-7520 5656

FBI AGENCY Ltd The
PO Box 250, Leeds LS1 2AZ
Website: www.fbi-agency.ltd.uk
e-mail: casting@fbi-agency.ltd.uk
Fax: 0113-279 7270   Tel/Fax: 07050 222747

FLETCHER ASSOCIATES
(Broadcast & Media)
25 Parkway, London N20 0XN
Fax: 020-8361 8866   Tel: 020-8361 8061

FOSTER Jill Ltd
9 Barb Mews, London W6 7PA
Fax: 020-7602 9336   Tel: 020-7602 1263

FOX ARTIST MANAGEMENT Ltd
Concorde House
101 Shepherds Bush Road, London W6 7LP
Website: www.foxartistmanagement.tv
e-mail: fox.artist@btinternet.com
Fax: 020-7603 2352   Tel: 020-7602 8822

GAY Noel ARTISTS
19 Denmark Street, London WC2H 8NA
Website: www.noelgay.com
Fax: 020-7287 1816   Tel: 020-7836 3941

GRANT James MANAGEMENT
Syon Lodge, 201 London Road
Isleworth, Middlesex TW7 5BH
Website: www.jamesgrant.co.uk
e-mail: darren@jamesgrant.co.uk
Fax: 020-8232 4101   Tel: 020-8232 4100

www.actorsheadshots.co.uk

STAR MANAGEMENT

Representing Artistes for UK Television and Radio

TELEPHONE 0870 242 2276

GURNETT J. PERSONAL MANAGEMENT Ltd
2 New Kings Road, London SW6 4SA
Website: www.jgpm.co.uk
e-mail: mail@jgpm.co.uk
Fax: 020-7736 5455   Tel: 020-7736 7828

HICKS Jeremy ASSOCIATES
11-12 Tottenham Mews, London W1T 4AG
Website: www.jeremyhicks.com
e-mail: info@jeremyhicks.com
Fax: 020-7636 8880   Tel: 020-7636 8008

HOBBS Liz GROUP Ltd
First Floor, 65 London Road, Newark, Notts NG24 1RZ
Website: www.lizhobbsgroup.com
e-mail: casting@lizhobbsgroup.com
Fax: 0870 3337009   Tel: 08700 702702

INTERNATIONAL ARTISTES Ltd
4th Floor, Holborn Hall
193-197 High Holborn, London WC1V 7BD
e-mail: (name)@intart.co.uk
Fax: 020-7404 9865   Tel: 020-7025 0600

IVELAW-CHAPMAN Julie
The Chase, Chaseside Close, Cheddington, Beds LU7 0SA
e-mail: jic@collectorsworldwide.co.uk
Fax: 01296 662451   Tel: 01296 662441

JAYMEDIA
(Nigel Jay)
171 Sandbach Road, Lawton Heath End
Church Lawton, Cheshire ST7 3RA
e-mail: media@jaymedia.co.uk
Fax: 0870 1209079   Tel: 01270 884453

JLA (Jeremy Lee Associates Ltd)
4 Stratford Place, London W1C 1AT
e-mail: talk@jla.co.uk
Fax: 020-7907 2801   Tel: 020-7907 2800

KBJ MANAGEMENT Ltd
(TV Presenters)
7 Soho Street, London W1D 3DQ
e-mail: elaine@kbjmgt.co.uk
Fax: 020-7287 1191   Tel: 020-7434 6767

KNIGHT AYTON MANAGEMENT
114 St Martin's Lane, London WC2N 4BE
Website: www.knightayton.co.uk
e-mail: info@knightayton.com
Fax: 020-7836 8333   Tel: 020-7836 5333

MARKS PRODUCTIONS Ltd
2 Gloucester Gate Mews, London NW1 4AD
Fax: 020-7486 2165   Tel: 020-7486 2001

MARSH Billy ASSOCIATES Ltd
76A Grove End Road, St. Johns Wood, London NW8 9ND
e-mail: talent@billymarsh.co.uk
Fax: 020-7449 6933   Tel: 020-7449 6930

MEDIA PEOPLE
12 Nottingham Place, London W1U 5NE
Website: www.celebrity.co.uk   e-mail: info@celebrity.co.uk
Fax: 020-7224 6060   Tel: 020-7224 5050

MILES John ORGANISATION
Cadbury Camp Lane, Clapton-in-Gordano, Bristol BS20 7SB
e-mail: john@johnmiles.org.uk
Fax: 01275 810186   Tel: 01275 854675

MONDI ASSOCIATES Ltd
30 Cooper House, 2 Michael Road, London SW6 2AD
e-mail: mondi.sw@virgin.net
Fax: 020-7351 7628   Mobile: 07817 133349

MPC ENTERTAINMENT
MPC House, 15-16 Maple Mews, London NW6 5UZ
e-mail: mpc@mpce.com
Fax: 020-7624 4220   Tel: 020-7624 1184

PRESENTING FOR TV AND VIDEO
By Joanne Zorian-Lynn

'A useful read for all wannabe presenters.' Bliss

'Anyone who's ever likely to appear in front of camera can learn from this terrific book.' Film & Video Maker

Packed with technical tips, illustrations, practical exercises and advice from professional presenters

£12.99

ISBN - 0-7136-5778-2 Available from bookshops or direct from
A&C Black Customer Services Tel: 01480 212666 sales@acblack.com

MTC (UK) Ltd
20 York Street, London W1U 6PU
Website: www.mtc-uk.com
e-mail: enquiries@mtc-uk.com
Fax: 020-7935 8066   Tel: 020-7935 8000

NCI MANAGEMENT Ltd
51 Queen Anne Street, London W1G 9HS
Website: www.nci-management.com
e-mail: info@nci-management.com
Fax: 020-7487 4258   Tel: 020-7224 3960

NOEL John MANAGEMENT
2nd Floor, 10A Belmont Street, London NW1 8HH
Website: www.johnnoel.com   e-mail: john@johnnoel.com
Fax: 020-7428 8401   Tel: 020-7428 8400

OFF THE KERB PRODUCTIONS
(Comedy Presenters & Comedians)
3rd Flr, Hammer Hse, 113-117 Wardour St, London W1F 0UN
Website: www.offthekerb.co.uk
e-mail: offthekerb@aol.com
Fax: 020-7437 0647   Tel: 020-7437 0607
22 Thornhill Crescent, London N1 1BJ
Website: www.offthekerb.co.uk
e-mail: info@offthekerb.co.uk
Fax: 020-7700 4646   Tel: 020-7700 4477

PHA CASTING
Tanzaro House, Ardwick Green North, Manchester M12 6FZ
Website: www.pha-agency.co.uk
e-mail: info@pha-agency.co.uk
Fax: 0161-273 4567   Tel: 0161-273 4444

PRINCESS TALENT MANAGEMENT
Princess Studios, Whiteleys Centre
151 Queensway, London W2 4SB
Website: www.princesstv.com
e-mail: talent@princesstv.com
Fax: 020-7985 1989   Tel: 020-7985 1985

PVA MANAGEMENT Ltd
Hallow Park, Hallow, Worcester WR2 6PG
e-mail: clients@pva.co.uk
Fax: 01905 641842   Tel: 01905 640663

RAZZAMATAZZ MANAGEMENT
Mulberry Cottage, Park Farm, Haxted Rd, Lingfield RH7 6DE
Website: fillmcgrogan@btconnect.com
e-mail: mcgrogan@tinyworld.co.uk   Tel/Fax: 01342 835359

RDF MANAGEMENT
The Gloucester Building, Kensington Village
Avonmore Road, London W14 8RF
e-mail: debi.allen@rdfmanagement.com
Fax: 020-7013 4101   Tel: 020-7013 4103

ADAM PARKER | Photographer

07710 787 708 - 020 7684 2005

High end digital photography
Central London Studio
Special rates for students

1 Hoxton House, 34 Hoxton Street
London N1 6LR

Member of the Association of Photographers

RHINO MANAGEMENT
Oak Porch House
5 Western Road
Nazeing, Essex EN9 2QN
Website: www.rhino-management.co.uk
e-mail: info@rhino-management.co.uk
Mobile: 07941 453043   Tel/Fax: 01992 893259

ROSEMAN ORGANISATION The
51 Queen Anne Street, London W1G 9HS
Website: www.therosemanorganisation.co.uk
e-mail: info@therosemanorganisation.co.uk
Fax: 020-7486 4600   Tel: 020-7486 4500

SINGER Sandra ASSOCIATES
21 Cotswold Road
Westcliff-on-Sea, Essex SS0 8AA
Website: www.sandrasinger.com
e-mail: sandrasingeruk@aol.com
Fax: 01702 339393   Tel: 01702 331616

SOMETHIN' ELSE
(Grant Michaels)
Units 1-4, 1A Old Nichol Street, London E2 7HR
e-mail: grant.michaels@somethin-else.com
Fax: 020-7739 9799   Tel: 020-7204 1969

SOUTHWEST MANAGEMENT & CASTING Ltd
The Courtyard, Whitchurch, Ross-on-Wye HR9 6DA
Website: www.southwestcasting.co.uk
e-mail: agent@southwestcasting.co.uk
Fax: 01600 891099   Tel: 01600 892005

SPEAK-EASY Ltd
1 Dairy Yard, High Street, Market Harborough
Leicestershire LE16 7NL
Website: www.speak-easy.co.uk
e-mail: enquiries@speak-easy.co.uk
Fax: 01858 461994   Tel: 0870 0135126

STAR MANAGEMENT Ltd
16A Winton Drive, Glasgow G12 0QA
Website: www.starmanagement.co.uk
e-mail: carol@starmanagement.co.uk   Tel: 0870 2422276

STORM ARTISTS MANAGEMENT
1st Floor, 5 Jubilee Place, London SW3 3TD
e-mail: info@stormartists.co.uk
Fax: 020-7376 5145   Tel: 020-7437 4313

TAKE THREE MANAGEMENT
110 Gloucester Avenue
Primrose Hill, London NW1 8HX
e-mail: info@take3management.co.uk
Fax: 020-7209 3770   Tel: 020-7209 3777

TALKBACK MANAGEMENT
20-21 Newman Street, London W1T 1PG
Fax: 020-7861 8061   Tel: 020-7861 8060

TF GROUP
(Tony Fitzpatrick)
Suite 104, Davina House
137-149 Goswell Road, London EC1V 7ET
Website: www.tfa-group.com
e-mail: tony@tfa-group.com
Fax: 07000 400707   Tel: 07000 300707

UNIQUE MANAGEMENT GROUP
Beaumont House, Kensington Village
Avonmore Road, London W14 8TS
Website: www.unique-management.co.uk
e-mail: celebrities@uniquegroup.co.uk
Fax: 020-7605 1101   Tel: 020-7605 1100

VAGABOND HEART
2 Grassmere Road
Hornchurch, Essex RM11 3DP
e-mail: vagabond@virgin.net   Tel: 01708 456703

V R M
Laser House
Waterfront Quay
Salford Quays, Manchester M50 3XW
Fax: 0161-888 2242   Tel: 0161-874 5741

WILLCOCKS John MEDIA AGENCY Ltd
34 Carisbrook Close
Enfield, Middlesex EN1 3NB
e-mail: john.willcocks@blueyonder.co.uk
Fax: 020-8292 5060   Tel: 020-8364 4556

ACCENT BANK
7 Great Jubilee Wharf
78-80 Wapping Wall, London E1W 3TH
Website: www.accentbank.co.uk
e-mail: info@accentbank.co.uk   Tel/Fax: 020-7702 1589

AD VOICE
Oxford House, 76 Oxford Street, London W1D 1BS
Website: www.advoice.co.uk
e-mail: info@advoice.co.uk
Fax: 020-7323 0101   Tel: 020-7323 2345

AMERICAN AGENCY VOICES The
14 Bonny Street, London NW1 9PG
e-mail: americanagency@btconnect.com
Fax: 020-7482 4666   Tel: 020-7485 8883

ANOTHER TONGUE VOICES Ltd
The Basement
10-11 D'Arblay Street, London W1F 8DS
Website: www.anothertongue.com
e-mail: info@anothertongue.com
Fax: 020-7494 7080   Tel: 020-7494 0300

ASQUITH & HORNER
Write with SAE
The Studio, 14 College Road, Bromley, Kent BR1 3NS
Fax: 020-8313 0443   Tel: 020-8466 5580

BURNETT GRANGER ASSOCIATES Ltd
3 Clifford Street, London W1S 2LF
e-mail: raphael@burnettgranger.co.uk
Fax: 020-7287 3239   Tel: 020-7437 8029

CALYPSO VOICES
25-26 Poland Street
London W1F 8QN
e-mail: calypso@calypsovoices.com
Fax: 020-7437 0410   Tel: 020-7734 6415

CAMPBELL ASSOCIATES
2 Chelsea Cloisters
Sloane Avenue
Chelsea, London SW3 3DW
e-mail: jack@campbellassociates.org.uk
Fax: 020-7584 8799   Tel: 020-7584 5586

CASTAWAY
7 Garrick Street
London WC2E 9AR
Website: www.castaway.org.uk
e-mail: sheila@castaway.org.uk
Fax: 020-7240 2772   Tel: 020-7240 2345

CONWAY VAN GELDER Ltd
(Kate Plumpton)
3rd Floor, 18-21 Jermyn Street, London SW1Y 6HP
e-mail: kate@conwayvg.co.uk
Fax: 020-7494 3324   Tel: 020-7287 1070

CYBER-ARTISTS
In The Can Ltd
The Studio, Kingsway Court
Queen's Gardens, Hove BN3 2LP
Website: www.cyberartists.co.uk
e-mail: cyber.1@btconnect.com
Fax: 01273 739984   Tel: 01273 821821

DIAMOND MANAGEMENT
31 Percy Street, London W1T 2DD
e-mail: lj@diman.co.uk
Fax: 020-7631 0500   Tel: 020-7631 0400

DOUBLEFVOICES
(Singers Agency)
1 Hunters Lodge, Bodiam
East Sussex TN32 2UE
e-mail: rob@doublefvoices.com
Mobile: 07976 927764   Tel: 01580 830071

DREW Bryan Ltd
Mezzanine, Quadrant House
80-82 Regent Street, London W1B 5AU
e-mail: bryan@bryandrewltd.com
Fax: 020-7437 0561   Tel: 020-7437 2293

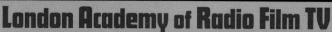

EVANS O'BRIEN
115 Humber Road
London SE3 7LW
Website: www.evansobrien.co.uk
e-mail: info@evansobrien.co.uk
Fax: 020-8293 7066   Tel: 020-8293 7077

EXCELLENT VOICE COMPANY
19-21 Tavistock Street
London WC2E 5PA
Website: www.excellentvoice.co.uk
e-mail: info@excellentvoice.co.uk   Tel: 020-7520 5656

FOREIGN VERSIONS Ltd
(Translation)
60 Blandford Street, London W1U 7JD
Website: www.foreignversions.com
e-mail: info@foreignversions.co.uk
Fax: 020-7935 0507   Tel: 020-7935 0993

GAY Noel VOICES
19 Denmark Street
London WC2H 8NA
Website: www.noelgay.com
Fax: 020-7287 1816   Tel: 020-7836 3941

fŏreignversions

GLOBAL LANGUAGE SERVICE

Voice Overs
Translations
Script Adaptation
Foreign Copywriting
Studio Production
Subtitles
Dubbing

Contact: Margaret Davies, Annie Geary
or Bérangère Capelle

On 020 7935 0993

Foreign Versions Ltd
60 Blandford Street
London W1U 7JD

e-mail: info@foreignversions.co.uk
www.foreignversions.com

GORDON & FRENCH
12-13 Poland Street, London W1F 8QB
e-mail: mail@gordonandfrench.net
Fax: 020-7734 4832   Tel: 020-7734 4818

HOBSON'S SINGERS
62 Chiswick High Road, London W4 1SY
Website: www.hobsons-international.com
e-mail: singers@hobsons-international.com
Fax: 020-8996 5350   Tel: 020-8995 3628

HOBSON'S VOICES
62 Chiswick High Road, London W4 1SY
Website: www.hobsons-international.com
e-mail: voices@hobsons-international.com
Fax: 020-8996 5350   Tel: 020-8995 3628

HOPE Sally ASSOCIATES
108 Leonard Street, London EC2A 4XS
e-mail: casting@sallyhope.biz
Fax: 020-7613 4848   Tel: 020-7613 5353

HOWARD Amanda ASSOCIATES
21 Berwick Street, London W1F 0PZ
Website: www.amandahowardassociates.co.uk
e-mail: mail@amandahowardassociates.co.uk
Fax: 020-7287 7785   Tel: 020-7287 9277

KIDZTALK Ltd
(Children's Voices aged 4-24)
Website: www.kidztalk.com
e-mail: studio@kidztalk.com
Fax: 01737 352456   Tel: 01737 350808

LIP SERVICE
60-66 Wardour Street, London W1F 0TA
Website: www.lipservice.co.uk
e-mail: bookings@lipservice.co.uk
Fax: 020-7734 3373   Tel: 020-7734 3393

MANSON Andrew
(Genuine Americans only)
288 Munster Road, London SW6 6BQ
Website: www.andrewmanson.com
e-mail: post@andrewmanson.com
Fax: 020-7381 8874   Tel: 020-7386 9158

MARKHAM & FROGGATT Ltd
4 Windmill Street, London W1T 2HZ
e-mail: charlie@markhamfroggatt.co.uk
Fax: 020-7637 5233   Tel: 020-7636 4412

MBA
3rd Floor Suite, 10-11 Lower John Street, London W1F 9EB
e-mail: info@braidman.com
Fax: 020-7439 3600   Tel: 020-7437 0817

McREDDIE Ken Ltd
21 Barrett Street, London W1U 1BD
Fax: 020-7408 0886   Tel: 020-7499 7448

NOEL John MANAGEMENT
2nd Floor, 10A Belmont Street, London NW1 8HH
Website: www.johnnoel.com
e-mail: john@johnnoel.com
Fax: 020-7428 8401   Tel: 020-7428 8400

NUTOPIA-CHANG VOICES
Number 8
132 Charing Cross Road, London WC2H 0LA
Website: www.nutopia.co.uk
Fax: 029-2070 9440   Mobile: 07801 493133

P F D
Drury House, 34-43 Russell Street
London WC2B 5HA
Fax: 020-7836 9544   Tel: 020-7344 1010

QVOICE
4th Floor, Holborn Hall
193-197 High Holborn, London WC1V 7BD
Website: www.qvoice.co.uk
e-mail: info@qvoice.co.uk
Fax: 020-7025 0659   Tel: 020-7025 0660

RABBIT VOCAL MANAGEMENT
2nd Floor, 18 Broadwick Street, London W1F 8HS
Website: www.rabbit.uk.net
e-mail: info@rabbit.uk.net
Fax: 020-7287 6566   Tel: 020-7287 6466

RHINO MANAGEMENT
Oak Porch House, 5 Western Road, Nazeing, Essex EN9 2QN
Website: www.rhino-management.co.uk
e-mail: info@rhino-management.co.uk
Mobile: 07941 453043   Tel/Fax: 01992 893259

RHUBARB
Bakerloo Chambers, 304 Edgware Road, London W2 1DY
Website: www.rhubarb.co.uk
e-mail: enquiries@rhubarb.co.uk
Fax: 020-7724 1030   Tel: 020-7724 1300

SHINING MANAGEMENT Ltd
82C Shirland Road
London W9 2EQ
Website: www.shiningvoices.com
e-mail: info@shiningvoices.com
Fax: 020-7286 6123   Tel: 020-7286 6092

SOUTHWEST MANAGEMENT & CASTING Ltd
The Courtyard
Whitchurch
Ross-on-Wye HR9 6DA
Website: www.southwestcasting.co.uk
e-mail: agent@southwestcasting.co.uk
Fax: 01600 891099   Tel: 01600 892005

SPEAK Ltd
59 Lionel Road North
Brentford, Middlesex TW8 9QZ
Website: www.speak.ltd.uk
e-mail: info@speak.ltd.uk
Fax: 020-8578 0333   Tel: 020-8578 0666

SPEAK-EASY Ltd
1 Dairy Yard
High Street
Market Harborough
Leicestershire LE16 7NL
Website: www.speak-easy.co.uk
e-mail: enquiries@speak-easy.co.uk
Fax: 01858 461994   Tel: 0870 0135126

STONE Richard PARTNERSHIP The
2 Henrietta Street
London WC2E 8PS
e-mail: all@richstonepart.co.uk
Fax: 020-7497 0869   Tel: 020-7497 0849

SUMMERS Mark MANAGEMENT & AGENCY
9 Hansard Mews
Kensington, London W14 8BJ
Website: www.marksummers.com
e-mail: mark@marksummers.com
Fax: 0870 4435623   Tel: 0870 4435621

TALKING HEADS
2-4 Noel Street
London W1F 8GB
Website: www.talkingheadsvoices.com
e-mail: voices@talkingheadsvoices.com
Fax: 020-7292 7576   Tel: 020-7292 7555

TERRY Sue VOICES Ltd
5th Floor
18 Broadwick Street
London W1F 8HS
Website: www.sueterryvoices.co.uk
e-mail: sue@sueterryvoices.co.uk
Fax: 020-7434 2042   Tel: 020-7434 2040

TONGUE & GROOVE
3 Stevenson Square, Manchester M1 1DN
Website: www.tongueandgroove.co.uk
e-mail: info@tongueandgroove.co.uk
Fax: 0161-237 1809   Tel: 0161-228 2469

VACCA Roxane VOICES
73 Beak Street
London W1F 9SR
Website: www.roxanevaccamanagement.com
e-mail: mail@roxanevaccavoices.com
Fax: 020-7734 8086   Tel: 020-7734 8085

VOCAL POINT
25 Denmark Street
London WC2H 8NJ
Website: www.vocalpoint.net
e-mail: enquiries@vocalpoint.net
Fax: 020-7419 0699   Tel: 020-7419 0700

VOICE & SCRIPT INTERNATIONAL
Aradco House
132 Cleveland Street, London W1T 6AB
Website: www.vsi.tv
e-mail: info@vsi.tv
Fax: 020-7692 7711   Tel: 020-7692 7700

VOICE BOX
Laser House, Waterfront Quay
Salford Quays, Manchester M50 3XW
Website: www.thevoicebox.co.uk
Fax: 0161-888 2242   Tel: 0161-874 5741

VOICE GALLERY The
34 Stockton Road
Manchester M21 9ED
Website: www.thevoicegallery.co.uk
e-mail: info@thevoicegallery.co.uk   Tel/Fax: 0161-718 1009

VOICE SHOP
Bakerloo Chambers, 304 Edgware Road, London W2 1DY
Website: www.voice-shop.co.uk
e-mail: info@voice-shop.co.uk
Fax: 020-7706 1002   Tel: 020-7402 3966

VOICE SQUAD
62 Blenheim Gardens, London NW2 4NT
Website: www.voicesquad.com
e-mail: bookem@voicesquad.com
Fax: 020-8452 7944   Tel: 020-8450 4451

VOICEBANK, THE IRISH VOICE-OVER AGENCY
The Barracks, 76 Irishtown Road, Dublin 4, Eire
Website: www.voicebank.ie
e-mail: voicebank@voicebank.ie
Fax: 00 353 1 6607850   Tel: 00 353 1 6687234

VOICECALL
67A Gondar Gardens
London NW6 1EP
e-mail: voices@voicecall-online.co.uk   Tel: 020-7209 1064

VOICEOVERS.CO.UK
6 Cleveland Road, Plymouth PL4 9DF
Website: www.voiceovers.co.uk
e-mail: info@voiceovers.co.uk
Fax: 01752 227141   Tel: 01752 207313

WOOTTON Suzy VOICES
75 Shelley Street, Kingsley, Northampton NN2 7HZ
e-mail: suzy@suzywoottonvoices.com
Fax: 0870 7659668   Tel: 0870 7659660

YAKETY YAK
8 Bloomsbury Square, London WC1A 2NE
Website: www.yaketyyak.co.uk
e-mail: info@yaketyyak.co.uk
Fax: 020-7404 6109   Tel: 020-7430 2600

A1 ANIMALS
(Farm, Domestic & Exotic Animals)
Folly Farm, Folly Lane
Bramley, Hants RG26 5BD
Website: www.a1animals.co.uk
e-mail: info@a1animals.freeserve.co.uk
Fax: 01256 880653   Tel: 01256 880993

ABBIE@JANIMALS Ltd
T/A Abbie's Animals
Naish Hill Cottage
Lacock, Wilts SN15 2QJ
Website: www.abbiesanimals.co.uk
e-mail: info@abbiesanimals.co.uk
Mobile: 07900 494028   Tel/Fax: 0870 2417693

ABNALLS HORSES
Abnalls Farm
Cross in Hand Lane
Lichfield, Staffs WS13 8DZ
e-mail: carolynsj@dial.pipex.com
Fax: 01543 417226   Tel: 01543 417075

ALTERNATIVE ANIMALS
(Animatronics/Taxidermy)
28 Greaves Road
High Wycombe, Bucks HP13 7JU
Website: www.animalworld.org.uk
e-mail: animalworld@bushinternet.com
Fax: 01494 441385   Tel: 01494 448710

AMAZING STUNT DOGS
18 Rosewood Avenue
Kingsway
Rugby, Warwickshire CV22 5PJ
Website: www.amazingstuntdogs.co.uk
Mobile: 07759 804813   Tel: 01788 812703

ANIMAL ACTING
(Stunts, Prop, Horse-Drawn Vehicles)
15 Wolstenvale Close
Middleton, Manchester M24 2HP
Website: www.animalacting.com
e-mail: information@animalacting.com
Fax: 0161-655 3700   Tel: 0800 387755

ANIMAL ACTORS
(Animals, Birds, Reptiles)
95 Ditching Road, Brighton
Sussex BN1 4ST   Tel: 020-8654 0450

ANIMAL AMBASSADORS
Old Forest
Hampstead Norreys Road
Hermitage, Berks RG18 9SA
e-mail: kayweston@tiscali.co.uk
Mobile: 07831 558594   Tel/Fax: 01635 200900

ANIMAL ARK
(Animals & Animal Prop Shop)
Studio, 29 Somerset Road
Brentford
Middlesex TW8 8BT
Website: www.animal-ark.co.uk
e-mail: info@animal-ark.co.uk
Fax: 020-8560 5762   Tel: 020-8560 3029

ANIMAL ARRANGERS
(Animal Suppliers & Co-ordinators)
28 Greaves Road
High Wycombe, Bucks HP13 7JU
Fax: 07930 439895   Tel: 01494 448710

ANIMAL CASTING
89 Tilehurst Road
Earlsfield, London SW1B 3EX
e-mail: silcresta@aol.com
Mobile: 07956 246450   Tel: 020-8874 9530

ANIMAL WELFARE FILMING FEDERATION
28 Greaves Road
High Wycombe, Bucks HP13 7JU
e-mail: animalworld@bushinternet.com
Fax: 07930 439895   Mobile: 07770 666088

ANIMAL WELFARE INSPECTION SERVICES
(Independent Consultancy of All Aspects of Use of Animals
in Media Productions)
15B St Anne's Road, Eastbourne BN21 2AJ
e-mail: animal.insp.svcs@amserve.net
                    Tel/Fax: 01323 726105

ANIMAL WORLD Ltd
(Trevor Smith)
19 Greaves Road
High Wycombe, Bucks HP13 7JU
Website: www.animalworld.org.uk
e-mail: animalworld@bushinternet.com
Fax: 01494 441385   Tel: 01494 442750

ANIMALATION
16 Wiltshire Avenue
Crowthorne, Berks RG45 6NG
Fax: 01344 779437   Tel: 01344 775244

ANIMALS GALORE
208 Smallfield Road
Horley, Surrey RH6 9LS
Fax: 01342 841546   Tel: 01342 842400

ANIMALS O KAY
3 Queen Street, Chipperfield
Kings Langley, Herts WD4 9BT
Website: www.animalsokay.com
e-mail: kay@animalsokay.com
Fax: 01923 269076   Tel: 01923 291277

A-Z ANIMALS Ltd
The Bell House, Bell Lane
Fetcham, Surrey KT22 9ND
e-mail: xlence@a-zanimals.com
Fax: 01372 377666   Tel: 01372 377111

A-Z DOGS
The Bell House, Bell Lane
Fetcham, Surrey KT22 9ND
e-mail: dogs@a-zanimals.com
Fax: 01372 377666   Tel: 020-7248 6222

BUGS & THINGS
28 Greaves Road, High Wycombe, Bucks HP13 7JU
Website: www.animalworld.org.uk
e-mail: animalworld@bushinternet.com
Fax: 01494 441385   Tel: 01494 448710

CANINE FILM ACADEMY The
57C Cheapside Road, Ascot, Berks SL5 7QR
Website: www.thecaninefilmacademy.com
e-mail: katie.cfa@virgin.net
Mobile: 07767 341424   Tel: 01344 291465

CHEESEMAN Virginia
21 Willow Close, Flackwell Heath
High Wycombe, Bucks HP10 9LH
Website: www.virginiacheeseman.co.uk
e-mail: virginia@virginiacheeseman.co.uk
                                      Tel: 01628 522632

CLIFT Pauline
15 Gwendale
Pinkneys Green
Maidenhead, Berks SL6 6SH
e-mail: paulineclift@btclick.com   Tel/Fax: 01628 788564

COTSWOLD FARM PARK
(Rare Breed Farm Animals)
Guiting Power, Cheltenham
Gloucestershire GL54 5UG
Fax: 01451 850423   Tel: 01451 850307

CREATURE FEATURE
(Animal Agent)
Gubhill Farm, Ae, Dumfries, Scotland DG1 1RL
Website: www.creaturefeature.co.uk
e-mail: david@creaturefeature.co.uk
Mobile: 07770 774866   Tel/Fax: 01387 860648

DOLBADARN FILM HORSES
Dolbadarn Hotel, High Street
Llanberis, Gwynedd
North Wales LL55 4SU
Website: www.filmhorses.co.uk
e-mail: info@filmhorses.co.uk
Mobile: 07710 461341   Tel: 01286 870277

DUDLEY Yvonne LRPS
(Glamour Dog)
55 Cambridge Park, Wanstead
London E11 2PR   Tel: 020-8989 1528

EAST NOLTON RIDING STABLES
Nolton, Nr Newgale, Haverfordwest
Pembrokeshire SA62 3NW
Website: www.noltonstables.com
e-mail: noltonstables@aol.com
Fax: 01437 710967   Tel: 01437 710360

FILM HORSES
(Horses, Saddlery, Equestrian Centre)
The Shire Horse Centre
Bath Road, Littlewick Green
Maidenhead, Berks SL6 3QA
Website: www.filmhorses.com
Mobile: 07831 629662   Tel/Fax: 01628 822770

FREE ANIMAL CONSULTANT SERVICES
28 Greaves Road
High Wycombe
Bucks HP13 7JU
Fax: 01494 441385   Tel: 08000 749383

GET STUFFED
(Taxidermy)
105 Essex Road
London N1 2SL
Website: www.thegetstuffed.co.uk
e-mail: taxidermy@thegetstuffed.co.uk
Fax: 020-7359 8253   Tel: 020-7226 1364

GRAY Robin COMMENTARIES
(Equestrian Equipment)
Comptons, Isington
Alton, Hants GU34 4PL
e-mail: gray@isington.fsnet.co.uk   Tel: 01420 23347

KNIGHTS OF ARKLEY The
Glyn Sylen Farm, Five Roads
Llanelli SA15 5BJ
Website: www.knightsofarkley.com
e-mail: penny@knightsofarkley.fsnet.co.uk
                                      Tel/Fax: 01269 861001

MABEL'S PLACE TV & FILM AQUATICS
114 Mill Lane
West Hampstead
London NW6 1NF
e-mail: mabelsplace14@hotmail.com
Mobile: 07960 152826   Tel/Fax: 020-7813 2644

MILLENNIUM BUGS
(Live Insects)
28 Greaves Road
High Wycombe, Bucks HP13 7JU
e-mail: animalworld@bushinternet.com
Fax: 01494 441385   Tel: 01494 448710

MORTON Geoff
(Shire Horse & Equipment)
Hasholme Carr Farm
Holme on Spalding Moor
York YO43 4BD   Tel: 01430 860393

OTTERS
(Tame Otters) (Daphne & Martin Neville)
Baker's Mill
Frampton Mansell
Stroud, Glos GL6 8JH
e-mail: martin.neville@ukgateway.net   Tel: 01285 760234

PATCHETTS EQUESTRIAN CENTRE
Hillfield Lane
Aldenham
Watford, Herts WD25 8PE
Website: www.patchetts.co.uk
Fax: 01923 859289   Tel: 01923 855776

PROP FARM Ltd
(Pat Ward)
Grange Farm, Elmton, Nr Creswell
North Derbyshire S80 4LX
e-mail: pat/les@propfarm.free-online.co.uk
Fax: 01909 721465   Tel: 01909 723100

ROCKWOOD ANIMALS ON FILM
Lewis Terrace, Llanbradach
Caerphilly CF83 3JZ
Website: www.rockwoodanimals.com
e-mail: rockwood@gxn.co.uk
Mobile: 07973 930983   Tel: 029-2088 5420

SCHOOL OF NATIONAL EQUITATION Ltd
(Sam Humphrey)
Bunny Hill Top, Costock
Loughborough
Leicestershire LE12 6XE
Website: www.bunny-hill.co.uk
e-mail: sam@bunny-hill.co.uk
Fax: 01509 856067   Tel: 01509 852366

STAR DOGS ROADSHOW
(Trick Performing Dogs for Stage & Television)
10 Edinburgh Road
Wallasey
Merseyside CH45 4LR
Website: www.star-dogs.co.uk
Mobile: 07818 263147   Tel/Fax: 0151-200 7174

STUDIO & TV HIRE
(Stuffed Animal Specialists)
3 Ariel Way, Wood Lane
White City, London W12 7SL
Website: www.stvhire.com
e-mail: enquiries@stvhire.com
Fax: 020-8740 9662   Tel: 020-8749 3445

STUNT DOGS
3 The Chestnuts
Clifton
Deddington, Oxon OX15 0PE
e-mail: gill@euro-stuntdogs.co.uk   Tel/Fax: 01869 338546

STUNTS APOCALYPSE
(Ian Van Temperley)
PO Box 11, Frodsham, Cheshire WA6 8GZ
Website: www.horsemen-of-the-apocalypse.co.uk
e-mail: ian@stuntsapocalypse.co.uk
Mobile: 07887 602749   Tel: 01766 819121

TAME WOLF SPECIALISTS The
The UK Wolf Conservation Trust
UK Wolf Centre, Butlers Farm, Beenham, Berks RG7 5NT
Website: www.ukwolf.org
e-mail: ukwct@ukwolf.org   Tel: 0118-971 3330

TATE Olive
(Trained Dogs & Cats)
49 Upton Road
Bexleyheath, Kent DA6 8LW
Mobile: 07731 781892   Tel/Fax: 020-8303 0683

TATE'S Nigel DOGSTARS
4 Hoads Wood Gardens
Ashford, Kent TN25 4QB
Website: www.dogstars.co.uk
e-mail: animals@dogstars.co.uk
Fax: 07092 031929   Tel: 01233 635439

THORNE'S OF WINDSOR
(Beekeeping & Other Insect Suppliers)
Oakley Green Farm
Oakley Green
Windsor, Berks SL4 4PZ
e-mail: mattallan@aol.com
Fax: 01753 830605   Tel: 01753 830256

WHITE DOVES COMPANY Ltd The
(Provision of up to 100 Doves for Release)
9-11 High Beech Road
Loughton, Essex IG10 4BN
Website: www.thewhitedovecompany.co.uk
e-mail: thewhitedovecompany@lineone.net
Fax: 020-8502 2461   Tel: 020-8508 1414

WOODS Sue
(Animal Promotions, Specializing in Dogs, Domestic Cats,
Rodents, Poultry & Farm Stock)
White Rocks Farm
Underriver, Sevenoaks, Kent TN15 0SL
Website: www.animalspromotions.co.uk
e-mail: happyhounds@yahoo.co.uk
Fax: 01732 763767   Tel: 01732 762913

ALDERSHOT
West End Centre
Queens Road, Aldershot, Hants GU11 3JD
Website: www.westendcentre.co.uk
BO: 01252 330040 Admin: 01252 408040

ANDOVER
Cricklade Theatre
Charlton Road, Andover, Hants SP10 1EJ
e-mail: ssharp@cricklade.ac.uk
Fax: 01264 360066 Tel: 01264 360063

BAMPTON
West Ox Arts
WOA Gallery, Market Square
Bampton, Oxfordshire OX18 2JH
Administrator: Olivia Thornton
e-mail: www.westoxarts@yahoo.co.uk Tel: 01993 850137

BANGOR
Theatr Gwynedd, Ffordd Deiniol, Bangor, Gwynedd LL57 2TL
Website: www.theatrgwynedd.co.uk
e-mail: theatr@theatrgwynedd.co.uk
BO: 01248 351708 Admin: 01248 351707

BILLERICAY
Billericay Arts Association
The Fold, 72 Laindon Road, Billericay, Essex CM12 9LD
Secretary: Edmond Philpott Tel: 01277 659286

BINGLEY
Bingley Arts Centre
Main Street, Bingley, West Yorkshire BD16 2LZ
Head of Halls: Mark Davies Tel: 01274 431576

BIRMINGHAM
The Custard Factory
Gibb Street, Digbeth, Birmingham B9 4AA
Website: www.custardfactory.com
e-mail: post@custardfactory.com
Fax: 0121-604 8888 Tel: 0121-224 7777

BIRMINGHAM
Midlands Arts Centre
Cannon Hill Park, Birmingham B12 9QH
Website: www.macarts.co.uk
Director: Dorothy Wilson
BO: 0121-440 3838 Admin: 0121-440 4221

BOSTON
Blackfriars Arts Centre
Spain Lane, Boston, Lincolnshire PE21 6HP
Contact: Andrew Rawlinson
Website: www.blackfriars.uk.com
e-mail: director@blackfriars.uk.com
Fax: 01205 358855 Tel: 01205 363108

BRACKNELL
South Hill Park Arts Centre
Bracknell, Ringmead, Berkshire RG12 7PA
Chef Executive: Ron McAllister
Fax: 01344 411427
BO: 01344 484123 Admin: 01344 484858

BRADFORD
Theatre in the Mill
University of Bradford
Shearbridge Road, Bradford, West Yorkshire BD7 1DP
e-mail: theatre@bradford.ac.uk Tel: 01274 233188

BRAINTREE
The Town Hall Centre, Market Square
Braintree, Essex CM7 3YG
General Manager: Jean Grice Tel: 01376 557776

BRENTFORD
Watermans, 40 High Street, Brentford TW8 0DS
Fax: 020-8232 1030
BO: 020-8232 1010 Admin: 020-8232 1020

BRIDGWATER
Bridgwater Arts Centre
11-13 Castle Street, Bridgwater, Somerset TA6 3DD
Website: www.bridgwaterartscentre.co.uk
e-mail: info@bridgwaterartscentre.co.uk Tel: 01278 422700

BRIGHTON
Gardner Arts Centre
University of Sussex, Falmer, Brighton BN1 9RA
Director: Sue Webster
Website: www.gardnerarts.co.uk
e-mail: info@gardnerarts.co.uk
Fax: 01273 678551
BO: 01273 685861 Admin: 01273 685447

BRISTOL
Arnolfini, 16 Narrow Quay, Bristol BS1 4QA
Operations Manager: Polly Cole
Director: Caroline Collier
e-mail: arnolfini@arnolfini.demon.org.uk
Fax: 0117-917 2303 Tel: 0117-917 2300

BUILTH WELLS
Wyeside Arts Centre
Castle Street, Builth Wells, Powys LD2 3BN
Fax: 01982 553995 Tel: 01982 553668

BURTON UPON TRENT
The Brewhouse
Union Street, Burton upon Trent, Staffs DE14 1EB
Arts Manager: Rachel Walker
Administrator: Mike Mear
Website: www.brewhouse.co.uk
e-mail: brewhousearts@btconnect.com
Fax: 01283 515106
BO: 01283 516030 Admin: 01283 567720

BURY
The Met Arts Centre
Market Street, Bury, Lancs BL9 0BW
Director: Ged Kelly
e-mail: post@themet.biz
Fax: 0161-763 5056
BO: 0161-761 2216 Admin: 0161-761 7107

CANNOCK
Prince of Wales Centre
Church Sreet, Cannock, Staffs WS11 1DE
General Manager: Richard Kay Tel: 01543 466453

CARDIFF
Chapter Arts Centre
Market Road, Canton, Cardiff CF5 1QE
Theatre Programmer: James Tyson
BO: 029-2030 4400 Admin: 029-2031 1050

CHESTERFIELD
The Arts Centre
Chesterfield College, Sheffield Road, Chesterfield
Derbyshire S41 7LL
Co-ordinator: Joe Littlewood Tel/Fax: 01246 500578

CHIPPING NORTON
The Theatre, 2 Spring St, Chipping Norton, Oxon OX7 5NL
Director: Caroline Sharman General Manager: Chris Durham
Website: www.chippingnortontheatre.co.uk
e-mail: admin@chippingnortontheatre.co.uk
Fax: 01608 642324
BO: 01608 642350 Admin: 01608 642349

CHRISTCHURCH
The Regent Centre
51 High Street, Christchurch, Dorset BH23 1AS
General Manager: Keith Lancing
Website: www.regentcentre.co.uk
e-mail: info@regentcentre.co.uk
Fax: 01202 479952
BO: 01202 499148   Admin: 01202 479819

CIRENCESTER
Brewery Arts, Brewery Court, Cirencester, Glos GL7 1JH
Artistic Director: Dan Scrivener
Website: www.breweryarts.org.uk
e-mail: admin@breweryarts.org.uk
Fax: 01285 644060
BO: 01285 655522   Admin: 01285 657181

COLCHESTER
Colchester Arts Centre
Church Street, Colchester, Essex CO1 1NF
Director: Anthony Roberts
Website: www.colchesterartscentre.com
e-mail: info@colchesterartscentre.com   Tel: 01206 500900

CORNWALL
Sterts Theatre & Arts Centre
Upton Cross, Liskeard, Cornwall PL14 5AZ
Tel/Fax: 01579 362382   Tel/Fax: 01579 362962

COVENTRY
Warwick Arts Centre
University of Warwick, Coventry CV4 7AL
Director: Alan Rivett
Website: www.warwickartscentre.co.uk
e-mail: arts.centre@warwick.ac.uk
BO: 024-7652 4524   Admin: 024-7652 3734

CUMBERNAULD
Cumbernauld Theatre, Kildrum, Cumbernauld G67 2BN
Administrator: Debra Jaffrey
Artistic Director: Simon Sharkey
Fax: 01236 738408
BO: 01236 732887   Admin: 01236 737235

DARLINGTON
Darlington Arts Centre
Vane Terrace, Darlington, County Durham DL3 7AX
BO: 01325 486555   Admin: 01325 483271

DORSET
The Coade Hall Theatre, Blandford Forum, Dorset DT11 0PX
Administrator: Claire Topping
Artistic Director: Jane Quan
e-mail: bac@bryanston.co.uk
Fax: 01258 484506   Tel: 01258 456533

EDINBURGH
Netherbow: Scottish Storytelling Centre
The Netherbow, 43-45 High Street, Edinburgh EH1 1SR
Director: Dr Donald Smith
Website: www.scottishstorytellingcentre.co.uk
e-mail: scottishstorytellingcentre@uk.uumail.com
                                    Tel: 0131-556 9579

EDINBURGH
Theatre Workshop, 34 Hamilton Place, Edinburgh EH3 5AX
Director: Robert Rae
Fax: 0131-220 0112   Tel: 0131-225 7942

EPSOM
Playhouse, Ashley Avenue, Epsom, Surrey KT18 5AL
Venues Manager: Trevor Mitchell
Website: www.epsomplayhouse.co.uk
e-mail: tmitchell@epsom-ewell.gov.uk
Fax: 01372 726228
BO: 01372 742555   Admin: 01372 742226

EVESHAM
Evesham Arts Centre
Victoria Avenue, Evesham, Worcestershire WR11 4QH
President: Lauri Griffith-Jones
BO: 01386 45567
Director: 01386 446067   Theatre: 01386 48883

EXETER
Exeter Phoenix
Bradninch Place, Gandy Street, Exeter, Devon EX4 3LS
Business Manager: Patrick Cunningham
e-mail: admin@exeterphoenix.org.uk
Fax: 01392 667599
BO: 01392 667080   Admin: 01392 667060

FAREHAM
Ashcroft Arts Centre
Osborn Road, Fareham, Hants PO16 7DX
Director/Programmer: Annabel Cook
Website: www.ashcroft.org.uk
e-mail: info@ashcroft.org.uk
Fax: 01329 825661
BO: 01329 310600   Tel: 01329 235161

FROME
Merlin Theatre, Bath Road, Frome, Somerset BA11 2HG
Website: www.merlintheatre.co.uk
BO: 01373 465949   Admin: 01373 461360

GAINSBOROUGH
Trinity Arts Centre
Trinity Street, Gainsborough, Lincolnshire DN21 2AL
e-mail: trinityarts@west-lindsey.gov.uk
Fax: 01427 811198
BO/Admin: 01427 676655   Admin: 01427 810298

GREAT TORRINGTON
The Plough Arts Centre
9-11 Fore Street, Great Torrington, Devon EX38 8HQ
Website: www.plough-arts.org
BO: 01805 624624   Admin: 01805 622552

HARLECH
Theatr Ardudwy, Harlech, Gwynedd LL46 2PU
Theatre Director: Rhian Jones   BO: 01766 780667

HAVANT
Havant Arts Centre
East Street, Havant, Hants PO9 1BS
Director: Amanda Eels
Website: www.havantartsactive.co.uk
e-mail: info@havantartsactive.co.uk
Fax: 023-9249 8577
BO: 023-9247 2700   Admin: 023-9248 0113

HEMEL HEMPSTEAD
Old Town Hall Arts Centre
High Street, Hemel Hempstead, Herts HP1 3AE
General Manager: Alison Young
Website: www.oldtownhall.co.uk
e-mail: othadmin@dacorum.gov.uk
BO: 01442 228091   Admin: 01442 228095

HEXHAM
Queens Hall Arts
Beaumont Street, Hexham
Northumberland NE46 3LS
Artistic Director: Geof Keys
Website: www.queenshall.co.uk
e-mail: boxoffice@queenshall.co.uk
Fax: 01434 652478   Tel: 01434 652476

HORSHAM
The Capitol
North Street, Horsham, West Sussex RH12 1RG
General Manager: Michael Gattrell
Website: www.thecapitolhorsham.com
Fax: 01403 756092   Tel: 01403 550220

HUDDERSFIELD
Kirklees (various venues)
Kirklees Cultural Services
Red Doles Lane, Huddersfield HD2 1YF
BO: 01484 223200   Admin: 01484 226300

INVERNESS
Eden Court Theatre, Bishop's Road, Inverness IV3 5SA
Director: Colin Marr
e-mail: admin@eden-court.co.uk
BO: 01463 234234   Admin: 01463 239841

JERSEY
Jersey Arts Centre
Phillips Street, St Helier, Jersey JE2 4SW
Director: Daniel Austin
Administrator: Graeme Humphries
Fax: 01534 726788
BO: 01534 700444   Admin: 01534 700400

KENDAL
Brewery Arts Centre
Highgate, Kendal, Cumbria LA9 4HE
Chief Executive: Sam Mason
Website: www.breweryarts.co.uk
e-mail: admin@breweryarts.co.uk
BO: 01539 725133   Admin: 01539 722833

KING'S LYNN
Corn Exchange
Tuesday Market Place, King's Lynn, Norfolk PE30 1JW
Marketing Manager: Suzanne Hopp
e-mail: suzanne.hopp@west-norfolk.gov.uk
Fax: 01553 762141
BO: 01553 764864   Tel: 01553 765565

KING'S LYNN
King's Lynn Arts Centre
27 King's Street, King's Lynn, Norfolk PE30 1HA
Website: www.kingslynnarts.co.uk
Fax: 01553 762141
BO: 01553 764864   Tel: 01553 765565

LEICESTER
Phoenix Arts Centre
21 Upper Brown Street, Leicester LE1 5TE
e-mail: vicky@phoenix.org.uk
BO: 0116-255 4854   Admin: 0116-224 7700

LICHFIELD
Lichfield District Arts Association
Donegal House, Bore Street, Lichfield WS13 6NE
Director: Brian Pretty
Website: www.lichfieldarts.org.uk
e-mail: info@lichfieldarts.org.uk
Fax: 01543 308211   Tel: 01543 262223

LIVERPOOL
Bluecoat Arts Centre, School Lane, Liverpool L1 3BX
e-mail: admin@bluecoatartscentre.com   Tel: 0151-709 5297

LONDON
Artsdepot
5 Nether Street, North Finchley, London N12
Website: www.artsdepot.co.uk
e-mail: info@artsdepot.co.uk
BO: 020-8449 0048   Tel: 020-8359 7767

LONDON
BAC
Lavender Hill, Battersea, London SW11 5TN
Website: www.bac.org.uk
e-mail: mailbox@bac.org.uk
Fax: 020-7978 5207
BO: 020-7223 2223   Admin: 020-7223 6557

LONDON
Chats Palace
42-44 Brooksby's Walk, Hackney, London E9 6DF
Administrator: Nick Reed
e-mail: chatspalace@hotmail.com
                                 BO/Admin: 020-8533 0227

LONDON
Cockpit Theatre
Gateforth Street, London NW8 8EH
e-mail: dave.wybrow@cwc.ac.uk
Fax: 020-7258 2921
BO: 020-7258 2925   Admin: 020-7258 2920

LONDON
The Drill Hall
16 Chenies Street, London WC1E 7EX
Website: www.drillhall.co.uk
e-mail: admin@drillhall.co.uk
Fax: 020-7307 5062   Tel: 020-7307 5061

LONDON
Hoxton Hall Arts Centre
130 Hoxton Street, London N1 6SH
Venue Manager: Jonathan Salisbury
Website: www.hoxtonhall.co.uk
e-mail: admin@hoxtonhall.co.uk
Fax: 020-7729 3815   Admin: 020-7684 0060

LONDON
Institute of Contemporary Arts
(No in-house productions or castings)
The Mall, London SW1Y 5AH
Performing Arts & International Projects Director:
Vivienne Gaskin
Website: www.ica.org.uk
e-mail: vivienneg@ica.org.uk
Fax: 020-7306 0122
BO: 020-7930 3647   Admin: 020-7930 0493

LONDON
Islington Arts Factory
2 Parkhurst Road, London N7 0SF
e-mail: islington@artsfactory.fsnet.co.uk
Fax: 020-7700 7229   Tel: 020-7607 0561

LONDON
Jacksons Lane
269A Archway Road, London N6 5AA
Fax: 020-8348 2424
BO: 020-8341 4421   Admin: 020-8340 5226

LONDON
Menier Chocolate Factory
51-53 Southwark Street, London SE1 1RU
Website: www.menierchocolatefactory.com
e-mail: office@menierchocolatefactory.com
Fax: 020-7378 1713   Admin: 020-7378 1712

LONDON
The Nettlefold, West Norwood Library Centre
1 Norwood High Street, London SE27 9JX
Fax: 020-7926 8071   Admin/BO: 020-7926 8070

LONDON
October Gallery
24 Old Gloucester Street, London WC1N 3AL
Contact: Chili Hawes
Website: www.theoctobergallery.com
e-mail: octobergallery@compuserve.com
Fax: 020-7405 1851   Tel: 020-7242 7367

LONDON
Oval House Theatre
52-54 Kennington Oval, London SE11 5SW
Programmer: Karena Johnson
Director: Deborah Bestwick
Website: www.ovalhouse.com
e-mail: info@ovalhouse.com   Tel: 020-7582 0080

LONDON
Polish Social & Cultural Association
238-246 King Street, London W6 ORF   Tel: 020-8741 1940

LONDON
Riverside Studios
Crisp Road, Hammersmith, London W6 9RL
Website: www.riversidestudios.co.uk
e-mail: admin@riversidestudios.co.uk
Fax: 020-8237 1001
BO: 020-8237 1111   Tel: 020-8237 1000

LONDON
The Stables Gallery & Arts Centre
Gladstone Park, Dollis Hill Lane, London NW2 6HT
e-mail: stablesgallery@msn.com   Tel: 020-8452 8655

LOWESTOFT
Seagull Theatre
Morton Road, Lowestoft, Suffolk NR33 0JH
Advisory Drama Teacher: Sandra Redsell
Fax: 01502 515338   Tel: 01502 562863

MAIDENHEAD
Norden Farm Centre For The Arts
Altwood Road, Maidenhead SL6 4PF
Director: Annabel Turpin
Website: www.nordenfarm.org
e-mail: admin@nordenfarm.org
Fax: 01628 682525
BO: 01628 788997   Admin: 01628 682555

MAIDSTONE
Corn Exchange Complex/Hazlitt Theatre
Earl Street, Maidstone, Kent ME14 1PL
Commercial Manager: Mandy Hare
Fax: 01622 602194
BO: 01622 758611   Admin: 01622 753922

MANCHESTER
Green Room
54-56 Whitworth Street West, Manchester M1 5WW
Artistic Director: Garfield Allen
Website: www.greenroomarts.org
e-mail: info@greenroomarts.org
Fax: 0161-615 0516
BO: 0161-615 0500   Admin: 0161-615 0515

MANCHESTER
The Lowry
Pier 8, Salford Quays M50 3AZ
Theatre Productions Bookings: Louise Ormerod
Website: www.thelowry.com
e-mail: info@thelowry.com
Fax: 0161-876 2021
BO: 0870 1112000   Admin: 0161-876 2020

MANSFIELD
New Perspectives Theatre Company
The Old Library, Leeming Street, Mansfield, Notts NG18 1NG
Website: www.newperspectives.co.uk
e-mail: info@newperspectives.co.uk   Tel: 01623 412570

MILFORD HAVEN
Torch Theatre, St Peter's Road, Milford Haven
Pembrokeshire SA73 2BU
Artistic Director: Peter Doran
Website: www.torchtheatre.org
e-mail: info@torchtheatre.co.uk
Fax: 01646 698919
BO: 01646 695267   Admin: 01646 694192

NEWPORT (Isle of Wight)
Quay Arts
Sea Street, Newport Harbour
Isle of Wight PO30 5BD
Fax: 01983 526606
BO: 01983 528825   Tel: 01983 822490

NORWICH
Norwich Arts Centre
St Benedicts Street, Norwich, Norfolk NR2 4PG
Website: www.norwichartscentre.co.uk
e-mail: stuarthobday@norwichartscentre.co.uk
BO: 01603 660352   Admin: 01603 660387

NUNEATON
Abbey Theatre & Arts Centre
Pool Bank Street, Nuneaton, Warks CV11 5DB
Chairman: Tony Deeming
Website: www.abbeytheatre.co.uk
e-mail: admin@abbeytheatre.co.uk
Tel: 024-7632 7359   BO: 024-7635 4090

PLYMOUTH
Plymouth Arts Centre
38 Looe Street, Plymouth, Devon PL4 0EB
Director: Ian Hutchinson
Website: www.plymouthac.org.uk
e-mail: arts@plymouthac.org.uk
Fax: 01752 206118   Tel: 01752 206114

POOLE
Lighthouse Poole Centre for The Arts
Kingland Road, Poole, Dorset BH15 1UG
Website: www.lighthousepoole.co.uk
BO: 01202 685222   Admin: 01202 665334

RADLETT
The Radlett Centre
1 Aldenham Avenue, Radlett, Herts WD7 8HL
Website: www.radlettcentre.co.uk
Fax: 01923 857592   Tel: 01923 857546

ROTHERHAM
Rotherham Theatres
Walker Place, Rotherham, South Yorkshire S65 1JH
Strategic Leader Culture/Leisure/Lifelong Learning:
Phil Rodgers
Website: www.rotherham.gov.uk
BO: 01709 823621   Admin: 01709 823641

SALISBURY
Salisbury Arts Centre
Bedwin Street, Salisbury
Wiltshire SP1 3UT
e-mail: info@salisburyarts.co.uk
Fax: 01722 331742
BO: 01722 321744   Admin: 01722 430700

SHREWSBURY
Shrewsbury & District Arts Association
The Gateway, Chester Street
Shrewsbury, Shropshire SY1 1NB
e-mail: gateway.centre@shropshire-cc.gov.uk
Tel: 01743 355159

SOUTHPORT
Southport Arts Centre
Lord Street, Southport, Merseyside PR8 1DB
Website: www.seftonarts.co.uk
e-mail: artsops@seftonarts.co.uk
BO: 01704 540011   Admin: 01704 540004

STAMFORD
Stamford Arts Centre
27 St Mary's Street
Stamford, Lincolnshire PE9 2DL
Website: www.stamfordartscentre.com
e-mail: boxoffice@stamfordartscentre.com
Fax: 01780 766690
BO: 01780 763203   Admin: 01780 480846

STIRLING
MacRobert
University of Stirling, Stirling FK9 4LA
Director: Liz Moran
Website: www.macrobert.org
BO: 01786 466666   Admin: 01786 467155

SWANSEA
Taliesin Arts Centre
University of Wales Swansea
Singleton Park, Swansea SA2 8PZ
General Manager: Sybil Crouch
Website: www.taliesinartscentre.co.uk
e-mail: s.e.crouch@swansea.ac.uk   Tel: 01792 295438

SWINDON
Wyvern Theatre
Theatre Square, Swindon, Wiltshire SN1 1QN
Website: www.wyverntheatre.org.uk
BO: 01793 524481   Admin: 01793 535534

TAUNTON
Brewhouse
Coal Orchard, Taunton, Somerset TA1 1JL
Artistic Director: Glenys Gill
Website: www.thebrewhouse.net
e-mail: brewhouse@btconnect.com
Fax: 01823 323116
BO: 01823 283244   Admin: 01823 274608

TOTNES
Dartington Arts
The Barn, Dartington Hall, Totnes, Devon TQ9 6DE
e-mail: info@dartingtonarts.co.uk
BO: 01803 847070   Admin: 01803 847074

TUNBRIDGE WELLS
Trinity Theatre, Church Road
Tunbridge Wells, Kent TN1 1JP
Director: Adrian Berry
BO: 01892 678678   Admin: 01892 678670

ULEY
Prema
South Street
Uley, Nr Dursley, Glos GL11 5SS
Director: Gordon Scott
Website: www.prema.demon.co.uk
e-mail: info@prema.demon.co.uk   Tel: 01453 860703

VALE OF GLAMORGAN
St Donats Arts Centre
St Donats Castle, The Vale of Glamorgan CF61 1WF
Artistic Director: David Ambrose
Fax: 01446 799101   Tel: 01446 799099

WAKEFIELD
Wakefield Arts Centre
Wakefield College
Thornes Park Campus, Thornes Park
Horbury Road, Wakefield WF2 8QZ
Facilities Officer: Carole Clark
e-mail: c.clark@wakcoll.ac.uk   Tel: 01924 789824

WALLSEND
Buddle Arts Centre
258B Station Road, Wallsend
Tyne & Wear NE28 8RG
Contact: Geoffrey A Perkins
Fax: 0191-200 7142   Tel: 0191-200 7132

WASHINGTON
The Arts Centre Washington
Biddick Lane, Fatfield, District 7
Washington, Tyne & Wear NE38 8AB
Fax: 0191-219 3466   Tel: 0191-219 3455

WELLINGBOROUGH
The Castle, Castle Way
Wellingborough, Northants NN8 1XA
Executive Director: Graham Brown
Artistic Director: Bart Lee
Website: www.thecastle.org.uk
e-mail: info@thecastle.org.uk
Fax: 01933 229888   Tel: 01933 229022

WIMBORNE
Layard Theatre
Canford School, Canford Magna
Wimborne, Dorset BH21 3AD
Director of Drama: Stephen Hattersley
e-mail: layardtheatre@canford.com
Fax: 01202 847525
BO: 01202 847525   Admin: 01202 847529

WINCHESTER
Tower Arts Centre
Romsey Road, Winchester, Hampshire SO22 5PW
Director: John Tellett
Website: www.towerarts.co.uk   Tel: 01962 867986

WINDSOR
Windsor Arts Centre
St Leonard's Road, Windsor, Berks SL4 3BL
Director: Debbie Stubbs
Website: www.windsorartscentre.org
e-mail: admin@windsorartscentre.org
Fax: 01753 621527
BO: 01753 859336   Admin: 01753 859421

WOLVERHAMPTON
Afro-Caribbean Cultural Centre
2 Clarence Street, Wolverhampton WV1 4JH
Arts Co-ordinator: R Diaram   Tel: 01902 420109

WREXHAM
Wrexham Arts Centre
Rhosddu Road, Wrexham LL11 1AU
e-mail: arts.centre@wrexham.gov.uk
Website: www.wrexham.gov.uk
Fax: 01978 292611   Tel: 01978 292093

ARTS COUNCIL ENGLAND, EAST
Norfolk, Suffolk, Bedfordshire, Cambridgeshire, Essex,
Hertfordshire and the unitary authorities of Luton,
Peterborough, Southend-on-Sea and Thurrock
Eden House, 48-49 Bateman Street, Cambridge CB2 1LR
Website: www.artscouncil.org.uk
Fax: 0870 2421271   Tel: 0845 3006200

ARTS COUNCIL ENGLAND, EAST MIDLANDS
Derbyshire, Leicestershire, Lincolnshire excluding North
and North East Lincolnshire, Northamptonshire,
Nottinghamshire and the Unitary Authorities of Derby and
Rutland
St Nicholas Court, 25-27 Castle Gate, Nottingham NG1 7AR
Website: www.artscouncil.org.uk
Fax: 0115-950 2467   Tel: 0845 3006200

ARTS COUNCIL ENGLAND, LONDON
The arts funding and development agency for the 32
London boroughs and the Corporation of London
2 Pear Tree Court, London EC1R 0DS
Website: www.artscouncil.org.uk
Fax: 020-7608 4100   Tel: 0845 3006200

ARTS COUNCIL ENGLAND, NORTH EAST
Teeside, Durham, Northumberland, Tyne and Wear
Central Square, Forth Street, Newcastle upon Tyne NE1 3PJ
Website: www.artscouncil.org.uk
Fax: 0191-230 1020   Tel: 0845 3006200

ARTS COUNCIL ENGLAND, NORTH WEST
Greater Manchester, Merseyside, Lancashire, Cheshire &
Cumbria
Manchester House, 22 Bridge Street, Manchester M3 3AB
Website: www.artscouncil.org.uk
Fax: 0161-834 6969   Tel: 0845 3006200

ARTS COUNCIL ENGLAND, SOUTH EAST
Sovereign House, Church Street, Brighton BN1 1RA
Website: www.artscouncil.org.uk
Fax: 0870 2421257   Tel: 0845 3006200

ARTS COUNCIL ENGLAND, SOUTH WEST
Cornwall, Devon, Dorset, Gloucestershire, Somerset and
Wiltshire and the Unitary Authorities of Bristol, Bath,
Torbay and Swindon
Bradninch Place, Gandy Street, Exeter, Devon EX4 3LS
Website: www.artscouncil.org.uk
Fax: 01392 229229   Tel: 0845 3006200

ARTS COUNCIL ENGLAND, WEST MIDLANDS
Herefordshire, Worcestershire, Staffordshire, Warwickshire
and Shropshire, Stoke-on-Trent, Telford and Wrekin and
districts of Birmingham, Coventry, Dudley, Sandwell,
Solihull, Walsall & Wolverhampton
82 Granville Street, Birmingham B1 2LH
Website: www.artscouncil.org.uk
Fax: 0121-643 7239   Tel: 0845 3006200

ARTS COUNCIL ENGLAND, YORKSHIRE
21 Bond Street, Dewsbury, West Yorkshire WF13 1AX
Website: www.artscouncil.org.uk
Fax: 01924 466522   Tel: 0845 3006200

ARTS COUNCIL OF WALES, MID & WEST WALES OFFICE
Ceredigion, Camarthenshire
Pembrokeshire, Powys, Swansea, Neath, Port Talbot
6 Gardd Llydaw, Jackson's Lane, Carmarthen SA31 1QD
Website: www.artswales.org
Fax: 01267 233084   Tel: 01267 234248

ARTS COUNCIL OF WALES, NORTH WALES OFFICE
Anglesey, Gwynedd, Conwy
Denbighshire, Flintshire, Wrexham
36 Prince's Drive, Colwyn Bay, Conwy LL29 8LA
Website: www.artswales.org
Fax: 01492 533677   Tel: 01492 533440

ARTS COUNCIL OF WALES, SOUTH WALES OFFICE
9 Museum Place
Cardiff CF10 3NX
Website: www.artswales.org
Fax: 029-2022 1447   Tel: 029-2037 6525

A C A CASTING
(Catherine Arton)
32A Edenvale Street, London SW6 2SF
e-mail: casting@acacasting.com   Tel/Fax: 020-7384 2635

ADAMSON Joanne CASTING
4 Hillthorpe Square, Leeds LS28 8NQ
e-mail: watts07@hotmail.com   Mobile: 07787 311270

AILION Pippa
3 Towton Road, London SE27 9EE
Tel/Fax: 020-8670 4816   Tel: 020-8761 7095

ALEXANDER Pam CDG
e-mail: pam.alexander@virgin.net   Mobile: 07715 119158

ALL DIRECTIONS OF LONDON
7 Rupert Court, Off Wardour Street
London W1D 6EB   Tel: 020-7437 5879

ALL KIDS CASTING
(Children & Young Performers)
5 Brook Place, Barnet, Herts EN5 2DL
Website: www.allkidscasting.com
e-mail: jenny@allkidscasting.com   Tel: 020-8441 5010

ANDREW Dorothy CASTING
Campus Manor, Childwall Abbey Road
Childwall, Liverpool L16 0JP
Fax: 0151-722 9079   Tel: 0151-722 9122

ARNELL Jane
Flat 2, 39 St Peter's Square, London W6 9NN

BAIG Shaheen
(Shaheen Baig & Abi Cohen Casting)
343B Archway Road, London N6 5AA
e-mail: loop@dircon.co.uk

BALDIES CASTING AGENCY
(The only agency purely for bald people)
6 Marlott Road, Poole, Dorset BH15 3DX
Mobile: 07860 29s0437   Tel: 01202 666001

BARBOUR Penny
Rosemary Cottage
Fontridge Lane, Etchingham, East Sussex TN19 7DD

BARNES Derek
BBC DRAMA SERIES CASTING
Centre House
Room DG20, 56 Wood Lane, London W12 7SB
Fax: 020-8225 6170   Tel: 020-8225 7266

BARNES Michael CDG
25 Old Oak Road, London W3 7HN
Fax: 020-8742 9385   Tel: 020-8749 1354

Casting Directors

For information regarding membership of
the Casting Directors' Guild (CDG) please contact

PO Box 34403
London W6 0YG
Tel/Fax: 020-8741 1951
Website: www.tcdg.co.uk

Concert & Exhibition Halls
Concert Promoters & Agents
Consultants
Costumes, Wigs & Make-up
Critics

[CONTACTS 2005]

BARTLETT Carolyn CDG
22 Barton Road, London W14 9HD

BATH Andrea
85 Brightwell Road, Watford WD18 0HR
e-mail: andreabath@btinternet.com   Tel: 01923 333067

BEARDSALL Sarah CDG
73 Wells Street, London W1T 3QG
e-mail: casting@beardsall.com
Fax: 020-7436 8859   Tel: 020-7323 4040

BEATTIE Victoria
Unit 19, The John Cotton Building
Sunnyside, Edinburgh EH7 5RA
e-mail: victoria@victoriabeattie.com
Fax: 0131-652 4001   Tel: 0131-652 4002

BERTRAND Leila CASTING
53 Hormead Road, London W9 3NQ
e-mail: leilabcasting@aol.com   Tel/Fax: 020-8964 0683

BEVAN Lucy
c/o Twickenham Studios, St Margaret's
Twickenham TW1 2AW   Tel: 020-8607 8888

BEWICK Maureen CASTING
104A Dartmouth Road, London NW2 4HB

BEXFIELD Glenn
BBC DRAMA SERIES CASTING
Centre House
Room DG20, 56 Wood Lane, London W12 7SB
Fax: 020-8225 6170   Tel: 020-8576 8172

BIG FISH CASTING
(See HAMILTON & CRAWFORD)

BILL The
Thames Television Ltd
Talkbackthames Studios
1 Deer Park Road, Merton
London SW19 3TL   Tel: 020-8540 0600

BIRD Sarah CDG
PO Box 32658, London W14 0XA
Fax: 020-7602 8601   Tel: 020-7371 3248

BIRKETT Hannah CASTING
19 Stanley Crescent, Notting Hill, London W11 2NA
Website: www.johndoeassociates.com
e-mail: hannahbirkettcasting@tiscali.co.uk
Fax: 07957 114175   Tel: 020-7229 4300

BOULTING Lucy CDG
7 Gravel Road, Twickenham Green, Middlesex TW2 6RH
e-mail: boultingcasting@btconnect.com

BRACKE Siobhan CDG
Basement Flat, 22A The Barons
St Margaret's TW1 2AP   Tel: 020-8891 5686

BROADCASTING
(Lesley Beastall, Sophie North & Jon Levene)
23 Canalot Studios, 222 Kensal Road, London W10 5BN
e-mail: casting@broad-casting.co.uk
Fax: 020-7460 5223   Tel: 020-7460 5220

BRUFFIN Susie CDG
133 Hartswood Road
London W12 9NG   Tel: 020-8740 9895

BRUSCHELLE Barbara
(See CASTING UNLIMITED LONDON & LOS ANGELES)

CAIRD Angela
PO Box MT 86, Leeds LS17 8YQ
e-mail: cairdlitt@aol.com
Fax: 0113-266 6068   Tel: 0113-288 8014

CAMERON Polly
BBC DRAMA SERIES CASTING
Centre House, Room DG20, 56 Wood Lane, London W12 7SB
Fax: 020-8225 6170   Tel: 020-8225 6640

CANDID CASTING
2nd Floor
111-113 Great Titchfield Street, London W1W 6RY
e-mail: mail@candidcasting.co.uk
Fax: 020-7636 5522   Tel: 020-7636 6644

CANNON DUDLEY & ASSOCIATES
43A Belsize Square, London NW3 4HN
e-mail: cdacasting@blueyonder.co.uk
Fax: 020-7433 3599   Tel: 020-7433 3393

CANNON John CDG
(See ROYAL SHAKESPEARE COMPANY)

CARLING Di CASTING CDG
1st Floor, 49 Frith Street, London W1D 4SG
Fax: 020-7287 6844   Tel: 020-7287 6446

CARROLL Anji CDG
4 Nesfield Drive, Winterley, Cheshire CW11 4NT
e-mail: anjicarrollcdg@yahoo.co.uk   Tel/Fax: 01270 250240

CASTING ANGELS The
(London & Paris)
Suite 4, 14 College Road, Bromley
Kent BR1 3NS   Tel/Fax: 020-8313 0443

CASTING COMPANY (UK) The
(Michelle Guish)
3rd Floor, 112-114 Wardour Street, London W1F 0TS
Fax: 020-7434 2346   Tel: 020-7734 4954

CASTING CONNECTION The
(Michael Syers)
Dalrossie House, 16 Victoria Grove
Stockport, Cheshire SK4 5BU
Fax: 0161-442 7280   Tel: 0161-432 4122

CASTING COUCH PRODUCTIONS Ltd
(Moira Townsend)
97 Riffel Road, London NW2 4PG
e-mail: moiratownsend@yahoo.co.uk
Fax: 020-8208 2373   Tel: 020-8438 9679

CASTING DIRECTORS The
(Gillian Hawser & Caroline Hutchings)
24 Cloncurry Street, London SW6 6DS,
e-mail: gillian.hawser@virgin.net
e-mail: carohutchings@hotmail.com
Fax: Gillian: 020-7731 0738
Fax: Caroline: 020-8336 1067   Tel: 020-7731 5988

CASTING UK
(Andrew Mann)
88-90 Gray's Inn Road, London WC1X 8AA
Website: www.castinguk.com
e-mail: info@castinguk.com
Fax: 020-7430 1155   Tel: 020-7430 1122

CASTING UNLIMITED (LONDON)
9 Hansard Mews, Kensington, London W14 8BJ
e-mail: info@castingdirector.co.uk
Fax: 0870 4435623   Tel: 0870 4435621

CASTING UNLIMITED (LOS ANGELES)
e-mail: info@castingdirector.co.uk

CATLIFF Suzy CDG
PO Box 32658, London W14 0XA
e-mail: soose@soose.co.uk
Fax: 020-7602 8601   Tel: 020-7371 3248

CELEBRITY MANAGEMENT Ltd
12 Nottingham Place, London W1U 5NE
Website: www.celebrity.co.uk
e-mail: info@celebrity.co.uk
Fax: 020-7224 6060   Tel: 020-7224 5050

CELEX CASTING Ltd
11 Glencroft Drive, Stenson Fields, Derby DE24 3LS
Website: www.celex.co.uk
e-mail: enquiries@celex.co.uk
Fax: 01332 232115   Tel: 01332 232445

CHARD Alison CDG
23 Groveside Court
4 Lombard Road, Battersea, London SW11 3RQ
e-mail: alisonchard@castingdirector.freeserve.co.uk
Tel/Fax: 020-7223 9125

Heather Peace

Stephen Tompkinson

Nicola Blackman

Claire Grogan
Photography

020 7272 1845
mobile 07932 635381
www.clairegrogan.co.uk
student rates

CHARKHAM CASTING (Beth Charkham)
Suite 07, 97 Mortimer Street
London W1W 7SU
e-mail: info@charkhamcasting.co.uk
Fax: 020-7927 8336   Tel: 020-7927 8335

CLARK Andrea
(See ZIMMERMANN Jeremy CASTING)

COGAN Ben
BBC DRAMA SERIES CASTING
Centre House, Room DG20, 56 Wood Lane, London W12 7SB
Fax: 020-8225 6170   Tel: 020-8576 9859

COHEN Abi CASTING
(Shaheen Baig & Abi Cohen Casting)
343B Archway Road, London N6 5AA
e-mail: cohencasting@tinyonline.co.uk

COHEN Yona
9 Seymour Road
Hampton Wick KT1 4HN   Mobile: 07754 198134

COLLINS Jayne CASTING
38 Commercial Street, London E1 6LP
Website: www.jaynecollinscasting.com
e-mail: info@jaynecollinscasting.com
Fax: 020-7422 0015   Tel: 020-7422 0014

COLLINS Katrina
BBC DRAMA SERIES CASTING
BBC Elstree, Room N418, Neptune House
Clarendon Road, Borehamwood, Herts WD6 1JF
Fax: 020-8228 8311   Tel: 020-8228 8621

CORDORAY Lin
66 Cardross Street, London W6 0DR

COTTON Irene CDG
25 Druce Road, Dulwich Village, London SE21 7DW
e-mail: oliver36@btopenworld.com
Tel/Fax: 020-8299 2787   Tel: 020-8299 1595

CRAMPSIE Julia
(Deputy Head of Casting)
BBC DRAMA SERIES CASTING
Centre House, Room DG20, 56 Wood Lane, London W12 7SB
Fax: 020-8225 6170   Tel: 020-8576 9726

CRANE Carole CASTING
9 Oakbrook Court
Sheffield S10 3HR
Mobile: 07976 869442   Tel: 0114-230 881

CROCODILE CASTING COMPANY The
(C. Gibbs & T. Saban)
9 Ashley Close, Hendon, London NW4 1PH
Website: www.crocodilecasting.com
e-mail: croccast@aol.com
Fax: 020-8203 7711   Tel: 020-8203 7009

CROWE Sarah CASTING
24 Poland Street, London W1F 8QL
e-mail: sarah@sarahcrowecasting.co.uk
Fax: 020-7287 2147   Tel: 020-7734 5464

CROWLEY POOLE CASTING
11 Goodwins Court, London WC2N 4LL
Fax: 020-7379 5971   Tel: 020-7379 5965

CROWLEY Suzanne CDG
(See CROWLEY POOLE CASTING)

CYBER-ARTISTS
(Marc Sinclair & Amanda Lucas)
In The Can Ltd, The Studio, Kingsway Court
Queen's Gardens, Hove BN3 2LP
Website: www.cyberartists.co.uk
e-mail: cyber.1@btconnect.com
Fax: 01273 739984   Tel/Fax: 01273 821821

DAVIES Jane CASTING Ltd
(Jane Davies CDG & John Connor CDG)
PO Box 680, Sutton, Surrey SM1 3ZG
e-mail: info@janedaviescasting.co.uk
Fax: 020-8644 9746   Tel: 020-8715 1036

DAVIS Leo (Miss)
(JUST CASTING)
20th Century Theatre
291 Westbourne Grove, London W11 2QA
Fax: 020-7792 2143   Tel: 020-7229 3471

DAVY Gary CDG
1B Wakeham Street
London N1 3HP   Tel: 020-7359 0880

DAY Kate CDG
Pound Cottage, 27 The Green South, Warborough
Oxon OX10 7DR Tel/Fax: 01865 858709

DE FREITAS Paul CDG
PO Box 4903, London W1A 7JZ

DEITCH Jane
(Head of Casting)
BBC DRAMA SERIES CASTING
Centre House, Room DG20, 56 Wood Lane, London W12 7SB
Fax: 020-8225 6170 Tel: 020-8225 6417

DENMAN Jack CASTING
Burgess House, Main Street, Farnsfield
Notts NG22 8EF Tel/Fax: 01623 882272

DENNISON Lee ASSOCIATES
Fushion (London Office)
27 Old Gloucester Street, London WC1N 3XX
e-mail: leedennison@fushion-uk.com
Fax: 08700 111020 Tel: 08700 111100

DICKENS Laura CDG
1st Floor, 54 Commercial Street, London E1 6LT
e-mail: dickenscasting@aol.com
Fax: 020-7247 5622 Tel: 020-7247 5717

DOWD Kate
117 Piccadilly, London W1J 7JS
Fax: 020-7493 8027 Tel: 020-7491 2090

DRURY Malcolm CDG
34 Tabor Road, London W6 0BW Tel: 020-8748 9232

DUDLEY Carol CDG
(See CANNON DUDLEY & ASSOCIATES)

DUFF Julia CDG
73 Wells Street, London W1T 3QG
Fax: 020-7436 8859 Tel: 020-7436 8860

DUFF Maureen CDG
PO Box 47340, London NW3 4TY
e-mail: belgrove@dircon.co.uk
Fax: 020-7681 7172 Tel: 020-7586 0532

DUFFY Jennifer CDG
42 Old Compton Street, London W1D 4TX
Fax: 020-7287 7752 Tel: 020-7287 7751

EAST Irene CASTING CDG
40 Brookwood Avenue, Barnes, London SW13 0LR
e-mail: irneast@aol.com Tel: 020-8876 5686

EJ CASTING
Lower Ground Floor, 86 Vassall Road, London SW9 6JA
e-mail: info@ejcasting.com
Mobile: 07976 726869 Tel: 020-7564 2688

EMMERSON Chloe
56 Abingdon Villas, London W8 6XD
e-mail: chloe@chloeemmerson.com
Fax: 020-7937 6109 Tel: 020-7937 8474

ET-NIK-A PMC Ltd
Prime Management & Castings
Ground Floor, 30 Great Portland Street, London W1W 7QU
Website: www.et-nik-a.com
e-mail: castings@et-nik-a.com
Fax: 020-7299 3558 Tel: 020-7299 3555

EVANS Richard CDG
10 Shirley Road, London W4 1DD
Website: www.evanscasting.co.uk
e-mail: contact@evanscasting.co.uk
Fax: 020-8742 1010 Tel: 020-8994 6304

FEARNLEY Ali
26 Goodge Street, London W1T 2QG
e-mail: katealicasting@btclick.com
Fax: 020-7636 8080 Tel: 020-7636 4040

Brenda
Fricker

Lucy
Gaskell

Arthur
White

FIGGIS Susie
19 Spencer Rise, London NW5 1AR   Tel: 020-7482 2200

FILDES Bunny CASTING CDG
56 Wigmore Street, London W1   Tel: 020-7935 1254

FINCHER Sally CDG
e-mail: sally.fincher@btinternet.com   Tel: 020-8347 5945

FOX Celestia
5 Clapham Common Northside, London SW4 0QW
e-mail: celestia.fox@virgin.net

FRAZER Janie CDG
London Weekend TV
Television Centre, South Bank, London SE1 9LT
e-mail: janie.frazer@granadamedia.com   Tel: 020-7261 3848

FRECK Rachel
e-mail: rachelfreck@btopenworld.com   Tel: 020-8673 2455

FRISBY Jane CASTING CDG
51 Ridge Road, London N8 9LJ
e-mail: jane.frisby@tiscali.co.uk

FUNNELL Caroline CDG
25 Rattray Road, London SW2 1AZ
Fax: 020-7274 7129   Tel: 020-7326 4417

GALLIE Joyce
37 Westcroft Square, London W6 0TA

GANE CASTING
(Natasha Gane)
52 Woodhouse Road, London N12 0RJ
e-mail: natasha@ganecasting.com
Fax: 020-8446 2508   Tel: 020-8446 2551

GB CASTING UK Ltd (Karin Grainger)
1 Charlotte Street, London W1T 1RD
e-mail: kggbuk@lineone.net
Fax: 020-7255 1899   Tel: 020-7636 2437

GILLHAM Tracey CDG
(Entertainment - Comedy)
BBC Television Centre
Wood Lane, London W12 7RJ
Fax: 020-8576 4414   Tel: 020-8225 8488

GILLON WOODWARD CASTING
(Tamara Gillon & Tara Woodward CDG)
93 Gloucester Avenue, London NW1 8LB
e-mail: gillonwoodward@yahoo.co.uk
Fax: 020-7681 8574   Tel: 020-7586 3487

GOLD Nina CDG
10 Kempe Road, London NW6 6SJ
e-mail: nina@ninagold.co.uk
Fax: 020-8968 6777   Tel: 020-8960 6099

GOLDWYN Lauren CASTING INC
14 Dean Street, London W1D 3RS
e-mail: entertainment@rentingeyeballs.com
Fax: 020-7437 4221   Tel: 020-7437 4188

GOOCH Miranda CASTING
102 Leighton Gardens, London NW10 3PR
e-mail: mirandagooch@hotmail.com
Fax: 020-8962 9579   Tel: 020-8962 9578

GREEN Jill CASTING CDG
Cambridge Theatre, Seven Dials
Earlham Street, London WC2H 9HU
Fax: 020-7379 4796   Tel: 020-7379 4795

GREENE Francesca CASTING
79 Ashworth Mansions, London W9 1LN
Fax: 020-7266 9001   Tel: 020-7286 5957

GRESHAM Marcia CDG
3 Langthorne Street, London SW6 6JT   Tel: 020-7381 2876

GROSVENOR CASTING
(Angela Grosvenor CDG)
27 Rowena Crescent, London SW11 2PT
Fax: 020-7652 6256   Tel: 020-7738 0449

GUISH Michelle CDG
See CASTING COMPANY (UK) The

HALL David CASTING
9 Falconet Court, 123 Wapping High St, London E1W 3NX
e-mail: davidhall@casting.wanadoo.co.uk
Fax: 020-7381 3288   Tel: 020-7488 9916

HALL Janet
1 Shore Avenue, Shaw, Oldham OL2 8DA
e-mail: stage@hall257.fsbusiness.co.uk
Mobile: 07780 783489   Tel: 01706 291459

HALL Pippa
(Children & Teenagers only)
Vine House, Blockley, Nr Moreton-in-Marsh, Glos GL56 9ET
e-mail: pippahall.casting@virgin.net   Tel/Fax: 01386 700227

HAMILTON & CRAWFORD
(Des Hamilton & Kahleen Crawford)
The Pearce Institute, 840 Govan Road, Glasgow G51 3UU
Website: www.hamiltonandcrawford.co.uk
Fax: 0141-445 6900   Tel: 0141-425 1725

HAMMOND Louis
30-31 Peter Street, London W1F 0AR
Fax: 020-7439 2522   Tel: 020-7734 0626

HANCOCK Gemma CDG
The Rosary, Broad Street, Cuckfield, West Sussex RH17 5DL
e-mail: gemma.hancock@virgin.net
Tel/Fax: 01444 441398

HARE Jackie
Top Floor, 30 High Street, Lymington, Hampshire SO41 9AF
e-mail: jackiehare@cast73.fsnet.co.uk   Tel: 01590 688664

HARKIN Julie
BBC DRAMA SERIES CASTING
BBC Elstree, Room N418, Neptune House, Clarendon Road
Borehamwood, Herts WD6 1JF
Fax: 020-8228 8311   Tel: 020-8228 8285

HARRIS Lisa
290 Coulsdon Road, Old Coulsdon
Surrey CR5 1EB   Mobile: 07956 561247

HAWSER Gillian CASTING
24 Cloncurry Street, London SW6 6DS
e-mail: gillian.hawser@virgin.net
Fax: 020-7731 0738   Tel: 020-7731 5988

Sarah-Jayne Steed

RUTH MULHOLLAND
Photographer
07939 516987

Rachel Ferjani

Leanne Rowe

Charlie Condou

Serena Evans

Charlie Carter
P H O T O G R A P H E R
0 2 0   7 7 5 1   0 5 7 5

HAYFIELD Judi CDG
Granada Television
Quay Street, Manchester M60 9EA
Fax: 0161-827 2853 Tel: 0161-832 7211

HILL Serena
Sydney Theatre Company
Pier 4, Hickson Road
Walsh Bay, NSW 2000, Australia
e-mail: shill@sydneytheatre.com.au Tel: 00 612 925 01700

HILTON Carrie CDG
BM306 Barley Mow Centre
10 Barley Mow Passage, Chiswick, London W4 4PH
Fax: 020-8747 4570 Tel: 020-8747 4590

HOOTKINS Polly CDG
PO Box 25191, London SW1V 2WN
e-mail: phootkins@clara.net
Fax: 020-7828 5051 Tel: 020-7233 8724

HORAN Julia CDG
26 Falkland Road, London NW5 2PX Tel: 020-7267 5261

HOWE Gary CASTING
34 Orbit Street, Roath
Cardiff CF24 0JX Tel/Fax: 029-2045 3883

HUBBARD CASTING
(Ros Hubbard, John Hubbard, Dan Hubbard CDG)
2nd Floor, 19 Charlotte Street, London W1T 1RL
e-mail: email@hubbardcasting.com
Fax: 020-7636 7117 Tel: 020-7636 9991

HUGHES Sarah
Stephen Joseph Theatre
Westborough, Scarborough
North Yorkshire YO11 1JW Tel: 01723 370540

HUGHES Sylvia
Casting Suite
The Deanwater, Wilmslow Road
Woodford, Cheshire SK7 1RJ
Mobile: 07770 520007 Tel: 01565 653777

HUTCHINGS Caroline
PO Box 1119, Kingston & Surbiton KT2 7WY
e-mail: carohutchings@hotmail.com
Fax: 020-8336 1067 Mobile: 07768 615343

INTERNATIONAL CASTING
(Elaine Grainger)
Flint Cottage, Duncton, Petworth, West Sussex GU28 0LT
e-mail: e.grainger@virgin.net
Mobile: 07932 741794 Tel: 01798 343556

Valerie Colgan

- For professional actors who need a voice production "MOT"
- Private individual classes
- Valerie Colgan and a consortium of tutors as appropriate.

Ex Head of Drama at the City Lit · 5 Drama Schools · The Actors Centre

Tel: 020 7267 2153 The Green, 17 Herbert Street, London NW5 4HA

JACKSON Sue
Yorkshire Television, The TV Centre, Leeds LS3 1JS

JAFFA Janis CASTING CDG
67 Starfield Road, London W12 9SN
e-mail: janis@janisjaffacasting.co.uk
Fax: 020-8743 9561   Tel: 020-7565 2877

JAFFREY Jennifer
136 Hicks Avenue, Greenford, Middlesex UB6 8HB
e-mail: jaffreymag@aol.com
Fax: 020-8575 0369   Tel: 020-8578 2899

JAY Jina CASTING CDG
Ofiice 4, Novello Lodge, Twickenham Film Studios
The Barons, St Margarets, Twickenham, Middlesex TW1 2AW
Fax: 020-8607 8982   Tel: 020-8607 8888

JELOWICKI Ilenka
(Mad Dog Casting Ltd)
Top Floor, 10 Warwick Street, London W1B 5LZ
e-mail: ilenka@maddogcasting.com
Fax: 020-7287 5983   Tel: 020-7434 1211

JENKINS Lucy CDG
74 High St, Hampton Wick, Kingston-upon-Thames KT1 4DQ
e-mail: lucy@littlejenkins.freeserve.co.uk
Fax: 020-8977 0466   Tel: 020-8943 5328

JN PRODUCTION
5A Penton Street, London N1 9PT
e-mail: james@jnproduction.net
Fax: 020-7278 8855   Tel: 020-7278 8800

JOHN Priscilla CDG
PO Box 22477, London W6 0GT
Fax: 020-8741 4005   Tel: 020-8741 4212

JOHNSON Alex CASTING
15 McGregor Road, London W11 1DE
e-mail: alex@alexjon.demon.co.uk
Fax: 020-7229 1665   Tel: 020-7229 8779

JOHNSON Marilyn CDG
1st Floor, 11 Goodwins Court, London WC2N 4LL
e-mail: marilynjohnson@lineone.net
Fax: 020-7497 5530   Tel: 020-7497 5552

JONES Doreen CDG
PO Box 22478, London W6 0WJ
Fax: 020-8748 8533   Tel: 020-8746 3782

JONES Sam CDG
6th Floor, International House
223 Regent Street, London W1R 7DB
e-mail: get@samjones.fsnet.co.uk
Fax: 020-7493 7890   Tel: 020-7493 5456

JONES Sue CDG
24 Nicoll Road, London NW10 9AB
Fax: 020-8838 1130   Tel: 020-8838 5153

KATE & ALI CASTING
(See FEARNLEY Ali)

KEOGH Beverley CASTING Ltd
29 Ardwick Green North, Ardwick, Manchester M12 6DL
e-mail: beverley@beverleykeogh.tv
Fax: 0161-273 4401   Tel: 0161-273 4400

KESTER Gaby
The CASTING COMPANY (UK)
3rd Floor, 112-114 Wardour Street, London W1F 0TS
Fax: 020-7434 2346   Tel: 020-7734 4954

KING Andrea
e-mail: andreaking.tv@ntlworld.com
Mobile: 07752 455510   Tel: 01204 456253

KNIGHT-SMITH Jerry CDG
Royal Exchange Theatre Company
St Ann's Square, Manchester M2 7DH
Fax: 0161-615 6691   Tel: 0161-615 6761

KOREL Suzy CDG
20 Blenheim Road, London NW8 0LX
e-mail: suzy@korel.org
Fax: 020-7372 3964   Tel: 020-7624 6435

KYLE CASTING
The Summerhouse, Thames House
54 Thames Street, Hampton TW12 2DX
Fax: 020-8274 8423   Tel: 020-8274 8096

LAYTON Claudie CASTING
(Claudie Layton & Alix Charpentier)
Unit 308, Canalot Studios
222 Kensal Road, London W10 5BN
e-mail: casting@claudielayton.com
Fax: 020-8968 1330   Tel: 020-8964 2055

LESSALL Matthew
Unit 5, Gun Wharf, 241 Old Ford Road, London E3 5QB
e-mail: matt@lessallcasting.com
Fax: 020-8980 2211   Tel: 020-8980 0117

LEVINSON Sharon
30 Stratford Villas, London NW1 9SG
e-mail: sharonlev@aol.com   Tel: 020-7485 2057

LINDSAY-STEWART Karen CDG
PO Box 2301, London W1A 1PT
Fax: 020-7439 0548   Tel: 020-7439 0544

LIP SERVICE CASTING
(Voice-overs only)
60-66 Wardour Street
London W1F 0TA
Website: www.lipservice.co.uk
e-mail: bookings@lipservice.co.uk
Fax: 020-7734 3373   Tel: 020-7734 3393

MAGSON Kay
PO Box 175, Pudsey, Leeds LS28 7WY
e-mail: kay.magson@btinternet.com   Tel/Fax: 0113-236 0251

MARCH Heather CASTING
The Aberdeen Centre
22-24 Highbury Grove, London N5 2EA
e-mail: hm@heathermarchcasting.com
Fax: 020-7704 6085   Tel: 020-7704 6464

McCANN Joan CDG
26 Hereford Road, London W3 9JW
Fax: 020-8992 8715   Tel: 020-8993 1747

McLEOD Carolyn
PO Box 26495, London SE10 0WO
e-mail: carolynmcleodcasting@hotmail.com
                               Tel/Fax: 0704 4001720

McMANUS Sarah Ltd
201 Canalot Studios, 222 Kensal Road, London W10 5BN
Fax: 020-8969 8860   Tel: 020-8969 8868

McMURRICH Chrissie
16 Spring Vale Avenue, Brentford
Middlesex TW8 9QH   Tel: 020-8568 0137

McSHANE Sooki CDG
8A Piermont Road, East Dulwich
London SE22 0LN   Tel/Fax: 020-8693 7411

McWILLIAMS Debbie
e-mail: debbiemcwilliams@hotmail.com
                               Mobile: 07785 575805

MOISELLE Frank
7 Corrig Avenue, Dun Laoghaire, Co. Dublin, Eire
Fax: 00 353 1 2803277   Tel: 00 353 1 2802857

MOISELLE Nuala
7 Corrig Avenue
Dun Laoghaire, Co. Dublin, Eire
Fax: 00 353 1 2803277   Tel: 00 353 1 2802857

MORRISON Melika
12A Rosebank, Holyport Road
London SW6 6LG   Tel/Fax: 020-7381 1571

MUGSHOTS
(Jacqui Morris)
50 Frith Street, London W1D 4SQ
Fax: 020-7437 0308   Tel: 020-7292 0555

NATIONAL THEATRE CASTING DEPARTMENT
(Casting Director: Toby Whale CDG, Deputy Casting
Director: Gabrielle Dawes CDG, Casting Assistant:
Alastair Coomer)
Upper Ground
South Bank, London SE1 9PX
Fax: 020-7452 3340   Tel: 020-7452 3336

Adrian and Neil Rayment

Daisy Bates

Photography by
ANGUS DEUCHAR
t. 020 8286 3303   m. 07973 600728
www.ActorsPhotos.co.uk

NEEDLEMAN Sue
19 Stanhope Gardens, London NW7 2JD
Fax: 020-8959 0225   Tel: 020-8959 1550

NOEL CASTING
(Specializing in Character Actors, Ethnic & Asian Actors)
Suite 501, International House
223 Regent Street, London W1B 2QD
e-mail: noelcasting@yahoo.com
Fax: 020-7544 1090   Tel: 020-7544 1010

NORCLIFFE Belinda
(Belinda Norcliffe & Matt Selby)
23 Brougham Road, London W3 6JD
e-mail: belinda@bncasting.co.uk
Fax: 020-8992 5533   Tel: 020-8992 1333

O'BRIEN Debbie
72 High Street, Ashwell, Nr Baldock, Herts SG7 5NS
Fax: 01462 743110   Tel: 01462 742919

PAIN David
BBC DRAMA SERIES CASTING
BBC Elstree, Room N418
Neptune House, Clarendon Road
Borehamwood, Herts WD6 1JF
Fax: 020-8228 8311   Tel: 020-8228 7322

PALMER Helena
(See CANNON DUDLEY & ASSOCIATES)

PARRISS Susie CASTING CDG
PO Box 40, Morden SM4 4WJ
Fax: 020-8543 3327   Tel: 020-8543 3326

PEARCE WOOLGAR CASTING
(Prop. Francesca Woolgar CDG)
Studio 4, 33 Chatsworth Road, London CR0 1HE
Website: www.pearcewoolgar.com

PERRYMENT Mandy CASTING
e-mail: mandy@perryment-cast.demon.co.uk
Fax: 01372 472795   Tel: 01372 472794

PETTS Tree CASTING
125 Hendon Way, London NW2 2NA
e-mail: casting@treepetts.co.uk
    Tel: 020-8458 8898

PLANTIN Kate
37 Albany Mews, Kingston-upon-Thames, Surrey KT2 5SL
e-mail: kateplantin@hotmail.com
Fax: 020-8549 7299   Tel: 020-8546 4577

POLENTARUTTI Tania CASTING CDG
Top Floor, 37 Berwick Street, London W1F 8RS
Fax: 020-7734 3549   Tel: 020-7734 1819

POOLE Gilly CDG
(See CROWLEY POOLE CASTING)

PROCTOR Carl CDG
15B Bury Place, London WC1A 2JB
e-mail: carlproctor@blueyonder.co.uk
Fax: 020-7916 2533   Tel: 020-7681 0034

PRYOR Andy CDG
7 Garrick Street, London WC2E 9AR
Fax: 020-7836 8299   Tel: 020-7836 8298

REICH Liora
25 Manor Park Road, London N2 0SN   Tel: 020-8444 1686

REYNOLDS Simone CDG
60 Hebdon Road, London SW17 7NN

RHODES JAMES Kate CDG
HG14, The Aberdeen Centre
22-24 Highbury Grove, London N5 2EA
e-mail: katerhodesjames@aol.com
Fax: 020-7359 5378   Tel: 020-7704 8186

ROBERTSON Sasha CASTING CDG
19 Wendell Road, London W12 9RS
e-mail: casting@sasharobertson.com
Fax: 020-8740 1396   Tel: 020-8740 0817

RODRIGUEZ Corinne
11 Lytton Avenue, London N13 4EH
Fax: 020-8886 5564

ROFFE Danielle CDG
71 Mornington Street, London NW1 7QE   Tel: 020-7388 1898

ROYAL SHAKESPEARE COMPANY
(Casting Director: John Cannon CDG, Casting Co-ordinator: Hannah Miller)
1 Earlham Street, London WC2H 9LL
e-mail: john.cannon@rsc.org.uk
Tel: 020-7845 0505   Tel: 020-7845 0500

SALBERG Jane
8 Halstow Road, Greenwich, London SE10 0LD
e-mail: janesalberg@aol.com
Fax: 020-8516 9365   Tel: 020-8858 1114

SBS Ltd
(The Casting Information Service Ltd)
Suite 1, 16 Sidmouth Road, London NW2 5JX
e-mail: casting@sbsltd.demon.co.uk
Fax: 020-8459 7442   Tel: 020-8451 2852

SCHILLER Ginny
180A Graham Road, London E8 1BS
e-mail: ginny.schiller@virgin.net
Fax: 020-8525 1049   Tel: 020-8525 1637

SCOTT Laura CDG
56 Rowena Crescent, London SW11 2PT
Website: www.castingdirectorsguild.co.uk
e-mail: laurascottcasting@mac.com
Fax: 020-7924 1907   Tel: 020-7978 6336

SEARCHERS The
70 Sylvia Court
Cavendish Street, London N1 7PG
e-mail: waynerw.searchers@blueyonder.co.uk
Fax: 020-7684 5763 Mobile: 07958 922829

SEECOOMAR Nadira
PO Box 167, Twickenham TW1 2UP
Fax: 020-8744 1274 Tel: 020-8892 8478

SHAW Philip
Suite 476, 2 Old Brompton Road
South Kensington, London SW7 3DQ
e-mail: shawcastlond@aol.com
Fax: 020-8408 1193 Tel: 020-8715 8943

SHEPHERD Debbie CASTING
Suite 16, 63 St Martin's Lane, London WC2N 4JS
e-mail: debbie@debbieshepherd.com
Fax: 020-7240 4640 Tel: 020-7240 0400

SINGER Sandra ASSOCIATES
21 Cotswold Road, Westcliff-on-Sea, Essex SS0 8AA
Website: www.sandrasinger.com
e-mail: sandrasingeruk@aol.com
Fax: 01702 339393 Tel: 01702 331616

SMITH Michelle CDG
220 Church Lane
Woodford, Stockport SK7 1PQ
Fax: 0161-439 0622 Tel: 0161-439 6825

SMITH Suzanne CDG
33 Fitzroy Street, London W1T 6DU
e-mail: zan@dircon.co.uk
Fax: 020-7436 9690 Tel: 020-7436 9255

SPON Wendy CDG
(Head of Casting)
Talkbackthames Studios
1 Deer Park Road, London SW19 3TL

STAFFORD Emma
33 Stopes Road, Radcliffe
Manchester M25 6TL Tel: 0161-748 7940

STARK CASTING
e-mail: stark.casting@virgin.net
Mobile: 07956 150689 Tel: 020-8800 0060

STEELE Mandy
89 Mayfield Road, London N8 9LN
e-mail: mandy@mandysteele.com
Fax: 0870 1329017 Tel: 020-8341 1918

MARTIN NIGEL DAVEY

1ST CLASS PHOTOGRAPHY
0121 457 8141
07813 282391

STEVENS Gail CASTING CDG
2 Sutton Lane, 54A Clerkenwell Road, London EC1M 5PS
Fax: 020-7253 6574 Tel: 020-7253 6532

STEVENSON Sam CDG
PO Box 50225
London EC1Y 8WD
e-mail: samstevenson@blueyonder.co.uk
Tel: 020-7256 5727

STEWART Amanda CASTING
Apartment 1, 35 Fortress Road
London NW5 1AD Tel: 020-7485 7973

STOLL Liz
BBC DRAMA SERIES CASTING
Centre House, Room DG20, 56 Wood Lane, London W12 7SB
Fax: 020-8225 6170 Tel: 020-8576 9897

STYLE Emma CDG
7 Chamberlain Cottages
Camberwell Grove, London SE5 8JD
Fax: 020-7701 7704 Tel: 020-7701 7750

SUMMERS Mark (LONDON)
See CASTING UNLIMITED (LONDON)

SUMMERS Mark (LOS ANGELES)
See CASTING UNLIMITED (LOS ANGELES)

SYERS Michael
(See CASTING CONNECTION The)

SYSON Lucinda CDG
11 Goodwins Court, London WC2N 4LL
e-mail: lscasting@yahoo.co.uk
Fax: 020-7240 7710 Tel: 020-7379 4868

TABAK Amanda CDG
(See CANDID CASTING)

TEECE Shirley
106 North View Road, London N8 7LP Tel: 020-8347 9241

TOPOLSKI Tessa
25 Clifton Hill, London NW8 0QE Tel: 020-7328 6393

TOPPS CASTING
(Nicola Topping)
The Media Centre
7 Northumberland Street, Huddersfield HD1 1RL
e-mail: topps.casting@btopenworld.com
Fax: 01484 320787 Tel: 01484 511988

TREVELLICK Jill CDG
123 Rathcoole Gardens, London N8 9PH
e-mail: jill@trevellick.force9.co.uk
Fax: 020-8348 7400 Tel: 020-8340 2734

TREVIS Sarah CDG
c/o Twickenham Studios, St Margaret's
Twickenham TW1 2AW   Tel: 020-8607 8888

TWIST & FLIC CASTING
(Penny Burrows)
1A Calton Avenue, Dulwich Village, London SE21 7DE
e-mail: info@sportsmodels.com
Fax: 020-8299 8600   Tel: 020-8299 8800

VAN OST & MILLINGTON CASTING
(Valerie Van Ost & Andrew Millington)
PO Box 115, Petersfield GU31 5BB
Fax: 020-7436 9858   Tel: 020-7436 9838

VAUGHAN Sally
2 Kennington Park Place
London SE11 4AS   Tel: 020-7735 6539

VITAL PRODUCTIONS
PO Box 26441, London SE10 9GZ
e-mail: mail@vital-productions.co.uk
                            Tel/Fax: 020-8858 8880

VOSSER Anne CASTING CDG
199 Piccadilly, London W1J 9HA
Fax: 020-7494 2232   Tel: 020-7434 1800

WATSON Tim
BBC DRAMA SERIES CASTING
Centre House, Room DG20, 56 Wood Lane, London W12 7SB
Fax: 020-8225 6170   Tel: 020-8225 6640

WEIR Fiona
c/o Twickenham Studios, St Margaret's
Twickenham TW1 2AW   Tel: 020-8607 8888

WEST June
Granada Television, Quay Street, Manchester M60 9EA
Fax: 0161-827 2853   Tel: 0161-832 7211

WESTERN Matt CASTING CDG
2nd Floor, 59-61 Brewer Street, London W1F 9UN
e-mail: matt@mattwestern.co.uk
Fax: 020-7439 1941   Tel: 020-7434 1230

WHALE Toby CDG
80 Shakespeare Road, London W3 6SN
Website: www.whalecasting.com
e-mail: toby@whalecasting.com
Fax: 020-8993 8096   Tel: 020-8993 2821

WHITALL Keith
(Theatre Only)
10 Woodlands Avenue, West Byfleet
Surrey KT14 6AT   Tel: 01932 343655

WHITTINGHAM Ian Zachary
c/o Manic Group, Room 112
Skyline Plaza, 80 Commercial Road, London E1 1NZ
Website: www.themanicgroup.com
e-mail: info@themanicgroup.com
Fax: 020-7481 1898   Tel: 020-7059 0498

WILLIS Catherine
BBC DRAMA SERIES CASTING
Centre House, Room DG20, 56 Wood Lane, London W12 7SB
Fax: 020-8225 6170   Tel: 020-8225 7906

WOODHAMS Keith CASTING
20 Lowther Hill, London SE23 1PY
e-mail: kwoodhams@mcmail.com
Fax: 020-8314 1950   Tel: 020-8314 1677

WOOLGAR Francesca CDG
(See PEARCE WOOLGAR CASTING)

ZIMMERMANN Jeremy CASTING
Clareville House, 26-27 Oxendon Street, London SW1Y 4EL
Fax: 020-7925 0708   Tel: 020-7925 0707

AMADEUS CENTRE The
50 Shirland Road, London W9 2JA
e-mail: amadeus@amadeuscentre.co.uk
Fax: 020-7266 1225   Tel: 020-7286 1686

BARBICAN EXHIBITION CENTRE
Barbican, Silk Street, London EC2Y 8DS
Fax: 020-7382 7263   Tel: 020-7382 7053

BIRMINGHAM SYMPHONY HALL
Broad Street, Birmingham B1 2EA
Website: www.symphonyhall.co.uk
e-mail: symphonyhall@necgroup.co.uk
BO: 0121-780 3333   Tel: 0121-200 2000

BLACKHEATH HALLS
23 Lee Road, Blackheath, London SE3 9RQ
Website: www.blackheathhalls.com
e-mail: mail@blackheathhalls.com
Fax: 020-8852 5154   BO: 020-8463 0100

CENTRAL HALL - WESTMINSTER
Storey's Gate, Westminster, London SW1H 9NH
Website: www.c-h-w.co.uk
e-mail: events@c-h-w.co.uk   Tel: 020-7222 8010

EARL'S COURT & OLYMPIA EXHIBITION CENTRES
Warwick Road, London SW5 9TA
Website: www.eco.co.uk
e-mail: marketing@eco.co.uk   Tel: 020-7385 1200

FAIRFIELD HALLS
Park Lane, Croydon CR9 1DG
BO: 020-8688 9291   Tel: 020-8681 0821

FERNEHAM HALL
Osborn Road, Fareham, Hants PO16 7DB
e-mail: boxoffice@fareham.gov.uk   Tel: 01329 824864

GORDON CRAIG THEATRE
Stevenage Arts & Leisure Centre
Lytton Way, Stevenage, Herts SG1 1LZ
Website: www.stevenage-leisure.co.uk
e-mail: gordoncraig@stevenage-leisure.co.uk
BO: 08700 131030   Admin: 01438 242642

HEXAGON The
Queen's Walk, Reading RG1 7UA
Website: www.readingarts.com
e-mail: boxoffice@readingarts.com
Fax: 0118-939 0028   Admin: 0118-939 0390

MINERVA STUDIO THEATRE
Oaklands Park, Chichester, West Sussex PO19 6AP
Website: www.cft.org.uk
Fax: 01243 787288   Tel: 01243 784437

NATIONAL CONCERT HALL OF WALES The
St David's Hall, The Hayes, Cardiff CF10 1SH
Website: www.stdavidshallcardiff.co.uk
Fax: 029-2087 8599   Tel: 029-2087 8500

OLYMPIA EXHIBITION CENTRES
Hammersmith Road, Kensington, London W14 8UX
Fax: 020-7598 2500   Tel: 020-7385 1200

RIVERSIDE STUDIOS
Crisp Road, London W6 9RL
Website: www.riversidestudios.co.uk
e-mail: online@riversidestudios.co.uk
BO: 020-8237 1111   Tel: 020-8237 1000

ROYAL ALBERT HALL
Kensington Gore, London SW7 2AP
Website: www.royalalberthall.com
e-mail: admin@royalalberthall.com
Fax: 020-7823 7725   Tel: 020-7589 3203

SOUTH BANK CENTRE
(Including The Royal Festival Hall, Queen Elizabeth Hall,
Purcell, Room & Hayward Gallery)
Royal Festival Hall
London SE1 8XX
Website: www.rfh.org.uk
BO: 0870 3800400   Tel: 020-7921 0601

ST JOHN'S
Smith Square, London SW1P 3HA
Website: www.sjss.org.uk
Fax: 020-7233 1618   Tel: 020-7222 1061

VENUES @ BAC
Battersea Arts Centre, Lavender Hill
Battersea, London SW11 5TP   Tel: 020-7326 8211

**WEMBLEY CONFERENCE & EXHIBITION CENTRE &
WEMBLEY ARENA**
Wembley HA9 0DW
Website: www.whatsonwembley.com
BO: 0870 0600870   Admin: 020-8902 8833

WIGMORE HALL
36 Wigmore Street
London W1U 2BP
e-mail: info@wigmore-hall.org.uk   BO: 020-7935 2141

ACORN ENTERTAINMENTS Ltd
PO Box 64
Cirencester, Glos GL7 5YD
Website: www.acornents.co.uk
e-mail: acornents@btconnect.com
Fax: 01285 642291   Tel: 01285 644622

ASKONAS HOLT Ltd
(Classical Music)
Lonsdale Chambers
27 Chancery Lane, London WC2A 1PF
Website: www.askonasholt.co.uk
e-mail: info@askonasholt.co.uk
Fax: 020-7400 1799   Tel: 020-7400 1700

AVALON PROMOTIONS Ltd
4A Exmoor Street, London W10 6BD
Fax: 020-7598 7334   Tel: 020-7598 7333

BARRUCCI LEISURE ENTERPRISES Ltd
(Promoters)
45-47 Cheval Place
London SW7 1EW
e-mail: barrucci@barrucci.com
Fax: 020-7581 2509   Tel: 020-7225 2255

BLOCK Derek ARTISTES AGENCY
70-76 Bell Street
Marylebone, London NW1 6SP
e-mail: dbaa@derekblock.demon.co.uk
Fax: 020-7724 2102   Tel: 020-7724 2101

CITY CONCERT ORGANISATION Ltd The
PO Box 3145
Lichfield WS13 6YN
Website: www.cityconcert.com
e-mail: admin@cityconcert.com   Tel/Fax: 01543 262286

FLYING MUSIC
110 Clarendon Road, London W11 2HR
Website: www.flyingmusic.com
e-mail: info@flyingmusic.com
Fax: 020-7221 5016   Tel: 020-7221 7799

GOLDSMITH Harvey PRODUCTIONS Ltd
(Concert Promotion)
65 Newman Street, London W1T 6EG
Website: www.harveygoldsmith.com
e-mail: mail@harveygoldsmith.com
Fax: 020-7224 0111   Tel: 020-7224 1992

GUBBAY Raymond Ltd
Dickens House
15 Tooks Court, London EC4A 1QH
Website: www.raymondgubbay.co.uk
e-mail: mail@raymondgubbay.co.uk
Fax: 020-7025 3751   Tel: 020-7025 3750

HOBBS Liz EVENTS
First Floor, 65 London Road
Newark, Nottinghamshire NG24 1RZ
Website: www.lizhobbsgroup.com
e-mail: events@lizhobbsgroup.com
Fax: 0870 3337009   Tel: 08700 702702

HOCHHAUSER Victor
4 Oak Hill Way
London NW3 7LR
Fax: 020-7431 2531   Tel: 020-7794 0987

IMG ARTS & ENTERTAINMENT
Pier House
Strand on the Green
Chiswick, London W4 3NN
Fax: 020-8233 5001   Tel: 020-8233 5000

KARUSHI PROMOTIONS
Fifth Floor
97-99 Dean Street, London W1D 3TE
Website: www.karushi.com
e-mail: ed@karushi.com
Fax: 020-7484 5151   Tel: 020-7484 5040

McINTYRE Phil ENTERTAINMENT
2nd Floor
35 Soho Square
London W1D 3QX
e-mail: reception@mcintyre-ents.com
Fax: 020-7439 2280   Tel: 020-7439 2270

RBM
(Comedy)
3rd Floor
18 Broadwick Street, London W1V 1FG
Website: www.rbmcomedy.com
e-mail: info@rbmcomedy.com
Fax: 020-7287 5020   Tel: 020-7287 5010

ZANDER Peter CONCERT MANAGEMENT
22 Romilly Street
London W1D 5AG
e-mail: peterzan.berlin@virgin.net   Tel: 020-7437 4767

ACE ARRANGEMENTS Ltd
(Entertainment Providers, Parties/Corporate Events)
7 Berghem Mews, Blythe Road, London W14 0US
e-mail: sally.allen@ace-uk.biz
Fax: 020-7751 1275   Tel: 020-7603 3444

ACTORS ILLUMINATED.COM
(A Service from Luminous Designs)
Website: www.actorsilluminated.com
e-mail: mail@actorsilluminated.com   Mobile: 07769 626074

ACTOR'S ONE-STOP SHOP The
(Showreels, Photographs, CV's)
54 Belsize Avenue, London N13 4TJ
Website: www.actorsone-stopshop.com
e-mail: info@actorsone-stopshop.com
Tel/Fax: 020-8888 9666   Tel: 020-8888 7006

AGENTFILE
(Software for Agents)
Website: www.agentfile.com
e-mail: info@agentfile.com   Mobile: 07956 544764

AON Ltd (Trading as AON/ALBERT G. RUBEN)
(Insurance Brokers)
Pinewood Studios, Pinewood Road, Iver, Bucks SL0 0NH
Website: www.aon.co.uk
Fax: 01753 653152   Tel: 01753 658200

ARTON Michael PhD
(Historical Research, Technical Advisor)
122 Sunningfields Road, London NW4 4RE
e-mail: miriarton@excite.com   Tel/Fax: 020-8203 2733

ARTS VA The
(Bronwyn Robertson) (Administrative Support for
Individuals & Organisations)
PO Box 2911, Stratford-upon-Avon CV37 9WU
Website: www.theartsva.com
e-mail: bronwyn@theartsva.com
Fax: 01789 552818   Tel: 01789 552559

ATKINS Chris & COMPANY
(Accountants & Business Consultants)
Astra House, Arklow Road, London SE14 6EB
e-mail: jerry@chrisatkins.co.uk   Tel: 020-8691 4100

BERGER Harvey FCA
(Chartered Accountant)
18 Chalk Lane, Cockfosters
Barnet, Herts EN4 9HJ
e-mail: harvey.berger@tesco.net   Tel/Fax: 020-8449 9328

BIG PICTURE
(Part-time Work in Computer Retail Industry)
13 Netherwood Road, London W14 0BL
e-mail: info@ebigpicture.co.uk   Tel: 020-7371 4455

BLACKMORE Lawrence
(Production Accountant)
Suite 5, 26 Charing Cross Road, London WC2H 0DG
Fax: 020-7836 3156   Tel: 020-7240 1817

BLOSSOM Matt
(Circus Skills Consultant)
5 Widworthy, Sylvan Way
Bognor Regis, West Sussex PO21 2RS
Website: www.mattblossom.com
e-mail: mail@mattblossom.com   Tel: 01243 862469

BOARDMAN Paul
(Script Writer)
14 Belsay Close
Elm Tree Farm, Stockton on Tees
Cleveland TS19 0UF
e-mail: scripts@paulboardman.co.uk   Mobile: 07986 504499

BOWKER ORFORD
(Chartered Accountants)
15-19 Cavendish Place, London W1G 0DD
e-mail: morford@bowkerorford.com
Fax: 020-7580 3909   Tel: 020-7636 6391

BREBNER ALLEN TRAPP
(Chartered Accountants)
180 Wardour Street, London W1F 8LB
Website: www.brebner.co.uk
e-mail: partners@brebner.co.uk
Fax: 020-7287 5315   Tel: 020-7734 2244

BRECKMAN & COMPANY
(Chartered Accountants)
49 South Molton Street
London W1K 5LH   Tel: 020-7499 2292

BRITISH ASSOCIATION FOR DRAMA THERAPISTS The
41 Broomhouse Lane, London SW6 3DP
e-mail: gillian@badth.demon.co.uk   Tel/Fax: 020-7731 0160

BROOK-REYNOLDS Natalie
(Freelance Stage Manager/Floor Manager TV & Theatre.
Member of SMA, Equity & BECTU)
Website: www.nataliebrookreynolds.com
e-mail: info@nataliebrookreynolds.com
Fax: 0871 2429919   Tel: 020-8350 0877

CADENZA ENTERTAINMENT SERVICES Ltd
Bedford Chambers, The Piazza
Covent Garden, London WC2E 8HA
Website: www.cadenzaservices.co.uk
e-mail: info@cadenzaservices.co.uk   Tel: 020-7836 3401

CARR Mark & Co
(Chartered Accountants)
63 Lansdowne Place, Hove, East Sussex BN3 1FL
Website: www.markcarr.co.uk
e-mail: mark@markcarr.co.uk
Fax: 01273 778822   Tel: 01273 778802

CASTLE MAGICAL SERVICES
(Magical Consultants) (Michael Shepherd)
Broompark, 131 Tadcaster Road
Dringhouses, York YO24 1QJ
e-mail: castle@evemail.net   Tel/Fax: 01904 709500

CAULKETT Robin DipSM, MIIRSM
(Abseiling, Rope Work)
3 Churchill Way, Mitchell Dean, Glos GL17 0AZ
Mobile: 07970 442003   Tel: 01594 825865

CELEBRITIES WORLDWIDE Ltd
(Celebrity on-line Media Database)
39-41 New Oxford Street, London WC1A 1BN
Website: www.celebritiesworldwide.com
e-mail: info@celebritiesworldwide.com
Fax: 020-7836 7701   Tel: 020-7836 7702

CIRCUS MANIACS
(Circus, Theatre, Dance, Extreme Sports)
Office 8A, The Kingswood Foundation
Britannia Road, Kingswood, Bristol BS15 8DB
e-mail: agency@circusmaniacs.com
Mobile: 07977 247287   Tel/Fax: 0117-947 7042

COBO MEDIA Ltd
(Performing Arts, Entertainment & Leisure Marketing)
43A Garthorne Road, London SE23 1EP
Website: www.theatrenet.com
e-mail: admin@cobomedia.com
Fax: 020-8291 4969   Tel: 020-8291 7079

COOPER Margaret
(Art Director)
c/o 75/1 Old College Street, Sleima, Malta
e-mail: mediacorp1@yahoo.com
Mobile: 00 356 9925 2925   Tel: 00 356 21 342338

COUNT AND SEE LIMITED
(Tax & Accountancy Services)
219 Macmillan Way, London SW17 6AW
Website: www.countandsee.com
e-mail: info@countandsee.com
Fax: 0870 130 5375   Tel: 020-8767 7882

CREATIVE INDUSTRIES DEVELOPMENT AGENCY (CIDA)
(Professional Development & Business Support for Artists
& Creative Businesses)
Media Centre, Northumberland Street
Huddersfield, West Yorkshire HD1 1RL
Website: www.cida.org
e-mail: info@cida.org
Fax: 01484 483150   Tel: 01484 483140

DYNAMIC FX Ltd
(Magical Entertainment Company)
Regent House, 291 Kirkdale, London SE26 4QD
e-mail: mail@dynamicfx.co.uk
Fax: 020-8659 8118   Tel: 020-8659 8130

EARLE Kenneth PERSONAL MANAGEMENT
214 Brixton Road, London SW9 6AP
Fax: 020-7274 9529   Tel: 020-7274 1219

EQUITY INSURANCE SERVICES
131-133 New London Road, Chelmsford, Essex CM2 0QZ
Website: www.equity-ins-services.com
e-mail: enquiries@equity-ins-services.com
Fax: 01245 491641   Tel: 01245 357854

EXECUTIVE AUDIO VISUAL
(Showreels for Actors & Presenters)
80 York St, London W1H 1QW   Tel/Fax: 020-7723 4488

FACADE
(Creation and Production of Musicals)
43A Garthorne Road
London SE23 1EP
e-mail: facade@cobomedia.com   Tel: 020-8291 7079

FILMANGEL
(Film Finance & Script Services)
110 Trafalgar Road
Portslade, East Sussex BN41 1GS
Website: www.filmangel.co.uk
e-mail: filmangels@freenetname.co.uk
Fax: 01273 705451
Tel: 01273 27733

FLAMES MARTIAL ARTS ACADEMY
Unit 2, 128 Milton Road Business Park
Gravesend, Kent DA12 2PG
Website: www.kuentao.com
e-mail: arstunts@yahoo.co.uk
Mobile: 07950 396389

FORD Jonathan & Co
(Chartered Accountants)
The Coach House
31 View Road
Rainhill, Merseyside L35 0LF
Website: www.jonathanford.co.uk
e-mail: info@jonathanford.co.uk
Tel: 0151-426 4512

FREE ELECTRON
(Website Design)
45 Alpha Street
Slough, Berks SL1 1RA
Website: www.free-electron.co.uk
e-mail: info@free-electron.co.uk
Tel/Fax: 01753 693074

FULL EFFECT The
(Live Event Producers including Choreographers)
4 Arkwright Industrial Estate
Arkwright Road, Bedford MK42 0LQ
Website: www.thefulleffect.co.uk
e-mail: mark.harrison@tfe.co.uk
Fax: 01234 214445
Tel: 01234 269099

GHOSTWRITER
(John Parker)
21 Hindsleys Place
London SE23 2NF
e-mail: parkerwrite@yahoo.co.uk
Tel: 020-8244 5816

GORDON LEIGHTON
(Chartered Accountants, Business Advisors)
3rd Floor, 20-23 Greville Street, London EC1N 8SS
Website: www.gordonl.co.uk
e-mail: gl@gordonl.com
Fax: 020-7831 0500
Tel: 020-7831 8300

HANDS UP PUPPETS
c/o Peter Charlesworth & Associates
68 Old Brompton Road, London SW7 3LD
Website: www.handsuppuppets.com
e-mail: handsuppuppets@btinternet.com
Tel: 020-7581 2478

HARVEY MONTGOMERY Ltd
(Chartered Accountants)
3 The Fairfield, Farnham, Surrey GU9 8AH
Website: www.harveymontgomery.co.uk
e-mail: peter@harveymontgomery.co.uk
Fax: 01252 734394
Tel: 01252 734388

HASLAM Dominic
(Arranger & Composer)
c/o Sandra Singer Associates
21 Cotswold Road, Westcliff-on-Sea, Essex SS0 8AA
Website: www.sandrasinger.com
e-mail: sandrasingeruk@aol.com
Fax: 01702 339393
Tel: 01702 331616

HATSTAND Helena
(Special Skills Performer, Circus, Whip Cracking,
Fire-eating, Juggling Solo/Double/Triple Group Acts)
39 Old Church Road, Stepney, London E1 0QB
Website: www.hatstandcircus.co.uk
e-mail: helenahatstand@btopenworld.com
Mobile: 07748 005839
Tel/Fax: 020-7791 2541

HAYES Susan
(Choreographer/Body Worker)
84A Shaftesbury Road, London N19 4QN
e-mail: susan.hayes@blueyonder.co.uk
Mobile: 07721 927714
Tel/Fax: 020-7686 0306

HERITAGE RAILWAY ASSOCIATION
7 Robert Close
Potters Bar, Herts EN6 2DH
Website: www.ukhrail.uel.ac.uk
Tel: 01707 643568

HOMEMATCH PROPERTY FINANCE
(Mortgages for Entertainers)
6 Shaw Street, Worcester WR1 3QQ
e-mail: chrisjcatchpole@aol.com
Fax: 01905 22121
Tel: 01905 22007

HONRI Peter
(Music Hall Consultant)
1 Evingar Road, Whitchurch
Hants RG28 7EY
Tel: 01256 892162

HUSSEY Daniel
(International Paranormal Occult
Investigator & Consultant)
PO Box 24250, London SE9 3ZH
Website: www.lifeafterdeath.net
e-mail: enquiries@paranormaloccultinvestigator.com
Mobile: 07764 428318
Tel: 020-8378 6844

IMAGE DIGGERS
(Slide/Stills/Audio/Video Library & Theme Research)
618B Finchley Road
London NW11 7RR
Website: http://imagediggers.netfirms.com
e-mail: lambhorn@tiscali.co.uk   Tel/Fax: 020-8455 4564

IMPACT AGENCY
(Public Relations)
3 Bloomsbury Place, London WC1A 2QL
Fax: 020-7580 7200   Tel: 020-7580 1770

I R A - INDEPENDENT REVIEWS ARTS SERVICES
(Stories from World of Film/Art/Showbiz))
12 Hemingford Close, London N12 9HF
e-mail: e.lovatt@btinternet.com
Mobile: 07956 212916   Tel/Fax: 020-8343 7437

JACKSON Kim
(Arts Education Consultancy)
1 Mellor Road
Leicester LE3 6HN
e-mail: jacksongillespie@hotmail.com   Tel: 0116-233 8432

JENKINS Andrew Ltd
(Venue & Production Consultancy)
63 Kidbrooke Park Road
Blackheath, London SE3 0EE
Website: www.andrewjenkinsltd.com
e-mail: info@andrewjenkinsltd.com
Fax: 020-8856 7106   Tel: 020-8319 3657

JFL
(Recruitment Consultants)
47 New Bond Street, London W1S 1DJ
Fax: 020-7493 7161   Tel: 020-7493 8824

JONES Melanie ASSOCIATES
(Deign & Print)
109 Highland Road, Bromley BR1 4AA
Website: www.mjassoc.co.uk
e-mail: melaniejones@designandprint.demon.co.uk
Tel/Fax: 020-8290 4999

JOSHI CLINIC The
57 Wimpole Street, London W1G 8YW
Fax: 020-7486 9622   Tel: 020-7487 5456

KEAN LANYON Ltd
(Graphic Designers, PR & Marketing Consultants)
Rose Cottage, Aberdeen Centre
22 Highbury Grove, London N5 2EA
Website: www.keanlanyon.com
e-mail: iain@keanlanyon.com
Fax: 020-7359 0199   Tel: 020-7354 3362

KELLER Don
(Marketing Consultancy & Project Management)
65 Glenwood Road, Harringay, London N15 3JS
e-mail: info@dakam.waitrose.com
Fax: 020-8809 6825   Tel: 020-8800 4882

KERR John CHARTERED ACCOUNTANTS
369-375 Eaton Road, West Derby, Liverpool L12 2AH
e-mail: advice@jkca.co.uk
Fax: 0151-228 3792   Tel: 0151-228 8977

KIEVE Paul
(Magical Effects for Theatre & Film)
23 Terrace Road
South Hackney, London E9 7ES
Website: www.stageillusion.com
e-mail: mail@stageillusion.com   Tel/Fax: 020-8985 6188

LAMBOLLE Robert
(Script Evaluation/Editing)
618B Finchley Road
London NW11 7RR
Website: http://readingandrighting.netfirms.com
e-mail: lambhorn@tiscali.co.uk   Tel/Fax: 020-8455 4564

LARK INSURANCE BROKING GROUP
(Insurance Brokers)
Wigham House, Wakering Road, Barking, Essex IG11 8PJ
Fax: 020-8557 2430   Tel: 020-8557 2300

LEEP MARKETING & PR
(Marketing, Press and Publicity)
5 Nassau House
122 Shaftesbury Avenue, London W1D 5ER
e-mail: philip@leep.biz
Fax: 020-7439 8833   Tel: 020-7439 9777

LINGUA FRANCA
(French Dialogue & Script Translators/Subtitlers)
12 Ack Lane West, Cheadle Hulme
Cheshire SK8 7EL   Tel: 0161-485 3357

LOCATION TUTORS NATIONWIDE
(Fully Qualified/Experienced Teachers working with
Children on Film Sets and Covering all Key Stages of
National Curriculum)
16 Poplar Walk, Herne Hill, London SE24 0BU
Fax: 020-7207 8794   Tel: 020-7978 8898

LOVE Billie HISTORICAL PHOTOGRAPHS
(Picture Research. Formerly 'Amanda' Theatrical
Portraiture)
3 Winton Street, Ryde
Isle of Wight PO33 2BX   Tel: 01983 812572

Daniel Hussey

Psychic International Occult Investigator & Consultant

PO Box 24250, London SE9 3ZH

Tel: 020 8378 6844

Mobile: 077 400 43156

E-mail: occultcentre@hotmail.com

Web page: www.lifeafterdeath.net

Psychic   Research   -   Paranormal   Phenomena

Practical   Ritual   Workings   -   Physical   Mediumship

Materialisation's   -   Haunting's   -   Exorcisms

Criminal   Paranormal   Investigation's

Spiritualism   -   Transcendental   Magic

Witchcraft   &   Occult   Esoteric   Problems

McKENNA Deborah Ltd
(Celebrity Chefs & Lifestyle Presenters)
Claridge House, 29 Barnes High Street, London SW13 9LW
Website: www.deborahmckenna.com
e-mail: info@deborahmckenna.com
Fax: 020-8392 2462   Tel: 020-8876 7566

MEDIA LEGAL
(Education Services)
West End House, 83 Clarendon Road
Sevenoaks, Kent TN13 1ET   Tel: 01732 460592

MILDENBERG Vanessa
(Choreographer/Movement Director)
30 Mount Ephraim Road
London SW16 1LW   Mobile: 07796 264828

MILITARY ADVISORY & INSTRUCTION SPECIALISTS
(John Sessions) (Advice on Weapons, Drill, Period to
Present. Ex-Army Instructors)
e-mail: higgins5889@ntlworld.com   Tel: 01904 491198

MILLER ALLAN Ann
(Private Lessons, Consultancy, Choreography)
The Belly Dance Centre, Mayfield
5 Rother Road, Seaford
East Sussex BN25 4HT   Tel: 01323 899083

MINISTRY OF FUN
(Provision of Performers/PR Marketing Campaigns)
Unit 1, Suffolk Studios
127-129 Great Suffolk Street, London SE1 1PP
Website: www.ministryoffun.net
e-mail: james@ministryoffun.net
Fax: 020-7407 5763   Tel: 020-7407 6077

MORGAN Jane ASSOCIATES
(Marketing & Media)
8 Heathville Road, London N19 3AJ
e-mail: morgans@dircon.co.uk
Fax: 020-7263 9877   Tel: 020-7263 9867

MULLEN Julie
(Improvisors/Comedy Consultancy)
The Impro Lab, 34 Watts Lane
Teddington Lock TW11 8HQ   Mobile: 07956 877839

NEATE Rodger PRODUCTION MANAGEMENT
15 Southcote Road, London N19 5BJ
e-mail: rneate@dircon.co.uk
Fax: 020-7697 8237   Tel: 020-7609 9538

NEOVISION
(Location & Production Services)
46 rue de Berne, 1201 Geneva, Switzerland
Website: www.neovisionprod.com
e-mail: info@neovisionprod.com
Fax: (41 22) 741 1208   Tel: (41 79) 357 5417

NUTOPIA CHANG MUSIC
(Music for Film & Television)
Number 8, 132 Charing Cross Road, London WC2H 0LA
Website: www.nutopia.co.uk
Fax: 029-2070 9440   Tel/Fax: 07801 493133

NWA-UK HAMMERLOCK
(Wrestling Events, Training & Promotion)
PO Box 282, Ashford, Kent TN23 7ZZ
e-mail: nwauk@hammerlockwrestling.com
Fax: 01233 336757   Tel: 01233 663828

NYMAN LIBSON PAUL
(Chartered Accountants)
Regina House, 124 Finchley Road, London NW3 5JS
Website: www.nymanlibsonpaul.co.uk
e-mail: entertainment@nymanlibsonpaul.co.uk
Fax: 020-7433 2401   Tel: 020-7433 2400

ORANGE TREE STUDIO & MUSIC SERVICES
(Original Music/Composition & Production)
PO Box 99, Kings Langley WD4 8FB
Website: www.orangetreestudio.com
e-mail: richard@orangetreestudio.com
Mobile: 07768 146200   Tel: 01923 440550

PEMART
(Artist Promotion, Image Consultancy, Business Seminars,
Copy Writing, Translation Services)
London - New York
Website: www.noraarmani.com
e-mail: info@noraarmani.com
Tel: (917) 318-2290   Mobile: 07766 706415

PHYSICALITY Ltd
(Physical Skills Specialist)
Unit 8, Hatherley Mews, Walthamstow, London E17 4QP
Fax: 020-8521 3744   Tel: 020-8521 5522

PRODUCTIONS & PROMOTIONS Ltd
2 Sharpcroft
Hemel Hempstead, Herts HP2 5YY
Website: www.prodmotions.com
e-mail: stuartw@prodmotions.com   Tel/Fax: 01442 236821

PUPPET CENTRE TRUST
(Development & Advocacy Agency for Puppetry
& Related Theatre)
BAC Lavender Hill
London SW11 5TN
Website: www.puppetcentre.com
e-mail: pct@puppetcentre.demon.co.uk   Tel: 020-7228 5335

RETROGRAPH NOSTALGIA ARCHIVE
(Nostalgia Picture Consultants 1870-1970)
10 Hanover Crescent
Brighton BN2 9SB
Website: www.retrograph.com
e-mail: retropix1@aol.com   Tel: 01273 687554

RIPLEY-DUGGAN PARTNERSHIP The
(Tour Booking)
52 Tottenham Street
London W1T 4RN
e-mail: info@ripleyduggan.com   Tel: 020-7436 1392

SEAGER Martin
(Composer/Lyricist for Film/TV/Theatre)
14 Neal's Yard
Covent Garden, London WC2H 9DP
e-mail: martin_seager@onetel.com   Tel: 020-8943 4145

SHAW Bernard
(Specialist in Recording and Directing Voice Tapes)
Horton Manor
Canterbury CT4 7LG
Website: www.bernardshaw.co.uk
e-mail: bernard@bernardshaw.co.uk Tel/Fax: 01227-730843

SHOWREEL The
(Voice-Over Showreels, Digital Editing etc)
Knightsbridge House, 229 Acton Lane
Chiswick, London W4 5DD
Fax: 020-8995 2144   Tel: 020-8995 3232

SINGER Sandra PUBLIC RELATIONS
(Entertainers, Promotions Staff & Events)
21 Cotswold Road, Westcliff-on-Sea, Essex SS0 8AA
e-mail: sandrasingeruk@aol.com
Fax: 01702 339393   Tel: 01702 331616

SPEAKERPOWER.CO.UK
48 Fellows Road, London NW3 3LH
Website: www.speakerpower.co.uk
e-mail: barbara@speakerpower.co.uk
Fax: 020-7722 5255   Tel: 020-7586 4361

SPENCER Ivor
(Professional Toastmaster, Events Organiser
& Head Butler)
12 Little Bornes, Dulwich, London SE21 8SE
Website: www.ivorspencer.com
e-mail: ivor@ivorspencer.com
Fax: 020-8670 0055   Tel: 020-8670 5585

SPORTS WORKSHOP PROMOTIONS Ltd
(Production Advisors, Sport, Stunts, Safety)
PO Box 878, Crystal Palace National Sports Centre
London SE19 2BH
e-mail: info@sportspromotions.co.uk
Fax: 020-8776 7772   Tel: 020-8659 4561

STUNT ACTION SPECIALISTS (S.A.S.)
(Corpoate & TV Stunt Work)
110 Trafalgar Road, Portslade, East Sussex BN41 1GS
Website: www.stuntactionspecialists.com
e-mail: wayne@stuntactionspecialists.co.uk
Fax: 01273 708699   Tel: 01273 230214

SUMMERS David & COMPANY
(Chartered Accountants)
Argo House, Kilburn Park Road, London NW6 5LF
e-mail: dsummersfca@hotmail.com
Fax: 020-7644 0678   Tel: 020-7644 0478

TAKE FIVE CASTING STUDIO
(Showreels)
37 Beak Street, London W1F 9RZ
Website: www.takefivestudio.co.uk
e-mail: info@takefivestudio.co.uk
Fax: 020-7287 3035   Tel: 020-7287 2120

TARLO LYONS
(Solicitors)
Watchmaker Court, 33 St John's Lane
London EC1M 4DB
Website: www.tarlolyons.com
e-mail: info@tarlolyons.com
Fax: 020-7814 9421   Tel: 020-7405 2000

TAYLOR Chris
(Arts Administration)
1 Chichester Terrace, Brighton BN2 1FG
e-mail: chris.taylor@clara.co.uk
Fax: 01273 675922   Tel: 01273 625132

TELESCRIPT Ltd
The Barn, Handpost Farmhouse
Maidens Green, Berkshire RG42 6LD
Fax: 01344 890655   Tel: 01344 890470

THEATRE PROJECTS CONSULTANTS
4 Apollo Studios, Charlton Kings Road, London NW5 2SW
Website: www.tpcworld.com
Fax: 020-7284 0636   Tel: 020-7482 4224

THORNTON W. M. Lt Cdr MBE RD RNR
(Military Adviser & Researcher)
37 Wolsey Close, Southall, Middlesex UB2 4NQ
e-mail: maitland@thornton44.fsnet.co.uk
          Tel: 020-8574 4425

TODD Carole
(Director/Choreographer)
c/o Chris Davis - International Artistes
4th Floor Holborn Hall, 193-195 High Holborn
London WC1V 7BD
Website: www.caroletodd.me.uk e-mail: chris@intart.co.uk
Fax: 020-7404 9865   Tel: 020-7025 0600

TODS MURRAY LLP
(Richard Findlay Entertainment Lawyer)
66 Queen Street
Edinburgh EH2 4NE
e-mail: richard.findlay@todsmurray.com
Fax: 0131-300 2202   Tel: 0131-226 4771

TV UK Ltd/LATITUDE MEDIA COURSES
(Voice-Over Courses, Alan Meyer)
PO Box 2183
London W1A 1UB
Website: www.tvuk.net
e-mail: alanmeyer@tvuk.net   Tel: 020-7727 7447

UC PRODUCTIONS
(Production & Event Management)
22 Freshfield Place
Brighton, East Sussex BN2 0BN
e-mail: byford@ucproductions.co.uk
Fax: 01273 606402   Tel: 01273 623972

UK THEATRE AVAILABILITY
(Bookings Service for Theatre Producers)
3 Grand Union Walk
Camden Town, London NW1 9LP
Website: www.uktheatreavailability.co.uk
e-mail: info@uktheatreavailability.co.uk
Fax: 020-7424 0877   Tel: 020-8455 3278

UNITED KINGDOM COPYRIGHT BUREAU
(Script Services)
110 Trafalgar Road, Portslade
East Sussex BN41 1GS
Website: www.copyrightbureau.co.uk
e-mail: info@copyrightbureau.co.uk
Fax: 01273 705451   Tel: 01273 277333

UPFRONT TELEVISION Ltd
(Celebrity Booking for Events)
39-41 New Oxford Street, London WC1A 1BN
Website: www.celebritiesworldwide.com
e-mail: info@upfronttv.com
Fax: 020-7836 7701   Tel: 020-7836 7702

VANTIS
(Accountants/Business Advisers)
Torrington House, 47 Holywell Hill
St Albans, Hertfordshire AL1 1HD
e-mail: ian.skelton@vantisplc.com
Fax: 01727 861052   Tel: 01727 838255

VENTURINO Antonio
(Commedia dell'arte, Mask Specialist & Movement Director)
Coup de Masque, 97 Moore Road,
Mapperley, Nottingham NG3 6EJ
e-mail: a-and-t@coup-de-masque.fsnet.co.uk
                                    Tel/Fax: 0115-985 8409

VERNON Doremy
(Author 'Tiller Girls'/Archivist/Dance Routines
Tiller Girl Style)
16 Ouseley Road
London SW12 8EF   Tel/Fax: 020-8767 6944

VSI
(Translation, Subtitling, Casting, Dubbing
Foreign Language Versions)
132 Cleveland Street, London W1T 6AB
Website: www.vsi.tv
e-mail: info@vsi.tv
Fax: 020-7692 7711   Tel: 020-7692 7700

WEB CREATIONS
(Tim Groves)
63 Clarence Road
Bounds Green, London N22 8PG
Website: www.tgwc.co.uk
e-mail: info@tgwc.co.uk   Mobile: 07764 740182

WELBOURNE Jacqueline
(Circus Trainer, Choreographer, Consultant)
c/o Circus Maniacs Agency
Office 8A, The Kingswood Foundation
Britannia Road
Kingswood, Bristol BS15 8DB
e-mail: jackie@circusmaniacs.com
Mobile: 07977 247287   Tel/Fax: 0117-947 7042

WHITE Leonard
(Production & Script Consultant)
Highlands
40 Hill Crest Road
Newhaven, Brighton
East Sussex BN9 9EG
e-mail: leoguy.white@virgin.net   Tel/Fax: 01273 514473

WIDDOWSON Alexis CHARTERED ACCOUNTANTS
1 High Street, Welford
Northants NN6 6HT
e-mail: alexiswiddowson@aol.com   Tel/Fax: 01858 575734

WILD DREAM CONSULTANCY
(Confidence Course Public Speaking, Creative
Development)   Tel: 020-8374 3924

WITCH FINDER GENERAL
(Occult Consultants)
BCM Akademia
London WC1N 3XX
e-mail: esbat@blueyonder.co.uk   Tel: 020-8683 2173

YOUNGBLOOD Ltd
(Dramatic Action Specialists)
16 Gunnersbury Close
Chiswick High Road
London W4 4AH
Website: www.youngblood.org.uk
e-mail: info@youngblood.org.uk
Mobile: 07813 463102   Tel: 0845 6449418

ACADEMY COSTUMES
50 Rushworth Street, London SE1 0RB
Website: www.academycostumes.com
e-mail: academyco@aol.com
Fax: 020-7928 6287   Tel: 020-7620 0771

ALL-SEWN-UP
Mechanics Institute, 7 Church Street
Heptonstall, West Yorks HX7 7NS
Website: www.allsewnup.org.uk
e-mail: nwheeler_allsewnup@hotmail.com
Fax: 01422 845070   Tel: 01422 843407

ANELLO & DAVIDE Ltd
(Bespoke, Bridal, Dance & Theatrical Footwear)
26-28 Standard Road, Park Royal, London NW10 6EU
Fax: 020-8965 4111   Tel: 020-8963 1220

ANGELS
(Fancy Dress & Revue)
119 Shaftesbury Avenue, London WC2H 8AE
Website: www.fancydress.com
e-mail: party@fancydress.com
Fax: 020-7240 9527   Tel: 020-7836 5678

ANGELS PARIS
(Costume and Uniform Hire)
Cap 18, 189 rue d'Aubervilles, 75018 Paris, France
Website: www.angels.fr
e-mail: angels@angels.fr
Fax: 00 33 1 44 729060   Tel: 00 33 1 44 728282

ANGELS THE COSTUMIERS
1 Garrick Road, London NW9 6AA
Website: www.angels.uk.com
e-mail: angels@angels.uk.com
Fax: 020-8202 1820   Tel: 020-8202 2244

ANGELS WIGS
(Wig Hire/Makers, Facial Hair Suppliers)
1 Garrick Road, London NW9 6AA
Website: www.angels.uk.com
e-mail: wigs@angels.uk.com
Fax: 020-8202 1820   Tel: 020-8202 2244

ARMS & ARCHERY
(Armour, Weaponry, Chain Mail, Warrior Costumes, Tents)
The Coach House, London Road
Ware, Herts SG12 9QU
e-mail: tgou104885@aol.com
Fax: 01920 461044   Tel: 01920 460335

BABOO William
(Theatrical Tailor)
46 Berwick Street
London W1F 8SG   Tel/Fax: 020-7434 1680

BAHADLY R
(Hair & Make-Up Specialist, incl. Bald Caps,
Ageing & Casualty)
48 Ivy Meade Road, Macclesfield, Cheshire
Mobile: 07973 553073   Tel: 01625 615878

BBC COSTUME & WIGS
172-178 Victoria Road, North Acton, London W3 6UL
Website: www.bbresources.co.uk/costumewig
e-mail: costume@bbc.co.uk
Fax: 020-8993 7040   Tel: 020-8576 1761

BERTRAND Henry
(London Stockhouse for Silk)
52 Holmes Road, London NW5 3AB
Website: www.henrybertrand.co.uk
e-mail: sales@henrybertrand.co.uk
Fax: 020-7424 7001   Tel: 020-7424 7000

BIBA LIVES VINTAGE CLOTHING
Alfies Antiques Market
13-25 Church Street, London NW8 8DT
Website: www.bibalives.com
e-mail: bibalives@aol.com   Tel: 020-7258 7999

BIRMINGHAM COSTUME HIRE
Suites 209-210, Jubilee Centre
130 Pershore Street
Birmingham B5 6ND
e-mail: info@birminghamcostumehire.co.uk
Fax: 0121-622 2758   Tel: 0121-622 3158

BISHOP Kerry
(Hair & Make-Up Artist)
Flat 4, 49 Upper Rock Gardens
Brighton, East Sussex BN2 1QF
e-mail: kerrybishop@email.com   Mobile: 07759 704394

BOSANQUET Pamela COSTUME SERVICES
2 Lebanon Park, Twickenham TW1 3DG
e-mail: pamelabosanquet@virgin.net
Fax: 020-8891 6259   Tel: 020-8891 4346

BRYAN PHILIP DAVIES COSTUMES
(Lavish Pantomime Revue Costumes)
68 Court Road, Lewes, East Sussex BN7 2SA
Website: www.bpdcostumes.co.uk
e-mail: bryan@bpdcostumes.force9.co.uk
Mobile: 07931 249097   Tel/Fax: 01273 481004

BURLINGTONS
(Hairdressers)
14 John Princes Street, London W1G 0JS
Website: www.burlingtonsuk.com   Tel: 0870 8701299

CALICO FABRICS
(Suppliers of Unbleached Calico & other Fabrics for Stage,
Costumes, Backdrops etc)
3 Ram Passage, High Street
Kingston-upon-Thames KT1 1HH
Website: www.calicofabrics.co.uk
e-mail: sales@calicofabrics.co.uk
Fax: 020-8546 7755   Tel: 020-8541 5274

CATCO MILLINERY
134 Mercers Road
London N19 4PV   Tel: 020-7272 4833

CAVALCADE COSTUMES
(Period & Light Entertainment Costumes, Single Outfits to
Full Productions)
57 Pelham Road
London SW19 1NW
Fax: 020-8540 2243   Tel: 020-8540 3513

CHRISANNE Ltd
(Specialist Fabrics & Accessories)
Chrisanne House, 14 Locks Lane
Mitcham, Surrey CR4 2JX
Website: www.chrisanne.co.uk
e-mail: sales@chrisanne.co.uk
Fax: 020-8640 2106   Tel: 020-8640 5921

COLTMAN Mike
(See COSTUME CONSTRUCTION)

COOK Sheila TEXTILES
(Vintage Textiles, Costumes & Accessories for Sale)
(By Appointment)
184 Westbourne Grove, London W11 2RH
Website: www.sheilacook@sheilacook.co.uk
e-mail: sheilacook@sheilacook.co.uk
Fax: 020-7243 1744   Tel: 020-7792 8001

COOPER Margaret
(Period Costumes)
75/1 Old College Street, Sliema, Malta
e-mail: g1greatdane@yahoo.com
Mobile: 00 356 9925 2925   Tel: 00 356 21 342338

COSPROP Ltd
(Costumes & Accessories)
26-28 Rochester Place, London NW1 9JR
Website: www.cosprop.com
e-mail: enquiries@cosprop.com
Fax: 020-7485 5942   Tel: 020-7485 6731

COSTUME COLLECTION
(Entire Costuming Service)
60 Viola Avenue, Stanwell, Middlesex TW19 7SB
e-mail: costumes4all@hotmail.com   Mobile: 07787 974857

COSTUME CONSTRUCTION
(Costumes, Masks, Props, Puppets)
21A Silchester Road, London W10 6SF
Website: www.costumeconstruction.co.uk
Tel/Fax: 020-8968 9136

COSTUME REPRODUCTIONS
(Costumiers)
200 Main Road
Goostrey, Cheshire CW4 8PD
Website: www.replicawarehouse.co.uk
e-mail: lesleyedwards@replicawarehouse.co.uk
Tel/Fax: 01477 534075

COSTUME STORE The Ltd
(Costume Accessories)
16 Station Street, Lewes
East Sussex BN7 2DB
Website: www.thecostumestore.co.uk
Fax: 01273 477191   Tel: 01273 479727

COSTUME STUDIO Ltd
(Costumes & Wigs)
Montgomery House, 159-161 Balls Pond Road, London N1 4BG
Website: www.costumestudio.co.uk
e-mail: costume.studio@easynet.co.uk
Tel/Fax: 020-7837 6576   Tel: 020-7275 9614

COUNTY DRAMA WARDROBE
(Costumes & Wigs. Hire only)
25 Gwydir Street, Cambridge CB1 2LG   Tel: 01223 313423

CRAZY CLOTHES CONNECTION
(1920's-1970's for Sale or Hire)
134 Lancaster Road, Ladbroke Grove
London W11 1QU   Tel: 020-7221 3989

DESIGNER ALTERATIONS
(Restyling & Remodelling of Clothes & Costumes)
220A Queenstown Road, Battersea, London SW8 4LP
Website: www.designeralterations.com
Fax: 020-7622 4148   Tel: 020-7498 4360

EASTON Derek
(Wigs For Theatre, Film & TV)
1 Dorothy Avenue, Peacehaven, East Sussex BN10 8LP
Website: www.derekeastonwigs.co.uk
Mobile: 07768 166733   Tel/Fax: 01273 588262

EDA ROSE MILLINERY
(Ladies' Model Hat Design & Manufacture)
Lalique, Mongewell, Wallingford
Oxon OX10 8BP   Tel/Fax: 01491 837174

FOX Charles H. Ltd
(Professional Make-Up & Wigs)
22 Tavistock Street, London WC2E 7PY
Website: www.charlesfox.co.uk
Fax: 0870 2001369   Tel: 0870 2000369

FREED OF LONDON
(Dancewear & Dance Shoes)
94 St Martin's Lane, London WC2N 4AT
Website: www.freedoflondon.com
e-mail: shop@freed.co.uk
Fax: 020-7240 3061   Tel: 020-7240 0432

FUNN Ltd
(Silk, Cotton Wool Stockings, Opaque Opera Tights & 40's
Rayon Stockings)
PO Box 102, Steyning, West Sussex BN44 3EB
e-mail: funn.biz@lycos.com
Fax: 0870 1361780   Tel: 0870 8810560

GAMBA THEATRICAL
(See THEATRICAL FOOTWEAR COMPANY Ltd)

GAV NICOLA THEATRICAL SHOES
1A Suttons Lane, Hornchurch, Essex RM12 6RD
e-mail: sales@gavnicola.freeserve.co.uk
Mobile: 07961 974278   Tel/Fax: 01708 438584

GILLHAM Felicite
(Wig Makers for Theatre, Opera & Film)
15 Newland, Sherborne, Dorset DT9 3JG
e-mail: f.gillham.wigs@gmx.net   Tel: 01935 814328

HAIRAISERS
(Wigs)
9-11 Sunbeam Road, Park Royal, London NW10 6JP
Website: www.hairaisers.com
Fax: 020-8963 1600   Tel: 020-8965 2500

HARVEYS OF HOVE
(Theatrical Costumes & Military Specialists)
110 Trafalgar Road, Portslade, Sussex BN41 1GS
e-mail: harveys.costume@ntlworld.com
Fax: 01273 708699   Tel: 01273 430323

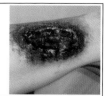
HERALD & HEART HATTERS
(Men's & Women's Hats & Headdresses - Period & Modern)
102 High Street, Rye, East Sussex TN31 7JN
Website: www.heraldandheart.com
e-mail: enquiries@heraldandheart.com   Tel: 01797 226798

HIREARCHY
(Classic & Contemporary Costume)
45-47 Palmerston Road
Boscombe, Bournemouth, Dorset BH1 4HW
Website: www.hirearchy.co.uk
e-mail: hirearchy1@aol.com   Tel: 01202 394465

HIYA COSTUME
(Hire of Theatre Costumes for Adults & Children)
1-3 Ham Road, Shoreham-by-Sea
Sussex BN43 6PA   Tel: 01273 453421

HODIN Annabel
(Costume Designer/Stylist)
12 Eton Avenue, London NW3 3EH
e-mail: annabelhodin@aol.com
Mobile: 07836 754079   Tel: 020-7431 8761

INCE Katie
(Wig Maker & Make-Up Artist)
Fairview Cottage, Main Street, Styrrup, Doncaster DN11 8NA
e-mail: katie@inces.freeserve.co.uk   Tel: 07900 250853

JULIETTE DESIGNS
(Diamante Jewellery Manufacturers)
90 Yerbury Road, London N19 4RS
Website: stagejewellery.com
Fax: 020-7281 7326   Tel: 020-7263 7878

K & D Ltd
(Footwear)
Unit 7A, Thames Road Industrial Estate
Thames Road, Silvertown, London E16 2EZ
Website: www.shoemaking.co.uk
e-mail: k&d@shoemaking.co.uk
Fax: 020-7476 5220   Tel: 020-7474 0500

LANDSFIELD Warren
(Period Legal Wigs)
47 Glenmore Road, London NW3 4DA   Tel: 020-7722 4581

LAURENCE CORNER THEATRICALS
(Theatrical Costumiers - Militaria, Uniforms - Hire & Sale)
62-64 Hampstead Road, London NW1 2NU
Website: www.laurencecorner.com
Fax: 020-7813 1413   Tel: 020-7813 1010

LEWIS HENRY Ltd
(Dress Makers)
3rd Floor, 42 Great Titchfield Street
London W1W 7PY   Tel: 020-7636 6683

LUISETTI Martina
(Professional Freelance Make-Up Artist for Film, TV,
Theatre, Fashion)
Flat 7, 468 Hornsey Road, London N19 4EE
e-mail: martola@virgilio.it   Mobile: 07919 652089

MADDERMARKET THEATRE COSTUME HIRE
(Period Clothing, Costume Hire & Wig Hire)
St John's Alley, Norwich NR2 1DR
Website: www.maddermarket.co.uk
e-mail: mmtheatre@btconnect.com
Fax: 01603 661357   Tel: 01603 626292

MAKEUP CENTRE The
(Make-Up Lessons & Supplies)
52A Walham Grove, London SW6 1QR
Website: www.themake-upcentre.co.uk
e-mail: info@themake-upcentre.co.uk   Tel: 020-7381 0213

MANNEE Nichola
(Make-Up Artist)
e-mail: nicola_mannee@yahoo.com   Mobile: 07984 644288

MASK Kim
(Costume & Make-up Protection Masks)
60 Winchester Road, St Margaret's, Twickenham TW1 1LD
Website: www.kimmask.com
e-mail: info@kimmask.com
Tel/Fax: 020-8891 3446   Tel: 08450 568482

MASON Sophia
(Hair & Make-Up Artist)
28 Watersmeet Close, Guildford, Surrey GU4 7NQ
Website: www.sophiamason.co.uk
e-mail: sophia@facetime.co.uk
Fax: 01483 832884   Tel: 01483 306700

MASTER CLEANERS The
(Theatrical Costumes & Antique Garments)
189 Haverstock Hill, London NW3 4QG   Tel: 020-7431 3725

MBA COSTUMES
Goodyear House, 52-56 Osnaburgh Street, London NW1 3ND
Website: alastair@handembroidery.com
e-mail: nhowarduk@aol.com
Fax: 020-7383 2038   Tel: 020-7388 4994

McKAY Glynn MASKS
(Specialists in Special Effect Make-Up)
11 Mount Pleasant, Framlingham, Suffolk IP13 9HQ
Mobile: 07780 865073   Tel/Fax: 01728 723865

MIDNIGHT
Costume Design & Wardrobe (Music, Theatre, Film, Tours)
e-mail: midnight_wardrobe@hotmail.com
Mobile: 07941 313223

MUMFORD Jean
(Costume Maker)
92B Fortess Road, London NW5 2HJ   Tel: 020-7267 5829

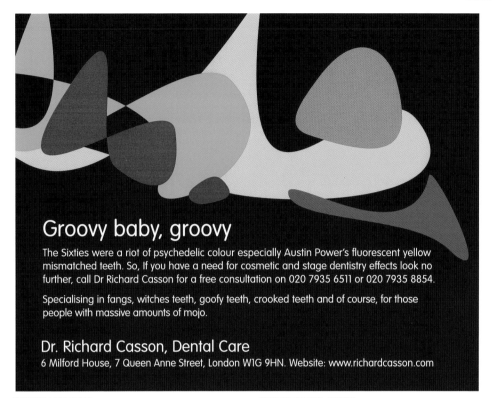

Groovy baby, groovy

The Sixties were a riot of psychedelic colour especially Austin Power's fluorescent yellow mismatched teeth. So, If you have a need for cosmetic and stage dentistry effects look no further, call Dr Richard Casson for a free consultation on 020 7935 6511 or 020 7935 8854.

Specialising in fangs, witches teeth, goofy teeth, crooked teeth and of course, for those people with massive amounts of mojo.

Dr. Richard Casson, Dental Care

6 Milford House, 7 Queen Anne Street, London W1G 9HN. Website: www.richardcasson.com

NATIONAL THEATRE
(Costume & Furniture Hire)
Chichester House, Kennington Park Estate
1-3 Brixton Road, London SW9 6DE
e-mail: costume_hire@nationaltheatre.org.uk
Tel: 020-7735 4774 (Costume)   Tel: 020-7820 1358 (Props)

NEW ID
(Makeover & Photographic Studios)
Third Floor, 17-18 Margaret Street, London W1W 8RP
Website: www.newidstudios.com
e-mail: bookings@newidstudios.co.uk   Tel: 0870 8701299

ORIGINAL KNITWEAR
(Inc. Fake Fur) (Gina Pinnick)
Avalon, Mevagissey, Cornwall PL26 6RG
Mobile: 07957 376855   Tel/Fax: 01726 844807

PATEY (LONDON) Ltd
Unit 1, 9 Gowlett Road, London SE15 4HX
Website: www.pateyhats.com
e-mail: pateyhats@aol.com
Fax: 020-7732 9538   Tel: 020-7635 0030

PINK POINTES DANCEWEAR
1A Suttons Lane, Hornchurch, Essex RM12 6RD
e-mail: sales@gavnicola.freeserve.co.uk
     Tel/Fax: 01708 438584

POLAND DENTAL STUDIO
(Film/Stage Dentistry)
1 Devonshire Place, London W1N 1PA
e-mail: polandslab@aol.com
Fax: 020-7486 3952   Tel: 020-7935 6919

PROBLOOD
11 Mount Pleasant, Framlingham
Suffolk IP13 9HQ   Tel/Fax: 01728 723865

PULLON PRODUCTIONS
(Costumiers)
St George's Studio, Wood End Lane
Fillongley, Coventry CV7 8DF
Website: www.pm-productions.co.uk   Tel/Fax: 01676 541390

RAINBOW PRODUCTIONS Ltd
(Manufacture & Handling of Costume Characters)
Rainbow House, 56 Windsor Avenue, London SW19 2RR
Website: www.rainbowproductions.co.uk
e-mail: info@rainbowproductions.co.uk
Fax: 020-8545 0777   Tel: 020-8545 0700

ROBBINS Sheila
(Costumes & Wigs)
Broombarn, 7 Ivy Cottages, Hinksey Hill
Oxford OX1 5BQ   Tel/Fax: 01865 735524

REALISTIC NON-STAIN BLOOD   TEL/FAX 01728 723865

ALLAN SCOTT COSTUMES *Costume Hire for* **STAGE FILM TV**
Offley Works, Unit F
Prima Road, London SW9 0NA (Oval Tube - 2 Mins)   **020 7793 1197**

ROYAL EXCHANGE THEATRE COSTUME HIRE
(Period Costumes, Wigs & Accessories)
47-53 Swan Street, Manchester M4 4JY
Website: www.royalexchange.co.uk
e-mail: costume.hire@royalexchange.co.uk
Tel/Fax: 0161-615 6800

ROYAL LYCEUM THEATRE COMPANY
(Theatrical Costume Hire)
29 Roseburn Street, Edinburgh EH12 5PE
Website: www.lyceum.org.uk
Fax: 0131-346 8072   Tel: 0131-337 1997

ROYAL SHAKESPEARE COMPANY COSTUME HIRE WARDROBE
Timothy's Bridge Road, Stratford-upon-Avon
Warwickshire CV37 9UY   Tel/Fax: 01789 205920

ROYER Hugo INTERNATIONAL Ltd
(Hair & Wig Materials)
10 Lakeside Business Park
Swan Lake, Sandhurst, Berkshire GU47 9DN
Website: www.royer.co.uk
e-mail: enquiries@royer.co.uk
Fax: 01252 878852   Tel: 01252 878811

RUMBLE Jane
(Masks, Millinery, Helmets Made to Order)
121 Elmstead Avenue, Wembley
Middlesex HA9 8NT   Tel: 020-8904 6462

RUSSELL HOWARTH Ltd
35 Hoxton Square, London N1 6NN
Fax: 020-7729 0107   Tel: 020-7739 6960

SCOTT Allan COSTUMES
(Costume Hire, Stage, Film & TV)
Offley Works, Unit F, Prima Road
London SW9 0NA   Tel: 020-7793 1197

SEXTON Sally Ann
(Hair & Make-Up Designer)
c/o 52 Forty Avenue, Wembley, Middlesex NW9
Mobile: 07973 802842   Tel: 020-8908 4451

SHOWBIZWIGS Ltd
(Theatrical Wigmakers & Hire)
7 Tumulus Close, Southampton SO19 6RL
Website: www.showbizwigs.co.uk   Tel/Fax: 023-8040 6699

Easton. Derek
WIGS FOR THEATRE, FILM & TV
1 Dorothy Avenue, PEACEHAVEN
East Sussex BN10 8LP
Mobile: 07768 166 733
www.derekeastonwigs.co.uk
Tel/Ans/Fax: 01273 588262

SIDE EFFECTS
(Custom-made Character/FX Costumes)
Unit 4, Camberwell Trading Estate
117 Denmark Road, London SE5 9LB
e-mail: sfx@lineone.net
Fax: 020-7738 5198   Tel: 020-7738 5199

SINGER Sandra ASSOCIATES
21 Cotswold Road, Westcliff-on-Sea, Essex SS0 8AA
Website: www.sandrasinger.com
e-mail: sandrasingeruk@aol.com
Fax: 01702 339393   Tel: 01702 331616

SKINNER Rachel MILLINERY
13 Princess Road, London NW1 8JR
Website: www.rachelskinner.co.uk
e-mail: rachel@rachelskinner.co.uk
Tel/Fax: 020-7209 0066

SLEIMAN Hilary
(Specialist & Period Knitwear)
72 Godwin Road, London E7 0LG
e-mail: hilary.sleiman@ntlworld.com
Mobile: 07940 555663   Tel: 020-8555 6176

SOFT PROPS
(Costume & Modelmakers)
Unit 4, Camberwell Trading Estate
117-119 Denmark Road, London SE5 9LB
e-mail: jackie@softprops.co.uk
Fax: 020-7738 5198   Tel: 020-7738 6324

STRIBLING DE LAUNAY Joan
(Make-Up and Hair Designer)
3 Richmond Avenue, Ilfracombe, Devon EX34 8DQ
Website: www.ilfracom.org.uk/stribling
e-mail: joanstribling@hotmail.com   Mobile: 07791 758480

SUMMERS Jane
(Animal Make-Up Artist)
c/o Firs Farm, Winston, Stowmarket, Suffolk IP14 6LQ
e-mail: janelouisemakeup@aol.com   Mobile: 07836 729800

SWINFIELD Rosemarie
(Make-Up Design & Training)
Rosie's Make-Up Box
6 Brewer Street, Soho, London W1R 3FS
Website: www.rosiesmake-up.co.uk
e-mail: rosemarie@rosiesmake-up.co.uk
Mobile: 07976 965520

THEATREKNITS
102C Belgravia Workshops
157-163 Marlborough Road, London N19 4NF
e-mail: trevorcollins@blueyonder.co.uk
Tel/Fax: 020-7561 0044

THEATRICAL FOOTWEAR COMPANY The Ltd
(Trading as GAMBA Theatrical)
Unit 14, Chingford Industrial Centre
Hall Lane, Chingford, London E4 8DJ
e-mail: gambatheatrical@yahoo.com
Fax: 020-8529 7995   Tel: 020-8529 9195

THREE KINGS THEATRICAL SUPPPLY CO
(Make-Up and Other Theatrical Services)
84 Queens Road, Farnborough, Hampshire GU14 6JR
Website: www.threekingstheatrical.com
e-mail: info@threekingstheatrical.com
Fax: 01252 515516   Tel: 01252 371123

TRENDS PRODUCTIONS Ltd
(Theatrical Costume Hire, Design & Making)
54 Lisson Street, London NW1 5DF
Website: www.trendsgroup.co.uk
e-mail: info@trendsgroup.co.uk
Fax: 020-7258 3591   Tel: 020-7723 8001

TRYFONOS Mary MASKS
(Designer and Maker of Masks and Headdresses)
59 Shaftesbury Road, London N19 4QW
Website: www.marysmasks.com
e-mail: marytryfonos@aol.com
Mobile: 07764 587433   Tel: 020-7561 9880

WAIN SHIELL & SON Ltd
(High Quality Cloth Merchants)
12 Savile Row, London W1S 3PQ
e-mail: wainshiell@compuserve.com
Fax: 020-7439 0093   Tel: 020-7734 1464

WEST YORKSHIRE FABRICS Ltd
(All Wool Venetian Crepe
Suiting, Barathea, Cut Lengths)
20 High Ash Drive, Leeds LS17 8RA
e-mail: info@stroud-brothers.demon.co.uk
Tel/Fax: 0870 4439842

WIG ROOM The
22 Coronation Road, Basingstoke, Hants RG21 4HA
e-mail: wigroom@fsbdial.co.uk   Tel/Fax: 01256 415737

WIG SPECIALITIES Ltd
(Wigs & Facial Hair, Hair Extensions etc)
First Floor, 173 Seymour Place, London W1H 4PW
Website: www.wigspecialites.co.uk
e-mail: wigspecialities@btconnect.com
Fax: 020-7723 1566   Tel: 020-7262 6565

WILLIAMS Emma
(Costume Designer & Stylist - Film, TV & Theatre)
e-mail: emmaw@costume.fsnet.co.uk
Mobile: 07710 130345   Tel/Fax: 01225 447169

WILSON Marian WIGS
(Theatrical & Film Wigmaker)
59 Gloucester Street, Faringdon, Oxon SN7 7JA
e-mail: wigmaker@wigmaker.screaming.net
Fax: 01367 242438   Tel: 01367 241696

WORLD OF FANTASY
(Costumes & Props)
Swansnest, Rear of 2 Windmill Road
Hampton Hill, Middlesex TW12 1RH
Fax: 020-8783 1366   Tel: 020-8941 1595

DAILY EXPRESS   Tel: 020-7928 8000
Ludgate House
245 Blackfriars Road, London SE1 9UX
Theatre: Sheridan Morley
Films: Ryan Gilbey, Alan Hunter
Television: Tim Hulse, Jeremy Novick
Saturday Magazine/Programmes: Pat Stoddart

DAILY MAIL   Tel: 020-7938 6000
Northcliffe House
2 Derry Street, Kensington, London W8 5TT
Films: Chris Tookey
Television: Peter Paterson, Christopher Matthew

DAILY STAR   Tel: 020-7928 8000
Ludgate House
245 Blackfriars Road, London SE1 9UX
Show Business & Television: Laura Benjamin
Julia Etherington, Sean Hamilton
Show Business & Television: Nigel Pauley, Debbie Pogue,
Gareth Morgan, Ben Todd
Show Business & Television: Amy Watts
Films & Video: Alan Frank

DAILY TELEGRAPH   Tel: 020-7538 5000
1 Canada Square, Canary Wharf, London E14 5DT
Theatre: Charles Spencer
Films: Sukhdev Sandhu
Radio: Gillian Reynolds   Art: Richard Dorment
Dance: Ismene Brown   Music: Geoffrey Norris

FINANCIAL TIMES   Tel: 020-7873 3000
1 Southwark Bridge, London SE1 9HL
Theatre: Alastair MacAulay
Films: Nigel Andrews
Television: Graham McCann

GUARDIAN   Tel: 020-7278 2332
119 Farringdon Road, London EC1R 3ER
Theatre: Michael Billington
Films: Peter Bradshaw
Television: Nancy Banks-Smith
Radio: Elisabeth Mahoney

INDEPENDENT   Tel: 020-7005 2000
191 Marsh Wall, London E14 9RS
Television: Tom Sutcliffe

LONDON EVENING STANDARD   Tel: 020-7938 6000
Northcliffe House, 2 Derry Street
Kensington, London W8 5EE
Theatre: Nicholas de Jong, Fiona Mountford
Films: Derek Malcolm   Opera: Fiona Maddocks
Television: Victor Lewis-Smith, Terry Ramsay
Classical Music: Barry Millington   Radio: Terry Ramsay

MAIL ON SUNDAY   Tel: 020-7938 6000
(Review Section), Northcliffe House
2 Derry Street, London W8 5TS
Theatre: Georgina Brown
Films: Jason Solomons, Matthew Bond
Television: Jaci Stephen
Radio: Simon Garfield

MIRROR   Tel: 020-7510 3000
Mirror Group Newspapers Ltd
1 Canada Square, Canary Wharf
London E14 5AP
Films: Kevin O'Sullivan
Television: Nicola Methven

MORNING STAR   Tel: 020-8510 0815
William Rust House
52 Beachy Road, London E3 2NS
Theatre & Films: Katie Gilmore
Television & Radio: Kate Gibney

NEWS OF THE WORLD   Tel: 020-7782 4000
News International plc
1 Virginia Street, London E98 1NW
Show Business: Rav Singh, Polly Graham
Films: Paul Ross, Shebah Ronay

OBSERVER   Tel: 020-7278 2332
119 Farringdon Road
London EC1R 3ER
Theatre: Susanna Clapp
Films: Philip French, Akin Ojumu
Radio: Sue Arnold

SPORT   Tel: 0161-238 8151
Sport Newspapers Ltd
19 Great Ancoats Street
Manchester M60 4BT
Show Business/Features: Tanya Jones

SUN   Tel: 020-7782 4000
News International plc
1 Virginia Street
Wapping, London E98 1SN
Television: Ally Ross

SUNDAY EXPRESS   Tel: 020-7928 8000
Express Newspapers
Ludgate House
245 Blackfriars Road, London SE1 9UX
Theatre: Sheridan Moley
Films: Henry Fitzherbert
Television: David Stephenson
Radio & Arts: Rachel Jane

SUNDAY MIRROR   Tel: 020-7510 3000
Mirror Group
1 Canada Square
Canary Wharf, London E14 5AP
Theatre & Television: Ian Hyland
Films: Mark Adams
Showbusiness: Suzanne Kerins

SUNDAY PEOPLE   Tel: 020-7510 3000
1 Canada Square
Canary Wharf, London E14 5AP
Television & Radio: Sarah Moolla
Films: Richard Bacon
Show Business: Sean O' Brien
Features: Katy Weitz

SUNDAY TELEGRAPH   Tel: 020-7538 5000
1 Canada Square
Canary Wharf, London E14 5DT
Theatre: John Gross
Films: Jenny McCartney
Television: John Preston
Radio: David Sexton

SUNDAY TIMES   Tel: 020-7782 5000
News International plc
1 Pennington Street, London E98 1ST
Theatre: John Peter
Films: Cosmo Landesman
Television: A.A. Gill
Radio: Paul Donovan

TIMES   Tel: 020-7782 5000
News International plc
1 Pennington Street
London E1 9XN
Theatre: Benedict Nightingale
Films: Barbara Ellen, James Christopher
Television: Joe Joseph
Video: Geoff Brown   Radio: Chris Campling

Abbreviations:

SS Stage School for Children
D Dramatic Art (incl Coaching. Audition Technique etc)
DS Full time Drama Training **E** Elocution Coaching
(incl Correction of Accents. Speech Therapy,
Dialects etc)
S Singing **Md** Modelling **Sp** Specialised Training

ADZIDO
Canonbury Business Centre
202 New North Road, London N1 7BJ
e-mail: info@adzido.co.uk
Fax: 020-7704 0300   Tel: 020-7359 7453

AKADEMI
(South Asian Dance in the UK)
Hampstead Town Hall, Haverstock Hill, London NW3 4QP
Website: www.akademi.co.uk
e-mail: info@akademi.co.uk
Fax: 020-7691 3211   Tel: 020-7691 3210

ALSTON Richard DANCE COMPANY
The Place, 17 Duke's Road, London WC1H 9PY
e-mail: radc@theplace.org.uk
Fax: 020-7383 5700   Tel: 020-7387 0324

BALLET CREATIONS
3 Blackbird Way, Bransgore
Nr Christchurch, Hampshire BH23 8LG
Website: www.ballet-creations.co.uk
e-mail: info@ballet-creations.co.uk   Tel/Fax: 01425 674163

BALLROOM - LONDON THEATRE OF
(Artistic Director - Paul Harris)
24 Ovett Close, Upper Norwood, London SE19 3RX
e-mail: paulharrisdance@hotmail.com
Mobile: 07958 784462   Tel/Fax: 020-8771 4274

BIRMINGHAM ROYAL BALLET
Thorp Street, Birmingham B5 4AU
Website: www.brb.org.uk
e-mail: administrator@brb.org.uk
Fax: 0121-245 3570   Tel: 0121-245 3500

BODY OF PEOPLE
(Jazz Theatre Company)
10 Stayton Road, Sutton, Surrey SM1 1RB
Website: www.bop.org.uk
e-mail: info@bop.org.uk   Tel: 020-8641 6959

BRITISH BALLET ORGANIZATION
(Dance Examining Society & Teacher Training)
Woolborough House, 39 Lonsdale Road, Barnes SW13 9JP
e-mail: info@bbo.org.uk   Tel: 020-8748 1241

CHOLMONDELEYS The
LF1.1
Lafone House, The Leathermarket
11-13 Leathermarket Street, London SE1 3HN
Website: www.thecholmondeleys.org
e-mail: admin@thecholmondeleys.org   Tel: 020-7378 8800

COMPANY OF CRANKS
1st Floor, 62 Northfield House
Frensham Street, London SE15 6TN
Website: www.brendanmime.freeuk.com
e-mail: mimetic16@yahoo.com   Mobile: 07802 805588

COUNCIL FOR DANCE EDUCATION & TRAINING
Toynbee Hall, 28 Commercial Street, London E1 6LS
Website: www.cdet.org.uk
e-mail: info@cdet.org.uk
Fax: 020-7247 3404   Tel: 020-7247 4030

DANCE FOR EVERYONE Ltd
30 Sevington Road, London NW4 3RX
e-mail: orders@dfe.org.uk   Tel: 020-8202 7863

DANCE UK
(Including the Healthier Dancer Programme)
Battersea Arts Centre, Lavender Hill, London SW11 5TN
Website: www.danceuk.org
e-mail: info@danceuk.org
Fax: 020-7223 0074   Tel: 020-7228 4990

[CONTACTS 2005]

DANCE UMBRELLA
20 Chancellors Street, London W6 9RN
Website: www.danceumbrella.co.uk
e-mail: mail@danceumbrella.co.uk
Fax: 020-8741 7902   Tel: 020-8741 4040

ENGLISH NATIONAL BALLET Ltd
Markova House, 39 Jay Mews, London SW7 2ES
Website: www.ballet.org.uk
e-mail: info@ballet.org.uk
Fax: 020-7225 0827   Tel: 020-7581 1245

FEATHERSTONEHAUGHS The
LF1 .1
Lafone House, The Leathermarket
11-13 Leathermarket Street, London SE1 3HN
Website: www.thecholmondeleys.org
e-mail: admin@thecholmondeleys.org   Tel: 020-7378 8800

GIELGUD BALLET The
Mulberry House, 583 Fulham Road, London SW6
Website: www.gielgud.com
e-mail: ballet@gielgud.com
Fax: 020-7471 1840   Tel: 020-7471 1740

**IDTA (INTERNATIONAL DANCE TEACHERS'
ASSOCIATION)**
International House, 76 Bennett Road
Brighton, East Sussex BN2 5JL
Website: www.idta.co.uk
e-mail: info@idta.co.uk
Fax: 01273 674388   Tel: 01273 685652

KOSH The
(Physical Theatre)
59 Stapleton Hall Road, London N4 3QF
e-mail: info@thekosh.com
Fax: 020-8374 5661   Tel: 020-8374 0407

LONDON CONTEMPORARY DANCE SCHOOL
The Place, 17 Duke's Road, London WC1H 9PY
Website: www.theplace.org.uk
e-mail: lcds@theplace.org.uk
Fax: 020-7387 3976   Tel: 020-7387 0152

LUDUS DANCE
Assembly Rooms, King Street, Lancaster LA1 1RE
e-mail: info@ludus.org
Fax: 01524 847744   Tel: 01524 35936

MUDRALAYA DANCE THEATRE
Formerly Pushkala Gopal Unnikrishnan & Co
(Classical Indian Dance-Theatre)
20 Brisbane Road, Ilford, Essex IG1 4SR
Fax: 020-8262 1984   Tel: 020-8554 4054

NATIONAL RESOURCE CENTRE FOR DANCE
University of Surrey, Guildford GU2 7XH
Website: www.surrey.ac.uk/nrcd
e-mail: nrcd@surrey.ac.uk   Tel: 01483 689316

NEW ADVENTURES
Sadler's Wells, Rosebery Avenue, London EC1R 4TN
e-mail: info@new-adventures.net   Tel/Fax: 020-7665 1039

NORTHERN BALLET THEATRE
West Park Centre, Spen Lane, Leeds LS16 5BE
e-mail: administration@northernballettheatre.co.uk
Fax: 0113-220 8007   Tel: 0113-274 5355

PHOENIX DANCE THEATRE
3 St Peter's Buildings, St Peter's Square, Leeds LS9 8AH
Website: www.phoenixdancetheatre.co.uk
e-mail: info@phoenixdancetheatre.co.uk
Fax: 0113-244 4736   Tel: 0113-242 3486

RAMBERT DANCE COMPANY
94 Chiswick High Road, London W4 1SH
Website: www.rambert.org.uk   e-mail: rdc@rambert.org.uk
Fax: 020-8747 8323   Tel: 020-8630 0600

ROYAL BALLET The
Royal Opera House, Covent Garden, London WC2E 9DD
Fax: 020-7212 9502   Tel: 020-7240 1200

RUSS Claire ENSEMBLE
(Choreography, Contemporary/Commerical)
74A Queens Road, Twickenham TW1 4ET
Website: www.clairerussensemble.com
e-mail: info@clairerussensemble.com
Mobile: 07932 680224   Tel/Fax: 020-8892 9281

SCOTTISH BALLET
261 West Princes Street, Glasgow G4 9EE
Website: www.scottishballet.co.uk
e-mail: sb@scottishballet.co.uk
Fax: 0141-331 2629   Tel: 0141-331 2931

SCOTTISH DANCE THEATRE
Dundee Repertory Theatre, Tay Square, Dundee DD1 1PB
Website: www.scottishdancetheatre.com
e-mail: achinn@dundeereptheatre.com
Fax: 01382 228609   Tel: 01382 342600

SOUTH-EAST DANCE - NATIONAL DANCE AGENCY
5 Palace Place, Castle Square
Brighton, East Sussex BN1 1EF
e-mail: info@southeastdance.org.uk
Fax: 01273 205540   Tel: 01273 202032

UNION DANCE COMPANY
Top Floor, 6 Charing Cross Road, London WC2H 0HG
Website: www.uniondance.co.uk
e-mail: info@uniondance.co.uk
Fax: 020-7836 7847   Tel: 020-7836 7837

YORKSHIRE DANCE CENTRE NATIONAL DANCE AGENCY
3 St Peter's Buildings, St Peter's Square, Leeds LS9 8AH
Website: www.everybodydances.com
e-mail: admin@everybodydances.com   Tel: 0113-243 9867

(020-8771 4274) PAUL HARRIS (07958-784462)

Choreographer / Mentor "Faking It" - BAFTA Winner 2003

Choreography and Coaching in Vintage and Contemporary Social Dance

* **Swing** * **Waltz** * **Salsa** * **Tango** * **Charleston** *etc.*

BALLROOM - LONDON THEATRE OF
(Artistic Director - Paul Harris)
24 Ovett Close, Upper Norwood, London SE19 3RX
e-mail: paulharrisdance@hotmail.com
Mobile: 07958 784462   Tel/Fax: 020-8771 4274

BELLYDANCE CENTRE The
(Private Lessons, Consultancy, Choreography)
Mayfield, 5 Rother Road, Seaford
East Sussex BN25 4HT   Tel: 01323 899083

BIRD COLLEGE OF PERFORMING ARTS
(Dance & Theatre Performance Diploma/BA (Hons))
Birkbeck Centre, Birkbeck Road, Sidcup, Kent DA14 4DE
Fax: 020-8308 1370   Tel: 020-8300 6004

BODENS STUDIOS
(Performing Arts Classes)
99 East Barnet Road, New Barnet, Herts EN4 8RF
Website: www.bodensstudios.com
e-mail: bodens2692@aol.com
Fax: 020-8449 5212   Tel: 020-8449 0982

CAPITAL ARTS THEATRE SCHOOL
Wyllyotts Centre, Darkes Lane, Potters Bar, Herts EN6 2HN
e-mail: capitalartstheatre@o2.co.uk
Mobile: 07885 232414   Tel/Fax: 020-8449 2342

CENTRAL SCHOOL OF BALLET
(Dance Classes & Professional Training)
10 Herbal Hill, Clerkenwell Road, London EC1R 5EG
Website: www.centralschoolofballet.co.uk
e-mail: info@csbschool.co.uk
Fax: 020-7833 5571   Tel: 020-7837 6332

CENTRE - PERFORMING ARTS COLLEGE The
Building 62, Level 4
37 Bowater Road, Charlton, London SE8 5TF
e-mail: dance@thecentrepac.com   Tel/Fax: 020-8855 6661

COLIN'S PERFORMING ARTS Ltd
The Studios, 219B North Street, Romford RM1 4QA
Website: www.colinsperformingarts.co.uk
e-mail: admin@colinsperformingarts.co.uk
Fax: 01708 766077   Tel: 01708 766007

COLLECTIVE DANCE & DRAMA
The Studio, Rectory Lane, Rickmansworth
Herts WD3 1FD   Tel/Fax: 020-8428 0037

CONTI Italia ACADEMY OF THEATRE ARTS
(Full-time 3 year Musical Theatre Course)
Italia Conti House, 23 Goswell Road, London EC1M 7AJ
e-mail: sca@italiaconti36.freeserve.co.uk
Fax: 020-7253 1430   Tel: 020-7608 0047

Founded in 1979, CDET promotes excellence in dance education and training. It accredits courses at vocational dance schools, advocates on behalf of the private dance teaching communities and provides an information service. CDET is a membership organisation, which includes vocational dance training institutions, teacher organisations, industry bodies and individuals.

The Conference of Professional Dance Schools (CPDS) exists to provide a forum in which representatives from vocational dance training institutions may discuss policy and recommend action in relation to vocational dance training.

- Arts Educational School, Tring
- ArtsEd London
- Bird College
- Central School of Ballet
- Elmhurst
- Hammond School
- Italia Conti Academy of Theatre Arts Ltd
- LABAN
- Laine Theatre Arts
- London Contemporary Dance School
- London Studio Centre
- Northern Ballet School
- Performers College
- SLP College
- Stella Mann College
- Urdang Academy

For more info on the CPDS and CDET:

Contact:

Council for Dance Education & Training
Toynbee Hall
28 Commercial Street, London E1 6LS
Tel: 020 7247 4030
Fax: 020 7247 3404
Email: info@cdet.org.uk
Website: www.cdet.org.uk

CUSTARD FACTORY
Gibb Street, Digbeth, Birmingham B9 4AA
e-mail: info@custardfactory.com
Fax: 0121-604 8888   Tel: 0121-224 7777

D & B SCHOOL OF PERFORMING ARTS
Central Studios, 470 Bromley Road, Bromley, Kent BR1 4PN
Website: www.dandbperformingarts.co.uk
e-mail: bonnie@dandbperformingarts.co.uk
Fax: 020-8697 8100   Tel: 020-8698 8880

DANCEWORKS
(Also Fitness, Yoga & Martial Arts Classes)
16 Balderton Street, London W1K 6TN   Tel: 020-7629 6183

DUFFILL Drusilla THEATRE SCHOOL
Grove Lodge, Oakwood Rd, Burgess Hill, W. Sussex RH15 0HZ
e-mail: drusilladschool@btclick.com
Fax: 01444 232680   Tel: 01444 232672

ELMHURST - SCHOOL FOR DANCE
Heathcote Road, Camberley, Surrey GU15 2EU
Website: www.elmhurstdance.co.uk
e-mail: elmhurst@cableol.co.uk
Fax: 01276 670320   Tel: 01276 65301

EXPRESSIONS ACADEMY OF PERFORMING ARTS
3 Newgate Lane, Mansfield, Nottingham NG18 2LB
e-mail: expressions-uk@btconnect.com
Fax: 01623 647337   Tel: 01623 424334

GREASEPAINT ANONYMOUS
4 Gallus Close, Winchmore Hill, London N21 1JR
e-mail: info@greasepaintanonymous.co.uk
Fax: 020-8882 9189   Tel: 020-8886 2263

HARRIS Paul
(Movement for Actors, Choreography, Coaching in
Traditional & Contemporary Social Dance)
24 Ovett Close, Upper Norwood, London SE19 3RX
e-mail: paulharrisdance@hotmail.com
Mobile: 07958 784462   Tel: 020-8771 4274

ISLINGTON ARTS FACTORY
2 Parkhurst Road, London N7 0SF
e-mail: islington@artsfactory.fsnet.co.uk
Fax: 020-7700 7229   Tel: 020-7607 0561

KIDZ IN THE BIZ
5 Brittendon Parade, Green Street Green, Kent BR6 6DD
e-mail: thebizmanagement@aol.com
Mobile: 07710 352889   Tel/Fax: 01689 882850

LEE Lynn THEATRE SCHOOL The
(Office) 126 Church Road, Benfleet, Essex SS7 4EP
e-mail: lynn@leetheatre.fsnet.co.uk   Tel: 01268 795863

LONDON CONTEMPORARY DANCE SCHOOL
The Place, 17 Duke's Road, London WC1H 9PY
Website: www.theplace.org.uk e-mail: lcds@theplace.org.uk
Fax: 020-7387 3976   Tel: 020-7387 0152

LONDON STUDIO CENTRE
42-50 York Way, London N1 9AB
Website: www.london-studio-centre.co.uk
e-mail: enquire@london-studio-centre.co.uk
Fax: 020-7837 3248   Tel: 020-7837 7741

MANN Stella COLLEGE
(Professional Dance Course for Performers & Teachers)
10 Linden Road, Bedford, Beds MK40 2DA
Website: www.stellamanncollege.co.uk
e-mail: info@stellamanncollege.co.uk
Fax: 01234 217284   Tel: 01234 213331

MILLENNIUM DANCE 2000 Ltd
Hampstead Town Hall Centre
213 Haverstock Hill, London NW3 4QP
Website: www.md2000.co.uk e-mail: md2000hampstead@aol.com
Fax: 020-7916 9334   Tel: 020-7916 9335

NORTH LONDON PERFORMING ARTS CENTRE
76 St James Lane, Muswell Hill, London N10 3DF
e-mail: nlpac@aol.com
Fax: 020-8444 4040   Tel: 020-8444 4544

PAUL'S THEATRE SCHOOL
Fairkytes Arts Centre, 51 Billet Lane, Hornchurch, RM11 1AX
Website: www.paulstheatreschool.co.uk
e-mail: info@paulstheatreschool.co.uk
Fax: 01708 475286   Tel: 01708 447123

PERFORMERS COLLEGE
Southend Road, Corringham, Essex SS17 8JT
Website: www.performerscollege.co.uk
e-mail: pdc@dircon.co.uk
Fax: 01375 672353   Tel: 01375 672053

PINEAPPLE DANCE STUDIOS
7 Langley Street, London WC2H 9JA
Website: www.pineapple.uk.com
e-mail: studios@pineapple.uk.com
Fax: 020-7836 0803   Tel: 020-7836 4004

PULLEY Rosina SCHOOL OF STAGE DANCING
5 Lancaster Road, London E11 3EH   Tel: 020-8539 7740

RIDGEWAY STUDIOS PERFORMING ARTS COLLEGE
Fairley House, Andrews Lane, Cheshunt, Herts EN7 6LB
Website: www.ridgewaystudios.co.uk
e-mail: info@ridgewaystudios.co.uk
Fax: 01992 633844   Tel: 01992 633775

ROEBUCK Gavin
51 Earls Court Square, London SW5 9DG Tel: 020-7370 7324

STEP ONE DANCE & DRAMA SCHOOL
Rear of 24 Penrhyn Road, Colwyn Bay
Conwy LL29 8LG   Tel: 01492 534424

URDANG ACADEMY The
20-22 Shelton Street
Covent Garden, London WC2H 9JJ
Website: www.theurdangacademy.com
e-mail: info@theurdangacademy.com
Fax: 020-7836 7010   Tel: 020-7836 5709

VALLÉ ACADEMY OF PERFORMING ARTS Ltd The
The Valle Academy Studios
Wilton House, Delamare Road
Cheshunt, Herts EN8 9SG
Website: www.valleacademy.co.uk
e-mail: enquiries@valleacademy.co.uk
Fax: 01992 622868   Tel: 01992 622862

WHITEHALL PERFORMING ARTS CENTRE
Rayleigh Road, Leigh-on-Sea
Essex SS9 5UU   Tel/Fax: 01702 529290

YOUNG Sylvia THEATRE SCHOOL
Rossmore Road, London NW1 6NJ
e-mail: sylvia@sylviayoungtheatreschool.co.uk
Fax: 020-7723 1040   Tel: 020-7402 0673

The Conference of Drama Schools comprises Britain's 21 leading Drama Schools. CDS exists to set and maintain the highest standards of training within the vocational drama sector and to make it easier for prospective students to understand the range of courses on offer and the application process. CDS member schools offer courses in Acting, Musical Theatre, Directing and Technical Theatre training.

CDS members offer courses which are:

• PROFESSIONAL – you will be trained to work in the theatre by staff with professional experience and by visiting professionals.

• INTENSIVE – courses are full-time

• WORK ORIENTATED – you are being trained to do a job – these courses are practical training for work.

CDS publishes the *Conference of Drama Schools: Guide to Professional Training in Drama and Technical Theatre 2005.*

For links to CDS schools please visit the website at www.drama.ac.uk

The full text of the guide is available on the website – if you would like a hard copy please send a SAE (at least C5 – that's half A4) with 75p in stamps to:

The Executive Secretary, CDS Ltd, P.O. Box 34252, London NW5 1XJ

Designed by Consider This UK Ltd. T: 01923 817 000

ALRA (ACADEMY OF LIVE AND RECORDED ARTS)
The Royal Victoria Patriotic Building
Fitzhugh Grove, Trinity Road, London SW18 3SX
Website: www.alra.demon.co.uk
e-mail: acting@alra.demon.co.uk
Fax: 020-8875 0789   Tel: 020-8870 6475

ARTS EDUCATIONAL SCHOOLS LONDON
14 Bath Road, London W4 1LY
Website: www.artsed.co.uk
e-mail: drama@artsed.co.uk
Fax: 020-8987 6699   Tel: 020-8987 6666

BIRMINGHAM SCHOOL OF ACTING
The Link Building, Paradise Place
Birmingham B3 3HJ
Website: www.bssd.ac.uk
e-mail: bssd@bssd.ac.uk
Fax: 0121-262 6801   Tel: 0121-262 6800

BRISTOL OLD VIC THEATRE SCHOOL
2 Downside Road, Clifton, Bristol BS8 2XF
Website: www.oldvic.ac.uk
e-mail: enquiries@oldvic.ac.uk
Fax: 0117-923 9371   Tel: 0117-973 3535

CENTRAL SCHOOL OF SPEECH & DRAMA
Embassy Theatre, 64 Eton Avenue
Swiss Cottage, London NW3 3HY
Website: www.cssd.ac.uk
e-mail: enquiries@cssd.ac.uk   Tel: 020-7722 8183

CONTI Italia ACADEMY OF THEATRE ARTS
Avondale, 72 Landor Road, London SW9 9PH
Website: www.italiaconti-acting.co.uk
e-mail: acting@lsbu.ac.uk
Fax: 020-7737 2728   Tel: 020-7733 3210

CYGNET TRAINING THEATRE
New Theatre, Friars Gate
Exeter, Devon EX2 4AZ
e-mail: cygnetarts@btinternet.com   Tel/Fax: 01392 277189

DRAMA CENTRE LONDON
Central Saint Martins College of Art & Design
Saffron House, 10 Back Hill, London EC1R 5LQ
Website: www.csm.arts.ac.uk/drama
e-mail: drama@arts.ac.uk
Fax: 020-7514 8777   Tel: 020-7514 8778

EAST 15 ACTING SCHOOL
The University of Essex
Hatfields & Corbett Theatre Rectory Lane
Loughton, Essex IG10 3RY
Website: www.east15.ac.uk
e-mail: east15@essex.ac.uk
Fax: 020-8508 7521   Tel: 020-8508 5983

GSA CONSERVATOIRE
Millmead Terrace
Guildford, Surrey GU2 4YT
Website: www.conservatoire.org
e-mail: enquiries@conservatoire.org   Tel: 01483 560701

GUILDHALL SCHOOL OF MUSIC & DRAMA
Silk Street, Barbican, London EC2Y 8DT
Website: www.gsmd.ac.uk
e-mail: info@gsmd.ac.uk
Fax: 020-7256 9438   Tel: 020-7382 7149

LAMDA
155 Talgarth Road
London W14 9DA
Website: www.lamda.org.uk
e-mail: enquiries@lamda.org.uk
Fax: 020-8834 0501   Tel: 020-8834 0500

**MANCHESTER METROPOLITAN UNIVERSITY
SCHOOL OF THEATRE**
The Mabel Tylecote Building
Cavendish Street
Manchester M15 6BG
Website: www.capitoltheatre.co.uk   Tel: 0161-247 1305

MOUNTVIEW
Academy of Theatre Arts
Ralph Richardson Memorial Studios
Clarendon Road
London N22 6XF
Website: www.mountview.ac.uk
e-mail: enquiries@mountview.ac.uk
Fax: 020-8829 0034   Tel: 020-8881 2201

OXFORD SCHOOL OF DRAMA The
Sansomes Farm Studios
Woodstock, Oxford OX20 1ER
Website: www.oxforddrama.ac.uk
e-mail: info@oxforddrama.ac.uk
Fax: 01993 811220   Tel: 01993 812883

QUEEN MARGARET UNIVERSITY COLLEGE
The Gateway Theatre
Elm Row, Edinburgh EH7 4AH
Website: www.qmuc.ac.uk
e-mail: admissions@qmuc.ac.uk
Fax: 0131-317 3902   Tel: 0131-317 3900

ROSE BRUFORD COLLEGE
Lamorbey Park
Burnt Oak Lane
Sidcup, Kent DA15 9DF
Website: www.bruford.ac.uk
Fax: 020-8308 0542   Tel: 020-8308 2600

ROYAL ACADEMY OF DRAMATIC ART
62-64 Gower Street
London WC1E 6ED
Website: www.rada.org
e-mail: enquiries@rada.ac.uk
Fax: 020-7323 3865   Tel: 020-7636 7076

ROYAL SCOTTISH ACADEMY OF MUSIC & DRAMA
100 Renfrew Street, Glasgow G2 3DB
Website: www.rsamd.ac.uk
e-mail: registry@rsamd.ac.uk   Tel: 0141-332 4101

ROYAL WELSH COLLEGE OF MUSIC & DRAMA
Drama Department
Castle Grounds
Cathays Park, Cardiff CF10 3ER
Website: www.rwcmd.ac.uk
e-mail: drama.admissions@rwcmd.ac.uk
Fax: 029-2039 1302   Tel: 029-2039 1327

WEBBER DOUGLAS ACADEMY OF DRAMATIC ART
30 Clareville Street
London SW7 5AP
e-mail: webberdouglas@btconnect.com
Fax: 020-7373 5639   Tel: 020-7370 4154

VOICE COACH PRESENTATION SKILLS

Alexandre HARRINGTON

Trained in Voice Studies **C.S.S.D.**
Voice Tutor, The Academy of Creative Training
Teaching experience in leading C.D.S. accredited Drama Schools
"Build up confidence, and strengthen your skills"

AUDITION SPEECH U.S. ACCENTS
020 7727 6421 alexhvoice@tiscali.co.uk

A & J THEATRE WORKSHOP
The Open Door Community Centre
Beaumont Road
London SW19
Website: www.ajmanagement.co.uk
Fax: 020-8342 0842 Tel: 020-8342 0542

A B ACADEMY OF PERFORMING ARTS
22 Greek Street
Stockport, Cheshire SK3 8AB
e-mail: ab22actout@aol.com Tel/Fax: 0161-429 7413

ACADEMY DRAMA SCHOOL The
DS (Day, Evening, Full-time 1 or 2 yr Courses, Preparatory
to Post-graduate)
189 Whitechapel Road, London E1 1DN
Website: www.the-academy.info
e-mail: ask@the-academy.info Tel: 020-7377 8735

ACADEMY OF CHILDREN'S THEATRE
(Part-time Children's Theatre School)
373 Lower Addiscombe Road
Croydon CR0 6RJ Tel: 020-8655 3438

ACE ACCOMPANIST - JACK HONEYBORNE
S (Coaching/Accompanist)
165 Gunnersbury Lane, London W3 8LJ Tel: 020-8993 2111

**ACKERLEY STUDIOS OF SPEECH, DRAMA & PUBLIC
SPEAKING**
Sp D Margaret Christina Parsons (Principal)
5th Floor, Hanover House
Hanover Street
Liverpool L1 3DZ Tel: 0151-709 5995

ACT @ SCHOOL
(Drama for Children & Young People)
Part of APM Training Group
PO Box 834
Hemel Hempstead HP3 9ZP
Website: www.apmtraining.co.uk
e-mail: info@apmtraining.co.uk
Fax: 01442 241099 Tel: 01442 252907

ACT ONE DRAMA STUDIO
31 Dobbin Hill, Sheffield S11 7JA
Website: www.actonedrama.co.uk
e-mail: casting@actonedrama.co.uk
Fax: 07971 112153 Tel: 0114-266 7209

ACT UP
(Acting Classes for Everyone)
Unit 88, Battersea Business Centre
99-109 Lavender Hill
London SW11 5QL
Website: www.act-up.co.uk
e-mail: info@act-up.co.uk
Fax: 020-7924 6606 Tel: 020-7924 7701

ACTING & AUDITION SUCCESS
(Philip Rosch LALAM, FVCM, ANEA, BA, Adv. Dip Acting)
(Associate Guildhall Teacher)
52 West Heath Court, North End Road
London NW11 7RG Tel: 020-8731 6686

ACTION LAB
(Part-time Acting Courses, Miranda French & Peter Irving)
18 Lansdowne Road
London W11 3LL
Mobile: 07979 623987 Tel: 020-7727 3473

ACTORCLUB Ltd
17 Inkerman Road
London NW5 3BT
Website: www.actorclub.co.uk
e-mail: johncunningham@actorclub.fsnet.co.uk
                                            Mobile: 07956 940453

ACTOR'S TEMPLE The
54 Paramount Court
University Street, London WC1E 6JP
Website: www.actorstemple.com
e-mail: info@actorstemple.com
Mobile: 07775 675499   Mobile: 07771 734670

ACTORS' THEATRE SCHOOL
(Foundation Course)
32 Exeter Road, London NW2 4SB
Website: www.mywebaddress.net
e-mail: ats@mywebaddress.net
Fax: 020-8450 1057   Tel: 020-8450 0371

ACTORSPACE.CO.UK
D E Sp (Auditions, Improvisation, Voice & Text)
6 Chandos Court, The Green
Southgate, London N14 7AA
Website: www.actorspace.co.uk
e-mail: drama@london.com   Tel: 020-8886 8870

ACTS
(Ayres-Clark Theatre School)
12 Gatward Close
Winchmore Hill, London N21   Tel: 020-8360 0352

ALEXANDER Helen
(Audition Technique/Drama School Entry)
14 Chestnut Road, Raynes Park
London SW20 8EB   Tel: 020-8543 4085

ALLSORTS - DRAMA FOR CHILDREN
(Part-time Courses - Kensington, Notting Hill, Hampstead,
Fulham ages 3-18 yrs) 34 Pember Road, London NW10 5LS
Website: www.allsortsdrama.com
e-mail: info@allsortsdrama.com
Fax: 020-8969 3196   Tel: 020-8969 3249

ALLSORTS THEATRE SCHOOL Ltd
Three Mills Film Studios, Unit 1, Sugar House Business Ctr,
24 Sugar House Lane, London E15 2QS
Website: www.allsortsagency.com
e-mail: bookings@allsortsagency.com
Fax: 020-8555 0909   Tel: 020-8555 0099

ALRA (ACADEMY OF LIVE & RECORDED ARTS)
See DRAMA SCHOOLS (Conference of)

AND ALL THAT JAZZ
(Eileen Hughes - Accompanist & Vocal Coaching)
165 Gunnersbury Lane
Acton Town, London W3 8LJ   Tel: 020-8993 2111

ARDEN SCHOOL OF THEATRE The
City Campus, Whitworth Street, Manchester M1 3HB
e-mail: ast@ccm.ac.uk   Tel/Fax: 0161-279 7257

ARTEMIS FOUNDATION The
25 Athelstan Road, Tuckton, Bournemouth BH6 5LY
Website: www.doorways2power.co.uk
e-mail: artemis@doorways2power.co.uk Tel: 01202 418880

ARTEMIS SCHOOL OF SPEECH & DRAMA
Peredur Centre of the Arts, West Hoathly Road
East Grinstead, West Sussex RH19 4NF
Website: www.artemisspeechanddrama.org.uk
e-mail: office@artemisspeechanddrama.org.uk
                                     Tel/Fax: 01342 321330

ARTS EDUCATIONAL SCHOOL
(Dance, Drama & Musical Theatre Training School
for 8-18 yrs)
Tring Park, Tring, Herts HP23 5LX
Website: www.aes-tring.com
e-mail: info@aes-tring.com   Tel: 01442 824255

ARTS EDUCATIONAL SCHOOLS LONDON
See DRAMA SCHOOLS (Conference of)

ASHCROFT ACADEMY OF DRAMATIC ART The
(Drama LAMDA, Dance ISTD, Singing, Age 4-18 yrs)
Malcolm Primary School
Malcolm Road, Penge, London SE20 8RH
Website: www.ashcroftacademy.co.uk
e-mail: geri.ashcroftacademy@tiscali.co.uk
Mobile: 07799 791586   Tel: 020-8693 8088

**ASHFORD Clare BSc, PGCE, LLAM, ALAM (Recital),
ALAM (Acting)**
D E
20 The Chase, Coulsdon, Surrey CR5 2EG
e-mail: clareashford@handbag.com   Tel: 020-8660 9609

BAC
(Young People's Theatre Workshops & Performance
Projects, 12-25 yrs)
Lavender Hill, London SW11 5TN
e-mail: mailbox@bac.org.uk
Fax: 020-7978 5207   Tel: 020-7223 6557

BARNES Bi Bi
(Feldenkrais Practitioner & Voice Coach)
Rose Cottage, Church Road
Ashmanhaugh, Norwich NR12 8YL
Website: www.bibibarnes.co.uk
e-mail: bibibarnes@aol.com
Mobile: 07770 375339   Tel: 01603 781281

**BATE Richard MA (Theatre) LGSM (TD), PGCE (FE),
Equity**
D E
31 Trafalgar Square, Scarborough
North Yorkshire YO12 7PZ
Mobile: 07956 172409   Tel: 01723 365654

BECK Eirene
D E (Specializing in Voice & Audition Pieces)
23 Rayne House, 170 Delaware Road
London W9 2LW   Tel: 020-7286 0588

BELCANTO LONDON ACADEMY Ltd
(Stage School & Agency)
Performance House, 20 Passey Place
Eltham, London SE9 5DQ
e-mail: enquiries@theatretraining.com
Fax: 020-8850 9944   Tel: 020-8850 9888

**BENCH Paul MEd, LGSM, ALAM, FRSA, LJBA, PGCE, ACP
(Lings) (Hons), MASC, MIFA (Reg)**
D E
1 Whitehall Terrace, Shrewsbury, Shropshire SY2 5AA
e-mail: pfbench@aol.com   Tel/Fax: 01743 233164

BENSKIN Eileen
(Dialect Coach)   Tel: 020-8455 9750

BERKERY Barbara
(Dialogue/Dialect Coach for Film & Television)
     Tel: 020-7281 3139

BEST SHOT YOUTH THEATRE COMPANY
(Weekly Drama Classes & Theatre Based Holiday Courses)
1 Queensland Avenue, Wimbledon SW19 3AD
Website: www.bestshot.org.uk
e-mail: enquiries@bestshot.org.uk   Tel: 020-8540 1238

BEST THEATRE ARTS
61 Marshalswick Lane, St Albans, Herts AL1 4UT
Website: www.besttheatrearts.com
e-mail: bestarts@aol.com   Tel: 01727 759634

BILLINGS Una
(Dance Training)
Methodist Church, Askew Road
London W12 9RN   Tel: 020-7603 8156

BIRD COLLEGE
(Drama/Musical Theatre College)
Birkbeck Centre, Birkbeck Road, Sidcup, Kent DA14 4DE
Website: www.birdcollege.co.uk
e-mail: admin@birdcollege.co.uk
Fax: 020-8308 1370   Tel: 020-8300 6004

BIRMINGHAM SCHOOL OF ACTING
See DRAMA SCHOOLS (Conference of)

BIRMINGHAM THEATRE SCHOOL
The Old Rep Theatre, Station Street, Birmingham B5 4DY
Website: www.the-birmingham-theatre-school.com
e-mail: info@birminghamts.demon.co.uk
                                           Tel/Fax: 0121-643 3300

BODENS STUDIOS
D S E SS DS
99 East Barnet Road, New Barnet, Herts EN4 8RF
Website: www.bodenstudios.com
e-mail: bodens2692@aol.com
Fax: 020-8449 5212   Tel: 020-8449 0982

BORLAND Denise MA Voice (Perf), LRAM, PG Dip RAM, Perf Dip GSMD
(Singing, Acting & Voice Coach)
25 Frogston Road West, Edinburgh EH10 7AB
e-mail: info@dbsvoicedevelopment.com   Tel: 0131-445 7491

BOURNEMOUTH YOUTH THEATRE The (BYT)
(Klair/Lucinda Spencer)
14 Cooper Dean Drive, Bournemouth BH8 9LN
Website: www.thebyt.com
e-mail: klair@thebyt.com
Fax: 01202 393290   Tel: 01202 854116

BOYD Beth
D S
10 Prospect Road, Long Ditton, Surbiton
Surrey KT6 5PY   Tel: 020-8398 6768

BRADSHAW Irene
(Private Coach. Voice & Audition Preparation)
Flat F, Welbeck Mansions, Inglewood Road
West Hampstead, London NW6 1QX
Website: www.voicepowerworks.com   Tel: 020-7794 5721

BRAITHWAITE'S ACROBATIC SCHOOL
8 Brookshill Avenue, Harrow Weald
Middlesex   Tel: 020-8954 5638

BRIDGE THEATRE TRAINING COMPANY The
Cecil Sharp House
2 Regent's Park Road, London NW1 7AY
Website: www.thebridge-ttc.org
Fax: 020-7424 9118   Tel: 020-7424 0860

BRIGHTON SCHOOL OF MUSIC & DRAMA
96 Claremont Road, Seaford
East Sussex BN25 2QA   Tel: 01323 492918

BRIGHTON STAGERS
(William Pool ARCM, Singing Tuition & Workshops)
31A Osmond Road, Hove, East Sussex BN3 1TD
Website: www.brightonstagers.co.uk
e-mail: brightonstagers@hotmail.com
                                          Mobile: 07973 518643

BRISTOL OLD VIC THEATRE SCHOOL
See DRAMA SCHOOLS (Conference of)
B.R.I.T. SCHOOL FOR PERFORMING ARTS & TECHNOLOGY The
60 The Crescent, Croydon CR0 2HN
Fax: 020-8665 8676   Tel: 020-8665 5242
BRITISH AMERICAN DRAMA ACADEMY
14 Gloucester Gate, Regent's Park, London NW1 4HG
Website: www.badaonline.com
Fax: 020-7487 0731   Tel: 020-7487 0730
BURTON Gwendolen MA, PG Dip (Performance)
(Singing Teacher)
70 Barnsbury Road
London N1
e-mail: singing@symbolic.net   Mobile: 07771 657261

CAMERON BROWN Jo PGDVS
(Dialect and Voice)
6 The Bow Brook, Gathorne Street, London E2 0PW
Agent: Representation Joyce Edwards 020-7735 5736
e-mail: jocameronbrown@hotmail.com
Mobile: 07970 026621   Tel: 020-8981 1005
CAMPBELL Kenneth
S E D
Parkhills, 6 Clevelands Park
Northam, Bideford, North Devon EX39 3QH
e-mail: kencam@tinyworld.co.uk   Tel: 01237 425217
CAMPBELL Ross ARCM, Dip RCM (Perf)
(Singing Coach, Accompanist & Music Director)
17 Oldwood Chase, Farnborough, Hants GU14 0QS
e-mail: rosscampbell@ntlworld.com   Tel: 01252 510228

CAPITAL ARTS THEATRE SCHOOL
(Kathleen Shanks)
Wyllyotts Centre, Darkes Lane
Potters Bar, Herts EN6 2HN
e-mail: capitalartstheatre@o2.co.uk
Mobile: 07885 232414   Tel/Fax: 020-8449 2342

CARSHALTON COLLEGE
DS
Nightingale Road, Carshalton, Surrey SM5 2EJ
Website: www.carshalton.ac.uk
e-mail: helpline@carshalton.ac.uk
Fax: 020-8770 6899   Tel: 020-8770 6800

CARTEURS THEATRICAL AGENCY
170A Church Road, Hove, East Sussex BN3 2DJ
Website: www.stonelandsschool.co.uk
e-mail: dianacarteur@stonelandsschool.co.uk
Fax: 01273 770444   Tel: 01273 770445

CASE Sarah BA Hons, PGDVS
(Voice, Text, Auditions)
14 Northern Heights, Crescent Road
Crouch End, London N8 8AS   Tel: 020-8347 6784

CELEBRATION THEATRE COMPANY FOR THE YOUNG
SS D E S Sp, 48 Chiswick Staithe
London W4 3TP   Tel: 020-8994 8886

CENTRAL SCHOOL OF SPEECH & DRAMA
See DRAMA SCHOOLS (Conference of)

CENTRE STAGE SCHOOL OF PERFORMING ARTS
(Students 4-18 yrs) (North London)
The Croft, 7 Cannon Road
Southgate, London N14 7HJ
Website: www.centrestageuk.com
Fax: 020-8886 7555   Tel: 020-8886 4264

CENTRESTAGE SCHOOL OF PERFORMING ARTS
(All Day Saturday Classes, Summer Courses, Private
Coaching for Professionals & Drama School Auditions)
7 Cavendish Square, London W1G 0PE
Website: www.centrestageschool.co.uk
e-mail: centrest@dircon.co.uk
Fax: 020-7372 2728   Tel: 020-7328 0788

CHARD Verona L.RAM, Dip RAM (Musical Theatre)
(Singing Tutor)
Ealing House, 33 Hanger Lane, London W5 3HJ
e-mail: verona.chard@vampevents.com   Tel: 020-8992 1571

CHARLTON Catherine
8 Tudor Gates, Highfield Avenue, London NW9 0QE
e-mail: info@catherine-charlton.com
Mobile: 07711 079292   Tel: + 36 204 118227

CHARRINGTON Tim
E D
54 Topmast Point
Strafford Street, London E14 8SN
e-mail: tim.charrington@lycos.co.uk
Mobile: 07967 418236   Tel: 020-7987 3028

CHRISKA STAGE SCHOOL
37-39 Whitby Road, Ellesmere Port
Cheshire L64 8AA   Tel: 01928 739166

CHRYSTEL ARTS THEATRE SCHOOL
(Edgware Branch)
38 Cavendish Road,
Chesham, Bucks HP5 1RW
e-mail: chrystelarts@beeb.net   Tel: 01494 785589

CHURCHER Mel MA
(Acting & Vocal Coach)
32 Denman Road, London SE15 5NP
e-mail: melchurcher@hotmail.com   Tel: 020-7701 4593

ArtsEd^{London}

SCHOOL OF MUSICAL THEATRE
Director Ian Watt-Smith
Tel 020 8987 6677   **Fax** 020 8987 6680   **email** mts@artsed.co.uk

SCHOOL OF ACTING
Director Jane Harrison
Associate Director Adrian James
Tel 020 8987 6655   **Fax** 020 8987 6656   **email** drama@artsed.co.uk

The Arts Educational Schools, 14 Bath Road, Chiswick, London W4 1LY
www.artsed.co.uk

BA (Hons) Acting
3 Year Acting Course. An NCDT Accredited Course.
Validated by City University.
A 3 yr course offering the full range of acting skills to adult students aged 18 or over. The emphasis is on the actor in performance and the relationship with the audience. Classes and tutorial work include: a range of textual, psychological and physical acting techniques, screen acting and broadcasting, voice and speech, movement and dance, mask and theatre history.

MA Acting
1 Year Course. An NCDT Accredited Course.
Validated by City University.
An intensive 1 yr post-graduate acting course offering a fully integrated ensemble training for mature students (aged 21 or over) with a degree or equivalent professional experience. Emphasis is on the pro-active contemporary performer.

Post Diploma BA (Hons) Acting
Validated by City University.
One-year part-time degree conversion course for anyone who has graduated since 1995 from a NCDT/CDET 3 yr acting or musical course: or for those who can offer appropriate professional experience.

BA (Hons) Musical Theatre
A CDET Accredited Course. Validated by City University.
A full-time 3 yr course (18+). A flexible approach providing outstanding training in dance, acting and singing by leading professionals. Training the Complete Performer with excellent employment opportunities for graduates.

Latest Government Inspection rated ArtsEd "outstanding".
Government funded Dance and Drama Awards available.

Member of the Conference of Drama Schools

CIRCOMEDIA
(Centre for Contemporary Circus & Physical Performance)
Britannia Road, Kingswood, Bristol BS15 8DB
Website: www.circomedia.com
e-mail: info@circomedia.com   Tel/Fax: 0117-947 7288

CIRCUS MANIACS SCHOOL OF CIRCUS ARTS
(Part-time Day & Evenings, Act Preparation, Private Tuition)
Office 8A, The Kingswood Foundation, Britannia Road
Kingswood, Bristol BS15 8DB
e-mail: info@circusmaniacs.com
Mobile: 07977 247287   Tel/Fax: 0117-947 7042

CITY LIT The
(Part-time Day & Evening)
16 Stukeley Street, Off Drury Lane
London WC2B 5LJ   Tel: 020-7430 0544

CLASS ACT THEATRE SCHOOL
(Schools in Herts, Bucks & London) (Part-time weekend
5-16 yrs) (Principal: Alice Hyde) (Singing, Musical Theatre
& Drama Training)
47 St Margaret's Road, Twickenham, Middlesex TW1 2LL
Fax: 020-8395 2808   Tel: 020-8891 6663

CLEMENTS Anne MA, LGSM, FRSA
(Drama/Speech/Auditions/Coaching)
293 Shakespeare Tower, Barbican
London EC2Y 8DR   Tel: 020-7374 2748

COLDIRON M J
(Private Coaching, Audition Preparation & Presentation
Skills)
21 Chippendale Street, London E5 0BB
e-mail: jiggs@blueyonder.co.uk
Fax: 020-8525 0687   Tel: 020-8533 1506

COLGAN Valerie
The Green, 17 Herbert Street
London NW5 4HA   Tel: 020-7267 2153

COLIN'S PERFORMING ARTS Ltd
(Full-time 3 yr Performing Arts College)
The Studios, 219B North Street, Romford, Essex RM1 4QA
Website: www.colinsperformingarts.co.uk
e-mail: college@colinsperformingarts.co.uk
Fax: 01708 766077   Tel: 01708 766007

COMBER Sharrone BA Hons MAVS (CSSD)
D E Sp (Voice & Speech, Text, Auditions)
122 Calabria Road, Highbury, London N5 1HT
Mobile: 07752 029422   Tel: 020-7704 9252

CONTI Dizi
D Sp E
4 Brentmead Place, London NW11 9LH   Tel: 020-8458 5535

CONTI Italia ACADEMY OF THEATRE ARTS
SS
Italia Conti House, 23 Goswell Road, London EC1M 7AJ
e-mail: sca@italiaconti36.freeserve.co.uk
Fax: 020-7253 1430   Tel: 020-7608 0047

CONTI Italia ACADEMY OF THEATRE ARTS
See DRAMA SCHOOLS (Conference of)

CORNER Clive AGSM LRAM
(Qualified Teacher, Private Coaching & Audition Training)
73 Gloucester Road, Hampton, Middlesex TW12 2UQ
e-mail: cornerclive@aol.com   Tel: 020-8287 2726

COURT THEATRE TRAINING COMPANY
The Courtyard Theatre
10 York Way, King's Cross, London N1 9AA
Website: www.thecourtyard.org.uk
e-mail: info@thecourtyard.org.uk   Tel/Fax: 020-7833 0870

CREATIVE PERFORMANCE
(Circus Skills, TIE/Workshops, Children 5-11 yrs Part-time)
20 Pembroke Road, North Wembley, Middlesex HA9 7PD
Website: www.jennymayers.co.uk
e-mail: mjennymayers@aol.com   Tel/Fax: 020-8908 0502

CYGNET TRAINING THEATRE
See DRAMA SCHOOLS (Conference of)

D & B SCHOOL OF PERFORMING ARTS
Central Studios, 470 Bromley Road, Bromley BR1 4PN
Website: www.dandbperformingarts.co.uk
e-mail: bonnie@dandbperformingarts.co.uk
Fax: 020-8697 8100   Tel: 020-8698 8880

DALLA VECCHIA Sara
(Italian Teacher)
549A Chiswick High Road
London W4 3AY   Mobile: 07774 703686

DAVIDSON Clare
D E
30 Highgate West Hill, London N6 6NP
Website: www.csf.edu
e-mail: cdavidson@csf.edu   Tel: 020-8348 0132

DE COURCY Bridget
S (Singing Teacher)
19 Muswell Road, London N10   Tel: 020-8883 8397

De FLOREZ Jane LGSM PG Dip
(Singing Teacher - Musical Theatre, Jazz, Classical)
70 Ipsden Buildings, Windmill Walk
Waterloo, London SE1 8LT   Tel: 020-7803 0835

DEBUT THEATRE SCHOOL & CASTING AGENCY Ltd
1 Thrice Fold, Thackley, Bradford, West Yorkshire BD10 8WW
Website: www.debuttheatreschool.co.uk
Fax: 01274 532353   Tel: 01274 532347

DI LACCIO Gabriela
S (Singing Teacher & Coach)
165 Gunnersbury Lane, London W3 8LJ   Tel: 020-8993 2111

DIGNAN Tess PDVS
(Audition, Text & Voice Coach)
60 Mereton Mansions, Brookmill Road
London SE8 4HS   Tel: 020-8691 4275

DONNELLY Elaine
(Children's Acting Coach)
The Talent Partnership, Riverside Studios
Crisp Road, London W6 9RL   Tel: 020-8237 1040

DRAGON DRAMA
(Drama for Children)
1B Station Road, Hampton Wick, Kingston KT1 4HG
Website: www.dragondrama.co.uk
e-mail: info@dragondrama.co.uk   Tel/Fax: 020-8943 1504

DRAMA ASSOCIATION OF WALES
(Summer Courses for Amateur Actors & Directors)
The Old Library, Singleton Road, Splott, Cardiff CF24 2ET
e-mail: aled.daw@virgin.net
Fax: 029-2045 2277   Tel: 029-2045 2200

DRAMA CENTRE LONDON
See DRAMA SCHOOLS (Conference of)

DRAMA STUDIO EDINBURGH The
(Children's weekly drama workshops)
19 Belmont Road, Edinburgh EH14 5DZ
Website: www.thedramastudio.co.uk
e-mail: thedra@thedramastudio.co.uk
Fax: 0131-453 3108   Tel: 0131-453 3284

DRAMA STUDIO LONDON
DS
Grange Court, Grange Road, London W5 5QN
Website: www.dramastudiolondon.co.uk
e-mail: admin@dramastudiolondon.co.uk
Fax: 020-8566 2035   Tel: 020-8579 3897

DUNMORE Simon
(Acting & Audition Tuition)
Website: www.simon.dunmore.btinternet.co.uk
e-mail: simon.dunmore@btinternet.com

DURRENT Peter
(Audition & Rehearsal Pianist & Vocal Coach)
Blacksmiths Cottage, Bures Road, Little Cornard
Sudbury, Suffolk CO10 0NR   Tel: 01787 373483

DYSON Kate LRAM
(Audition Coaching - Drama)
28 Victoria Street, Brighton BN1 3FQ   Tel: 01273 746505

EARNSHAW Susi THEATRE SCHOOL
SS
5 Brook Place, Barnet EN5 2DL
Website: www.susiearnshaw.co.uk
e-mail: casting@susiearnshaw.co.uk
Fax: 020-8364 9618   Tel: 020-8441 6005

EAST 15 ACTING SCHOOL
See DRAMA SCHOOLS (Conference of)

ECOLE INTERNATIONALE DE THEATRE JACQUES LECOQ
57 rue du Faubourg Saint-Denis, 75010 Paris
Website: www.ecole-jacqueslecoq.com
e-mail: contact@ecole-jacqueslecoq.com
Fax: 00 331 45 234014   Tel: 00 331 47 704478

ELLIOTT CLARKE SCHOOL
(Saturday & Evening Classes in Dance, Drama & Singing
RAD, ISTD, LAMDA)
75A Bold Street, Liverpool L1 4EZ   Tel: 0151-709 3323

Drama Studio London

* **One year full time ACTING Course**
Established 1966 (Accredited by NCDT)

* **One year full time DIRECTING Course**
Established 1978

* **Excellent graduate employment record**

* **For postgraduate and mature students**

* **Comprehensive training includes regular productions of classical and modern texts, TV acting and employment classes**

Drama Studio London,
Grange Court, Grange Road, London W5 5QN
Tel: 020 8579 3897 Fax: 020 8566 2035
e-mail: Admin@dramastudiolondon.co.uk
www.dramastudiolondon.co.uk

DSL is supported by Friends of Drama Studio London
a registered charity: no 1051375 - President Dame Judi Dench

EXPRESSIONS ACADEMY OF PERFORMING ARTS
3 Newgate Lane, Mansfield, Notts NG18 2LB
Website: www.expressions-uk.com
e-mail: expressions-uk@btconnect.com
Fax: 01623 474820   Tel: 01623 647337

FAIRBROTHER Victoria MA, CSSD, LAMDA Dip
15A Devenport Road, Shepherd's Bush, London W12 8NZ
e-mail: victoriafairbrother1@hotmail.com
Mobile: 07789 430535   Tel: 020-8743 6449

FAITH Gordon BA, IPA Dip, REM Sp, MCHC (UK), LRAM
Sp
1 Wavel Mews, Priory Road
London NW6 3AB   Tel: 020-7328 0446

FAME FACTORY
4 Dawes Lane, The Meads, Wheathampstead
Herts AL4 8FF   Tel: 01582 831020

FBI AGENCY Ltd
(Acting Classes for Everyone)
PO Box 250, Leeds LS1 2AZ
e-mail: j.spencer@fbi-agency.ltd.uk   Tel/Fax: 07050 222747

FERRIS Anna MA (Voice Studies, CSSD)
D E
Gil'cup Leaze, Hilton, Blandford Forum, Dorset DT11 0DB
e-mail: atcferris@aol.com
Mobile: 07905 656661   Tel: 01258 881098

FINBURGH Nina
D Sp
1 Buckingham Mansions
West End Lane, London NW6 1LR   Tel/Fax: 020-7435 9484

FOOTSTEPS THEATRE SCHOOL
145 Bolton Lane, Bradford BD2 4AA
e-mail: helen@footsteps.fslife.co.uk   Tel/Fax: 01274 626353

FORD Carole Ann ADVS
E D Sp
59 Grove Avenue, Muswell Hill, London N10 2AL
Fax: 020-8365 3248   Tel: 020-8815 1832

FORREST Dee
(Voice/Dialects, Film & TV)
602A High Road, Leytonstone, London E11 3DA
e-mail: dee_forrest@yahoo.com
Tel: 01273 204779   Tel: 020-8556 3828

FOX Betty STAGE SCHOOL
The Friends Institute
220 Moseley Road, Birmingham B12 0DG
e-mail: bettyfox.school@virgin.net   Tel/Fax: 0121-440 1635

FRANKLIN Michael
(Meisner Technique)
Correspondence: c/o The Spotlight
7 Leicester Place, London WC2H 7RJ Tel/Fax: 020-8979 9185

FRIEZE Sandra
D E Sp (English & Foreign Actors)
London Area NW3/NW6   Mobile: 07802 865305

FURNESS Simon
(Actor Training/Audition Coaching)
203A Waller Road, New Cross Gate, London SE14 5LX
e-mail: sfurness@tiscali.co.uk
Mobile: 07931 681173   Tel: 020-7640 9968

GLYNNE Frances THEATRE STUDENTS
SS
12 Stoneleigh Close, Leeds LS17 8FH
e-mail: franandmo@yahoo.co.uk
Fax: 0113-237 1038   Tel: 0113-266 4286

GO FOR IT THEATRE SCHOOL
47 North Lane, Teddington, Middlesex TW11 0HU
Website: www.goforitts.com
e-mail: agency@goforitts.com
Fax: 020-8287 9405   Tel: 020-8943 1120

GRAYSON John
(Vocal Tuition)
14 Lile Crescent, Hanwell, London W7 1AH
e-mail: john@bizzybee.freeserve.co.uk
Mobile: 07702 188031   Tel: 020-8578 3384

GREASEPAINT ANONYMOUS
(Youth Theatre & Training Company)
4 Gallus Close, Winchmore Hill, London N21 1JR
e-mail: info@greasepaintanonymous.co.uk
Fax: 020-8882 9189   Tel: 020-8886 2263

GREGORY Lynda SCHOOL OF SPEECH & DRAMA
(Speech and drama classes, All ages)
23 High Ash Avenue, Leeds LS17 8RS   Tel: 0113-268 4519

GREGORY Paul
(Drama Coach)
133 Kenilworth Court, Lower Richmond Road
Putney, London SW15 1HB   Tel: 020-8789 5726

GREVILLE Jeannine THEATRE SCHOOL
Melody House, Gillott's Corner
Henley-on-Thames, Oxon RG9 1QU   Tel: 01491 572000

GROUT Philip
(Theatre Director, Drama Coaching)
81 Clarence Road, London N22 8PG
e-mail: philipgrout@hotmail.com   Tel: 020-8881 1800

GSA CONSERVATOIRE
See DRAMA SCHOOLS (Conference of)

GUILDHALL SCHOOL OF MUSIC & DRAMA
See DRAMA SCHOOLS (Conference of)

HALEY Jennifer STAGE SCHOOL
(Dance RAD, ISTD, Drama LAMDA)
Toad Hall, 67 Poppleton Road
London E11 1LP   Tel: 020-8989 8364

HALL Michael THEATRE SCHOOL & CASTING AGENCY
Performing Arts Centre
19 Preston Old Road, Blackpool, Lancs FY3 9PR
e-mail: frances@thehalls.force9.co.uk   Tel: 01253 696990

HANCOCK Allison LLAM
D E (Dramatic Art, Acting, Voice, Audition Coaching,
Elocution, Speech Correction etc)
38 Eve Road, Isleworth
Middlesex TW7 7HS   Tel/Fax: 020-8891 1073

HARLEQUIN STUDIOS PERFORMING ARTS SCHOOL
(Drama & Dance Training)
223 Southcoast Road, Peacehaven
East Sussex BN10 8LB   Tel: 01273 581742

The Actors Company
Auditioning now for October 2005

Not a drama school...
...but an acclaimed company in training

Quality training for a vocation

The Actors Company is a one year programme for mature
and post-graduates – 21+ to no upper age limit. The Company
offers intensive vocational training (40 hours per week) and
a six week repertory season at the Jermyn Street Theatre
in the West End of London. The course is 46 weeks in length
– 36 of which is arranged so that Company members support
themselves in employment during training.

Flare Path – "Top Notch"
The Stage

Jermyn Street Repertory Season 2003

Photographs courtesy of Phil R Daniels

Some recent
successful
graduates

Bill Ward
Charlie Stubbs
Coronation Street

Kate Brown
Round the Horne,
West End

Phillip Edgerley
RSC Julius Caesar
2004/5

Robin Sebastian
Round the Horne,
West End

Lloyd Morris
Pier Pressure
Theatre Royal Plymouth

LONDON CENTRE FOR THEATRE STUDIES

For a prospectus contact:
The London Centre for Theatre Studies, 12–18 Hoxton Street, London N1 6NG
T/F 020 7739 5866 E ldncts@aol.com

HARRINGTON Alexandre
(Audition Coach, Voice Consultant)
20 Princes Square, London W2 4NP
e-mail: alexhvoice@tiscali.co.uk   Mobile: 07979 963410

HARRIS Sharon NCSD, LRAM, LAM, STSD, IPA Dip DA
(London Univ)
The Harris Drama School, 52 Forty Avenue
Wembley, Middlesex HA9 8LQ
e-mail: sharrisltd@aol.com
Fax: 020-8908 4455   Tel: 020-8908 4451

HARRISON Joy
(Coaching in Audition Technique, Confidence Building, Text
Work & Drama School Entry)
e-mail: joyh@london.com   Tel: 020-7226 8377

HERTFORDSHIRE THEATRE SCHOOL
40 Queen Street, Hitchin, Herts SG4 9TS
Website: www.htstheatreschool.co.uk
e-mail: info@htstheatreschool.co.uk   Tel: 01462 421416

HESTER John LLCM (TD)
D E (Member of The Society of Teachers of Speech &
Drama)
105 Stoneleigh Park Road, Epsom, Surrey KT19 0RF
e-mail: hjohnhester@aol.com   Tel: 020-8393 5705

HEWITT PERFORMING ARTS
160 London Road, Romford, Essex RM7 9QL
Website: www.hewittperformingarts.com
e-mail: hewittstudios@aol.com   Tel: 01708 727784

HIGGS Jessica
(Voice)
41A Barnsbury Street, London N1 1PW
Mobile: 07940 193631   Tel/Fax: 020-7359 7848

HONEYBORNE Jack
S (Accompanist & Coach)
The Studio, 165 Gunnersbury Lane
London W3 8LJ   Tel: 020-8993 2111

HOPE STREET Ltd
DS Sp (Theatre, Culture & Communities Programme,
University Certificate)
13A Hope Street, Liverpool L1 9BQ
Website: www.hope-street.org
e-mail: arts@hope.u-net.org
Fax: 0151-709 3242   Tel: 0151-708 8007

HOPNER Ernest LLAM
E D Public Speaking
70 Banks Road
West Kirby CH48 0RD   Tel: 0151-625 5641

HOUSEMAN Barbara
(Ex-RSC Voice Dept, Associate Director Young Vic,
Voice/Text/Acting/Confidence)
e-mail: barbarahouseman@hotmail.com
                    Mobile: 07767 843737

HUGHES Dewi
(Voice, Accents, Bodywork, Text, Auditions)
Flat 2, 4 Fielding Road, London W14 0LL
e-mail: dewih@onetel.net.uk   Mobile: 07836 545717

IMPULSE COMPANY The
PO Box 158, Twickenham TW1 3WG
e-mail: info@impulsecompany.co.uk   Tel/Fax: 020-8892 7292

INDEPENDENT THEATRE WORKSHOP The
2 Mornington Road, Ranelagh, Dublin 6, Eire
Website: www.independent-theatre-workshop.com
e-mail: itw@esatclear.ie   Tel/Fax: 00 353 1 4968808

IVES-CAMERON Elaine BA, MA
(Private Coaching, Dialect (USA, European & RP), Drama
School Entrance/Auditions)
29 King Edward Walk, London SE1 7PR
Mobile: 07980 434513   Tel: 020-7928 3814

JACK Andrew
Vrouwe Johanna, PO Box 412, Weybridge, Surrey KT13 8WL
Website: www.andrewjack.com   Mobile: 07836 615839

JAMES Linda RAM Dip Ed, IPD, LRAM
(Dialect Coach)
25 Clifden Road, Brentford
Middlesex TW8 0PB   Tel: 020-8568 2390

JIGSAW PERFORMING ARTS SCHOOL
64-66 High Street, Barnet, Herts EN5 5SJ
e-mail: admin@jigsaw-arts.co.uk   Tel: 020-8447 4530

JONES Desmond SCHOOL OF MIME AND PHYSICAL THEATRE The
20 Thornton Avenue, London W4 1QG
Website: www.desmondjones.co.uk
e-mail: enquiries@desmondjones.co.uk   Tel: 020-8747 3537

JUSTICE Herbert ACADEMY The
PO Box 253, Beckenham
Kent BR3 3WH   Tel: 020-8650 8878

KASTKIDZ
40 Sunnybank Road
Unsworth, Bury BL9 8HF
Website: www.kastkidz.com
e-mail: kastkidz@ntlworld.com
Mobile: 07905 646832   Tel/Fax: 0161-796 7073

K-BIS THEATRE SCHOOL
Clermont Hall, Cumberland Road
Brighton BN1 6SL
e-mail: k-bis@zoom.co.uk
Mobile: 07798 610010   Tel/Fax: 01273 564366

KENT YOUTH THEATRE & AGENCY
Pinks Hill House, Briton Road, Faversham, Kent ME13 8QH
e-mail: richard@kyt.org.uk   Tel/Fax: 01795 534395

KERR Louise
(Voice Coach)
20A Rectory Road, London E17 3BQ
Website: www.louisekerr.com
e-mail: louise@louisekerr.com
Mobile: 07780 708102   Tel: 020-8509 2767

VOICE CONSULTANT & COACH

Tel/Fax: 020-7359 7848   Mobile: 079-4019 3631

Basic vocal technique - text and acting -
Consultancy in all areas of voice use.

KERSLAKE Kelli
137A Culford Road, London N1 4HX
e-mail: noochie05@aol.com
Fax: 020-7684 8091   Mobile: 07833 694743

KIDS AHEAD STAGE SCHOOL OF TOTTENHAM
Johnston & Mathers Associates Ltd
PO Box 3167, Barnet EN5 2WA
e-mail: joinkidsahead@aol.com
Fax: 020-8449 2386   Tel: 020-8449 4968

KIDZ IN THE BIZ
5 Brittendon Parade, Green Street Green, Kent BR6 6DD
Website: www.kidzinthebiz.co.uk
e-mail: thebizmanagement@aol.com
Mobile: 07763 958096   Tel: 01689 882850

LAINE THEATRE ARTS
(Betty Laine)
The Studios, East Street, Epsom, Surrey KT17 1HH
Website: www.laine-theatre-arts.co.uk
e-mail: info@laine-theatre-arts.co.uk
Fax: 01372 723775   Tel: 01372 724648

LAMDA
See DRAMA SCHOOLS (Conference of)

LAMONT DRAMA SCHOOL & CASTING AGENCY
94 Harington Road, Formby, Liverpool L37 1PQ
Website: www.lamontcasting.co.uk
e-mail: diane@lamontcasting.co.uk
Fax: 01704 872422   Tel: 01704 877024

LAURIE Rona
(Coach for Auditions & Voice & Speech Technique)
21 New Quebec Street
London W1H 7SA   Tel: 020-7262 4909

LEAN David Lawson BA Hons, PGCE
(Acting Tuition, LAMDA Exams, Licensed Chaperone)
72 Shaw Drive, Walton-on-Thames
Surrey KT12 2LS   Tel: 01932 230273

LEE STAGE SCHOOL The
(Office)
126 Church Road, Benfleet, Essex SS7 4EP
e-mail: lynn@leetheatre.fsnet.co.uk   Tel: 01268 795863

LESLIE Maeve
(Singing, Voice Production, Presentation)
60 Warwick Square
London SW1V 2AL   Tel: 020-7834 4912

LEVENTON Patricia BA Hons
D E Sp
113 Broadhurst Gardens, West Hampstead, London NW6 3BJ
e-mail: patricia@lites2000.com
Mobile: 07703 341062   Tel: 020-7624 5661

LINTON MANAGEMENT
Carol Godby Theatre Workshop
21 The Rock, Bury, Lancs BL9 0JP
Fax: 0161-761 1999   Tel: 0161-763 6420

LIVE & LOUD
(Children & Teenage Drama Coaching)
The S.P.A.C.E., 2nd Floor
188 St Vincent's Street, Glasgow G2 5SP
e-mail: info@west-endmgt.com
Fax: 0141-226 8983   Tel: 0141-222 2942

LIVERPOOL INSTITUTE FOR PERFORMING ARTS The
Mount Street, Liverpool L1 9HF
e-mail: reception@lipa.ac.uk
Fax: 0151-330 3131   Tel: 0151-330 3000

LIVINGSTON Dione LRAM, FETC
Sp E D
7 St Luke's Street
Cambridge CB4 3DA   Tel: 01223 365970

LOCATION TUTORS NATIONWIDE
(Fully Qualified/Experienced Teachers Working with
Children on Film Sets and Covering all Key Stages of
National Curriculum)
16 Poplar Walk, Herne Hill SE24 0BU
Fax: 020-7207 8794   Tel: 020-7978 8898

LONDON ACADEMY OF PERFORMING ARTS (LAPA)
St Matthew's Church, St Petersburgh Place, London W2 4LA
Website: www.lapadrama.com
e-mail: admin@lapadrama.com
Fax: 020-7727 0330   Tel: 020-7727 0220

LONDON ACTORS WORKSHOPS
Pinewood Film Studios Room 131, Pinewood Road
Iver Heath, Bucks SL0 0NH
Website: www.londonactorsworkshop.co.uk
e-mail: info@londonactorsworkshop.co.uk
Fax: 01753 785162   Tel: 01753 655514

LONDON DRAMA SCHOOL
(Acting, Speech Training, Singing)
30 Brondesbury Park, London NW6 7DN
Website: www.startek-uk.com
e-mail: enquiries@startek-uk.com
Fax: 020-8830 4992   Tel: 020-8830 0074

LONDON FILMMAKERS STUDIO The
10 Brunswick Centre, off Bernard Street, London WC1N 1AE
e-mail: business@skoob.com
Mobile: 07712 880909   Tel: 020-7278 8760

LONDON SCHOOL OF MUSICAL THEATRE
83 Borough Road, London SE1 1DN
e-mail: enquiries@lsmt.co.uk   Tel/Fax: 020-7407 4455

TIM CHARRINGTON
Dip. C.S.S.D., A.D.V.S., ACTOR & TEACHER
THEATRE, TV & FILM
Accents, Dialects & Standard English
020 7987 3028   mobile 07967 418 236

MEL CHURCHER Voice & Acting Coach

R.S.C., Regent's Park, Royal Court, Young Vic.

'King Arthur', 'Tomb Raider', 'The Count Of Monte Cristo', 'The Hole', 'The Fifth Element', '102 Dalmatians'.

'Acting for Film: Truth 24 Times a Second' Virgin Books 2003.

Tel/Fax: 020 7701 4593   Mobile: 07778 773019

Email: melchurcher@hotmail.com

LONDON STUDIO CENTRE
42-50 York Way, London N1 9AB
Website: www.london-studio-centre.co.uk
e-mail: enquire@london-studio-centre.co.uk
Fax: 020-7837 3248   Tel: 020-7837 7741

LYTTON Gloria
E D
22 Green Road, Oakwood, Southgate
London N14 4AU   Tel: 020-8441 3118

MADDERMARKET THEATRE
(Education Officer)
Education and Training Department, St John's Alley,
Norwich NR2 1DR
Website: www.maddermarket.freeserve.co.uk
e-mail: mmtheatre@btconnect.com
Fax: 01603 661357   Tel: 01603 628600

**MANCHESTER METROPOLITAN UNIVERSITY
SCHOOL OF THEATRE**
See DRAMA SCHOOLS (Conference of)

MANCHESTER SCHOOL OF ACTING
29 Ardwick Green North, Manchester M12 6DL
Website: www.manchesterschoolofacting.com
e-mail: actorclass@aol.com   Tel/Fax: 0161-273 4738

MARLOW Jean LGSM
D E
32 Exeter Road, London NW2 4SB   Tel: 020-8450 0371

MARSHALL Elizabeth Tracey LGSM, GSMD, LGSMD
(Training for Corporates)
23 Gynsills Hall, Stelle Way, Glenfield, Leicester LE3 8HP
e-mail: marshall@grenedan.demon.co.uk
                Mobile: 07788 420578

MARTIN Liza GRSM ARMCM (Singing), ARMCM (Piano)
(Singing Tuition, Sounds Sensational)   Tel: 020-8348 0346

MASTERS PERFORMING ARTS COLLEGE Ltd
(Musical Theatre/Dance Course)
Arterial Rd, Rayleigh, Essex SS6 7UQ   Tel: 01268 777351

McCALLION Michael
D E
Flat 2, 11 Sinclair Gdns, London W14 0AU Tel: 020-7602 5599

McCRACKEN Jenny
First Floor Flat, 316A Chiswick High Road
London W4 5TA   Tel: 020-8747 6724

McDAID Marj
1 Chesholm Road, Stoke Newington, London N16 0DP
e-mail: marjmcdaid@hotmail.com
Fax: 020-7502 0412   Tel: 020-7923 4929

McKELLAN Martin
P2 Abbey Orchard Street, London SW1P 2DP
e-mail: m.mckellan@macunlimited.net   Tel: 020-7222 1875

MELLECK Lydia
S (Accompanist & Coach for Auditions & Repertoire - RADA)
10 Burgess Park Mansions
London NW6 1DP   Tel: 020-7794 8845

METHOD STUDIO, LONDON The
Conway Hall, 25 Red Lion Square, London WC1R 4RL
Website: www.themethodstudio.com
e-mail: info@themethodstudio.com
Fax: 020-7831 8319   Tel: 020-7831 7335

MICHEL Hilary ARCM
(Singing Teacher, Vocal Coaching, Accompanist, Auditions,
Technique)
82 Greenway, Totteridge, London N20 8EJ
Mobile: 07775 780182   Tel: 020-8343 7243

MIDDLESEX UNIVERSITY
(Singing Teaching, Vocal Coaching, Accompanist, Audition Technique)
Bramley Road, Oakwood, Trent Park, London N14 4YZ
Fax: 020-8441 4672   Tel: 020-8362 5000

MILNER Jack COMEDY WORKSHOPS
88 Pearcroft Road, London E11 4DR
Website: www.jackmilner.com
e-mail: jack@jackmilner.com   Tel: 020-8556 9768

MONTAGE THEATRE ARTS
(Dance, Drama, Singing - Children & Adults)
(Artistic Director Judy Gordon)
441 New Cross Gate, London SE14 6TA
Website: www.montagetheatre.com
e-mail: info@montagetheatre.com   Tel: 020-8692 7007

MORLEY ADULT EDUCATION COLLEGE
(LOCN Accredited Evening Theatre School, Daytime
Performing Arts Programme)
61 Westminster Bridge Road, London SE1 7HT
Website: www.morleycollege.ac.uk
e-mail: keith.brazil@morleycollege.ac.uk
Fax: 020-7928 4074   Tel: 020-7450 1832

MORRIS David SCHOOL FOR PERFORMING ARTS The
6 Sussex Close, Redbridge, Essex IG4 5DP
Mobile: 07973 129130   Tel: 020-8924 0197

MOUNTVIEW
See DRAMA SCHOOLS (Conference of)

MRS WORTHINGTON'S WORKSHOPS
SS S Md (Part-time Performing Arts for Children 6-15 yrs)
16 Ouseley Road, London SW12 8EF   Tel: 020-8767 6944

MURRAY Barbara LGSM, LALAM
129 Northwood Way, Northwood
Middlesex HA6 1RF   Tel: 01923 823182

NATHENSON Zoe
(Film Acting, Audition Technique & Sight Reading)
66E Priory Road, London N8 7EX
e-mail: zoe.nathenson@which.net
Mobile: 07956 833850   Tel: 020-8347 7799

NATIONAL PERFORMING ARTS SCHOOL & AGENCY The
The Factory Rehearsal Studios
35A Barrow Street, Dublin 4, Eire
e-mail: info@npas.ie   Tel/Fax: 00 353 1 6684035

NEIL Andrew
2 Howley Place, London W2 1XA
e-mail: andrewneil@surf3.net
Mobile: 07979 843984   Tel/Fax: 020-7262 9521

NEWNHAM Caryll
(Singing Teacher)
35 Selwyn Crescent, Hatfield, Herts AL10 9NL
e-mail: caryll@ntlworld.com
Mobile: 07976 635745   Tel: 01707 267700

NORTH LONDON PERFORMING ARTS CENTRE
(Performing Arts Classes 3-19 yrs, Dance, Drama, Music.
GCSE Courses & LAMDA)
76 St James Lane, Muswell Hill, London N10 3DF
e-mail: nlpac@aol.com
Fax: 020-8444 4040   Tel: 020-8444 4544

NORTHERN FILM & DRAMA
21 Low Street, South Milford, North Yorks LS25 5AR
Website: www.northernfilmanddrama.com
e-mail: alyson@connew.com   Tel/Fax: 01977 681949

NORTHERN THEATRE SCHOOL OF PERFORMING ARTS
The Studios, Madeley Street, Hull, East Yorkshire HU3 2AH
e-mail: northco75@aol.com
Fax: 01482 212280   Tel: 01482 328627

NUTOPIA-CHANG ACTORS STUDIO LONDON
(Camera Acting & Presenting Courses)
Number 8, 132 Charing Cross Road, London WC2H 0LA
Website: www.nutopia.co.uk
Fax: 029-2070 9440   Mobile: 07801 493133

O'FARRELL STAGE & THEATRE SCHOOL
(Dance, Drama, Singing)
36 Shirley Street
Canning Town, London E16 1HU
Fax: 020-7476 0010   Tel: 020-7511 9444

OLLERENSHAW Maggie BA (Hons), Dip Ed
D Sp (TV & Theatre Coaching, Career Guidance)
151D Shirland Road, London W9 2EP
e-mail: maggieoll@aol.com   Tel: 020-7286 1126

OLSON Lise
(American Accents, Voice & Text)
North West Based, LIPA, Mount Street, Liverpool
e-mail: l.olson@lipa.ac.uk
Mobile: 07790 877145   Tel: 0151-330 3032

OMOBONI Lino
Sp
2nd Floor, 12 Weltje Road, London W6 9TG
Website: www.bluewand.co.uk
e-mail: lino@bluewand.co.uk
Mobile: 07885 528743   Tel/Fax: 020-8741 2038

OPEN VOICE
(Consultancy, Auditions, Personal Presentation
- Catherine Owen)
9 Bellsmains, Gorebridge
Near Edinburgh EH23 4QD   Tel: 01875 820175

ORTON Leslie LRAM, ALAM, ANEA
E D Sp
141 Ladybrook Lane, Mansfield
Notts NG18 5JH   Tel: 01623 626082

OSBORNE HUGHES John
(Art & Craft of Acting)
Venus Productions Training Department
51 Church Road, London SE19 2TE
e-mail: johughes@loveray.demon.co.uk
Mobile: 07801 950916   Tel: 020-8653 7735

OSCARS COLLEGE OF PERFORMANCE ARTS Ltd
103 Fitzwilliam Street, Huddersfield HD1 5PS
e-mail: oscarscollege@smartone.co.uk
Fax: 01484 545036   Tel: 01484 545519

OVERSBY William
(Singing & Vocal Projection)
Streatham
e-mail: bill@ward-thomas.co.uk   Mobile: 07811 946663

OXFORD SCHOOL OF DRAMA The
See DRAMA SCHOOLS (Conference of)

PALMER Jackie STAGE SCHOOL
30 Daws Hill Lane, High Wycombe, Bucks HP11 1PW
Website: www.jackiepalmer.co.uk
e-mail: jackie.palmer@btinternet.com
Fax: 01494 510479   Tel: 01494 510597

PARKES Frances MA, AGSM
(Voice & Acting Coach)
451A Kingston Road, London SW20 8JP
Agent: Representation Joyce Edwards 020-7735 5736
e-mail: frances25@blueyonder.co.uk
                                     Tel/Fax: 020-8542 2777

PAUL'S THEATRE SCHOOL
Fairkytes Arts Centre
51 Billet Lane
Hornchurch, Essex RM11 1AX
Website: www.paulstheatreschool.co.uk
e-mail: info@paulstheatreschool.co.uk
Fax: 01708 475286   Tel: 01708 447123

PEMART
(Voice, Acting, Audition Preparation, Accent, Diction,
Speech & Language Coaching)
London & New York
Website: www.noraarmani.com
e-mail: info@noraarmani.com
Mobile: 07766 706415   Tel: (917) 318-2290

PERFORM
SS
66 Churchway, London NW1 1LT
Fax: 020-7691 4822   Tel: 020-7209 3805

CHARLES VERRALL
Formerly Co-Director of Anna Scher Theatre
IMPROVISATION
Saturday morning workshops for renewal, confidence building and enjoyment
1:1 sessions on voice work, auditions and preparation for drama school entrance

Leo Information Limited 19 Matilda Street N1 0LA Tel: 020 7833 1971 e-mail: charles.verrall@virgin.net

---

PERFORMANCE BUSINESS The
15 Montrose Walk, Weybridge, Surrey KT13 8JN
Website: www.theperformance.biz
e-mail: michael@theperformance.biz   Tel: 01932 888885

PERFORMERS COLLEGE
(Brian Rogers - Susan Stephens)
Southend Road, Corringham, Essex SS17 8JT
Website: www.performerscollege.co.uk
e-mail: pdc@dircon.co.uk
Fax: 01375 672353   Tel: 01375 672053

PERFORMERS THEATRE SCHOOL
3 Benmore Road, Liverpool L18 4QJ
Website: www.performerstheatre.co.uk
e-mail: info@performerstheatre.co.uk
Tel: 0151-708 4000   Tel: 020-8874 0700

PETHICK Fiona & Claire BA Hons ADB LRAM LGSM
D Sp (Audition Technique & Musical Theatre)
31 Grove Road, Chertsey, Surrey
Website: www.ata-productions.com
e-mail: atatheatre@aol.com   Tel: 01932 702174

PHELPS Neil
D Sp (Private Coaching for Auditions, Schools, Showbiz, etc)
61 Parkview Court, London SW6 3LL
e-mail: nphelps@usa.com   Tel: 020-7731 3419

PILATES INTERNATIONAL
(Physical Coaching, Stage, Film & Dance)
Unit 1, Broadbent Close
20-22 Highgate High Street, London N6 5JG
Website: www.pilatesinternational.co.uk
Tel/Fax: 020-8348 1442

POLLYANNA CHILDREN'S TRAINING THEATRE
PO Box 30661, London E1W 3GG
Website: www.eada.demon.co.uk/pollyanna
e-mail: pollyanna-mgmt@btinternet.com
Fax: 020-7480 6761   Tel: 020-7702 1937

POLYDOROU Anna MA Voice Studies (CSSD)
(Accents, Voice & Text)
147C Fernhead Road, London W9 3ED
e-mail: annahebe@yahoo.com
Mobile: 07947 071714   Tel: 020-8969 8881

POOR SCHOOL
242 Pentonville Road, London N1 9JY
Website: www.thepoorschool.com
e-mail: acting@thepoorschool.com
Fax: 020-7837 5330   Tel: 020-7837 6030

PRECINCT THEATRE The
Units 2/3 The Precinct
Packington Square, London N1 7UP
Website: www.breakalegman.com
e-mail: theatre@breakalegman.com
Fax: 020-7359 3660   Tel: 020-7359 3594

QUEEN MARGARET UNIVERSITY COLLEGE
See DRAMA SCHOOLS (Conference of)

QUESTORS THEATRE EALING The
12 Mattock Lane, London W5 5BQ
Website: www.questors.org.uk
e-mail: admin@questors.org.uk
Fax: 020-8567 8736   Admin: 020-8567 0011

RADCLIFFE Tom
(Sanford Meisner Technique/Actor Training)
203A Waller Road, New Cross Gate
London SE14 5LX   Tel: 020-7207 0499

RAVENSCOURT THEATRE SCHOOL Ltd
Tandy House, 30-40 Dalling Road, London W6 0JB
Website: www.ravenscourt.net
e-mail: info@ravenscourt.net
Fax: 020-8741 1786   Tel: 020-8741 0707

RED ONION PERFORMING ARTS CENTRE
(Drama, Dance & Vocal Training, Age 8 yrs to Adult)
Hilton Grove Business Centre, 25 Hilton Grove
Hatherley Mews, London E17 4QP
Website: www.redonion.uk.com
e-mail: info@redonion.uk.com
Fax: 020-8521 6646   Tel: 020-8520 3975

REDROOFS THEATRE SCHOOL
DS SS D S Sp
Littlewick Green, Maidenhead, Berks SL6 3QY
Website: www.redroofs.co.uk   Tel: 01628 822982

REP COLLEGE The
17 St Mary's Avenue, Purley on Thames, Berks RG8 8BJ
Website: www.repcollege.com
e-mail: tudor@repcollege.co.uk   Tel/Fax: 0118-942 1144

REYNOLDS Sandra COLLEGE
(Modelling & Grooming School)
35 St Georges Street, Norwich NR3 1DA
Website: www.sandrareynolds.co.uk
e-mail: recruitment@sandrareynolds.co.uk
Fax: 01603 219825   Tel: 01603 623842

RICHMOND DRAMA SCHOOL
DS (One Year Course)
Parkshot Centre, Parkshot, Richmond, Surrey TW9 2RE
e-mail: david.whitworth@racc.ac.uk   Tel: 020-8439 8944

 Dee Forrest PGDVS Dip.DV. *VOICE & SINGING COACH*
DIALECTS: FILMS & TV
AUDITIONS-PROJECTION-DIALECTS-INTERPRETATION-
VOCAL PROBLEMS-PHONETICS-PRESENTATION SKILLS.
Tel: 01273-204779   Mob: 07957 211065

RIDGEWAY STUDIOS PERFORMING ARTS COLLEGE
Fairley House, Andrews Lane, Cheshunt, Herts EN7 6LB
Website: www.ridgewaystudios.co.uk
e-mail: info@ridgewaystudios.co.uk
Fax: 01992 633844   Tel: 01992 633775

ROSE BRUFORD COLLEGE
See DRAMA SCHOOLS (Conference of)

ROSSENDALE DANCE & DRAMA CENTRE
52 Bridleway, Waterfoot, Rossendale, Lancs BB4 9DS
e-mail: rddc@btinternet.com   Tel: 01706 211161

ROYAL ACADEMY OF DRAMATIC ART
See DRAMA SCHOOLS (Conference of)

ROYAL ACADEMY OF MUSIC
Marylebone Road, London NW1 5HT   Tel: 020-7873 7373

ROYAL SCOTTISH ACADEMY OF MUSIC & DRAMA
See DRAMA SCHOOLS (Conference of)

ROYAL WELSH COLLEGE OF MUSIC & DRAMA
See DRAMA SCHOOLS (Conference of)

SCHER Anna THEATRE The
70-72 Barnsbury Road, London N1 OES
e-mail: info@astm.co.uk
Fax: 020-7833 9467   Tel: 020-7278 2101

SCHOOL OF THE SCIENCE OF ACTING The
67-83 Seven Sisters Road, London N7 6BU
Website: www.scienceofacting.org.uk
e-mail: find@scienceofacting.org.uk
Fax: 020-7272 0026   Tel: 020-7272 0027

SCREENWRITERS' WORKSHOP The
Screenwriters' Centre, Suffolk House
1-8 Whitfield Place, London W1T 5JU
Website: www.lsw.org.uk
e-mail: screenoffice@tiscali.co.uk   Tel/Fax: 020-7387 5511

SETTELEN Peter
181 Jersey Road, Osterley, Middlesex TW7 4QJ
Website: www.settelen.com
e-mail: talk@settelen.net
Fax: 020-8737 2987   Tel: 020-8737 1616

SHARP Judith
(Career Consultant & Coach)
e-mail: sharp.judith@talk21.com
Mobile: 07941 863499   Tel/Fax: 020-7263 1403

SHAW Philip
(Actors Consultancy Service, Acting/Voice Coaching)
Suite 476, 2 Old Brompton Road
South Kensington, London SW7 3DQ
e-mail: shawcastlond@aol.com
Fax: 020-8408 1193   Tel: 020-8715 8943

SHENEL Helena
(Singing Teacher)
80 Falkirk House, 165 Maida Vale
London W9 1QX   Tel: 020-7328 2921

SHERRIFF David
(Vocal Coaching, Accompanist, Act Preparation,
Musical Services)
106 Mansfield Drive, Merstham, Surrey RH1 3JN
Fax: 01737 271231   Tel: 01737 642829

SINGER Sandra ASSOCIATES
21 Cotswold Road, Westcliff-on-Sea, Essex SS0 8AA
Website: www.sandrasinger.com
e-mail: sandrasingeruk@aol.com
Fax: 01702 339393   Tel: 01702 331616

**SKILLSBASE - THE NORTH WEST ACADEMY OF MEDIA
AND PERFORMING ARTS**
24-25 Booth House, Featherstall Road
Oldham OL9 7QT   Tel/Fax: 0161-652 2651

Louise Kerr MA

TV Voice Expert
Channel Five "Celebrity Swap" 2004
Voice Coaching and Training Consultant

▸ Professional Delivery
▸ Personal Impact
▸ Public Speaking
▸ Presentation Skills

For more information see
www.louisekerr.com
email: louise@louisekerr.com
mob: 07780 708102

SOCIETY OF TEACHERS OF SPEECH & DRAMA The
73 Berry Hill Road, Mansfield, Notts NG18 4RU
Website: www.stsd.org.uk
e-mail: ann.k.jones@btinternet.com   Tel: 01623 627636

SPEAKE Barbara STAGE SCHOOL
East Acton Lane, London W3 7EG
e-mail: speakekids4@aol.com   Tel/Fax: 020-8743 1306

SPEAKERPOWER.CO.UK
48 Fellows Road, London NW3 3LH
Website: www.speakerpower.co.uk
e-mail: barbara@speakerpower.co.uk
Fax: 020-7722 5255   Tel: 020-7586 4361

SPEED Anne-Marie Hon ARAM, MA (Voice Studies), CSSD, ADVS, BA
(Vocal Technique, Coaching, Auditions, Accents)
31 Nether Close, Finchley, London N3 1AA
e-mail: anne-marie.speed@virgin.net
Mobile: 07957 272554   Tel: 020-8349 9639

STAGE 84 YORKSHIRE SCHOOL OF PERFORMING ARTS
(Evening & Weekend Classes & Summer Schools)
Old Bell Chapel, Town Lane, Bradford, West Yorks BD10 8PR
e-mail: valeriejackson@stage84.com
Mobile: 07785 244984   Tel: 01274 569197

STAGE DOOR THEATRE SCHOOL
The Stage Door Centre, 27 Howard Business Park
Waltham Abbey, Essex EN9 1XE
Website: www.stagedoorschool.co.uk
e-mail: stagedoorschool@aol.com
Fax: 01992 652171   Tel: 01992 717994

STAGE ONE THEATRE PRODUCTION SCHOOL
32 Westbury Lane, Buckhurst Hill, Essex IG9 5PL
Website: www.stage01.com
e-mail: stage01@lineone.net
Mobile: 07939 121154   Tel/Fax: 020-8506 0949

STAGECOACH TRAINING CENTRES FOR THE PERFORMING ARTS
The Courthouse, Elm Grove
Walton-on-Thames, Surrey KT12 1LZ
Website: www.stagecoach.co.uk
e-mail: mail@stagecoach.co.uk
Fax: 01932 222894   Tel: 01932 254333

STEP ONE DANCE AND DRAMA SCHOOL
Rear of 24 Penrhyn Road, Colwyn Bay
Conwy LL29 8LG   Tel: 01492 534424

STEPHENSON Sarah
(Vocal Coach, Pianist, Musical Director, Estil Voice Pratitioner)
8A Edgington Road, Streatham, London SW16 5BS
e-mail: sarahjane.stephenson@ntlworld.com
Mobile: 07957 477642   Tel: 020-8425 1225

STOCKTON RIVERSIDE COLLEGE
(Education & Training)
Harvard Avenue, Thornaby
Stockton TS17 6FB   Tel: 01642 865566

STOMP! THE SCHOOL OF PERFORMING ARTS
Holcombe House, The Ridgeway, Mill Hill, London NW7 4HY
Website: www.stompschool.com
e-mail: stompschoolnw7@aol.com
Fax: 020-8446 4049   Tel: 020-8446 4079

STONELANDS SCHOOL
(Full-time Training in Ballet & Theatre Arts)
170A Church Road, Hove BN3 2DJ
e-mail: dianacarteur@stonelandsschool.co.uk
Fax: 01273 770444   Tel: 01273 770445

STREETON Jane
(Singing Teacher - RADA)
24 Richmond Road, Leytonstone
London E11 4BA   Tel: 020-8556 9297

SWINDON YOUNG ACTORS
65 Stafford Street, Old Town, Swindon, Wiltshire SN1 3PF
e-mail: young.actorsfile@virgin.net   Tel: 01793 423688

SWINFIELD Rosemarie
(Make-Up Design & Training)
Rosie's Make-Up Box, 6 Brewer St, Soho, London W1R 3FS
Website: www.rosiesmake-up.co.uk
e-mail: rosemarie@rosiesmake-up.co.uk
Mobile: 07976 965520

TALENTED KIDS PERFORMING ARTS SCHOOL
(Drama, Musical Theatre, Dance Classes For All Ages)
17 Monastery Gate Villas, Monastery Road
Clondalkin, Dublin 22, Eire
e-mail: talentedkids@hotmail.com
Tel/Fax: 00 353 1 4642160

TEAM ACTIVATE
(Performance & Presentation Skills)
38 Highbury Hill, London N5 1AL
Website: www.islington.org.uk/business/tapps
e-mail: teamactivate@fastmail.fm   Mobile: 07837 712323

THEATRE ARTS (WEST LONDON)
(Agency & Part-time Classes in Drama, Dance & Singing)
18 Kingsdale Gardens, Notting Hill, London W11 4TZ
e-mail: theatreartswestlondon@hotmail.com
Tel/Fax: 020-7603 3471

THEATRETRAIN
(6 -18 yrs, Annual West End Productions involving all Pupils)
PO Box 117, Ilford, Essex IG3 8PN
Website: www.theatretrain.co.uk
e-mail: info@theatretrain.co.uk   Tel: 01992 560000

Rose Bruford College

Providing training and education in theatre and related arts
to the highest level through the following range of programmes

Theatre
Acting BA (Hons)
Actor Musicianship BA (Hons)
American Theatre Arts BA (Hons)
Directing BA (Hons)
European Theatre Arts BA (Hons)
Theatre Arts Acting (Part-time)
Theatre Practices MA (Hons)

Design & Production
Costume Production BA (Hons)
Lighting Design BA (Hons)
Multimedia Design BA (Hons)
Music Technology BA (Hons)
Scenic Arts (Construction & Scenic Painting) BA (Hons)
Stage Management BA (Hons)
Theatre Design BA (Hons)

Distance Learning
Theatre Studies BA (Hons)
Opera Studies BA (Hons)
Theatre & Performance Studies MA
Dramatic Writing MA

Places are limited and entry is based on audition
or interview which take place throughout the year

The College is committed to equality of opportunity

For further information please contact:
Telephone: 020 8308 2600
Fax: 020 8308 0542
Email: enquiries@bruford.ac.uk
Website: www.bruford.ac.uk
Lamorbey Park, Burnt Oak Lane, Sidcup, Kent DA15 9DF

A University Sector Institution and a Member of the Conference of Drama Schools CDS

THORN Barbara
D Sp (TV & Theatre Coaching, Career Guidance)
51 Parkside, Vanbrugh Park, Blackheath
London SE3 7QF   Tel: 020-8305 0094

TIP TOE STAGE SCHOOL
For correspondence only:
45 Viola Close, South Ockendon, Essex RM15 6JF
Website: www.tiptoestageschool.com
e-mail: tiptoestageschool@blueyonder.co.uk
                                    Mobile: 07969 909284

TO BE OR NOT TO BE
(TV/Film Acting Techniques. Showreels, Theatre/Audition pieces. LAMDA Exams) (Anthony Barnett)
48 Northampton Road, Kettering, Northants NN15 7JU
Website: www.tobeornottobe.tv
e-mail: tobeornottobe@ntlworld.com   Mobile: 07958 996227

TREMAINE Sally
17 Dartington, Plender Street, London NW1 0PE
Website: www.voiceset.co.uk
e-mail: sally@voiceset.co.uk
Fax: 07970 188945   Tel: 020-7813 9218

TROTTER William BA, MA, PGDVS
D E Sp
25 Thanet Lodge, Mapesbury Road, London NW2 4JA
Website: www.ukspeech.co.uk
e-mail: william.trotter@ukspeech.co.uk
                                    Tel/Fax: 020-8459 7594

TUCKER John
Flat 503, Mountjoy House, Barbican, London EC2Y 8BP
Website: www.johntucker.org.uk
e-mail: tucker_roher@onetel.net.uk
Mobile: 07903 269409   Tel/Fax: 020-7638 8109

TV ACTING CLASSES
(Elisabeth Charbonneau)
14 Triangle Place, Clapham, London SW4 7HS
e-mail: ejcharbonneau@aol.com
Mobile: 07885 621061   Tel: 020-7627 8036

TWICKENHAM THEATRE WORKSHOP FOR CHILDREN
22 Butts Crescent, Hanworth
Middlesex TW13 6HQ   Tel: 020-8898 5882

URQUHART Moray
D Sp (Private Coaching for Auditions)
Write, 61 Parkview Court, London SW6 3LL
e-mail: nphelps@usa.com

VALLÉ ACADEMY OF PERFORMING ARTS Ltd The
The Valle Academy Studios
Wilton House, Delamare Road, Cheshunt, Herts EN8 9SG
Website: www.valleacademy.co.uk
e-mail: enquiries@valleacademy.co.uk
Fax: 01992 622868   Tel: 01992 622862

VERRALL Charles
D
19 Matilda Street, London N1 0LA
e-mail: charles.verrall@virgin.net   Tel: 020-7833 1971

VOCAL CONFIDENCE FOR SPEECH & SINGING
(Alix Longman)
Flat 2, 1A The Boulevard, London SW17 7BW
Website: www.vocalconfidence.com
e-mail: info@vocalconfidence.com   Mobile: 07958 450382

VOICE & THE ALEXANDER TECHNIQUE
(Robert Macdonald)
Flat 5, 17 Hatton Street, London NW8 8PL
Website: www.voice.org.uk   Mobile: 07956 852303

VOICE BODY COMMUNICATION
(Patricia Perry)
65 Castelnau, Barnes SW13 9RT
e-mail: ppvoice@blueyonder.co.uk   Tel/Fax: 020-8748 9699

VOICE IN ACTION
(Gary Owston)
65 Trym Side, Sea Mills, Bristol BS9 2HD
e-mail: owston@madasafish.com   Mobile: 07712 444374

VOICE MASTER
(Specialized Training for Voice-Overs & TV Presenters)
Website: www.voicemaster.info
e-mail: info@voicemaster.info
Fax: 020-8455 2344   Tel: 020-8455 2211

VOICE TAPE SERVICES INTERNATIONAL Ltd
(Professional Voice-Over Direction & CDs)
80 Netherlands Road, New Barnet, Herts EN5 1BS
e-mail: info@vtsint.co.uk
Fax: 020-8441 4828   Tel: 020-8440 4848

VOXTRAINING Ltd
(Voice-Over Training and Demo CDs)
20 Old Compton Street, London W1D 4TW
Website: www.voxtraining.com
e-mail: info@voxtraining.com
Fax: 020-7434 4414   Tel: 020-7434 4404

WALLACE Elaine BA
D Sp Voice
249 Goldhurst Terrace, London NW6 3EP
e-mail: im@voicebiz.biz   Tel: 020-7625 4049

WALSH Anne
(Accents, Dialect, Speech)
45B Windsor Road, Willesden Green, London NW2 5DT
e-mail: annewalsh.voice@virgin.net   Tel: 020-8459 8071

Royal Welsh College of Music & Drama

SPACE
TO EXPLORE

Three-Year Degree &
One-Year Diploma
Programmes in:

- **Acting** †
- **Theatre Design**
- **Stage Management/**
  Technical Theatre †

† Accredited by the National Council for Drama Training

CDS A Member of the Conference of Drama Schools

For a prospectus, contact:
Tel   029 2039 1327
Email   drama.admissions@rwcmd.ac.uk
Royal Welsh College of Music & Drama,
Castle Grounds, Cathays Park, Cardiff, CF10 3ER

www.rwcmd.ac.uk

WALTZER Jack
(Professional Acting Workshops)
5 Minetta Street Apt 2B
New York NY 10012
Website: www.jackwaltzer.com
e-mail: jackwaltzer@yahoo.co.uk
Tel: 001 (212) 840-1234   Tel: 020-8347 6598

WEBB Bruce
S
Abbots Manor, Kirby Cane
Bungay, Suffolk NR35 2HP   Tel: 01508 518703

WEBBER DOUGLAS ACADEMY OF DRAMATIC ART
See DRAMA SCHOOLS (Conference of)

WELBOURNE Jacqueline
(Circus Trainer, Choreographer, Consultant)
c/o Circus Maniacs Agency
Office 8A, Britannia Road
The Kingswood Foundation
Kingswood, Bristol BS15 8DB
e-mail: jackie@circusmaniacs.com
Mobile: 07977 247287   Tel/Fax: 0117-947 7042

WESTMINSTER KINGSWAY COLLEGE
(Performing Arts)
Regent's Park Centre
Longford Street
London NW1 3HB
Website: www.westking.ac.uk
e-mail: courseinfo@westking.ac.uk
Fax: 020-7391 6400   Tel: 020-7556 8001

WHITEHALL PERFORMING ARTS CENTRE
Rayleigh Road
Leigh-on-Sea, Essex SS9 5UU   Tel: 01702 529290

WHITWORTH Geoffrey LRAM, MA
S (Piano Accompanist)
789 Finchley Road
London NW11 8DP   Tel: 020-8458 4281

WILD CREATIVE ARTS THEATRE SCHOOL
(& Private Coaching)
PO Box 222
Rainham, Essex RM13 7WQ
e-mail: wildtm@lineone.net   Tel 01708 505543

WILDER Andrea
D E
23 Cambrian Drive
Colwyn Bay, Conwy LL28 4SL
Website: www.awagency.co.uk
e-mail: andrea@awagency.co.uk
Fax: 07092 249314   Tel: 01492 547542

WILMER Elizabeth J.
E D
34 Campden Street, London W8 7ET   Tel: 020-7727 6624

WILSON Holly
3 Worple Street, Mortlake
London SW14 8HE   Tel: 020-8878 0015

WIMBUSH Martin Dip GSMD
D E Sp (Audition Coaching)
Flat 4, 289 Trinity Road
Wandsworth Common
London SW18 3SN   Tel: 020-8877 0086

WINDSOR Judith MA
(American Accents/Dialects)
Woodbine, Victoria Road, Deal, Kent CT14 7AS
e-mail: joyce.edwards@virgin.net
Fax: 020-7820 1845   Tel: 020-7735 5736

WOOD Tessa Teach Cert AGSM, CSSD, PGVDS
(Voice Coach)
11 Chaucer Road, Poets' Corner
London W3 6DR
e-mail: tessaroswood@aol.com   Tel: 020-8896 2659

WOODHOUSE Alan AGSM ADVS
(Voice & Acting Coach)
33 Burton Road, Kingston upon Thames, Surrey KT2 5TG
e-mail: alanwoodhouse50@hotmail.com
Website: www.woodhousevoice.co.uk
          Tel/Fax: 020-8549 1374

WOODHOUSE Nan (Playwright & LAMDA Examiner)
LGSM (Hons Medal) LLAM, LLCM (TD), ALCM
Write
2 New Street, Morecambe, Lancashire LA4 4BW
e-mail: nan.woodhouse@amserve.com

WORTMAN Neville
(Voice Training & Speech Coach)
48 Chiswick Staithe, London W4 3TP
e-mail: nevillewortman@beeb.net
Mobile: 07976 805976   Tel: 020-8994 8886

Philip Grout - Theatre Director / Actor

40 Years Experience * Private Coaching For Professionals & Students

Tel: 020 8881 1800 * Close to Bounds Green Tube * Full CV on application

WYNN Madeleine
(Director & Acting Coach)
40 Barrie Hse, Hawksley Court, Albion Rd, London N16 0TX
e-mail: madeleine@onetel.net.uk
Tel: 01394 450265   Tel: 020-7249 4487

YOUNG BLOOD Ltd
16 Gunnersbury Close, Chiswick High Road, London W4 4AH
Website: www.youngblood.org.uk
e-mail: info@youngblood.org.uk
Mobile: 07813 463102   Tel: 0845 6449418

YOUNG PERFORMERS THEATRE & POP SCHOOL
SS
Unit 3, Ground Floor, Clements Court
Clements Lane, Ilford, Essex IG1 2QY
e-mail: sara@tots-twenties.co.uk
Fax: 020-8553 1880   Tel: 020-8478 1848

YOUNG STARS
(Part-time Children's Theatre School, Age 5-16 yrs, Drama,
Singing, Dancing)
4 Haydon Dell, Bushey, Herts WD23 1DD
e-mail: youngstars@bigfoot.com
Mobile: 07966 176756   Tel: 020-8950 5782

YOUNG Sylvia THEATRE SCHOOL
SS
Rossmore Road
London NW1 6NJ
e-mail: sylvia@sylviayoungtheatreschool.co.uk
Fax: 020-7723 1040   Tel: 020-7402 0673

YOUNG VICTORIA The
Correspondence: 35 Thorpes Crescent
Skelmanthorpe
Huddersfield HD8 9DH   Tel: 01484 866401

YOUNGSTAR DRAMA SCHOOL
(Evening, Saturday & Holiday Classes, Film, Television &
Theatre 6-20 yrs)
5 Union Castle House, Canute Road
Southampton SO14 3FJ
e-mail: louisayoungstar@aol.com
Fax: 023-8045 5816   Tel: 023-8033 9322

ZANDER Peter
D E SP (German)
22 Romilly Street
London W1D 5AG
e-mail: peterzan.berlin@virgin.net   Tel: 020-7437 4767

European Trades' & Actor's Unions

For information on the FIA please contact
International Federation of Actors
Guild House, Upper St Martin's Lane
London WC2H GEG
Tel: 020-7379 0900 Fax: 020-7379 8260
e-mail: office@fia-actors.com

BELGIUM
ACV - TransCom
Galerie Agora
Rue du Marche aux Herbes 105
Bte 38-40, B-1000 Brussels
e-mail: mhendrickx.transcom@acv-csc.be
Fax: 00 32 2 512 8591   Tel: 00 32 2 549 0769

BELGIUM
CGSP
Confédération Générale des Services Publics
Place Fontainas 9-11, B-1000 Brussels
Fax: 00 32 2 508 59 02   Tel: 00 32 2 508 58 11

DENMARK
DANSK ARTIST FORBUND
Vendersgade 24, DK-1363 Copenhagen K
Website: www.artisen.dk
e-mail: artisten@artisten.dk
Fax: 00 45 33 33 73 30   Tel: 00 45 33 32 66 77

DENMARK
DANSK SKUESPILLERFORBUND
Sankt Knuds Vej 26, DK-1903 Frederiksberg C
Website: www.skuespillerforbundet.dk
e-mail: dsf@skuespillerforbundet.dk
Fax: 00 45 33 24 81 59   Tel: 00 45 33 24 22 00

FINLAND
SNL - SUOMEN NAYTTELIJALIITTO
Temppelikatu 3-5 A 11, SF-00100 Helsinki
e-mail: suomen.nayttelijaliitto@co.inet.fi
Fax: 00 358 9 4342 7350   Tel: 00 353 9 4342 7311

FRANCE
SFA
Syndicat Francais des Artistes-Interpretes
21 bis, rue Victor Masse, F-75009 Paris
Website: www.sfa-cgt.fr
e-mail: international@sfa-cgt.fr
Fax: 00 33 1 53 25 09 01   Tel: 00 33 1 53 25 09 09

GERMANY
GDBA
Genossenschaft Deutscher Bühnen-Angehöriger
Feldbrunnenstrasse 74, D-20148 Hamburg
Website: www.buehnengenossenschaft.de
e-mail: gdba@buehnengenossenschaft.de
Fax: 00 49 40 45 93 52   Tel: 00 49 40 44 51 85

GREECE
HAU - HELLENIC ACTORS' UNION
33 Kaniggos Street, GR-106 82 Athens
Website: www.sei.gr
e-mail: sei@greektour.com
Fax: 00 30 10 380 8651   Tel: 00 30 10 383 3742

GREECE
UGS - UNION OF GREEK SINGERS
130 Patission Street
GR-112 57 Athens
Fax: 00 30 10 823 8321   Tel: 00 30 10 823 8335/6

IRELAND
SIPTU - IRISH ACTORS' EQUITY GROUP
Liberty Hall, Dublin 1
Website: www.siptu.ie
e-mail: equity@siptu.ie
Fax: 00 353 1 874 3691   Tel: 00 353 1 874 0081

[CONTACTS2005]

ITALY
SAI
Sindacato Attori Italiani, Via Ofanto 18, I-00198 Rome
Website: www.cgil.it/sai-slc
e-mail: sai-slc@cgil.it
Fax: 00 39 06 854 6780   Tel: 00 39 06 841 7303/1288

LUXEMBOURG
OGB-L
Onofhängege Gewerkschaftsbond Lëtzebuerg
19 rue d'Epernay, B.P. 2031, L-1020 Luxembourg
Website: www.ogb-l.lu
e-mail: joel.jung@ogb-l.lu
Fax: 00 352 486 949   Tel: 00 352 496 005 Ext 213

NETHERLANDS
FNV KIEM
Kunsten Informatie en Media
Postbus 9354, NL-1006 AJ Amsterdam
Website: www.fnv-kiem.nl
e-mail: fnvkiem@worldonline.nl
Fax: 00 31 20 355 3737   Tel: 00 31 20 355 3636

NORWAY
NSF
Norsk Skuespillerforbund
Welhavensgate 3, N-0166 Oslo
Website: www.skuespillerforbund.no
e-mail: nsf@skuespillerforbund.no
Fax: 00 47 21 02 71 91   Tel: 00 47 21 02 71 90

PORTUGAL
STE
Sindicato dos Trabalhadores de Espectáculos
Rua Da Fe, 23, 2° Piso, P-1050 Lisbon
e-mail: sind.trab.espect@mail.telepac.pt
Fax: 00 351 1 885 3787   Tel: 00 351 1 885 2728

SPAIN
CC.OO.
Plaza Cristino Martos 4
6a Planta, E-28015 Madrid
e-mail: internacional.fct@fct.ccoo.es
Fax: 00 34 91 548 1613   Tel: 00 34 91 540 9295/37

SPAIN
FAEE
Federación de Actores del Estado Español
C/Montera 34, I Piso - D, 28013 Madrid
Website: www.faee.net
e-mail: faee@wanadoo.es
Fax: 00 34 91 522 6055   Tel: 00 34 91 522 2804

SWEDEN
TF TEATERFORBUNDET
Box 12 710, S-112 94 Stockholm
Website: www.teaterforbundet.se
e-mail: info@teaterforbundet.se
Fax: 00 46 8 653 9507   Tel: 00 46 8 441 1300

UK
EQUITY
Guild House
Upper St Martin's Lane
London WC2H 9EG
Website: www.equity.org.uk
e-mail: info@equity.org.uk
Fax: 020-7379 7001   Tel: 020-7379 6000

F

Festivals
Film & Television Distributors
Film Preview Theatres
Film & Video Facilities
Film, Radio, Television & Video Production
   Companies

Key to areas of specialization:
F Films **FF** Feature Films **CV** Corporate Video
D Drama **Ch** Children's Entertainment
Co Comedy & Light Entertainment
Docs Documentaries

Film & Television Schools
Film & Television Studios

[CONTACTS2005]

ALDEBURGH FESTIVAL OF MUSIC AND THE ARTS
(10 - 26 June 2005)
Aldeburgh Productions, Snape Maltings Concert Hall
Snape Bridge, Nr Saxmundham, Suffolk IP17 1SP
Website: www.aldeburgh.co.uk
e-mail: enquiries@aldeburgh.co.uk
Fax: 01728 687120
BO: 01728 687110   Admin: 01728 687100

ALMEIDA OPERA
(Late June - End of July 2005)
Almeida Street, Islington, London N1 1TA
Website: www.almeida.co.uk
e-mail: pdickie@almeidatheatre.demon.co.uk
Fax: 020-7288 4901
BO: 020-7359 4401   Admin: 020-7288 4900

ARUNDEL FRINGE FESTIVAL
(October)
Dramazone, Arundel Town Hall
Arundel, West Sussex BN18 9AP
Director: Kevin Williams
Website: www.arundelfestival.org.uk
e-mail: arundelfringe@aol.com   Tel/Fax: 01963 889821

BARBICAN INTERNATIONAL THEATRE EVENT (BITE)
(Year Round Festival)
Barbican Theatre, Silk Street, London EC2Y 8DS
Website: www.barbican.org.uk
e-mail: lclark@barbican.org.uk
Fax: 020-7382 7377   Tel: 020-7382 7372

BATH INTERNATIONAL MUSIC FESTIVAL
(20 May - 5 June 2005)
Bath Festivals Trust, 5 Broad Street, Bath BA1 5LJ
Website: www.bathfestivals.org.uk
e-mail: info@bathfestivals.org.uk
Fax: 01225 445551
BO: 01225 463362   Tel: 01225 462231

BATH LITERATURE FESTIVAL
(26 February - 6 March 2005)
Bath Festivals Trust
5 Broad Street, Bath BA1 5LJ
Website: www.bathlitfest.org.uk
e-mail: info@bathfestivals.org.uk
Fax: 01225 445551   Tel: 01225 462231

BELFAST FESTIVAL AT QUEEN'S
(21 October - 6 November 2005)
25 College Gardens, Belfast BT9 6BS
Website: www.belfastfestival.com
e-mail: festival@qub.ac.uk
Fax: 028-9097 2630   Tel: 028-9097 2600

BRIGHTON FESTIVAL
(7 - 29 May 2005)
12A Pavilion Buildings
Castle Square, Brighton BN1 1EE
Website: www.brighton-festival.org.uk
e-mail: info@brighton-festival.org.uk
BO: 01273 709709   Admin: 01273 700747

BUXTON FESTIVAL
(8 - 24 July 2005)
5 The Square, Buxton, Derbyshire SK17 6AZ
Website: www.buxtonfestival.co.uk
e-mail: info@buxtonfestival.co.uk
BO: 0845 1272190   Admin: 01298 70395

CARDIFF INTERNATIONAL FESTIVAL OF
MUSICAL THEATRE
(1 - 17 April 2005)
4th Floor, Market Chambers
5/7 St Mary Street
Cardiff CF10 1AT
Website: www.cardiffmusicals.com
e-mail: enquiries@cardiffmusicals.com
Fax: 029-2037 2011   Tel: 029-2034 6999

CHESTER FESTIVALS
(Events July - October 2005)
8 Abbey Square, Chester CH1 2HU
Website: www.chesterfestivals.co.uk   BO: 01244 320700

CHICHESTER FESTIVITIES
(Not Chichester
Festival Theatre)
(3 - 17 July 2005)
Canon Gate House
South Street, Chichester
West Sussex PO19 1PU
Website: www.chifest.org.uk
Fax: 01243 528356   Tel: 01243 785718

CULT TV
(October Annually)
PO Box 1701, Peterborough PE7 1ER
Website: www.cult.tv
e-mail: enquiries@cult.tv   Tel: 01733 205009

DANCE UMBRELLA
(Autumn 2005)
Annual Contemporary Dance Festival
20 Chancellors Street
London W6 9RN
Website: www.danceumbrella.co.uk
e-mail: mail@danceumbrella.co.uk
Fax: 020-8741 7902   Tel: 020-8741 4040

DUBLIN THEATRE FESTIVAL
(26 September - 8 October 2005)
44 East Essex Street
Temple Bar, Dublin 2, Eire
Website: www.dublintheatrefestival.com
e-mail: info@dublintheatrefestival.com
Fax: 00 353 1 6797709   Tel: 00 353 1 6778439

EDINBURGH FESTIVAL FRINGE
(7 - 29 Aug 2005)
Festival Fringe Society Ltd
180 High Street
Edinburgh EH1 1QS
Website: www.edfringe.com
e-mail: admin@edfringe.com
Fax: 0131-226 0016   Tel: 0131-226 0026

EDINBURGH INTERNATIONAL FESTIVAL
(14 August - 4 September 2005)
The Hub, Castlehill
Edinburgh EH1 2NE
Website: www.eif.co.uk
e-mail: eif@eif.co.uk
Tickets: 0131-473 2000   Admin: 0131-437 2099

GREENWICH & DOCKLANDS FESTIVALS
(July 2005)
Festival Office, 6 College Approach
Greenwich, London SE10 9HY
Website: www.festival.org
e-mail: info@festival.org
Fax: 020-8305 1188   Tel: 020-8305 1818

HARROGATE INTERNATIONAL FESTIVAL
(21 July - 6 August 2005)
1 Victoria Avenue, Harrogate
North Yorkshire HG1 1EQ
Website: www.harrogate-festival.org.uk
e-mail: info@harrogate-festival.org.uk
Fax: 01423 521264   Tel: 01423 562303

KING'S LYNN FESTIVAL
(17 - 30 July 2005)
5 Thoresby College, Queen Street
King's Lynn, Norfolk PE30 1HX
Website: www.kl-festival.freeserve.co.uk
Fax: 01553 767688   Tel: 01553 767557

LIFT - LONDON INTERNATIONAL FESTIVAL OF THEATRE
(Events Year Round)
19-20 Great Sutton Street, London EC1V 0DR
Website: www.liftfest.org
e-mail: info@liftfest.org.uk
Fax: 020-7490 3976   Tel: 020-7490 3964

LLANDOVERY THEATRE ARTS FESTIVAL
(July 2005)
Llandovery Theatre
Stone Street, Llandovery
Carmarthenshire SA20 0DQ   Tel: 01550 720113

LUDLOW FESTIVAL SOCIETY Ltd
(18 June - 10 July 2005)
Festival Office, Castle Square, Ludlow, Shropshire SY8 1AY
Website: www.ludlowfestival.co.uk
e-mail: admin@ludlowfestival.co.uk
Fax: 01584 877673
BO: 01584 872150   Admin: 01584 875070

NORWICH FORUM/VAMP STREET THEATRE FESTIVAL
Vamp Street Theatre Productions
Ealing House, 33 Hanger Lane, London W5 3HJ
e-mail: info@vampevents.com   Tel: 020-8997 3355

THE 50th SUNDAY TIMES NATIONAL STUDENT
DRAMA FESTIVAL
(18 - 25 March 2005)
D14, The Foxhole centre
Dartington, Totnes, Devon TQ9 6EB
Website: www.nsdf.org.uk
e-mail: admin@nsdf.org.uk
Fax: 01803 847711   Tel: 01803 864836

VISIONS - FESTIVAL OF VISUAL PERFORMANCE
(21 - 30 October 2004. Next Festival 2006)
University of Brighton Gallery, & Sallis Benney Theatre
University of Brighton, Grand Parade, Brighton BN2 2JY
Website: www.vision-festival.com
e-mail: visions.fest@bton.ac.uk
Fax: 01273 643038   Tel: 01273 643194

FILM & TELEVISION DISTRIBUTORS

ASIAN PICTURES INTERNATIONAL
1st Floor
787 High Road, London E11 4QS
e-mail: enquiries@asianpicturesinternational.com
Fax: 020-8558 9891   Tel: 020-8539 6529

BLUE DOLPHIN FILM AND VIDEO
(Film Production/Video Distribution)
40 Langham Street, London W1W 7AS
Website: www.bluedolphinfilms.com
e-mail: info@bluedolphinfilms.com
Fax: 020-7580 7670   Tel: 020-7255 2494

CONTEMPORARY FILMS
24 Southwood Lawn Road
London N6 5SF
Website: www.contemporaryfilms.com
e-mail: inquiries@contemporaryfilms.com
Fax: 020-8348 1238   Tel: 020-8340 5715

GUERILLA FILMS Ltd
35 Thornbury Road, Isleworth
Middlesex TW7 4LQ
Website: www.guerilla-films.com
e-mail: david@guerilla-films.com
Fax: 020-8758 9364   Tel: 020-8758 1716

HIGH POINT FILMS & TV
(International Sales)
25 Elizabeth Mews, London NW3 4UH
Website: www.highpointfilms.co.uk
e-mail: sales@highpointfilms.co.uk
Fax: 020-7586 3117   Tel: 020-7586 3686

JACKSON Brian FILMS Ltd
39-41 Hanover Steps
St George's Fields
Albion Street, London W2 2YG
e-mail: brianjfilm@aol.com
Fax: 020-7262 5736   Tel: 020-7402 7543

NBC/UNIVERSAL INTERNATIONAL TELEVISION SERVICES Ltd
5-7 Mandeville Place, London W1U 3AR
Fax: 020-7957 0107   Tel: 020-7535 3500

PATHÉ DISTRIBUTION Ltd
Kent House, 14-17 Market Place
Great Titchfield Street, London W1W 8AR
Website: www.pathe.co.uk
Fax: 020-7631 3568   Tel: 020-7323 5151

SONY PICTURES EUROPE HOUSE
25 Golden Square, London W1F 9LU
Fax: 020-7533 1015   Tel: 020-7533 1000

SOUTHERN STAR SALES
45-49 Mortimer Street, London W1W 8HX
Fax: 020-7436 7426   Tel: 020-7636 9421

SQUIRREL FILMS DISTRIBUTION Ltd
Grice's Wharf, 119 Rotherhithe Street, London SE16 4NF
Website: www.sandsfilms.co.uk
Fax: 020-7231 2119   Tel: 020-7231 2209

UIP (UK)
12 Golden Square, London W1A 2JL
Website: www.uip.co.uk
Fax: 020-7534 5202   Tel: 020-7534 5200

UNIVERSAL PICTURES INTERNATIONAL
Oxford House
76 Oxford Street, London W1D 1BS
Fax: 020-7307 1301   Tel: 020-7307 1300

WARNER BROS PICTURES
Warner House
98 Theobald's Road
London WC1X 8WB
Fax: 020-7984 5001   Tel: 020-7984 5000

FILM PREVIEW THEATRES

BRITISH ACADEMY OF FILM & TELEVISION ARTS The
195 Piccadilly, London W1J 9LN
Fax: 020-7734 1792   Tel: 020-7734 0022

BRITISH FILM INSTITUTE
21 Stephen Street, London W1P 1LM
e-mail: roger.young@bfi.org.uk
Fax: 020-7957 4832   Tel: 020-7957 8976

CENTURY THEATRE
(Twentieth Century Fox)
31 Soho Square, London W1D 3AP
e-mail: projection@fox.com   Tel: 020-7437 7766

COLUMBIA TRI STAR FILMS (UK)
25 Golden Square, London W1F 9LU
Fax: 020-7533 1015   Tel: 020-7533 1111

DE LANE LEA
75 Dean Street
London W1D 3PU
Website: www.delanelea.com
e-mail: dll@delanelea.com
Fax: 020-7432 3838   Tel: 020-7432 3800

EXECUTIVE THEATRE
(Twentieth Century Fox)
31 Soho Square
London W1D 3AP
e-mail: projection@fox.com   Tel: 020-7437 7766

MR YOUNG'S PREVIEW THEATRE
14 D'Arblay Street
London W1F 8DY
Fax: 020-7734 4520   Tel: 020-7437 1771

RSA
(Royal Society of Arts)
8 John Adam Street
London WC2N 6EZ
Website: www.theplacetomeet.org.uk
e-mail: conference@rsa.org.uk
Fax: 020-7321 0271   Tel: 020-7839 5049

TRICYCLE CINEMA
269 Kilburn High Road
London NW6 7JR
Website: www.tricycle.co.uk
e-mail: cinema@tricycle.co.uk   Tel: 020-7328 1000

7LA STUDIOS Ltd
(Photographic Services)
42B Medina Road, London N17 7LA
Website: www.7lastudios.co.uk
e-mail: sevenla@blueyonder.co.uk
Mobile: 07960 726957   Tel/Fax: 020-7281 5908

AC ARTS VIDEO PRODUCTION & EQUIPMENT HIRE
(Showreels, CV-CD Roms & Websites)
57 East Dulwich Road, London SE22 9AP
Website: www.ac-arts.co.uk
e-mail: admin@ac-arts.co.uk   Mobile: 07957 750246

ACTIVE PHOTOGRAPHY
(Showreels & Production)
Unit 13, Acton Business Centre,
School Road, London NW10 6TD
Website: www.activephotography.co.uk
e-mail: chris@activephotography.co.uk
Mobile: 07831 541342   Tel: 0800 7812412

ACTOR'S ONE-STOP SHOP The
(Showreels, Photographs, CVs)
54 Belsize Avenue, London N13 4TJ
Website: www.actorsone-stopshop.com
e-mail: info@actorsone-stopshop.com
Tel/Fax: 020-8888 9666   Tel: 020-8888 7006

ANVIL POST PRODUCTION
(Studio Manager - Mike Anscombe)
Denham Media Park, North Orbital Road
Uxbridge, Middlesex UB9 5HL
Website: www.anvilpost.com
e-mail: mike.anscombe@thomson.net
Fax: 01895 835006   Tel: 01895 833522

ARK STUDIO Ltd
(Stills - Studio & Location)
Unit 5, 9 Park Hill, London SW4 9NS
Website: www.arkstudio.co.uk
e-mail: info@arkstudio.co.uk
Fax: 020-7498 9497   Tel: 020-7622 4000

ARRI MEDIA
3 Highbridge, Oxford Road, Uxbridge, Middlesex UB8 1LX
Website: www.arri.com   e-mail: info@arrimedia.com
Fax: 01895 457101   Tel: 01895 457100

ASCENT MEDIA Ltd
(Post-Production Facilities)
Film House, 142 Wardour Street, London W1F 8DD
Website: www.ascentmedia.co.uk
e-mail: sally.hart.info@ascentmedia.co.uk
Fax: 020-7878 7800   Tel: 020-7878 0000

ASCENT MEDIA CAMDEN Ltd
(Post Production Film Facilities)
13 Hawley Crescent, London NW1 8NP
Website: www.ascentmedia.co.uk
Fax: 020-7284 1018   Tel: 020-7284 7900

ASCENT MEDIA GROUP Ltd
(Video & Satellite, Music & Agency)
Video House, 48 Charlotte Street, London W1T 2NS
Website: www.ascentmedia.co.uk
Fax: 020-7208 2227   Tel: 020-7208 2200

AUTOMOTIVE ACTION STUNTS
(Stunt Rigging & Supplies/Camera Tracking Vehicles)
2 Sheffield House, Park Road
Hampton Hill, Middlesex TW12 1HA
Website: www.carstunts.co.uk
Mobile: 07974 919589   Tel: 020-8977 6186

AXIS FILMS
(Film Equipment Rental)
Shepperton Studios, Studios Road
Middlesex TW17 0QD
Website: www.axisfilms.co.uk
e-mail: info@axisfilms.co.uk
Fax: 01932 592246   Tel: 01932 592244

BEWILDERING PICTURES
(Showreel Service) (Graeme Kennedy)
110-116 Elmore Street, London N1 3AH
Website: www.bewildering.co.uk
e-mail: gk@bewildering.co.uk
Mobile: 07974 916258   Tel: 020-7354 9101

CENTRAL FILM FACILITIES
(Camera Tracking Specialists)
c/o The High House, Horderley
Craven Arms, Shropshire SY7 8HT
Website: www.centralfilmfacilities.com   Tel/Fax: 0870 7941418

CHANNEL 20-20 Ltd
Flint House, 91-93 Gray's Inn Road, London WC1X 8TX
Website: www.channel2020.co.uk
e-mail: info@channel2020.co.uk
Fax: 020-7242 4386   Tel: 020-7242 4328

CINE TO VIDEO & FOREIGN TAPE CONVERSION
& DUPLICATING
(Peter J Snell Enterprises)
Amp House, Grove Road
Rochester, Kent ME2 4BX
e-mail: pjstv@blueyonder.co.uk
Fax: 01634 726000   Tel: 01634 723838

CLEAR CUT VIDEO EDITING & FILMING
(Peter J Snell Enterprises)
Amp House, Grove Road, Rochester, Kent ME2 4BX
e-mail: pjstv@blueyonder.co.uk
Fax: 01634 726000   Tel: 01634 723838

CRYSTAL MEDIA
28 Castle Street, Edinburgh EH2 3HT
Website: www.crystal.tv
e-mail: info@crystal-media.co.uk
Fax: 0131-240 0989   Tel: 0131-240 0988

CURIOUS YELLOW Ltd
17 Sugarhouse Lane, Stratford, London E15 2QS
Website: www.curiousyellow.co.uk
e-mail: paul@curiousyellow.co.uk   Tel: 020-8534 0101

DBUG MULTIMEDIA
(Showreels)
50 Weston Park, London N8 9TD
Website: www.dbug.info
e-mail: info@dbug.info   Tel: 020-8342 9143

DE LANE LEA
(Film & TV Sound Dubbing & Editing Suite)
75 Dean Street, London W1D 3PU
Website: www.delanelea.com
e-mail: dll@delanelea.com
Fax: 020-7432 3838   Tel: 020-7432 3800

DENMAN PRODUCTIONS
(3D Computer Animation, Film/Video CD
Business Card Showreels)
60 Mallard Place, Strawberry Vale, Twickenham TW1 4SR
Website: www.denman.co.uk
e-mail: info@denman.co.uk   Tel: 020-8891 3461

DIVERSE PRODUCTIONS
(Pre & Post-Production)
6 Gorleston Street, London W14 8XS
Website: www.diverse.tv
e-mail: reception@diverse.tv
Fax: 020-7603 2148   Tel: 020-7603 4567

EXECUTIVE AUDIO VISUAL
(Showreels for Actors & TV Presenters)
80 York Street, London W1H 1QW   Tel: 020-7723 4488

FARM DIGITAL POST PRODUCTION The
27 Upper Mount Street, Dublin 2, Eire
Website: www.thefarm.ie
e-mail: info@thefarm.ie
Fax: 353 1 676 8816   Tel: 353 1 676 8812

FLYING DUCKS GROUP The Ltd
(Conference, Multimedia & Video Production)
Oakridge, Weston Road, Staffordshire ST16 3RS
Website: enquiries@flyingducks.biz
e-mail: mail@contactgroup.co.uk
Fax: 01785 610955   Tel: 01785 610966

FWF PRODUCTIONS
(Crews & Equipment, Full Beta SP Kit & Chip Mini DV Kit)
71 Ashburnham Road, Ham
Richmond-upon-Thames, Surrey TW10 7NJ
e-mail: david@fwfilms.freeserve.co.uk
Fax: 020-8715 5014   Tel: 020-8715 4861

GREENPARK PRODUCTIONS Ltd
(Film Archives)
Illand, Launceston, Cornwall PL15 7LS
Website: www.greenparkimages.co.uk
e-mail: info@greenparkimages.co.uk
Fax: 01566 782127   Tel: 01566 782107

HULK PRODUCTIONS
(TV Showreels)
PO Box 35762, London E14 8WG
Website: www.hulkproductions.com
e-mail: hulkproductions@aol.com
Fax: 0870 4601686   Mobile: 07970 279277

HUNKY DORY PRODUCTIONS Ltd
(Facilities & Crew)
Cambridge House
135 High Street
Teddington, Middlesex TW11 8HH
Website: www.hunkydory.tv   Tel: 020-8440 0820

HUNTER Ewan
(Freelance Cameraman)
The Cottage To Be
2B East Street, Herne Bay, Kent CT6 5HN
e-mail: ewan.hunter@ukonline.co.uk   Tel: 01227 742843

KINGSTON INMEDIA
Studio K, PO Box 2287
Gerrards Cross, Bucks SL9 8BF
Fax: 01494 876006   Tel: 01494 878297

MAGPIE FILM PRODUCTIONS
31-32 Cheapside, Birmingham B5 6AY
Website: www.magpiefilms.co.uk
Fax: 0121-666 6077   Tel: 0121-622 5884

MINAMON PRODUCTIONS
(Specialist in Showreels)
117 Downton Avenue, London SW2 3TX
e-mail: info@minamonfilm.co.uk
Fax: 020-8674 1779   Tel: 020-8674 3957

MOVING PICTURE COMPANY The
(Post-Production)
127-133 Wardour Street, London W1F 0NL
Website: www.moving-picture.com
e-mail: mailbox@moving-picture.com
Fax: 020-7287 5187   Tel: 020-7434 3100

OCEAN OPTICS
(Underwater Camera Sales & Operator Rental)
13 Northumberland Avenue, London SW2N 5AQ
Betacam SP, Digi Beta & DVCam Digital
e-mail: optics@oceanoptics.co.uk
Fax: 020-7839 6148   Tel: 020-7930 8408

PANAVISION UK
Bristol Road, Greenford, Middlesex UB6 8GD
Website: www.panavision.co.uk
Fax: 020-8839 7300   Tel: 020-8839 7333

PANTECHNICON
(Audio Visual, Video, Conference Production,
Design for Print)
90 Lots Road, London SW10 0QD
Website: www.pantechnicon.co.uk
e-mail: info@pantechnicon.co.uk
Fax: 020-7351 0667   Tel: 020-7351 7579

PEDIGREE PUNKS
(Interactive CD-Rom & DVD Showreels)
49 Woolstone Road, Forest Hill, London SE23 2TR
Website: www.pedigree-punks.com
e-mail: info@pedigree-punks.com   Tel/Fax: 020-8291 5801

PRO-LINK RADIO SYSTEMS Ltd
(Radio Microphones & Communications)
4 Woden Court, Saxon Business Park, Hanbury Road
Bromsgrove, Worcestershire B60 4AD
Website: http://prolink-radio.com
e-mail: service@prolink-radio.com
Fax: 01527 577757   Tel: 01527 577788

Q SOUND
(Voice Recording Studio)
Queen's Studios, 117-121 Salusbury Road, London NW6 6RG
Website: www.qsound.co.uk
e-mail: queries@qsound.uk.com
Fax: 020-7625 5355   Tel: 020-7625 5359

REEL BREAKS
Unit 10 Eurolink Business Centre
49 Effra Road, Brixton SW2 1BZ   Mobile: 07903 408007

REPLAY Ltd
(Showreels & Performance Recording)
199 Piccadilly, London W1J 9HA
Website: www.replayfilms.co.uk
e-mail: sales@replayfilms.co.uk
Fax: 020-7287 5348   Tel: 020-7287 5334

REYNOLDS George F
(Videographer & Editor, Video Production)
12 Mead Close, Grays, Essex RM16 2TR
e-mail: g.f.reynolds@talk21.com   Tel: 01375 373886

SALON Ltd
(Post Production & Editing Equipment Hire)
12 Swainson Road, London W3 7XB
Website: www.salonrentals.com
e-mail: hire@salonrentals.com   Tel: 020-8746 7611

SHOWREEL SERVICES
35 Bedfordbury, Covent Garden, London WC2N 4DU
Fax: 020-7379 5210   Tel: 020-7379 6082

SHOWREELS 1
Qd Studios, 45 Poland Street, London W1F 7NA
Website: www.ukscreen.com/company/showreels1
e-mail: showreels1@aol.com
Fax: 020-7437 2830   Tel: 020-7436 6289

STAR PRODUCTIONS
(Facilities)
Star Studios, 36 Lea Bridge Road
London E5 9QD   Tel: 020-8986 4470

TAKE FIVE
(Showreels)
37 Beak Street, London W1F 9RZ
Website: www.takefivestudio.co.uk
e-mail: info@takefivestudio.co.uk
Fax: 020-7287 3035   Tel: 020-7287 2120

TO BE OR NOT TO BE
(Showreels, Corporate Films) (Anthony Barnett)
48 Northampton Road, Kettering, Northants NN15 7JU
Website: www.tobeornottobe.tv
e-mail: tobeornottobe@ntlworld.com
Mobile: 07958 996227   Tel/Fax: 01536 359631

TVMS (SCOTLAND)
(Video & Broadcast Facilities)
3rd Floor, 420 Sauchiehall Street, Glasgow G2 3JD
e-mail: tvmsmail@aol.com
Fax: 0141-332 9040   Tel: 0141-331 1993

VFG HIRE Ltd
(Film & TV Equipment Hire)
8 Beresford Avenue, Wembley, Middlesex HA0 1LA
e-mail: info@vfg.co.uk
Fax: 020-8795 3366   Tel: 020-8795 7000

VIDEO CASTING DIRECTORY Ltd
(Production of Performers Showreels) (Simon Hicks)
27B Great George Street, Bristol BS1 5QT
e-mail: simon@fightingfilms.com   Mobile: 07958 007231

VIDEO INN PRODUCTION
(AV Equipment Hire)
Glebe Farm, Wooton Road
Quinton, Northampton NN7 2EE
Website: www.videoinn.co.uk
e-mail: andy@videoinn.co.uk   Tel: 01604 864868

VIDEOSONICS CINEMA SOUND
(Film & Television Dubbing Facilities)
68A Delancey Street
London NW1 7RY
Website: www.videosonics.com
e-mail: info@videosonics.com
Fax: 020-7419 4470   Tel: 020-7209 0209

VOICE & SCRIPT INTERNATIONAL
132 Cleveland Street, London W1T 6AB
Website: www.vsi.tv
e-mail: info@vsi.tv
Fax: 020-7692 7711   Tel: 020-7692 7700

VOICE CLINIC The
(Demo's)
99 Cobold Road, London NW10 9SL
e-mail: ptmellor@yahoo.co.uk   Tel: 020-8451 7003

VOICE MASTER
(Digital Studio & Video Editing)
Website: www.voicemaster.info
e-mail: info@voicemaster.info   Tel: 020-8455 2211

VOICE TAPE SERVICES INTERNATIONAL Ltd
(Professional Voice-Over Direction & CDs)
80 Netherlands Road
New Barnet, Herts EN5 1BS
Website: www.vtsint.co.uk
e-mail: info@vtsint.co.uk
Fax: 020-8441 4828   Tel: 020-8440 4848

W6 STUDIO
(Video Production & Editing Facilities)
359 Lillie Road
Fulham, London SW6 7PA
Website: www.w6studio.co.uk
Fax: 020-7381 5252   Tel: 020-7385 2272

WILD IRIS FILMS
59 Brewer Street, London W1R 3FB
e-mail: joe@wildiris.co.uk
Fax: 020-7494 1764   Tel: 020-8374 4536

30 BIRD PRODUCTIONS
138A Kingswood Road, Brixton, London SW2 4JL
e-mail: thirtybirdproductions@ntlworld.com
Tel/Fax: 020-8678 7034

303 PRODUCTIONS
11 D'Arblay Street, London W1F 8DT
e-mail: philburgess@mac.com
Fax: 020-7494 0956 Tel: 020-7494 0955

ACADEMY
16 West Central Street, London WC1A 1JJ
Fax: 020-7240 0355 Tel: 020-7395 4155

AGE FILM & VIDEO
F CV
Fyletts Barn, The Green, Hawstead, Bury St Edmunds
Suffolk INP 5NP Tel: 01284 386629

ALGERNON Ltd
15 Cleveland Mansions, Widley Road, London W9 2LA
Website: www.algernonproductions.com
e-mail: info@algernonproductions.com
Fax: 0870 1388516 Tel: 020-7266 1582

ALIBI PRODUCTIONS Plc
35 Long Acre, London WC2E 9JT
Website: www.alibifilms.co.uk
Fax: 020-7379 7035 Tel: 020-7845 0400

ALIVE EVENTS
Fulton House, Fulton Road
Wembley Park, Middlesex HA9 0TF
Website: www.aliveevents.co.uk
e-mail: simon@aliveevents.co.uk
Fax: 020-8584 0443 Tel: 020-8584 0444

AN ACQUIRED TASTE TV CORP
51 Croham Road, South Croydon CR2 7HD
e-mail: cbennetttv@aol.com
Fax: 020-8686 5928 Tel: 020-8686 1188

APT FILMS
225A Brecknock Road, London N19 5AA
Website: www.aptfilms.com e-mail: admin@aptfilms.com
Fax: 020-7482 1587 Tel: 020-7284 1695

APTN
The Interchange, Oval Road, Camden Lock, London NW1 7DZ
Fax: 020-7413 8312 Tel: 020-7482 7400

ARENA FILMS Ltd
TV D
2 Pelham Road, London SW19 1SX
Fax: 020-8540 3992 Tel: 020-8543 3990

ARIEL PRODUCTIONS Ltd
46 Melcombe Regis Court, 59 Weymouth Street
London W1G 8NT Tel/Fax: 020-7935 6636

ARLINGTON PRODUCTIONS Ltd
TV D Co
Cippenham Court, Cippenham Lane
Cippenham, Nr Slough, Berkshire SL1 5AU
Fax: 01753 691785 Tel: 01753 516767

ART BOX PRODUCTIONS
10 Heatherway, Crowthorne
Berkshire RG45 6HG Tel/Fax: 01344 773638

ASCENT MEDIA Ltd
Film House, 142 Wardour Street, London W1F 8DD
Website: www.ascentmedia.co.uk
e-mail: sally.hart-ives@ascentmedia.co.uk
Fax: 020-7878 7870 Tel: 020-7878 0000

ASF PRODUCTIONS Ltd
38 Clunbury Crt, Manor St, Berkhamsted, Herts HP4 2FF
e-mail: asfc@genmail.net
Fax: 01442 870838 Tel: 01422 872999

ASHFORD ENTERTAINMENT CORPORATION Ltd The
20 The Chase, Coulsdon, Surrey CR5 2EG
Website: www.ashford-entertainment.co.uk
e-mail: info@ashford-entertainment.co.uk
Tel: 020-8660 9609

ATLANTIC SEVEN PRODUCTIONS Ltd
52 Lancaster Road, London N4 4PR
Fax: 020-7436 9233 Tel: 020-7263 4435

ATTICUS TELEVISION Ltd
5 Clare Lawn, London SW14 8BH
e-mail: attwiz@aol.com
Fax: 020-8878 3821 Tel: 020-8487 1173

AVALON TELEVISION Ltd
4A Exmoor Street, London W10 6BD
Fax: 020-7598 7281 Tel: 020-7598 7280

BAILEY Catherine Ltd
110 Gloucester Avenue, Primrose Hill, London NW1 8JA
Fax: 020-7483 2155 Tel: 020-7483 2681

BANANA PARK Ltd
(Animation Production Company)
Banana Park, 6 Cranleigh Mews, London SW11 2QL
Website: www.bananapark.co.uk
e-mail: studio@bananapark.co.uk
Fax: 020-7738 1887 Tel: 020-7228 7136

BARFORD FILM COMPANY The
35 Bedfordbury, London WC2N 4DU
Website: www.barford.co.uk
e-mail: info@barford.co.uk
Fax: 020-7379 5210 Tel: 020-7836 1365

BARRATT Michael
Field House, Ascot Road, Maidenhead, Berkshire SL6 3LD
e-mail: mbarratt@compuserve.com
Fax: 01628 627737 Tel: 01628 770800

BBC WORLDWIDE Ltd
Woodlands, 80 Wood Lane, London W12 0TT
Fax: 020-8749 0538 Tel: 020-8433 2000

BIRD Martin PRODUCTIONS
TV
Saucelands Barn, Coolham
Horsham, West Sussex RH13 8QG
Website: www.mbptv.com
e-mail: info@mbptv.com
Fax: 01403 741647 Tel: 01403 741620

BIZMANE ENTERTAINMENT Ltd
1st Floor, 787 High Road, London E11 4QS
e-mail: enquiries@bizmane.com
Fax: 020-8558 9891 Tel: 020-8558 4488

BLACKBIRD PRODUCTIONS
6 Molasses Row, Plantation Wharf
Battersea, London SW11 3TW
e-mail: enquiries@blackbirdproductions.co.uk
Tel: 020-7924 6440

BLUE FISH MEDIA
39 Ratby Close, Lower Earley, Reading RG6 4ER
Website: www.bfmedia.co.uk
e-mail: ideas@bfmedia.co.uk
Fax: 0118-962 0748 Tel: 0118-975 0272

BLUE WAND PRODUCTIONS Ltd
2nd Floor, 12 Weltje Road, London W6 9TG
Website: www.bluewand.co.uk
e-mail: lino@bluewand.co.uk
Mobile: 07885 528743 Tel/Fax: 020-8741 2038

BLUELINE PRODUCTIONS Ltd
16 Five Oaks Close, Woking, Surrey GU21 8TU
e-mail: david@blue-line.tv Tel: 01483 797002

BOWE TENNANT PRODUCTIONS
(Specialist Animal Pet Productions & Supply of Animals for
Film & TV)
Applewood House Studio, Ringshall Road
Dagnall, Berkhamsted, Herts HP4 1RN
Fax: 01442 842453 Tel: 01923 213008

BRIDGE LANE THEATRE COMPANY Ltd
(Film Production & Script Development)
The Studio, 49 Ossulton Way
London N2 0JY Tel: 020-8444 0505

BRONCO FILMS
F TV D
The Producers' Centre, 61 Holland Street, Glasgow G2 4NJ
Website: www.broncofilms.co.uk
e-mail: broncofilm@btinternet.com
Fax: 0141-287 6815 Tel: 0141-287 6817

BROOKSIDE PRODUCTIONS Ltd
TV
Campus Manor, Childwall, Abbey Road, Liverpool L16 0JP
Fax: 0151-722 6839   Tel: 0151-722 9122

BRUNSWICK FILMS Ltd
(Formula One Grand Prix Film Library)
26 Macroom Road, Maida Vale, London W9 3HY
Website: www.brunswickfilms.com
e-mail: brunswick.films@virgin.net
Fax: 020-8960 4997   Tel: 020-8960 0066

BUCKMARK PRODUCTIONS
Commer House, Station Road
Tadcaster, North Yorkshire LS24 9JF
Website: www.buckmark.co.uk
e-mail: ed@buckmark.co.uk
Fax: 01937 835901   Tel: 01937 835900

BUENA VISTA PRODUCTIONS
3 Queen Caroline Street, Hammersmith, London W6 9PE
Fax: 020-8222 2795   Tel: 020-8222 1000

BURDER FILMS
37 Braidley Road, Meyrick Park, Bournemouth BH2 6JY
Website: www.johnburder.co.uk
e-mail: burderfilms@aol.com   Tel: 01202 295395

CALDERDALE TELEVISION
Dean Clough, Halifax HX3 5AX
e-mail: ctv@calderdaletv.co.uk
Fax: 01422 384532   Tel: 01422 253100

CAMBRIDGE FILM & TELEVISION PRODUCTIONS
Middlewhite Barn, St Georges Way
Impington, Cambridge CB4 9AF
Website: www.cftp.co.uk   e-mail: contact@cftp.co.uk
Fax: 01223 237555   Tel: 01223 236007

CARAVEL FILM TECHNIQUES Ltd
The Great Barn Studios, Cippenham Lane
Slough, Berkshire SL1 5AU
e-mail: ajjcaraveltv@aol.com
Fax: 01494 446662   Tel: 01753 534828

CARDINAL BROADCAST
Bray Film Studios, Down Place, Water Oakley, Windsor,
Berkshire SL4 5UG   Tel: 01628 622111

CARNIVAL (FILMS & THEATRE) Ltd
12 Raddington Road, London W10 5TG
Website: www.carnival-films.co.uk
Fax: 020-8968 0177   Tel: 020-8968 0968

CASE TV.COM
204 Mare Street Studios
203-213 Mare Street, London E8 3QE
e-mail: case@casetv.com
Fax: 020-7296 0011   Tel: 020-7296 0010

CASPIAN PRODUCTIONS
28A Great King Street, Edinburgh EH3 6QH
e-mail: nigel.h@blueyonder.co.uk
Fax: 0131-557 5525   Tel: 0131-556 6667

CELADOR PRODUCTIONS Ltd
39 Long Acre, London WC2E 9LG
Fax: 020-7845 6975   Tel: 020-7240 8101

CELANDINE PRODUCTIONS
39 Pemberton Road, Molesey KT8 9LG
e-mail: producers@celandine.tv   Tel: 020-8941 9991

CELTIC FILMS Ltd
22 Grafton Street, London W1S 4EX
e-mail: info@celticfilms.co.uk
Fax: 020-7409 2383   Tel: 020-7409 2080

CENTRE SCREEN PRODUCTIONS
Eastgate, Castle Street, Castlefield, Manchester M3 4LZ
Website: www.centrescreen.co.uk
e-mail: info@centrescreen.co.uk
Fax: 0161-832 8934   Tel: 0161-832 7151

CENTRELINE VIDEO PRODUCTIONS
138 Westwood Road, Tilehurst, Reading RG31 6LL
Website: www.centrelinevideo.com   Tel: 0118-941 0033

CHANNEL 20/20 Ltd
20/20 House, 26-28 Talbot Lane, Leicester LE1 4LR
Fax: 0116-222 1113   Tel: 0116-233 2220

CHANNEL X Ltd
2nd Floor, Highgate Business Centre
33 Greenwood Place, London NW5 1LB
e-mail: firstname.lastname@channelx.co.uk
Fax: 020-7428 3998   Tel: 020-7428 3999

CHATSWORTH TELEVISION Ltd
D Co
4 Great Chapel Street, London W1F 8FD
Website: www.chatsworth-tv.co.uk
e-mail: television@chatsworth-tv.co.uk
Fax: 020-7437 3301   Tel: 020-7734 4302

CHILDREN'S FILM & TELEVISION FOUNDATION Ltd
Elstree Film & TV Studios, Borehamwood, Herts WD6 1JG
e-mail: annahome@cftf.onyxnet.co.uk
Fax: 020-8207 0860   Tel: 020-8953 0844

CINEMA VERITY PRODUCTIONS Ltd
F TV D Co
11 Addison Avenue, London W11 4QS
Fax: 020-7371 3329   Tel: 020-7460 2777

CLARION TELEVISION
The 1929 Building, Merton Abbey Mills
Watermill Way, London SW19 2RD
Website: www.clariontv.com
e-mail: info@clariontv.com   Tel: 020-8540 0110

CLASSIC PICTURES ENTERTAINMENT Ltd
Shepperton Studios, Studios Road
Shepperton, Middlesex TW17 0QD
e-mail: lyn.beardsall@classicpictures.co.uk
Fax: 01932 592046   Tel: 01932 592016

COLLINGWOOD O'HARE ENTERTAINMENT Ltd
10-14 Crown Street, Acton, London W3 8SB
e-mail: info@crownstreet.co.uk
Fax: 020-8993 9595   Tel: 020-8993 3666

COMMERCIAL BREAKS
Anglia House, Norwich NR1 3JG
Website: www.commercialbreaks.co.uk
e-mail: commercialbreaks@itv.com
Fax: 01603 752610   Tel: 01603 752600

COMMUNICATOR Ltd
199 Upper Street, London N1 1RQ
e-mail: info@communicator.ltd.uk
Fax: 020-7704 8444   Tel: 020-7704 8333

COMTEC Ltd
Unit 19, Tait Road, Croydon, Surrey CR0 2DP
Website: www.comtecav.co.uk e-mail: info@comtecav.co.uk
Fax: 020-8684 6947   Tel: 020-8684 6615

CONVERGENCE PRODUCTIONS Ltd
10-14 Crown Street, Acton, London W3 8SB
e-mail: info@crownstreet.co.uk
Fax: 020-8993 9595   Tel: 020-8993 3666

COURTYARD PRODUCTIONS
TV Ch Co
Little Postlings Farmhouse, Four Elms, Kent TN8 6NA
Fax: 01732 700534   Tel: 01732 700324

COWBOY FILMS
2nd Floor, 87 Notting Hill Gate, London W11 3JZ
Website: www.cowboyfilms.co.uk
e-mail: info@cowboyfilms.co.uk
Fax: 020-7792 0592   Tel: 020-7792 5400

CREATE TV & FILM
33 Bath Road, Slough, Berkshire SL1 3UF
Website: www.createtvandfilm.com
e-mail: info@createtvandfilm.com
Fax: 01753 495225   Tel: 08700 949400

CREATIVE CHANNEL Ltd
The Television Centre, La Pouquelaye
St Helier, Jersey JE1 3ZD
e-mail: creative@channeltv.co.uk
Fax: 01534 816889   Tel: 01534 816888

CREATIVE FILM MAKERS Ltd
Pottery Lane House, 34A Pottery Lane, London W11 4LZ
Fax: 020-7229 4999   Tel: 020-7229 5131

CREATIVE FILM PRODUCTIONS
68 Conway Road, London N14 7BE   Tel: 020-8447 8187

CREATIVE MEDIA
(Part of the ITM Group)
Latimer Square, White Lion Road, Amersham
Buckinghamshire HP7 9JQ   Tel: 0870 8712233

CREATIVE PARTNERSHIP The
13 Bateman Street, London W1D 3AF
Website: www.creativepartnership.co.uk
Fax: 020-7437 1467   Tel: 020-7439 7762

CROFT TELEVISION & GRAPHICS
Croft House, Progress Business Centre
Whittle Parkway, Slough, Berkshire SL1 6DQ
Fax: 01628 668791   Tel: 01628 668735

CTVC
Hillside, Merry Hill Road, Bushey, Herts WD23 1DR
Website: www.ctcv.co.uk
e-mail: ctvc@ctvc.co.uk
Fax: 020-8950 1437   Tel: 020-8950 7919

CUTHBERT Tony PRODUCTIONS
7A Langley Street, London WC2H 9JA
Website: www.tonycuthbert.com
e-mail: info@tonycuthbert.com
Fax: 020-7734 6579   Tel: 020-7437 8884

DALTON FILMS Ltd
127 Hamilton Terrace, London NW8 9QR
Fax: 020-7624 4420   Tel: 020-7328 6169

DARLOW SMITHSON PRODUCTIONS Ltd
4th Floor, Highgate Business Centre
33 Greenwood Place, London NW5 1LB
e-mail: mail@darlowsmithson.com
Fax: 020-7482 7039   Tel: 020-7482 7027

DAWKINS ASSOCIATES Ltd
PO Box 615, Boughton Monchelsea, Kent ME17 4RN
e-mail: da@ccland.demon.co.uk
Fax: 01622 741731   Tel: 01622 741900

DAWSON FILMS
67 Hillfield Park, London N10 3QU
Website: www.dawsonfilms.com
e-mail: mail@dawsonfilms.com
Fax: Tel: 020-8444 6854

DIALOGICS
Square Red Studio, 249-251 Kensal Road, London W10 5DB
e-mail: peter@dialogics.com
Fax: 020-8968 1517   Tel: 020-8960 6069

DIFFERENT FILMS
Website: www.differentfilms.co.uk
e-mail: info@differentfilms.co.uk
Fax: 0845 4585791   Tel: 0845 4585790

DLT ENTERTAINMENT UK Ltd
10 Bedford Square, London WC1B 3RA
Fax: 020-7636 4571   Tel: 020-7631 1184

DON PRODUCTIONS Ltd
26 Shacklewell Lane, London E8 2EZ
Website: www.donproductions.com
e-mail: info@donproductions.com
Fax: 020-7690 4333   Tel: 020-7690 0108

DRAGONFLY FILMS Ltd
King's Head Theatre, 115 Upper Street, London N1 1QN
e-mail: silencego@aol.com   Tel: 020-7354 9259

DRAMA HOUSE The
Coach Road Cottages, Little Saxham
Bury St Edmunds, Suffolk IP29 5LE
Website: www.dramahouse.co.uk
e-mail: jack@dramahouse.co.uk
Fax: 01284 811425   Tel: 01284 810521

DRAMATIS PERSONAE Ltd
(Nathan Silver, Nicolas Kent)
19 Regency Street, London SW1P 4BY
e-mail: nathan.silver@btconnect.com   Tel: 020-7834 9300

DREAMING WILL INITIATIVE The
PO Box 38155, London SE17 3XP
Website: www.londonshakespeare.org.uk/dw.htm
e-mail: londonswo@europe.com   Tel/Fax: 020-7793 9755

DUCK LANE FILM COMPANY The
5 Carlisle Street, London W1D 3BL
Fax: 020-7437 2260   Tel: 020-7439 3912

DVA
8 Campbell Court, Bramley, Hampshire RG26 5EG
Website: www.dvafacilities.co.uk
e-mail: barrieg@dva.co.uk
Fax: 01256 882024   Tel: 01256 882032

ECOSSE FILMS Ltd
Brigade House, 8 Parsons Green, London SW6 4TN
Website: www.ecossefilms.com
e-mail: info@ecossefilms.com
Fax: 020-7736 3436   Tel: 020-7371 0290

EDGE PICTURE COMPANY Ltd The
7 Langley Street, London WC2H 9JA
Website: www.edgepicture.com
e-mail: ask.us@edgepicture.com
Fax: 020-7836 6949   Tel: 020-7836 6262

EDUCATIONAL TRAINING FILMS
17 West Hill, London SW18 1RB   Tel: 020-8870 9933

ELEPHANT PRODUCTIONS
The Studio, 2 Rothamsted Ave, Harpenden, Herts AL5 2DB
e-mail: elephant@elephant-productions.com
Fax: 01582 767532   Tel: 01582 621425

ENDEMOL PRODUCTIONS Ltd
(Formerly BAZAL PRODUCTIONS Ltd)
Shepherds Building Central, Charecroft Way
Shepherds Bush, London W14 0EE
Fax: 0870 3331800   Tel: 0870 3331700

ENLIGHTENMENT PRODUCTIONS
CV
East End House, 24 Ennerdale, Skelmersdale WN8 6AJ
Website: www.trainingmultimedia.co.uk   Tel: 01695 727555

EON PRODUCTIONS Ltd
Eon House, 138 Piccadilly, London W1J 7NR
Fax: 020-7408 1236   Tel: 020-7493 7953

EPA INTERNATIONAL MULTIMEDIA Ltd
31A Regent's Park Road, London NW1 7TL
Fax: 020-7267 8852   Tel: 020-7267 9198

EXCELSIOR GROUP PRODUCTIONS
Dorking Road, Tadworth, Surrey KT20 7TJ
Fax: 01737 813163   Tel: 01737 812673

EYE FILM & TELEVISION
9/11A Dove Street, Norwich, Norfolk NR2 1DE
Website: www.eyefilmandtv.co.uk
e-mail: production@eyefilmandtv.co.uk
Fax: 01603 762420   Tel: 01603 762551

FANTASY FILM COMPANY
74 Vivian Avenue, London NW4 3XG   Tel: 020-8202 4935

FARNHAM FILM COMPANY The
34 Burnt Hill Road, Lower Bourne, Farnham GU10 3LZ
Website: www.farnfilm.com   e-mail: info@farnfilm.com
Fax: 01252 725855   Tel: 01252 710313

FEELGOOD FICTION Ltd
49 Goldhawk Road, London W12 8QP
e-mail: feelgood@feelgoodfiction.co.uk
Fax: 020-8740 6177   Tel: 020-8746 2535

FESTIVAL FILM & TELEVISION Ltd
Festival House, Tranquil Passage
Blackheath Village, London SE3 0BJ
Website: www.festivalfilm.com   e-mail: info@festivalfilm.com
Fax: 020-8297 1155   Tel: 020-8297 9999

FILM & GENERAL PRODUCTIONS Ltd
4 Bradbrook House, Studio Place, London SW1X 8EL
Fax: 020-7245 9853   Tel: 020-7235 4495

FILMS OF RECORD Ltd
2 Elgin Avenue, London W9 3QP
e-mail: films@filmsofrecord.com
Fax: 020-7286 0444   Tel: 020-7286 0333

FIREDOG MOTION PICTURE CORPORATION Ltd The
20 The Chase, Coulsdon, Surrey CR5 2EG
Website: www.firedogfilms.co.uk
e-mail: info@firedogfilms.co.uk   Tel: 020-8660 9609

FIRST WRITES RADIO COMPANY
(Radio Drama Company)
Lime Kiln Cottage, High Starlings
Banham, Norfolk NR16 2BS
Website: www.first-writes.co.uk
e-mail: ellen@firstwrites.fsnet.co.uk
Fax: 01953 888874   Tel: 01953 888525

FLASHBACK TELEVISION Ltd
11 Bowling Green Lane, London EC1R 0BG
Website: www.flashbacktv.com
e-mail: mailbox@flashbacktv.co.uk
Fax: 020-7490 5610   Tel: 020-7490 8996

FLYING DUCKS GROUP The
(Conference Production)
Oakridge, Weston Road, Staffordshire ST16 3RS
Website: www.flyingducks.biz
e-mail: enquiries@flyingducks.biz
Fax: 01785 610955   Tel: 01785 610966

FLYNN PRODUCTIONS Ltd
64 Charlotte Road, London EC2A 3PE
Website: www.flynnproductions.com
e-mail: info@flynnproductions.com
Fax: 020-7729 7279   Tel: 020-7729 7291

FOCUS PRODUCTIONS Ltd
PO Box 173, Stratford-upon-Avon
Warwickshire CV37 7ZA
e-mail: maddern@focusproductions.co.uk
Fax: 01789 294845   Tel: 01789 298948

FORSTATER Mark PRODUCTIONS
27 Lonsdale Road, London NW6 6RA
Fax: 020-7624 1124   Tel: 020-7624 1123

FREEHAND PRODUCTIONS Ltd
97 Clacton Road, London E17 8AP
e-mail: freehanduk@yahoo.com   Tel/Fax: 020-8520 7777

FREMANTLEMEDIA TALKBACKTHAMES
1 Stephen Street, London W1T 1AL
Fax: 020-7691 6100   Tel: 020-7691 6000

FRONT PAGE & CHARISMA FILMS Ltd
Riverbank House, 1 Putney Bridge Approach
London SW6 3JD
Fax: 020-7610 6836   Tel: 020-7610 6830

FULL WORKS The
Mill Studio, Crane Mead
Ware, Herts SG12 9PY   Tel: 01920 444399

FULMAR TELEVISION & FILM Ltd
Pascoe House, 54 Bute Street, Cardiff Bay, Cardiff CF10 5AF
Fax: 029-2045 5111   Tel: 029-2045 5000

GALA PRODUCTIONS Ltd
25 Stamford Brook Road, London W6 0XJ
Website: www.gala-productions.co.uk
e-mail: info@galaproductions.co.uk
Fax: 020-8741 2323   Tel: 020-8741 4200

GALLEON FILMS
Greenwich Playhouse, Station Forecourt
189 Greenwich High Road, London SE10 8JA
Website: www.galleonfilms.co.uk
e-mail: alice@galleontheatre.co.uk   Tel/Fax: 020-8310 7276

GAMMOND Stephen ASSOCIATES
24 Telegraph Lane, Claygate, Surrey KT10 0DU
e-mail: stephengammond@hotmail.com   Tel: 01372 460674

GATEWAY TELEVISION PRODUCTIONS
Gemini House, 10 Bradgate
Cuffley, Herts EN6 4RL   Tel: 01707 872054

GAY Noel TELEVISION Ltd
TV D Ch Co
Shepperton Studios, Studios Road, Middlesex TW17 0QD
e-mail: charles.armitage@virgin.net
Fax: 01932 592172   Tel: 01932 592569

GHA GROUP
1 Great Chapel Street, London W1F 8FA
Website: www.ghagroup.co.uk
e-mail: sales@ghagroup.co.uk
Fax: 020-7437 5880   Tel: 020-7439 8705

GLASS PAGE Ltd The
15 De Montfort Street, Leicester LE1 7GE
Fax: 0116-249 2188   Tel: 0116-249 2199

GRADE COMPANY The
17 Albermarle Street, Mayfair, London W1S 4HP
Fax: 020-7408 2042   Tel: 020-7409 1925

GRANT NAYLOR PRODUCTIONS Ltd
Rooms 950-951, The David Lean Building
Shepperton Studios, Studios Road
Shepperton, Middlesex TW17 0QD
Fax: 01932 592484   Tel: 01932 592175

GREAT GUNS Ltd
43-45 Camden Road, London NW1 9LR
e-mail: greatguns@greatguns.com
Fax: 020-7692 4422   Tel: 020-7692 4444

GREENPOINT FILMS
F TV D
7 Denmark Street, London WC2H 8LZ
Website: www.greenpointfilms.co.uk
e-mail: info@greenpointfilms.co.uk
Fax: 020-7240 7088   Tel: 020-7240 7066

GUERILLA FILMS Ltd
35 Thornbury Road, Isleworth, Middlesex TW7 4LQ
Website: www.guerilla-films.com
e-mail: david@guerilla-films.com
Fax: 020-8758 9364   Tel: 020-8758 1716

HAMMERWOOD FILM PRODUCERS
110 Trafalgar Road, Portslade, Sussex BN41 1GS
Website: www.filmangel.co.uk
e-mail: filmangels@freenetname.co.uk
Fax: 01273 705451   Tel: 01273 277333

HARBOUR PICTURES
11 Langton Street, London SW10 0JL
Website: www.harbourpictures.com
e-mail: info@harbourpictures.com
Fax: 020-7352 3528   Tel: 020-7351 7070

HARTSWOOD FILMS
Twickenham Studios, The Barons
St Margaret's, Twickenham, Middlesex TW1 2AW
Fax: 020-8607 8744   Tel: 020-8607 8736

HASAN SHAH FILMS Ltd
153 Burnham Towers, Adelaide Road, London NW3 3JN
Fax: 020-7483 0662   Tel: 020-7722 2419

HAT TRICK PRODUCTIONS Ltd
TV Co
10 Livonia Street, London W1F 8AF
Fax: 020-7287 9791   Tel: 020-7434 2451

HAWK EYE FILMS
82 Kenley Road, St Margarets
Twickenham TW1 1JU   Tel: 020-8241 7089

HEAD Sally PRODUCTIONS
Twickenham Film Studios, The Barons, St Margaret's
Twickenham, Middlesex TW1 2AW
e-mail: admin@shpl.demon.co.uk
Fax: 020-8607 8964   Tel: 020-8607 8730

HEAVY ENTERTAINMENT Ltd
222 Kensal Road, London W10 5BN
Website: www.heavy-entertainment.com
e-mail: info@heavy-entertainment.com
Fax: 020-8960 9003   Tel: 020-8960 9001

HENSON Jim COMPANY
30 Oval Road, Camden, London NW1 7DE
Website: www.henson.com
Fax: 020-7428 4001   Tel: 020-7428 4000

UK FILM | COUNCIL

The UK Film Council is the lead agency for film in the UK ensuring that the economic, cultural and educational aspects of film are effectively represented at home and abroad.

Co-production and international partnerships are vital to the growth of every part of our industry.

Young Adam

Lara Croft: Tomb Raider

Anita & Me

A selection of films made in the UK

Please visit our web site or contact us for further information.

UK Film Council
10 Little Portland Street, London W1W 7JG
Tel: +44 (0)20 7861 7861, Fax: +44 (0)20 7861 7862
Email: info@ukfilmcouncil.org.uk
Web: www.ukfilmcouncil.org.uk

HEWETT Yvonne
Optimum Productions, 32 Thames Eyot, Cross Deep
Twickenham TW1 4QL   Tel: 020-8892 1403

HINCHLIFFE Barrie PRODUCTIONS Ltd
Unit 2A, Utopia Village, 7 Chalcot Road, London NW1 8LH
Fax: 020-7722 6229   Tel: 020-7722 2261

HIT ENTERTAINMENT Plc
5th Flr, Maple Hse, 149 Tottenham Crt Rd, London W1T 7NF
Website: www.hitentertainment.com
e-mail: creative@hitentertainment.com
Fax: 020-7388 9321   Tel: 020-7554 2500

HOLMES ASSOCIATES & OPEN ROAD FILMS
F TV D
The Studio, 37 Redington Road, London NW3 7QY
e-mail: holmesassociates@blueyonder.co.uk
Fax: 020-7813 4334   Tel: 020-7813 4333

HUDSON FILM Ltd
24 St Leonard's Terrace
London SW3 4QG   Tel: 020-7730 0002

HUNGRY MAN Ltd
19 Grafton Mews, London W1T 5JB
Website: www.hungryman.com
e-mail: receptionuk@hungryman.com
Fax: 020-7380 8299   Tel: 020-7380 8280

HUNKY DORY PRODUCTIONS Ltd
TV D Co
Cambridge Hse, 135 High St, Teddington, Middx TW11 8HH
Fax: 020-8977 4464   Tel: 020-8440 0820

HURLL Michael TELEVISION Ltd
3rd Floor, Beaumont House
Kensington Village, Avonmore Road, London W14 8TS
e-mail: sgraff@uniquegroup.co.uk
Fax: 020-7605 1201   Tel: 020-7605 1200

HURRICANE FILMS Ltd
19 Hope Street, Liverpool L1 9BQ
Website: www.hurricanefilms.net
e-mail: sol@hurricanefilms.co.uk
Fax: 0151-707 9149   Tel: 0151-707 9700

IAMBIC PRODUCTIONS Ltd
1st Floor, 31 Eastcastle Street, London W1W 8DL
e-mail: team@iambicproductions.com
Fax: 020-7637 7084   Tel: 020-7436 1400

ICON FILMS Ltd
4 West End, Somerset Street, Bristol BS2 8NE
Fax: 0117-942 0386   Tel: 0117-924 8535

IMMEDIA TELEVISION COMMUNICATIONS Ltd
Carlton Studios, Lenton Lane, Nottingham NG7 2NA
Website: www.immediagroup.co.uk
e-mail: info@immediagroup.co.uk
Fax: 0115-964 5502   Tel: 0115-964 5505

IMPEY Jason FILM & VIDEO PRODUCTIONS
10 Linden Grove, Great Linford
Milton Keynes, Bucks MK14 5HF
Website: www.jasonimpey.co.uk
e-mail: jason.impey@freeuk.com
Mobile: 07732 476409   Tel: 01408 676081

INFORMATION TRANSFER Ltd
CV (Training Video Packages)
Burleigh House, 15 Newmarket Road, Cambridge CB5 8EG
Fax: 01223 310200   Tel: 01223 312227

INTERESTING TELEVISION Ltd
Oakslade Studios, Station Road, Hatton, Warwick CV35 7LH
Fax: 01926 844045   Tel: 01926 844044

ISIS PRODUCTIONS Ltd
106 Hammersmith Grove, London W6 7HB
Website: www.isisproductions.co.uk
e-mail: isis@isis-productions.com
Fax: 020-8748 3046   Tel: 020-8748 3042

IWC MEDIA
3-6 Kenrick Place, London W1U 6HD
e-mail: info@iwcmedia.co.uk
Fax: 020-7317 2231   Tel: 020-7317 2230

JACKSON Brian FILMS Ltd
F TV Ch
39-41 Hanover Steps, St George's Fields
Albion Street, London W2 2YG
e-mail: brianjfilm@aol.com
Fax: 020-7262 5736   Tel: 020-7402 7543

JMS GROUP Ltd
Hethersett, Norwich, Norfolk, NR9 3DL
Website: www.jms-group.com
e-mail: info@jmsradio.co.uk
Fax: 01603 812255   Tel: 01603 811855

KCD FILMS Ltd
6 Eglon Mews, Primrose Hill, London NW1 8YS
e-mail: bill@eglon.freeserve.co.uk   Tel: 020-7586 4813

KELPIE FILMS
227 St Andrews Road, Glasgow G41 1PD
Website: www.kelpiefilms.com
e-mail: info@kelpiefilms.com
Fax: 0141-429 8438   Tel: 0141-429 3565

KICK PRODUCTION Ltd
50 Greek Street, Soho, London W1D 4EQ
e-mail: admin@kickproduction.co.uk
Fax: 020-7437 0125   Tel: 020-7287 3757

KINGFISHER TELEVISION PRODUCTIONS Ltd
Carlton Studios, Lenton Lane, Nottingham NG7 2NA
Fax: 0115-964 5263   Tel: 0115-964 5262

KNOWLES Dave FILMS
(Also Multimedia Interactive CD-Roms)
34 Ashleigh Close, Hythe SO45 3QP
Website: www.dkfilms.co.uk
e-mail: mail@dkfilms.co.uk
Fax: 023-8084 1600   Tel: 023-8084 2190

LANDSEER PRODUCTIONS Ltd
140 Royal College Street, London NW1 0TA
Website: www.landseerfilms.com
e-mail: mail@landseerfilms.com
Fax: 020-7485 7573   Tel: 020-7485 7333

LARGE BEAST PRODUCTIONS Ltd
Number 1, 38 Rowallan Road, London SW6 6AG
Website: www.largebeastproductions.com
e-mail: email@largebeastproductions.com
    Tel: 020-7381 8228

LE PARK TV Ltd
Windmill Studios, 49-51 York Rd, Brentford, Middx TW8 0QP
Website: www.leparktv.com   e-mail: ian@leparktv.com
Fax: 020-8568 4151   Tel: 020-8568 5855

LINK ENTERTAINMENT Ltd
Colet Court, 100 Hammersmith Road, London W6 7JP
Fax: 020-8762 6299   Tel: 020-8762 6200

LITTLE BIRD COMPANY Ltd
9 Grafton Mews, London W1T 5HZ
e-mail: info@littlebird.co.uk
Fax: 020-7380 3981   Tel: 020-7380 3980

LITTLE KING COMMUNICATIONS
The Studio, 2 Newport Road, Barnes, London SW13 9PE
Fax: 020-8653 2742   Tel: 020-8741 7658

LITTLE WING FILMS Ltd
The Old Laundry, Ossington Buildings, London W1V 4JZ
Website: www.lwf.info   e-mail: lwf@info
Fax: 020-7935 1970   Tel: 020-7486 6550

LIVE IN FIVE PRODUCTIONS
14 Kingsmead Road, London SW2 3JB
Website: www.liveinfive.co.uk
e-mail: enquiries@liveinfive.co.uk
Fax: 020-8674 0543   Tel: 020-8674 5964

LONDON COLLEGE OF COMMUNICATION
(Film & Video Division)
Elephant & Castle, London SE1 6SB
Fax: 020-7514 6848   Tel: 020-7514 6500

LONDON FILMS
71 South Audley Street, London W1K 1JA
Website: www.londonfilms.com
Fax: 020-7499 7994   Tel: 020-7499 7800

LONDON SCIENTIFIC FILMS
Mill Studio, Crane Mead, Ware
Herts SG12 9PY   Tel: 01920 444399

LOOKING GLASS FILMS Ltd
103 Brittany Point, Ethelred Estate
Kennington, London SE11 6UH
e-mail: lookingglassfilm@aol.com   Tel/Fax: 020-7735 1363

LOOP COMMUNICATION AGENCY The
Hanover House, Queen Charlotte Street, Bristol BS1 4EX
e-mail: info@theloopagency.com
Fax: 0117-311 2041   Tel: 0117-311 2040

MAGICIAN PICTURES Ltd
Suite 2E, Horseshoe Business Park
Upper Lye Lane, Bricket Wood, Herts AL2 3TA
Website: www.magician-pictures.co.uk
e-mail: admin@magician-pictures.co.uk
Fax: 01923 673808   Tel: 01923 661499

MAGPIE FILM PRODUCTIONS Ltd
31-32 Cheapside, Birmingham B5 6AY
Fax: 0121-666 6077   Tel: 0121-622 5884

MALLINSON TELEVISION PRODUCTIONS
(TV Commercials)
29 Lynedoch Street, Glasgow G3 6EF
e-mail: shoot@mtp.co.uk
Fax: 0141-332 6190   Tel: 0141-332 0589

MALONE GILL PRODUCTIONS Ltd
27 Campden Hill Road, London W8 7DX
e-mail: malonegill@aol.com
Fax: 020-7376 1727   Tel: 020-7937 0557

MANIC TELEVISION & FILM
112 Skyline Plaza, 80 Commercial Road, London E1 1NZ
Website: www.themanicgroup.com
e-mail: info@themanicgroup.com
Fax: 020-7059 0498   Tel: 020-7481 1898

MANS Johnny PRODUCTIONS Ltd
PO Box 196, Hoddesdon, Herts EN10 7WG
Fax: 01992 470516   Tel: 01992 470907

MANSFIELD Mike TELEVISION Ltd
5th Floor, 41-42 Berners Street, London W1T 3NB
e-mail: mikemantv@aol.com
Fax: 020-7580 2582   Tel: 020-7580 2581

MAP FILMS
3 Bourlet Close, London W1W 7BQ
e-mail: mail@mapfilms.com
Fax: 020-7291 7841   Tel: 020-7291 7840

MARTIN William PRODUCTIONS
The Studio, Tubney Warren Barns
Tubney, Oxfordshire OX13 5QJ
Website: www.wmproductions.co.uk
e-mail: info@wmproductions.co.uk
Fax: 01865 390234   Tel: 01865 390258

MAVERICK MEDIA Ltd
5th Floor, 74 Newman Street, London W1T 3EL
Website: www.maverickmedia.co.uk
e-mail: info@maverickmedia.co.uk
Fax: 020-7323 4143   Tel: 020-7291 3450

MAVERICK TELEVISION
Progress Works, The Custard Factory
Heath Mill Lane, Birmingham B9 4AL
e-mail: mail@mavericktv.co.uk
Fax: 0121-771 1550   Tel: 0121-771 1812

MAX MEDIA
The Lilacs, West End, Woodhurst
Huntingdon, Cambridge PE28 3BH
Website: www.therealmaxmedia.com
e-mail: therealmaxmedia@aol.com
Fax: 01487 823468   Tel: 01487 823608

MAYA VISION INTERNATIONAL
43 New Oxford Street, London WC1A 1BH   Tel: 020-7836 1113

MEANPEACH
11 Coniston Court, Hanger Hill, Weybridge, Surrey KT13 9YR
Website: www.meanpeach.com
e-mail: info@meanpeach.com
Fax: 01932 855598   Tel: 01932 858724

MENTORN
43 Whitfield Street, London W1T 4HA
Fax: 020-7258 6888   Tel: 020-7258 6800

MERCHANT IVORY PRODUCTIONS
46 Lexington Street, London W1F 0LP
Website: www.merchantivory.com
e-mail: miplondon@merchantivory.demon.co.uk
Fax: 020-7734 1579   Tel: 020-7437 1200

MERSEY TELEVISION COMPANY Ltd The
TV
Campus Manor, Childwall, Abbey Road, Liverpool L16 0JP
Fax: 0151-722 6839   Tel: 0151-722 9122

MIGHTY MEDIA
Long Boyds House, PO Box 73, Bourne End
Buckinghamshire SL8 5FJ
Fax: 01628 526530   Tel: 01628 522002

MINAMON PRODUCTIONS
117 Downton Avenue, London SW2 3TX
Website: www.minamonfilm.co.uk
e-mail: info@minamonfilm.co.uk
Fax: 020-8674 1779   Tel: 020-8674 3957

MISTRAL FILM LONDON
31 Oval Road, London NW1 7EA
e-mail: info@mistralfilm.co.uk
Fax: 020-7284 0547   Tel: 020-7284 2300

MODUS OPERANDI FILMS
10 Soho Square, London W1V 6NT
Fax: 020-7243 8199   Tel: 020-7434 1440

MOONLIGHT COMMUNICATIONS Ltd
48 Vyse Street, Hockley, Birmingham B18 6HF
e-mail: norman.moonlight@btclick.com
Fax: 0121-551 6455   Tel: 0121-523 6221

MORE Alan FILMS
Pinewood Studios, Pinewood Road, Iver, Bucks SL0 0NH
e-mail: almorefilm@aol.com
Fax: 01753 650988   Tel: 01753 656789

MORRISON COMPANY The
302 Clive Court, Maida Vale, London W9 1SF
e-mail: don@morrisonco.com
Fax: 0870 1275065   Tel: 020-7289 7976

MOSAIC FILMS
The Old Butcher's Shop
St Briavels, Gloucestershire GL15 6TA
e-mail: info@mosaicfilms.com
Fax: 01594 530094   Tel: 01594 530708

MOVE A MOUNTAIN PRODUCTIONS
5 Ashchurch Park Villas, London W12 9SP
Website: www.moveamountain.com
e-mail: mail@moveamountain.com   Tel: 020-8743 3017

MURPHY Patricia FILMS Ltd
Lock Keepers Cottage, Lyme Street, London NW1 0SF
e-mail: office@patriciamurphy.co.uk
Fax: 020-7485 0555   Tel: 020-7267 0007

NEBRASKA PRODUCTIONS
12 Grove Avenue, London N10 2AR
e-mail: nebraskaprods@aol.com
Fax: 020-8444 2113   Tel: 020-8444 5317

NEW MOON TELEVISION
8 Ganton Street, London W1F 7QP
Website: www.new-moon.co.uk
e-mail: production@new-moon.co.uk
Fax: 020-7479 7011   Tel: 020-7479 7010

NEWGATE COMPANY
(Radio)
40 Wellington Court, Weymouth
Dorset DT4 8UA   Tel: 01305 770015

NEXUS PRODUCTIONS Ltd
(Animation for Commercials, Pop Promos & Title Sequences)
113-114 Shoreditch High Street, London E1 6JN
Website: www.nexusproductions.com
e-mail: info@nexusproductions.com
Fax: 020-7749 7501   Tel: 020-7749 7500

N F D PRODUCTIONS Ltd
21 Low Street, South Milford LS25 5AR
Website: www.nfdproductions.com
e-mail: info@nfdproductions.com
Mobile: 07932 653466   Tel/Fax: 01977 681949

NUTOPIA-CHANG FILMS
Number 8, 132 Charing Cross Road, London WC2H 0LA
Website: www.nutopia.co.uk
Fax: 029-2070 9440   Mobile: 07801 493133

OMNI PRODUCTIONS Ltd
Studio 44, Easton Business Centre
Felix Road, Bristol BS5 0HE
Website: www.omniproductions.co.uk
e-mail: creation@omniproductions.co.uk   Tel: 0117-941 5820

ON COMMUNICATION/ON TV
(Work across all Media in Business Communications,
Museum Prods & Broadcast Docs)
5 East St Helen Street, Abingdon, Oxford OX14 5EG
Website: www.oncomms-tv.co.uk
e-mail: on@oncomms-tv.co.uk
Fax: 01235 530581   Tel: 01235 537400

ON SCREEN PRODUCTIONS Ltd
Ashbourne House, 33 Bridge Street
Chepstow, Monmouth NP16 5GA
Website: www.onscreenproductions.co.uk
e-mail: action@onscreenproductions.co.uk
Fax: 01291 636301   Tel: 01291 636300

OPEN DOORS ASSOCIATES COMPANY Ltd
2 Rathmore Road, Chelston, Torquay, Devon TQ2 6NY
e-mail: barrygout@tiscali.co.uk
Mobile: 07899 965420   Tel: 01803 200558

OPEN DOORS PRODUCTIONS Ltd
2 Rathmore Road, Chelston, Torquay, Devon TQ2 6NY
e-mail: barrygout@tiscali.co.uk   Tel/Fax: 01803 212892

OPEN MIND PRODUCTIONS
6 Newburgh Street, London W1F 7RQ
e-mail: production.manager@openmind.co.uk
Fax: 020-7434 9256   Tel: 020-7437 0624

OPEN SHUTTER PRODUCTIONS Ltd
100 Kings Road, Windsor
Berkshire SL4 2AP   Tel/Fax: 01753 841309

ORIGINAL FILM & VIDEO PRODUCTIONS Ltd
84 St Dionis Road, London SW6 4TU
e-mail: original.films@btinternet.com
Fax: 020-7731 0027   Tel: 020-7731 0012

OVC MEDIA Ltd
88 Berkeley Court, Baker Street, London NW1 5ND
Website: www.ovcmedia.com
e-mail: eliot@ovcmedia.co.uk
Fax: 020-7723 3064   Tel: 020-7402 9111

PALADIN INVISION
8 Barb Mews, London W6 7PA
Fax: 020-7371 2160   Tel: 020-7371 2123

PALIN Barry ASSOCIATES
Unit 10, Princeton Court, 55 Felsham Rd, London SW15 1AZ
e-mail: mail@barrypalinassociates.com
Fax: 020-8785 0440   Tel: 020-8394 5660

PANTECHNICON
90 Lots Road, London SW10 0QD
e-mail: info@pantechnicon.co.uk
Fax: 020-7351 0667   Tel: 020-7351 7579

PAPER MOON PRODUCTIONS
Wychwood House, Burchetts Green Lane, Littlewick Green
Maidenhead, Berkshire SL6 3QW
e-mail: david@paper-moon.co.uk
Fax: 01628 825949   Tel: 01628 829819

PARADINE David PRODUCTIONS Ltd
1st Floor, 5 St Mary Abbot's Pl, Kensington, London W8 6LS
Fax: 020-7602 0411   Tel: 020-7371 3111

PARALLAX INDEPENDENT Ltd
7 Denmark Street, London WC2H 8LZ
Fax: 020-7497 8062   Tel: 020-7836 1478

PARAMOUNT FILM SERVICES Ltd
UIP House, 45 Beadon Road, London W6 0EG
Fax: 020-8563 4266   Tel: 020-8563 4158

PARK VILLAGE Ltd
1 Park Village East, London NW1 7PX
e-mail: reception@parkvillage.co.uk
Fax: 020-7388 3051   Tel: 020-7387 8077

PARLIAMENTARY FILMS Ltd
11A Enterprise House, 59-65 Upper Ground, London SE1 9PQ
Fax: 020-7827 9511   Tel: 020-7827 9514

PASSION PICTURES Ltd
Animation
3rd Floor, 33-34 Rathbone Place, London W1T 1JN
e-mail: info@passion-pictures.com
Fax: 020-7323 9030   Tel: 020-7323 9933

PATHÉ PICTURES Ltd
Kent House, 14-17 Market Place
Great Titchfield Street, London W1W 8AR
Website: www.pathe.co.uk
Fax: 020-7631 3568   Tel: 020-7323 5151

PCI LIVE DESIGN
(Live Events, Live Design Exhibitions, Film & Video,
2D & 3D Design)
G4 Harbour Yard, Chelsea Harbour, London SW10 0XD
Fax: 020-7352 7906   Tel: 020-7544 7500

PERSONIFICATION FILMS Ltd
97 Choumert Road, London SE15 4AP
Website: www.personificationfilms.com
e-mail: rabbie@personificationfilms.com
                          Tel/Fax: 020-7639 9295

PICTURE PALACE FILMS Ltd
13 Egbert Street, London NW1 8LJ
Website: www.picturepalace.com
e-mail: info@picturepalace.com
Fax: 020-7586 9048   Tel: 020-7586 8763

PIE FILMS
Write: PO Box 42301, London N12 9YR
Website: www.pie.uk.net   e-mail: film@pie.uk.net

PIER PRODUCTIONS Ltd
Lower Ground Floor, 1 Marlborough Place, Brighton BN1 1TU
e-mail: pieradmin@mistral.co.uk
Fax: 01273 693658   Tel: 01273 691401

PIEREND PRODUCTIONS
34 Fortis Green, London N2 9EL
e-mail: russell@pierend.fsnet.co.uk   Tel: 020-8444 0138

POKER Ltd
143B Whitehall Court
London SW1A 2EL   Tel/Fax: 020-7839 6070

POSITIVE IMAGE Ltd
25 Victoria Street, Windsor, Berkshire SL4 1HE
Fax: 01753 830878   Tel: 01753 842248

POZZITIVE TELEVISION Ltd
Paramount House, 162-170 Wardour Street, London W1F 8AB
e-mail: pozzitive@pozzitive.demon.co.uk
Fax: 020-7437 3130   Tel: 020-7734 3258

PRETTY CLEVER PICTURES
Iping Mill, Iping, Midhurst, West Sussex GU29 0PE
e-mail: pcpics@globalnet.co.uk
Mobile: 07836 616981   Tel: 01730 817899

PRINCIPAL PICTURES Ltd
Picture House, 65 Hopton Street, London SE1 9LR
e-mail: pictures@principalmedia.com
Fax: 020-7928 9886   Tel: 020-7928 9287

PRISM ENTERTAINMENT
1-2 Grand Union Centre
West Row Courtyard, London W10 5AS
Website: www.prismentertainment.co.uk
e-mail: info@prism-e.com
Fax: 020-8969 1012   Tel: 020-8969 1212

PRODUCERS The
8 Berners Mews, London W1T 3AW
Website: www.theproducersfilms.co.uk
Fax: 020-7636 4099   Tel: 020-7636 4226

PRODUCTION LINKS
68 Oakfield Road, Clifton, Bristol BS8 2BG
Website: www.productionlinks.tv
e-mail: info@productionlinks.tv
Fax: 0117-973 6038   Tel: 0117-973 6037

PRODUCTIONS & PROMOTIONS Ltd
2 Sharpcroft, Hemel Hempstead, Herts HP2 5YY
Website: www.prodmotions.com
e-mail: stuartw@prodmotions.com   Tel/Fax: 01442 236821

PROFESSIONAL MEDICAL COMMUNICATIONS Ltd
Grosvenor House, 1 High Street, Edgware
Middlesex HA8 7TA   Tel: 020-8381 1819

PROMENADE ENTERPRISES Ltd
6 Russell Grove, London SW9 6HS
e-mail: promenadeproductions@msn.com
Fax: 020-7564 3026   Tel: 020-7582 9354

PSA Ltd
52 The Downs, Altrincham WA14 2QJ
e-mail: info@psafilms.co.uk
Fax: 0161-924 0022   Tel: 0161-924 0011

PURPLE FROG MEDIA Ltd
19 Westbourne Gardens, Hove BN3 5PL
e-mail: julie@purplefrogmedia.com
Fax: 01273 775787   Tel: 01273 735475

PVA MANAGEMENT Ltd
Hallow Park, Hallow, Worcs WR2 6PG
e-mail: films@pva.co.uk
Fax: 01905 641842   Tel: 01905 640663

QUADRANT TELEVISION Ltd
17 West Hill, London SW18 1RB
Website: www.quadrant-tv.com
e-mail: quadranttv@aol.com   Tel: 020-8870 9933

QUADRILLION
The Old Barn, Kings Lane
Cookham Dean, Berkshire SL6 9AY
Website: www.quadrillion.tv
e-mail: enq@quadrillion.net
Fax: 01628 487523   Tel: 01628 487522

QUARK TV Ltd
5 Broadway Market Mews, Benjamin Close, London E8 4TS
Website: www.quarktv.co.uk
e-mail: quarktv@btclick.com
Fax: 020-7241 1451   Tel: 020-7254 5049

RAW CHARM Ltd
Ty Cefn, Rectory Road, Cardiff CF5 1QL
Website: www.rawcharm.tv
e-mail: kate@rawcharm.co.uk
Fax: 029-2066 8220   Tel: 029-2064 1511

READ Rodney
45 Richmond Road, Twickenham, Middlesex TW1 3AW
e-mail: rodney_read@blueyonder.co.uk
Fax: 020-8744 9603   Tel: 020-8891 2875

RECORDED PICTURE COMPANY Ltd
24-26 Hanway Street, London W1T 1UH
Fax: 020-7636 2261   Tel: 020-7636 2251

RED KITE Animation
89 Giles Street, Edinburgh EH6 6BZ
Website: www.redkite-animation.com
e-mail: info@redkite-animation.com
Fax: 0131-554 6007   Tel: 0131-554 0060

RED ROSE CHAIN
1 Fore Hamlet, Ipswich IP3 8AA
Website: www.redrosechain.co.uk
e-mail: info@redrosechain.co.uk   Tel: 01473 288886

REDWEATHER PRODUCTIONS
Easton Business Centre, Felix Road, Bristol BS5 0HE
Website: www.redweather.co.uk
e-mail: info@redweather.co.uk
Fax: 0117-941 5851   Tel: 0117-941 5854

REEL THING Ltd The
20 The Chase, Coulsdon, Surrey CR5 2EG
Website: www.reelthing.tv
e-mail: info@reelthing.tv   Tel: 020-8668 8188

REPLAY Ltd
199 Piccadilly, London W1J 9HA
Website: www.replayfilms.co.uk
e-mail: sales@replayfilms.co.uk
Fax: 020-7287 5348   Tel: 020-7287 5334

RESOURCE BASE
Television Centre, Southampton SO14 0PZ
Website: www.resource-base.co.uk
e-mail: post@resource-base.co.uk
Fax: 023-8023 6816   Tel: 023-8023 6806

REUTERS TELEVISION
85 Fleet Street, London EC4P 4AJ   Tel: 020-7250 1122

REVERE ENTERTAINMENT
91 Berwick Street, London W1F 0NE
Fax: 020-7292 8372   Tel: 020-7292 8370

RIVERSIDE TV STUDIOS
Riverside Studios, Crisp Road, London W6 9RL
e-mail: info@riversidetv.co.uk
Fax: 020-8237 1121   Tel: 020-8237 1123

RM ASSOCIATES DISTRIBUTION Ltd
Shepherds West, Rockley Road, London W14 0DA
Website: www.rmassociates.co.uk
e-mail: rma@rmassociates.co.uk
Fax: 020-7605 6610   Tel: 020-7605 6600

ROCLIFFE
PO Box 37344, London N1 8YB
Website: www.rocliffe.com
e-mail: info@rocliffe.com   Tel: 020-7221 7669

ROGERS Peter PRODUCTIONS Ltd
Pinewood Studios, Iver Heath
Buckinghamshire SL0 0NH   Tel: 01753 651700

ROOKE Laurence PRODUCTIONS
14 Aspinall House, 155 New Park Road, London SW2 4EY
Mobile: 07765 652058   Tel: 020-8674 3128

ROSE HACKNEY BARBER Ltd
5-6 Kingly Street, London W1B 5PF
Fax: 020-7434 4102   Tel: 020-7439 6697

ROUGE VIDEO
(Video Production)
53 Nightingale Road, London E5 8NB
Website: www.rougevideo.com
e-mail: info@rougevideo.com
Mobile: 07711 863573   Tel/Fax: 020-8533 3877

RSA FILMS
42-44 Beak Street, London W1F 9RH
Fax: 020-7734 4978   Tel: 020-7437 7426

RUSSO Denis ASSOCIATES
F TV Animation
161 Clapham Road, London SW9 0PU
Fax: 020-7582 2725   Tel: 020-7582 9664

SAMUELSON PRODUCTIONS Ltd
13 Manette Street, London W1D 4AW
e-mail: samuelsonp@aol.com
Fax: 020-7439 4901   Tel: 020-7439 4900

SANDS FILMS
Grice's Wharf, 119 Rotherhithe Street, London SE16 4NF
Website: www.sandsfilms.co.uk
Fax: 020-7231 2119   Tel: 020-7231 2209

SCALA PRODUCTIONS Ltd
4th Floor, Portland House
4 Great Portland Street, London W1W 8QJ
e-mail: scalaprods@aol.com
Fax: 020-7437 3248   Tel: 020-7734 7060

SCIMITAR FILMS Ltd
219 Kensington High Street, London W8 6BD
e-mail: winner@ftech.co.uk
Fax: 020-7602 9217   Tel: 020-7734 8385

SCREEN FIRST Ltd
The Studios, Funnells Farm
Down Street, Nutley, East Sussex TN22 3LF
e-mail: paul.madden@virgin.net
Fax: 01825 713511   Tel: 01825 712034

SCREEN VENTURES
49 Goodge Street, London W1T 1TE   Tel: 020-7580 7448

SEDDON FILMS
(Commercials)
51-53 Mount Pleasant, London WC1X 0AE
Website: www.tabletp.com
e-mail: alison@julianseddonfilms.com
Fax: 020-7405 3721   Tel: 020-7831 3033

SEPTEMBER FILMS Ltd
Glen Hse, 22 Glenthorne Rd, Hammersmith, London W6 0NG
Fax: 020-8741 7214   Tel: 020-8563 9393

SEVENTH ART PRODUCTIONS
63 Ship Street, Brighton BN1 1AE
Website: www.seventh-art.com
e-mail: info@seventh-art.com
Fax: 01273 323777   Tel: 01273 777678

SHART BROS Ltd
52 Lancaster Road, London N4 4PR
Fax: 020-7436 9233   Tel: 020-7263 4435

SHELL FILM & VIDEO UNIT
F CV Docs
Shell Centre, York Road, London SE1 7NA
Fax: 020-7934 7490   Tel: 020-7934 3318

SHELL LIKE
Whitfield House, 81 Whitfield Street, London W1T 4HG
Website: www.shelllike.com
e-mail: enquiries@shelllike.com
Fax: 020-7255 5255   Tel: 020-7255 5204

SIGHTLINE
(Videos, Commercials, CD-Rom, DVD, Websites)
Dylan House, Town End Street, Godalming, Surrey GU7 1BQ
Website: www.sightline.co.uk
e-mail: action@sightline.co.uk
Fax: 01483 861516   Tel: 01483 861555

SILK PRODUCTION
13 Berwick Street, London W1F 0PW
Website: www.silkproduction.com
e-mail: production@silkproduction.com
Fax: 020-7494 1748   Tel: 020-7434 3461

SILVER PRODUCTIONS Ltd
Bridge Farm, Lower Road, Britford
Salisbury, Wilthsire SP5 4DY
Website: www.silver.co.uk
Fax: 01722 336227   Tel: 01722 336221

SINDIBAD FILMS Ltd
5th Floor, 5 Princes Gate, London SW7 1QJ
Website: www.sindibad.co.uk
e-mail: sindibad@lineone.net
Fax: 020-7823 9137   Tel: 020-7823 7488

SMITH & WATSON PRODUCTIONS
The Gothic House, Fore Street, Totnes, Devon TQ9 5EH
Website: www.smithandwatson.com
e-mail: info@smithandwatson.com
Fax: 01803 864219   Tel: 01803 863033

SNEEZING TREE FILMS
C
1-2 Bromley Place, London W1T 6DA
e-mail: firstname@sneezingtree.com
Fax: 020-7927 9909   Tel: 020-7927 9900

SONY PICTURES EUROPE HOUSE
25 Golden Square, London W1F 9LU
Fax: 020-7533 1015   Tel: 020-7533 1000

SOREL STUDIOS
10 Palace Court, Palace Road, London SW2 3ED
e-mail: info@sorelstudios.co.uk   Tel/Fax: 020-8671 2168

SOUTHERN STAR
45-49 Mortimer Street, London W1W 8HX   Tel: 020-7636 9421

SPACE CITY PRODUCTIONS
77 Blythe Road, London W14 0HP
Website: www.spacecity.co.uk   e-mail: info@spacecity.co.uk
Fax: 020-7371 4001   Tel: 020-7371 4000

SPEAKEASY PRODUCTIONS Ltd
Wildwood House, Stanley, Perth PH1 4PX
Website: www.speak.co.uk   e-mail: info@speak.co.uk
Fax: 01738 828419   Tel: 01738 828524

SPECIFIC FILMS Ltd
25 Rathbone Street, London W1T 1NQ
e-mail: info@specificfilms.com
Fax: 020-7494 2676   Tel: 020-7580 7476

SPELLBOUND PRODUCTIONS Ltd
90 Cowdenbeath Path, Islington, London N1 0LG
e-mail: phspellbound@hotmail.com   Tel/Fax: 020-7713 8066

SPINSTER Ltd
71 Whinney Hill, Holywood, County Down
Northern Ireland BT18 0HG
Website: www.spinster-associates.com
e-mail: info@spinster-associates.com
Fax: 028-9042 2888   Tel: 028-9042 2088

SPIRAL PRODUCTIONS Ltd
Aberdeen Studios, 22 Highbury Grove, London N5 2EA
Fax: 020-7359 6123   Tel: 020-7354 5492

SPIRIT FILMS Ltd
1 Wedgwood Mews, 12-13 Greek Street, London W1D 4BA
e-mail: producer@spiritfilms.co.uk
Fax: 020-7734 9850   Tel: 020-7734 6642

STAFFORD Jonathan Ltd
1 The Limes, St Nicholas Hill, Leatherhead, Surrey KT22 8NH
Fax: 01372 383060   Tel: 01372 383050

STANDFAST FILMS
F TV D
The Studio, 14 College Road, Bromley, Kent BR1 3NS
Fax: 020-8313 0443   Tel: 020-8466 5580

STANTON MEDIA
6 Kendal Close, Aylesbury, Bucks
Website: www.stantonmedia.com
e-mail: info@stantonmedia.com   Tel/Fax: 01296 489539

STEEL SPYDA Ltd
96-98 Undley, Lakenheath, Suffolk IP27 9BY
Website: www.steelspyda.com
e-mail: kay.hill@steelspyda.com
Fax: 01842 862875   Tel: 01842 862880

STONE PRODUCTIONS
Lakeside Studio, 62 Mill Street, St Osyth, Essex CO16 8EW
e-mail: info@stone-productions.co.uk
Fax: 01255 822160   Tel: 01255 822172

STREETWISE TV
11-15 Betterton Street, Covent Garden, London WC2H 9BP
e-mail: streetwisetv@hotmail.com
Fax: 020-7379 0801   Tel: 020-7470 8825

STUDIO AKA
(Animation)
30 Berwick Street, London W1F 8RH
Website: www.studioaka.co.uk   e-mail: info@studioaka.co.uk
Fax: 020-7437 2309   Tel: 020-7434 3581

SUN DANCE FILMS Ltd
6 Glamorgan Road, Hampton Wick
Kingston, Surrey KT1 4HP
Fax: 020-8977 9441   Tel: 020-8977 1791

SUNFLOWER PRODUCTIONS
(Docs TV)
106 Mansfield Drive, Merstham, Surrey RH1 3JN
Fax: 01737 271231   Tel: 01737 642829

TABARD PRODUCTIONS
Adam House, 7-10 Adam Street, London WC2N 6AA
e-mail: info@tabard.co.uk
Fax: 020-7497 0830   Tel: 020-7497 0850

TABLE TOP PRODUCTIONS
1 The Orchard, Bedford Park, Chiswick, London W4 1JZ
e-mail: berry@tabletopproductions.com
    Tel/Fax: 020-8742 0507

TAILOR-MADE FILMS
Units 16 & 17, Waterside
44-48 Wharf Road, London N1 7UX
Website: www.tailormadefilms.net
e-mail: info@tailormadefilms.net
Fax: 020-7253 1117   Tel: 020-7566 0280

TAKE 3 PRODUCTIONS Ltd
72-73 Margaret Street, London W1W 8ST
Website: www.take3.co.uk   e-mail: mail@take3.co.uk
Fax: 020-7637 4678   Tel: 020-7637 2694

TAKE FIVE PRODUCTIONS
CV Docs
37 Beak Street, London W1F 9RZ
Website: www.takefivestudio.co.uk
e-mail: info@takefivestudio.co.uk
Fax: 020-7287 3035   Tel: 020-7287 2120

TALISMAN FILMS Ltd
7 Alan Road, London SW19 7PT
e-mail: email@talismanfilms.com
Fax: 020-8947 0446   Tel: 020-7603 7474

TALKBACK PRODUCTIONS Ltd
20-21 Newman Street, London W1T 1PG
Fax: 020-7861 8001   Tel: 020-7861 8000

TALKING PICTURES
Pinewood Studios, Pinewood Road
Iver Heath, Bucks SL0 0NH
Website: www.talkingpictures.co.uk
e-mail: info@talkingpictures.co.uk
Fax: 01753 650048   Tel: 01753 655744

TANDEM TV & FILM Ltd
Charleston House, 13 High Street
Hemel Hempstead, Herts HP1 3AA
Website: www.tandemtv.com
e-mail: ttv@tandemtv.com
Fax: 01442 219250   Tel: 01442 261576

TAYLOR David ASSOCIATES Ltd
F CV D Ch
83 Westholme Close, Congleton
Cheshire CW12 4FZ   Tel/Fax: 01260 279406

TB TV - TONY BASTABLE TELEVISION
The White House, Church Road, Lingfield, Surrey RH7 6AH
e-mail: tony@tbtv.tv
Fax: 01342 834600   Tel: 01342 834588

TELEVIRTUAL Ltd
Thorpe House, 7G Thorpe Road, Norwich NR1 1UA
Website: www.televirtual.com
e-mail: tim@televirtual.com
Fax: 01603 764946   Tel: 01603 767493

THIN MAN FILMS
9 Greek Street, London W1D 4DQ
e-mail: info@thinman.co.uk
Fax: 020-7287 5228   Tel: 020-7734 7372

TIGER ASPECT PRODUCTIONS
7 Soho Street, London W1D 3DQ
Website: www.tigeraspect.co.uk
e-mail: website@tigeraspect.co.uk
Fax: 020-7434 1798   Tel: 020-7434 6700

TKO COMMUNICATIONS Ltd
PO Box 130, Hove, Sussex BN3 6QU
e-mail: tkoinc@tkogroup.com
Fax: 01273 540969   Tel: 01273 550088

TMB MARKETING COMMUNICATIONS
Milton Heath Hse, Westcott Rd, Dorking, Surrey RH4 3NB
Website: www.tmbmmarcom.com
e-mail: mail@motivation.co.uk
Fax: 01306 877777   Tel: 01306 877000

TOP BANANA
Wassell Grove Business Centre, Wassell Grove Lane,
Stourbridge, West Midlands DY9 9JH
Website: www.top-b.com   e-mail: talk@top-b.com
Fax: 01562 881011   Tel: 01562 881010

TOPICAL TELEVISION
TV Centre, Southampton SO14 0PZ
Fax: 023-8033 9835   Tel: 023-8071 2233

TV MEDIA SERVICES Ltd/TVMS
3rd Floor, 420 Sauchiehall Street, Glasgow G2 3JD
e-mail: mail@tvms.fsnet.co.uk
Fax: 0141-332 9040   Tel: 0141-331 1993

TV PRODUCTION PARTNERSHIP Ltd
4 Fullerton Manor, Fullerton, Hants SP11 7LA
e-mail: dbj@tvpp.tv   Tel: 01264 861440

TVE Ltd
(Broadcast Facilities, Non-Linear Editing)
TVE House, Wick Drive, New Milton, Hampshire BH25 6RH
e-mail: enquiries@tvehire.com
Fax: 01425 625021   Tel: 01425 625020

TVF
375 City Road, London EC1V 1NB
Fax: 020-7833 2185   Tel: 020-7837 3000

TWENTIETH CENTURY FOX TELEVISION Ltd
Twentieth Century Hse, 31-32 Soho Square, London W1D 3AP
Fax: 020-7434 2170   Tel: 020-7437 7766

TWO SIDES TV Ltd
53A Brewer Street, London W1F 9UH
e-mail: info@2sidestv.co.uk
Fax: 020-7287 2289   Tel: 020-7439 9882

TWOFOUR PRODUCTIONS Ltd
Quay West Studios, Old Newnham, Plymouth PL7 5BH
e-mail: enq@twofour.co.uk
Fax: 01752 344224   Tel: 01752 333900

TWOTHREEFIVE Ltd
107-109 Temple Chambers
3-7 Temple Avenue, London EC4Y 0HP
Website: www.twothreefivepictures.com
e-mail: info@twothreefivepictures.com   Tel: 020-7936 3888

TYBURN FILM PRODUCTIONS Ltd
F
Cippenham Court, Cippenham Lane
Cippenham, Nr Slough, Berkshire SL1 5AU
Fax: 01753 691785   Tel: 01753 516767

TYRO PRODUCTIONS
The Coach House, 20A Park Road
Teddington, Middlesex TW11 0AQ
Fax: 020-8943 4901   Tel: 020-8943 4697

UMTV Ltd
Clearwater Yard, 35 Inverness Street, London NW1 7HB
Website: www.umtv.tv
e-mail: production@umtv.tv
Fax: 020-7267 3730   Tel: 020-7428 5740

UNGER Kurt
112 Portsea Hall, Portsea Place, London W2 2BZ
Fax: 020-7706 4818   Tel: 020-7262 9013

UNIQUE TELEVISION
3rd Floor, Beaumont House, Kensington Village
Avonmore Road, London W14 8TS
e-mail: sgraff@uniquegroup.co.uk
Fax: 020-7605 1101   Tel: 020-7605 1100

UNIVERSAL PICTURES/UNIVERSAL STUDIOS Ltd
UIP House, 45 Beadon Road, London W6 0EG
Fax: 020-8563 4331   Tel: 020-8563 4329

VERA
3rd Floor, 66-68 Margaret Street, London W1W 8SR
e-mail: cree@vera.co.uk
Fax: 020-7436 6117   Tel: 020-7436 6116

VERA MEDIA
(Video Production & Training Company)
30-38 Dock Street, Leeds LS10 1JF
e-mail: vera@vera-media.co.uk
Fax: 0113-242 8739   Tel: 0113-242 8646

VIDEO & FILM PRODUCTION
Robin Hill, The Ridge
Lower Basildon, Reading, Berks
Website: www.videoandfilm.co.uk
e-mail: david.fisher@videoandfilm.co.uk
Mobile: 07836 544955   Tel: 0118-984 2488

VIDEO ARTS
6-7 St Cross Street, London EC1N 8UA
e-mail: sales@videoarts.co.uk
Fax: 020-7400 4900   Tel: 020-7400 4800

VIDEO ENTERPRISES
12 Barbers Wood Road, High Wycombe
Buckinghamshire HP12 4EP
Website: www.videoenterprises-uk.co.uk
e-mail: videoenterprises@btconnect.com
Fax: 01494 534145   Tel: 01494 534144

VIDEOTEL PRODUCTIONS
84 Newman Street, London W1T 3EU
Fax: 020-7299 1818   Tel: 020-7299 1800

VILLAGE PRODUCTIONS
4 Midas Business Centre, Wantz Road
Dagenham, Essex RM10 8PS
e-mail: village000@btclick.com
Fax: 020-8593 0198   Tel: 020-8984 0322

VISAGE TELEVISION Ltd
c/o Instrumental Media
40 New Bond Street, London W1S 2RX
e-mail: television@visagegroup.com
Fax: 020-7629 8785   Tel: 020-7659 1140

W3KTS Ltd
10 Portland Street, York YO31 7EH
e-mail: chris@w3kts.demon.co.uk
Fax: 08700 554863   Tel: 01904 647822

W6 STUDIO
(The Complete Video Service)
359 Lillie Road, Fulham, London SW6 7PA
Website: www.w6studio.co.uk
Fax: 020-7381 5252   Tel: 020-7385 2272

WALKOVERS VIDEO PRODUCTION
Brook Cottage, Silver Street, Kington Langley
Nr Chippenham, Wiltshire SN15 5NU
e-mail: walkoversvideo@btinternet.com   Tel: 01249 750428

WALNUT MEDIA COMMUNICATIONS Ltd
Crown House, Armley Road, Leeds LS12 2EJ
Website: www.walnutmedia.com
e-mail: mail@walnutmedia.com
Fax: 08707 427080   Tel: 08707 427070

WALSH BROS Ltd
24 Redding House, Harlinger Street
King Henry's Wharf, London SE18 5SR
Website: www.walshbros.co.uk
e-mail: info@walshbros.co.uk
Tel/Fax: 020-8854 5557   Tel/Fax: 020-8858 6870

WALSH Steve PRODUCTIONS Ltd
78 Fieldview, London SW18 3HF
Website: www.steve-walsh.com
e-mail: info@steve-walsh.com
Fax: 020-7924 7461   Tel: 020-7223 6070

WARD BECHMAN Ltd
118 Clonmore Street, London SW18 5HB
e-mail: film@creativewizard.com   Tel: 020-8637 0955

WARNER BROS PRODUCTIONS Ltd
FF
Warner Suite, Pinewood Studios, Iver Heath
Buckinghamshire SL0 0NH
Fax: 01753 655703   Tel: 01753 654545

WARNER SISTERS PRODUCTIONS Ltd
Ealing Studios, Ealing Green, London W5 5EP
e-mail: ws@warnercini.com   Tel: 020-8567 6655

WATER BABIES
73 Holmcroft, Crawley
West Sussex RH10 6TP   Tel: 01293 516886

WEST DIGITAL Ltd
65 Goldhawk Road, London W12 8EG
Fax: 020-8743 2345   Tel: 020-8743 5100

WEST ONE FILM PRODUCERS Ltd
c/o Richard Hatton Ltd
29 Roehampton Gate, London SW15 5JR
Fax: 020-8876 8278   Tel: 020-8876 6699

WHITE Michael
48 Dean Street, London W1D 5BF
e-mail: contact@michaelwhite.co.uk
Fax: 020-7734 7727   Tel: 020-7734 7707

WHITEHALL FILMS
10 Lower Common South, London SW15 1BP
e-mail: mwhitehall@msn.com
Fax: 020-8788 2340   Tel: 020-8785 3737

WICKES COMPANY The
F TV D
10 Abbey Orchard Street, London SW1P 2LD
e-mail: wickesco@aol.com
Fax: 020-7222 0822   Tel: 020-7222 0820

WILD IRIS FILMS
59 Brewer Street, London W1R 3FB
e-mail: joe@wildiris.co.uk
Fax: 020-7494 1764   Tel: 020-8374 4536

WILD WEST PRODUCTIONS
4 Greenacre Close
Walderslade, Chatham, Kent ME5 7JJ
Website: www.wildwestproductions.com
e-mail: philip@wildwestproductions.com
Mobile: 07904 177937   Tel: 01634 201865

WINNER Michael Ltd
219 Kensington High Street, London W8 6BD
e-mail: winner@ftech.co.uk
Fax: 020-7602 9217   Tel: 020-7734 8385

WORKING TITLE FILMS Ltd
Oxford House, 76 Oxford Street, London W1D 1BS
Fax: 020-7307 3001   Tel: 020-7307 3000

WORLD PRODUCTIONS & WORLD FILM SERVICES Ltd
Eagle House, 50 Marshall Street, London W1F 9BQ
Website: www.world-productions.com
Fax: 020-7758 7000   Tel: 020-7734 3536

WORLD WIDE PICTURES
21-25 St Anne's Court, London W1F 0BJ
Website: www.worldwidegroup.ltd.uk
e-mail: info@worldwidegroup.ltd.uk
Fax: 020-7734 0619   Tel: 020-7434 1121

WORLD'S END
35 Harwood Road, London SW6 4QP
Website: www.worldsendproductions.com
e-mail: info@worldsendproductions.com
Fax: 020-7731 0406   Tel: 020-7751 9880

WORTHWHILE MOVIE Ltd
(Providing the services of Bruce Pittman as Film Director)
25 Tolverne Road, London SW20 8RA
Fax: 00 1 (416) 4695894   Tel: 00 1 (416) 4690459

WORTHWHILE WATCHING PRODUCTIONS Ltd
The Car Barn, Worth Farm
Little Horsted, Nr Uckfield
East Sussex TN22 5TT
Website: www.3wp.net   e-mail: info@3wp.net
Fax: 01825 750277   Tel: 01825 750788

XINGU FILMS
12 Cleveland Row, London SW1A 1DH
Fax: 020-7451 0601   Tel: 020-7451 0600

YOUNGER Greg ASSOCIATES
Baron's Croft, Hare Lane
Blindley Heath, Surrey RH7 6JA
Fax: 01342 833768   Tel: 01342 832515

ZAHRA & REMICK
186 Albert Road, London N22 7AH   Tel/Fax: 020-8889 6225

ZENITH ENTERTAINMENT Plc
43-45 Dorset Street, London W1U 7NA
Fax: 020-7224 3194   Tel: 020-7224 2440

ZEPHYR FILMS Ltd
33 Percy Street, London W1T 2DL
e-mail: info@zephyrfilms.co.uk
Fax: 020-7255 3777   Tel: 020-7255 3555

ARTTS SKILLCENTRE
Highfield Grange
Bubwith
North Yorkshire YO8 6DP
Website: www.artts.co.uk
e-mail: admin@artts.co.uk
Fax: 01757 288253   Tel: 01757 288088

BLAZE THE TRAIL Ltd
2nd Floor
241 High Street, London E17 7BH
Website: www.blaze-the-trail.com
e-mail: training@coralmedia.co.uk
Fax: 020-8520 2358   Tel: 020-8520 4569

BRIGHTON FILM SCHOOL
(Member of the National Association for Higher Education
in the Moving Image (NAHEMI) and the University Film and
Video Association (UFVA). Part-time Day or Evening Film
Directors' Courses includes Screenwriting, Cinematography
and Avid Editing. 1-Yr course and 3-week summer school.
Senior Lecturer: Franz von Habsburg FBKS (BAFTA)
Website: www.brightonfilmschool.org.uk
e-mail: info@brightonfilmschool.org.uk
Fax: 01273 302163   Tel: 01273 302166

LEEDS METROPOLITAN UNIVERSITY
(PG Dip/MA's in Film & Moving Image Production or Fiction
Screenwriting, HND in Moving Image Production)
The Leeds School of Art, Architecture and Design
H505, Calverley Street, Leeds LS1 3HE
Website: www.leedsmet.ac.uk
Fax: 0113-283 1901   Tel: 0113-283 2600

LONDON ACADEMY OF RADIO, FILM & TV
1 Lancing Street
London NW1 1NA
Website: www.media-courses.com
e-mail: help@radio321.com   Tel: 0870 7276677

LONDON FILM ACADEMY
The Old Church, 52A Walham Grove, London SW6 1QR
Website: www.londonfilmacademy.com
e-mail: info@londonfilmacademy.com
Fax: 020-7381 6116   Tel: 020-7386 7711

LONDON FILM SCHOOL The
(2-year MA Course in Film Making)
24 Shelton Street, London WC2H 9UB
e-mail: film.school@lfs.org.uk
Fax: 020-7497 3718   Tel: 020-7836 9642

MIDDLESEX UNIVERSITY
(School of Arts)
Cat Hill, Barnet
Herts EN4 8HT
Website: www.mdx.ac.uk
Fax: 020-8440 9541   Tel: 020-8411 5000

NATIONAL FILM & TELEVISION SCHOOL
(2-Year MA courses in Directing (Animation, Fiction or
Documentary), Cinematography, Composing for Film & TV,
Editing, Producing, Production Design, Post-Production
Sound and Screenwriting. 1-Yr Sound Recording Diploma
and many short courses.
Beaconsfield Studios, Station Road
Beaconsfield
Bucks HP9 1LG
Website: www.nfts-tv.ac.uk
e-mail: admin@nftsfilm-tv.ac.uk
Fax: 01494 674042   Tel: 01494 671234

RE:ACTORS
15 Montrose Walk, Weybridge, Surrey KT13 8JN
Website: www.reactors.co.uk
e-mail: michael@reactors.co.uk
Fax: 01932 830248   Tel: 01932 888885

**SURREY INSTITUTE OF ART & DESIGN UNIVERSITY
COLLEGE**
(3-year BA (Hons) Photography, Film & Video, Digital
Screen Arts, Arts & Media, Animation)
Falkner Road
Farnham, Surrey GU9 7DS
Website: www.surrart.ac.uk   Tel: 01252 722441

**UNIVERSITY OF WESTMINSTER SCHOOL OF MEDIA ARTS
& DESIGN**
(Degree courses in Film and Television/Contemporary
Media Practice)
Watford Road, Northwick Park
Harrow, Middlesex HA1 3TP
Website: www.wmin.ac.uk   Tel: 020-7911 5000

ARDMORE STUDIOS Ltd
Herbert Road, Bray
Co. Wicklow, Eire
Website: www.ardmore.ie
e-mail: film@ardmore.ie
Fax: 00 353 1 2861894   Tel: 00 353 1 2862971

BBC SOUTH (Elstree)
BBC Elstree Centre
Clarendon Road
Borehamwood, Herts WD6 1JF   Tel: 020-8953 6100

BBC TELEVISION
Television Centre
Wood Lane, Shepherds Bush
London W12 7RJ   Tel: 020-8743 8000

BRAY STUDIOS
Down Place
Water Oakley
Windsor Road
Windsor, Berkshire SL4 5UG
Fax: 01628 770381   Tel: 01628 622111

BRIGHTON FILM STUDIOS
Fax: 01273 302163   Tel: 01273 302166

CAPITAL STUDIOS
Wandsworth Plain
London SW18 1ET
Website: www.capitalstudios.com
e-mail: info@capitalstudios.com
Fax: 020-8877 0234   Tel: 020-8877 1234

CHELTENHAM FILM STUDIOS Ltd
Arle Court
Hatherley Lane
Cheltenham
Gloucestershire GL51 6PN
Website: www.cheltstudio.com
e-mail: info@cheltstudio.com
Fax: 01242 542 701   Tel: 01242 542 700

EALING STUDIOS
Ealing Green
London W5 5EP
Website: www.ealingstudios.com
e-mail: info@ealingstudios.com
Fax: 020-8758 8658   Tel: 020-8567 6655

ELSTREE FILM & TELEVISION STUDIOS
Shenley Road
Borehamwood
Herts WD6 1JG
Website: www.elstreefilmtv.com
e-mail: info@elstreefilmtv.com
Fax: 020-8905 1135   Tel: 020-8953 1600

FILMLAB UK Ltd The
Unit 415 Pilot Close
Fulmar Way, Wickford
Essex SS11 8YW
Website: www.thefilmlab.com
e-mail: janice@trickylight.com
Fax: 01268 571221   Tel: 01268 571408

HILLSIDE
Merry Hill Road
Bushey, Herts WD23 1DR
Website: www.hillside-studios.co.uk
e-mail: info@hillside-studios.co.uk
Fax: 020-8421 8085   Tel: 020-8950 7919

LONDON STUDIOS The
London Television Centre
Upper Ground
London SE1 9LT
Website: www.londonstudios.co.uk
Fax: 020-7928 8405   Tel: 020-7737 8888

PINEWOOD STUDIOS
Pinewood Road, Iver Heath
Buckinghamshire SL0 0NH
Website: www.pinewoodshepperton.com
Fax: 01753 656844   Tel: 01753 651700

REUTERS TELEVISION
85 Fleet Street, London EC4P 4AJ   Tel: 020-7250 1122

RIVERSIDE STUDIOS
Crisp Road, London W6 9RL
Website: www.riversidestudios.co.uk
e-mail: online@riversidestudios.co.uk
Fax: 020-8237 1001   Tel: 020-8237 1000

SANDS FILMS/ROTHERHITHE STUDIOS
119 Rotherhithe Street
London SE16 4NF
Fax: 020-7231 2119   Tel: 020-7231 2209

SHEPPERTON STUDIOS
Studios Road
Shepperton
Middlesex TW17 0QD
Website: www.pinewoodshepperton.com
Fax: 01932 592555   Tel: 01932 592000

TEDDINGTON STUDIOS
Broom Road
Teddington, Middlesex TW11 9NT
Website: www.teddington.tv
e-mail: sales@teddington.tv   Tel: 020-8977 3252

TWICKENHAM FILM STUDIOS Ltd
The Barons, St Margaret's
Twickenham, Middlesex TW1 2AW
Fax: 020-8607 8889   Tel: 020-8607 8888

G

GOOD DIGS GUIDE
Compiled By JANICE CRAMER & DAVID BANKS

This is a list of digs recommended by
those who have used them. To keep the list
accurate please send recommendations for
inclusion to GOOD DIGS GUIDE at The Spotlight.
Thanks to all who did so over the last year. Entries
in Bold have been paid for by the Digs concerned.

ABERDEEN
Milne, Mrs A
5 Sunnyside Walk, Aberdeen AB2 3NZ   Tel: 01224 638951

Woods, Pat
62 Union Grove, Aberdeen AB10 6RX   Tel: 01224 586324

AYR
Dunn, Sheila
The Dunn-Thing Guest House
13 Park Circus, Ayr KA7 2DJ
Mobile: 07887 928685   Tel: 01292 284531

BATH
Hutton, Celia Mrs
Bath Holiday Homes, Terranova
Shepherds Walk, Bath BA2 5QT
Website: www.bathholidayhomes.co.uk
e-mail: bhh@virgin.net   Tel: 01225 830830

Porter, Mrs G
95 Shakespeare Avenue
Bath, Avon BA2 4RQ   Tel: 01225 420166

Tapley, Jane
Camden Lodgings,
3 Upper Camden Place, Bath BA1 5HX   Tel: 01225 446561

BELFAST
Greer, Nora
59 Rugby Road, Belfast BT7 1PT
Mobile: 07760 370344   Tel: 028-9032 2120

McCully, Mrs S
28 Eglantine Avenue
Belfast BT9 6DX
Mobile: 07711 309534   Tel: 028-9068 2031

Murray, Mrs
Eglantine Guest House
21 Eglantine Avenue, Belfast BT9 6DW   Tel:028-9066 7585

BILLINGHAM
Farminer, Anna
168 Kennedy Gardens, Billingham, Cleveland TS23 3RJ
Mobile: 07946 237381   Tel: 01642 530205

Gibson, Mrs S
Northwood, 61 Tunstall Avenue, Billingham TS23 3QB
Mobile: 07813 407674   Tel: 01642 561071

Newton, Mrs Edna
97 Brendon Crescent
Billingham, Cleveland TS23 2QU   Tel: 01642 647958

BIRMINGHAM
Baker, Mr N K
41 King Edward Road
Mosley, Birmingham B13 8EL   Tel: 0121-449 8220

Eccles, John
18 Holly Road, Edgbaston
Birmingham B16 9NH   Tel: 0121-454 4853

Matusiak-Varley, Ms B T
Red Gables
69 Handsworth Wood Road, Handsworth Wood
Birmingham B20 2DH
Mobile: 07711 751105   Tel/Fax: 0121-686 5942

Mountain, Marlene P
268 Monument Road, Edgbaston
Birmingham B16 8XF   Tel: 0121-454 5900

Wilson, Mrs
17 Yew Tree Road, Edgbaston
Birmingham B15 2LX   Tel: 0121-440 5182

[CONTACTS 2005]

BLACKPOOL

Somerset Apartments

VERY HIGH STANDARD - en suite studios & apartments
• Central Heating • Cooker • Fridge • Microwave & TV - all new
Beds • Linen provided • 'Highly recommended' by members of the profession
• 10 minutes walk to the Theatre
Irene Chadderton, 22 Barton Avenue, Blackpool FY1 6AP • Tel/Fax: 01253 346743

BLACKPOOL

Chapman, Brian & Liz
Hollywood Apartments
2-4 Wellington Road, Blackpool FY1 6AR Tel: 01253 341633

Lees, Jean
Ascot Flats, 6 Hull Road
Central Blackpool FY1 4QB Tel: 01253 621059

The Proprietor
The Brooklyn Hotel,
7 Wilton Parade, Blackpool FY1 2HE Tel: 01253 627003

The Somerset & Dorset Apartments
22 Barton Avenue, Blackpool FY1 6AP Tel: 01253 346743

BOLTON

Duckworth, Paul
19 Burnham Avenue, Bolton BL1 6DB
Mobile: 07762 545129 Tel: 01204 495732

BOURNEMOUTH

Sitton, Martin
Flat 2, 9 St Winifreds Road
Meyrick Park, Bournemouth BH2 6NX Tel: 01202 293318

BRADFORD

Smith, Theresa
8 Moorhead Terrace,
Shipley, Bradford BD18 4LA Tel: 01274 778568

BRIGHTON

Benedict, Peter
19 Madeira Place, Brighton BN2 1TN Tel: 020-7703 4104

Cleveland, Carol
13 Belgrave Street
Brighton BN2 9NS
Mobile: 07973 363939 Tel: 01273 602607

Dyson, Kate
28 Victoria Street, Brighton BN1 3FQ Tel: 01273 746505

Hamlin, Corinne
Flat 6, Preston Lodge
Little Preston Street
Brighton BN1 2HQ Tel: 01273 321346

Merrin, Kate
2a Exton House, 4 Second Avenue
Hove BN3 2LG Mobile: 07714 672233

BRISTOL

Rozario, Jean
Manor Lodge
21 Station Road
Keynsham, N Somerset BS31 2BH
e-mail: stay@manorlodge.co.uk Tel: 0117-986 2191

BURTON ON TRENT

Boddy, Susan
St Wilfrid's, Barrow-upon-Trent
Derbyshire DE73 1HB Tel: 01332 701384

BURY ST EDMUNDS

Bird, Mrs S
30 Crown Street, Bury St Edmunds
Suffolk IP33 1QU Tel: 01284 754492

Harrington-Spie, Sue
39 Well Street, Bury St Edmunds
Suffolk IP33 1EQ Tel: 01284 768986

BUXTON

Kitchen, Mrs M
Flat 1, 17 Silverlands,
Buxton, Derbyshire SK17 6QH Tel: 01298 78898

Scruton, Anne & Colin
Griff Guest House
2 Compton Road, Buxton SK17 9DN Tel: 01298 23628

CANTERBURY

Dolan, Mrs A
12 Leycroft Close
Canterbury, Kent CT2 7LD Tel: 01227 450064

Ellen, Nikki
Crockshard Farmhouse
Wingham, Canterbury CT3 1NY
Website: www.crockshard.com
e-mail: crockshard_bnb@yahoo.com Tel: 01227 720464

Stockbridge, Doris
Tudor House, 6 Best Lane
Canterbury, Kent CT1 2JB Tel: 01227 765650

CARDIFF

Blade, Mrs Anne
25 Romilly Road
Canton, Cardiff CF5 1FH Tel: 029-2022 5860

Lewis, Nigel
66 Donald Street, Roath, Cardiff CF24 4TR
e-mail: nigel.lewis66@btinternet.com
Mobile: 07813 069822 Tel: 029-2049 4008

Nelmes, Michael
12 Darran Street, Cathays
Cardiff, South Glamorgan CF24 4JF Tel: 029-2034 2166

Taylor, T & Chichester, P
32 Kincraig Street, Roath
Cardiff, South Glamorgan CF24 3HW Tel: 029-2048 6785

CHESTERFIELD

Cook, Linda & Chris
27 Tennyson Avenue
Chesterfield, Derbyshire
Mobile: 07929 850561 Tel: 01246 202631

Forsyth, Mr & Mrs
Anis Louise Guest House, 34 Clarence Road
Chesterfield S40 1LN Tel: 01246 235412

Popplewell, Mr & Mrs
23 Tennyson Avenue, Chesterfield
Derbyshire S40 4SN Tel: 01246 201738

The one-stop
Website for digs
listings across
the UK.

CHICHESTER
Potter, Iain & Lyn
Hunston Mill Cottages, Selsey Road
Chichester PO20 6AU   Tel: 01243 783375

COVENTRY
Snelson, Paddy & Bob
Banner Hill Farmhouse, Rouncil Lane
Kenilworth CV8 1NN   Tel: 01926 852850

DARLINGTON
Bird, Mrs
Gilling Old Mill, Gilling West
Richmond, N Yorks DL10 5JD   Tel: 01748 822771

Evans, Jean
26a Pierremont Crescent
Darlington DL3 9PB   Tel: 01325 252032

Graham, Anne
Holme House, Piercebridge
Darlington DL2 3SY   Tel: 01325 374280

Kernon, Mr G
George Hotel, Piercebridge
Darlington DL2 3SW   Tel: 01325 374576

DUNDEE
Hill, Mrs J
Ash Villa, 216 Arbroath Road
Dundee DD4 7RZ   Tel: 01382 450831

EASTBOURNE
Allen, Peter
Flat 1, 16 Enys Road, Eastbourne BN21 2DN
Mobile: 07712 439289   Tel: 01323 730235

Chant, David E J
Hamdon, 49 King's Drive
Eastbourne BN21 2NY   Tel: 01323 722544

Dawson, Jacqui
Lavender House, 14 New Upperton Road
Eastbourne   Tel: 01323 729988

Weaver, Mr & Mrs
Meads Lodge Holiday Flats, 1 Jevington Gardens
Eastbourne BN21 4HR   Tel: 01323 724362

EDINBURGH
Glen Miller, Edna
25 Bellevue Road
Edinburgh EH7 4DL   Tel: 0131-556 4131

Stobbart, Joyce
84 Bellevue Road, Edinburgh EH7 4DE
Mobile: 07740 503951   Tel: 0131-222 9889

Tyrrell, Helen
9 Lonsdale Terrace, Edinburgh EH3 9HN
e-mail: helen.tyrrell@vhscotland.org.uk
Tel: 0131-652 5912   **Tel: 0131-229 7219**

GLASGOW
Baird, David W
6 Beaton Road, Maxwell Park, Glasgow G41 4LA
Mobile: 07752 954176   Tel: 0141-423 1340

Leslie-Carter, Simon
52 Charlotte Street, Glasgow G1 5DW
Website: www.52charlottestreet.co.uk
e-mail: slc@52charlottestreet.co.uk
Fax: 01436 810520   Tel: 0845 2305252

Lloyd Jones, David
3 Whittinghame Drive, Kelvinside
Glasgow G12 0XS   Tel: 0141-339 3331

Robinson, Lesley
28 Marywood Square, Glasgow G41 2BJ
Mobile: 07957 188922   Tel: 0141-423 6920

GRAVESEND
Greenwood, Mrs S
8 Sutherland Close, Chalk
Gravesend, Kent DA12 4XJ   **Tel: 01474 350819**

HULL
The Arches Guesthouse
38 Saner Street, Hull HU3 2TR   Tel: 01482 211558

INVERNESS
Blair, Mrs
McDonald House Hotel
1 Ardross Terrace, Inverness IV3 5NQ Tel: 01463 232878

Kerr-Smith, Jennifer
Ardkeen Tower, 5 Culduthel Road
Inverness   Tel: 01463 233131

IPSWICH
Ball, Bunty
56 Henley Road, Ipswich IP1 3SA   Tel: 01473 256653

Bennett, Liz
Gayfers, Playford, Ipswich IP6 9DR Tel: 01473 623343

Hyde-Johnson, Anne
64 Benton Street, Hadleigh
Ipswich, Suffolk IP7 5AT   Tel: 01473 823110

ISLE OF WIGHT
Ogston, Sue
Windward House, 69 Mill Hill Road
Cowes, Isle of Wight PO31 7EQ   Tel: 01983 280940

KESWICK
Bell, Mrs A
Flat 4, Skiddaw View, Penrith Road
Keswick CA12 5HF   Mobile: 07740 949250

KIRKCALDY
Nicol, Mrs
44 Glebe Park, Kirkcaldy
Fife KY1 1BL   Tel: 01592 264531

LEEDS

Baker, Mrs M
2 Ridge Mount, (off Cliff Road)
Leeds LS6 2HD Tel: 0113-275 8735

Gibbs, Mr
52 Stanningley Road, Upper Armley
Leeds LS12 2QS Tel: 0113-263 3112

Hannelore, N
52 Stanningley Road
Leeds LS12 2QS Mobile: 07905 261030

LINCOLN

Carnell, Andrew
Tennyson Court Cottages
3 Tennyson Street, Lincoln LN1 1LZ Tel: 01522 569892

Sharpe, Mavis S
Bight House, 17 East Bight
Lincoln LN2 1QH Tel: 01522 534477

Ye Olde Crowne Inn (Theatre Pub)
Clasketgate, Lincoln LN2 1JS Tel: 01522 542896

LIVERPOOL

De Leng, Ms S
7 Beach Lawn, Waterloo
Liverpool L22 8QA Tel: 0151-476 1563

Double, Ross
5 Percy Street, Liverpool L8 7LT Tel: 0151-708 8821

Maloney, Anne
16 Sandown Lane, Wavertree
Liverpool L15 8HY Tel: 0151-734 4839

McGuinness, Damian
Seapark Apartments, (office) 51 Alexandra Road
Southport, Merseyside PR9 9HD Tel: 01704 500444

LLANDUDNO

Bell, Alan
Quinton Hotel, 36 Church Walks
Llandudno LL30 2HN Tel: 01492 876879

LONDON

Allen, Mrs I
Flat 2, 9 Dorset Square
London NW1 6QB Tel: 020-7723 3979

Broughton, Mrs P A
31 Ringstead Road, Catford
London SE6 2BU Tel: 020-8461 0146

Cardinal, Maggie
17a Gaisford Street, London NW5 Tel: 020-7681 7376

Cobban, Carole
138 Tottenham Road, London N1 4DY Tel: 020-7249 4627

Guess, Maggie
36 Federal Road
Perivale, Middlesex UB6 7AW Tel: 020-8991 0918

Maya, Ms Y
7 Cornwall Road, Edmonton N18 Mobile: 07958 461468

Mesure, Nicholas
16 St Alfege Passage
Greenwich, London SE10 9JS Tel: 020-8853 4337

Montagu, Beverley
13 Hanley Road, London N4 3DU Tel: 020-7263 3883

Rothner, Dora
23 The Ridgeway
Finchley, London N3 2PG Tel: 020-8346 0246

Quinton Hotel AA B&B ☆☆☆

Comfortable warm rooms, most en-suite with TV, radio, direct dial phones, tea/coffee facilities. Flexible breakfasts, late bar, pool table, darts, piano and karaoke. Free light suppers. Mini-bus service to and from Theatre. Railway and Bus.

36 Church Walks, Llandudno. Tel/Fax: 01492-876879 Email: susanmarybell@yahoo.co.uk

Rothner, Stephanie
44 Grove Road, North Finchley, London N12 0AP
Mobile: 07956 406446   Tel: 020-8446 1604

Shaw, Lindy
11 Baronsmede
Acton, London W5 4LS   Tel: 020-8567 0877

Walsh, Genevieve
37 Kelvedon House, Guildford Road
Stockwell, London SW8 2DN   Tel: 020-7627 0024

Warren, Sally
28 Prebend Gardens, Chiswick W4 1TW   Tel: 020-8994 0560

MALVERN
Emuss, Mrs
Priory Holme
18 Avenue Road, Malvern WR14 3AR   Tel: 01684 568455

McLeod, Mr & Mrs
Sidney House, 40 Worcester Road
Malvern WR14 4AA
Website: www.sidneyhouse.co.uk
e-mail: len@sidneyhouse.co.uk   Tel: 01684 574994

MANCHESTER
Dyson, Mrs Edwina
33 Danesmoor Road
West Didsbury, Manchester M20 3JT   Tel: 0161-434 5410

Heaton, Miriam
58 Tamworth Avenue
Whitefield, Manchester M45 6UA   Tel: 0161-773 4490

Jones, P M
375 Bury New Road
Whitefield, Manchester M45 7SU   Tel: 0161-766 9243

Martin, David & Dolan, Jez
86 Stanley Road
Old Trafford, Manchester M16 9DH   Tel: 0161-848 9231

Prichard, Fiona & John
45 Bamford Road
Didsbury, Manchester M20 2QP   Tel: 0161-434 4877

Twist, Susan
45 Osborne Road
Levenshulme, Manchester M19 2DU   Tel: 0161-225 1591

MILFORD HAVEN
Henricksen, Bruce & Diana
Belhaven House Hotel Ltd, 29 Hamilton Terrace
Milford Haven SA73 3JJ
Website: www.westwaleshotels.com
e-mail: bruce@westwaleshotels.com
Fax: 01646 690787   Tel: 01646 695983

NEWCASTLE UPON TYNE
Charlton, Tot
Ryton Grange, Ryton
Tyne and Wear NE40 3UN   Tel: 0191-413 3878

Guy, Thomas
2 Pine Avenue, Fawdon
Newcastle upon Tyne NE3 2AJ
e-mail: thomas-guy@freeuk.com   Tel: 0191-285 7057

Kalaugher, Mary & Cross, Dave
4 Tankerville Terrace, Jesmond
Newcastle upon Tyne NE2 3AH   Tel: 0191-281 0475

Moffatt, Madaleine
9 Curtis Road, Fenham NE4 9BH   Tel: 0191-272 5318

Stansfield, Mrs P
Rosebery Hotel, 2 Rosebery Crescent
Jesmond, Newcastle upon Tyne NE2 1ET
Website: www.roseberyhotel.co.uk   Tel: 0191-281 3363

Steele, Miss M E
7 Stoneyhurst Road, South Gosforth
Newcastle upon Tyne NE3 1PR   Tel: 0191-285 7771

NEWPORT
Price, Miss Dinah
Great House, Isca Road, Old Village
Caerleon, Gwent NP18 1QG
Website: www.visitgreathouse.co.uk
e-mail: dinah.price@amserve.net   Tel: 01633 420216

NORWICH
Busch, Julia
8 Chester Street, Norwich NR2 2AY
Mobile: 07786 304211   Tel: 01603 612833

Calver, Michael
14 Binyon Gardens
Taverham, Norwich NR8 6SS   Tel: 01603 869260

Moore, Maureen
63 Surrey Street, Norwich NR1 3PG   Tel: 01603 621979

Mutch, Cathy
128 Southwell Road
Norwich NR1 3RS   Tel: 01603 632787

Youd, Cherry
Whitegates, 181 Norwich Road
Wroxham, NR12 8RZ   Tel: 01603 781037

NOTTINGHAM
Davis, Barbara
3 Tattershall Drive
The Park, Nottingham NG7 1BX   Tel: 0115-947 4179

Offord, Mrs
5 Tattershall Drive
The Park, Nottingham NG7 1BX   Tel: 0115-947 6924

Santos, Mrs S
Eastwood Farm, Hagg Lane
Epperstone
Nottingham NG14 6AX   Tel: 0115-966 3018

Walker, Christine
18a Cavendish Cresent North
The Park, Nottingham NG7 1BA   Tel: 0115-947 2485

OXFORD
Petty, Susan
74 Corn St, Witney, Oxford OX28 6BS   Tel: 01993 703035

PLYMOUTH

Carson, Mr & Mrs
6 Beech Cottages, Parsonage Road
Newton Ferrers, Nr Plymouth PL8 1AX   Tel: 01752 872124

Humphreys, John & Sandra
Lyttleton Guest House (Self-Catering)
4 Crescent Avenue, Plymouth PL1 3AN   Tel: 01752 220176

Mead, Teresa
Ashgrove Hotel, 218 Citadel Road
The Hoe, Plymouth PL1 3BB   Tel: 01752 664046

Spencer, Hugh & Eloise
10 Grand Parade, Plymouth PL1 3DF   Tel: 01752 664066

POOLE

Burnett, Mrs
63 Orchard Avenue, Parkstone
Poole, Dorset BH14 8AH   Tel: 01202 743877

Moore, Sarah
Harbour View, 11 Harbour View Road
Poole BH14 0PD   Tel: 01202 734763

Saunders, Mrs
1 Harbour Shallows,
15 Whitecliff Road, Poole BH14 8DU   Tel: 01202 741637

READING

Estate Office
Mapledurham House and Watermill
Mapledurham Estate, Reading RG4 7TR   Tel: 0118-972 3350

SHEFFIELD

Craig, J & Rosen, B
59 Nether Edge Road, Sheffield S7 1RW   Tel: 0114-258 1337

Gillespie, Carole
251 Western Road, Crookes
Sheffield S10 1LE   Mobile: 07791 484320

Godfrey, Liz
12 Victoria Road, Sheffield S10 2DL   Tel: 0114-266 9389

Horton, Jane & Cullumbine, Lynn
223 Cemetery Road, Sheffield S11 8FQ   Tel: 0114-255 6092

Slack, Penny
Rivelin Glen Quarry, Rivelin Valley Road, Sheffield S6 5SE
Website: www.quarryhouse.org.uk
e-mail: pennyslack@aol.com
Fax: 0114-234 7630   Tel: 0114-234 0382

SOUTHAMPTON

Cuzzolin, Sandrea
15 Methuen Street, Inner Avenue
Southampton SO14 6FL   Tel: 023-8063 7345

SOUTHPORT

Best, Mr & Mrs S
Sandcroft Holiday Flats
13 Albany Road, Southport PR9 0JF   Tel: 01704 537497

SOUTHSEA & PORTSMOUTH

Tyrell, Wendy
Douglas Cottage, 27 Somerset Road
Southsea PO5 2NL   Tel: 023-9282 1453

STOKE-ON-TRENT

Griffiths, Dorothy
40 Princes Road, Hartshill, Stoke-on-Trent
Mobile: 07719 925345   Tel: 01782 416198

Hindmoor, Mrs
Verdon Guest House, 44 Charles Street, Hanley
Stoke-on-Trent ST1 3JY   Tel: 01782 264244

Meredith, Mr & Mrs K
Bank End Farm Cottages
Hammond Ave, Brown Edge
Stoke-on-Trent Staffs ST6 8QU   **Tel: 01782 502160**

STRATFORD-UPON-AVON

Caterham House Hotel
58-59 Rother Street
Stratford-upon-Avon CV37 6LT   Tel: 01789 267309

TORQUAY

Lovsey, Frank & Irena
Silverton Holiday Apts
217 St Marychurch Road
Torquay TQ1 3JT   Tel: 01803 327147

WESTCLIFF

Hussey, Joy
42a Ceylon Road
Westcliff-on-Sea SS0 7HP   Mobile: 07946 413496

Moulding, Mark
24a Elderton Road
Westcliff-on-Sea, Essex   Tel: 01702 344965

Swan, Nicola
7 Old Leigh Road, Leigh, Essex   Tel: 01702 471600

WINCHESTER

Fetherston-Dilke, Mrs
85 Christchurch Road
Winchester SO23 9QY   Tel: 01962 868661

WOKING

Goodson, Pat
1a Horsell Moor, Woking   Tel: 01483 760208

WOLVERHAMPTON

Bell, Julia
Treetops, The Hem
Shifnal, Shropshire TF11 9PS   Tel: 01952 460566

Nixon, Sonia
39 Stubbs Road, Pennfields
Wolverhampton WV3 7DJ   Tel: 01902 339744

Riggs, Peter A
'Bethesda', 56 Chapel Lane
Codsall, Nr Wolverhampton WV8 2EJ
Mobile: 07930 967809   Tel: 01902 844068

WORTHING

Stewart, Mollie
School House, 11 Ambrose Place
Worthing BN11 1PZ   Tel: 01903 206823

Symonds, Val
23 Shakespeare Rd, Worthing BN11 4AR   Tel: 01903 201557

YORK

Abbey Apts, 7 St Marys
Bootham, York YO30 7DD   Tel: 01904 636154

Blacklock, Tom
155 Lowther Street, York YO3 7LZ   Tel: 01904 620487

Blower, Iris & Dennis
Dalescroft Guest House
10 Southlands Road, York YO23 1NP
Website: www.dalescroft-york.co.uk
e-mail: info@dalescroft-york.co.uk   Tel: 01904 626801

Harrand, Greg
Hedley House Hotel & Apts
3 Bootham Terrace, York YO3 7DH   Tel: 01904 637404

Health & Wellbeing

ALEXANDER ALLIANCE
(Alexander Technique, Voice & Audition Coaching)
3 Hazelwood Drive, St Albans, Herts
Website: www.alextech.co.uk
e-mail: bev.keech@ntlworld.com   Tel: 01727 843633

ALEXANDER CENTRE The Bloomsbury
(Alexander Technique)
Bristol House
80A Southampton Row, London WC1B 4BB
Website: www.alexcentre.com
e-mail: bloomsbury.alexandercentre@btinternet.com
                                        Tel: 020-7404 5348

ALEXANDER TECHNIQUE
(Jackie Coote MSTAT)
27 Britannia Road, London SW6 2HJ   Tel: 020-7731 1061

ALEXANDER TECHNIQUE AND VOICE
(Robert Macdonald)
Flat 5, 17 Hatton Street, London NW8 8PL
Website: www.voice.org.uk   Mobile: 07956 852303

ARTS CLINIC The
(Psychological Counselling, Personal & Professional
Development)
14 Devonshire Place, London W1G 6HX
e-mail: mail@artsclinic.co.uk
Fax: 020-7224 6256   Tel: 020-7935 1242

ASPEY ASSOCIATES
(Management & Team Training, Counselling,
Human Resources)
8 Bloomsbury Square, London WC1A 2LQ
Website: www.aspey.com
e-mail: hr@aspey.com
Fax: 020-7405 5541   Tel: 020-7405 0500

BODYMINDED PERSONAL FITNESS TRAINING
The Ability Gym
29 Crawford Street
London W1H 1LW
Website: www.bodyminded.com
e-mail: edouard@bodyminded.com   Mobile: 07855 254252

BODYWISE
(Yoga and Alternative Therapies)
119 Roman Road, London E2 0QN
Website: ww.bodywisehealth.org
e-mail: info@bodywisehealth.org   Tel: 020-8981 6938

BURGESS Chris
(Counselling for Performing Artists)
81 Arne House, Tyers Street
London SE11 5EZ   Tel: 020-7582 8229

CENTRE OF HOLISTIC WELLBEING
(Holistic Therapies)
228 Wood Street, Middleton, Manchester M24 5RT
Website: www.prideradio.co.uk
e-mail: pma@prideradio.co.uk   Tel/Fax: 0161-643 6266

CHOUT DR
(Cosmetic Surgeon)
27 Wellbeck Street, London W1G 8EN
Website: www.philippechout.com
email: philippechout75@yahoo.com   Tel: 020-7863 1715

[CONTACTS2005]

CONSTRUCTIVE TEACHING CENTRE Ltd
(Alexander Technique Teacher Training)
18 Lansdowne Road, London W11 3LL
Website: www.alexandertek.com
e-mail: info@alexandertek.com   Tel: 020-7727 7222

CORTEEN Paola MSTAT
(Alexander Technique)
10A Eversley Park Road, London N21 1JU
e-mail: pmcorteen@yahoo.co.uk   Tel: 020-8882 7898

COURTENAY Julian
(NLP Master Practitioner)
42 Langdon Park Road, London N6 5QG
e-mail: julian@mentalfitness.uk.com   Tel: 020-8348 9033

CUSSONS Nicola Dip ITEC
(Holistic Massage Therapist, Qualified & Insured)
The Factory Fitness & Dance Centre
407 Hornsey Road
London N19 4DX
e-mail: nicolacussons@freeuk.com
Mobile: 07713 629952   Tel: 020-7272 6262

DAWN ELIZABETH
(Professional Haircare)
Unit 3, Crown House
71 High Street
Wickham Market
Woodbridge, Suffolk IP13 0RA   Tel: 01728 746168

DREAM
(Reflexology, Head, Neck & Shoulder Massage in the Workplace)
117B Gaisford Street
London NW5 2EG
Website: www.dreamtherapies.co.uk
e-mail: dreamtherapies@hotmail.com   Mobile: 07973 731026

EDWARDS Simon MCA Hyp
(Hypnotherapy for Professionals in Film, TV & Theatre)
15 Station Road
Quainton
Nr Aylesbury
Buckinghamshire HP22 4BW
e-mail: hypnotherapisttothestars@o2.co.uk
Mobile: 07889 333680   Tel: 01296 651259

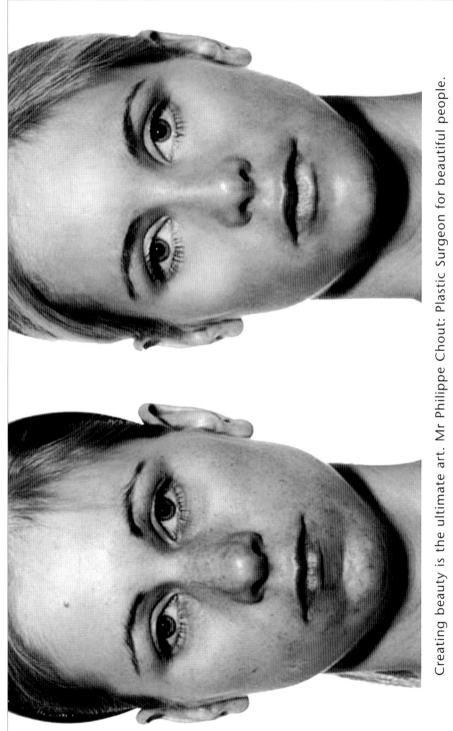

FAITH Gordon BA DHC MCHC (UK)
(Hypnotherapy, Obstacles to Performing, Positive
Affirmation, Focusing)
1 Wavel Mews, Priory Road
London NW6 3AB   Tel: 020-7328 0446

FITNESS COACH The
(Jamie Baird)
Agua at The Sanderson
50 Berners Street, London W1T 4AT
e-mail: jamie@thefitnesscoach.com
Mobile: 07970 782476   Tel: 020-7300 1414

FOAD Gene Dip Hyp GHR Reg GQHP
(Clinical Hypnotherapy, Creativity & Performance
Enhancement for Adults & Children)
23 Windsor Road
Kingston-upon-Thames
Surrey KT2 5EY
e-mail: genefoad@hotmail.com   Mobile: 07903 261214

GIRAUDON Olivier
(Alexander Technique Teacher)
22 Lake Road, Verwood
Dorset BH31 6BX   Tel: 01202 813636

HAMMOND John B. Ed (Hons) ICHFST
(Fitness Consultancy, Sports & Relaxation Massage)
4 Glencree, Billericay, Essex CM11 1EB
Mobile: 07703 185198   Tel/Fax: 01277 632830

HEIDELBACH Sabine MSTAT
(Alexander Technique)
50 Hillside Grove, London N14 6HE   Tel: 020-8882 8562

HYPNOSIS WORKS
Tulip House
70 Borough High Street
London SE1 1XE
Website: www.hypnosisdoeswork.net
e-mail: sssp@hypnosisdoeswork.net   Tel: 020-7237 5815

HYPNOTHERAPY & PSYCHOTHERAPY
(Including Performance Improvement,
Karen Mann DCH DHP)
9 Spencer House
Vale of Health
Hampstead, London NW3 1AS
Website: www.karenmann.co.uk   Tel: 020-7794 5843

MAGIC KEY PARTNERSHIP The
(Lyn Burgess - Life Coach)
4 Bewley Street
London SW19 1XB
Website: www.magickey.biz
e-mail: lyn@magickey.co.uk   Tel: 0845 1297401

MATRIX ENERGY FIELD THERAPY
121 Church Road
Wimbledon, London SW19 5AH
e-mail: donnie@lovingorganization.org
Mobile: 07762 821828   Tel: 020-8946 8534

McCALLION Anna
(Alexander Technique)
Flat 2, 11 Sinclair Gardens
London W14 0AU   Tel: 020-7602 5599

MINDSCI CLINIC
(Clinical Hypnotism)
34 Willow Bank
Ham, Richmond, Surrey TW10 7QX
Website: http://mindsci-clinic.com
e-mail: info@mindsci-clinic.com   Tel/Fax: 020-8948 2439

MONSHIN Deborah J. MNSPH
(Healing with Hypnosis)
Kitley House Hotel, Yealmpton, Devon
Website: www.devon-hypnosis.co.uk
e-mail: debmonshin@yahoo.co.uk   Tel: 01752 880880

NORTON Michael R
(Implant/Reconstructive Dentistry)
98 Harley Street
London W1G 7HZ
Website: www.nortonimplants.com
e-mail: drnorton@nortonimplants.com
Fax: 020-7486 9119   Tel: 020-7486 9229

PEAK PERFORMANCE TRAINING
(Tina Reibl, Hypnotherapy, NLP, Success Strategies)
42 The Broadway
Maidenhead, Berkshire SL6 1LU
e-mail: tina.reibl@tesco.net   Tel: 01628 633509

POLAND DENTAL STUDIOS
(Film/Stage Dentistry)
1 Devonshire Place
London W1N 1PA
Fax: 020-7486 3952   Tel: 020-7935 6919

PRYCE Jacqui-Lee OCR ABA BAWLA GKFO
(Personal Training & Group Sessions, Boxing, Kick/Muay
Thai Boxing)
e-mail: getfitquick@hotmail.com   Mobile: 07930 304809

REID Elspeth COACHING
(Life/Career Coaching)
Website: www.elspethreid.com
e-mail: coach@elspethreid.com   Tel: 020-8879 7676

SHER SYSTEM The
(Helping Skin with Acne & Rosacea)
30 New Bond Street
London W1S 2RN
Website: www.sher.co.uk
e-mail: skincare@sher.co.uk
Fax: 020-7629 7021   Tel: 020-7499 4022

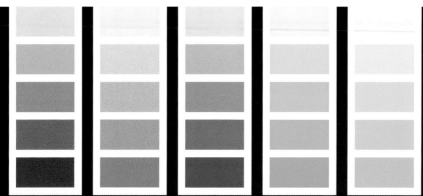

SHIATSU HEALTH CENTRE
21 Warren Bank
Simpson
Milton Keynes
Bucks MK6 3AQ
Website: www.shiatsuhealth.com
e-mail: shiatsuhealth@aol.com   Mobile: 07905 504418

SMILE SOLUTIONS
(Dental Practice)
24 Englands Lane
London NW3 4TG
Website: www.smile-solutions.info
e-mail: beeta@smile-solutions.info
Fax: 020-7449 1769   Tel: 020-7449 1760

STAT
(The Society of Teachers of the Alexander Technique)
1st Floor Linton House
39-51 Highgate Road
London NW5 1RS
Website: www.stat.org.uk
e-mail: enquiries@stat.org.uk
Fax: 020-7482 5435   Tel: 020-7284 3338

THEATRICAL DENTISTRY
(Richard D Casson)
6 Milford House
7 Queen Anne Street
London W1G 9HN
Website: www.richardcasson.com
Tel/Fax: 020-7935 6511   Tel/Fax: 020-7935 8854

THEGILMOURCENTRE.COM
(Rev/Dr Glenn J Gilmour, MSc D) (Clairvoyant, Healer,
Personal Consultant, Investigator of Psychic Phenomena)
Website: www.sandrasinger.com   Tel: 01702 331616

TRUEWAYS
(Tasha Sangster, Holistic Practitioner in Indian Head
Massage, Facelift Massage & Feng Shui)
8 Brangton Road
London SE11 5PY   Tel: 020-7735 2238

TURNER Jeff
(Psychotherapy, Counselling & Performance Coaching)
Life Management Systems
14 Randell's Road
London N1 0DH
Website: www.lifemanagement.co.uk
e-mail: info@lifemanagement.co.uk   Tel: 020-7837 9871

VITAL TOUCH The
(On-Site Massage Company)
11 Evering Road
London N16 7PX
Website: www.thevitaltouch.com
e-mail: suzi@thevitaltouch.com
Mobile: 07976 263691   Tel: 020-7249 4209

WELLBEING
(Leigh Jones)
86 Beaufort Street
London SW3 6BU
e-mail: fitness4upersonaltraining@hotmail.com
Mobile: 07957 333921

O

Opera Companies
Organisations

BROOMHILL OPERA
Wiltons Music Hall, Graces Alley, Ensign St, London E1 8JB
e-mail: opera@broomhill.demon.co.uk
Fax: 020-7702 1414   Tel: 020-7702 9555

CARL ROSA OPERA
359 Hackney Road, London E2 8PR
e-mail: mail@carlrosaopera.co.uk
Fax: 020-7613 0859   Tel: 020-7613 0777

DUAL CONTROL THEATRE COMPANY
The Admiral's Offices
The Historic Dockyard, Chatham, Kent ME4 4TZ
Website: www.ellenkent.com
e-mail: info@ellenkentinternational.co.uk
Fax: 01634 819149   Tel: 01634 819141

ENGLISH NATIONAL OPERA
London Coliseum, St Martin's Lane, London WC2N 4ES
Website: www.eno.org
Fax: 020-7845 9277   Tel: 020-7836 0111

ENGLISH TOURING OPERA
(James Conway)
1st Floor, 52-54 Rosebery Avenue, London EC1R 4RP
Website: www.englishtouringopera.org.uk
e-mail: admin@englishtouringopera.org.uk
Fax: 020-7713 8686   Tel: 020-7833 2555

GLYNDEBOURNE FESTIVAL OPERA
Glyndebourne, Lewes, E. Sussex BN8 5UU   Tel: 01273 812321

GRANGE PARK OPERA
The Coach Hse, 12 St Thomas Street, Winchester SO23 9HF
Website: www.grangeparkopera.co.uk
e-mail: info@grangeparkopera.co.uk
Fax: 01962 868968   Tel: 01962 868600

GUBBAY Raymond Ltd
Dickens House, 15 Tooks Court, London EC4A 1QH
Website: www.raymondgubbay.co.uk
e-mail: mail@raymondgubbay.co.uk
Fax: 020-7025 3751   Tel: 020-7025 3750

KENTISH OPERA
Watermede, Wickhurst Rd, Sevenoaks, Weald, Kent TN14 6LX
Website: www.kentishopera.fsnet.co.uk   Tel: 01732 463284

LONDON OPERA PLAYERS
32 Trinity Court, 170A Gloucester Terrace, London W2 6HN
Website: www.operaplayers.co.uk
e-mail: info@operaplayers.co.uk
Fax: 0700 5802121   Mobile: 07779 225921

MUSIC THEATRE LONDON
Chertsey Chambers, 12 Mercer St, London WC2H 9QD
Website: www.mtl.org.uk
e-mail: musictheatre.london@virgin.net
Fax: 020-7240 0805   Tel: 020-7240 0919

OPERA DELLA LUNA
7 Cotmore Hse, Fringford, Bicester, Oxfordshire OX27 8RQ
Website: www.operadellaluna.org
e-mail: operadellaluna@aol.com
Fax: 01869 323533   Tel: 01869 325131

OPERA NORTH
Grand Theatre, 46 New Briggate, Leeds LS1 6NU
Website: www.operanorth.co.uk
Fax: 0113-244 0418   Tel: 0113-243 9999

PEGASUS OPERA COMPANY Ltd
The Brix, St Matthew's, Brixton Hill, London SW2 1JF
Website: www.pegopera.org   Tel/Fax: 020-7501 9501

PIMLICO OPERA
The Coach Hse, 12 St Thomas St, Winchester SO23 9HF
e-mail: pimlico@grangeparkopera.co.uk
Fax: 01962 868968   Tel: 01962 868600

ROYAL OPERA The
Royal Opera House, Covent Garden, London WC2E 9DD
Website: www.royaloperahouse.org.uk   Tel: 020-7240 1200

SCOTTISH OPERA
39 Elmbank Crescent, Glasgow G2 4PT
Website: www.scottishopera.org.uk   Tel: 0141-248 4567

WELSH NATIONAL OPERA
John Street, Cardiff CF10 5SP
Website: www.wno.org.uk   e-mail: marketing@wno.org.uk
Fax: 029-2048 3050   Tel: 029-2046 4666

[CONTACTS2005]

ACTING POSITIVE
22 Chaldon Road
London SW6 7NJ
e-mail: ianflintoff@aol.com   Tel: 020-7385 3800

ACTORCLUB Ltd
17 Inkerman Road, London NW5 3BT
Website: www.actorclub.co.uk
e-mail: johncunningham@actorclub.fsnet.co.uk
                                          Tel: 020-7267 2759

ACTORS CENTRE (NORTHERN)
(See NORTHERN ACTORS CENTRE)

ACTORS CENTRE The (LONDON)
1A Tower Street, London WC2H 9NP
Website: www.actorscentre.co.uk
e-mail: admin@actorscentre.co.uk
Fax: 020-7240 3896   Tel: 020-7240 3940

ACTORS CENTRE The NORTH-EAST
2nd Floor, 1 Black Swan Court, Westgate Road
Newcastle upon Tyne NE1 1SG
Website: www.actorscentrene.co.uk
e-mail: allan@actorscentrene.co.uk   Tel: 0191-221 0158

ACTORS' ADVISORY SERVICE
29 Talbot Road, Twickenham
Middlesex TW2 6SJ   Tel: 020-8287 2839

ACTORS' BENEVOLENT FUND
6 Adam Street, London WC2N 6AD
Website: www.actorsbenevolentfund.co.uk
e-mail: office@abf.org.uk
Fax: 020-7836 8978   Tel: 020-7836 6378

ACTORS' CHARITABLE TRUST
Africa House, 64-78 Kingsway, London WC2B 6BD
e-mail: robert@tactactors.org
Fax: 020-7242 0234   Tel: 020-7242 0111

ACTORS' CHURCH UNION
St Paul's Church, Bedford Street, London WC2E 9ED
e-mail: actors_church_union@yahoo.co.uk
                                          Tel: 020-7240 0344

ADVERTISING ASSOCIATION
Abford House, 15 Wilton Road, London SW1V 1NJ
Website: www.adassoc.org.uk
e-mail: aa@adassoc.org.uk
Fax: 020-7931 0376   Tel: 020-7828 2771

AFTRA
(American Federation of Television & Radio Artists)
5757 Wilshire Boulevard, 9th Floor
Los Angeles CA 90036   Tel: (323) 634-8100

260 Madison Avenue, New York NY 10016
Fax: (212) 545-1238   Tel: (212) 532-0800

AGENTS' ASSOCIATION (Great Britain)
54 Keyes House, Dolphin Square, London SW1V 3NA
Website: www.agents-uk.com
e-mail: association@agents-uk.com
Fax: 020-7821 0261   Tel: 020-7834 0515

ARTS & BUSINESS
Nutmeg House, 60 Gainsford Street
Butlers Wharf, London SE1 2NY
Website: www.aandb.org.uk
e-mail: head.office@aandb.org.uk
Fax: 020-7407 7527   Tel: 020-7378 8143

ARTS & ENTERTAINMENT TECHNICAL
TRAINING INITIATIVE (AETTI)
261 Baker Street, Derby DE24 8SG
e-mail: aetti@sumack.freeserve.co.uk
Fax: 020-7328 5035   Tel: 01332 751740

ARTS CENTRE GROUP The
ACG, St Saviours Church, Walton Place, London SW3 1SA
Website: www.artscentregroup.org.uk
e-mail: info@artscentregroup.org.uk
Fax: 0870 7060964   Tel: 020-7581 2777

ARTS COUNCIL ENGLAND
14 Great Peter Street, London SW1P 3NQ
Website: www.artscouncil.org.uk
e-mail: enquiries@artscouncil.org.uk
Fax: 020-7973 6590   Tel: 0845 300 6200

ARTS COUNCIL NORTHERN IRELAND
MacNeice House, 77 Malone Road, Belfast BT9 6AQ
Website: www.artscouncil-ni.org
Fax: 028-9066 1715   Tel: 028-9038 5200

ARTS COUNCIL WALES
9 Museum Place, Cardiff CF10 3NX
Website: www.artswales.org.uk
e-mail: info@artswales.org.uk
Fax: 029-2022 1447   Tel: 029-2037 6500

ARTSLINE
(Disability Access Information Service)
54 Chalton Street, London NW1 1HS
Website: www.artslineonline.com
e-mail: access@artsline.com
Fax: 020-7383 2653   Tel: 020-7388 2227

ASSITEJ UK
(UK Centre of the International Association of Theatre for
Children and Young People)
c/o Kevin Lewis, Secretary, Theatre Iolo
The Old School Building, Cefn Road
Mynachdy, Cardiff CF14 3HS
Website: www.childrenstheatre.org.uk
e-mail: info@assitej.org.uk   Tel: 029-2061 3782

ASSOCIATION OF BRITISH THEATRE TECHNICIANS
4th Floor, 55 Farringdon Road, London EC1M 3JB
Website: www.abtt.org.uk
e-mail: office@abtt.org.uk
Fax: 020-7242 9303   Tel: 020-7242 9200

ASSOCIATION OF LIGHTING DESIGNERS
PO Box 89, Welwyn Garden City AL7 1ZW
Website: www.ald.org.uk   e-mail: office@ald.org.uk
Fax: 020-7622 4148   Tel/Fax: 01707 891848

ASSOCIATION OF MODEL AGENTS
122 Brompton Road, London SW3 1JE
Info. Line: 09068 517644   Tel: 020-7584 6466

BECTU
(See BROADCASTING ENTERTAINMENT CINEMATOGRAPH &
THEATRE UNION)

BRITISH ACADEMY OF COMPOSERS &
SONGWRITERS The
2nd Floor, British Music House
26 Berners Street, London W1T 3LR
Website: www.britishacademy.com
e-mail: info@britishacademy.com
Fax: 020-7636 2212   Tel: 020-7636 2929

BRITISH ACADEMY OF FILM & TELEVISION ARTS The
195 Piccadilly, London W1J 9LN
Website: www.bafta.org
e-mail: membership@bafta.org
Fax: 020-7292 5868   Tel: 020-7734 0022

BRITISH ACADEMY OF FILM & TELEVISION ARTS/
LOS ANGELES The
8533 Melrose Avenue, Suite D, West Hollywood, CA 90069
e-mail: info@baftala.org
Fax: (310) 854-6002   Tel: (310) 652-4121

WE CAN HELP ACTORS' CHILDREN

Are you:

- a professional actor?
- the parent of a child under 21?
- having trouble with finances?

Please get in touch for a confidential chat.

The Actors' Charitable Trust
020 7242 0111
admin@tactactors.org

TACT can help in many ways: with regular monthly payments, one-off grants, and long-term support and advice.
We help with clothing, child-care, music lessons, school trips, special equipment and adaptations, and in many other ways.

Our website has a link to a list of all the theatrical and entertainment charities which might be able to help you if you do not have children: www.tactactors.org

TACT, Africa House, 64 Kingsway, London WC2B 6BD.
Registered charity number 206809.

TACT

BRITISH ACADEMY OF STAGE & SCREEN COMBAT
Suite 280, 14 Tottenham Court Road, London W1T 1JY
Website: www.bassc.org
e-mail: info@bassc.org   Tel: 020-8352 0605

**BRITISH ASSOCIATION FOR PERFORMING
ARTS MEDICINE**
4th Floor, Totara Park House, 34-36 Gray's Inn Road
London WC1X 8HR   Tel: 020-7404 5888

BRITISH ASSOCIATION OF DRAMA THERAPISTS The
41 Broomhouse Lane, London SW6 3DP
Website: www.badth.co.uk
e-mail: gillian@badth.demon.co.uk   Tel/Fax: 020-7731 0160

BRITISH BOARD OF FILM CLASSIFICATION
3 Soho Square, London W1D 3HD
Website: www.bbfc.co.uk
Fax: 020-7287 0141   Tel: 020-7440 1570

BRITISH COUNCIL The
(Performing Arts Department)
10 Spring Gardens, London SW1A 2BN
Website: www.britishcouncil.org/arts
e-mail: theatredance@britishcouncil.org   Tel: 020-7389 3010

BRITISH FILM INSTITUTE
21 Stephen Street, London W1T 1LN
e-mail: library@bfi.org.uk
Fax: 020-7436 2338   Tel: 020-7255 1444

BRITISH LIBRARY SOUND ARCHIVE
96 Euston Road, London NW1 2DB
Website: www.bl.uk/nsa   e-mail: sound-archive@bl.uk
Fax: 020-7412 7794   Tel: 020-7412 7000

BRITISH MUSIC HALL SOCIETY
(Secretary: Daphne Masterton)
82 Fernlea Road, London SW12 9RW
Tel: 020-8673 2175   Tel: 01727 768878

**BROADCASTING ENTERTAINMENT CINEMATOGRAPH &
THEATRE UNION (BECTU) (Formerly BETA & ACTT)**
375-377 Clapham Road, London SW9 9BT
e-mail: smacdonald@bectu.org.uk
Fax: 020-7346 0901   Tel: 020-7346 0900

CASTING DIRECTORS' GUILD
PO Box 34403, London W6 0YG
Website: www.tcdg.co.uk   Tel/Fax: 020-8741 1951

CATHOLIC STAGE GUILD
(Write SAE)
Ms Molly Steele (Hon Secretary)
1 Maiden Lane, London WC2E 7NB   Tel: 020-7240 1221

CELEBRATE
(Creative Events Development)
1 Hill Street, Jackson Bridge
Holmfirth, West Yorkshire HD9 1LZ
e-mail: info@celebrateprojects.co.uk   Tel: 01484 688219

CELEBRITY SERVICE Ltd
4th Floor, Kingsland House, 122-124 Regent Street W1B 5SA
e-mail: celebritylondon@aol.com
Fax: 020-7494 3500   Tel: 020-7439 9840

CHILDREN'S FILM & TELEVISION FOUNDATION Ltd
Elstree Film & Television Studios
Borehamwood, Herts WD6 1JG
e-mail: annahome@cftt.onyxnet.co.uk
Fax: 020-8207 0860   Tel: 020-8953 0844

CINEMA & TELEVISION BENEVOLENT FUND (CTBF)
22 Golden Square, London W1F 9AD
Website: www.ctbf.co.uk
e-mail: charity@ctbf.co.uk
Fax: 020-7437 7186   Tel: 020-7437 6567

CINEMA EXHIBITORS' ASSOCIATION
22 Golden Square, London W1F 9JW
e-mail: cea@cinemauk.ftech.co.uk
Fax: 020-7734 6147   Tel: 020-7734 9551

CLUB FOR ACTS & ACTORS
(Incorporating Concert Artistes Association)
20 Bedford Street, London WC2E 9HP
Office: 020-7836 3172   Members: 020-7836 2884

COI COMMUNICATIONS
(Television)
Hercules House
Hercules Road, London SE1 7DU
e-mail: eileen.newton@coi.gsi.gov.uk
Fax: 020-7261 8776   Tel: 020-7261 8220

COMPANY OF CRANKS
1st Floor, 62 Northfield House
Frensham Street, London SE15 6TN
e-mail: mimetic16@yahoo.com   Mobile: 07802 805588

CONCERT ARTISTES ASSOCIATION
(See CLUB FOR ACTS & ACTORS)

CONFERENCE OF DRAMA SCHOOLS
(Saul Hyman, Executive Secretary)
PO Box 34252, London NW5 1XJ
Website: www.drama.ac.uk
e-mail: info@cds.drama.ac.uk

**COUNCIL FOR DANCE EDUCATION &
TRAINING (CDET) The**
Toynbee Hall
28 Commercial Street, London E1 6LS
Website: www.cdet.org.uk
e-mail: info@cdet.org.uk
Fax: 020-7247 3404   Tel: 020-7247 4030

CPMA
(Co-operative Personal Management Association)
The Secretary, c/o 1 Mellor Road, Leicester LE3 6HN
e-mail: cpmauk@yahoo.co.uk   Mobile: 07981 902525

CREATIVE INDUSTRIES DEVELOPMENT AGENCY (CIDA)
(Professional development & business support for artists &
creative businesses)
Media Centre, Northumberland Street
Huddersfield, West Yorkshire HD1 1RL
Website: www.cida.org
e-mail: info@cida.org
Fax: 01484 483150   Tel: 01484 483140

CRITICS' CIRCLE The
c/o 69 Marylebone Lane, London W1U 2PH
Website: www.criticscircle.org.uk   Tel: 020-7224 1410

DANCE UK
(Including the Healthier Dancer Programme & 'The UK
Choreographers' Directory')
Battersea Arts Centre
Lavender Hill, London SW11 5TN
Website: www.danceuk.org
e-mail: info@danceuk.org
Fax: 020-7223 0074   Tel: 020-7228 4990

DENVILLE HALL
(Nursing Home)
62 Ducks Hill Road
Northwood, Middlesex HA6 2SB
Website: www.denvillehall.org
e-mail: denvillehall@yahoo.com
Fax: 01923 841855
Residents: 01923 820805   Office: 01923 825843

DEVOTEES of HAMMER FILMS PRESERVATION SOCIETY The
(Fan Club)
14 Kingsdale Road
London SE18 2DG   Tel: 020-8244 8640

DIRECTORS' & PRODUCERS' RIGHTS SOCIETY
Victoria Chambers
16-18 Strutton Ground, London SW1P 2HP
Website: www.dprs.org
e-mail: info@dprs.org
Fax: 020-7227 4755   Tel: 020-7227 4757

DIRECTORS GUILD OF GREAT BRITAIN
The Directors Centre
8 Flitcroft Street, London WC2H 8DL
Website: www.dggb.org
e-mail: guild@dggb.org
Fax: 020-7836 3603   Tel: 020-7836 3602

D'OYLY CARTE OPERA COMPANY
The Powerhouse, 6 Sancroft Street, London SE11 5UD
Website: www.doylycarte.org.uk
e-mail: mail@doylycarte.org.uk
Fax: 020-7793 7300   Tel: 020-7793 7100

DRAMA ASSOCIATION OF WALES
(Specialist Drama Lending Library)
The Old Library, Singleton Road, Splott, Cardiff CF24 2ET
e-mail: aled.daw@virgin.net
Fax: 029-2045 2277   Tel: 029-2045 2200

DRAMATURGS' NETWORK
(Network of Professional Dramaturgs)
139B Tooting Bec Road, London SW17 8BW
Website: www.dramaturgy.co.uk
e-mail: info@dramaturgy.co.uk   Tel: 020-8767 6004

ENGLISH FOLK DANCE & SONG SOCIETY
Cecil Sharp House, 2 Regent's Park Road, London NW1 7AY
Website: www.efdss.org.info
e-mail: info@efdss.org
Fax: 020-7284 0534   Tel: 020-7485 2206

EQUITY inc Variety Artistes' Federation
Guild House, Upper St Martin's Lane, London WC2H 9EG
Website: www.equity.org.uk
e-mail: info@equity.org.uk
Fax: 020-7379 7001   Tel: 020-7379 6000

(North West)
Conavon Court, 12 Blackfriars Street, Salford M3 5BQ
e-mail: info@manchester-equity.org.uk
Fax: 0161-839 3133   Tel: 0161-832 3183

(Scotland & Northern Ireland)
114 Union Street, Glasgow G1 3QQ
e-mail: igilchrist@glasgow.equity.org.uk
Fax: 0141-248 2473   Tel: 0141-248 2472

(Wales & South West)
Transport House, 1 Cathedral Road, Cardiff CF11 9SD
e-mail: info@cardiff-equity.org.uk
Fax: 029-2023 0754   Tel: 029-2039 7971

ETF (Equity Trust Fund)
Suite 222, Africa House, 64 Kingsway, London WC2B 6BD
Fax: 020-7831 4953   Tel: 020-7404 6041

FAA
(See FILM ARTISTS ASSOCIATION)

FILM ARTISTS ASSOCIATION
(Amalgamated with BECTU)
373-377 Clapham Road, London SW9
Fax: 020-7346 0925   Tel: 020-7346 0900

FILM LONDON
20 Euston Centre, Regent's Place, London NW1 3JH
Website: www.filmlondon.org.uk
e-mail: info@filmlondon.org.uk
Fax: 020-7387 8788　　　　Tel: 020-7387 8787

GLASGOW FILM FINANCE
(Production Finance for Feature Films)
City Chambers, Glasgow G2 1DU
Fax: 0141-287 0311　　　　Tel: 0141-287 0424

GRAND ORDER OF WATER RATS
328 Gray's Inn Road, London WC1X 8BZ
Website: www.gowr.net
e-mail: water.rats@virgin.net
Fax: 020-7278 1765　　　　Tel: 020-7278 3248

GROUP LINE
(Group Bookings for London Theatre)
22-24 Torrington Place, London WC1E 7HJ
Website: www.groupline.com
e-mail: tix@groupline.com
Fax: 020-7436 6287　　　　Tel: 020-7580 6793

GUY Gillian ASSOCIATES
84A Tachbrook Street, London SW1V 2NB
Website: www.show-pairs.co.uk
Fax: 020-7976 5885　　　　Tel: 020-7976 5888

INDEPENDENT THEATRE COUNCIL (ITC)
12 The Leathermarket, Weston Street, London SE1 3ER
Website: www.itc-arts.org
e-mail: admin@itc-arts.org
Fax: 020-7403 1745　　　　Tel: 020-7403 1727

INSIGHT ARTS
7-15 Greatorex Street, London E1 5NF
e-mail: info@insightarts.org
Fax: 020-7247 8077　　　　Tel: 020-7247 0778

INTERNATIONAL FEDERATION OF ACTORS (FIA)
Guild House, Upper St Martin's Lane, London WC2H 9EG
Website: www.fia-actors.com
e-mail: office@fia-actors.com
Fax: 020-7379 8260　　　　Tel: 020-7379 0900

INTERNATIONAL THEATRE INSTITUTE
Goldsmiths College, University of London, Lewisham Way
New Cross, London SE14 6NW
Website: http://iti.gold.ac.uk
e-mail: iti@gold.ac.uk
Fax: 020-7919 7277　　　　Tel: 020-7919 7276

**INTERNATIONAL VISUAL COMMUNICATION
ASSOCIATION (IVCA)**
19 Pepper Street, Glengall Bridge, London E14 9RP
Website: www.ivca.org
e-mail: info@ivca.org
Fax: 020-7512 0591　　　　Tel: 020-7512 0571

IRISH EQUITY GROUP (SIPTU)
9th Floor, Liberty Hall, Dublin 1, Eire
Website: www.irishequity.ie
e-mail: equity@siptu.ie
Fax: 00 353 1 8743691　　　　Tel: 00 353 1 8586403

IRVING SOCIETY The
(Michael Kilgarriff, Hon. Secretary)
10 Kings Avenue, London W5 2SH
e-mail: secretary@theirvingsociety.org.uk
　　　　　　　　　　　　Tel: 020-8566 8301

ITC
(See INDEPENDENT THEATRE COUNCIL)

ITV PLC
200 Gray's Inn Road, London WC1X 8HF
Website: www.itv.com
Fax: 020-7843 8158　　　　Tel: 020-7843 8000

**LIAISON OF ACTORS, MANAGEMENTS & PLAYWRIGHTS
(LAMP)**
(W Robi)
86A Elgin Avenue, London W9　　　　Tel: 020-7289 3031

LONDON SCHOOL OF CAPOEIRA The
Units 1 & 2 Leeds Place, Tollington Park, London N4 3RQ
Website: www.londonschoolofcapoeira.co.uk
　　　　　　　　　　　　Tel: 020-7281 2020

LONDON SHAKESPEARE WORKOUT The
181A Faunce House
Doddington Grove, Kennington, London SE17 3TB
Website: www.londonshakespeare.org.uk
e-mail: londonswo@hotmail.com　　Tel/Fax: 020-7793 9755

MANDER & MITCHENSON THEATRE COLLECTION
Jerwood Library of the Performing Arts
King Charles Building, Old Royal Naval College
Greenwich, London SE10 9JF
e-mail: rmangan@tcm.ac.uk
Fax: 020-8305 3993　　　　Tel: 020-8305 4426

MUSICIANS' UNION
60-64 Clapham Road, London SW9 0JJ
Website: www.musiciansunion.org.uk
Fax: 020-7582 9805　　　　Tel: 020-7582 5566

**NATIONAL ASSOCIATION OF SUPPORTING ARTISTES
AGENTS (NASAA)**
Website: www.nasaa.org.uk
e-mail: extrasagencies@hotmail.com

NATIONAL ASSOCIATION OF YOUTH THEATRES (NAYT)
Arts Centre, Vane Terrace
Darlington, County Durham DL3 7AX
Website: www.nayt.org.uk
e-mail: nayt@btconnect.com
Fax: 01325 363313　　　　Tel: 01325 363330

NATIONAL CAMPAIGN FOR THE ARTS
Pegasus House
37-43 Sackville Street
London W1S 3EH
Website: www.artscampaign.org.uk
e-mail: nca@artscampaign.org.uk
Fax: 020-7333 0660　　　　Tel: 020-7333 0375

NATIONAL COUNCIL FOR DRAMA TRAINING
1-7 Woburn Walk
Bloomsbury, London WC1H 0JJ
Website: www.ncdt.co.uk
e-mail: info@ncdt.co.uk
Fax: 020-7387 3860　　　　Tel: 020-7387 3650

NATIONAL ENTERTAINMENT AGENTS COUNCIL
PO Box 112, Seaford, East Sussex BN25 2DQ
Website: www.neac.org.uk
e-mail: wfo@neac.org
Fax: 0870 7557613　　　　Tel: 0870 7557612

NATIONAL FILM THEATRE
South Bank, London SE1 8XT
Website: www.bfi.org.uk　　　　Tel: 020-7928 3535

NATIONAL RESOURCE CENTRE FOR DANCE
University of Surrey
Guildford, Surrey GU2 7XH
Website: www.surrey.ac.uk/nrcd
e-mail: nrcd@surrey.ac.uk　　　　Tel: 01483 689316

NODA (National Operatic & Dramatic Association)
Noda House, 58-60 Lincoln Road, Peterborough PE1 2RZ
Website: www.noda.org.uk
e-mail: everyone@noda.org.uk
Fax: 0870 7702490　　　　Tel: 0870 7702480

the actors centre

A space of energy and inspiration where professional actors can experiment, share creativity, meet new challenges and pursue excellence.

A meeting place where professional actors can develop ideas, exchange information and support one another.

Subsidised Classes

- audition technique
- dialect
- sight reading
- singing
- voice

- film
- musical theatre
- poetry reading
- radio
- television
- writing

- Alexander technique
- fencing/stage combat
- movement
- dance

- career advice
- casting sessions
- financial advice

Tristan Bates Theatre

A vibrant and varied programme of new and developing work

The Green Room Bar and Restaurant

Drinks & Snacks

Audition Rooms

Available for hire - ranging from 10 x 15 ft to 22 x 29 ft
Line-Learning service available

If you would like a copy of our current programme please telephone:

020 7240 3940

1A Tower Street Covent Garden WC2H 9NP

or

admin@actorscentre.co.uk

Founding Patron: Lord Olivier
Patron: 1983-94: Sir Alec Guinness
Patron: Sir Alan Bates
Artistic Director: Matthew Lloyd

NORTH AMERICAN ACTORS ASSOCIATION
1 De Vere Cottages, Canning Place, London W8 5AA
Website: www.naaa.org.uk
e-mail: americanactors@aol.com   Tel/Fax: 020-7938 4722

NORTH WEST PLAYWRIGHTS
18 St Margaret's Chambers
5 Newton Street, Manchester M1 1HL
Website: www.newplaysnw.com
e-mail: newplaysnw@hotmail.com   Tel/Fax: 0161-237 1978

NORTHERN ACTORS CENTRE
21-23 Oldham Street, Manchester M1 1JG
Website: www.northernactorscentre.co.uk
e-mail: info@northernactorscentre.co.uk
    Tel/Fax: 0161-819 2513

OFCOM
Ofcom Media Office, Riverside House
2A Southwark Bridge Road, London SE1 9HA
Website: www.ofcom.org.uk
e-mail: mediaoffice@ofcom.org.uk   Tel: 020-7981 3033

PACT (PRODUCERS ALLIANCE FOR CINEMA & TELEVISION)
(Trade Association for Independent Television, Feature
Film & New Media Production Companies)
45 Mortimer Street, London W1W 8HJ
Website: www.pact.co.uk
e-mail: enquiries@pact.co.uk
Fax: 020-7331 6700   Tel: 020-7331 6000

PERFORMING RIGHT SOCIETY Ltd
29-33 Berners Street, London W1T 3AB
Website: www.mcps-prs-alliance.co.uk
Fax: 020-7306 4455   Tel: 020-7580 5544

PERSONAL MANAGERS' ASSOCIATION Ltd
Rivercroft, 1 Summer Road
East Molesey, Surrey KT8 9LX
e-mail: info@thepma.com   Tel/Fax: 020-8398 9796

ROYAL TELEVISION SOCIETY
Holborn Hall, 100 Gray's Inn Road, London WC1X 8AL
Website: www.rts.org.uk
e-mail: info@rts.org.uk
Fax: 020-7430 0924   Tel: 020-7430 1000

ROYAL THEATRICAL FUND
11 Garrick Street, London WC2E 9AR
e-mail: admin@trtf.com
Fax: 020-7379 8273   Tel: 020-7836 3322

S A G
(Screen Actors Guild)
5757 Wilshire Boulevard, Los Angeles, CA 90036-3600
Fax: (323) 549-6656   Tel: (323) 954-1600

360 Madison Avenue, 44th Floor, New York NY 10017
Website: www.sag.org   Tel: (212) 944-1030

SAMPAD SOUTH ASIAN ARTS DEVELOPMENT
(Promotes the appreciation & practice of South Asian Arts)
c/o Mac Cannon Hill Park, Birmingham B12 9QH
Website: www.sampad.org.uk
e-mail: info@sampad.org.uk
Fax: 0121-440 8667   Tel: 0121-446 4312

SAVE LONDON'S THEATRES CAMPAIGN
Guild House, Upper St Martin's Lane, London WC2H 9EG
Website: www.savelondonstheatres.org.uk
e-mail: contactus@savelondonstheatres.org.uk
Fax: 020-7379 7001   Tel: 020-7670 0270

SCOTTISH ARTS COUNCIL
12 Manor Place, Edinburgh EH3 7DD
Website: www.scottisharts.org.uk
Fax: 0131-225 9833   Tel: 0131-226 6051

SCOTTISH SCREEN PRODUCTION & DEVELOPMENT
249 West George Street, Glasgow G2 4QE
Website: www.scottishscreen.com
e-mail: info@scottishscreen.com
Fax: 0141-302 1711   Tel: 0141-302 1700

SCREENWRITER'S WORKSHOP The
Screenwriters' Centre, Suffolk House
1-8 Whitfield Place, London W1T 5JU
Website: www.lsw.org.uk
e-mail: screenoffice@tiscali.co.uk   Tel: 020-7387 5511

SCRIPT
(West Midlands Playwrights, Scriptwriters - Training & Support)
Unit 107 The Greenhouse, The Custard Factory, Gibb Street
Birmingham B9 4AA   Tel/Fax: 0121-224 7415

SOCIETY FOR THEATRE RESEARCH The
c/o The Theatre Museum
1E Tavistock Street, London WC2E 7PR
Website: www.blot.co.uk/str
e-mail: e.cottis@btinternet.com

SOCIETY OF AUTHORS
84 Drayton Gardens, London SW10 9SB
Website: www.societyofauthors.org
e-mail: info@societyofauthors.org   Tel: 020-7373 6642

SOCIETY OF BRITISH THEATRE DESIGNERS
4th Floor, 55 Farringdon Road, London EC1M 3JB
Website: www.theatredesign.org.uk
e-mail: office@abtt.org.uk
Fax: 020-7242 9303   Tel: 020-7242 9200

SOCIETY OF LONDON THEATRE (SOLT)
32 Rose Street, London WC2E 9ET
e-mail: enquiries@solttma.co.uk
Fax: 020-7557 6799   Tel: 020-7557 6700

SOCIETY OF TEACHERS OF SPEECH & DRAMA The
Registered Office:
73 Berry Hill Road, Mansfield, Nottinghamshire NG18 4RU
Website: www.stsd.org.uk
e-mail: ann.k.jones@btinternet.com   Tel: 01623 627636

SOCIETY OF THEATRE CONSULTANTS
4th Floor, 55 Farringdon Road, London EC1M 3JB
e-mail: office@abtt.org.uk
Fax: 020-7242 9303   Tel: 020-7242 9200

STAGE CRICKET CLUB
39-41 Hanover Steps, St George's Fields
Albion Street, London W2 2YG
Website: www.stagecc.co.uk
e-mail: brianjfilm@aol.com
Fax: 020-7262 5736   Tel: 020-7402 7543

STAGE GOLFING SOCIETY
Sudbrook Park, Sudbrook Lane
Richmond, Surrey TW10 7AS   Tel: 020-8940 8861

STAGE MANAGEMENT ASSOCIATION
55 Farringdon Road
London EC1M 3JB
Website: www.stagemanagementassociation.co.uk
e-mail: admin@stagemanagementassociation.co.uk
Fax: 020-7242 9303   Tel: 020-7242 9250

THEATRE INVESTMENT FUND Ltd
32 Rose Street, London WC2E 9ET
Fax: 020-7557 6799   Tel: 020-7557 6737

THEATRE MUSEUM The
1E Tavistock Street, London WC2E 7PR
Website: http://theatremuseum.org
Fax: 020-7943 4777   Tel: 020-7943 4700

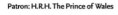

THEATRE WRITING PARTNERSHIP
Nottingham Playhouse
Wellington Circus
Nottingham NG1 5AF
e-mail: esther@theatrewritingpartnership.com
Fax: 0115-953 9055 Tel: 0115-947 4361

THEATRECARES
(Theatre Arm of Crusaid - the National Fundraiser for HIV & Aids)
1st Floor, 1-5 Curtain Road
London EC2A 3JX
Website: www.theatrecares.org.uk
e-mail: info@theatrecares.org.uk
Fax: 020-7539 3890 Tel: 020-7539 3880

THEATRES TRUST The
22 Charing Cross Road
London WC2H 0QL
Website: www.theatrestrust.org.uk
e-mail: info@theatrestrust.org.uk
Fax: 020-7836 3302 Tel: 020-7836 8591

THEATRICAL GUILD The
PO Box 22712
London N22 5WQ
Website: www.the-theatrical-guild-org-uk
e-mail: admin@the-theatrical-guild.org.uk
Tel: 020-8889 7570

THEATRICAL MANAGEMENT ASSOCIATION
(See TMA)

TMA
(Theatrical Management Association)
32 Rose Street
London WC2E 9ET
Website: www.tmauk.org
e-mail: enquiries@solttma.co.uk
Fax: 020-7557 6799 Tel: 020-7557 6700

TOOTING & BALHAM WRITERS' CIRCLE
(Write)
1A Gambole Road
Tooting Broadway
London SW17 0QJ
Website: www.writers-circles.com/tooting.html
e-mail: jasonyoung72@yahoo.com

UK CHOREOGRAPHERS' DIRECTORY The
(See DANCE UK)

UK FILM COUNCIL INTERNATIONAL
10 Little Portland Street, London W1W 7JG
Website: www.ukfilmcouncil.org.uk
e-mail: internationalinfo@ukfilmcouncil.org.uk
Fax: 020-7861 7864 Tel: 020-7861 7861

UK THEATRE CLUBS
54 Swallow Drive
London NW10 8TG
e-mail: uktheatreclubs@aol.com Tel/Fax: 020-8459 3972

UNITED KINGDOM COPYRIGHT BUREAU
110 Trafalgar Road
Portslade
East Sussex BN41 1GS
Website: www.copyrightbureau.co.uk
e-mail: info@copyrightbureau.co.uk
Fax: 01273 705451 Tel: 01273 277333

VARIETY & LIGHT ENTERTAINMENT COUNCIL
54 Keyes House
Dolphin Square, London SW1V 3NA
Fax: 020-7821 0261 Tel: 020-7798 5622

VARIETY CLUB OF GREAT BRITAIN
Variety Club House
93 Bayham Street
London NW1 0AG
Website: www.varietyclub.org.uk
e-mail: info@varietyclub.org.uk
Fax: 020-7428 8111 Tel: 020-7428 8100

VOICE GUILD OF GREAT BRITAIN The
c/o 4 Turner Close
London SW9 6UQ
Fax: 020-7820 1845 Tel: 020-7735 5736

WOLFF Peter THEATRE TRUST The
(Peter Wolff)
Flat 22, 7 Princess Gate, London SW7 1QL
Website: www.peterwolfftheatretrust.org
e-mail: pmwolff@msn.com Mobile: 07767 242552

WOMEN IN FILM AND TELEVISION
6 Langley Street
London WC2H 9JA
e-mail: info@wftv.org.uk
Fax: 020-7379 1625 Tel: 020-7240 4875

WRITERNET
Cabin V
Clarendon Buildings
25 Horsell Road, London N5 1XL
Website: www.writernet.org.uk
e-mail: writernet@btinternet.com
Fax: 020-7609 7557 Tel: 020-7609 7474

WRITERS' GUILD OF GREAT BRITAIN The
15 Britannia Street
London WC1X 9JN
Website: www.writersguild.org.uk
e-mail: admin@writersguild.org.uk
Fax: 020-7833 4777 Tel: 020-7833 0777

P

Photographers (Advertisers Only)

Each photographer listed in this section has taken an advertisement in this edition. Also see Index to Advertisers pages 346-347.

Press Cutting Agencies
Properties & Trades
Publications
Publicity & Press Representatives

[CONTACTS 2005]

1ST CLASS PHOTOGRAPHY
Mobile: 07813 282391   Tel: 0121-457 8141

ACTIVE PHOTOGRAPHY
Website: www.activephotography.co.uk
e-mail: chrishall@activephotography.co.uk
Mobile: 07831 541342   Tel: 0800 781 2412

ACTORSHEADSHOTS.CO.UK
Website: www.actorsheadshots.co.uk

ACTOR'S ONE-STOP SHOP
Website: www.actorsone-stopshop.com
Tel: 020-8888 7006

ALLEN Rafe
Mobile: 07980 840757

ALLEN Stuart
Website: www.stuartallenphotos.com
Mobile: 07776 258829

ANNAND Simon
e-mail: simonannand@blueyonder.co.uk
Mobile: 07884 446776   Tel: 020-7241 6725

ARTSHOT.CO.UK
e-mail: angela@artshot.co.uk
Mobile: 07931 537363   Tel: 020-8521 7654

BACON Ric
Website: www.ricbacon.co.uk
Mobile: 07970 970799

BAKER Chris
e-mail: chrisbaker@photos2000.demon.co.uk
Tel: 020-8441 3851

BAKER Sophie
Tel: 020-8340 3850

BLAKE Coral
e-mail: coralblake@ntlworld.com
Mobile: 07949 702563   Tel: 020-7652 1108

BRIERLEY Marcus
Tel: 01695 555014

BURNETT Sheila
Website: www.sheilaburnett-photography.com
Tel: 020-7289 3058

CAREY Richenda
Mobile: 07980 393866

CARPENTER TURNER Robert
Website: www.carpenterturner.co.uk
e-mail: robert@carpenterturner.co.uk
Mobile: 07956 222596   Tel: 020-7624 2225

CARROLL Scott Michael
Mobile: 07802 918238   Tel: 0161-273 7277

CARTER Charlie
Tel: 020-7751 0575

CASTING-IMAGE.COM
e-mail: photo@casting-image.com
Mobile: 07905 311408   Tel: 020-8533 3126

CHAPMAN Linda
Website: www.lcphotography.demon.co.uk
e-mail: lindachapman@lcphotography.demon.co.uk
Mobile: 07931 592560   Tel: 020-8678 6373

CICCHELLI Carlos
Website: 7LAstudios.co.uk
Mobile: 07960 726957   Tel: 020-7686 2324

CLARK John
Website: www.johnclarkphotography.com
e-mail: info@johnclarkphotography.com
Mobile: 07702 627237   Tel: 020-8854 4069

COOK Mark
Website: www.markcookphotography.com
Tel: 0121-240 8950

COX Melanie
Website: www.melaniecoxphoto.com
Mobile: 07973 450424   Tel: 020-7254 1449

CUNNINGHAM Kim
Website: www.kimcunningham.co.uk
Mobile: 07941 227729

DANCE SCENE PHOTOGRAPHIC
Mobile: 07702 747123   Tel: 01737 552874

DEBAL
e-mail: debal@abeautifulimage.com
Tel: 020-8568 2122

DE LENG Stephanie
Website: www.stephaniedeleng.co.uk
e-mail: deleng@blueyonder.co.uk
Mobile: 07740 927765   Tel: 0151-476 1563

DEUCHAR Angus
Website: www.actorsphotos.co.uk
Mobile: 07973 600728   Tel: 020-8286 3303

DILLON Harry
Website: www.harrydillon.com
Mobile: 07941 503166

DOCKAR-DRYSDALE Jonathan
e-mail: j.d-d@lineone.net
Mobile: 07711 006191   Tel: 020-8560 1077

DUNKIN Mary
Website: www.marydunkinphotography.co.uk
Tel: 020-8969 8043

DYE Debbie
Website: www.debbiedye.com
Mobile: 07957 653913

EDDOWES Mike
Website: www.theatre-photography.co.uk
e-mail: mike@photo-publicity.co.uk
Mobile: 07970 141005

EVANS Owen
Mobile: 07940 700294

EYRE Anne
Website: www.eyrephoto.co.uk
Tel: 020-7638 1289

FERNANDES David
Website: www.image2film.com
Mobile: 07958 272333   Tel: 01273 549967

FLETCHER John
Tel: 020-8203 4816

FLETCHER Julian
Mobile: 07949 637551   Tel: 020-7485 6861

GILL James
Tel: 020-7735 5632

GREENBERG Natasha
Mobile: 07932 618111   Tel: 020-7642 5468

GREGAN Nick
Website: www.nickgregan.com
Mobile: 07774 421878   Tel: 020-7538 1249

GROGAN Claire
Website: www.clairegrogan.co.uk
Mobile: 07932 635381   Tel: 020-7272 1845

HARWOOD-STAMPER Daniel
e-mail: dan_stamper@hotmail.com
Tel: 020-7930 1372

HASTINGS Magnus
Website: www.magnushastings.co.uk
Mobile: 07905 304705 Tel: 020-7033 9757

HUGHES Jamie
Mobile: 07850 122977

HUNTER Remy
Website: www.remyhunter.co.uk
Mobile: 07766 760724   Tel: 020-7431 8055

JEFFERSON Paris
Mobile: 07876 586601   Tel: 020-7252 0328

JOHNSON Olyden
Website: www.olyden.com
e-mail: oj@olyden.com
Mobile: 07739 172399   Tel: 020-8733 8229

KELLY Luke
Tel: 020-8878 2823

KENDALL Neil
Website: neilkendallphotography.com
Mobile: 07776 198332

KING Simon
Website: www.simonking.com
Mobile: 07885 201404   Tel: 0161-272 6808

LATIMER Carole
Fax: 020-7229 9306   Tel: 020-7727 9371

LAWTON Steve
Website: www.stevelawton.com
Mobile: 07973 307487

LB PHOTOGRAPHY (Lisa Bowerman)
Mobile: 07885 966192   Tel: 01737 224578

LIFEIMAGE
Website: www.lifeimage.org
Mobile: 07950 7333993

MACKLE John
Mobile: 07808 298860

M.A.D. PHOTOGRAPHY
Website: www.mad-photography.co.uk
Mobile: 07949 581909   Tel: 020-8363 4182

MARSHALL Chris
e-mail: marshallini152@yahoo.com
Tel: 07830 115123

MARTIN Murray
Tel: 020-8952 6198

MOORE Casey
Website: www.caseymoore.com
e-mail: casey@caseymoore.com
Mobile: 07974 188105

MULHOLLAND Ruth
Mobile: 07939 516987

MY CV ONLINE
Website: www.mycvonline.co.uk

NAMDAR Fatimah
Website: www.fatimahnamdar.com
Tel: 020-8341 1332

NEW ID
Website: www.newidstudios.com
Tel: 0870 870 1299

NEWMAN-WILLIAMS Claire
Website: www.clairenewmanwilliams.com
e-mail: claire@newmanwilliams.com
Mobile: 07963 967444

O'SHEA Louise
www.louiseoshea.com
Mobile: 07966 236188   Tel: 020-8348 6101

PARKER Adam
Mobile: 07710 787708   Tel: 020-7684 2005

PASSMORE George
e-mail: georgepassmore@mac.com
Mobile: 07775 658515

PASSPORT PHOTO SERVICE
Tel: 020-7629 8540

POLLARD Michael
Website: www.michaelpollard.co.uk
e-mail: info@michaelpollard.co.uk
Tel: 0161-456 7470

PR PHOTOGRAPHY
Website: www.pr-photography.com
e-mail: penny@pr-photography.com
Tel: 01483 755837

PRICE David
Website: www.davidpricephotography.co.uk
Mobile: 07950 542494

RUSSELL Tony
e-mail: tonyrussellphoto@hotmail.com
Mobile: 07831 103843   Tel: 020-8530 4030

SAYER Howard
Website: www.howardsayer.co.uk
e-mail: howardsayer@btconnect.com
Mobile: 07860 559891

SHAKESPEARE LANE Catherine
Tel: 020-7226 7694

SHIRKÉ Milind
Website: www.milindshirke.com
Mobile: 07930 462589

SIMPKIN Peter
Website: www.petersimpkin.co.uk
e-mail: petersimpkin@aol.com
Tel: 020-8883 2727

SMITH Lucy
Website: www.thatlucy.co.uk
Tel: 020-8521 1347

SMITH Richard H.
Tel: 020-7490 2090

SPENCER CLAMP Paul
Tel: 01273 323782

STILL Rosie
Website: www.rosiestillphotography.com
Mobile: 07957 318919   Tel: 020-8857 6920

STONE Deborah
Tel: 0845 6445225

STRAEGER Anthony
Website: www.straegerphoto.co.uk
e-mail: straeger@hotmail.com
Mobile: 07963 838633

STUDIO 64
Website: www.studio64headshots.com
Tel: 020-7243 3115

SUMMERS Caroline
Tel: 020-7223 7669

TAKE THE POSE
Website: www.takethepose.co.uk
e-mail: markeady@takethepose.co.uk
Mobile: 07775 711114   Tel: 020-8429 4810

TM PHOTOGRAPHY
Website: www.tmphotography.co.uk
e-mail: tm.photography@ntlworld.com
Mobile: 07931 755252   Tel: 020-8924 4694

TWINNING John
Mobile: 07976 165109   Tel: 0121-515 2906

ULLATHORNE Steve
Website: www.ullapix.com
e-mail: steve@ullapix.com
Mobile: 07961 380969

VANDYCK Katie
Website: www.iphotou.co.uk
Mobile: 07941 940259

WATSON Robin
Website: www.robinwatson.biz
e-mail: robin@robinwatson.biz
Mobile: 07956 416943   Tel: 020-7833 1982

WILL C
Website: www.billysnapper.com
e-mail: billy_snapper@hotmail.com
Mobile: 07712 669953   Tel/Fax: 020-8438 0202

WOOLNOUGH Laura
Mobile: 07941 018957   Tel: 020-8693 9596

WORKMAN Robert
Website: www.robertworkman.demon.co.uk
Tel: 020-7385 5442

PRESS CUTTING AGENCIES

DURRANTS
(Media Monitoring Agency)
Discovery House
28-42 Banner Street
London EC1Y 8QE
Website: www.durrants.co.uk
e-mail: sales@durrants.co.uk
Fax: 020-7674 0222   Tel: 020-7674 0200

INFORMATION BUREAU The
51 The Business Centre
103 Lavender Hill
London SW11 5QL
Website: www.informationbureau.co.uk
e-mail: info@informationbureau.co.uk
Fax: 020-7738 2513   Tel: 020-7924 4414

INTERNATIONAL PRESS-CUTTING BUREAU
224-236 Walworth Road
London SE17 1JE
e-mail: ipcb2000@aol.com
Fax: 020-7701 4489   Tel: 020-7708 2113

McCALLUM MEDIA MONITOR
Tower House
10 Possil Road
Glasgow G4 9SY
Website: www.press-cuttings.com
Fax: 0141-333 1811   Tel: 0141-333 1822

TNS MEDIA INTELLIGENCE
6th Floor
292 Vauxhall Bridge Road
London SW1V 1AE
Fax: 020-7963 7609   Tel: 020-7963 7605

07000 BIG TOP
(Big Top, Seating, Circus)
The Arts Exchange, Congleton, Cheshire CW12 1JG
Website: www.arts-exchange.com
e-mail: phillipgandey@netcentral.co.uk
Fax: 01260 270777 Tel: 01260 276627

10 OUT OF 10 PRODUCTIONS Ltd
(Lighting, Sound, AV Hire, Sales & Installation)
Unit 14 Forest Hill Business Centre
Clyde Vale, London SE23 3JF
Website: www.10outof10.co.uk
e-mail: sales@10outof10.co.uk
Fax: 020-8699 8968 Tel: 0845 1235664

20TH CENTURY FUNFAIR FACTORY
(Fun Fair Locations, Equipment and Prop Hire)
5 Bonds Drive, Pennypot Lane, Chobham, Surrey GU24 8DJ
Mobile: 07976 297735 Tel: 01276 485893

3D CREATIONS
(Production Design, Scenery Contractors, Prop Makers &
Scenic Artists)
9A Bells Road, Gorleston-on-Sea
Great Yarmouth, Norfolk NR31 6BB
Website: www.3dcreations.co.uk
e-mail: 3dcreations@rjt.co.uk
Fax: 01493 443124 Tel: 01493 652055

ACROBAT PRODUCTIONS
(Artistes & Advisors)
The Circus Space, Coronet Street, Hackney, London N1 6HD
Website: www.acrobatproductions.co.uk
e-mail: info@acrobatproductions.co.uk Tel: 020-7613 5259

ADAMS ENGRAVING
Unit G1A, The Mayford Centre
Mayford Green, Woking GU22 0PP
Website: www.adamsengraving.co.uk
e-mail: adamsengraving@pncl.co.uk
Fax: 01483 751787 Tel: 01483 725792

AFX (UK) Ltd
(Incorporating Kirby's Flying Ballets)
8 Greenford Avenue, Hanwell, London W7 3QP
Website: www.kirbysflying.co.uk
e-mail: mail@afxuk.com
Mobile: 07958 285608 Tel/Fax: 020-8723 8552

AIRBOURNE SYSTEMS INTERNATIONAL
(All Skydiving Requirements Arranged. Parachute Hire -
Period & Modern)
8 Burns Crescent
Chelmsford, Essex CM2 0TS Tel: 01245 268772

ALCHEMICAL LABORATORIES ETC
(Medieval Science & Technology Recreated for
Museums & Films)
2 Stapleford Lane, Coddington
Newark, Nottinghamshire NG24 2QZ
Website: www.jackgreene.co.uk Tel: 01636 707836

ALL SCENE ALL PROPS
(Props, Masks, Painting & Scenery Makers)
443-445 Holloway Road, London N7 6LW
Website: www.allscene.net
e-mail: info@allscene.net Tel/Fax: 020-7561 9231

ANCHOR MARINE FILM & TELEVISION
(Boat Location, Charter, Maritime Co-ordinators)
Spikemead Farm, Poles Lane
Lowfield Heath, West Sussex RH11 0PX
e-mail: amsfilm@aol.com
Fax: 01293 551558 Tel: 01293 538188

ANELLO & DAVIDE Ltd
(Bridal Footwear)
Shop: 47 Beauchamp Place, Chelsea, London SW3 1NX
Website: www.handmadeshoes.co.uk
Fax: 020-7225 3375 Tel: 020-7225 2468

ANGLO PACIFIC INTERNATIONAL Plc
(Freight Forwarders & Removal Services)
Unit 1, Bush Industrial Estate
Standard Road, North Acton, London NW10 6DF
Website: www.anglopacific.co.uk
Fax: 020-8965 4954 Tel: 020-8965 1234

ANIMAL ARK
(Animals & Natural History Props)
The Studio, 29 Somerset Road
Brentford, Middlesex TW8 8BT
Website: www.animal-ark.co.uk
e-mail: info@animal-ark.co.uk
Fax: 020-8560 5762 Tel: 020-8560 3029

ANNUAL CLOWNS DIRECTORY The
(Salvo The Clown)
13 Second Avenue, Kingsleigh Park
Thundersley, Essex SS7 3QD Tel: 01268 745791

AQUARIUS
(Film & TV Stills Library)
PO Box 5, Hastings TN34 1HR
Website: www.aquariuscollection.com
e-mail: aquarius.lib@clara.net
Fax: 01424 717704 Tel: 01424 721196

AQUATECH
(Camera Boats)
Epney, Gloucestershire GL2 7LN
Website: www.aquatech-uk.com
e-mail: office@aquatech-uk.com
Fax: 01452 741958 Tel: 01452 740559

ARCHERY CENTRE The
PO Box 39, Battle
East Sussex TN33 0ZT — Tel: 01424 777183

ARMS & ARCHERY
(Armour, Weaponry, Chainmail, X-bows, Longbows)
The Coach House, London Road
Ware, Herts SG12 9QU
e-mail: tgou104885@aol.com
Fax: 01920 461044 — Tel: 01920 460335

ART*
(Art Consultant, Supplier of Paintings & Sculpture)
66 Josephine Avenue
London SW2 2LA
Website: www.artstar.clara.net
e-mail: h_artstar@hotmail.com
Fax: 07970 455956 — Tel: 07967 294985

ART DIRECTORS & TRIP PHOTO LIBRARY
(Colour Slides - All Subjects)
57 Burdon Lane, Cheam, Surrey SM2 7BY
Website: www.artdirectors.co.uk
e-mail: images@artdirectors.co.uk
Fax: 020-8395 7230 — Tel: 020-8642 3593

A. S. DESIGNS
(Theatrical Designer, Sets, Costumes, Heads, Masks, Puppets etc)
Website: www.astheatricaldesign.co.uk
e-mail: maryannscadding@btinternet.com
Fax: 01279 435642 — Tel: 01279 722416

ASH Riky
(Equity Registered Stunt Performer/Co-ordinator)
c/o 65 Britania Avenue, Nottingham NG6 0EA
Website: www.fallingforyou.tv
Mobile: 07850 471227 — Tel: 0115-849 3470

ATP EUROPE Ltd
(Design, Print & Repro)
ATP House, 12 Sovereign Park
London NW10 7QP
e-mail: info@atpeurope.com
Fax: 020-8961 7743   Tel: 020-8961 0001

BAD DOG DESIGN/3D PRODUCTIONS
(3D Productions, 3D Models, Props, Sets)
Fir Tree Cottage, Fish Pool Hill, Brentry, Bristol BS10 6SW
e-mail: info@baddogdesign.co.uk
Fax: 0117-959 1245   Tel: 0117-959 2011

BAPTY 2000 Ltd
(Weapons, Dressing, Props etc)
Witley Works, Witley Gardens
Norwood Green, Middlesex UB2 4ES
e-mail: hire@bapty.demon.co.uk
Fax: 020-8571 5700   Tel: 020-8574 7700

BARNES CATERERS Ltd
8 Ripley Drive, Normanton, Wakefield
West Yorkshire WF6 1QT   Tel/Fax: 01924 892332

BARTON Joe
(Puppeteer, Model & Prop Maker)
7 Brands Hill Avenue, High Wycombe
Buckinghamshire   Tel: 01494 439056

BASINGSTOKE PRESS The
Digital House, The Loddon Centre, Wade Road
Basingstoke, Hampshire RG24 8QW
Website: www.basingstokepress.co.uk
e-mail: sales@baspress.co.uk
Fax: 01256 840383   Tel: 01256 467771

BEAT ABOUT THE BUSH Ltd
(Musical Instruments)
Unit 23, Enterprise Way, Triangle Business Centre
Salter Street, London NW10 6UG
Website: www.beataboutthebush.com
e-mail: info@beataboutthebush.com
Fax: 020-8969 2281   Tel: 020-8960 2087

BENSON'S JUMPAROUND ACTIVITY CENTRES
(Chester Benson Inflatables & Soft Play Equipment, Bouncy
Castles)
PO Box 4227, Worthing BN11 5ST
Website: www.davebensonphillips.co.uk   Tel: 01903 248258

BIANCHERI The
(Wingbolt Spanner)
T & D House, 7 Woodville Road, London E17 7ER
Mobile: 07973 663154   Tel: 020-8521 6408

BIANCHI AVIATION FILM SERVICES
(Historic & Other Aircraft)
Wycombe Air Pk, Booker Marlow, Buckinghamshire SL7 3DP
Website: www.bianchiaviation.com
e-mail: info@bianchiaviation.com
Fax: 01494 461236   Tel: 01494 449810

BIDDLES Ltd
(Quality Book Binders & Printers)
Unit 26, Rollesby Road, Hardwick Industrial Estate
King's Lynn, Norfolk PE30 4LS
Website: www.biddles.co.uk
e-mail: enquiries@biddles.co.uk
Fax: 01553 764633   Tel: 01553 764728

BLACKOUT Ltd
280 Western Road, London SW19 2QA
Website: www.blackout-ltd.com
e-mail: info@blackout-ltd.com
Fax: 020-8687 8500   Tel: 020-8687 8400

BLUEBELL RAILWAY Plc
(Steam Locomotives, Pullman Coaches, Period Stations,
Much Film Experience)
Sheffield Park Station, East Sussex TN22 3QL
Website: www.bluebell-railway.co.uk
Fax: 01825 720804   Tel: 01825 720800

BOLDGATE Ltd
The Crossbow Centre, 40 Liverpool Road, Berks SL1 4QZ
Fax: 01753 696401   Tel: 01753 696410

BOSCO LIGHTING
(Design/Technical Consultancy)
63 Nimrod Road, London SW16 6SZ
e-mail: boscolx@lineone.net   Tel: 020-8769 3470

BRISTOL (UK) Ltd
(Scenic Paint & StageFloor Duo Suppliers)
Unit 3, Sutherland Court, Tolpits Lane, Watford WD18 9SP
Website: www.bristolpaint.com
Fax: 01923 779666   Tel: 01923 779333

BRITISH-FOOD-GROCERIES
(British Food Export Service for British People Working
Overseas)
46 Burrage Place, Plumstead, London SE18 7BE
Website: www.british-food-groceries.co.uk
e-mail: sales@directfoods.uk.com   Tel/Fax: 01322 448272

BRODIE & MIDDLETON Ltd
(Theatrical Suppliers, Paints, Powders, Glitter etc)
68 Drury Lane, London WC2B 5SP
Website: www.brodies.net
e-mail: info@brodies.net
Fax: 020-7497 8425   Tel: 020-7836 3289

BROOK-REYNOLDS Natalie
(Freelance Stage Manager/Floor Manager. Member of SMA,
Equity & BECTU)
Website: www.nataliebrookreynolds.com
e-mail: info@nataliebrookreynolds.com
Fax: 0871 2429919   Tel: 020-8350 0877

CANDLE MAKERS SUPPLIES
The Wax & Dyecraft Centre, 28 Blythe Rd, London W14 0HA
Website: www.candlemakers.co.uk
e-mail: candles@candlemakers.co.uk
Fax: 020-7602 2796   Tel: 020-7602 4031

CHALFONT CLEANERS & DYERS Ltd
(Dry Cleaners, Launderers & Dyers, Stage Curtains &
Costumes)
222 Baker Street, London NW1 5RT   Tel: 020-7935 7316

CHEVALIER EVENT DESIGN
(Corporate Hospitality Caterers)
Studio 4-5, Garnett Close, Watford, Herts WD24 7GN
Website: www.chevalier.co.uk
e-mail: enquiries@chevalier.co.uk
Fax: 01923 211704   Tel: 01923 211703

CHRISANNE Ltd
(Specialist Fabrics & Accessories for Theatre & Dance)
Chrisanne House, 14 Locks Lane, Mitcham, Surrey CR4 2JX
Website: www.chrisanne.co.uk
e-mail: sales@chrisanne.co.uk
Fax: 020-8640 2106   Tel: 020-8640 5921

CIRCUS MANIACS
(Circus Equipment, Rigging & Training)
Office 8A, The Kingswood Foundation, Britannia Road
Kingswood, Bristol BS15 8DB
e-mail: info@circusmaniacs.com
Mobile: 07977 247287   Tel/Fax: 0117-947 7042

CIRCUS PROMOTIONS
(Entertainers)
36 St Lukes Road, Tunbridge Wells
Kent TN4 9JH   Tel: 01892 537964

CLARK DAVIS
(Stationery & Office Equipment)
Units 5 & 6, Meridian Trading Estate, 20 Bugsbys Way
Charlton, London SE7 7SJ
e-mail: info@clarkdavis.co.uk
Fax: 020-8331 2091   Tel: 020-8331 2090

CLARKE Donald
(Historical Interpreter, Role Playing)
80 Warden Avenue, Rayners Lane
Harrow, Middlesex HA2 9LW
Mobile: 07811 606285   Tel: 020-8866 2997

CLEANING & FLAME RETARDING SERVICE The
Grove Farm, Grove Farm Road, Tolleshunt Major
Maldon, Essex CM4 8LR
Website: www.flameretarding.co.uk
e-mail: email@flameretarding.co.uk
Fax: 01621 819803   Tel: 01621 818477

COBO MEDIA Ltd
(Performing Arts, Entertainment & Leisure Marketing)
43A Garthorne Road, London SE23 1EP
Website: www.theatrenet.com
e-mail: admin@cobomedia.com
Fax: 020-8291 4969   Tel: 020-8291 7079

COLE MANSON
(Ex-Grenadier Guards. Drill Instructor)
3 Bond Street, London W4 1QZ   Tel: 020-8747 3510

COMPTON Mike & Rosi
(Costumes, Props & Models)
11 Woodstock Road
Croydon, Surrey CR0 1JS
e-mail: mikeandrosicompton@btopenworld.com
Fax: 020-8681 3126   Tel: 020-8680 4364

CONCEPT ENGINEERING Ltd
(Smoke, Fog, Snow etc)
7 Woodlands Business Park, Woodlands Park Avenue,
Maidenhead, Berkshire SL6 3UA
Website: www.concept-smoke.co.uk
Fax: 01628 826261   Tel: 01628 825555

COOK Sheila
(Textiles, Costumes & Accessories for Hire/Sale)
283 Westbourne Grove, London W11 2QA
e-mail: sheilacook@sheilacook.co.uk
Fax: 020-7229 3855   Tel: 020-7792 8001

CRESTA BLINDS Ltd
(Supplier of Vertical Blinds)
Crown Works, Tetnall Street, Dudley DY2 8SA
Website: www.crestablindsltd.co.uk
e-mail: info@crestablindsltd.co.uk
Fax: 01384 457675   Tel: 01384 255523

CROCKSHARD FARMHOUSE
(Bed & Breakfast, Contact: Nicola Ellen)
Wingham, Canterbury, Kent CT3 1NY
e-mail: crockshard_bnb@yahoo.com   Tel: 01227 720464

CROFTS Andrew
(Book Writing Services)
Westlands Grange, West Grinstead
Horsham, West Sussex RH13 8LZ
Website: www.andrewcrofts.com   Tel/Fax: 01403 864518

CUE ACTION POOL PROMOTIONS
(Advice for UK & US Pool, Snooker, Trick Shots)
PO Box 3941, Colchester, Essex CO2 8HN
Website: www.cueaction.com
e-mail: sales@cueaction.com
Fax: 01206 729480   Tel: 07000 868689

DARK SIDE
(Photographic Repro Service)
4 Helmet Row, London EC1V 3QJ
Website: www.darksidephoto.co.uk
e-mail: info@darksidephoto.co.uk
Fax: 020-7250 1771   Tel: 020-7250 1200

DAVEY Brian
(See NOSTALGIA AMUSEMENTS)

DEAN Audrey Vincente
(Soft Dolls, Toys & Figures to Order, No Hire)
76 Burlington Avenue, Kew, Surrey TW9 4DH
e-mail: audreymiller@waitrose.com   Tel: 020-8876 6441

DESIGN ASYLUM
(Design, Web & Print)
Crown House, North Circular Road
Park Royal, London NW10 7PN
Website: www.designasylum.co.uk
e-mail: info@designasylum.co.uk   Tel/Fax: 020-8838 3555

DESIGN PROJECTS
Perrysfield Farm, Broadham Green
Old Oxted, Surrey RH8 9PG
Fax: 01883 723707   Tel: 01883 730262

DEVEREUX K W & Sons
(Removals)
Daimler Drive, Cowpen Industrial Estate
Billingham, Cleveland TS23 4JD
Fax: 01642 566664   Tel: 01642 560854

DONOGHUE Phil
(Film & Television Production Designer)
6 Harbour House, Harbour Way
Shoreham Beach, West Sussex BN43 5HZ
Mobile: 07802 179801   Tel/Fax: 01273 465165

DORANS PROPMAKERS/SET BUILDERS
53 Derby Road, Ashbourne, Derbyshire DE6 1BH
Website: www.doransprops.com
e-mail: props@dorans.demon.co.uk   Tel/Fax: 01335 300064

DRIVING CENTRE The
(Expert Driving Instructors on All Vehicles)
6 Marlott Road, Poole, Dorset BH15 3DX
Mobile: 07860 290437   Tel: 01202 666001

DURRENT Peter
(Audition & Rehearsal Pianist, Cocktail Pianist, Composer, Vocal Coach)
Blacksmiths Cottage, Bures Road, Little Cornard
Sudbury, Suffolk CO10 0NR   Tel: 01787 373483

EAT TO THE BEAT
(Production & Location Caterers)
Studio 4-5, Garnett Close, Watford, Herts WD24 7GN
Website: www.eattothebeat.com
e-mail: enquiries@eattothebeat.com
Fax: 01923 211704   Tel: 01923 211702

ECCENTRIC TRADING COMPANY Ltd
(Antique Furniture & Props) incorporating COMPUHIRE
(Computer Hire)
Unit 2, Frogmore Estate, Acton Lane, London NW10 7NQ
Website: www.compuhire.com
e-mail: info@compuhire.com   Tel: 020-8453 1125

ELECTRO SIGNS Ltd
97 Vallentin Road, London E17 3JJ
Fax: 020-8520 8127   Tel: 020-8521 8066

ELMS LESTERS PAINTING ROOMS
(Scenic Painting)
1-3-5 Flitcroft Street, London WC2H 8DH
e-mail: office@elmslesters.co.uk
Fax: 020-7379 0789   Tel: 020-7836 6747

ENCHANTING FOREST
(Bespoke Props)
Nottingham
Website: www.enchantingforest.co.uk
e-mail: info@enchantingforest.co.uk   Tel/Fax: 0115-983 0777

ESCORT GUNLEATHER
(Custom Leathercraft)
602 High Road, Benfleet, Essex SS7 5RW
Website: www.escortgunleather.com
e-mail: info@escortgunleather.com
Fax: 01268 566775   Tel: 01268 792769

EVANS Peter STUDIOS Ltd
(Scenic Embellishment, Vacuum Forming) (Catalogue Available)
12-14 Tavistock Street, Dunstable, Bedfordshire LU6 1NE
e-mail: peter@peterevansstudios.co.uk
Fax: 01582 481329   Tel: 01582 725730

FAB 'N' FUNKY
(Prop Hire Specialist 50's - 70's)
18-20 Brunel Road, London W3 7XR
Website: www.superhire.com
Fax: 020-8743 2662   Tel: 020-8746 7746

FACADE
(Musical Production Services)
43A Garthorne Road, London SE23 1EP
e-mail: facade@cobomedia.com   Tel: 020-8291 7079

FAIRGROUNDS TRADITIONAL
Halstead, Fovant, Salisbury, Wiltshire SP3 5NL
Website: www.pozzy.co.uk
e-mail: s-vpostlethwaite@fovant.fsnet.co.uk
Mobile: 07710 287251   Tel: 01722 714786

FALCONS STUNT DISPLAY TEAM COMBAT THROUGH THE AGES
(Medieval Displays, Combat Display Team, Stunt Action Specialists)
110 Trafalgar Road, Portslade, East Sussex BN41 1GS
Fax: 01273 708699   Tel: 01273 411862

FILM MEDICAL SERVICES
Units 5 & 7, Commercial Way, Park Royal, London NW10 7XF
Website: www.filmmedical.co.uk
e-mail: filmmed@aol.com
Fax: 020-8961 7427   Tel: 020-8961 3222

FIND ME ANOTHER
(Theatrical Prop Hire & Services. Gardenalia, Kitchenalia,
Dairy & Farming Bygones. Some 1960's)
Mills Barns, c/o 10 Tenzing Grove
Luton, Bedfordshire LU1 5JJ
Website: www.findmeanother.co.uk
e-mail: info@findmeanother.co.uk
Mobile: 07885 777751   Tel/Fax: 01582 415834

FIREBRAND
(Flambeaux Hire & Sales)
Leac na ban, By Lochgilphead, Argyll PA31 8PF
e-mail: alex@firebrand.fsnet.co.uk   Tel/Fax: 01546 870310

FLAMENCO PRODUCTIONS
(Entertainers)
Sevilla 4 Cormorant Rise, Lower Wick
Worcester WR2 4BA   Tel: 01905 424083

FLINT HIRE & SUPPLY Ltd
Queen's Row, London SE17 2PX
Website: www.flints.co.uk
e-mail: sales@flints.co.uk
Fax: 020-7708 4189   Tel: 020-7703 9786

FLYING BY FOY
(Flying Effects for Theatre, TV, Corporate Events etc)
Unit 4, Borehamwood Enterprise Centre, Theobald Street
Borehamwood, Herts WD6 4RQ
Website: www.flyingbyfoy.co.uk
e-mail: mail@flyingbyfoy.co.uk
Fax: 020-8236 0235   Tel: 020-8236 0234

FOXTROT PRODUCTIONS Ltd
(Armoury Services, Firearms, Weapons & Costume Hire)
Unit 46 Canalot Production Studios, 222 Kensal Road,
London W10 5BN   Tel: 020-8964 3555

FREEDALE PRESS
(Printing)
36 Hedley Street, Maidstone, Kent ME14 5AD
e-mail: freedalepress@blueyonder.co.uk
Fax: 01622 200131   Tel: 01622 200123

FROST John NEWSPAPERS
(Historical Newspaper Service)
22B Rosemary Avenue, Enfield, Middlesex EN2 0SS
Website: www.johnfrostnewspapers.com
e-mail: andrew@johnfrostnewspapers.com
            Tel: 020-8366 1392

GAMBA
(Dancewear & Ballet Shoes)
3 Garrick Street, Covent Garden, London WC2E 9BF
Fax: 020-7497 0754   Tel: 020-7437 0704

GARRATT Jonathan
(Suppliers of Unusual Garden Pots & Installations)
Hare Lane Farmhouse, Cranborne, Dorset BH21 5QT
Website: www.jonathangarratt.com
e-mail: jonathan.garratt@talk21.com   Tel: 01725 517770

GAV NICOLA THEATRICAL SHOES
1A Suttons Lane, Hornchurch, Essex RM12 6RD
e-mail: sales@gavnicola.freeserve.co.uk
Mobile: 07961 974278   Tel/Fax: 01708 438584

GET STUFFED
(Taxidermy)
105 Essex Road, London N1 2SL
Website: www.thegetstuffed.co.uk
e-mail: taxidermy@thegetstuffed.co.uk
Fax: 020-7359 8253   Tel: 020-7226 1364

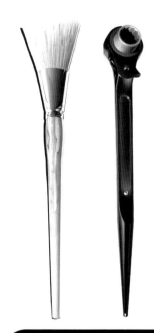

GLOBAL CEILINGS & TILES
(Designers, Suppliers, Installers)
1B Argyle Road, Argyle Corner, Ealing, London W13 OLL
Website: www.globalceiling.co.uk
Mobile: 07976 159402   Tel: 020-8810 5914

GORGEOUS GOURMETS
(Caterers & Equipment Hire)
Gresham Way, Wimbledon SW19 8ED
Website: www.gorgeousgourmets.co.uk
e-mail: events@gorgeousgourmets.co.uk
Fax: 020-8946 1639   Tel: 020-8944 7771

GOULD Gillian ANTIQUES
(Scientific & Marine Antiques & Collectables)
18A Belsize Park Gardens, Belsize Park, London NW3 4LH
e-mail: gillgould@dealwith.com
Mobile: 07831 150060   Tel: 020-7419 0500

GRADAV HIRE & SALES Ltd
(Lighting & Sound Hire/Sales)
Units C6 & C9 Hastingwood Trading Estate, Harbet Road
Edmonton, London N18 3HU
e-mail: office@gradav.co.uk
Fax: 020-8803 5060   Tel: 020-8803 7400

GRAY Robin COMMENTARIES
(Saddles, Bridles, Racing Colours & Hunting Attire)
Comptons, Isington, Alton, Hampshire GU34 4PL
e-mail: gray@isington.fsnet.co.uk   Tel/Fax: 01420 23347

GREENPROPS
(Prop Suppliers, Artificial Trees, Plants, Flowers, Fruit,
Grass etc)
West Bovey Farm, Waterrow, Somerset TA4 2BA
Website: www.greenprops.com
e-mail: trevor@greenprops.com
Fax: 01398 361307   Tel: 01398 361531

HAMPTON COURT HOUSE
(1857 Country House & Grounds)
East Molesey KT8 9BS
Website: www.hamptoncourthouse.com
Fax: 020-8977 5357   Tel: 020-8943 0889

HARLEQUIN Plc
(Floors for Stage, Opera, Dance, Concert, Shows & Events)
Festival House, Chapman Way
Tunbridge Wells, Kent TN2 3EF
Website: www.harlequinfloors.com
e-mail: sales@harlequinfloors.com
Fax: 01892 514222   Tel: 01892 514888

HARLEQUIN PROMOTIONS
(Fun Casinos, Scalextric & Race Nights)
Harlequin House, 13 Gurton Road
Coggleshall, Essex CO6 1QL
Website: www.harlequin-casinos.co.uk
e-mail: john@harlequin-casinos.co.uk   Tel: 01376 563385

HAWES Joanne
(Children's Administrator for Theatre, Film & TV)
21 Westfield Road, Maidenhead, Berkshire SL6 5AU
e-mail: jo.hawes@virgin.net
Fax: 01628 672884   Tel: 01628 773048

HERON & DRIVER
(Scenic Furniture & Prop Makers)
Unit 7, Dockley Road Industrial Estate
Rotherhithe, London SE16 3SF
Website: www.herondriver.co.uk
e-mail: mail@herondriver.co.uk
Fax: 020-7394 8680   Tel: 020-7394 8688

HEWER Richard
(Props Maker)
7 Sion Lane, Bristol BS8 4BE   Tel/Fax: 0117-973 8760

HI-FLI (Flying Effects)
2 Boland Drive, Manchester M14 6DS
e-mail: mikefrost@hi-fli.co.uk   Tel/Fax: 0161-224 6082

HOWARD Rex DRAPES Ltd
Acton Park Industrial Estate, Eastman Road
The Vale, London W3 7QS
Fax: 020-8740 5994   Tel: 020-8740 5881

IMPACT DISTRIBUTION & MARKETING
(Leaflet & Poster Distribution & Display)
Tuscany Wharf, 4B Orsman Road, London N1 5QJ
Website: www.impact.uk.com
e-mail: admin@impact.uk.com
Fax: 020-7729 5994   Tel: 020-7729 5978

IMPACT PERCUSSION
(Percussion Instruments for Sale)
Unit 7 Goose Green Trading Estate
47 East Dulwich Road, London SE22 9BN
e-mail: sales@impactpercussion.com
Fax: 020-8299 6704   Tel: 020-8299 6700

JAPAN PROMOTIONS
(Organise Japanese Events)
200 Russell Court, 3 Woburn Place
London WC1H OND   Tel/Fax: 020-7278 4099

JESSAMINE Bob
(Scene Painting, Prop Making)
4 Matlock Avenue, Birkdale
Southport, Merseyside PR8 5EZ
e-mail: rscsjessamine@supanet.com   Tel: 01704 564521

JONES Melanie ASSOCIATES
(Design & Print)
109 Highland Road, Bromley BR1 4AA
Website: www.mjassocs.co.uk
e-mail: melaniejones@designandprint.demon.co.uk
    Tel/Fax: 020-8290 4999

JULIETTE DESIGNS
(Diamante Jewellery Manufacturer, Necklaces, Crowns etc)
90 Yerbury Road, London N19 4RS
Website: www.stagejewellery.com
Fax: 020-7281 7326   Tel: 020-7263 7878

K & D Ltd
(Footwear)
Unit 7A, Thames Road Industrial Estate, Thames Road
Silvertown, London E16 2EZ
Website: www.shoemaking.co.uk
e-mail: k&d@shoemaking.co.uk
Fax: 020-7476 5220   Tel: 020-7474 0500

KEW BRIDGE STEAM MUSEUM
(Steam Museum)
Green Dragon Lane, Brentford, Middlesex TW8 OEN
Website: www.kbsm.org
e-mail: corporate@kbsm.org
Fax: 020-8569 9978   Tel: 020-8568 4757

KIRKLAND Cindy at CREATIVE WORKS UK Ltd
(Freelance Floral Designer)
Website: www.ckworks.net   e-mail: info@ckworks.net
Mobile: 07976 449681   Tel: 01737 226595

KNEBWORTH HOUSE, GARDENS & PARK
(Knebworth)
Herts SG3 6PY   Tel: 01438 812661

LAREDO Alex
(Expert with Ropes, Bullwhips, Shooting, Riding)
29 Lincoln Road, Dorking
Surrey RH4 1TE   Tel: 01306 889423

LAREDO WILD WEST TOWN
(Wild West Entertainments)
19 Surrenden Road, Staplehurst, Tonbridge, Kent TN12 OLY
Website: www.laredo.org.uk
e-mail: enquiries@laredo.org.uk
Tel: 01474 706129   Tel: 01580 891790

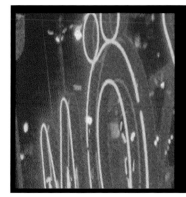
LEES-NEWSOME Ltd
(Manufacturers of Flame Retardant Fabrics)
Ashley Street, Westwood, Oldham, Lancashire OL9 6LS
e-mail: info@leesnewsome.co.uk
Fax: 0161-627 3362   Tel: 0161-652 1321

LEIGHTON HALL
(Historic House)
Carnforth, Lancashire LA5 9ST
Website: www.leightonhall.co.uk
e-mail: leightonhall@yahoo.co.uk
Fax: 01524 720357   Tel: 01524 734474

LEVRANT Stephen - HERITAGE ARCHITECTURE Ltd
(Historic Buildings & Interiors Consultants)
363 West End Lane, West Hampstead, London NW6 1LP
e-mail: levrant@aol.com
Fax: 020-7794 9712   Tel: 020-7435 7502

LONDON BUSINESS EQUIPMENT
(Authorised Canon Dealer)
527-529 High Road, Leytonstone, London E11 4PB
Website: www.londonbusinessequipment.com
e-mail: sales@londonbusinessequipment.com
Fax: 020-8556 4865   Tel: 020-8558 0024

LONO DRINKS COMPANY The
The Hawthorns, Driffield, Cirencester, Glos GL7 5PY
Website: www.lono.co.uk
e-mail: info@lono.co.uk   Tel/Fax: 01285 850682

LOS KAOS
(Entertainment, Circus Skills, Puppetry & Animatronics)
Kaos Towers, 346 Tunbridge Road
Maidstone, Kent ME16 8TG
Website: www.loskaos.co.uk   Tel/Fax: 01622 727433

LYON EQUIPMENT
(Petzl & Beal Rope Access Equipment (PPE) for Industrial & Theatrical Work)
Rise Hill Mill, Dent, Sedbergh, Cumbria LA10 5QL
Website: www.lyon.co.uk   e-mail: info@lyon.co.uk
Fax: 01539 625454   Tel: 01539 625493

M A C
(Sound Hire)
1-2 Attenburys Park
Park Road, Altrincham, Cheshire WA14 5QE
Website: www.macsound.co.uk
e-mail: hire@macsound.co.uk
Fax: 0161-962 9423   Tel: 0161-969 8311

MACKIE Sally LOCATIONS
(Location Finding & Management)
Cownham Farm, Broadwell, Moreton-in-Marsh
Gloucestershire GL56 0TT
Website: www.sallymackie-locations.com
e-mail: info@lokations.fsnet.co.uk
Fax: 01451 832442   Tel: 01451 830294

MADDERMARKET THEATRE
(Furniture, Props, Costumes & Accessories)
(Contact Rhett Davies, Resident Stage Manager)
St John's Alley, Norwich NR2 1DR
Website: www.maddermarket.co.uk
e-mail: mmtheatre@btconnect.com
Fax: 01603 661357   Tel: 01603 626560

MAGICAL MART
(Magic, Ventriloquists' Dolls, Punch & Judy, Hire & Advising. Callers by Appointment)
42 Christchurch Road, Sidcup, Kent DA15 7HQ
Website: www.johnstylesentertainer.co.uk
Tel/Fax: 020-8300 3579

MARKSON PIANOS
8 Chester Court, Albany Street, London NW1 4BU
Website: www.pianosuk.co.uk
e-mail: info@pianosuk.co.uk
Fax: 020-7224 0957   Tel: 020-7935 8682

McDONALD ROWE (SCULPTURE) Ltd
20 Southfield Way, St Albans, Herts AL4 9JJ
e-mail: mcdonald@stalbans01.freeserve.co.uk
Tel: 01727 765277

MIDNIGHT ELECTRONICS
(Sound Hire)
Off Quay Building, Foundry Lane
Newcastle upon Tyne NE6 1LH
Website: www.midnightelectronics.co.uk
e-mail: info@midnightelectronics.co.uk
Fax: 0191-224 0080   Tel: 0191-224 0088

MILITARY, MODELS & MINATURES
(Model Figures)
38A Horsell Road, London N5 1XP
Website: www.modelsculpture.com
e-mail: figsculpt@aol.com
Fax: 020-7700 4624   Tel: 020-7700 7036

MODEL BOX Ltd
(Computer Aided Design & Design Services)
2 Saddlers Way, Okehampton, Devon EX20 1TL
Website: www.modelbox.co.uk
e-mail: info@modelbox.co.uk   Tel/Fax: 01837 54026

MODERNEON LONDON Ltd
(Sign Makers)
Cromwell House, 27 Brabourne Rise
Park Langley, Beckenham, Kent BR3 6SQ
Website: www.moderneon.co.uk
e-mail: moderneon@tiscali.co.uk
Fax: 020-8658 2770   Tel: 020-8650 9690

MOORFIELDS PHOTOGRAPHIC Ltd
2 Old Hall Street, Liverpool L3 9RQ
Website: www.moorfieldsphoto.com
e-mail: info@moorfieldsphoto.com
Fax: 0151-236 1677   Tel: 0151-236 1611

MORTON G & L
(Horses/Farming)
Hashome Carr, Holme-on-Spalding Moor
Yorkshire YO43 4BD   Tel: 01430 860393

MOULDART
(Mouldmaking, Props, Sculpture)
Nile House Studios, Nile Street
Burslem, Stoke-on-Trent ST6 2BA
Website: www.mouldart.co.uk
e-mail: mouldart@aol.com
Mobile: 07786 473443   Tel: 01782 577727

NEWENS Chas MARINE COMPANY Ltd
(Boats for Sale, Marine Props etc)
The Boathouse, Embankment
Putney, London SW15 1LB
Fax: 020-8780 2339   Tel: 020-8788 4587

NEWMAN HIRE COMPANY
16 The Vale, Acton
London W3 7SB
e-mail: info@newman-hire-company.co.uk   Tel: 020-8743 0741

NORTHERN LIGHT
Assembly Street, Leith, Edinburgh EH6 7RG
Website: www.northernlight.co.uk
e-mail: enquiries@northernlight.co.uk
Fax: 0131-622 9101   Tel: 0131-622 9100

NOSTALGIA AMUSEMENTS
(Brian Davey)
22 Greenwood Close, Thames Ditton, Surrey KT7 0BG
Mobile: 07973 506869   Tel: 020-8398 2141

NOTTINGHAM JOUSTING ASSOCIATION SCHOOL OF NATIONAL EQUITATION Ltd
(Jousting & Medieval Tournaments, Horses & Riders for Films & TV)
Bunny Hill Top, Costock, Loughborough
Leicestershire LE12 6XE
Website: www.bunny-hill.co.uk
e-mail: info@bunny-hill.co.uk
Fax: 01509 856067   Tel: 01509 852366

OCEAN LEISURE
(Scuba Diving, Watersports Retail)
11-14 Northumberland Avenue, London WC2N 5AQ
e-mail: info@oceanleisure.co.uk
Fax: 020-7930 3032   Tel: 020-7930 5050

OFFSTAGE
(Theatre & Film Bookshop)
37 Chalk Farm Road, London NW1 8AJ
e-mail: offstagebookshop@aol.com
Fax: 020-7916 8046   Tel: 020-7485 4996

P. A . LEISURE
(Specialists in Amusements & Fairground Equipment)
Delph House, Park Bridge Road
Towneley Park, Burnley, Lancs BB10 4SD
Website: www.p-a-leisure.co.uk
e-mail: paleisure@btconnect.com
Fax: 01282 420467   Tel: 01282 453939

PALAVA ARTS
(Digital Media, Musical Composition & Production Services)
43 Kingsway Avenue, Kingswood, Bristol BS15 8DB
e-mail: sam@palava-arts.com   Tel/Fax: 0117-961 6858

PATERSON Helen
(Typing Services)
40 Whitelands House, London SW3 4QY
e-mail: pater@waitrose.com   Tel: 020-7730 6428

PENDLEBURYS CANDLE COMPANY
(Church Candles & Requisites)
Church House, Portland Avenue
Stamford Hill, London N16 6HJ
e-mail: books@pendleburys.com   Tel/Fax: 020-8809 4922

PERIOD PETROL PUMP CO
c/o Diss Ironworks, 7 St Nicholas Street
Diss, Norfolk IP22 4LB
Website: www.periodpetrolpump.co.uk   Tel: 01379 643978

PHOSPHENE
(Lighting, Sound & Accessories. Design, Sales, Hire)
Milton Road South
Stowmarket, Suffolk IP14 1EZ
Website: www.phosphene.co.uk
e-mail: cliff@phosphene.freeserve.co.uk   Tel: 01449 770011

PICKFORDS Ltd
Heritage House
345 Southbury Road
Enfield EN1 1UP
Fax: 020-8219 8001   Tel: 020-8219 8000

PICTURES PROPS CO Ltd
(TV, Film & Stage Hire)
12-16 Brunel Road, London W3 7XR
Fax: 020-8740 5846   Tel: 020-8749 2433

PINK POINTES DANCEWEAR
1A Suttons Lane
Hornchurch, Essex RM12 6RD
e-mail: sales@gavnicola.freeserve.co.uk
Tel/Fax: 01708 438584

PLAYBOARD PUPPETS
2 Ockendon Mews
London N1 3JL
Tel/Fax: 020-7226 5911

POLAND Anna: SCULPTOR AND MODELMAKER
(Sculpture, Models, Puppets, Masks etc)
Salterns, Old Bursledon
outhampton, Hampshire SO31 8DH
e-mail: polandanna@hotmail.com   Tel: 023-8040 5166

POLLEX PROPS / FIREBRAND
(Prop Makers)
Leac na Ban, Tayvallich
Lochgilphead, Argyll PA31 8PF
e-mail: alex@firebrand.fsnet.co.uk   Tel/Fax: 01546 870310

PRAETORIAN ASSOCIATES
(Personal Safety & Anti-Stalking Consultancy)
Suite 501, 2 Old Brompton Road, London SW7 3DG
Website: www.praetorianasc.com
e-mail: info@praetorianasc.com
Fax: 020-8923 7177   Tel: 020-8923 9075

PRAETORIAN PROCUREMENT SERVICES - SA
(Providing Services for the Film/TV Industry
within South Africa)
Suite 501, 2 Old Brompton Road, London SW7 3DG
Website: www.praetorianasc.com
e-mail: info@praetorianasc.com
Fax: 020-8923 7177   Tel: 020-8923 9075

PROBLOOD
11 Mount Pleasant, Framlingham
Suffolk IP13 9HQ   Tel/Fax: 01728 723865

PROFESSOR PATTEN'S PUNCH & JUDY
(Hire & Performances/Advice on Traditional Show)
14 The Crest, Goffs Oak, Hertfordshire EN7 5NP
Website: www.dennispatten.co.uk   Tel: 01707 873262

PROFILE PRINTS
(Photographic Processing)
Courtwood Film Service Ltd
Freepost TO55, Penzance
Cornwall TR18 2DQ
Website: www.courtwood.co.uk
e-mail: people@courtwood.co.uk
Fax: 01736 350203   Tel: 01736 365222

PROP FARM Ltd
(Pat Ward)
Grange Farm, Elmton
Nr Creswell, North Derbyshire S80 4LX
e-mail: pat/les@propfarm.free-online.co.uk
Fax: 01909 721465   Tel: 01909 723100

PROP ROTATION
41 Trelawney Road, Cotham
Bristol BS6 6DY   Tel: 0117-974 1058

PROPS GALORE
(Period Textiles/Jewellery)
15 Brunel Road, London W3 7XR
e-mail: propsgalore@farley.co.uk
Fax: 020-8354 1866   Tel: 020-8746 1222

PUNCH & JUDY PUPPETS & BOOTHS
(Hire & Advisory Service, Callers by Appointment)
42 Christchurch Road, Sidcup, Kent DA15 7HQ
Website: www.johnstylesentertainer.co.uk
Tel/Fax: 020-8300 3579

Q2Q Ltd
(Production Solutions)
7 Portland Mews, London W1F 8JQ
Website: www.q-2-q.com
e-mail: kvg@q-2-q.com   Tel/Fax: 0870 9505727

RAINBOW PRODUCTIONS Ltd
(Manufacture & Handling of Costume Characters)
Rainbow House, 56 Windsor Avenue, London SW19 2RR
Website: www.rainbowproductions.co.uk
e-mail: info@rainbowproductions.co.uk
Fax: 020-8545 0777   Tel: 020-8545 0700

RENT-A-CLOWN
(Mattie Faint)
37 Sekeforde Street, Clerkenwell
London EC1R 0HA   Tel/Fax: 020-7608 0312

RENT-A-SWORD
(Alan M Meek)
180 Frog Grove Lane, Wood Street Village
Guildford, Surrey GU3 3HD
Fax: 01483 236684   Tel: 01483 234084

REPLAY Ltd
(Showreels & TV Facilities Hire)
199 Piccadilly, London W1J 9HA
Website: www.replayfilms.co.uk
e-mail: sales@replayfilms.co.uk
Fax: 020-7287 5348   Tel: 020-7287 5334

RETROGRAPH NOSTALGIA ARCHIVE
(Posters & Packaging 1880-1970, Picture Library/Photo
Stills/
Ephemera/Fine Arts 1870-1970), 10 Hanover Crescent
Brighton, East Sussex BN2 9SB
Website: www.retrograph.com
e-mail: retropix1@aol.com   Tel: 01273 687554

ROBERTS Chris INTERIORS
(Film Set & Property Maintenance)
420G, Sims House
Commercial Road
London E1 1LD   Mobile: 07956 512074

ROOTSTEIN Adel Ltd
(Mannequin Hire)
9 Beaumont Avenue, London W14 9LP
Fax: 020-7381 3263   Tel: 020-7381 1447

ROYAL HORTICULTURAL HALLS & CONFERENCE CENTRE
(Film Location: Art Deco & Edwardian Buildings)
80 Vincent Square, London SW1P 2PE
Website: www.horticultural-halls.co.uk
e-mail: maugiel@rhs.org.uk
Fax: 020-7834 2072   Tel: 020-7828 4125

RR DESIGN
(Theatre Posters, CD, 2-D Cards, Publicity)
e-mail: r.r.studio@btinternet.com   Tel: 01243 389758

RUDKIN DESIGN
(Design Consultants, Brochures, Advertising
Corporate etc)
10 Cottesbrooke Park
Heartlands Business Park, Daventry
Northamptonshire NN11 5YL
e-mail: studio@rudkindesign.com
Fax: 01327 872728   Tel: 01327 301770

RUMBLE Jane
(Props to Order, No Hire)
121 Elmstead Avenue, Wembley
Middlesex HA9 8NT   Tel: 020-8904 6462

GREENPROPS
Trees ▪ Plants ▪ Flowers ▪ Fruit & Grass
Tel: 01398 361531
Fax 01398 361307 www.greenprops.com
e mail:trevor@greenprops.com
The artificial STAGE SUPPLIERS, serving The West End, The UK and Europe

S + H TECHNICAL SUPPORTS Ltd
(Starcloths, Drapes)
Starcloth Way, Mullacourt Industrial Estate
Ilfracombe, Devon EX34 9PL
Website: www.starcloth.co.uk
e-mail: enquiries@starcloth.co.uk
Fax: 01271 865423   Tel: 01271 866832

SABAH
(Stylist, Costumes, Wardrobe, Sets, Props)
2841 N. Ocean Blvd, Apt 501
Fort Lauderdale, Florida 33308 USA
e-mail: sabah561@aol.com
Mobile: (954) 383-2179   Tel/Fax: (954) 566-6219

SAPEX SCRIPTS
Millennium Studios, 5 Elstree Way
Borehamwood, Herts WD6 1SF
Website: www.sapex.co.uk
e-mail: scripts@sapex.co.uk
Fax: 020-8236 1591   Tel: 020-8236 1600

SCENA PROJECTS Ltd
240 Camberwell Road, London SE5 0DP
e-mail: scena@pro.com
Fax: 020-7703 7012   Tel: 020-7703 4444

SCENE TWO HIRE
(Film & TV Props Hire)
18-20 Brunel Road, Acton, London W3 7XR
Website: www.superhire.com
e-mail: sales@scene2hire.co.uk
Fax: 020-8743 2662   Tel: 020-8740 5544

SCENICS
Copse Field Farm, Cawlow Lane
Warslow, Buxton SK17 0HE   Tel: 01298 84762

SCHULTZ & WIREMU FABRIC EFFECTS
(Dyeing/Printing/Distressing)
Unit B202 Faircharm Studios
8-12 Creekside, London SE8 3DX
Website: www.schultz-wiremufabricfx.co.uk
e-mail: swfabricfx@tiscali.co.uk   Tel/Fax: 020-8469 0151

SCRIPTRIGHT
(S.C. Hill - Script/Manuscript Typing Services/Script
Reading Services)
6 Valetta Road, London W3 7TN
e-mail: samc.hill@virgin.net
Fax: 020-8740 6486   Tel: 020-8740 7303

SCRIPTS BY ARGYLE
(Play, Film & Book. Word Processing, Copying & Binding)
St John's Buildings, 43 Clerkenwell Road, London EC1M 5RS
Website: www.scriptsbyargyle.co.uk
e-mail: scripts.typing@virgin.net
Fax: 020-7608 1642   Tel: 020-7608 2095

SHAOLIN WAY
(Martial Arts Supplies, Lion Dance & Kung Foo Instruction)
10 Little Newport Street, London WC2H 7JJ
e-mail: shaolinway@btclick.com
Fax: 020-7287 6548   Tel: 020-7734 6391
21 Baron Street, Angel, London N1 9EX   Tel: 020-7837 1118

SHIRLEY LEAF & PETAL COMPANY Ltd
(Flower Makers Museum)
58A High Street
Old Town, Hastings
East Sussex TN34 3EN   Tel/Fax: 01424 427793

SHOP FITTINGS DIRECT
Unit 3, The Interchange
Colonial Way
Watford, Herts WD24 4PR
Fax: 01923 232326   Tel: 01923 232425

SIDE EFFECTS
(Props, Models & FX)
Unit 4, Camberwell Trading Estate
117 Denmark Road
London SE5 9LB
e-mail: sfx@lineone.net
Fax: 020-7738 5198   Tel: 020-7738 5199

SILVER Sam KENSINGTON Ltd
(Special Eye Effects)
37 Kensington Church Street
London W8 4LL
e-mail: admin@samsilveropticians.com
Fax: 020-7937 8969   Tel: 020-7937 8282

SMITH Tom
(Blacksmith)
Unit 2, Lopen Works, Lopen Road
Edmonton, London N18 1PU Tel/Fax: 020-8884 2626

SNOW BUSINESS
(Snow/Winter Effects on Any Scale)
The Snow Mill, Bridge Road, Ebley, Stroud, Glos GL5 4TR
Website: www.snowfx.com
e-mail: snow@snowbusiness.com Tel/Fax: 01453 840077

SOFT PROPS
(Costume & Modelmakers)
Unit 4, Camberwell Trading Estate
117-119 Denmark Road, London SE5 9LB
e-mail: jackie@softprops.co.uk
Fax: 020-7738 5198 Tel: 020-7738 6324

STEELDECK RENTALS
(Theatre & Staging Equipment)
King's Cross Freight Depot, York Way, London N1 0UZ
e-mail: steeldeck@aol.com
Fax: 020-7278 3403 Tel: 020-7833 2031

STEELDECK SALES Ltd
(Modular Staging)
King's Cross Freight Depot, York Way, London N1 0UZ
e-mail: steeldeck@aol.com
Fax: 020-7278 3403 Tel: 020-7833 2031

STEVENSON Scott
(Prop Maker)
Flat 2, 100 Vaughan Road, Harrow, Middlesex HA1 4ED
Website: www.bodymechprops.co.uk
e-mail: scott@bodymechprops.co.uk Mobile: 07739 378579

STIRLING Rob
(Carpentry & Joinery)
Copse Field Farm, Cawlow Lane
Warslow, Buxton SK17 0HE Tel: 01298 84762

STUDIO & TV HIRE
3 Ariel Way, Wood Lane, White City, London W12 7SL
Website: www.stvhire.com
e-mail: enquiries@stvhire.com
Fax: 020-8740 9662 Tel: 020-8749 3445

SUPERSCRIPTS
(Audio Typing, Rushes, Post-Prod Scripts)
56 New Road, Hanworth, Middlesex TW13 6TQ
e-mail: jackie@superscripts.fsnet.co.uk
Mobile: 07971 671011 Tel: 020-8898 7933

SUPERSCRIPTS
14 Cambridge Grove Road, Kingston, Surrey KT1 3JJ
Mobile: 07793 160138 Tel: 020-8546 9824

TAYLOR Charlotte
(Stylist/Props Buyer)
18 Eleanor Grove, Barnes, London SW13 0JN
e-mail: charlotte-taylor@tiscali.co.uk
Mobile: 07836 708904 Tel/Fax: 020-8876 9085

TECHNIQUES
(Property Makers)
15 Danehurst Avenue
Leicester LE3 6DB Tel/Fax: 0116-285 7294

TELESCRIPT PROMPTING Ltd
The Barn, Handpost Farmhouse
Maidens Green, Bracknell, Berkshire RG42 6LD
Fax: 01344 890655 Tel: 01344 890470

TESTMAN P.A.T.
(Portable Electrical Appliance Testing, Specialists in Theatre)
7 Woodville Road, London E17 7ER
Mobile: 07973 663154 Tel: 020-8521 6408

THEATRESEARCH
(Theatre Consultants)
Dacre Hall, Dacre, North Yorkshire HG3 4ET
Website: www.theatresearch.co.uk
e-mail: info@theatresearch.co.uk
Fax: 01423 781957 Tel: 01423 780497

THEME TRADERS Ltd
(Props)
The Stadium, Oaklands Road, London NW2 6DL
Website: www.themetraders.com
e-mail: mailroom@themetraders.com
Fax: 020-8450 7322 Tel: 020-8452 8518

TOP SHOW
(Props & Scenery, Conference Specialists)
North Lane, Huntington
Yorks YO32 9SU Tel/Fax: 01904 750022

TRANSCRIPTS
(Audio + LTC/Post-prod)
#2, 6 Cornwall Gardens, London SW7 4AL
e-mail: lucy@transcripts.demon.co.uk
Mobile: 07973 200197 Tel: 020-7584 9758

TRAPEZE & AERIAL COACH/CHOREOGRAPHER
(Jacqueline Welbourne)
c/o Circus Maniacs Agency, Office 8A
The Kingswood Foundation, Britannia Road
Kingswood, Bristol BS15 8DB
e-mail: jackie@circusmaniacs.com
Mobile: 07977 247287 Tel/Fax: 0117-947 7042

TROPICAL SURROUNDS Ltd
(Distributors & Installers of Natural Fencing & Screening Materials)
The Old Stables, Redenham Park Farm, Redenham
Nr Andover, Hampshire SP11 9AQ
Fax: 01264 773660 Tel: 01264 773009

TRYFONOS Mary MASKS
(Mask, Headdress & Puppet Specialist)
59 Shaftesbury Road, London N19 4QW
e-mail: marytryfonos@aol.com
Mobile: 07764 587433 Tel: 020-7561 9880

TURN ON LIGHTING
(Antique Lighting c1840-1940)
116-118 Islington High Street, Camden Passage
London N1 8EG Tel/Fax: 020-7359 7616

UPSTAGE
(Event Design & Production Management)
Studio A, Flat Iron Yard
14 Ayres Street, London SE1 1ES
Website: www.upstagelivecom.co.uk
e-mail: post@upstagelivecom.co.uk
Fax: 020-7403 6511 Tel: 020-7403 6510

VENTRILOQUIST DOLLS HOME
(Hire & Helpful Hints, Callers by Appointment)
42 Christchurch Road
Sidcup, Kent DA15 7HQ
Website: www.johnstylesentertainer.co.uk
Tel/Fax: 020-8300 3579

VENTRILOQUIST DUMMY HIRE
(Dennis Patten - Hire & Advice)
14 The Crest, Goffs Oak, Herts EN7 5NP
Website: www.dennispatten.co.uk Tel: 01707 873262

VINMAG ARCHIVE Ltd
84-90 Digby Road, London E9 6HX
Website: www.vinmagarchive.com
e-mail: piclib@vinmag.com
Fax: 020-8533 7283 Tel: 020-8533 7588

VISUALEYES IMAGING SERVICES
(Photographic Reproduction)
11 West Street, London WC2H 9NE
Website: www.visphoto.co.uk
e-mail: imaging@visphoto.co.uk
Fax: 020-7240 0050
Tel: 020-7836 3004

VOCALEYES
(Suppliers of Audio Description for Theatrical
Performance)
1st Floor, 54 Commercial Street
London SE1 6LT
Website: www.vocaleyes.co.uk
e-mail: enquiries@vocaleyes.co.uk
Fax: 020-7247 5622
Tel: 020-7375 1043

WEBBER Peter HIRE/RITZ STUDIOS
(Music Equipment Hire, Rehearsal Studios)
110-112 Disraeli Road
London SW15 2DX
e-mail: lee@ritzstudios.com
Fax: 020-8877 1036
Tel: 020-8870 1335

WESTED LEATHERS COMPANY
(Suede & Leather Suppliers/Manufacturers)
Little Wested House
Wested Lane, Swanley
Kent BR8 8EF
e-mail: wested@wested.com
Fax: 01322 667039
Tel: 01322 660654

WESTWARD Lynn BLINDS
(Window Blind Specialist)
458 Chiswick High Road
London W4 5TT
Fax: 020-8742 8444
Tel: 020-8742 8333

WHITEHORN Simon
(Sound Design)
57 Acre Lane, London SW2 5TN
Website: www.orbitalsound.co.uk
e-mail: simon.whitehorn@orbitalsound.co.uk
Fax: 020-7501 6869
Tel: 020-7501 6868

WILLIAMS Frank
(Bottles, Jars, Footwarmers & Flagons, Spitoons, Poisons,
Beers & Inks 1870-1940)
33 Enstone Road
Ickenham
Uxbridge, Middlesex
e-mail: wllmsfrn4@aol.com
Tel: 01895 672495

WILTSHIRE A. F.
(Agricultural Vehicle Engineers, Repairs, etc)
The Agricultural Centre
Alfold Road
Dunsfold, Surrey GU8 4NP
e-mail: team@afwiltshire.fsnet.co.uk
Fax: 01483 200491
Tel: 01483 200516

WINSHIP Geoff
The Knights of Merrie England Ltd
153 Salisbury Road
Burton
Christchurch BH23 7JS
Website: www.jousting.biz
e-mail: geoff@jousting.biz
Tel: 01202 483777

WOODEN CANAL BOAT SOCIETY
(Historic Canal Boats)
5 Oaken Clough Terrace
Limehurst, Ashton-under-Lyne
Lancashire OL7 9NY
Website: www.wcbs.org.uk
e-mail: chris-wcbs@people-link.net
Mobile: 07931 952037
Tel: 0161-330 2315

WORBEY Darryl STUDIOS
(Specialist Puppet Design)
Ground Floor, 33 York Grove, London SE15 2NY
e-mail: dworbey@freewire.co.uk
Fax: 020-7635 6397
Tel: 020-7639 8090

WORLD OF FANTASY
(Props and Costumes)
Swansnest, Rear of 2 Windmill Road
Hampton Hill, Middlesex TW12 1RH
Website: www.swansflight.com
e-mail: swansflight@aol.com
Fax: 020-8783 1366
Tel: 020-8941 1595

WORLD OF ILLUSION
4 Sunnyside, Wimbledon SW19 4SL
Website: www.parasoltheatre.co.uk
e-mail: parasoltheatre@waitrose.com
Fax: 020-8946 0228
Tel: 020-8946 9478

WWW.PUPPETSPRESENT.COM
c/o Peter Charlesworth & Associates
68 Old Brompton Road, London SW7 3LD
Website: www.puppetspresent.com
e-mail: puppetspresent@btinternet.com   Tel: 020-7581 2478

A & C BLACK (Publicity Dept)
37 Soho Square, London W1D 3QZ
e-mail: publicity@acblack.com
Fax: 020-7758 0222   Tel: 020-7758 0200

A C I D PUBLICATIONS
Room 7, Minus One House, Lyttelton Road, London E10 5NQ
e-mail: acidnews@aol.com   Tel/Fax: 07050 205206

ACADEMY PLAYERS DIRECTORY
Pickford Center for Motion Picture Study
1313 N. Vine Street, Los Angeles CA 90028
Website: www.playersdirectory.com
e-mail: players@oscars.org
Fax: (310) 550-5034   Tel: (310) 247-3058

ACTING: A DRAMA STUDIO SOURCE BOOK
(Peter Owen Publishers)
73 Kenway Road, London SW5 ORE
Website: www.peterowen.com
e-mail: admin@peterowen.com   Tel: 020-7373 5628

ACTORS' YEARBOOK 2005 The
(A&C Black Publishers)
37 Soho Square, London W1D 3QZ
Website: www.acblack.com
e-mail: actorsyearbook@acblack.com
Fax: 020-7758 0222   Tel: 020-7758 0200

AMATEUR STAGE MAGAZINE & COMMUNITY ARTS DIRECTORY
(Platform Publications Ltd)
Hampden House, 2 Weymouth Street, London W1W 5BT
e-mail: cvtheatre@aol.com
Fax: 020-7636 2323   Tel: 020-7636 4343

ANNUAIRE DU CINEMA BELLEFAYE
(French Actors' Directory, Production, Technicians & All Technical Industries & Suppliers)
38 rue Etienne Marcel, 75002 Paris
Website: www.bellefaye.com
e-mail: contact@bellefaye.com
Fax: 00 331 42 33 39 00   Tel: 00 331 42 33 52 52

ARTISTES & AGENTS
(Richmond House Publishing Co)
70-76 Bell Street, Marylebone, London NW1 6SP
Website: www.rhpco.co.uk   e-mail: sales@rhpco.co.uk
Fax: 020-7224 9688   Tel: 020-7224 9666

AUDIENCE TODAY
(Dance, Opera, Film)
51 Earls Court Square, London SW5 9DG   Tel: 020-7370 7324

AUDITION NOW
(Weekly Casting Publication)
Lifegroup Ltd, Garden Studios
11-15 Betterton Street, Covent Garden
London WC2H 9BP   Tel: 0800 0966144

AURORA METRO PRESS (1989)
(Drama, Fiction, Reference & International Literature in English Translation)
4 Osier Mews, Chiswick, London W4 2NT
Website: www.aurorametro.com
e-mail: ampress@netcomuk.co.uk
Fax: 020-8742 8316   Tel: 020-8747 1953

BIRTH OF THEATRE The - STAGE BY STAGE
(Drama/Theatre Studies/History/Reference)
(Peter Owen Publishers), 73 Kenway Road, London SW5 ORE
e-mail: admin@peterowen.com
Fax: 020-7373 6760   Tel: 020-7373 5628

BRITISH NATIONAL FILM & VIDEO CATALOGUE
(British Film Institute)
21 Stephen Street, London W1T 1LN
Website: www.bfi.org.uk
e-mail: maureen.brown@bfi.org.uk
Fax: 020-7436 7950   Tel: 020-7957 4706

BRITISH PERFORMING ARTS YEARBOOK
(Rhinegold Publishing)
241 Shaftesbury Avenue
London WC2H 8TF
Website: www.rhinegold.co.uk
e-mail: bpay@rhinegold.co.uk   Tel: 01832 270333

BRITISH THEATRE DIRECTORY
(Richmond House Publishing Co)
70 -76 Bell Street, Marylebone, London NW1 6SP
Website: www.rhpco .co.uk   e-mail: sales@rhpco.co.uk
Fax: 020-7224 9688   Tel: 020-7224 9666

BROADCAST
33-39 Bowling Green Lane, London EC1R 0DA
Website: www.broadcastnow.co.uk
Fax: 020-7505 8020   Tel: 020-7505 8014

CALDER PUBLICATIONS
51 The Cut, London SE1 8LF
e-mail: info@calderpublications.com
Fax: 020-7928 5930   Tel: 020-7633 0599

CASTCALL & CASTFAX
(Casting Information Services)
106 Wilsden Avenue, Luton LU1 5HR
Website: www.castcall.co.uk   e-mail: admin@castcall.co.uk
Fax: 01582 480736   Tel: 01582 456213

CASTWEB
7 St Luke's Avenue, London SW4 7LG
Website: www.castweb.co.uk
e-mail: castweb@netcomuk.co.uk
Fax: 020-7720 3097   Tel: 020-7720 9002

CELEBRITY BULLETIN The
4th Flr, Kingsland Hse, 122-124 Regent St, London W1B 5SA
e-mail: celebritylondon@aol.com
Fax: 020-7494 3500   Tel: 020-7439 9840

CELEBRITY SERVICE Ltd
4th Floor, Kingsland House
122-124 Regent Street, London W1B 5SA
e-mail: celebritylondon@aol.com
Fax: 020-7494 3500   Tel: 020-7439 9840

CHAPPELL OF BOND STREET
(Sheet Music, Musical Instruments, Pianos, Synthesizers, Keyboards)
50 New Bond Street, London W1S 1RD
Fax: 020-7491 0133   Tel: 020-7491 2777

CONFERENCE & INCENTIVE TRAVEL MAGAZINE
174 Hammersmith Road, London W6 7JP
Website: www.citmagazine.com   e-mail: cit@haynet.com
Fax: 020-8267 4192   Tel: 020-8267 4307

CREATIVE HANDBOOK
(Reed Business Information)
Windsor Court, East Grinstead House
East Grinstead, West Sussex RH19 1XA
Website: www.chb.com   e-mail: chb.mktg@reedinfo.co.uk
Fax: 01342 332072   Tel: 01342 332034

DANCE EXPRESSION
(A. E. Morgan Publications Ltd)
9 West Street, Epsom, Surrey KT18 7RL
Website: www.danceexpressionmag.co.uk
          Tel: 020-7370 7324

DIRECTING DRAMA
(Peter Owen Publishers)
73 Kenway Road, London SW5 ORE
Website: www.peterowen.com
e-mail: admin@peterowen.com   Tel: 020-7373 5628

EQUITY JOURNAL
Guild House, Upper St Martin's Lane, London WC2H 9EG
Website: www.equity.org.uk
e-mail: info@equity.org.uk
Fax: 020-7379 6074   Tel: 020-7379 5185

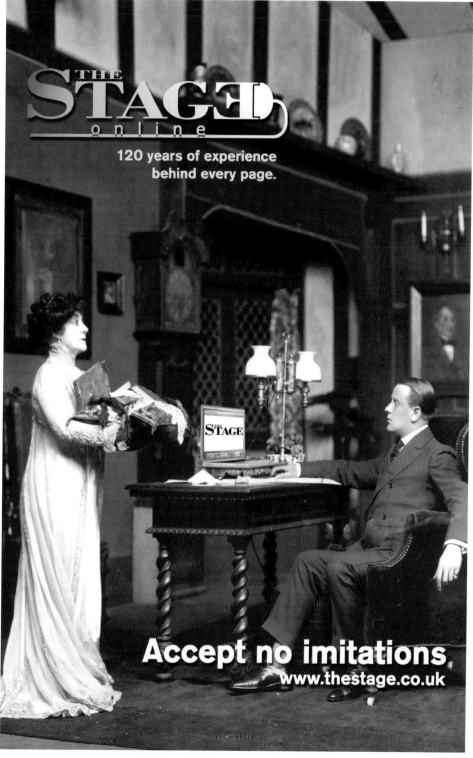

FILMLOG
(Subscriptions)
PO Box 100, Broadstairs, Kent CT10 1UJ
Tel: 01843 860885   Tel: 01843 866538

FIRST NIGHT NEWS
21 Hindsleys Place, London SE23 2NF
e-mail: firstnightnews@yahoo.co.uk   Tel: 020-8244 5816

FORESIGHT
(The Profile Group (UK) Ltd)
Dragon Court
27-29 Macklin Street, London WC2B 5LX
Website: www.foresightonline.co.uk
Fax: 020-7190 7858   Tel: 020-7190 7780

HOLLYWOOD REPORTER The
Endeavour Hse, 189 Shaftesbury Ave, London WC2H 8TJ
Website: www.hollywoodreporter.com
e-mail: london_one@eu.hollywoodreporter.com
Fax: 020-7420 6054   Tel: 020-7420 6000

KAY'S UK & EUROPEAN PRODUCTION MANUALS
Trinity Mews, Cambridge Gardens, London W10 6JH
Website: www.kays.co.uk
e-mail: info@kays.co.uk
Fax: 020-8960 6700   Tel: 020-8960 6900

KEMP'S FILM, TV & VIDEO
(Reed Business Information)
East Grinstead House, East Grinstead, W. Sussex RH19 1XA
Website: www.kftv.com
e-mail: phewson@reedinfo.co.uk
Fax: 01342 332072   Tel: 01342 332022

KNOWLEDGE The
Riverbank House, Angel Lane, Tonbridge, Kent TN9 1SE
Website: www.theknowledgeonline.com
e-mail: knowledge@cmpinformation.com
Fax: 01732 377454   Tel: 01732 377591

LIMELIGHT The
(Limelight Publications, Contacts & Casting Directory)
Postal Address: PO Box 760, Randpark Ridge, 2156,
Gauteng, South Africa
Website: www.limelight.co.za
e-mail: barbara@limelight.co.za   Tel/Fax: 00 27 11 793 7231

MAKING OF THE PROFESSIONAL ACTOR The
(Peter Owen Publishers)
73 Kenway Road, London SW5 ORE
Website: www.peterowen.com
e-mail: admin@peterowen.com   Tel: 020-7373 5628

MUSIC WEEK DIRECTORY/MUSIC WEEK
CPMI
United Business Media, 8th Floor, Ludgate House
245 Blackfriars Road, London SE1 9UR
Website: www.musicweek.com   Tel: 020-7921 8314

MUSICAL STAGES
(Musical Theatre Magazine)
Box 8365, London W14 OCL
Website: www.musicalstages.co.uk
e-mail: editor@musicalstages.co.uk   Tel/Fax: 020-7603 2221

OFFICIAL LONDON SEATING PLAN GUIDE The
(Richmond House Publishing Co)
70-76 Bell Street Marylebone, London NW1 6SP
Website: www.rhpco.co.uk
e-mail: sales@rhpco.co.uk
Fax: 020-7224 9668   Tel: 020-7224 9666

PA LISTINGS Ltd
292 Vauxhall Bridge Road, Victoria, London SW1V 1AE
Website: www.pa.press.net   e-mail: arts@listings.press.net
Fax: 020-7963 7801   Tel: 020-7963 7707

PANTOMIME BOOK The
(Peter Owen Publishers)
73 Kenway Road, London SW5 ORE
Website: www.peterowen.com
e-mail: admin@peterowen.com   Tel: 020-7373 5628

PCR
(See PRODUCTION & CASTING REPORT)

PERFORMING ARTS YEARBOOK FOR EUROPE (PAYE)
(Alain Charles Arts Publishing Ltd)
27 Wilfred Street, London SW1E 6PR
Website: www.api.co.uk
e-mail: paye@alaincharles.com
Fax: 020-7973 0076   Tel: 020-7834 7676

PLAYS INTERNATIONAL
33A Lurline Gardens
London SW11 4DD   Tel/Fax: 020-7720 1950

PRESENTER'S CONTACT FILE The/PRESENTER'S YEAR PLANNER The
Presenter Promotions
123 Corporation Road, Gillingham, Kent ME7 1RG
Website: www.presenterpromotions.com
e-mail: info@presenterpromotions.com
          Tel/Fax: 01634 851077

PRESENTERS SPOTLIGHT
7 Leicester Place, London WC2H 7RJ
Website: www.spotlight.com
e-mail: info@spotlight.com
Fax: 020-7437 5881   Tel: 020-7437 7631

PRESENTING FOR TV & VIDEO
(Joanne Zorian-Lynn, published by A & C Black)
A & C Black Customer Services
e-mail: mdl@macmillan.co.uk   Tel: 01256 302692

PRODUCERS ALLIANCE FOR CINEMA & TELEVISION
(Pact Directory of Independent Producers/Art of the Deal/Rights Clearance)
45 Mortimer Street, London W1W 8HJ
Website: www.pact.co.uk
e-mail: enquiries@pact.co.uk
Fax: 020-7331 6700   Tel: 020-7331 6000

PRODUCTION & CASTING REPORT
(Subscriptions)
PO Box 100, Broadstairs, Kent CT10 1UJ
Website: www.pcrnewsletter.com
Tel: 01843 860885   Tel: 01843 866538
(Editorial)
PO Box 11, London N1 7JZ
Fax: 020-7566 8284   Tel: 020-7566 8282

RADIO TIMES
80 Wood Lane, London W12 OTT
e-mail: radio.times@bbc.co.uk
Fax: 020-8433 3160   Tel: 020-8433 3400

RICHMOND HOUSE PUBLISHING COMPANY Ltd
70-76 Bell Street, Marylebone, London NW1 6SP
Website: www.rhpco.co.uk
e-mail: sales@rhpco.co.uk
Fax: 020 7224 9600   Tel: 020-7224 9666

SCREEN INTERNATIONAL
33-39 Bowling Green Lane, London EC1R ODA
Website: www.screendaily.com
e-mail: sade.sharp@emap.com
Fax: 020-7505 8117   Tel: 020-7505 8080

SCRIPT BREAKDOWN SERVICE Ltd
Suite 1, 16 Sidmouth Road, London NW2 5JX
e-mail: casting@sbsltd.demon.co.uk
Fax: 020-8459 7442   Tel: 020-8451 2852

SHOWCALL
47 Bermondsey Street, London SE1 3XT
Website: www.showcall.co.uk   e-mail: info@thestage.co.uk
Fax: 020-7378 0480   Tel: 020-7403 1818

Casting Directories for Film, TV, Theatre and Commercials

Over 30,000 professional actors, presenters and child artists
Photos and agent contact details for every performer

THE SPOTLIGHT [R]

t: 020 7437 7631   w: www.spotlight.com   e: info@spotlight.com

SHOWCAST: The AUSTRALASIAN CASTING DIRECTORY
PO Box 2001, Leumeah, NSW 2560 Australia
Website: www.showcast.com.au
e-mail: brian@showcast.com.au
Fax: 02 4647 4167   Tel: 02 4647 4166

SHOWDIGS.CO.UK
PO Box 29307, Glasgow G20 0YQ
Website: www.showdigs.co.uk
e-mail: info@showdigs.co.uk   Tel: 0845 4582896

SIGHT & SOUND
(British Film Institute)
21 Stephen Street, London W1T 1LN
Website: www.bfi.org.uk/sightandsound
e-mail: s&s@bfi.org.uk
Fax: 020-7436 2327   Tel: 020-7255 1444

SPEECH FOR THE SPEAKER
(Peter Owen Publishers)
73 Kenway Road
London SW5 0RE
Website: www.peterowen.com
e-mail: admin@peterowen.com   Tel: 020-7373 5628

SPOTLIGHT CASTING DIRECTORY The
7 Leicester Place, London WC2H 7RJ
Website: www.spotlight.com
e-mail: info@spotlight.com
Fax: 020-7437 5881   Tel: 020-7437 7631

STAGE NEWSPAPER Ltd The
47 Bermondsey Street, London SE1 3XT
Website: www.thestage.co.uk
e-mail: editorial@thestage.co.uk
Fax: 020-7357 9287   Tel: 020-7403 1818

TELEVISUAL
12-26 Lexington Street, London W1F 0LE
Website: www.televisual.com
Fax: 020-7970 6733   Tel: 020-7970 6541

THEATRE RECORD
P O Box 38159, London W10 6WN
Website: www.theatrerecord.com
e-mail: editor@theatrerecord.com
Fax: 020-8962 0655   Tel: 020-8960 0740

THEATRE REPORT
(Subscriptions)
PO Box 100, Broadstairs, Kent CT10 1UJ
Website: www.pcrnewsletter.com
Tel: 01843 860885   Tel: 01843 866538

TIME OUT GROUP Ltd
Universal Hse, 251 Tottenham Court Road, London W1T 7AB
Website: www.timeout.com
Fax: 020-7813 6001   Tel: 020-7813 3000

TV TIMES
IPC Media
Kings Reach Tower, Stamford Street, London SE1 9LS
Fax: 020-7261 7888   Tel: 020-7261 7000

VARIETY NEWSPAPER
7th Floor, 84 Theobalds Road, London WC1X 8RR
Website: www.variety.com
Fax: 020-7611 4581   Tel: 020-7611 4580

VOICE BOOK The
(Michael McCallion, published by Faber & Faber)
TBS Distribution
e-mail: sales@tbs-ltd.co.uk   Tel: 01206 255678

WHITE BOOK The
Bank House, 23 Warwick Road
Coventry CV1 2EW   Tel: 024-7657 1171

ABM
226 Seven Sisters Road, Finsbury Park, London N4 3GG
Fax: 0870 770 8814 Tel: 0870 770 8818
ARTHUR Anna PRESS & PR
52 Tottenham Street, London W1T 4RN
Website: www.aapr.co.uk e-mail: name@aapr.co.uk
Fax: 020-7637 2984 Tel: 020-7637 2994
ASSOCIATES The
(Film & DVD Specialists)
39-41 North Road, London N7 9DP
Website: www.the-associates.co.uk
e-mail: info@the-associates.co.uk
Fax: 020-7609 2249 Tel: 020-7700 3388
AVALON PUBLIC RELATIONS
(Marketing/Arts)
4A Exmoor Street, London W10 6BD
e-mail: edt@avalonuk.com
Fax: 020-7598 7223 Tel: 020-7598 7222
BARLOW Tony ASSOCIATES
(Press & Marketing for Music, Dance & Theatre)
13 Burns Court, Park Hill Road, Wallington SM6 0SF
Website: www.tonybarlowarts.com
e-mail: artspublicity@hotmail.com
Mobile: 07774 407385 Tel: 020-8773 8012
BOLTON Erica & QUINN Jane Ltd
10 Pottery Lane, London W11 4LZ
e-mail: e.mail@boltonquinn.com
Fax: 020-7221 8100 Tel: 020-7221 5000
BORKOWSKI Mark PR & IMPROPERGANDA Ltd
71 Kingsway, Holborn, London WC2B 6ST
Website: www.borkowski.co.uk
e-mail: larry@borkowski.co.uk
Fax: 020-7404 5000 Tel: 020-7404 3000
CAHOOTS PRODUCTION & PR
32 Champion Grove, London SE5 8BW
Website: www.cahootstheatre.co.uk
e-mail: cahootstheatreco@aol.com Tel/Fax: 020-7738 4250
CENTRESTAGE PUBLIC RELATIONS
Yeates Cottage, 27 Wellington Terrace
Knaphill, Woking, Surrey GU21 2AP
e-mail: dellaedwards@centrestagepr.com Tel: 01483 487808
CHAPMAN Guy ASSOCIATES
(Marketing & Press Support)
33 Southampton Street, Covent Garden, London WC2E 7HE
e-mail: admin@g-c-a.co.uk
Fax: 020-7379 8484 Tel: 020-7379 7474
CHESTON Judith PUBLICITY
30 Telegraph Street, Shipston-on-Stour
Warwickshire CV36 4DA
e-mail: cheston@shipstononstour1.freeserve.co.uk
Fax: 01608 663772 Tel: 01608 661198
COLE STEVENS
c/o 139 Belmont Road
Harrow Weald, Middlesex HA3 7PL
Website: www.mobiledj.co.uk
e-mail: info@mobiledj.co.uk
Mobile: 07956 511051 Tel: 020-8861 5223
CUE CONSULTANTS
18 Barrington Court, London N10 1QG
e-mail: cueconsultants@hotmail.com
Fax: 020-8883 4197
Mobile: 07974 704909 Tel: 020-8444 6533
DAVEY Christine ASSOCIATES
29 Victoria Road, Eton Wick, Windsor, Berkshire SL4 6LY
Fax: 01753 851123 Tel: 01753 852619

DDA PUBLIC RELATIONS Ltd
192-198 Vauxhall Bridge Road, London SW1V 1DX
Website: www.ddapr.com
e-mail: info@ddapr.com
Fax: 020-7932 4950 Tel: 020-7932 9800
EILENBERG Charlotte ASSOCIATES
6 Balfour Road, London N5 2HB
e-mail: charlotte.eilenberg@dsl.pipex.com
Tel/Fax: 020-7354 2155
ELSON Howard PROMOTIONS
16 Penn Avenue, Chesham, Buckinghamshire HP5 2HS
e-mail: helson1029@aol.com
Fax: 01494 784760 Tel: 01494 785873
GADABOUTS Ltd
(Theatre Marketing & Promotions)
54 Friary Road, London N12 9PB
Website: www.gadaboutstravel.com
e-mail: info@gadabouts.co.uk
Fax: 0870 7059140 Tel: 020-8445 5450
GAYNOR Avril ASSOCIATES
32 Brunswick Sqaure, Hove, East Sussex BN3 1ED
e-mail: gaynorama@aol.com Tel/Fax: 01273 821946
GOODMAN Deborah PUBLICITY Ltd
25 Glenmere Avenue, London NW7 2LT
e-mail: publicity@dgpr.co.uk
Fax: 020-8959 7875 Tel: 020-8959 9980
HYMAN Sue ASSOCIATES Ltd
St Martin's House, 59 Martin's Lane, London WC2N 4JS
e-mail: sue.hyman@btinternet.com
Fax: 020-7379 4944 Tel: 020-7379 8420
IMPACT AGENCY The
3 Bloomsbury Place, London WC1A 2QL
e-mail: mail@impactagency.co.uk
Fax: 020-7580 7200 Tel: 020-7580 1770
KEAN LANYON Ltd
(Sharon Kean)
Rose Cottage, The Aberdeen Centre
22 Highbury Grove, London N5 2EA
Website: www.keanlanyon.com
e-mail: sharon@keanlanyon.com
Fax: 020-7359 0199 Tel: 020-7354 3574
KELLER Don ARTS MARKETING
65 Glenwood Road, Harringay, London N15 3JS
e-mail: info@dakam.waitrose.com
Fax: 020-8809 6825 Tel: 020-8800 4882
KWPR
(Kevin Wilson Public Relations)
187 Drury Lane, London WC2B 5QD
Website: www.kwpr.co.uk
e-mail: kwpr@kwpr.co.uk
Fax: 020-7430 0364 Tel: 020-7430 2060
LAKE-SMITH GRIFFIN ASSOCIATES
Walter House, 418 Strand, London WC2R 0PT
e-mail: lakesmithgriffin@aol.com
Fax: 020-7836 1040 Tel: 020-7836 1020
LAVER Richard PUBLICITY
3 Troy Court, High Street Kensington, London W8 7RA
e-mail: richardlaver@btconnect.com Tel: 020-7937 7322
LEEP MARKEING & PR
(Marketing, Press and Publicity)
5 Nassau House, 122 Shaftesbury Avenue, London W1D 5FR
e-mail: philip@leep.biz
Fax: 020-7439 8833 Tel: 020-7439 9777
MAYER Anne PR
82 Mortimer Road, London N1 4LH
e-mail: annemayer@btopenworld.com
Fax: 020-7254 8227 Tel: 020-7254 7391

   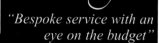
McDONALD & RUTTER
34 Bloomsbury Street, London WC1B 3QJ
e-mail: info@mcdonaldrutter.com
Fax: 020-7637 3690   Tel: 020-7637 2600

MITCHELL Jackie
(JM Communications)
4 Sims Cottages, The Green Claygate, Surrey KT10 0JH
Website: www.jackiem.com   e-mail: pr@jackiem.com
Fax: 01372 471073   Tel: 01372 465041

MITCHELL Sarah PARTNERSHIP The
Third Floor, 87 Wardour Street, London W1F 0UA
Website: www.thesmp.com   e-mail: sarah@thesmp.com
Fax: 020-7434 1954   Tel: 020-7434 1944

MORGAN Jane ASSOCIATES (JMA)
(Marketing & Media)
8 Heathville Road, London N19 3AJ
e-mail: morgans@dircon.co.uk
Fax: 020-7263 9877   Tel: 020-7263 9867

MORGAN Kim MEDIA & MARKETING
2 Averill Street, Hammersmith, London W6 8EB
e-mail: kim@kimmorgan-pr.com
Mobile: 07939 591403   Tel/Fax: 020-7381 4115

NELSON BOSTOCK COMMUNICATIONS
Compass House, 22 Redan Place, London W2 4SA
Website: www.nelsonbostock.com
e-mail: sue.skeats@nelsonbostock.com
Fax: 020-7727 2025   Tel: 020-7229 4400

NEWLEY Patrick ASSOCIATES
45 Kingscourt Road, London SW16 1JA
e-mail: patricknewley@yahoo.com   Tel/Fax: 020-8677 0477

PARKER James ASSOCIATES
67 Richmond Park Road, London SW14 8JY
e-mail: jimparkerjpa@hotmail.com   Tel/Fax: 020-8876 1918

POWELL Martin COMMUNICATIONS
1 Lyons Court, Long Ashton Business Park
Yanley Lane, Bristol BS41 9LB
e-mail: info@martin-powell.com
Fax: 01275 393933   Tel: 01275 394400

PR CONTACT Ltd The
Garden Studio, 32 Newman Street, London W1T 1PU
e-mail: pressoffice@theprcontact.com
Fax: 020-7323 1070   Tel: 020-7323 1200

PR PEOPLE The
1 St James Drive, Sale, Cheshire M33 7QX
e-mail: pr.people@btinternet.com
Fax: 0161-976 2758   Tel: 0161-976 2729

PREMIER PR
91 Berwick Street, London W1F 0NE
Website: www.premierpr.com
Fax: 020-7734 2024   Tel: 020-7292 8330

PUBLIC EYE COMMUNICATIONS Ltd
Suite 313, Plaza, 535 Kings Road, London SW10 0SZ
e-mail: ciara@publiceye.co.uk
Fax: 020-7351 1010   Tel: 020-7351 1555

RKM PUBLIC RELATIONS Ltd
(London. Los Angeles)
Suite 201, Erico House
93-99 Upper Richmond Road, London SW15 2TG
Website: www.rkmpr.com   e-mail: info@rkmpr.com
Fax: 020-8785 5641   Tel: 020-8785 5640

S & X MEDIA
(Contact: Roulla Xenides)
405F The Big Peg, Vyse Street, Birmingham B18 6NF
Website: www.sx-media.com   e-mail: roulla@sx-media.com
Fax: 0121-694 6494   Tel: 0121-604 6366

SAVIDENT Paul
(Marketing & Press Management)
199 Wardour Street, London W1F 8JN
Website: www.savident.com   e-mail: info@savident.com
Fax: 020-7734 3007   Tel: 020-8567 2089

SHIPPEN Martin MARKETING & MEDIA
91 Dyne Road, London NW6 7DR
e-mail: m.shippen@virgin.net
Mobile: 07956 879165   Tel/Fax: 020-7372 3788

SINGER Sandra ASSOCIATES
(Corporate Services)
21 Cotswold Road
Westcliff-on-Sea, Essex SS0 8AA
Website: www.sandrasinger.com
e-mail: sandrasingeruk@aol.com
Fax: 01702 339393   Tel: 01702 331616

TAYLOR HERRING COMMUNICATIONS Ltd
11 Westbury Centre
69 St Marks Road
London W10 6JG
Website: www.taylorherring.com
e-mail: james.herring@taylorherring.com
Fax: 020-8206 5155   Tel: 020-8206 5151

THOMPSON Peter ASSOCIATES
Flat One, 12 Bourchier Street, London W1V 5HN
Fax: 020-7439 1202   Tel: 020-7439 1210

THORNBORROW Bridget
110 Newark Street, London E1 2ES
e-mail: b.thornborrow@btinternet.com
Fax: 020-7247 4144   Tel: 020-7247 4437

TOWN HOUSE PUBLICITY Ltd
(Theatre & Television PR)
45 Islington Park Street, London N1 1QB
e-mail: thp@townhousepublicity.co.uk
Fax: 020-7359 6026   Tel: 020-7226 7450

TRE-VETT Eddie
Brink House, Avon Castle, Ringwood
Hampshire BH24 2BL   Tel: 01425 475544

WILLIAMS Tei PRESS & ARTS MARKETING
Kensel Green Mooring
Ladbroke Grove, London W10 4SR
e-mail: artsmarketing@btconnect.com
Mobile: 07957 664116   Tel: 020-8964 5289

WILSON Stella PUBLICITY
130 Calabria Road, London N5 1HT
e-mail: stella@stellawilson.com   Tel: 020-7354 5672

WINGHAM Maureen PRESS & PUBLIC RELATIONS
PO Box 125, Stowmarket, Suffolk IP14 1PB
e-mail: mjw.wingham@virgin.net
Fax: 01449 771400   Tel: 01449 771200

WRIGHT Peter
(See CUE CONSULTANTS)

Radio
BBC Radio London
BBC Local Radio Stations
Independent Local Radio

Recording Studios
Rehearsal Rooms & Casting Suites
Role Play Companies/Theatre Skills
in Business
Routes to Film & Television Studios

It is essential that anyone undertaking a journey to the studios listed in the Routes section, double checks these routes. Owing to constant changes of rail/bus companies/operators routes may change.

BBC RADIO, Broadcasting House
London W1A 1AA
Tel: 020-7580 4468 (Main Switchboard)

• DRAMA
BBC Radio Drama
Bush House
The Aldwych, London WC2B 4PH
Tel: 020-7580 4468 (Main Switchboard)

Production
Head	Gordon House
Production Executive	Rebecca Wilmshurst
Co-ordinator Radio Drama Company	Cynthia Fagan

Executive Producers
World Service	Marion Nancarrow
London	Sally Avens
	Jeremy Mortimer
Manchester	Sue Roberts
Birmingham	Vanessa Whitburn

Senior Producers
Cherry Cookson	David Hitchinson (Westway)
	James Peries (Silver Street)

Producers – London
Marc Beeby	Tracey Neale
Pam Fraser Solomon	Jonquil Panting
Claire Grove	Mary Peate
Peter Kavanagh	Janet Whitaker
Duncan Minshull	Rishi Sankar (World Service)

Producers – Manchester
Pauline Harris	Jim Poyser
Nadia Molinari	Polly Thomas

Producers Birmingham
Naylah Ahmed (Silver Street)	Jenny Stephens
Julie Beckett (Archers)	Deborah Sathe (Silver Street)
Kate Oates (Archers)	Peter Wild

Diversity Development
Director	Shabina Aslam

Development Producers
Howard Belgrad	Pam Marshall
Steven Canny	Toby Swift
Janet Hampson (Birmingham)	Liz Webb

Writersroom
Director	Kate Rowland
Co-ordinator	Jessica Dromgoole

BROADCAST

Radio Drama – BBC Scotland
Head	Patrick Rayner
Editor, Radio Drama	Bruce Young
Management Assistant	Sue Meek

Producers
Gaynor Macfarlane	David Jackson Young
Lu Kemp	

Radio Drama – BBC Wales
Alison Hindell

Radio Drama – BBC Northern Ireland
All enquiries to Anne Simpson

[CONTACTS 2005]

• LIGHT ENTERTAINMENT/RADIO PRODUCTION

Head, Light Entertainment Radio	John Pidgeon
Finance Manager	David Goodfellow

Producers

Colin Anderson	Ed Morrish
Adam Bromley	Simon Nicholls
Dawn Ellis	Will Saunders
Tilusha Ghelani	Carol Smith
Claire Jones	Katie Tyrrell
Katie Marsden	Helen Williams

Radio Administrator	Sarah Wright
Radio Administrator Asst	Mel Almond

• NEWS AND CURRENT AFFAIRS

BBC News (Television & Radio)
Television Centre
Wood Lane, London W12 7RJ
Tel: 020-7580 4468 (Main Switchboard)

Director News	Helen Boaden
Head of Newsgathering	Adrian Van Klaveren
Head of Political Programmes	Fran Unsworth
Head of Radio News	Steve Mitchell
Head of TV News	Roger Mosey
Head of Interactive News	Richard Deverell
Head of TV Current Affairs	Peter Horrocks
Head of Radio Current Affairs	Gwyneth Williams
Head of Research	Sue Inglish
Head of News Production Facilities	Peter Coles
Head of Communications	Janie Ironside Wood

• RADIO SPORT

Head of Sport	Gordon Turnbull

• CONTROLLERS

Director of Radio & Music	Jenny Abramsky

RADIO 1

Controller	Andy Parfitt

RADIO 2

Controller	Lesley Douglas

RADIO 3

Controller	Roger Wright

RADIO 4

Controller	Mark Damazer

RADIO 5 LIVE

Controller	Bob Shennan

• BBC NEW WRITING

BBC Writersroom
1 Mortimer Street
London W1T 3JA   Tel: 020-7765 2703
e-mail: new.writing@bbc.co.uk
Website: www.bbc.co.uk/writersroom

Creative Director	Kate Rowland
New Writing Co-ordinator	Jessica Dromgoole

BBC RADIO BRISTOL
PO Box 194, Bristol BS99 7QT
Website: www.bbc.co.uk/bristol
e-mail: radio.bristol@bbc.co.uk
Fax: 0117-923 8323　　　　　　　Tel: 0117-974 1111
Managing Editor: Jenny Lacey
News Editor: Dawn Trevett

BBC CAMBRIDGE
Broadcasting House, 104 Hills Road, Cambridge CB2 1LD
Fax: 01223 460832　　　　　　　Tel: 01223 259696
Managing Editor: David Martin
Assistant Editor: Patrick Davies

BBC RADIO CLEVELAND
PO Box 95 FM, Middlesbrough TS1 5DG
Website: www.bbc.co.uk/tees
Fax: 01642 211356　　　　　　　Tel: 01642 225211
Managing Editor: Andrew Glover

BBC RADIO CORNWALL
Phoenix Wharf, Truro, Cornwall TR1 1UA
Website: www.bbc.co.uk/cornwall
Fax: 01872 275045　　　　　　　Tel: 01872 275421
Managing Editor: Pauline Causey

BBC COVENTRY & WARWICKSHIRE
1 Holt Court, Greyfriars Road, Coventry CV1 2WR
Website: www.bbc.co.uk/coventry
Fax: 024-7657 0100　　　　　　　Tel: 024-7686 0086
Senior Broadcast Journalist: Sue Curtis

BBC RADIO CUMBRIA
Annetwell Street, Carlisle, Cumbria CA3 8BB
Website: www.bbc.co.uk/radiocumbria
Fax: 01228 511195　　　　　　　Tel: 01228 592444
Managing Editor: Nigel Dyson

BBC RADIO DERBY
PO Box 104.5, Derby DE1 3HL
Website: www.bbc.co.uk/derby　　　Tel: 01332 361111
Managing Editor: Simon Cornes

BBC RADIO DEVON
PO Box 1034, Plymouth PL3 5YQ
Website: www.bbc.co.uk/devon
Fax: 01752 234564　　　　　　　Tel: 01752 260323
Managing Editor: Robert Wallace

BBC ESSEX
PO Box 765, Chelmsford
Essex CM2 9XB　　　　　　　　Tel: 01245 616000
Managing Editor: Margaret Hyde

BBC RADIO GLOUCESTERSHIRE
London Road, Gloucester GL1 1SW　Tel: 01452 308585
Managing Editor: Mark Hurrell

BBC RADIO GUERNSEY
Broadcasting House, Bulwer Avenue
St Sampsons, Channel Islands GY2 4LA
Website: www.bbc.co.uk/guernsey
e-mail: radio.guernsey@bbc.co.uk
Fax: 01481 200361　　　　　　　Tel: 01481 200600
Senior Broadcast Journalist: Simon Alexander

BBC HEREFORD & WORCESTER
Hylton Road, Worcester WR2 5WW　Tel: 01905 748485
Managing Editor: James Coghill

BBC RADIO HUMBERSIDE
Queens Court, Queens Gardens, Hull HU1 3RH
e-mail: radio.humberside@bbc.co.uk
Fax: 01482 314403　　　　　　　Tel: 01482 323232
Editor: Simon Pattern

BBC RADIO JERSEY
18 Parade Road, St Helier, Jersey JE2 3PL
Website: www.bbc.co.uk/jersey
Fax: 01534 732569　　　　　　　Tel: 01534 870000
Assistant Editor: Matthew Price
News Editor: Sarah Scriven

BBC RADIO KENT
The Great Hall, Mount Pleasant Road
Tunbridge Wells, Kent TN1 1QQ
Website: www.bbc.co.uk/kent　　　Tel: 01892 670000
Managing Editor: Robert Wallis

BBC RADIO LANCASHIRE
20-26 Darwen Street, Blackburn, Lancashire BB2 2EA
Website: www.bbc.co.uk/lancashire　Tel: 01254 262411
Editor: John Clayton

BBC RADIO LEEDS
BBC Broadcasting Centre
2 St Peter's Square, Leeds LS9 8AH
Website: www.bbc.co.uk/leeds
Fax: 0113-242 0652　　　　　　　Tel: 0113-244 2131
Managing Editor: John Ryan

BBC RADIO LEICESTER
Epic House, Charles Street, Leicester LE1 3SH
Fax: 0116-251 1463　　　　　　　Tel: 0116-251 6688
Managing Editor: Kate Squire

BBC RADIO LINCOLNSHIRE
PO Box 219, Newport, Lincoln LN1 3XY
Website: www.bbc.co.uk/lincolnshire
Fax: 01522 511058　　　　　　　Tel: 01522 511411
Managing Editor: Charlie Partridge

BBC LONDON 94.9 FM
35 Marylebone High Street
London W1U 4QA
Website: www.bbc.co.uk/london
Fax: 020-7208 9660　　　　　　　Tel: 020-7224 2424
Managing Editor: David Robey
Assistant News Editor: Wyn Baptist
Assistant Editor General Programmes: Paul Leaper

BBC GMR (MANCHESTER)
PO Box 951, Oxford Road
Manchester M60 1SD
Website: www.bbc.co.uk/manchester　Tel: 0161-200 2000
Editor: Mike Briscoe

BBC RADIO MERSEYSIDE
55 Paradise Street, Liverpool L1 3BP
Website: www.bbc.co.uk/merseyside
e-mail: radio.merseyside@bbc.co.uk　Tel: 0151-708 5500
Managing Editor: Mick Ord

BBC RADIO NEWCASTLE
Broadcasting Centre, Barrack Road
Newcastle upon Tyne NE99 1RN
Website: www.bbc.co.uk/radionewcastle
Fax: 0191-232 5082　　　　　　　Tel: 0191-232 4141
Editor: Sarah Drummond

BBC RADIO NORFOLK
The Forum, Millennium Plain, Norwich NR2 1BH
Website: www.bbc.co.uk/norfolk
e-mail: radionorfolk@bbc.co.uk
Fax: 01603 667949　　　　　　　Tel: 01603 617411
Managing Editor: David Clayton

BBC NORTHAMPTON
Broadcasting Hse, Abington St, Northampton NN1 2BH
Website: www.bbc.co.uk/northamptonshire
e-mail: northamptonshire@bbc.co.uk
Fax: 01604 230709　　　　　　　Tel: 01604 239100
Manager: Laura Moss

BBC RADIO NOTTINGHAM
London Road, Nottingham NG2 4UU
Website: www.bbc.co.uk/nottingham
Fax: 0115-902 1985　　　　　　　Tel: 0115-955 0500
Editor: Mike Bettison
Editor News Gathering: Emma Agnew

BBC RADIO SHEFFIELD
54 Shoreham Street
Sheffield S1 4RS
Website: www.bbc.co.uk/sheffield
Fax: 0114-267 5454   Tel: 0114-273 1177
Managing Editor: Gary Keown
Senior Broadcast Journalist News: Mike Woodcock

BBC RADIO SHROPSHIRE
2-4 Boscobel Drive
Shrewsbury
Shropshire SY1 3TT
Website: www.bbc.co.uk/shropshire
e-mail: radio.shropshire@bbc.co.uk
Fax: 01743 271702   Tel: 01743 248484
Editor: Tim Pemberton
Senior Broadcast Journalist News: John Shone

BBC RADIO SOLENT
Broadcasting House
Havelock Road
Southampton SO14 7PW
Website: www.bbc.co.uk/solent
e-mail: solent@bbc.co.uk
Fax: 023-8033 9648   Tel: 023-8063 1311
Managing Editor: Mia Costello

BBC SOUTHERN COUNTIES
Broadcasting Centre
Guildford, Surrey GU2 7AP
e-mail: southern.counties.radio@bbc.co.uk
Fax: 01483 304952   Tel: 01483 306306
Managing Editor: Mike Hapgood
Assistant Editor: Sara David

BBC RADIO STOKE
Cheapside, Hanley, Stoke-on-Trent, Staffordshire ST1 1JJ
Website: www.bbc.co.uk/stoke
e-mail: radio.stoke@bbc.co.uk
Fax: 01782 289115   Tel: 01782 208080
Managing Editor: Sue Owen

BBC RADIO SUFFOLK
Broadcasting House, St Matthews Street, Ipswich IP1 3EP
Website: www.bbc.co.uk/suffolk
e-mail: radiosuffolk@bbc.co.uk   Tel: 01473 250000
Editor: Gerald Main

BBC RADIO SWINDON & BBC RADIO WILTSHIRE
Broadcasting House
56-58 Prospect Place, Swindon SN1 3RW
Fax: 01793 513650   Tel: 01793 513626
Manager: Tony Worgan

BBC THREE COUNTIES RADIO
1 Hastings Street, Luton LU1 5XL
Website: www.bbc.co.uk/threecountries
e-mail: 3cr@bbc.co.uk
Fax: 01582 401467   Tel: 01582 637400
Managing Editor: Mark Norman

BBC RADIO WM (West Midlands)
PO Box 206, Birmingham B5 7SD
Website: www.bbc.co.uk/westmidlands
Fax: 0121-472 3174   Tel: 0121-432 9000
Editor Local Services: Keith Beech

BBC RADIO YORK
20 Bootham Row, York YO30 7BR
Website: www.bbc.co.uk/radioyork
e-mail: radio.york@bbc.co.uk
Fax: 01904 610937   Tel: 01904 641351
Managing Editor: Matt Youdale

RADIO (INDEPENDENT LOCAL)

ABERDEEN
Northsound Radio
Abbotswell Road
West Tullos, Aberdeen AB12 3AG
Website: www.northsound.co.uk
e-mail: northsound@srh.co.uk   Tel: 01224 337000

AYR
South West Sound FM
Radio House
54A Holmston Road, Ayr KA7 3BE
e-mail: westfm@srh.co.uk   Tel: 01292 283662

BELFAST
City Beat 96.7 FM
PO Box 967, Belfast BT9 5DF
Website: www.citybeat.co.uk
Fax: 028-9020 0023   Tel: 028-9020 5967

BELFAST
Downtown Radio
Newtownards, Co Down BT23 4ES
e-mail: alastair.mcdowell@downtown.co.uk
Tel: 028-9181 5555

BERKSHIRE & NORTH HAMPSHIRE
2-Ten FM
PO Box 2020
Reading
Berkshire RG31 7FG
Website: www.musicradio.com   Tel: 0118-945 4400

BIRMINGHAM
96.4 BRMB & Capital Gold
4 Oozells Square, Birmingham B1 2DJ
Website: www.brmb.co.uk
Fax: 0121-245 5245   Tel: 0121-245 5000

BORDERS The
Radio Borders Ltd
Tweedside Park, Galashiels TD1 3TD
Website: www.radioborders.com
Fax: 0845 3457080   Tel: 01896 759444

BRADFORD
Sunrise Radio
30 Chapel Street, Little Germany, Bradford BD1 5DN
Website: www.sunriseradio.fm
Fax: 01274 728534   Tel: 01274 735043

BRADFORD, HUDDERSFIELD, HALIFAX, KEIGHLEY, DEWSBURY
Pulse Classic Gold
Forster Square, Bradford BD1 5NE
e-mail: general@pulse.co.uk   Tel: 01274 203040

BRIGHTON, EASTBOURNE & HASTINGS
Southern FM
Radio House, PO Box 2000, Brighton BN41 2SS
Website: www.southernfm.com
Fax: 01273 430098   Tel: 01273 430111

BRISTOL
GWR FM & Classic Gold 1260
1 Passage Street, PO Box 2000, Bristol BS99 7SN
Website: www.musicradio.com
Fax: 0117-984 3202   Tel: 0117-984 3200

CAMBRIDGE & NEWMARKET
Q103 FM
Q103, The Vision Park
Chivers Way
Histon, Cambridge CB4 4WW   Tel: 01223 235255

CARDIFF & NEWPORT
Red Dragon FM & Capital Gold
Atlantic Wharf
Cardiff Bay, Cardiff CF10 4DJ
Website: www.reddragonfm.com
e-mail: mail@reddragonfm.co.uk   Tel: 029-2066 2066

CHESTER, NORTH WALES & WIRRAL
Marcher Radio Group Ltd
The Studios Mold Road, Wrexham LL11 4AF
Website: www.musicradio.com
e-mail: sarah.smithard@musicradio.com
Managing Director: Sarah Smithard   Tel: 01978 752202

COVENTRY
KIX 96.2 FM
Watch Close, Spon Street, Coventry CV1 3LN
Website: www.kix.fm
Fax: 024-7655 1744   Tel: 024-7652 5656

COVENTRY
Mercia FM
Hertford Place, Coventry CV1 3TT
Website: www.musicradio.com
Fax: 024-7686 8203   Tel: 024-7686 8200

DUMFRIES
South West Sound FM
Unit 40, The Loreburn Centre
High Street, Dumfries DG1 2BD
Website: www.southwestsound.co.uk
Fax: 01387 265629   Tel: 01387 250999

DUNDEE & PERTH
Tay FM & Radio Tay AM
PO Box 123, 6 North Isla Street, Dundee DD3 7JQ
Website: www.radiotay.co.uk
e-mail: tayfm@radiotay.co.uk   Tel: 01382 200800

EDINBURGH
Radio Forth Ltd
Forth House, Forth Street, Edinburgh EH1 3LE
Website: www.forthonline.co.uk
e-mail: info@radioforth.co.uk   Tel: 0131-556 9255

EXETER & TORBAY
Gemini Radio Ltd
Hawthorn House, Exeter Business Park, Exeter EX1 3QS
Website: www.musicradio.com
Fax: 01392 354202   Tel: 01392 444444

FALKIRK
Central FM
201-203 High Street, Falkirk FK1 1DU
Website: www.centralfm.co.uk
Fax: 01324 611168   Tel: 01324 611164

GLASGOW
Radio Clyde FM1 & Clyde 2 AM
3 South Avenue
Clydebank Business Park, Glasgow G81 2RX
Website: www.clydeonline.co.uk
Fax: 0141-565 2265   Tel: 0141-565 2200

GLOUCESTER & CHELTENHAM
Severn Sound, FM & Classic Gold
Bridge Studios, Eastgate Centre
Gloucester GL1 1SS
Website: www.musicradio.com
Fax: 01452 572409   Tel: 01452 313200

GREAT YARMOUTH & NORWICH
Broadland 102 & Classic Gold Amber
St Georges Plain, 47-49 Colegate, Norwich NR3 1DB
Website: www.musicradio.com
Fax: 01603 671167   Tel: 01603 630621

GUILDFORD
96.4 Eagle FM & County Sound 1566 MW
Eagle Radio Ltd, Dolphin House
3 North Street, Guildford, Surrey GU1 4AA
e-mail: eagle@countysound.co.uk   Tel: 01483 300964

HEREFORD & WORCESTER
Wyvern FM
5-6 Barbourne Terrace, Worcester WR1 3JZ
Website: www.musicradio.com   Tel: 01905 612212

INVERNESS
Moray Firth Radio
PO Box 271, Scorguie Place, Inverness IV3 8UJ
Website: www.mfr.co.uk   e-mail: mfr@mfr.co.uk
Fax: 01463 243224   Tel: 01463 224433

IPSWICH
SGR-FM
Radio House, Alpha Business Park
Whitehouse Road, Ipswich IP1 5LT
Website: www.musicradio.com
Fax: 01473 467549   Tel: 01473 461000

ISLE OF WIGHT
Isle of Wight Radio
Dodnor Park Newport, Isle of Wight PO30 5XE
Website: www.iwradio.co.uk   e-mail: admin@iwradio.co.uk
Fax: 01983 821690   Tel: 01983 822557

KENT
Invicta FM & Capital Gold
Radio House, John Wilson Business Park
Whitstable, Kent CT5 3QX
Website: www.invictafm.com
e-mail: info@invictafm.com   Tel: 01227 772004

LEEDS
96.3 Radio Aire & Magic 828
PO Box 2000, 51 Burley Road, Leeds LS3 1LR
Website: www.radioaire.com
Fax: 0113-283 1303   Tel: 0113-283 5500

LEICESTER
Leicester Sound
6 Dominus Way, Meridian Business Park, Leicester LE19 1RP
Website: www.musicradio.com
Fax: 0116-256 1303   Tel: 0116-256 1300

LEICESTER, NOTTINGHAM & DERBY
96 Trent FM & Classic Gold GEM
29-31 Castle Gate, Nottingham NG1 7AP
Website: www.musicradio.com
Fax: 0115-912 9333   Tel: 0115-952 7000

LIVERPOOL
Radio City
St Johns Beacon, 1 Houghton Street, Liverpool L1 1RL
Website: www.radiocity.co.uk   Tel: 0151-472 6800

LONDON
Capital Radio Plc
30 Leicester Square, London WC2H 7LA
Website: www.capitalradiogroup.com
Fax: 020-7766 6100   Tel: 020-7766 6000

LONDON
Choice FM
291-299 Borough High Street, London SE1 1JG
Website: www.choicefm.com
Fax: 020-7378 3911   Tel: 020-7378 3969

LONDON
Classic FM
7 Swallow Place, Oxford Circus, London W1B 2AG
Website: www.classicfm.com
Fax: 020-7493 0750   Tel: 020-7343 9000

LONDON
Heart 106.2 FM
The Chrysalis Building, Bramley Road, London W10 6SP
Website: www.heart1062.co.uk
Fax: 020-7470 1066   Tel: 020-7468 1062

LONDON
(Independent Radio News) ITN Radio
200 Gray's Inn Road, London WC1X 8XZ
Website: www.irn.co.uk
e-mail: irn@itn.co.uk
Fax: 020-7430 4834   Tel: 020-7430 4814

LONDON
Jazz FM 102.2
26-27 Castlereagh Street, London W1H 5DL
Website: www.jazzfm.com
e-mail: info@jazzfm.com   Tel: 020-7706 4100

LONDON
London Greek Radio
437 High Road, Finchley, London N12 0AP
Website: www.lgr.co.uk   Tel: 020-8349 6950

LONDON
Magic 105.4 FM
Mappin House, 4 Winsley Street, London W1W 8HF
Website: www.magic1054.co.uk   Tel: 020-7955 1054

LONDON
Time 106.8 FM
2-6 Basildon Road, London SE2 0EW   Tel: 020-8311 3112

LONDON
Virgin Radio
1 Golden Square, London W1F 9DJ
Website: www.virginradio.co.uk
Fax: 020-7434 1197   Tel: 020-7434 1215

LUTON & BEDFORD
97.6 Chiltern FM & Classic Gold Digital 792/828
Broadcast Centre, Chiltern Road, Dunstable LU6 1HQ
Website: www.musicradio.com
Fax: 01582 676251   Tel: 01582 676200

MANCHESTER
Key 103 FM & Magic 1152
Piccadilly Radio Ltd, Castle Quay
Castle Field, Manchester M15 4PR
Website: www.key103.co.uk
Fax: 0161-288 5071   Tel: 0161-288 5000

MILTON KEYNES
FM 103 Horizon
14 Vincent Avenue
Milton Keynes Broadcast Centre
Crownhill, Milton Keynes MK8 0AD
Website: www.musicradio.com   Tel: 01908 269111

NORTHAMPTON
Northhants 96/Classic Gold 1557 Northamptonshire Digital
19-21 St Edmunds Road, Northampton NN1 5DY
Website: www.musicradio.com
e-mail: reception@northants96.musicradio.com
                                     Tel: 01604 795600

NORTHAMPTONSHIRE
Connect FM 97.2 & 107.4 FM
Centre 2000, Robinson Close, Telford Way Industrial
Estate, Kettering, Northamptonshire NN16 8PU
Website: www.connectfm.com
Fax: 01536 517390   Tel: 01536 412413

NOTTINGHAM & DERBY
96 Trent FM
29-31 Castle Gate, Nottingham NG1 7AP
e-mail: admin@musicradio.com   Tel: 0115-952 7000

OXFORD & BANBURY
Fox FM
Brush House, Pony Road, Oxford OX4 2XR
Website: www.foxfm.co.uk   Tel: 01865 871000

PETERBOROUGH
102.7 Hereward FM & Classic Gold
PO Box 225, Queensgate Centre
Peterborough PE1 1XJ   Tel: 01733 460460

PLYMOUTH
Plymouth Sound Radio
Earl's Acre, Alma Road, Plymouth PL3 4HX
Website: www.musicradio.com   Tel: 01752 275600

PORTSMOUTH & SOUTHAMPTON
Capitol Radio Group South
Radio House, Whittle Avenue, Segensworth West, Fareham
Hampshire PO15 5SH   Tel: 01489 589911

SOMERSET
Orchard FM
Haygrove House
Shoreditch, Taunton TA3 7BT
Website: www.musicradio.com   Tel: 01823 338448

SOUTH MANCHESTER
Imagine FM
Regent House
Heaton Lane, Stockport, Cheshire SK4 1BX
Website: www.imaginefm.co.uk
e-mail: ashley.byrne@imaginefm.net   Tel: 0161-609 1400

STOKE-ON-TRENT & STAFFORD
Signal Radio
Stoke Road
Stoke-on-Trent, Staffordshire ST4 2SR
Website: www.signalone.co.uk
e-mail: info@signalradio.com   Tel: 01782 441300

SWANSEA
96.4 FM The Wave
Victoria Road, Gowerton, Swansea SA4 3AB
Website: www.thewave.co.uk   Tel: 01792 511964

TEESSIDE
TFM 96.6 & Magic 1170
Yale Crescent Thornaby
Stockton on Tees, Cleveland TS17 6AA
Website: www.tfmradio.com   Tel: 01642 888222

TYNE & WEAR & NORTHUMBERLAND, DURHAM
Metro Radio
Newcastle upon Tyne NE99 1BB
Website: www.metroradio.co.uk   Tel: 0191-420 0971

WEST SUSSEX & SURREY
102.7 Mercury FM
9 The Stanley Centre, Kelvin Way
Manor Royal, Crawley
West Sussex RH10 9SE
Website: www.musicradio.com
e-mail: name@musicradio.com
Fax: 01293 636009   Tel: 01293 636101

WOLVERHAMPTON & BLACK COUNTRY/SHREWSBURY & TELFORD
West Midlands Beacon FM
267 Tettenhall Road, Wolverhampton WV6 0DE
Website: www.musicradio.com   Tel: 01902 461300

YORKSHIRE
Hallam FM & Magic AM
Radio House, 900 Herries Road
Hillsborough, Sheffield S6 1RH
Website: www.hallamfm.co.uk   Tel: 0114-209 1000

YORKSHIRE & LINCOLNSHIRE
96.9 Viking FM & Magic 1161 AM
Commercial Road, Hull HU1 2SG
Website: www.vikingfm.co.uk   Tel: 01482 325141

A1 VOX Ltd
(Spoken Word Audio, ISDN Links, Demo CDs & Audio Clips)
20 Old Compton Street, London W1D 4TW
Website: www.a1vox.com
e-mail: info@a1vox.com
Fax: 020-7434 4414   Tel: 020-7434 4404

ABBEY ROAD STUDIOS
3 Abbey Road, St John's Wood, London NW8 9AY
Website: www.abbeyroad.com
e-mail: info@abbeyroad.com
Fax: 020-7266 7250   Tel: 020-7266 7000

AIR-EDEL RECORDING STUDIOS Ltd
18 Rodmarton Street, London W1U 8BJ
e-mail: trevorbest@air-edel.co.uk
Fax: 020-7224 0344   Tel: 020-7486 6466

ANGEL RECORDING STUDIOS Ltd
311 Upper Street, London N1 2TU
e-mail: angel@angelstudio.co.uk
Fax: 020-7226 9624   Tel: 020-7354 2525

ASCENT MEDIA Ltd
Film House, 142 Wardour Street, London W1F 8DD
Website: www.ascentmedia.co.uk
e-mail: sally.hart-wb@ascentmedia.co.uk
Fax: 020-7878 7870   Tel: 020-7878 0000

AUDIOLAB WEST STREET
3 West Street, Buckingham MK18 1HL
Website: www.alab.co.uk
e-mail: studio@copysound.co.uk
Mobile: 07739 807159   Tel/Fax: 01280 822814

BLACKHEATH HALLS
23 Lee Road
Blackheath, London SE3 9RQ
Website: www.blackheathhalls.com
e-mail: mail@blackheathhalls.com
Fax: 020-8852 5154   Tel: 020-8318 9758

BRIGHT LIGHTS STUDIO
6 Brantwood Gardens, Oakwood
Enfield EN2 7LZ   Tel: 020-8367 8480

CHANNEL 20/20 Ltd
20/20 House, 26-28 Talbot Lane, Leicester LE1 4LR
Website: www.channel2020.co.uk
Fax: 0116-222 1113   Tel: 0116-233 2220

CRYING OUT LOUD
(Voice-Over Specialists/Voice-over Demo CDs)
Website: www.cryingoutloud.co.uk
e-mail: simon@cryingoutloud.co.uk
Mobile: 07946 533108   Mobile: 07796 266265

DE LANE LEA SOUND
(Post Production, Re-Recording Studios)
75 Dean Street, London W1D 3PU
Website: www.delanelea.com
e-mail: dll@delanelea.com
Fax: 020-7432 3838   Tel: 020-7432 3800

ELMS STUDIOS DIGITAL
(Mac G4/Logic Platinum/Emu Systems, 02R
Music Composing/Scoring & VOs)
Addiscombe, 10 Empress Avenue, London E12 5ES
Website: www.impulse-music.co.uk/elms-studio
e-mail: phillawrence@elmsstudios.com   Tel: 020-8518 8629

ESSENTIAL MUSIC
20 Great Chapel Street, London W1F 8FW
e-mail: admin@essentialmusic.com
Fax: 020-7287 3597   Tel: 020-7439 7113

FARM DIGITAL POST PRODUCTION The
27 Upper Mount Street, Dublin 2, Eire
Website: www.thefarm.ie
e-mail: info@thefarm.ie
Fax: 353 1 676 8816   Tel: 353 1 676 8812

HEAVY ENTERTAINMENT Ltd
222 Kensal Road, London W10 5BN
Website: www.heavy-entertainment.com
e-mail: info@heavy-entertainment.com
Fax: 020-8960 9003   Tel: 020-8960 9001

ISLAND 41
(Voice-over Recording Studio)
29 Ash Grove, London W5 4AX
Website: www.island41.com
e-mail: enquiries@island41.com
Fax: 020-8567 5183   Tel: 020-8567 5140

JMS GROUP Ltd
3 Montagu Row, London W1U 6DY
Website: www.jms-group.com
e-mail: info@jmslondon.co.uk
Fax: 020-7224 4035   Tel: 020-7224 1031

JMS GROUP Ltd
Hethersett, Norwich
Norfolk NR9 3DL
Website: www.jms-group.com
e-mail: info@jmsradio.co.uk
Fax: 01603 812255   Tel: 01603 811855

KONK STUDIOS
84-86 Tottenham Lane, London N8 7EE
e-mail: linda@konkstudios.com
Fax: 020-8348 3952   Tel: 020-8340 7873

LANSDOWNE RECORDING STUDIOS Ltd
Lansdowne House, Lansdowne Road, London W11 3LP
Website: www.cts-lansdowne.co.uk
e-mail: info@cts-lansdowne.co.uk
Fax: 020-7792 8904 Tel: 020-7727 0041

MOTIVATION SOUND STUDIOS
35A Broadhurst Gardens, London NW6 3QT
Website: www.motivationsound.co.uk
e-mail: info@motivationsound.co.uk
Fax: 020-7624 4879 Tel: 020-7328 8305

ORANGE ROOM MUSIC
(Recording Studios & Artist Management)
4 Kendal Court, Railway Road
Newhaven, East Sussex BN9 0AY
Website: www.orangeroommusic.co.uk
e-mail: office@orangeroommusic.co.uk
Fax: 01273 612811 Tel: 01273 612825

OTHERWISE STUDIOS
61D Gleneldon Road
London SW16 2BH
Website: www.otherwisestudios.com
e-mail: info@otherwisestudios.com Tel: 020-8769 7793

RED FACILITIES
61 Timberbush, Leith, Edinburgh EH6 6QH
Website: www.redfacilities.com
e-mail: doit@redfacilities.com
Fax: 0131-555 0088 Tel: 0131-555 2288

SARM STUDIOS WEST Ltd
8-10 Basing Street, London W11 1ET
Fax: 020-7221 9247 Tel: 020-7229 1229

SHAW Bernard
(Specialist in Recording & Directing Voice Tapes)
Horton Manor
Canterbury CT4 7LG
Website: www.bernardshaw.co.uk
e-mail: bernard@bernardshaw.co.uk Tel/Fax: 01227 730843

SHOWREEL The
(Voice-Over Showreels, Digital Editing etc)
Knightsbridge House, 229 Acton Lane
Chiswick, London W4 5DD
Website: www.theshowreel.com
e-mail: info@theshowreel.com
Fax: 020-8995 2144 Tel: 020-8995 3232

SILVER-TONGUED PRODUCTIONS
(Specializing in Voice Reels)
Website: www.silver-tongued.co.uk
e-mail: contact-us@silver-tongued.co.uk
Tel/Fax: 0870 2407408

SOUND CONCEPTION
82-84 York Road, Bristol BS3 4AL
e-mail: k-dubb@talk21.com
Fax: 0117-963 5059 Tel: 0117-966 2932

SOUND HOUSE POST PRODUCTION Ltd The
10th Floor, Astley House, Quay Street, Manchester M3 4AE
Website: www.thesoundhouse.tv
e-mail: suekean@thesoundhouse.tv
Fax: 0161-832 7266 Tel: 0161-832 7299

STERLING SOUND
(Voice-over, Demo CDs, Jingles & Commercials)
8A Barry Road
London SE22 0HU
e-mail: bob@mintman.co.uk Tel: 020-8693 2976

STUDIO AVP
82 Clifton Hill, London NW8 0JT
Fax: 020-7624 9112 Tel: 020-7624 9111

TOUCHWOOD AUDIO PRODUCTIONS
6 Hyde Park Terrace
Leeds, West Yorkshire LS6 1BJ
e-mail: brucetouchwood@hotmail.com Tel: 0113-278 7180

UNIVERSAL SOUND (JUST PLAY) Ltd
Old Farm Lane
London Road East
Amersham Buckinghamshire HP7 9DH
Website: www.universalsound.co.uk
e-mail: foley@universalsound.co.uk
Fax: 01494 723500 Tel: 01494 723400

VOICE OVER DEMOS
61 Cropley Street
London N1 7JB
Website: www.voiceoverdemos.co.uk
e-mail: daniel@voiceoverdemos.co.uk Tel: 020-7684 1645

WFS Ltd
(Sound Transfer/Optical & Magnetic)
Warwick Sound, 111A Wardour Street, London W1F 0UJ
Website: www.warwicksound.com
e-mail: info@warwicksound.com
Fax: 020-7439 0372 Tel: 020-7437 5532

WHITFIELD STREET STUDIOS
31-37 Whitfield Street, London W1T 2SS
Fax: 020-7580 2219 Tel: 020-7636 3434

WORLDWIDE SOUND Ltd
21-25 St Anne's Court, Soho, London W1F 0BJ
Website: www.worldwidegroup.ltd.uk
e-mail: sound@worldwidegroup.ltd.uk
Fax: 020-7734 0619 Tel: 020-7434 1121

Height 5 feet 10 inches (Equity/M.U.) Photo: *Stephen Hough*

Peter Durrent

Pianist ~ Accompanist ~ Composer ~ Vocalist
Audition & Rehearsal Pianist Cocktail Pianist

Tel: 01787 373483 Mob: 07810 613 938

or c/o The Spotlight

ACTORS CENTRE The (LONDON)
(Audition Space Only)
1A Tower Street, London WC2H 9NP
e-mail: admin@actorscentre.co.uk
Fax: 020-7240 3896   Tel: 020-7240 3940

ADI The
218 Lambeth Road, London SE1 7JY
e-mail: playltd@btconnect.com
Fax: 020-7401 2816   Tel: 020-7928 6160

ALFORD HOUSE
Aveline Street, London SE11 5DQ
Website: tim@alfordhouse.org.uk   Tel: 020-7735 1519

ALRA (Academy of Live and Recorded Arts)
Royal Victoria Patriotic Building, Fitzhugh Grove
Trinity Road, London SW18 3SX
Website: www.alra.co.uk
e-mail: enquiries@alra.co.uk
Fax: 020-8875 0789   Tel: 020-8870 6475

AMADEUS CENTRE The
50 Shirland Road, Little Venice, London W9 2JA
Website: www.amadeuscentre.co.uk
e-mail: amadeus@amadeuscentre.co.uk
Fax: 020-7266 1225   Tel: 020-7286 1686

AMERICAN CHURCH IN LONDON The
Whitefield Memorial Church
79A Tottenham Court Road, London W1T 4TD
Website: www.americanchurchinlondon.org
e-mail: latchcourt@amchurch.fsnet.co.uk
Fax: 020-7580 5013   Tel: 020-7580 2791

ARTSADMIN
(Toynbee Studios), 28 Commercial Street, London E1 6AB
Website: www.artsadmin.co.uk/aaresources
e-mail: admin@artsadmin.co.uk
Fax: 020-7247 5103   Tel: 020-7247 5102

BAC
Lavender Hill, London SW11 5TN
Website: www.bac.org.uk
e-mail: mailbox@bac.org.uk
Fax: 020-7978 5207   Tel: 020-7223 6557

BELSIZE MUSIC ROOMS
(Casting, Auditioning, Filming)
67 Belsize Lane, Hampstead, London NW3 5AX
Website: www.belsize-music-rooms.co.uk
e-mail: info@belsize-music-rooms.co.uk
Fax: 020-7916 0222   Tel: 020-7916 0111

BIG CITY STUDIOS
Montgomery House
159-161 Balls Pond Road, Islington, London N1 4BG
Website: www.pineapple-agency.com
Fax: 020-7241 3006   Tel: 020-7241 6655

BRIXTON ST VINCENT'S COMMUNITY CENTRE
Talma Road, London SW2 1AS
Website: www.bsvcc.org
e-mail: carofunnell@bsvcc.org
Fax: 020-7274 7129   Tel: 020-7326 4417

CASTING AT SWEET
Sweet Entertainments Ltd
42 Theobalds Road, London WC1X 8NW
e-mail: info@sweet-uk.net
Fax: 020-7404 6412   Tel: 020-7404 6411

CASTING CABIN The
19 Denmark Street, London WC2H 8NA
Website: www.castinspace.com
e-mail: thecastingcabin@btconnect.com
Fax: 020-7379 5444   Tel: 020-7379 0444

CASTING STUDIOS INTERNATIONAL Ltd
Ramillies House, 1-2 Ramillies Street, London W1F 7LN
Website: www.castingstudios.com
e-mail: info@castingstudios.com
Fax: 020-7437 2080   Tel: 020-7437 2070

THE SPOTLIGHT ROOMS

Six spacious casting rooms in the heart of the West End

- TV, VHS & camcorder facilities
- Free receptionist service
- Large waiting room
- Central London
- Video-casting on any format

www.spotlight.com/rooms

For bookings:

t: 020 7440 5030

e: casting@spotlight.com

THE SPOTLIGHT®
7 Leicester Place, London WC2H 7RJ

⊖ **Piccadilly Circus / Leicester Square**

CASTING SUITE The
10 Warwick Street, London W1R 5RA
Website: www.thecastingsuite.com
e-mail: info@thecastingsuite.com
Fax: 020-7494 0803   Tel: 020-7434 2331

CECIL SHARP HOUSE
(Pat Nightingale)
2 Regent's Park Road, London NW1 7AY
Website: www.efdss.org   e-mail: hire@efdss.org
Fax: 020-7284 0534   Tel: 020-7485 2206

CENTRAL CASTING FACILITIES
Website: www.sexypeople.tv   Tel: 0870 7276677

CENTRAL LONDON GOLF CENTRE
Burntwood Lane, London SW17 0AT
Website: www.clgc.co.uk
Fax: 020-8874 7447   Tel: 020-8871 2468

CENTRAL STUDIOS
470 Bromley Road, Bromley, Kent BR1 4PN
Website: www.dandbperformingarts.co.uk
e-mail: bonnie@dandbperformingarts.co.uk
Fax: 020-8697 8100   Tel: 020-8698 8880

CHATS PALACE ARTS CENTRE
42-44 Brooksby's Walk, Hackney, London E9 6DF
Fax: 020-8985 6878   Tel: 020-8533 0227

CHELSEA THEATRE
World's End Place, King's Road, London SW10 0DR
Website: www.chelseatheatre.org.uk
Fax: 020-7352 2024   Tel: 020-7352 1967

CIRCUS MANIACS SCHOOL OF CIRCUS ARTS
(Circus Skills Rehearsal & Casting Facilities)
Office 8A, The Kingswood Foundation, Britannia Road
Kingswood, Bristol BS15 8DB
e-mail: rehearse@circusmaniacs.com
Mobile: 07977 247287   Tel/Fax: 0117-947 7042

CLAPHAM COMMUNITY PROJECT
St Anne's Hall, Venn Street, London SW4 0BN
Website: www.rehearseatccp.co.uk
e-mail: admin@claphamcommunityproject.org.uk
                              Tel/Fax: 020-7720 8731

CLEAN BREAK THEATRE COMPANY
2 Patshull Road, London NW5 2LB
Website: www.cleanbreak.org.uk
e-mail: general@cleanbreak.org.uk
Fax: 020-7482 8611   Tel: 020-7482 8600

CLUB FOR ACTS & ACTORS
(Incorporating Concert Artistes Association)
20 Bedford Street, London WC2E 9HP Tel: 020-7836 3172

COPTIC STREET STUDIO Ltd
9 Coptic Street, London WC1A 1NH
Fax: 020-7636 1414   Tel: 020-7636 2030

COVENT GARDEN CASTING SUITES & AUDITION ROOMS
29 Maiden Lane, Covent Garden
London WC2E 7JS   Tel: 020-7240 1438

CRAGRATS Ltd
The Mill, Dunford Road, Holmfirth, Huddersfield HD9 2AR
Website: www.cragrats.com
e-mail: lindsay@cragrats.com
Fax: 01484 686212   Tel: 01484 686451

CUSTARD FACTORY The
Gibb Street, Digbeth, Birmingham B9 4AA
Website: www.custardfactory.com
e-mail: post@custardfactory.com
Fax: 0121-604 8888   Tel: 0121-693 7777

DANCE ATTIC STUDIOS
368 North End Road, London SW6   Tel: 020-7610 2055

DANCE COMPANY The
(Sue Hann)
76 High Street, Beckenham, Kent BR3 1ED
e-mail: dancecomp@aol.com
Fax: 020-8402 1414   Tel: 020-8402 2424

DANCEWORKS
16 Balderton Street, London W1K 6TN
Website: www.danceworks.net
Fax: 020-7629 2909   Tel: 020-7318 4100

DIGI_CAST
Unit 2, Sugar House Business Centre
24 Sugar House Lane, London E15 2QS
Website: www.digicastcards.co.uk
e-mail: gary@digicastcards.co.uk
Fax: 020-8555 0909   Tel: 020-8555 0005

DIORAMA ARTS
34 Osnaburgh Street, London NW1 3ND
Website: www.diorama-arts.org.uk
e-mail: admin@diorama-arts.org.uk
                             Tel: 020-7916 5467

DRILL HALL The
16 Chenies Street
London WC1E 7EX
Website: www.drillhall.co.uk
e-mail: admin@drillhall.co.uk
Fax: 020-7307 5062   Tel: 020-7307 5061

EALING STUDIOS
Ealing Green, London W5 5EP
Website: www.ealingstudios.com
e-mail: bookings@ealingstudios.com
Fax: 020-8758 8658   Tel: 020-8567 6655

ELMS LESTERS PAINTING ROOMS
1-3-5 Flitcroft Street, London WC2H 8DH
e-mail: info@elmslester.co.uk
Fax: 020-7379 0789   Tel: 020-7836 6747

ENGLISH FOLK DANCE & SONG SOCIETY
Cecil Sharp House
2 Regent's Park Road, London NW1 7AY
Website: www.efdss.org   e-mail: info@efdss.org
Fax: 020-7284 0534   Tel: 020-7485 2206

ENGLISH NATIONAL OPERA
Lilian Baylis House
165 Broadhurst Gardens, London NW6 3AX
Website: www.eno.org
e-mail: receptionlbh@eno.org
Fax: 020-7625 3398   Tel: 020-7624 7711

ESSEX HALL
Unitarian Headquarters
1-6 Essex Street, London WC2R 3HY
Fax: 020-7240 3089   Tel: 020-7240 2384

ETCETERA THEATRE
265 Camden High Street, London NW1 7BU
Website: www.etceteratheatre.com
e-mail: etc@etceteratheatre.com
Fax: 020-7482 0378   Tel: 020-7482 4857

EUROKIDS & ADULTS AGENCY CASTING STUDIOS
The Warehouse Studios, Glaziers Lane, Culcheth
Warrington, Cheshire WA3 4AQ
Website: www.eka-agency.com
e-mail: info@eka-agency.com
Fax: 01925 767563   Tel: 0871 7501575

FACTORY DANCE CENTRE
407 Hornsey Road, London N19 4DX
e-mail: info@tangolondon.com
Fax: 020-7272 1327   Tel: 020-7272 1122

FSU LONDON STUDY CENTRE
98-104 Great Russell Street, London WC1B 3LA
Fax: 020-8202 6797   Tel: 020-7813 3223

GARDEN STUDIOS The
1 Fitzroy Road, Primrose Hill, London NW1 8TU
Website: www.thegardenstudios.com
e-mail: donnaking@btopenworld.com
Mobile: 07802 939601   Tel/Fax: 020-7722 9304

HAMILTON ROAD CENTRE
1 Hamilton Road, Stratford, London E15 3AE
Fax: 020-7476 0050   Tel: 020-7473 0395

HAMPSTEAD THEATRE
Eton Avenue, Swiss Cottage, London NW3 3EU
Website: www.hampsteadtheatre.com
e-mail: info@hampsteadtheatre.com
Fax: 020-7449 4201   Tel: 020-7449 4200

HEN & CHICKENS THEATRE
Unrestricted View, Above Hen & Chickens Theatre Bar
109 St Paul's Road, London N1 2NA
Website: www.henandchickens.com
e-mail: james@henandchickens.com   Tel: 020-7704 2001

HER MAJESTY'S THEATRE
(Michael Townsend)
Haymarket, London SW1Y 4QL
Website: www.rutheatres.com
e-mail: mike.townsend@rutheatres.com Tel: 020-7494 5200

HOLY INNOCENTS CHURCH
Paddenswick Road, London W6 0UB
e-mail: innocent@fish.co.uk
Fax: 020-8563 8735   Tel: 020-8748 2286

HOPE STREET Ltd
13A Hope Street, Liverpool L1 9BQ
Website: www.hope-street.org
e-mail: arts@hopest.u-net.com
Fax: 0151-709 3242   Tel: 0151-708 8007

HOXTON HALL THEATRE & ARTS CENTRE
130 Hoxton Street, London N1 6SH
Website: www.hoxtonhall.co.uk
e-mail: admin@hoxtonhall.co.uk
Fax: 020-7729 3815   Tel: 020-7684 0060

ISLINGTON ARTS FACTORY
2 Parkhurst Road, London N7 0SF
Website: www.islingtonartsfactory.org.uk
e-mail: iaf@islingtonartsfactory.fsnet.co.uk
Fax: 020-7700 7229   Tel: 020-7607 0561

JACKSONS LANE ARTS CENTRE
(Various Spaces incl Rehearsal Rooms & Theatre Hire)
269A Archway Road, London N6 5AA
Website: www.jacksonslane.org.uk
e-mail: mail@jacksonslane.org.uk   Tel: 020-8340 5226

JERWOOD SPACE
171 Union Street, London SE1 0LN
Website: www.jerwoodspace.co.uk
e-mail: space@jerwoodspace.co.uk
Fax: 020-7654 0172   Tel: 020-7654 0171

K M C AGENCIES
PO Box 122, 48 Great Ancoats Street
Manchester M4 5AB
Website: www.kmcagencies.co.uk
e-mail: casting@kmcagencies.co.uk
Fax: 0161-237 9812   Tel: 0161-237 3009

LA MAISON VERTE
31 Avenue Henri Mas, 34320 Roujan, France
Website: www.lamaisonverte.co.uk
e-mail: nicole.russell@wanadoo.fr   Tel: 00 334 67248852

LIVE THEATRE
27 Broad Chare, Quayside
Newcastle upon Tyne NE1 3DQ
Website: www.live.org.uk
e-mail: info@live.org.uk   Tel: 0191-261 2694

LONDON BUBBLE THEATRE COMPANY Ltd
5 Elephant Lane, London SE16 4JD
Website: www.londonbubble.org.uk
e-mail: admin@londonbubble.org.uk
Fax: 020-7231 2366   Tel: 020-7237 4434

LONDON SCHOOL OF CAPOEIRA
Units 1 & 2 Leeds Place
Tollington Park, London N4 3RQ
Website: www.londonschoolofcapoeira.co.uk
                                      Tel: 020-7281 2020

LONDON STUDIO CENTRE
42-50 York Way, London N1 9AB
e-mail: enquire@london-studio-centre.co.uk
Fax: 020-7837 3248   Tel: 020-7837 7741

LONDON WELSH TRUST Ltd
157-163 Gray's Inn Road, London WC1X 8UE
Fax: 020-7837 6268   Tel: 020-7837 3722

LYRIC THEATRE HAMMERSMITH
Lyric Square, King Street, London W6 0QL
Website: www.lyric.co.uk   e-mail: enquiries@lyric.co.uk
Fax: 08700 5005811   Tel: 020-8741 5965

MACKINTOSH Cameron REHEARSAL STUDIO
The Tricycle, 269 Kilburn High Road, London NW6 7JR
Website: www.tricycle.co.uk   e-mail: foh@tricycle.co.uk
Fax: 020-7328 0795   Tel: 020-7372 6611

MADDERMARKET THEATRE
St John's Alley, Norwich, Norfolk NR2 1DR
Website: www.maddermarket.co.uk
e-mail: mmtheatre@btconnect.com
Fax: 01603 661357   Tel: 01603 626560

MARIA ASSUMPTA CENTRE
23 Kensington Square, Kensington, London W8 5HN
Fax: 020-7361 4710   Tel: 020-7361 4700

MARYMOUNT COLLEGE OF FORDHAM UNIVERSITY LONDON CENTRE
22 Brownlow Mews, London WC1N 2LA
Fax: 020-7831 7185   Tel: 020-7242 7004

MOBERLY SPORTS & EDUCATION CENTRE
Kilburn Lane, London W10 4AH
Fax: 020-7641 5878   Tel: 020-7641 4807

MOUNTVIEW
Academy of Theatre Arts
Ralph Richardson Memorial Studios, Kingfisher Place
Clarendon Road, London N22 6XF
Website: www.mountview.ac.uk
e-mail: enquiries@mountview.ac.uk
Fax: 020-8829 0034   Tel: 020-8881 2201

NATIONAL YOUTH THEATRE OF GREAT BRITAIN
443-445 Holloway Road, London N7 6LW
Website: www.nyt.org.uk   e-mail: info@nyt.org.uk
Fax: 020-7281 8246   Tel: 020-7281 3863

NEAL'S YARD MEETING ROOMS
14B Neal's Yard, Covent Garden, London WC2H 9DP
Website: www.nealsyardmeetingrooms.com
e-mail: nealsyardmeetingrooms@btconnect.com
Tel: 020-7379 0141

NETTLEFOLD The
West Norwood Library Centre
1 Norwood High Street, London SE27 9JX
e-mail: thenettlefold@lambeth.co.uk
Fax: 020-7926 8071   Tel: 020-7926 8070

NORTH LONDON PERFORMING ARTS CENTRE
(Production & Casting Office Facilities)
76 St James Lane, Muswell Hill, London N10 3DF
Website: www.nlpac.co.uk   e-mail: nlpac@aol.com
Fax: 020-8444 4040   Tel: 020-8444 4544

OCTOBER GALLERY
24 Old Gloucester Street, London WC1N 3AL
Website: www.theoctobergallery.com
e-mail: rentals@octobergallery.co.uk
Fax: 020-7405 1851   Tel: 020-7831 1618

OLD VIC THEATRE
The Cut, Waterloo Road, London SE1 8NB
Website: www.oldvictheatre.com   Tel: 020-7928 2651

OPEN DOOR COMMUNITY CENTRE
Beaumont Road, Wimbledon SW19 6TF
Website: www.wandsworth.gov.uk
e-mail: opendoor@wandsworth.gov.uk   Tel/Fax: 020-8871 8174

OUT OF JOINT
7 Thane Works, Thane Villas, London N7 7PH
Website: www.outofjoint.co.uk   e-mail: ojo@outofjoint.co.uk
Fax: 020-7609 0203   Tel: 020-7609 0207

OVAL HOUSE
52-54 Kennington Oval, London SE11 5SW
Website: www.ovalhouse.com
e-mail: info@ovalhouse.com   Tel: 020-7582 0080

PAINES PLOUGH AUDITION SPACE
4th Floor, 43 Aldwych, London WC2B 4DN
Website: www.painesplough.com
e-mail: office@painesplough.com
Fax: 020-7240 4534   Tel: 020-7240 4533

PEOPLE SHOW
People Show Studios, Pollard Row, London E2 6NB
Website: www.peopleshow.co.uk
e-mail: people@peopleshow.co.uk
Fax: 020-7739 0203   Tel: 020-7729 1841

PHA
Tanzaro House, Ardwick Green North, Manchester M12 6FZ
Website: www.pha-agency.co.uk
e-mail: info@pha-agency.co.uk
Fax: 0161-273 4567   Tel: 0161-273 4444

PINEAPPLE STUDIOS
7 Langley Street, London WC2H 9JA
Website: www.pineapple.uk.com
e-mail: studios@pineapple.uk.com
Fax: 020-7836 0803   Tel: 020-7836 4004

PLACE The (Contemporary Dance Trust)
17 Duke's Road, London WC1H 9PY
Website: www.theplace.org.uk
Fax: 020-7383 4851   Tel: 020-7387 0161

PLAYGROUND PERFORMING ARTS STUDIO The
Unit 8, Latimer Road, London W10 6RQ
Website: www.the-playground.co.uk
e-mail: info@the-playground.co.uk   Tel/Fax: 020-8960 0110

POOR SCHOOL The
242 Pentonville Road, London N1 9JY   Tel: 020-7837 6030

PRECINCT THEATRE The
Units 2/3 The Precinct, Packington Square, London N1 7UP
Website: www.breakalegman.com
e-mail: reima@breakalegman.com
Fax: 020-7359 3660   Tel: 020-7359 3594

Qd CASTING STUDIO
Qd Studios, 45 Poland Street, London W1F 7NA
e-mail: alicia.w@qotd.co.uk
Fax: 020-7437 2830   Tel: 020-7437 2823

QUESTORS THEATRE EALING The
12 Mattock Lane, London W5 5BQ
Website: www.questors.org.uk   e-mail: alice@questors.org.uk
Fax: 020-8567 8736   Tel: 020-8567 0011

QUICKSILVER THEATRE
The Glass House, 4 Enfield Road, London N1 5AZ
Website: www.quicksilvertheatre.org
e-mail: talktous@quicksilvertheatre.org
Fax: 020-7254 3119   Tel: 020-7241 2942

RAMBERT DANCE COMPANY
(Claire Drakeley)
94 Chiswick High Road, London W4 1SH
Website: www.rambert.org.uk   e-mail: rdc@rambert.org.uk
Fax: 020-8747 8323   Tel: 020-8630 0601

REALLY USEFUL THEATRES
(Michael Townsend)
Manor House, 21 Soho Square, London W1D 3QP
Website: www.rutheatres.com
e-mail: mike.townsend@rutheatres.com
Fax: 020-7434 1217   Tel: 020-7494 5200

RED ONION DANCE STUDIO
25 Hilton Grove, Hilton Grove Business Centre
Hatherley Mews, London E17 4QP
Website: www.redonion-uk.com
e-mail: info@redonion-uk.com
Fax: 020-8521 6646   Tel: 020-8520 3975

Are you looking for an outside venue for...

- Performances
- Workshops
- Product launches
- AGMs
- Rehearsals
- Auditions
- Conferences
- Private Parties

...if so, give **RADA** a call. RADA's newly rebuilt and refurbished premises in central London has three in-house theatres and several rehearsal studios which are all available for hire at very competitive rates.
The Academy catering team offers a variety of menu choices to enhance any occasion.

For further details and to arrange a site visit contact:
020 7908 4754 or genevieve@rada.ac.uk

RADA 62-64 Gower Street, London WC1E 6ED

RIDGEWAY STUDIOS
Fairley House, Andrews Lane, Cheshunt, Herts EN7 6LB
Fax: 01992 633844   Tel: 01992 633775

ROOFTOP STUDIO THEATRE
Rooftop Studio, Somerfield Arcade
Stone, Staffordshire ST15 8AU
Website: www.rooftopstudio.co.uk
Fax: 01785 818176   Tel: 01785 761233

ROTHERHITHE STUDIOS
119 Rotherhithe Street, London SE16 4NF
Website: www.sandsfilms.co.uk
e-mail: ostockman@sandsfilms.co.uk
Fax: 020-7231 2119   Tel: 020-7231 2209

ROYAL ACADEMY OF DANCE
36 Battersea Square, London SW11 3RA
Website: www.rad.org.uk   e-mail: info@rad.org.uk
Fax: 020-7924 3129   Tel: 020-7326 8000

ROYAL SHAKESPEARE COMPANY
35 Clapham High Street, London SW4 7TW
e-mail: london@rsc.org.uk
Fax: 020-7845 0505   Tel: 020-7845 0500

SAAM HOUSE
5 Gordon Road, London N11 2PA
e-mail: saamhouse@ukf.net   Tel/Fax: 020-8889 6945

SCHER Anna THEATRE
70-72 Barnsbury Road
Islington, London N1 0ES
Website: www.astm.co.uk   e-mail: info@astm.co.uk
Fax: 020-7833 9467   Tel: 020-7278 2101

SCREEN WEST
136-142 Bramley Road, London W10 6SR
e-mail: sarah.alliston@jbcp.co.uk
Fax: 020-7565 3077   Tel: 020-7565 3102

NEAL'S YARD MEETING ROOMS
c o v e n t   g a r d e n

Abuzz-CASTING
Also great space for
REHEARSALS & SHOW CASING. TWO ROOMS FOR HIRE!

ph: 020 7379 0141 mob: 07876 461018
website: www.nealsyardmeetingrooms.com

SEA CADET DRILL HALL
Fairways, Off Broom Road, Teddington   Tel: 01784 241020
SEBBON STREET COMMUNITY CENTRE
Sebbon Street, Islington, London N1 2DZ
e-mail: sebbon@ukf.net   Tel: 020-7354 2015
SHARED EXPERIENCE THEATRE
The Soho Laundry, 9 Dufours Place, London W1F 7SJ
Website: www.sharedexperience.org.uk
e-mail: admin@sharedexperience.org.uk
Fax: 020-7287 8763   Tel: 020 7734 8570
SMALLHOUSE CASTING
3rd Floor, 21 Foley Street, London W1W 6DR
e-mail: smallhouse@actonum.com   Tel/Fax: 020-7636 6975
SOHO GYMS
Earl's Court Gym, 254 Earl's Court Road, London SW5 9AD
Website: www.sohogyms.com
Fax: 020-7244 6893   Tel: 020-7370 1402
Camden Town Gym, 193 Camden High St, London NW1 7JY
Fax: 020-7267 0500   Tel: 020-7482 4524
Clapham Common Gym
95-97 Clapham High Street, London SW4 7TB
Fax: 020-7720 6510   Tel: 020-7720 0321
Covent Garden Gym, 12 Macklin Street, London WC2B 5NF
Fax: 020-7242 0899   Tel: 020-7242 1290
SOHO THEATRE & WRITERS' CENTRE
21 Dean Street, London W1D 3NE
Website: www.sohotheatre.com
e-mail: mail@sohotheatre.com
Fax: 020-7287 5061   Tel: 020-7478 0117
SOUTHALL COMMUNITY CENTRE
(Rehearsal/Location Work)
20 Merrick Road, Southall, London UB2 4AU
Fax: 020-8574 3459   Tel: 020-8574 3458
SPACE @ CLARENCE MEWS
40 Clarence Mews, London E5
e-mail: frith.salem@virgin.net   Tel: 020-8986 5260
SPACE PRODUCTIONS
Media Centre, 67 Dulwich Road, London SE24 0NJ
e-mail: space_productions@yahoo.com
Mobile: 07957 249911   Tel/Fax: 020-7924 9766
S.P.A.C.E. The
(Studio for Performing Arts & Creative Enterprise)
188 St Vincent Street, 2nd Floor, Glasgow G2 5SP
Website: www.west-endmgt.co.uk
e-mail: info@west-end-management.co.uk
Fax: 0141-226 8983   Tel: 0141-222 2942
SPOTLIGHT The
2nd Floor, 7 Leicester Place WC2H 7RJ
Website: www.spotlight.com/rooms
e-mail: info@spotlight.com
Fax: 020-7437 5881   Tel: 020-7437 7631
ST GEORGE'S CHURCH BLOOMSBURY
Vestry Hall, 7 Little Russell Street, London WC1E 6DP
Website: www.stgeorgesbloomsbury.org.uk
e-mail: holmado@aol.com   Tel: 020-7405 3044
ST JAMES'S CHURCH PICCADILLY
197 Piccadilly, London W1J 9LL
Website: www.st-james-piccadilly.org
Fax: 020-7734 7449   Tel: 020-7734 4511
ST JOHN'S CHURCH
Waterloo Road, Southbank, London SE1 8TY
Fax: 020-7928 4470   Tel: 020-7633 9819
ST JOHN'S METHODIST CHURCH
9-11 East Hill, Wandsworth, London SW18 2HT
Tel: 020-8874 4780   Tel: 020-8871 9124
ST MARY ABBOTS HALL
Vicarage Gate, Kensington, London W8 4HN
Website: www.stmaryabbots.freeserve.co.uk
e-mail: terry.pritchard@gmx.net
Fax: 020-7368 6505   Tel: 020-7937 8885

ST MARY NEWINGTON CHURCH HALL
The Parish Office, 57 Kennington Park Road
London SE11 4JQ   Tel: 020-7735 1894
ST MARY'S CHURCH HALL PADDINGTON
c/o Bill Kenwright Ltd, 106 Harrow Road, London W2 1RR
e-mail: info@kenwright.com
Fax: 020-7446 6222   Tel: 020-7446 6200
STABLES GALLERY & ARTS CENTRE The
The Hayloft, Gladstone Pk, Dollis Hill Lane, London NW2 6HT
e-mail: stablesgallery@msn.com   Tel: 020-8452 8655
TAKE FIVE CASTING STUDIO
(Casting Suite)
37 Beak Street, London W1F 9RZ
Website: www.takefivestudio.co.uk
e-mail: info@takefivestudio.co.uk
Fax: 020-7287 3035   Tel: 020-7287 2120
THEATRE ROYAL DRURY LANE
(Michael Townsend)
Catherine Street, London WC2B 5JF
Website: www.rutheatres.com
e-mail: mike.townsend@rutheatres.com   Tel: 020-7494 5200
TRESTLE ARTS BASE
(Home of Trestle Theatre Company)
Russet Drive, St Albans, Herts AL4 0JQ
Website: www.trestle.org.uk   e-mail: admin@trestle.org.uk
Fax: 01727 855558   Tel: 01727 850150
TRICYCLE The
269 Kilburn High Road, London NW6 7JR
Website: www.tricycle.co.uk   e-mail: foh@tricycle.co.uk
Fax: 020-7328 0795   Tel: 020-7372 6611
TWICKENHAM SEA CADETS
Fairways, Off Broom Road
Middlesex TW11 9PL   Tel: 01784 241020
UCL BLOOMSBURY The
15 Gordon Street, London WC1H 0AH
Website: www.thebloomsbury.com
e-mail: blooms.theatre@ucl.ac.uk   Tel: 020-7679 2777
UNION CHAPEL PROJECT
Compton Avenue, London N1 2XD
Website: www.unionchapel.org.uk
e-mail: spacehire@unionchapel.org.uk
Fax: 020-7354 8343   Tel: 020-7226 3750
URDANG ACADEMY The
20-22 Shelton Street
Covent Garden, London WC2H 9JJ
Website: www.theurdangacademy.com
e-mail: info@theurdangacademy.com
Fax: 020-7836 7010   Tel: 020-7836 5709
WATERMANS
40 High Street, Brentford TW8 0DS
Website: www.watermans.org.uk
e-mail: info@watermans.org.uk
Fax: 020-8232 1030   Tel: 020-8232 1020

WILDITCH COMMUNITY CENTRE
48 Culvert Road
Battersea, London SW11 5BB
Website: www.wandsworth.gov.uk/playservices/community/htm
e-mail: wilditch@wandsworth.gov.uk   Tel/Fax: 020-8871 8172
Y TOURING
10 Lennox Road
Finsbury Park, London N4 3JQ
e-mail: d.jackson@ytouring.org.uk
Fax: 020-7272 8413   Tel: 020-7272 5755
YOUNG Sylvia THEATRE SCHOOL
Rossmore Road, Marylebone, London NW1 6NJ
e-mail: sylvia@sylviayoungtheatreschool.co.uk
Fax: 020-7723 1040   Tel: 020-7723 0037

ACT UP
Unit 88, 99-109 Lavender Hill
London SW11 5QL
Website: www.act-up.co.uk
e-mail: info@act-up.co.uk
Fax: 020-7924 6606   Tel: 020-7924 7701

ACTIVATION ROLE PLAY
83-85 Bridge Court Road
Hampton Court, Surrey KT8 9HH
Website: www.activation.co.uk
e-mail: info@activation.co.uk
Fax: 020-8783 9345   Tel: 020-8783 9494

CRAGRATS Ltd
Cragrats Mill, Dunford Road
Holmfirth, Huddersfield HD9 2AR
Website: www.cragrats.com
e-mail: clairerowlands@cragrats.com
Fax: 01484 686212   Tel: 01484 686451

DRAMA FOR TRAINING
Impact Universal, Hopebank House
Woodhead Road, Honley, Huddesfield HD6 6PF
Website: www.impactonlearning.com
e-mail: lisa.riordan@impactonlearning.com
Fax: 01484 660088   Tel: 01484 660077

INTERACT
Bowden House, 14 Bowden Street, London SE11 4DS
Website: www.interact.eu.com
e-mail: info@interact.eu.com
Fax: 020-7793 7755   Tel: 020-7793 7744

NV MANAGEMENT Ltd
Central Office
4 Carters Leaze, Great Wolford
Warwickshire CV36 5NS
Website: www.nvmanagement.co.uk
e-mail: enquiries@nvmanagement.co.uk
Fax: 01608 674203   Tel: 0800 0830281

OFF THE CUFF THEATRE COMPANY
2nd Floor, 91A Rivington Street
London EC2A 3AY
e-mail: otctheatre@aol.com   Tel: 020-7739 2857

ROLEPLAY UK
2 St Mary's Hill, Stamford PE9 2DW
Website: www.roleplayuk.com
Fax: 01780 764436   Tel: 01780 761960

STEPS DRAMA LEARNING DEVELOPMENT
Unit 13.2.2, The Leathermarket
Weston Street, London SE1 3ER
Website: www.stepsdrama.com
e-mail: mail@stepsdrama.com
Fax: 020-7403 0909   Tel: 020-7403 9000

TURNING POINT THEATRE COMPANY
(Role Play, Filmed Training Dramas)
West Bank, Healthy Living Centre
off Farmhouse Rise, Exminster, Devon EX2 7TF
Website: www.eclipse.co.uk/turningpointtheatreco
e-mail: turningpoint@eclipse.co.uk
Fax: 01392 446279   Tel: 01392 446818

BBC TELEVISION
UNDERGROUND – CENTRAL LINE to WHITE CITY. Turn left from tube, cross zebra crossing. Studios outside station.

BBC South (Elstree) – BOREHAMWOOD
Trains from KINGS CROSS - Thames Link. Take stopping train to Elstree then walk (7/8 mins down Shenley High St.) UNDERGROUND – NORTHERN LINE to EDGWARE or HIGH BARNET.
107 & 292 BUSES FROM EDGWARE VIA HIGH BARNET TO BOREHAMWOOD.

BRAY STUDIOS (BRAYSWICK)
BR Train from PADDINGTON to MAIDENHEAD. Then take taxi to studios
BR WATERLOO - WINDSOR RIVERSIDE. Take taxi. Coach from VICTORIA to WINDSOR. Take taxi.

HILLSIDE STUDIOS
Train from EUSTON (Network SE) – WATFORD JUNCTION, then taxi. UNDERGROUND – METROPOLITAN LINE to WATFORD, then taxi. Fast Trains from the Midlands & the North also stop at Watford Junction.
If catching slow train get off at Bushey/Oxhey then catch taxi from rank outside, or JUBILEE LINE to STANMORE then a taxi. Metropolitan Line, change at Baker Street or Wembley.

THE LONDON STUDIOS
(LONDON TELEVISION CENTRE)
UNDERGROUND (Bakerloo, Jubilee and Northern Lines) to WATERLOO, take South Bank exit, follow signs to National Theatre then two buildings along.

PINEWOOD
UNDERGROUND – METROPOLITAN or PICCADILLY LINE to UXBRIDGE. Taxi rank outside station takes about 10 minutes. BRITISH RAIL WESTERN REGION – PADDINGTON to SLOUGH. Taxis from SLOUGH or BUS TO IVER HEATH.

RIVERSIDE STUDIOS
UNDERGROUND – HAMMERSMITH and CITY, DISTRICT or PICCADILLY LINE to HAMMERSMITH – then short walk to studios (behind the London Apollo Hammersmith). Numerous BUS ROUTES from the WEST END. 5 minutes from Hammersmith Broadway.

ROTHERHITHE STUDIOS
UNDERGROUND – DISTRICT LINE to WHITECHAPEL – then change to EAST LONDON LINE to ROTHERHITHE. JUBILEE LINE to CANADA WATER then EAST LONDON LINE to ROTHERHITHE.
(5 mins walk) BUS – 188 from EUSTON STATION via WATERLOO or 47 from LONDON BRIDGE or 381 from WATERLOO (best one to catch stops outside Studios).

SHEPPERTON STUDIOS
BRITISH RAIL – SOUTHERN REGION WATERLOO to SHEPPERTON then BUS Route 218 to studios

TEDDINGTON STUDIOS
(THAMES TELEVISION)
BRITISH RAIL – WATERLOO to TEDDINGTON. Cross over footbridge at station. Come out of Station Road entrance. Left past Garden Centre. Nat West at right hand side TURN RIGHT walk 10 mins, then to set of lights, go over into Ferry Road, follow road then come to Studios (next to Anglers Pub on river).
UNDERGROUND – DISTRICT LINE to RICHMOND – then take taxi or Bus R68 to TEDDINGTON to top of Ferry Road. Ask for Landmark Centre. Then go back to traffic lights, go across, past the Tide End Public House to Anglers Pub etc.

TWICKENHAM
BRITISH RAIL – SOUTHERN REGION – WATERLOO to ST MARGARET'S. UNDERGROUND – DISTRICT LINE to RICHMOND then SOUTHERN REGION or BUS 37 to ST MARGARET'S.

S

Set Construction, Lighting, Sound & Scenery

3D SET COMPANY
(Sets, Scenery Design & Construction)
106 Temperance Street, Manchester M12 6HR
Fax: 0161-273 6786   Tel: 0161-273 8831

ALBEMARLE OF LONDON
(Suppliers of Scenery & Costumes Construction/Hire)
74 Mortimer Street, London W1N 7DF
Website: www.freespace.virgin.net/albemarle.productions
e-mail: albemarle.productions@virgin.net
Fax: 020-7323 3074   Tel: 020-7631 0135

ALL SCENE ALL PROPS
(Scenery, Props, Painting Contractors)
443-445 Holloway Road, London N7 6LW
e-mail: info@allscene.net   Tel/Fax: 020-7561 9231

BLACKOUT Ltd
(Unitrack Track Systems, Automation, Drape & Rigging)
280 Weston Road, London SW19 2QA
Website: www.blackout-ltd.com
e-mail: info@blackout-ltd.com
Fax: 020-8687 8500   Tel: 020-8687 8400

BRISTOL (UK) Ltd
(Scenic Paint & StageFloor Duo Suppliers)
Unit 3, Southerland Court, Tolpits Lane, Watford WD18 9SP
Website: www.bristolpaint.com
e-mail: tech.sales@bristolpaint.com
Fax: 01923 779666   Tel: 01923 779333

CCT LIGHTING Ltd
(Lighting, Dimmers, Sound & Stage Machinery)
Hindle House, Traffic Street, Nottingham NG2 1NE
Website: www.cctlighting.com
e-mail: office@cctlighting.co.uk
Fax: 0115-986 2546   Tel: 0115-986 2722

DESIGN 1 INSIGHT
(Sound & Lighting Designs, Theatre Conferences
& Live Events)
6 Richmond Close, Shaw, Oldham OL2 8TA
Website: www.1insight.co.uk
e-mail: phil@1insight.co.uk
Tel: 07984 436617   Tel: 07984 717898

DISCO ENTERTAINMENTS
(Disc Jockeys/Mobile Discos)
12 Mead Close, Grays, Essex RM16 2TR
e-mail: disco-entertainments@talk21.com   Tel: 01375 373886

DOBSON SOUND PRODUCTION Ltd
(Sound Hire, Design & Installation)
66 Windsor Avenue, Merton, London SW19 2RR
e-mail: enquiries@dobsonsound.co.uk
Fax: 020-8543 3636   Tel: 020-8545 0202

DOVETAIL SPECIALIST SCENERY
(Scenery, Prop & Furniture Builders)
42-50 York Way, London N1 9AB
e-mail: daria@ntlworld.com   Tel/Fax: 020-7278 7379

FISHER Charles STAGING Ltd
Unit 4 Redhouse Farm, Bridgehewick
Ripon, North Yorkshire HG4 5AY
Website: www.charlesfisher.co.uk
e-mail: info@charlesfisher.co.uk   Tel: 01765 601604

FUTURIST PROJECTS Ltd
136 Thorns Lane, Wakefield, West Yorkshire WF2 7RE
Fax: 01924 298700   Tel: 01924 298900

HARLEQUIN (British Harlequin Plc)
Festival House, Chapman Way
Tunbridge Wells, Kent TN2 3EF
Website: www.harlequinfloors.com
e-mail: sales@harlequinfloors.co.uk
Fax: 01892 514222   Tel: 01892 514888

HENSHALL John
(Director of Lighting & Photography)
68 High Street, Stanford in the Vale, Oxfordshire SN7 8NL
e-mail: john@epi-centre.com   Tel: 01367 710191

HERON & DRIVER
(Scenic Furniture & Structural Prop Makers)
Unit 7, Dockley Road Industrial Estate
Rotherhithe, London SE16 3SF
Website: www.herondriver.co.uk
e-mail: mail@herondriver.co.uk
Fax: 020-7394 8680   Tel: 020-7394 8688

KNIGHT Robert/TOP OF THE BILL
1-2 Wyvern Way, Henwood, Ashford, Kent TN24 8DW
Fax: 01233 634999   Tel: 01233 634777

LEE LIGHTING Ltd
Wycombe Road, Wembley, Middlesex HA0 1QD
e-mail: info@lee.co.uk
Fax: 020-8902 5500   Tel: 020-8900 2900

LIGHT WORKS Ltd
2A Greenwood Road, London E8 1AB
Fax: 020-7254 0306   Tel: 020-7249 3627

MALTBURY Ltd
(Portable Staging Sales & Consultancy)
11 Hollingbury Terrace, Brighton BN1 7JE
Website: www.maltbury.com
e-mail: info@maltbury.com
Fax: 01273 504748   Tel/Fax: 0845 1308881

MARPLES Ken CONSTRUCTION
(Set Construction)
Honeybee Cottage, Millers Lane
Hornton, Banbury, Oxfordshire OX15 6BS
e-mail: ken@marplesk.freeserve.co.uk
Mobile: 07831 281574   Tel/Fax: 01295 670302

MASSEY Bob ASSOCIATES
(Electrical & Mechanical Stage Consultants)
9 Worrall Avenue, Arnold, Nottinghamshire NG5 7GN
Website: www.bobmasseyassociates.co.uk
e-mail: bm.associates@virgin.net   Tel/Fax: 0115-967 3969

MODELBOX
(Computer Aided Design & Design Services)
2 Saddlers Way, Okehampton, Devon EX20 1TL
Website: www.modelbox.co.uk
e-mail: info@modelbox.co.uk   Tel/Fax: 01837 54026

NEED Paul J
(Lighting Designer)
Unit 14, Forest Hill Business Centre
Clyde Vale, London SE23 3JF
Website: www.10outof10.co.uk
e-mail: paul@10outof10.co.uk
Fax: 020-8699 8968   Tel: 020-8291 6885

NORTHERN LIGHT
(Lighting, Sound, Communications & Stage Equipment)
Assembly Street, Leith, Edinburgh EH6 7RG
Website: www.northernlight.co.uk
e-mail: enquiries@northernlight.co.uk
Fax: 0131-553 3296   Tel: 0131-553 2383

ORBITAL
(Sound Hire & Design)
57 Acre Lane, Brixton, London SW2 5TN
e-mail: hire@orbitalsound.co.uk
Fax: 020-7501 6869   Tel: 020-7501 6868

P.L. PARSONS SCENERY MAKERS
King's Cross Freight Depot
York Way, London N1 0UZ
Fax: 020-7278 3403   Tel: 020-7833 2031

RED SHIFT LIGHTING
(Lighting Design & Hire Services)
South-east London
Website: www.redshiftlighting.co.uk
e-mail: ben@redshiftlighting.co.uk   Mobile: 07816 879561

RETROGRAPH NOSTALGIA ARCHIVE
(Posters/Prints/Ephemera for Interiors/Exteriors 1870-1970)
10 Hanover Cresent, Brighton BN2 9SB
Website: www.retrograph.com
e-mail: retropix1@aol.com   Tel: 01273 687554

RWS ELECTRICAL & AUDIO CONTRACTORS Ltd
(Lighting & Sound, All Aspects of Electrical Services, Design
& Consultancy)
1 Spinners Close
Biddenden, Kent TN27 8AY
Website: www.rwselectrical.com   Tel: 01580 291764

S2 EVENTS
(Production - Lighting, Set Construction & Scenery)
3-5 Valentine Place, London SE1 8QH
Fax: 020-7928 6082   Tel: 020-7928 5474

SCENERY JESSEL
(Scenery Builders/Stage Supplies)
Unit B
New Baltic Wharf, Oxestalls Road
Deptford, London SE8 5RJ
e-mail: sceneryjessel@ntlworld.com
Fax: 020-8694 2430   Tel: 020-8469 2777

SCOTT FLEARY Ltd
(Creative Construction Company)
Unit 2, Southside Industrial Estate
Havelock Terrace
London SW8 4AS
e-mail: matt@scottflearyltd.com
Fax: 020-7622 0322   Tel: 020-7978 1787

SCOTT MYERS
(Sound Design & Original Music for Theatre)
36 Madras Road, Cambridge CB1 3PX
Website: www.sound.design.freeuk.com
e-mail: scott.myers@freeuk.com
Mobile: 07780 856215   Tel: 01223 415633

STAGE SYSTEMS
(Designers & Suppliers of Modular Staging
Tiering & Auditorium Seating)
Stage House, Prince William Road
Loughborough LE11 5GU
Website: www.stagesystems.co.uk
e-mail: info@stagesystems.co.uk
Fax: 01509 233146   Tel: 01509 611021

STAGECRAFT Ltd
(Hire & Sales of Lighting, Sound, Audio Visual
& Staging for Conference & Live Events)
Ashfield Trading Estate
Salisbury, Wiltshire SP2 7HL
Website: www.stagecraft.co.uk
e-mail: hire@stagecraft.co.uk
Fax: 01722 414076   Tel: 01722 326055

STORM LIGHTING Ltd
Unit 6 Wintonlea Industrial Estate
Monument Way West
Woking, Surrey GU21 5EN
e-mail: info@stormlighting.co.uk
Fax: 01483 757710   Tel: 01483 757211

STRAND LIGHTING Ltd
(Lighting Equipment for Stage, Studio, Film & TV)
Unit 3, Hammersmith Studios
Yeldham Road, London W6 8JF
e-mail: sales@stranduk.com
Fax: 020-8735 9799   Tel: 01592 652333

SUFFOLK SCENERY
28 The Street, Brettenham
Ipswich, Suffolk IP7 7QP
Website: www.suffolkscenery.co.uk
e-mail: piehatch@aol.com
Fax: 01449 737620   Tel: 01449 736679

THEME PARTY COMPANY The
(Set Design Backdrops & Props)
21-37 Third Avenue, London E13 8AW
Fax: 020-8471 2111   Tel: 020-8471 3111

TMS INTERNATIONAL Ltd
(Scenic Construction)
Western Wharf, Livesey Place
Peckham Park Road, London SE15 6SL
e-mail: admin@tmsi.co.uk
Fax: 020-7277 5147   Tel: 020-7277 5156

TOBEM SERVICES
(Theatrical Lighting)
Glen Orrin, Felcourt
East Grinstead, West Sussex RH19 2LE
e-mail: valerieandterry@btclick.com   Tel: 01342 870438

TOP SHOW
(Props, Scenery, Conference Specialists)
North Lane, Huntington
York YO32 9SU   Tel: 01904 750022

VAMPEVENTS
(Theme Party Decor & Cabaret)
Ealing House
33 Hanger Lane, London W5 3HJ
e-mail: info@vampevents.com   Tel: 020-8997 3355

WEST John ASSOCIATES
(Designers & Scenic Artists - Film, TV & Display)
103 Abbotswood Close
Winyates Green
Redditch, Worcestershire B98 0QF
e-mail: johnwest@blueyonder.co.uk
Mobile: 07753 637451   Tel/Fax: 01527 516771

WHITE LIGHT (Electrics) Ltd
(Stage & TV Lighting)
20 Merton Industrial Park
Jubilee Way, London SW19 3WL
Website: www.whitelight.ltd.uk
e-mail: info@whitelight.ltd.uk
Fax: 020-8254 4601   Tel: 020-8254 4600

WHITEHORN Simon
(Sound Design)
57 Acre Lane, London SW2 5TN
e-mail: simon.whitehorn@orbitalsound.co.uk
Fax: 020-7501 6869   Tel: 020-7501 6868

WOOD Rod
(Scenic Artist, Backdrops, Scenery, Props,
Design & Fine Art Copies)
41 Montserrat Road, London SW15 2LD
Mobile: 07887 697646   Tel: 020-8788 1941

BBC Television
Wood Lane, London W12 7RJ
Tel: 020-8743 8000

• TALENT RIGHTS GROUP

BBC Finance, Property & Business Affairs
172 - 178 Victoria Road, W3 6UL

Head of Talent Rights Group   Simon Hayward-Tapp

LITERARY COPYRIGHT

Rights Manager	Neil Hunt
Rights Executives	Sharon Cowley
	Sue Dickson
	James Dundas
	Gail Finn
	Julie Gallagher
	Hazel King
	David Knight
	Kate Loveys
	Catriona Macloughlin
	Sally Millwood
	Hilary Sagar
	Emma Smart
	Catriona Taylor
	Carolyn Tutt
	Zoë Walker

FACTUAL, ARTS & CLASSICAL MUSIC

Rights Manager	Simon Brown
Rights Executives	Lorraine Clark
	Penelope Davies
	Hilary Dodds
	Caroline Edwards
	Tristan Evans
	Selena Harvey
	John Hunter
	Alison Johnston
	Ken McHale
	Shirley Noel
	Shelagh Morrison
	Costas Tanti
	Pamela Wise

MUSICAL COPYRIGHT

Senior Rights Manager, Music	Nicky Bignell
Rights Executives	Peter Bradbury
	Sally Dunsford
	Liz Evans
	Catherine Grimes
	Wendy Neilson
	Victoria Payne
	Debbie Rogerson

DRAMA ENTERTAINMENT & CHILDRENS

Rights Manager Performance	John Holland
	Stephanie Beynon
	Mike Bickerdike
	Sally Dean
	Matthew Hickling
	Amanda Kimpton
	Lesley Longhurst
	David Marum
	Annie Pollard
	Thalia Reynolds
	Lloyd Shepherd

Television
Television (BBC London)
BBC Television & Sound (Regional)
Independent
Theatre Producers
Theatre
Alternative & Community
Children's, Young People's & TIE
English Speaking in Europe
London
Outer London, Fringe & Venues
Provincial/Touring
Puppet Theatre Companies
Repertory (Regional)

Where appropriate, Rep periods are indicated,
e.g. (4 Weekly) and matinee times e.g. Th 2.30 for
Thursday 2.30pm.
SD Stage Door
BO Box Office
TIE Theatre in Education (For further details of
TIE/YPT
See Theatre - Children's, Young People's & TIE

[CONTACTS2005]

ENGLISH REGIONS:

BIRMINGHAM

Contracts Manager   Andrea Coles

BRISTOL

Rights Manager   Annie Thomas

MANCHESTER

Rights Manager   Shirley Chadwick

• DRAMA

Controller, Continuing Drama Series   Mal Young
Head of Films & Single Drama   David Thompson
Head of Drama Serials   Laura Mackie
Head of Development, Drama Serials   Sarah Brown

Executive Producers, Drama Series

Louise Berridge   Will Trotter
Serena Cullen   Mervyn Watson
Kathleen Hutchison

Producers, Drama Series

Beverley Dartnall   Annie Tricklebank
Peter Rose   Emma Turner

Executive Producers, Drama Serials

Ruth Caleb   Sally Haynes
Simon Curtis   Jessica Pope
Phillippa Giles   Hilary Salmon
Kate Harwood

Producers, Drama Serials

Kate Bartlett   Paul Rutman
Manda Levin   Diederick Santer
Kate Lewis   David Snodin
Liza Marshall   Pier Wilkie

• COMMISSIONING

Controller Factual Commissioning   Glenwyn Benson
Controller Entertainment Commissioning   Jane Lush
Controller Drama Commissioning   Jane Tranter
Genre Executive
   Drama Commissioning   Sarah Brandeist
Head of Drama Commissioning   Gareth Neame
Head of Development,
   Drama Commissioning   Sally Woodward Gentle
Arts Commissioner   Franny Moyle
Current Affairs Commissioner   Peter Horrocks
Documentaries & Contemporary
   Factual Commissioner   Nicola Moody
Specialist Factual Commissioner   Emma Swain

• NEWS AND CURRENT AFFAIRS

BBC News (Television & Radio)
Television Centre
Wood Lane, London W12 7RJ
Tel: 020-7580 4468 (Main Switchboard)

Director News   Helen Boaden
Head of Newsgathering   Adrian Van Klaveren
Head of Political Programmes   Fran Unsworth
Head of Radio News   Steve Mitchell
Head of TV News   Roger Mosey
Head of Interactive News   Richard Deverell
Head of TV Current Affairs   Peter Horrocks
Head of Radio Current Affairs   Gwyneth Williams
Head of Research   Sue Inglish

Head of News Production Facilities   Peter Coles
Head of Communications   Janie Ironside Wood

• DOCUMENTARIES & CONTEMPORARY
   FACTUAL GROUP

Controller of DCFG   Anne Morrison
Deputy Controller   Donna Taberer
Head of Production   Steve Wallis
Head of Programmes, Birmingham   Tessa Finch
Head of Programmes, Bristol   Tom Archer
Head of Documentaries   Alan Hayling

• ARTS

BBC Television (Arts)
201 Wood Lane
London W12 7TS   **Tel: 020-8752 5490**

Creative Director   Mark Harrison
Editor, Arena   Antony Wall
Editor, Arts Series   Kim Thomas
Editor, Arts Features   Basil Comely
Series Producer, Imagine   Ian MacMillan
Editor, Reports & Events   David Okuefuna
Executive Editor, Topical Arts Unit   George Entwistle

• MUSIC

Head of Television Classical Music
   & Performance   Peter Maniura

• CHILDREN'S PROGRAMMES

Head of CBBC   Elaine Sperber
Head of Entertainment, CBBC   Anne Gilchrist
Head of CBBC News & Factual programmes   Roy Milani
Head of Pre-School, CBBC   Clare Elstow
Head of Acquisitions &
   Co-Productions, CBBC   Michael Carrington
Head of CBBC, Scotland   Claire Mundell

• SPORT

Director of Sport   Peter Salmon
Director, Sports Rights & Finance   Dominic Coles
Controller Radio Five Live   Bob Shennan
Head of Major Events   Dave Gordon
Head of Football & Boxing   Niall Sloane
Head of Programmes & Planning   Pat Younge
Head of General Sports   Barbara Slater
Head of Radio Sport   Gordon Turnbull
Head of New Media, Sports News
   & Development   Andrew Thompson

• SCIENCE

Editor, Horizon   Mathew Barrett
Head of Development, Science   Michael Mosley
Executive Producers   Jessica Cecil
                                               Jill Fullerton-Smith
                                               Anne Laking

• NEW WRITING

BBC Writersroom
1 Mortimer Street
London W1T 3JA   **Tel: 020-7765 2703**
e-mail: new.writing@bbc.co.uk
Website: www.bbc.co.uk/writersroom

Creative Director   Kate Rowland
New Writing Co-ordinator   Jessica Dromgoole

• BBC BRISTOL

Broadcasting House
Whiteladies Road
Bristol BS8 2LR   Tel: 0117-973 2211

NETWORK TELEVISION AND RADIO FEATURES

Creative Directors	Andy Batten-Foster
	Mark Hill
Executive Producers	Dick Colthurst
	Jane Lomas
	Michael Poole
	Julia Simmons

TELEVISION

Producers

Lyn Barlow	Christopher Lewis
Robert Bayley	Kim Littlemore
Mark Bristow	Susan McDermott
Kathryn Broome	Julian Mercer
Michelle Burgess	Kathryn Moore
Roy Chapman	Helen Nabarro
Linda Cleeve	Martin Paithorpe
Hannah Corneck	Ian Pye
Peter Firstbrook	Amanda Reilly
Steve Greenwood	Kelly Richardson
Trevor Hill	Peter Smith
Jeremy Howe	Ben Southwell
Chris Hutchins	Miranda Steed
David Hutt	Jonny Young
Sarah Johnson	Jo Vale
Peter Lawrence	Tom Ware

RADIO

Unit Manager, Radio	Kate Chaney
Editors	Elizabeth Burke
	Fiona Cooper

Producers

Viv Beeby	Jane Greenwood
John Byrne	Jeremy Howe
Frances Byrnes	Kate McCall
Sara Davies	David Olusoga
Tim Dee	Lucy Willmore
Paul Dodgson	

NATURAL HISTORY UNIT

Head of Natural History Unit	Neil Nightingale
Editor The Natural World	Tim Martin

Television Producers

Paul Appleby	Liz Green
Melinda Barker	Martin Hughes-Games
Miles Barton	Mark Jacobs
Karen Bass	Hilary Jeffkins
Vanessa Belowitz	Mark Linfield
Mike Beynon	Neil Lucas
Lucy Bowden	Patrick Morris
Andrew Byatt	Stephen Moss
Paul Chapman	Mike Salisbury
Mary Colwell	Jo Sarsby
Huw Cordey	Tim Scoones
Yvonne Ellis	Mary Summerhill
Mark Flowers	James Walton
Sara Ford	
Managing Editor NHU Radio	Julian Hector
Director of Development	Martin Hughes-Games

• BBC WEST

Whiteladies Road
Bristol BS8 2LR   Tel: 0117-973 2211

Head of Regional & Local Programmes,
including BBC West, Radio Bristol & Somerset Sound
Radio Gloucestershire
& BBC Wiltshire Sound   Andrew Wilson
Series Producer, Current Affairs
Documentaries   James MacAlpine
Editor, Political Unit   Paul Bartrop
Editors, Output   Jane Kinghorn
                    Stephanie Marshall

• BBC SOUTH WEST

Seymour Road
Mannamead
Plymouth PL3 5BD   Tel: 01752 229201

Acting Head of Local & Regional
Programmes   John Lilley
Editor TV Current Affairs   Simon Willis
Acting News Editor   David Farwig

• BBC SOUTH

Havelock Road
Southampton SO14 7PU Tel: 023-8022 6201

Head of Regional & Local Programmes	Eve Turner
Managing Editor, BBC Oxford	Steve Taschini
Managing Editor, Radio Solent	Mia Costello
Managing Editor, Radio Berkshire	Marianne Bell

• BBC LONDON

PO Box 94.9
London W1A 6FL Tel: 020-7224 2424

BBC London News:
TV: The Politics Show
Radio: BBC London Radio 94.9FM
Online: BBC London online

Executive Editor	Michael MacFarlane
News/Output Editor	Catherine Herne
Executive Producer, Inside Out	Dippy Chaudhray
Managing Editor BBC Radio London 94.9FM	David Robey
Political Editor	Tim Donovan
Editor, BBC London Online	Claire Timms

• BBC SOUTH EAST

c/o BBC Radio Kent
The Great Hall, Mount Pleasant Road
Tunbridge Wells
Kent TN1 1QQ Tel: 01892 670000

Head of Regional & Local Programmes BBC South East	Leo Devine
Managing Editor BBC Radio Kent	Robert Wallace
Managing Editor BBC Southern Counties	Mike Hapgood
News Gathering Editor BBC South East Today	Tayla Roberson
Editor BBC South East Today	Quentin Smith

• BBC NORTH WEST

New Broadcasting House
Oxford Road
Manchester M60 1SJ Tel: 0161-200 2020
Website: www.bbc.co.uk/manchester

Entertainment & Features

Managing Editor, Entertainment & Features	Helen Bullough

Religion & Ethics

Head of Religion & Ethics	Alan Bookbinder

Network News & Current Affairs

Editor, Network News & Current Affairs	Dave Stanford
Editor, R&M Factual	Ian Bent

Regional & Local Programmes

Acting Head of Regional & Local Programmes North West	Leo Devine
Head of Regional & Local Programmes Yorkshire	Tamsin O'Brien (Leeds)

Head of Regional & Local Programmes Yorkshire & Lincolnshire	Helen Thomas (Hull)
Head of Regional & Local Programmes North East & Cumbria	Wendy Pilmer

• BBC BIRMINGHAM

BBC Birmingham
Pebble Mill Road
Birmingham B5 7QQ
Fax: 0121-432 8634 Tel: 0121-432 8888

From December 2004
BBC Birmingham
The Mailbox
Birmingham B1 1RF
Fax: 0121-567 6875 Tel: 0121-567 6767

English Regions

Controller, English Regions. Head of Centre (Birmingham)	Andy Griffee
Head of New Services, English Regions	John Allen
Head of Finance, English Regions	Julie Bertolini
Manager, Press & PR	Una Carlin
Secretary, English Regions	Louise Hall
Head of Regional & Local Programmes West Midlands	David Holdsworth
Director, Mailbox Project	Paresh Solanki

Factual & Learning
BBC Birmingham

Head of Programmes	Tessa Finch
Managing Editor	Jane Booth

Network Radio

Editor, Factual Radio & Rural Affairs	Andrew Thorman
Editor, Specialist Programmes, Radio 2	David Barber

Drama

Head of Production BBC Birmingham	Trevor West
Editor Radio Drama & The Archers	Vanessa Whitburn

• SCOTLAND

Glasgow
Broadcasting House
Queen Margaret Drive
Glasgow G12 8DG Tel: 0141-339 8844

SCOTTISH DIRECTION GROUP

Controller Scotland	Ken MacQuarrie
Controller, Network Development, Nations & Regions	Colin Cameron
Head of New Media	Julie Adair
Head of Comedy & Entertainment	Mike Bolland
Executive Editor New Media	Julie Adair
Commissioning Editor, TV	Ewan Angus

Head of Radio, Scotland	Maggie Cunningham
Head of TV Drama, Scotland	Barbara Mckissack
Head of Gaelic & Children's	Donalda Mackinnon
Head of News and Current Affairs	Blair Jenkins
Head of Factual, Scotland	Andrea Millar
Head of Sport & Leisure	Neil Fraser
Head of North	Andrew Jones
Head of Finance & Business Affairs	Irene Tweedie
Head of Production	Nancy Braid
Head of Human Resources and Internal Communications	Steve Ansell
Head of Marketing, Communications & Audiences	Mairead Ferguson
Secretary & Head of Public Policy	Ian Small

Edinburgh

The Tun
Holyrood Road
Edinburgh EH8 8JF   Tel: 0131-557 5677

Aberdeen

Broadcasting House
Beechgrove Terrace
Aberdeen AB15 5ZT   Tel: 01224 625233

Dumfries

BBC Dumfries
Elmbank, Lovers Walk
Dumfries DG1 1NZ   Tel: 01387 268008

Dundee

66 Nethergate
Nethergate Centre
Dundee DD1 4ER   Tel: 01382 202481

Inverness

BBC Inverness
Broadcasting House
7 Culduthel Road
Inverness IV2 4AD   Tel: 01463 720720

Orkney

BBC Radio Orkney
Castle Street
Kirkwall
Orkney KW15 1DF   Tel: 01856 873939

Portree

Clydesdale Bank Buildings
Somerled Square
Portree
Isle of Skye IV51 9BT   Tel: 01478 612005

Selkirk

BBC Selkirk
Old Municipal Buildings
High Street
Selkirk TD7 4JX   Tel: 01750 21884

Shetland

BBC Shetland
Pitt Lane
Lerwick
Shetland ZE1 0DW   Tel: 01595 694747

Stornoway

Radio nan Gaidheal
Rosebank
Church Street
Stornoway
Isle of Lewis HS1 2LS   Tel: 01851 705000

• WALES

Broadcasting House
Llandaff
Cardiff CF5 2YQ   Tel: 029-2032 2000

Controller	Menna Richards
Head of Programmes (Welsh)	Keith Jones
Head of Programmes (English)	Clare Hudson
Head of Marketing, Communications & Public Policy	Huw Roberts
Head of News & Current Affairs	Mark O'Callaghan
Head of Personnel	Keith Rawlings
Head of Finance	Gareth Powell
Head of Drama	Julie Gardner
Head of Sport	Nigel Walker
Head of North Wales	Marian Wyn Jones
Head of Factual	Adrian Davies
Head of Education	Eleri Wyn-Lewis
Editor Radio Wales	Julie Barton
Editor Radio Cymru	Aled Glynne Davies

• NORTHERN IRELAND

Belfast

Ormeau Avenue
Belfast BT2 8HQ   Tel: 028-9033 8000

Controller	Anna Carragher
Head of Broadcasting	Peter Johnston
Head of Creative Development	Bruce Batten
Head of Drama	Patrick Spence
Head of Finance	Crawford MacLean
Head of HR	Liz Torrans
Head of Learning & Interactive Services	Kieran Hegarty
Head of Marketing, Communications & Audiences	Kathy Bruce
Head of News & Current Affairs	Andrew Colman
Head of Programme Operations	Stephen Beckett
Head of Programme Production	Mike Edgar

Londonderry

BBC Radio Foyle   Tel: 028-7137 8600
Editor Foyle   Ana Leddy

ITV ANGLIA

Head Office

Anglia House Norwich NR1 3JG
Fax: 01603 631032　　　　　　　Tel: 01603 615151
East of England: Weekday & Weekend

Regional News Centres

Cambridge

26 Newmarket Road, Cambridge CB5 8DT
Fax: 01223 467106　　　　　　　Tel: 01223 467076
Reporters: Matthew Hudson, Phillipa Heap

Chelmsford

64-68 New London Road
Chelmsford CM1 0YU
Fax: 01245 267228　　　　　　　Tel: 01245 357676
Reporters: Timothy Evans, Diane Stradling

Luton

16 Park Street, Luton LU1 3EP
Fax: 01582 401214　　　　　　　Tel: 01582 729666
Reporters: Charlotte Fisher, Mike Cartwright

Northampton

77B Abington Street, Northampton NN1 2BH
Fax: 01604 629856　　　　　　　Tel: 01604 624343
Reporter: Karl Heidel

Peterborough

6 Bretton Green Village
Rightwell, Bretton, Peterborough PE3 8DY
Fax: 01733 269424　　　　　　　Tel: 01733 269440
Reporter: Piers Hopkirk

Ipswich

Hubbard House
Civic Drive, Ipswich IP1 2QA
Fax: 01473 233279　　　　　　　Tel: 01473 226157
Reporters: Rebecca Atherstone, Simon Newton,
Diane Stradling

ITV BORDER

Head Office & Studios

The Television Centre
Carlisle CA1 3NT　　　　　　　Tel: 01228 525101
Cumbria, South West Scotland,
Scottish Border Region
North Northumberland and the Isle of Man;
Weekday and Weekend

Chairman　　　　　　　　　　　Charles Allen
Managing Director　　　　　　　Paddy Merrall
Head Controller of Programmes　Jane Bolesworth

CHANNEL TELEVISION Ltd

Registered Office

The Television Centre
La Pouquelaye, St Helier, Jersey JE1 3ZD
Channel Islands
Fax: 01534 816817　　　　　　　Tel: 01534 816816
Channel Islands: Weekday and Weekend

Managing Director　　　　　　　　　　　Michael Lucas
Director of Programmes　　　　　　　　Karen Rankine
Head of Sales　　　　　　　　　　　　Don Miller
Director of Transmission & Resources　Kevin Banner
Director of Finance　　　　　　　　　　Amanda Trotman
News Editor　　　　　　　　　　　　　Allan Watts

CHANNEL FOUR TELEVISION CORPORATION

London Office

124 Horseferry Road
London SW1P 2TX
Fax: 020-7306 8116　　　　　　　Tel: 020-7396 4444

Members of the Board

Chairman　　　　　　　　　　　　　Luke Johnson
Deputy Chairman　　　　　　　　　Barry Cox
Chief Executive　　　　　　　　　　Andy Duncan
Deputy Chief Executive　　　　　　David Scott
Director of Programmes　　　　　　Tim Gardam
Sales Director　　　　　　　　　　Andy Barnes
Commercial Director　　　　　　　Rob Woodward

Non-Executive Directors

Karen Brady　　　　　　　　　　　Andy Mollett
Barry Cox　　　　　　　　　　　　Joe Sinyor

Heads of Department

Head of Airtime Management　　　　　　　　　Merlin Inkley
Head of Commercial & Marketing Strategy　Hugh Johnson
Head of Information Systems　　　　　　　　Ian Dobb
Director of Human Resources　　　　　　　Peter Meier
Head of Presentation　　　　　　　　　　　Steve White
Head of Business Affairs　　　　　　　　　Andrew Brann
Head of Legal & Compliance　　　　　　　　Jan Tomalin
Group Controller of Finance　　　　　　　　Tony Moore
Managing Director of 4Learning　　　　　Heather Rabbatts
Managing Editor Commissioning　　　　　Janey Walker
Director of Nations and Regions　　　　　Stuart Cosgrove
Controller of Programme Acquisitions　June Dromgoole
Acting Head of News and Current Affairs　Dorothy Byrne
Head of Entertainment　　　　　　　　　Andrew Newman

CHANNEL FOUR TELEVISION CORPORATION *Cont'd*

Head of Drama	John Yorke
Director of Marketing	Polly Cochrane
Head of Corporate Relations	John Newbigin
Controller of Broadcasting	Rosemary Newell
Head of Press and Publicity	Matt Baker
Chief Executive - FilmFour Ltd	Paul Webster
Head of Corporate Relations	John Newbigin
Controller Broadcasting	Rosemary Newell
Deputy Commercial Director & Managing Director of 4 Services	Anmar Kawash
Head of Features	Sue Murphy
Head of Marketing	Bill Griffin
Head of Market Planning	Claire Grimmond
Managing Director 4 Channels	Dan Brooke
Head of Sponsorship	David Charlesworth
Head of Factual Entertainment	Julian Belamy
Chief Engineer	Jim Hart
Head of Strategy	Jonathan Thompson
Head of Facilities Management	Julie Bunn
Head of Scheduling	Julie Oldroyd
Head of Client & Strategic Sales	Mike Parker
Managing Director of 4 Rights	Paul Sowerbutts
Finance Director	Sue Ford
Head of Film	Tessa Ross
Head of Documentaries	Peter Dale

Commissioning Editors

Entertainment	Caroline Leddy
Drama	Lucy Richer

five

CHANNEL 5 BROADCASTING

22 Long Acre, London WC2E 9LY

Fax: 020-7550 5554   Tel: 020-7550 5555

Website: www.five.tv

Chief Executive	Jane Lighting
Director of Programmes	Dan Chambers
Director of Strategy & Marketing	tba
Deputy Chief Executive/Director of Sales	Nick Milligan
Director of Finance	Grant Murray
Director of Legal & Business Affairs	Colin Campbell
Director of Broadcasting	Susanna Dinnage
Managing Editor & Director of Acquisitions	Jeff Ford
Director of Sales	Mark White
Senior Programme Controller	
News & Current Affairs	Chris Shaw

Controller of Entertainment & Features	Ben Frow
Controller of Factual	Dan Chambers
Controller of Factual Entertainment	Steve Gowens
Controller, Youth & Music	Sham Sandhu
Controller of Drama	Corinne Hollingworth
Controller of Sport	Robert Charles
Controller, Children's	Nick Wilson
Controller, Daytime Arts & Religion	Kim Peat

GMTV

London Television Centre
Upper Ground, London SE1 9TT

Fax: 020-7827 7001   Tel: 020-7827 7000

Chairman	Donald Emslie
Managing Director	Paul Corley
Director of Programmes	Peter McHugh
Finance Director	Rhian Walker
Director of Sales	Clive Crouch
Head of Press	Nikki Johnceline
Managing Editor	John Scammell
Editor	Martin Frizell
Chief Engineer	Geoff Wright

GRAMPIAN TELEVISION LTD

Television Centre
Craigshaw Business Park
West Tullos
Aberdeen AB12 3QH

Fax: 01224 848800   Tel: 01224 848848

Website: www.grampiantv.co.uk

Managing Director	Derrick Thomson
Head of News & Current Affairs	Henry Eagles
Production Resources Manager	Iain Macdonald

ITN

INDEPENDENT TELEVISION NEWS

200 Gray's Inn Rd, London WC1X 8XZ   Tel: 020-7833 3000

Chief Executive	Mark Wood
Editor-in-Chief, ITV News	David Mannian
Editor, ITV Networks News	Deborah Tumess
Editor, Channel 4 News	Jim Gray
Editor, 5 News	Gary Rogers
Director of Corporate Affairs	Sophie Cohen

ITV plc

The London Television Centre
Upper Ground
London SE1 9LT

Executive Board:

Chief Executive	Charles Allen
Finance Director	Henry Staunton
Chief Executive - Granada	Simon Shaps
Chief Executive - ITV Broadcasting	Mick Desmond
Chief Executive - ITV News Group	Clive Jones
Chief Operating Officer - Granada	John Creswell
Managing Director - ITV Sales	Graham Duff

Three divisions:
1. ITV Broadcasting
2. Granada
3. ITV News Group

Licence Companies:
- Anglia Television Limited
- Border Television Limited
- Carlton Broadcasting Limited
- Central Independent Television Limited
- Granada Television Limited
- HTV Group Limited
- LWT (Holdings) Limited
- Meridian Broadcasting Limited
- Tyne Tees Television Limited
- Westcountry Television Limited
- Yorkshire Television Limited

MERIDIAN BROADCASTING Ltd

Television Centre, Southampton, Hants SO14 0PZ
Fax: 023-8033 5050   Tel: 023-8022 2555
Website: www.meridiantv.com

MERIDIAN BOARD

Chairman	Charles Allen
Chief Executive, ITV Broadcasting	Mick Desmond
Financial Director, ITV News	Mike Fegan
Director of Regional Sales	David Croft
Managing Director, ITV Meridian	Lindsay Charlton
Controller of Regional Programmes	Mark Southgate

EXECUTIVES

Managing Director	Lindsay Charlton
Controller of Regional Programmes	Mark Southgate
General Manager	Jan Beal
Head of News	Andy Cooper
Head of Personnel	Richard Thurstin
Finance Manager	Dan Spencer
Head of Regional Affairs	Alison Pope

Meridian is part of the Granada Group

ITV - WALES

Television Centre, Culverhouse Cross
Cardiff CF5 6XJ   Tel: 029-2059 0590

Television Centre, Bath Road
Bristol BS4 3HG   Tel: 0117-972 2722

Wales/West of England: All week	
Group Managing Director	Jeremy Payne
Controller, Wales &	
Director of Programmes, ITV 1 Wales	Elis Owen
Director of Programmes ITV 1 West	Jane McCloskey
ITV Wales Head of Drama Development	Peter Edwards
ITV Wales Head of Factual Development	Paul Calverley

S4C

S4C-THE WELSH FOURTH CHANNEL

Parc Tŷ Glas, Llanishen, Cardiff CF14 5DU
Fax: 029-2075 4444   Tel: 029-2074 7444
e-mail: s4c@s4c.co.uk

The Welsh Fourth Channel Authority

Chair	Prof. Elan Closs Stephens CBE
Members:	Dr. Christopher Llewelyn
Eira Davies	Enid Rowlands
Carys Howell	Dafydd Wigley
Roger Jones	

Senior Staff

Chief Executive	Huw Jones
Director of Programming	Iona Jones
Director of Engineering & Technology	Arshad Rasul
Head of Marketing	Eleri Twynog Davies
Director of Finance & Human Resouces	Kathryn Morris
Managing Director S4C Masnachol	Wyn Innes
Head of Press	Hannah Thomas
Head of Human Resources	Kay Walters

scottish tv

SCOTTISH TV (Part of SMG Group)
Glasgow Office

200 Renfield Street, Glasgow G2 3PR
Fax: 0141-300 3030   Tel: 0141-300 3000
Website: www.scottishtv.co.uk

Chief Executive (SMG Television)	Donald Emslie
Managing Director	Bobby Hain
Head of News & Current Affairs	Paul McKinney

London Office

1st Flr, 3 Waterhouse Sq, 138-142 Holborn, London EC1N 2NY
Fax: 020-7882 1111   Tel: 020-7882 1010

SMG TV PRODUCTIONS

Glasgow Office

200 Renfield Street
Glasgow G2 3PR
Fax: 0141-300 3030   Tel: 0141-300 3000

Chief Executive   Donald Emslie (SMG Television)
Managing Director   Elizabeth Partyka
Head of Drama   Eric Coulter
Head of Factual   Helen Alexander

London Office
1 Golden Square
London W1F 9DJ   Tel: 020-7663 2300

TYNE TEES TELEVISION

The Television Centre, City Road
Newcastle upon Tyne NE1 2AL
Fax: 0191-261 2302   Tel: 0191-261 0181

Teesside Studio

Colman's Nook
Belasis Hall Technology Park
Billingham
Cleveland TS23 4EG
Fax: 01642 566560   Tel: 01642 566999

North East and North Yorkshire:
Weekday and Weekend

Chairman   Charles Allen
Managing Director,
  Controller of Programmes   Graeme Thompson
Managing Editor, News   Graham Marples
Head of Network Features   Mark Robinson
Head of Sport   Roger Tames
Head of New Media   Malcolm Wright
Editor, Current Affairs & Features Jane Bolesworth

ULSTER TELEVISION

Ormeau Road
Belfast BT7 1EB
Fax: 028-9024 6695   Tel: 028-9032 8122

Northern Ireland: Weekday and Weekend

Chairman   J B McGuckian BSc (Econ)
Group Chief Executive   J McCann BSc, FCA
Group Financial Director   Jim Downey
Director of Television   A Bremner
Head of Press & Public Relations   Orla McKibbin
Head of News & Current Affairs   R Morrison
Sales Director   P Hutchinson

ITV - YORKSHIRE
The Television Centre, Leeds LS3 1JS
Fax: 0113-244 5107　　　　　　　　Tel: 0113-243 8283

London Office
London Television Centre
Upperground, London SE1 9LT　　　　Tel: 020-7620 1620

Hull Office
23 Brook Street
The Prospect Centre, Hull HU2 8PN　　Tel: 01482 24488

Sheffield Office
Charter Square, Sheffield S1 3EJ　　　Tel: 0114-272 3262

Lincoln Office
88 Bailgate, Lincoln LN1 3AR　　　　Tel: 01522 530738

Grimsby Office
Margaret Street, Immingham
North East Lincs DN40 1LE　　　　　Tel: 01469 510661

York Office
8 Coppergate, York YO1 1NR　　　　Tel: 01904 610066

Executives
Managing Director　　　　　　　　　　David M B Croft
Controller of Regional Programmes (YTV)　　Clare Morrow
Controller, Features　　　　　　　　　　Sam Anthony
Director of Business Affairs　　　　　　Filip Cieslik
Head of News　　　　　　　　　　　　Will Venters
Controller of Drama, YTV　　　　　Carolyn Reynolds
Controller of Comedy Drama
　& Drama Features　　　　　　　　David Reynolds
Controller of Drama, Yorkshire-Tyne Tees
　Productions　　　　　　　　　Keith Richardson
Director of Finance, Yorkshire-Tyne Tees
　Productions　　　　　　　　　　　　Ian Roe
Director of Programmes　　　　　　John Whiston
Head of Regional Features　　　　　Mark Witty

SKY Satellite Television
BRITISH SKY BROADCASTING LIMITED (BSkyB)
6 Centaurs Business Park
Grant Way
Isleworth
Middlesex TW7 5QD
Fax: 020-7705 3030　　　　　　　　Tel: 020-7705 3000

Chief Executive　　　　　　　　　　James Murdoch
Chief Operating Officer　　　　　Richard Freudenstein
Managing Director, Sky Networks　　　　Dawn Airey
Managing Director, Sky Sports　　　　Vic Wakeling
Head of Sky News　　　　　　　　　Nick Pollard
Director of Public Affairs　　　　　Ray Gallagher
Director of Communications　　　　Julian Eccles
Deputy Managing Director,
　Sky Networks　　　　　　　Sophie Turner-Laing

30 BIRD PRODUCTIONS
138A Kingswood Road, Brixton, London SW2 4JL
e-mail: thirtybirdproductions@ntlworld.com
Tel: 020-8678 7034

ACORN ENTERTAINMENTS Ltd
PO Box 64, Cirencester, Glos GL7 5YD
Website: www.acornents.co.uk
e-mail: acornents@btconnect.com
Fax: 01285 642291
Tel: 01285 644622

ACT OUT THEATRE
36 Lord Street, Radcliffe, Manchester M26 3BA
e-mail: nigeladams@talk21.com   Tel/Fax: 0161-724 6625

ACT PRODUCTIONS Ltd
20-22 Stukeley Street, London WC2B 5LR
Website: www.actproductions.co.uk
e-mail: info@act.tt
Fax: 020-7242 3548
Tel: 020-7438 9500

AJTC THEATRE COMPANY
28 Rydes Hill Crescent, Guildford, Surrey GU2 9UH
Website: www.ajtctheatre.co.uk
e-mail: ajtc@ntlworld.com   Tel/Fax: 01483 232795

AKA PRODUCTIONS
First Floor, 115 Shaftesbury Avenue, Cambridge Circus
London WC2H 8AF
Website: www.akauk.com
e-mail: aka@akauk.com
Fax: 020-7836 8787
Tel: 020-7836 4747

AMBASSADOR THEATRE GROUP
Duke of York's Theatre
104 St Martin's Lane, London WC2N 4BG
e-mail: atglondon@theambassadors.com
Fax: 020-7854 7001
Tel: 020-7854 7000

AOD - ACTORS OF DIONYSUS
44-46 Old Steine, Brighton BN1 1NH
Website: www.actorsofdionysus.com
e-mail: info@actorsofdionysus.com
Fax: 01273 220025
Tel: 01273 320396

ARTS MANAGEMENT
Pinewood Studios, Iver Heath
Buckinghamshire SL0 0NH
Fax: 01753 785443
Tel: 01753 785444

ATC
Malvern House, 15-16 Nassau Street, London W1W 7AB
Website: www.atc-online.com
e-mail: atc@atc-online.com
Fax: 020-7580 7724
Tel: 020-7580 7723

ATP Ltd
PO Box 24182, London SW18 2WY
e-mail: atpmedia@btconnect.com   Tel/Fax: 020-7738 9886

ATTIC THEATRE COMPANY (LONDON) Ltd
Wimbledon Theatre, The Broadway, London SW19 1QG
Website: www.attictheatre.com
e-mail: info@attictheatre.com   Tel/Fax: 020-8543 7838

BACCHAI PRODUCTIONS
(Write)
10-12 High Street, Great Wakering, Essex SS3 0EQ
e-mail: mail@bacchai.com

BACKGROUND Ltd
167 Wardour Street, London W1F 8WP
e-mail: insight@background.co.uk
Fax: 020-7479 4710
Tel: 020-7479 4700

BAMBOO GROVE THEATRE COMPANY
Crogo Mains, Corsock
Castle Douglas, Kirkcudbrightshire DG7 3DR
Website: www.bamboogrovetheatre.co.uk
e-mail: cally@bamboogrovetheatre.co.uk   Tel: 07810 514622

BARKING PRODUCTIONS/INSTANT WIT
(Comedy Improvisation/Corporate Entertainment &
Training)
PO Box 597, Bristol BS99 2BB
Website: www.barkingproductions.co.uk
e-mail: info@barkingproductions.co.uk
Fax: 0117-908 5384
Tel: 0117-939 3171

BEE & BUSTLE ENTERPRISES
32 Exeter Road
London NW2 4SB
Website: www.beeandbustle.co.uk
e-mail: info@beeandbustle.co.uk
Fax: 020-8450 1057
Tel: 020-8450 0371

BIG DOG PRODUCTIONS Ltd
(Martin Roddy)
16 Kirkwick Avenue
Harpenden, Herts AL5 2QN
e-mail: bigdog@kirkwick.demon.co.uk
Fax: 01582 467349
Tel: 01582 467344

BIG NOSE PRODUCTIONS Ltd
220-222 High Street
Barnet, Herts EN5 5SZ
Website: www.bignoseproductions.net
e-mail: helga@bignoseproductions.net
Tel/Fax: 020-8441 3060

BIRMINGHAM STAGE COMPANY The
Suite 228 The Linen Hall
162 Regent Street
London W1B 5TG
Website: www.birminghamstage.net
e-mail: info@birminghamstage.net
Fax: 020-7437 3395
Tel: 020-7437 3391

BLUE BOX ENTERTAINMENT Ltd
The Penthouse, 7 Leicester Place, London WC2H 7BY
Website: www.blue-box.biz
e-mail: info@blue-box.biz
Fax: 020-7734 7185   Tel: 020-7434 4214

BORDER CROSSINGS
13 Laburnham Close
Poplar Grove, London N11 3NR
Website: www.bordercrossings.org.uk
e-mail: borcross@aol.com   Tel/Fax: 020-8361 2308

BORDERLINE THEATRE COMPANY
North Harbour Street, Ayr KA8 8AA
e-mail: enquiries@borderlinetheatre.co.uk
                                     Tel: 01292 281010

B & R PRODUCTIONS
32 Priory Road, Hastings
Kent TN34 3JH   Tel: 01424 200728

BREAKWITH PRODUCTIONS
7 London Court
Frogmore, London SW18 1HH
e-mail: breakwith@aol.com
Fax: 020-8871 4999   Tel: 020-8870 4431

BRIDGE LANE THEATRE COMPANY Ltd
The Studio, 49 Ossulton Way
London N2 0JY   Tel: 020-8444 0505

BRITISH STAGE PRODUCTIONS
Victoria Buildings, 1B Sherwood Street
Scarborough
North Yorkshire YO11 1SR
e-mail: britishstage@giomail.co.uk
Fax: 01723 501328   Tel: 01723 507186

BRIT-POL THEATRE Ltd
10 Bristol Gardens, London W9 2JG
Website: www.britpol.net
e-mail: admin@britpol.net   Tel: 020-7266 0323

BROADHOUSE PRODUCTIONS Ltd
38 Stourcliffe Close
Stourcliffe Street, London W1H 5AR
e-mail: admin@broadhouse.co.uk
Fax: 020-7402 2173   Tel: 020-7402 0624

BROOKE Nick Ltd
The Penthouse
7 Leicester Place, London WC2H 7BY
e-mail: info@nickbrooke.com
Fax: 020-7734 7185   Tel: 020-7851 0393

BROOKS Sacha Ltd
3rd Floor, 55 Greek Street, London W1D 3DT
e-mail: info@sacha.com
Fax: 020-7437 0930   Tel: 020-7437 2900

BUSH THEATRE
Shepherd's Bush Green, London W12 8QD
Website: www.bushtheatre.co.uk
e-mail: info@bushtheatre.co.uk
Fax: 020-7602 7614   Tel: 020-7602 3703

CAHOOTS PRODUCTION & PR
32 Champion Grove, London SE5 8BW
Website: www.cahootstheatre.co.uk
e-mail: cahootstheatreco@aol.com   Tel/Fax: 020-7738 4250

CAPRICORN STAGE (& SCREEN) DIRECTIONS
9 Spencer House, Vale of Health
Hampstead, London NW3 1AS   Tel: 020-7794 5843

CARP DIEM THEATRE COMPANY
PO Box 107, Camberley, Surrey GU15 4ZE
e-mail: terry@terryturbo.com   Tel/Fax: 01344 870475

CARPENTER Earl CONCERTS Ltd
PO Box 745, Guildford, Surrey GU3 1XJ
e-mail: earl@earlcarpenterconcerts.com
                                   Tel/Fax: 01483 813294

CASSANDRA THEATRE COMPANY
(Vanessa Mildenberg, Clare Bloomer)
Flat 3, 30 Ephraim Road, London SW16 1LW
e-mail: vm_cassandratc@yahoo.co.uk
                                   Mobile: 07796 264828

CAVALCADE THEATRE COMPANY
(Plays, Musicals & Tribute Shows, Cabaret, Children's Shows)
57 Pelham Road, London SW19 1NW
Fax: 020-8540 2243   Tel: 020-8540 3513

CELEBRATION
(Theatre Company for the Young)
48 Chiswick Staithe, London W4 3TP   Tel: 020-8994 8886

CENTRELINE PRODUCTIONS
Unit 7, 93 Paul Street, London EC2A 4NY
Website: www.centrelinenet.com
e-mail: info@centrelinenet.com
Fax: 020-7251 9255   Tel: 020-7251 9251

CHANNEL THEATRE COMPANY
Central Studios, 36 Park Place, Margate, Kent CT9 1LE
Website: www.channel-theatre.co.uk
e-mail: info@channel-theatre.co.uk
Fax: 01843 280088   Tel: 01843 280077

CHAPMAN Duggie ASSOCIATES
(Pantomime, Concerts, Musicals)
The Old Coach House
202 Common Edge Road, Blackpool FY4 5DG
Website: www.duggiechapman.co.uk
e-mail: duggie@chapmanassociates.fsnet.co.uk
                                   Tel/Fax: 01253 691823

CHAPMAN Guy PRODUCTIONS
33 Southampton Street, London WC2E 7HE
e-mail: admin@g-c-a.co.uk
Fax: 020-7379 8484   Tel: 020-7379 7474

CHEEK BY JOWL
Website: www.cheekbyjowl.com

CHICHESTER FESTIVAL THEATRE
Oaklands Park, Chichester, West Sussex PO19 6AP
Website: www.cft.org.uk
e-mail: admin@cft.org.uk
Fax: 01243 787288   Tel: 01243 784437

CHICKEN SHED THEATRE
Chase Side, Southgate, London N14 4PE
Website: www.chickenshed.org.uk
e-mail: info@chickenshed.org.uk
Minicom: 020-8350 0676   Tel: 020-8351 6161

CHURCHILL THEATRE BROMLEY Ltd
Churchill Theatre, High Street, Bromley, Kent BR1 1HA
Website: www.churchilltheatre.co.uk
Fax: 020-8290 6968   Tel: 020-8464 7131

CLASSIC REACTION THEATRE COMPANY
Clovelly, Cagefoot Lane, Henfield, West Sussex BN5 9HD
e-mail: crtcproductions@aol.com   Tel/Fax: 01273 492612

CLEAR CHANNEL ENTERTAINMENT (CCE)
35/36 Grosvenor Street, London W1K 4QX
Website: www.clearchanneleurope.co.uk
e-mail: enquiries@clearchannel.co.uk
Fax: 08707 490517   Tel: 020-7529 4300

CLOSE FOR COMFORT THEATRE COMPANY
34 Boleyn Walk, Leatherhead, Surrey KT22 7HU
Website: www.hometown.aol.com/close4comf
e-mail: close4comf@aol.com   Tel: 01372 378613

CLUBWEST PRODUCTIONS
Dramazone, Arundel Town Hall
Arundel, West Sussex BN18 9AP
Website: www.clubwest.co.uk
e-mail: admin@clubwest.co.uk   Tel/Fax: 01903 889821

CODRON Michael PLAYS Ltd
Aldwych Theatre Offices, London WC2B 4DF
Fax: 020-7240 8467   Tel: 020-7240 8291

COGO-FAWCETT Robert
58 Hythe Road, Brighton BN1 6JS
e-mail: robertcogo_fawcett@hotmail.com
    Mobile: 07973 938634

COLE KITCHENN Ltd
Nederlander House
7 Great Russell Street, London WC1B 3NH
Fax: 020-7580 2992   Tel: 020-7580 2772

COMPASS THEATRE COMPANY
Carver Street Institute
24 Rockingham Lane, Sheffield S1 4FW
Website: www.compasstheatrecompany.com
e-mail: info@compasstheatrecompany.com
Fax: 0114-278 6931   Tel: 0114-275 5328

COMPLICITE
14 Anglers Lane, London NW5 3DG
e-mail: email@complicite.org
Fax: 020-7485 7701   Tel: 020-7485 7700

CONCORDANCE
(Neil McPherson)
Finborough Theatre
118 Finborough Road, London SW10 9ED
Website: www.concordance.org.uk
e-mail: admin@concordance.org.uk
Fax: 020-7835 1853   Tel: 020-7244 7439

CONTEMPORARY STAGE COMPANY
3 Etchingham Park Road, Finchley, London N3 2DU
Website: www.contemporarystage.co.uk
e-mail: contemp.stage@britishlibrary.net
Fax: 020-8349 2458   Tel: 020-8349 4402

CONWAY Clive CELEBRITY PRODUCTIONS Ltd
32 Grove Street, Oxford OX2 7JT
Website: www.celebrityproductions.info
e-mail: clive.conway@ntlworld.com
Fax: 01865 514409   Tel: 01865 514830

COONEY Ray PLAYS
Everglades, 29 Salmons Road
Chessington, Surrey KT9 2JE
Website: www.raycooneyplays.co.uk
e-mail: alan@raycooneyplays.co.uk
Fax: 020-8397 0070   Tel: 020-8397 0021

CRISP THEATRE
8 Cornwallis Crescent
Clifton, Bristol BS8 4PL
Website: www.crisptheatre.co.uk
e-mail: crisptheatre@btconnect.com   Tel: 0117-973 7106

DAVIES Alma
2857 Paradise Road
Las Vegas NV 89109
e-mail: divaalmadavies@aol.com
Fax: (702) 341-5681   Tel: (702) 254-3775

DEAD EARNEST THEATRE
57 Burton Street, Sheffield S6 2HH
Website: www.deadearnest.co.uk
e-mail: info@deadearnest.co.uk   Tel: 0114-233 4579

DEAN Lee
PO Box 10703, London WC2H 9ED
e-mail: admin@leedean.co.uk
Fax: 020-7836 6968   Tel: 020-7497 5111

DELFONT MACKINTOSH THEATRES Ltd
(Theatre Owners)
Strand Theatre, Aldwych, London WC2B 4LD
e-mail: info@delfont-mackintosh.com
Fax: 020-7240 3831   Tel: 020-7379 4431

DISNEY THEATRICAL PRODUCTIONS (UK)
Lyceum Theatre, 21 Wellington Street, London WC2E 7RQ
Fax: 020-7845 0999   Tel: 020-7845 0900

DOODAH THEATRE
28 St Peter's Way, Ealing, London W5 2QR
e-mail: doodahtc@aol.com   Tel: 020-8991 5903

DRAMATIS PERSONAE Ltd
(Nathan Silver, Nicolas Kent)
19 Regency Street, London SW1P 4BY
e-mail: nathansilver@btconnect.com   Tel: 020-7834 9300

DUAL CONTROL THEATRE COMPANY
The Admiral's Offices
The Historic Dockyard, Chatham, Kent ME4 4TZ
Website: www.ellenkent.com
e-mail: info@ellenkentinternational.co.uk
Fax: 01634 819149   Tel: 01634 819141

EASTERN ANGLES THEATRE COMPANY
(Touring)
Sir John Mills Theatre
Gatacre Road, Ipswich, Suffolk IP1 2LQ
Website: www.easternangles.co.uk
e-mail: admin@easternangles.co.uk
Fax: 01473 384999   Tel: 01473 218202

ELLIOTT Paul Ltd
(Triumph Entertainment Ltd)
Suite 3 Waldorf Chambers, 11 Aldwych, London WC2B 4DG
e-mail: pelliott@paulelliott.ltd.uk
Fax: 020-7379 4860   Tel: 020-7379 4870

ENGLISH CHAMBER THEATRE
93 Camberwell Grove, London SE5 8JH
Website: www.englishchambertheatre.co.uk
email: jane@janemcculloch.com   Tel: 020-7703 0201

ENGLISH NATIONAL OPERA
London Coliseum
St Martin's Lane, London WC2N 4ES
Website: www.eno.org
Fax: 020-7845 9277   Tel: 020-7836 0111

ENGLISH STAGE COMPANY Ltd
Royal Court, Sloane Square, London SW1W 8AS
Website: www.royalcourttheatre.com
e-mail: info@royalcourttheatre.com
Fax: 020-7565 5001   Tel: 020-7565 5050

ENGLISH THEATRE COMPANY Ltd The
(TMA Member)
Nybrogatan 35, 114 39 Stockholm, Sweden
Website: www.englishtheatre.se
e-mail: etc.ltd@telia.com
Fax: 00 46 8660 1159   Tel: 00 46 8662 4133

ENGLISH TOURING THEATRE
25 Short Street, London SE1 8LJ
Website: www.englishtouringtheatre.co.uk
e-mail: admin@englishtouringtheatre.co.uk
Fax: 020-7450 1991   Tel: 020-7450 1990

ENTERTAINMENT BUSINESS Ltd The
199 Piccadilly, London W1J 9HA
Fax: 020-7287 5144   Tel: 020-7734 8555

EUROPEAN THEATRE COMPANY The
39 Oxford Avenue, London SW20 8LS
Website: www.europeantheatre.co.uk
e-mail: admin@europeantheatre.co.uk
Fax: 020-8544 1999   Tel: 020-8544 1994

FACADE
(Musicals)
43A Garthorne Road, London SE23 1EP
e-mail: facade@cobomedia.com   Tel: 020-8291 7079

FACE TO FACE THEATRE PRODUCTIONS Ltd
(Write)
10 St Fillans Road, Stepps, Glasgow G33 6LW
e-mail: robinfacetoface@hotmail.com

FAHODZI Tiata
AH 112 Aberdeen Centre
22-24 Highbury Grove, London N5 2EA
Website: www.tiatafahodzi.com
e-mail: info@tiatafahodzi.com   Tel/Fax: 020-7226 3800

FELL Andrew Ltd
4 Ching Court, 49-51 Monmouth Street, London WC2H 9EY
e-mail: hq@andrewfell.co.uk
Fax: 020-7240 2499   Tel: 020-7240 2420

FIERY ANGEL Ltd
22-24 Torrington Place, London WC1E 7HJ
Website: www.fiery-angel.com
e-mail: admin@fiery-angel.com
Fax: 020-7580 6652   Tel: 020-7907 7040

FORBIDDEN THEATRE COMPANY
Diorama Arts Centre
34 Osnaburgh Street, London NW1 3ND
Website: www.forbidden.org.uk
e-mail: info@forbidden.org.uk   Tel/Fax: 020-7813 1025

FORD Vanessa PRODUCTIONS Ltd
Upper House Farm, Upper House Lane
Shamley Green, Surrey GU5 0SX
Website: www.vfpltd.com
e-mail: vanessa@vfpltd.fsnet.co.uk
Fax: 01483 271509   Tel: 01483 278203

FOX Robert Ltd
6 Beauchamp Place, London SW3 1NG
Website: www.robertfoxltd.com
e-mail: info@robertfoxltd.com
Fax: 020-7225 1638   Tel: 020-7584 6855

FREEDMAN Bill Ltd
Room 311, Bedford Chambers
The Piazza, Covent Garden, London WC2E 8HA
Fax: 020-7836 9903   Tel: 020-7836 9900

FREEFLOW PRODUCTIONS Ltd
The Wilde Theatre, South Hill Park Arts Centre
Ringmead, Bracknell, Berks RG12 7PA
Website: www.freeflowproductions.co.uk
e-mail: info@freeflowproductions.co.uk   Tel: 01344 426464

FRIEDMAN Sonia PRODUCTIONS
New Ambassadors Theatre, West Street, London WC2H 9ND
Website: www.soniafriedman.com
e-mail: mail@soniafriedman.com
Fax: 020-7395 5455   Tel: 020-7395 5454

FUTURA MUSIC (PRODUCTIONS) Ltd
(Write only)
29 Emanuel House, Rochester Row, London SW1P 1BS

GALE PRODUCTIONS
24 Wimbledon Park Road, London SW18 1LT
e-mail: gale.prod@which.net
Fax: 020-8875 1582   Tel: 020-8870 1149

GALLEON THEATRE COMPANY Ltd
(Alice De Sousa)
Greenwich Playhouse, Greenwich BR Station Forecourt
189 Greenwich High Road, London SE10 8JA
Website: www.galleontheatre.co.uk
e-mail: boxoffice@galleontheatre.co.uk
Fax: 020-8310 7276   Tel: 020-8858 9256

GBM PRODUCTIONS Ltd
Bidlake Toft, Roadford Lake
Germansweek, Devon EX21 5BD
Website: www.musicaltheatrecreations.com
e-mail: gbm@bidlaketoft.com
Fax: 01837 871123   Tel: 01837 871522

GLASS David ENSEMBLE
59 Brewer Street, London W1F 9UN
Website: www.davidglassensemble.com
e-mail: matthew.dge@virgin.net   Tel/Fax: 020-7734 6030

GODOT COMPANY
51 The Cut, London SE1 8LF
e-mail: godot@calderpublications.com
Fax: 020-7928 5930   Tel: 020-7633 0599

GOOD COMPANY
at St Michaels, Powis Road, Brighton BN1 3HJ
Fax: 01273 779955   Tel: 01273 771777

GOSS Gerald Ltd
19 Gloucester Street, London SW1V 2DB
Fax: 020-7592 9301   Tel: 020-7592 9202

GOUCHER Mark Ltd
2nd Floor, 20-22 Stukeley Street
London WC2B 5LR
e-mail: info@markgoucher.com
Fax: 020-7438 9577   Tel: 020-7438 9570

GRAEAE THEATRE COMPANY
LVS Resource Centre, 356 Holloway Road, London N7 6PA
Website: www.graeae.org
e-mail: info@graeae.org
Fax: 020-7609 7324   Tel: 020-7700 2455

GRAHAM David ENTERTAINMENT Ltd
72 New Bond Street, London W1S 1RR
Website: www.davidgraham.co.uk
e-mail: info@davidgraham.co.uk
Fax: 0870 3211700   Tel: 0870 3211600

GREAT WESTERN STAGE
East Trevelmond Farm
Trevelmond, Liskeard, Cornwall PL14 4LT
e-mail: admin@greatwesternstage.fsnet.co.uk
Fax: 01579 321858   Tel: 01579 320328

GREEN & LENAGAN Ltd
(Write)
140 Buckingham Palace Road, London SW1W 9SA

HALE Ivan Ltd
5 Denmark Street, London WC2H 8LP
e-mail: ivanhaleltd@hotmail.com
Fax: 020-7240 6949   Tel: 020-7240 9800

HAMPSTEAD THEATRE PRODUCTIONS Ltd
Eton Avenue, Swiss Cottage, London NW3 3EU
Website: www.hampsteadtheatre.com
e-mail: info@hampsteadtheatre.com
Fax: 020-7449 4201   Tel: 020-7449 4200

HANDSTAND PRODUCTIONS
13 Hope Street, Liverpool L1 9BH
Website: www.handstand-uk.com
e-mail: info@handstand-uk.com
Fax: 0151-709 3515　　　　　Tel: 0151-708 7441

HARLEY (CINE LIBRE) PRODUCTIONS
68 New Cavendish Street, London W1G 8TE
e-mail: harleyprods@aol.com
Fax: 020-8202 8863　　　　　Tel: 020-7580 3247

HAYMARKET THEATRE COMPANY Ltd
Wote Street, Basingstoke, Hampshire RG21 7NW
Website: www.haymarket@org.uk
e-mail: info@haymarket.org.uk
Fax: 01256 357130　　　　　Tel: 0870 7701029

HENDERSON Glynis PRODUCTIONS
69 Charlotte Street, London W1T 4PJ
e-mail: info@ghmp.co.uk
Fax: 020-7436 1489　　　　　Tel: 020-7580 9644

HESTER John PRODUCTIONS
(Intimate Mysteries Theatre Company)
105 Stoneleigh Park Road, Epsom, Surrey KT19 0RF
e-mail: hjohnhester@aol.com　　Tel/Fax: 020-8393 5705

HEWITT-JONES Brian Ltd
Curlews House, Crowle DN17 4JS
Fax: 01724 711088　　　　　Tel: 01724 712459

HISS & BOO COMPANY Ltd The
(Ian Liston)
Nyes Hill, Wineham Lane, Bolney, West Sussex RH17 5SD
Website: www.hissboo.co.uk
e-mail: ian@hissboo.co.uk
Fax: 01444 882057　　　　　Tel: 01444 881707

HISTORIA THEATRE COMPANY
8 Cloudesley Square, London N1 0HT
Website: www.historiatheatre.com
e-mail: kateprice@lineone.net
Fax: 020-7278 4733　　　　　Tel: 020-7837 8008

HOLMAN Paul ASSOCIATES Ltd
20 Deane Avenue, South Ruislip, Middlesex HA4 6SR
Website: www.paulholmanassociates.co.uk
e-mail: paulholmanassociates@blueyonder.co.uk
Fax: 020-8582 2557　　　　　Tel: 020-8845 9408

HOLT Thelma Ltd
Waldorf Chambers, 11 Aldwych, London WC2B 4DG
Website: www.thelmaholt.co.uk
e-mail: thelma@dircon.co.uk
Fax: 020-7836 9832　　　　　Tel: 020-7379 0438

HOUSE OF GULLIVER Ltd
(Write)
55 Goldfield Road, Tring, Herts HP23 4BA

HULL TRUCK THEATRE
Spring Street, Hull HU2 8RW
Website: www.hulltruck.co.uk
e-mail: admin@hulltruck.co.uk
Fax: 01482 581182　　　　　Tel: 01482 224800

HUTT RUSSELL PRODUCTIONS Ltd
PO Box 64, Cirencester, Glos GL7 5YD
Website: www.huttrussellorg.com
e-mail: shows@huttrussellorg.com
Fax: 01285 642291　　　　　Tel: 01285 644622

IMAGE MUSICAL THEATRE
23 Sedgeford Road, Shepherd's Bush, London W12 0NA
Website: www.imagemusicaltheatre.co.uk
e-mail: brian.thresh@btconnect.com
Fax: 020-8749 9294　　　　　Tel: 020-8743 9380

Richard Jordan Productions Ltd

- **Producing**

- **General Management**
  UK and International Productions,
  and International Festivals

- **Consultancy**

Richard Jordan Productions Ltd
Mews Studios, 16 Vernon Yard
London W11 2DX

Tel:　　　020 7243 9001
Fax:　　　020 7313 9667
e-mail:　　richard.jordan@virgin.net

IMAGINATION ENTERTAINMENTS
25 Store Street
South Crescent, London WC1E 7BL
Website: www.imagination.com
e-mail: entertainments@imagination.com
Fax: 020-7323 5801　　　　　Tel: 020-7323 3300

INCISOR
30 Brondesbury Park
London NW6 7DN
Website: www.festival-edinburgh.com
e-mail: sarah.mann7@ntlworld.com
Fax: 020-8830 4992　　　　　Tel: 020-8830 0074

INDIGO ENTERTAINMENTS
Tynymynydd, Bryneglwys, Corwen, Denbighshire LL21 9NP
Website: www.indigoentertainments.co.uk
e-mail: info@indigoentertainments.com　Tel: 01978 790211

INSIDE INTELLIGENCE
(Theatre, Contemporary Opera & Music)
13 Athlone Close, London E5 8HD
Website: www.inside-intelligence.org.uk
e-mail: admin@inside-intelligence.org.uk
　　　　　　　　　　　　Tel/Fax: 020-8985 7211

INTERNATIONAL THEATRE & MUSIC Ltd
(Piers Chater Robinson)
Shakespeare House, Theatre Street, London SW11 5ND
Website: www.internationaltheatreandmusic.com
e-mail: inttheatre@aol.com
Fax: 020-7801 6317　　　　　Tel: 020-7801 6316

ISLEWORTH ACTORS COMPANY
38 Eve Road, Isleworth
Middlesex TW7 7HS　　　　Tel/Fax: 020-8891 1073

JACKSON Richard
48 William Mews
London SW1X 9HQ　　　　　Tel/Fax: 020-7235 3759

JAMES Bruce PRODUCTIONS Ltd
68 St Georges Park Ave
Westcliff-on-Sea, Essex SS0 9UD
Website: www.brucejamesproductions.co.uk
e-mail: info@brucejamesproductions.co.uk
　　　　　　　　　　　　Tel/Fax: 01702 335970

JENKINS Andrew Ltd
63 Kidbrooke Park Road, Blackheath, London SE3 0EE
Website: www.andrewjenkinsltd.com
e-mail: info@andrewjenkinsltd.com
Fax: 020-8856 7106　　　　　Tel: 020-8319 3657

JOHNSON David
85B Torriano Avenue, London NW5 2RX
e-mail: david@johnsontemple.co.uk　Tel: 020-7284 3733

JOHNSON Gareth Ltd
Plas Hafren, Eglwyswrw, Crymych, Pembrokeshire SA41 3UL
e-mail: gjltd@mac.com
Fax: 07779 007845   Tel: 07770 225227

JORDAN Andy PRODUCTIONS Ltd
5 Underwood Cottages
The Coombe, Streatley-on-Thames, Berkshire RG8 9RA
e-mail: ANDYJAndyjordan@aol.com
Mobile: 07775 615205   Tel/Fax: 01491 871411

JORDAN Richard PRODUCTIONS Ltd
Mews Studios, 16 Vernon Yard, London W11 2DX
e-mail: richard.jordan@virgin.net
Fax: 020-7313 9667   Tel: 020-7243 9001

KARUSHI PROMOTIONS
Fifth Floor, 97-99 Dean Street, London W1D 3TE
Website: www.karushi.com
e-mail: ed@karushi.com
Fax: 020-7484 5151   Tel: 020-7484 5040

KELLY Robert C Ltd
The Alhambra Suite
82 Mitchell Street, Glasgow G1 3NA
Website: www.robertckelly.co.uk
e-mail: robert@robertckelly.co.uk
Fax: 0141-229 1441   Tel: 0141-229 1444

KENWRIGHT Bill Ltd
BKL House, 106 Harrow Road
Off Howley Place, London W2 1RR
e-mail: info@kenwright.com
Fax: 020-7446 6222   Tel: 020-7446 6200

KING'S HEAD THEATRE PRODUCTION Ltd
115 Upper Street, London N1 1QN
Website: www.kingsheadtheatre.org
Fax: 020-7226 8507   Tel: 020-7226 8561

KIRK David PRODUCTIONS
11A Marwick Terrace, St Leonards-on-Sea
East Sussex TN38 ORE   Tel: 01424 445081

LHP Ltd
58 Hythe Road, Brighton BN1 6JS
e-mail: robertcogo_fawcett@hotmail.com
                                     Mobile: 07973 938634

LIMELIGHT ENTERTAINMENT PRODUCTIONS Ltd
The Gateway, 2A Rathmore Road, London SE7 7QW
e-mail: enquiries@limelightents.co.uk
Fax: 020-8305 2684   Tel: 020-8858 6141

LINNIT PRODUCTIONS Ltd
123A King's Road, London SW3 4PL
Fax: 020-7352 3450   Tel: 020-7352 7722

LIVE THEATRE
7-8 Trinity Chare, Quayside, Newcastle upon Tyne NE1 3DF
Website: www.live.org.uk   Tel: 0191-261 2694

LLOYD-JAMES Adrian
36 Fleece Road, Long Ditton, Surrey KT6 5JN
e-mail: adrianmljames@aol.com
Fax: 08714 332938   Tel: 020-8398 6746

LONDON BUBBLE THEATRE COMPANY Ltd
5 Elephant Lane, London SE16 4JD
Website: www.londonbubble.org.uk
e-mail: admin@londonbubble.org.uk
Fax: 020-7231 2366   Tel: 020-7237 4434

LONDON COMPANY INTERNATIONAL PLAYS Ltd The
(No CV's please)
6th Floor, Empire House, 175 Piccadilly, London W1J 9TB
e-mail: derek@glynnes.co.uk
Fax: 020-7486 2164   Tel: 020-7486 3166

LONDON PRODUCTIONS Ltd
PO Box 10703, London WC2H 9ED
e-mail: admin@leedean.co.uk
Fax: 020-7836 6968   Tel: 020-7497 5111

MACKINTOSH Cameron Ltd
1 Bedford Square, London WC1B 3RB
Fax: 020-7436 2683   Tel: 020-7637 8866

MACNAGHTEN PRODUCTIONS Ltd
Dundarave, Bushmills, Co. Antrim
Northern Ireland BT57 8ST
Fax: 028-2073 2575   Tel: 028-2073 1215

MALCOLM Christopher Ltd
1 Calton Road, Bath BA2 4PP
Website: www.christophermalcolm.co.uk
e-mail: christopher.malcolm@btconnect.com
Fax: 01225 427778   Tel: 01225 445459

MANS Johnny PRODUCTIONS Ltd
PO Box 196, Hoddesdon, Herts EN10 7WG
Fax: 01992 470516   Tel: 01992 470907

MASTERSON Guy PRODUCTIONS
(Write)
The Bull Theatre
68 High Street, Barnet, Herts EN5 5SJ
Website: www.guymasterson.com
e-mail: admin@guymasterson.com
Fax: 020-8449 5252   Tel: 020-8449 7800

MEADOW Jeremy
(See TEG PRODUCTIONS Ltd)

MENZIES Lee Ltd
118-120 Wardour Street, London W1F 0TU
Website: www.leemenzies.co.uk
e-mail: leemenzies@leemenzies.co.uk
Fax: 020-7734 4224   Tel: 020-7734 9559

MIDDLE GROUND THEATRE COMPANY
3 Gordon Terrace, Malvern Wells
Malvern, Worcestershire WR14 4ER
e-mail: middleground@tinyworld.co.uk
Fax: 01684 574472   Tel: 01684 577231

MITCHELL Matthew Ltd
The Penthouse, 7 Leicester Place, London WC2H 7RJ
e-mail: matthew@matthewmitchell.org
Fax: 020-7734 7185   Tel: 020-7287 2791

MONSTER PRODUCTIONS
Buddle Arts Centre, 258B Station Road
Wallsend, Tyne & Wear NE28 8RG
Website: www.monsterproductions.co.uk
e-mail: info@monsterproductions.co.uk
Fax: 0191-240 4016   Tel: 0191-240 4011

MORNING VICAR PRODUCTIONS Ltd
43B Camberwell New Road, London SE5 0RZ
Website: www.morningvicar.co.uk
e-mail: info@morningvicar.co.uk   Tel/Fax: 020-7582 2242

MOVING TALENT
Ground Floor
29 Ardwick Green North, Manchester M12 6DL
e-mail: movingtalent@aol.com   Tel: 0161-273 4738

MOVING THEATRE
16 Laughton Lodge, Laughton
Nr Lewes, East Sussex BN8 6BY
Website: www.movingtheatre.com
e-mail: info@movingtheatre.com
Fax: 01323 815736   Tel: 01323 815726

MUSIC THEATRE LONDON
Chertsey Chambers, 12 Mercer Street, London WC2H 9QD
Website: www.mtl.org.uk
e-mail: musictheatre.london@virgin.net
Fax: 020-7240 0805   Tel: 020-7240 0919

MUZIKANSKY
The Forum, Fonthill, The Common
Tunbridge Wells TN4 8YU
Website: www.mzky.co.uk
e-mail: admin@mzky.co.uk   Tel/Fax: 01892 542260

MU-LAN THEATRE COMPANY
The Albany, Douglas Way, London SE8 4AG
Website: www.mu-lan.org
e-mail: mailbox@mu-lan.org
Fax: 020-8694 0618   Tel: 020-8694 0557

NATIONAL THEATRE
South Bank, London SE1 9PX
Website: www.nt-online.org
Fax: 020-7452 3344   Tel: 020-7452 3333

NEW END THEATRE
27 New End, Hampstead, London NW3 1JD
Website: www.newendtheatre.co.uk
e-mail: briandaniels@newendtheatre.co.uk
Fax: 020-7472 5808   Tel: 020-7472 5800

NEW SHAKESPEARE COMPANY Ltd The
Open Air Theatre, The Iron Works, Inner Circle
Regent's Park, London NW1 4NR
Website: www.openairtheatre.org
Fax: 020-7487 4562   Tel: 020-7935 5756

NEW VIC THEATRE OF LONDON Inc
Suite 42, 91 St Martin's Lane
London WC2H 0DL   Tel/Fax: 020-7240 2929

NEW VIC WORKSHOP Ltd
56 Lansdowne Place, Brighton BN3 1FG
e-mail: newvicworkshop@lineone.net
Fax: 01273 776663   Tel: 01273 775126

NEWPALM PRODUCTIONS
26 Cavendish Avenue, London N3 3QN
Fax: 020-8346 8257   Tel: 020-8349 0802

NITRO
(Formerly Black Theatre Co-operative)
6 Brewery Road, London N7 9NH
Website: www.nitro.co.uk
e-mail: info@nitro.co.uk
Fax: 020-7609 1221   Tel: 020-7609 1331

NORTHERN BROADSIDES THEATRE COMPANY
Dean Clough, Halifax HX3 5AX
e-mail: sue@northern-broadsides.co.uk
Fax: 01422 383175   Tel: 01422 369704

NORTHERN STAGE (THEATRICAL PRODUCTIONS) Ltd
Barras Bridge, Newcastle upon Tyne NE1 7RH
Website: www.northernstage.com
e-mail: info@northernstage.com
Fax: 0191-261 8093   Tel: 0871 7000124

NORWELL LAPLEY ASSOCIATES
Lapley Hall, Lapley, Staffs ST19 9JR
Website: www.norwelllapley.co.uk
e-mail: norwelllapley@freeuk.com
Fax: 01785 841992   Tel: 01785 841991

NOT THE NATIONAL THEATRE
(Write) (Small/Mid-Scale Touring - UK & Abroad)
101 Broadhurst Gardens, London NW6 3BJ

NOTIONAL THEATRE
PO Box 130, Hexham NE46 4WA
e-mail: chris.mccullough@virgin.net   Tel: 07900 303576

NTC TOURING THEATRE COMPANY
The Playhouse, Bondgate Without, Alnwick
Northumberland NE66 1PQ
Website: www.ntc-touringtheatre.co.uk
e-mail: admin@ntc-touringtheatre.co.uk
Fax: 01665 605837   Tel: 01665 602586

O'BRIEN Barry (1968) Ltd
26 Cavendish Avenue, London N3 3QN
Fax: 020-8346 8257   Tel: 020-8346 8011

OFF THE CUFF THEATRE COMPANY
2nd Floor, 91A Rivington Street, London EC2A 3AY
e-mail: otctheatre@aol.com   Tel: 020-7739 2857

OLD VIC PRODUCTIONS Plc
The Old Vic Theatre, The Cut, Waterloo, London SE1 8NB
e-mail: ovp@oldvictheatre.com
Fax: 020-7261 9161   Tel: 020-7928 2651

ONE FOR THE ROAD
(Simon Fielder)
PO Box 256, Bicester, Oxfordshire OX26 3UZ
e-mail: enquiries@simonfielder.com   Tel/Fax: 01869 354854

ONE NIGHT BOOKING COMPANY The
3 Grand Union Walk, Camden Town, London NW1 9LP
e-mail: email@onenightbooking.com   Tel: 020-8455 3278

OPEN AIR THEATRE
(See NEW SHAKESPEARE COMPANY Ltd The)

OUT OF JOINT
7 Thane Works, Thane Villas, London N7 7PH
Website: www.outofjoint.co.uk
e-mail: ojo@outofjoint.co.uk
Fax: 020-7609 0203   Tel: 020-7609 0207

OUT OF THE BOX PRODUCTIONS Ltd
48 New Cavendish Street, London W1G 8TG
Website: www.outoftheboxproductions.org
e-mail: info@outoftheboxproductions.org
          Tel/Fax: 020-7935 1360

OVATION
1 Prince of Wales Passage, London NW1 3EF
Website: www.ovationtheatres.com
e-mail: events@ovationproductions.com
Fax: 020-7380 0404   Tel: 020-7387 2342

OXFORD STAGE COMPANY
Chertsey Chambers, 12 Mercer Street, London WC2H 9QD
Website: www.oxfordstage.co.uk
e-mail: info@oxfordstage.co.uk
Fax: 020-7438 9941   Tel: 020-7438 9940

P&S PRODUCTIONS
Top Flat, 51 Norroy Road, London SW15 1PQ
e-mail: timsawers@msn.com
Fax: 020-8780 9115   Tel: 020-8788 8521

PAINES PLOUGH
Fourth Floor, 43 Aldwych, London WC2B 4DN
Website: www.painesplough.com
e-mail: office@painesplough.com
Fax: 020-7240 4534   Tel: 020-7240 4533

PARASOL PRODUCTIONS
Garden House, 4 Sunnyside, Wimbledon SW19 4SL
Website: www.parasoltheatre.co.uk
e-mail: parasoltheatre@waitrose.com
Fax: 020-8946 0228   Tel: 020-8946 9478

PENDLE PRODUCTIONS
Bridge Farm, 249 Hawes Side Lane, Blackpool FY4 4AA
Website: www.pendleproductions.co.uk
e-mail: admin@pendleproductions.co.uk
          Tel/Fax: 01253 839375

PENTABUS
(National Touring Company for New Writing)
Bromfield, Ludlow, Shropshire SY8 2JU
Website: www.pentabus.co.uk
e-mail: firstname@pentabus.co.uk
Fax: 01584 856254   Tel: 01584 856564

PEOPLE SHOW
People Show Studios, Pollard Row, London E2 6NB
Website: www.peopleshow.co.uk
e-mail: people@peopleshow.co.uk
Fax: 020-7739 0203   Tel: 020-7729 1841

PERFORMANCE BUSINESS The
15 Montrose Walk, Weybridge, Surrey KT13 8JN
Website: www.theperformance.biz
e-mail: info@theperformance.biz   Tel: 01932 888885

PILOT THEATRE COMPANY
(New Writing & Multi Media YPT)
York Theatre Royal, St Leonards Place, York YO1 7HD
Website: www.pilot-theatre.com
e-mail: info@pilot-theatre.com
Fax: 01904 656378   Tel: 01904 635755

PLANTAGENET PRODUCTIONS
Westridge (Open Centre), (Drawing Room Recitals)
Star Lane, Highclere
Nr Newbury RG20 9PJ   Tel: 01635 253322

PLUNGE PRODUCTIONS Ltd
9 Whittington Road, London N22 8YS
Website: www.plungeproductions.com
e-mail: info@plungeproductions.com
                        Tel/Fax: 020-8888 6608

POLKA THEATRE
240 The Broadway, Wimbledon SW19 1SB
Website: www.polkatheatre.com
e-mail: admin@polkatheatre.com
Fax: 020-8545 8365   Tel: 020-8545 8320

POSTER Kim
The Penthouse, Charles House
7 Leicester Place, London WC2H 7BY
e-mail: office@stanhopeprod.com
Fax: 020-7734 7185   Tel: 020-7734 0710

PROMENADE ENTERPRISES Ltd
6 Russell Grove, London SW9 6HS
Website: www.promenadeproductions.com
e-mail: info@promenadeproductions.com
Fax: 020-7564 3026   Tel: 020-7582 9354

PUGH David Ltd
Canaletto Yard, 41 Beak Street, London W1F 9SB
e-mail: dpl@davidpughltd.com
Fax: 020-7287 8856   Tel: 020-7434 9757

PURSUED BY A BEAR PRODUCTIONS
4A Nelson Road, London SE10 9JB
Website: www.pbab.org
e-mail: pbab@pbab.org   Tel/Fax: 020-8480 9514

PW PRODUCTIONS Ltd
The Penthouse, 7 Leicester Place, London WC2H 7BP
Website: www.pwprods.co.uk
Fax: 020-7734 7185   Tel: 020-7734 7184

QDOS ENTERTAINMENT (THEATRE) Ltd
8 King Street, London WC2E 8HN
Fax: 020-7379 4892   Tel: 020-7836 2795

Qdos House, Queen Margaret's Road, Scarborough
North Yorkshire YO11 2SA
Fax: 01723 361958   Tel: 01723 500038

QUANTUM THEATRE
The Old Button Factory
1-11 Bannockburn Road, Plumstead, London SE18 1ET
Website: www.quantumtheatre.co.uk
e-mail: quantumtheatre@btinternet.com
                                     Tel: 020-8317 9000

RAGGED RAINBOW PRODUCTIONS Ltd
45 Nightingale Lane, Crouch End, London N8 7RA
e-mail: rainbowrp@onetel.net.uk   Tel/Fax: 020-8341 6241

RAGS & FEATHERS THEATRE COMPANY
80 Summer Road, Thames Ditton, Surrey KT7 0QP
e-mail: jill@ragsandfeathers.freeserve.co.uk
Mobile: 07958 724374   Tel: 020-8224 2203

RAIN OR SHINE THEATRE COMPANY
25 Paddock Gardens, Longlevens, Gloucester GL2 0ED
Website: www.rainorshine.co.uk
e-mail: theatre@rainorshine.co.uk   Tel/Fax: 01452 521575

REALLY USEFUL GROUP Ltd The
22 Tower Street, London WC2H 9TW
Fax: 020-7240 1204   Tel: 020-7240 0880

REALLY USEFUL THEATRES
(Theatre Operators)
Manor House, 21 Soho Square, London W1D 3QP
Website: www.rutheatres.com
e-mail: info@rutheatres.com
Fax: 020-7434 1217   Tel: 020-7494 5200

RED ROOM The
Cabin Q, Clarendon Buildings
11 Ronalds Road, London N5 1XJ
Website: www.theredroom.org.uk
e-mail: info@theredroom.org.uk
Fax: 020-7607 8451   Tel: 020-7697 8685

RED ROSE CHAIN
1 Fore Hamlet, Ipswich IP3 8AA
Website: www.redrosechain.co.uk
e-mail: info@redrosechain.co.uk   Tel: 01473 288886

RED SHIFT THEATRE COMPANY
Trowbray House, 108 Weston Street, London SE1 3QB
Website: www.redshifttheatreco.co.uk
e-mail: mail@redshifttheatreco.co.uk
Fax: 020-7378 9789   Tel: 020-7378 9787

REDINGTON Michael Ltd
10 Maunsel Street, London SW1P 2QL
Fax: 020-7828 6947   Tel: 020-7834 5119

REVEAL THEATRE COMPANY
40 Pirehill Lane, Walton, Stone, Staffs ST15 0JN
e-mail: revealtheatre@hotmail.com
Fax: 0115-878 0651   Tel: 01785 814052

RHO DELTA Ltd
(Greg Ripley-Duggan)
52 Tottenham Street, London W1T 4RN
e-mail: info@ripleyduggan.com   Tel: 020-7436 1392

RICHMOND PRODUCTIONS
47 Moor Mead Road
St Margaret's, Twickenham TW1 1JS
e-mail: alister@richmondproductions.co.uk
Mobile: 07968 026768   Tel/Fax: 020-8891 2280

ROCKET THEATRE COMPANY
245 Broadfield Road, Manchester M14 7JT
Website: www.rockettheatre.co.uk
e-mail: martin@rockettheatre.co.uk
Mobile: 07788 723570   Tel: 0161-226 8788

Stage Presence

PO Box 7579 London NW3 1WA

020-7794-9140

ROSE Michael Ltd
The Old Dairy, Throop Road
Holdenhurst, Bournemouth, Dorset BH8 0DL
e-mail: mrl@mrltheatre.u-net.com
Fax: 01202 522311 Tel: 01202 522711

ROSENTHAL Suzanna Ltd
PO Box 40001, London N6 4YA
e-mail: admin@suzannarosenthal.com
Tel/Fax: 020-8340 4421

ROYAL COURT THEATRE PRODUCTIONS Ltd
Sloane Square, London SW1W 8AS
Website: www.royalcourttheatre.com
e-mail: info@royalcourttheatre.com
Fax: 020-7565 5001 Tel: 020-7565 5050

ROYAL EXCHANGE THEATRE COMPANY
St Ann's Square, Manchester M2 7DH
Website: www.royalexchange.co.uk Tel: 0161-833 9333

ROYAL SHAKESPEARE COMPANY
1 Earlham Street, London WC2H 9LL
Website: www.rsc.org.uk
Fax: 020-7845 0505 Tel: 020-7845 0500

ROYAL SHAKESPEARE THEATRE
Waterside, Stratford-upon-Avon CV37 6BB
Website: www.rsc.org.uk
Fax: 01789 294810 Tel: 01789 296655

RUBINSTEIN Mark Ltd
25 Short Street, London SE1 8LJ
e-mail: info@mrluk.com
Fax: 0870 7059731 Tel: 020-7021 0787

SALBERG & STEPHENSON Ltd
18 Soho Square, London W1D 3QL
e-mail: soholondon@aol.com
Fax: 020-7025 8100 Tel: 020-7025 8701

SANDIS PRODUCTIONS
Suite 365
78 Marylebone High Street, London W1V 5AP
Website: www.sandisproductions.com
e-mail: info@sandisproduction.com
Fax: 020-7224 2777 Tel: 020-7644 5912

SANDPIPER PRODUCTIONS Ltd
49A Ossington Street, London W2 4LY
e-mail: harold@sanditen.fsworld.co.uk
Fax: 020-7229 6710 Tel: 020-7229 6708

SCAMP
Sutherland Callow Arts Management and Production
46 Church Lane, Arlesley, Beds SG15 6UX
Website: www.scamptheatre.com
e-mail: admin@scamptheatre.com
Mobile: 07710 49111 Tel: 01462 734843

SCARLET THEATRE
Studio 4, The Bull, 68 High Street, Barnet, Herts EN5 5SJ
Website: www.scarlettheatre.co.uk
e-mail: admin@scarlettheatre.co.uk
Fax: 020-8447 0075 Tel: 020-8441 9779

SECOND SIGHT PRODUCTIONS
(Second Productions of Plays)
TEG Productions (Second Sight) Ltd
11-15 Betterton Street, London WC2H 9BP
Fax: 020-7836 9454 Tel: 020-7379 1066

SETTLE FESTIVAL THEATRE
(Theatre in The Dales)
The Mains, Giggleswick, Settle, North Yorkshire BD24 0AX
e-mail: sft@giggleswick301.fsnet.co.uk
Tel/Fax: 01729 822058

SGRIPT CYMRU CONTEMPORARY DRAMA WALES
Chapter, Market Road, Canton, Cardiff CF5 1QE
Website: www.sgriptcymru.com
e-mail: sgriptcymru@sgriptcymru.com
Fax: 029-2023 6651 Tel: 029-2023 6650

SHARED EXPERIENCE THEATRE
(National/International Touring)
The Soho Laundry, 9 Dufour's Place, London W1F 7SJ
Website: www.sharedexperience.org.uk
e-mail: admin@sharedexperience.org.uk
Fax: 020-7287 8763 Tel: 020-7434 9248

SHARLAND Elizabeth
Suite 12, 30 New Compton Street
London WC2H 8DN Tel: 020-7836 4203

SHOW OF STRENGTH
74 Chessel Street, Bedminster, Bristol BS3 3DN
Website: www.showofstrength.org.uk
Fax: 0117-902 0196 Tel: 0117-902 0235

SINDEN Marc PRODUCTIONS
11 Garrick Street, London WC2E 9AR
Website: www.sindenproductions.com
e-mail: mail@sindenproductions.com
Tel/Fax: 020-8455 3278

SOHO THEATRE COMPANY
21 Dean Street, London W1D 3NE
Website: www.sohotheatre.com
e-mail: mail@sohotheatre.com
Fax: 020-7287 5061 Tel: 020-7287 5060

SPHINX THEATRE COMPANY The
25 Short Street, London SE1 8LJ
Website: www.sphinxtheatre.co.uk
Fax: 020-7401 9995 Tel: 020-7401 9993

SPIEGEL Adam PRODUCTIONS
2nd Floor, 20-22 Stukeley Street, London WC2B 5LR
e-mail: enquiries@adamspiegel.com
Fax: 020-7438 9577 Tel: 020-7438 9565

SPLATS ENTERTAINMENT
5 Denmark Street, London WC2H 8LP
e-mail: admin@splatsentertainment.com
Fax: 020-7240 8409 Tel: 020-7240 8400

STACEY Barrie UK PRODUCTIONS Ltd
Flat 8, 132 Charing Cross Road, London WC2H 0LA
Website: www.barriestacey.com
e-mail: hopkinstacey@aol.com
Fax: 020-7836 2949 Tel: 020-7836 4128

STAGE FURTHER PRODUCTIONS Ltd
Westgate, Stansted Road
Eastbourne, East Sussex BN22 8LG
e-mail: info@stagefurther.co.uk
Fax: 01323 736127   Tel: 01323 739478

STAGE HOLDING UK
Swan House, 52 Poland Street, London W1F 7NH
Fax: 020-7025 6971   Tel: 020-7025 6970

STAGE PRESENCE
PO Box 7579, London NW3 1WA
e-mail: contact@stage-presence.co.uk   Tel: 020-7794 9140

STANHOPE PRODUCTIONS Ltd
The Penthouse, Charles House
7 Leicester Place, London WC2H 7BY
e-mail: office@stanhopeprod.com
Fax: 020-7734 7185   Tel: 020-7734 0710

STEAM INDUSTRY The
The Finborough Theatre
118 Finborough Road, London SW10 9ED
Website: www.steamindustry.co.uk
e-mail: admin@steamindustry.co.uk
Fax: 020-7835 1853   Tel: 020-7244 7439

STRAIGHT LINE PRODUCTIONS
58 Castle Avenue, Epsom, Surrey KT17 2PH
e-mail: info@straightlineproductions.com
Fax: 020-8393 8079   Tel: 020-8393 4220

STRANGE CAPERS
110 Woodside Avenue South, Coventry CV3 6BE
Website: www.strangecapers.co.uk   Tel: 024-7641 8912

SUSPECT CULTURE
CCA, 350 Sauchiehall Street, Glasgow G2 3JD
Website: www.suspectculture.com
e-mail: info@suspectculture.com
Fax: 0141-332 8823   Tel: 0141-332 9775

SWALLOW PRODUCTIONS (UK) Ltd
32 Blenheim Gardens, Wembley Park, Middlesex HA9 7NP
e-mail: swproduk@aol.com   Tel/Fax: 020-8904 7024

TABS PRODUCTIONS
36 Fleece Road, Long Ditton, Surrey KT6 5JN
e-mail: adrianmljames@aol.com
Fax: 08714 332938   Tel: 020-8398 6746

TALAWA THEATRE COMPANY
23-25 Great Sutton Street, London EC1V 0DN
Website: www.talawa.com
e-mail: hq@talawa.com
Fax: 020-7251 5969   Tel: 020-7251 6644

TAMASHA THEATRE COMPANY Ltd
Unit 220, 30 Great Guildford Street, London SE1 0HS
Website: www.tamasha.org.uk
e-mail: info@tamasha.org.uk
Fax: 020-7021 0421   Tel: 020-7633 2270

TAMBAR Ltd
PO Box LB689, London W1A 9LB
e-mail: tambarltd@hotmail.com   Tel: 020-8342 8882

TBA MUSIC Ltd
24 Clifton Hill, London NW8 0QG
e-mail: mail@tbamusic.freeserve.co.uk
Fax: 020-7372 0802   Tel: 0845 1203722

TEG PRODUCTIONS Ltd
11-15 Betterton Street, London WC2H 9BP
Fax: 020-7836 9454   Tel: 020-7379 1066

Winnington Hall, Winnington, Northwich, Cheshire CW8 4DU
Fax: 01606 872701   Tel: 01606 872700

TENTH PLANET PRODUCTIONS
75 Woodland Gardens, London N10 3UD
Website: www.tenthplanetproductions.com
e-mail: admin@tenthplanetproductions.com
Fax: 020-8883 1708   Tel: 020-8442 2659

THEATRE ABSOLUTE
57-61 Corporation Street, Coventry CV1 1GQ
Website: www.theatreabsolute.co.uk
e-mail: info@theatreabsolute.co.uk   Tel: 024-7625 7380

THEATRE OF COMEDY COMPANY Ltd
Shaftesbury Theatre
210 Shaftesbury Avenue, London WC2H 8DP
Fax: 020-7836 8181   Tel: 020-7379 3345

THEATRE ROYAL HAYMARKET PRODUCTIONS
Theatre Royal Haymarket, London SW1Y 4HT
e-mail: amc@trh.co.uk
Fax: 020-7389 9698   Tel: 020-7389 9669

THEATRE ROYAL STRATFORD EAST
Gerry Raffles Square, Stratford, London E15 1BN
Website: www.stratfordeast.com
e-mail: theatreroyal@stratfordeast.com   Tel: 020-8534 7374

THEATRE SANS FRONTIERES
The Queen's Hall Arts Centre
Beaumont Street, Hexham NE46 3LS
Website: www.theatresansfrontieres.co.uk
e-mail: admin@tsfront.co.uk
Fax: 01434 607206   Tel: 01434 652484

THEATRE SET-UP Ltd
(International Touring)
12 Fairlawn Close, Southgate, London N14 4JX
Website: www.ts-u.co.uk   Tel/Fax: 020-8886 9572

THEATRE TOURS INTERNATIONAL
The Bull Theatre, 68 The High Street, Barnet, Herts EN5 5SJ
Website: www.theatretoursinternational.com
e-mail: mail@theatretoursinternational.com
Fax: 020-8449 5252   Tel: 020-8449 7800

TOWER THEATRE COMPANY
(Full-time non-professional)
11 Canonbury Place, Islington, London N1 2NQ
Website: www.towertheatre.org.uk
e-mail: info@towertheatre.freeserve.co.uk
     Tel/Fax: 020-7226 5111

TRADING FACES
(Mask & Physical Theatre)
2 Bridge View, Bridge Street, Abingdon OX14 3HN
Website: www.tradingfaces.org.uk
e-mail: admin@tradingfaces.org.uk
Fax: 01235 553403   Tel: 01235 550829

TRENDS PRODUCTIONS Ltd
54 Lisson Street, London NW1 5DF
e-mail: info@trendsgroup.co.uk
Fax: 020-7258 3591   Tel: 020-7723 8001

TRESTLE THEATRE COMPANY
(Touring Mask Theatre)
Trestle Arts Base
Russet Drive, Herts, St Albans AL4 0JQ
Website: www.trestle.org.uk
e-mail: admin@trestle.org.uk
Fax: 01727 855558   Tel: 01727 850950

TRIUMPH ENTERTAINMENT Ltd (DUNCAN C WELDON)
Suite 4, Waldorf Chambers, 11 Aldwych, London WC2B 4DG
e-mail: dcwtpp@aol.com
Fax: 020-7343 8801   Tel: 020-7343 8800

TURTLE KEY ARTS
Ladbroke Hall, 79 Barlby Road, London W10 6AZ
e-mail: admin@turtlekeyarts.org.uk
Fax: 020-8964 4080 Tel: 020-8964 5060

TWIST & CHEETHAM
39 Rosslyn Crescent, Edinburgh EH6 5AT
e-mail: ben.twist@blueyonder.co.uk Tel/Fax: 0131-477 7425

TWO'S COMPANY
244 Upland Road, London SE22 0DN
e-mail: 2scompany@britishlibrary.net
Fax: 020-8299 3714 Tel: 020-8299 4593

UK ARTS INTERNATIONAL
Second Floor, 6 Shaw Street, Worcester WR1 3QQ
Website: www.ukarts.com
e-mail: ukarts@ukarts.com
Fax: 01905 22868 Tel: 01905 26424

UK PRODUCTIONS Ltd
Lime House, 78 Meadrow
Godalming
Surrey GU7 3HT
Website: www.ukproductions.co.uk
e-mail: mail@ukproductions.co.uk
Fax: 01483 418486 Tel: 01483 423600

UNRESTRICTED VIEW
Above Hen & Chickens Theatre Bar
109 St Paul's Road, London N1 2NA
Website: www.henandchickens.com
e-mail: james@henandchickens.com Tel: 020-7704 2001

VANCE Charles
CV Productions Ltd
Hampden House
2 Weymouth Street, London W1W 5BT
e-mail: cvtheatre@aol.com
Fax: 020-7636 2323 Tel: 020-7636 4343

VANDER ELST Anthony PRODUCTIONS
The Studio
14 College Road
Bromley, Kent BR1 3NS
Fax: 020-8313 0443 Tel: 020-8466 5580

VOLCANO THEATRE COMPANY Ltd
Swansea Institute
Townhill Road, Swansea SA2 0UT
Website: www.volcanotheatre.co.uk
e-mail: volcano.tc@virgin.net Tel/Fax: 01792 281280

WALLACE Kevin Ltd
10 (H) St Martin's Place, London WC2N 4JL
e-mail: enquiries@kevinwallace.co.uk
Fax: 020-7836 9587 Tel: 020-7836 9586

WALLBANK John ASSOCIATES
60 Barclay Road, London E11 3DG
e-mail: john.wallbank2@ntlworld.com
Fax: 020-8928 0339 Tel: 020-8530 7386

WAREHOUSE THEATRE COMPANY
Dingwall Road, Croydon CR0 2NF
Website: www.warehousetheatre.co.uk
e-mail: info@warehousetheatre.co.uk
Fax: 020-8688 6699 Tel: 020-8681 1257

WAVE ENTERTAINMENT Ltd
308 Desborough Avenue
High Wycombe, Bucks HP11 2TJ
Website: www.wave-entertainment.co.uk
e-mail: paul@wave-entertainment.co.uk
Mobile: 07736 309290 Tel/Fax: 0870 7606263

WAX Kenneth H Ltd
The Penthouse, 7 Leicester Place, London WC2H 7RJ
e-mail: k.wax@virgin.net
Fax: 020-7734 7185 Tel: 020-7734 7184

WEAVER-HUGHES ENSEMBLE
12B Carholme Road, London SE23 2HS
Website: www.weaverhughesensemble.co.uk
e-mail: ensemble@weaverhughesensemble.co.uk
Tel/Fax: 020-8291 0514

WHITALL Keith
10 Woodlands Avenue, West Byfleet
Surrey KT14 6AT Tel: 01932 343655

WHITE Michael
48 Dean Street, London W1D 5BF
e-mail: contact@michaelwhite.co.uk
Fax: 020-7734 7727 Tel: 020-7734 7707

WHITEHALL FILMS
10 Lower Common South, London SW15 1BP
e-mail: mwhitehall@msn.com
Fax: 020-8788 2340 Tel: 020-8785 3737

WILDCARD THEATRE COMPANY
Suite A, Swan House
White Hart Street, High Wycombe, Bucks HP11 2HL
Website: www.wildcardtheatre.org.uk
e-mail: admin@wildcardtheatre.org.uk
Fax: 07092 024967 Tel: 01494 439375

WILLIAMSON R J COMPANY Ltd
8 Adelaide Grove, London W12 0JJ
Website: www.openairshakespeare.com
e-mail: robert@openairshakespeare.co.uk
Tel/Fax: 020-8749 4427

WILLS Newton MANAGEMENT
The Studio, 29 Springvale Ave, Brentford, Middx TW8 9QH
e-mail: newtoncttg@aol.com
Fax: 00 33 2418 23108 Mobile: 07989 398381

WINGATE Olivia PRODUCTIONS Ltd
68 Delancey Street, London NW1 7RY
e-mail: info@owproductions.co.uk Tel/Fax: 020-7485 1861

WISHBONE
40 Pilgrims' Cloisters, 116 Sedgmoor Place, London SE5 7RQ
Website: www.wishbonetheatre.org.uk
e-mail: karen@wishbonetheatre.org.uk
Tel/Fax: 020-7708 2897

WIZARD PRESENTS
2 Lord Hills Road, London W2 6PD
e-mail: info@wizardpresents.co.uk
Fax: 020-7286 7377 Tel: 020-7286 7277

WOOD Kevin PRODUCTIONS
5 Archery Square, Walmer, Deal, Kent CT14 7JA
e-mail: kevin.wood.organisation@dial.pipex.com
Fax: 01304 381192 Tel: 01304 365515

WRESTLING SCHOOL The
(The Howard Baker Company)
42 Durlston Road, London E5 8RR
Website: www.thewrestlingschool.co.uk
Tel/Fax: 020-8442 4229

YELLOW EARTH THEATRE
Diorama Arts Centre, 34 Osnaburgh St, London NW1 3ND
Website: www.yellowearth.org
e-mail: admin@yellowearth.org
Fax: 020-7209 2327 Tel: 020-7209 2326

YOUNG VIC
Kennington Park, 2nd Floor
Chester House, 1-3 Brixton Road, London SW9 6DE
Website: www.youngvic.org
e-mail: info@youngvic.org
Fax: 020-7820 3355 Tel: 020-7820 3550

7:84 THEATRE COMPANY (SCOTLAND) Ltd
333 Woodlands Road, Glasgow G3 6NG
Website: www.784theatre.com
e-mail: admin@784theatre.com
Fax: 0141-334 3369   Tel: 0141-334 6686

ABERYSTWYTH ARTS CENTRE
Penglais, Aberystwyth, Ceredigion SY23 3DE
Website: www.aber.ac.uk/artscentre
e-mail: lla@aber.ac.uk
Fax: 01970 622883   Tel: 01970 622882

ACTORCLUB Ltd
17 Inkerman Road, London NW5 3BT   Tel: 020-7267 2759

AGE EXCHANGE THEATRE TRUST
The Reminiscence Centre
11 Blackheath Village, London SE3 9LA
Website: www.age-exchange.org.uk
e-mail: administrator@age-exchange.org.uk
Fax: 020-8318 0060   Tel: 020-8318 9105

ALTERNATIVE ARTS
Top Studio, Bethnal Green Training Centre
Deal Street, London E1 5HZ
Website: www.alternative arts.co.uk
e-mail: info@alternativearts.co.uk
Fax: 020-7375 0484   Tel: 020-7375 0441

ANGLES THEATRE The
Alexandra Road, Wisbech, Cambridgeshire PE13 1HQ
e-mail: angeltheatre@aol.com
Fax: 01945 481768   Tel: 01945 585587

ASHTON GROUP THEATRE The
Old Fire Station, Abbey Road
Barrow-in-Furness, Cumbria LA14 1XH
Website: www.ashtongroup.co.uk
e-mail: admin@ashtongroup.co.uk   Tel/Fax: 01229 430636

ATTIC THEATRE COMPANY (LONDON) Ltd
Wimbledon Theatre, The Broadway, London SW19 1QG
Website: www.attictheatre.com
e-mail: info@attictheatre.com   Tel/Fax: 020-8543 7838

BANNER THEATRE
Friends Institute, 220 Moseley Road
Highgate, Birmingham B12 0DG
e-mail: banneroffice2@btinternet.com   Tel: 0121-440 0460

BECK THEATRE
Grange Road, Hayes, Middx UB3 2UE   Tel: 020-8561 7506

BLUE CRAZE
(Sharon Kennet, Siobhan O'Neill)
24 Wykeham Roadd, London NW4 2SU   Tel/Fax: 020-8203 1916

BLUNDERBUS THEATRE COMPANY Ltd
1st Floor, The Brook Theatre
Old Town Hall, Chatham, Kent ME4 4SE
Website: www.blunderbus.co.uk
e-mail: admin@blunderbus.co.uk
Fax: 01634 818138   Tel: 01634 818136

BORDERLINE THEATRE COMPANY
(Eddie Jackson)
North Harbour Street, Ayr KA8 8AA
Website: www.borderlinetheatre.co.uk
e-mail: enquiries@borderlinetheatre.co.uk
Fax: 01292 263825   Tel: 01292 281010

BRAVE NEW WORLD THEATRE COMPANY
Write
Second Floor, 79 Highbury Hill, London N5 1SX
e-mail: bravenewworld@onetel.com

BRUVVERS THEATRE COMPANY
(Touring on Tyneside)
The Fun Palace, 36 Lime Street
Ouseburn, Newcastle upon Tyne NE1 2PQ
Website: www.thefunpalace.co.uk
e-mail: mikeofbruvvers@hotmail.com   Tel: 0191-261 9230

CAPITAL ARTS YOUTH THEATRE
Wyllyotts Centre, Darkes Lane, Potters Bar, Herts EN6 2HN
e-mail: capitalartstheatre@o2.co.uk
Mobile: 07885 232414   Tel/Fax: 020-8449 2342

CARIB THEATRE COMPANY
73 Lancelot Road, Wembley, Middlesex HA0 2AN
e-mail: caribtheatre@aol.com   Tel/Fax: 020-8795 0576

CAVALCADE THEATRE COMPANY
(Touring Shows - Musicals, Pantomimes, Music Hall
Comedy & Rock 'n' Roll)
Write
57 Pelham Road, London SW19 1NW
Fax: 020-8540 3513

CENTRE FOR PERFORMANCE RESEARCH
6 Science Park, Aberystwyth SY23 3AH
Website: www.thecpr.org.uk
e-mail: cprwww@aber.ac.uk
Fax: 01970 622132   Tel: 01970 622133

CHALKFOOT THEATRE ARTS
Central Studios, 36 Park Place, Margate, Kent CT9 1LE
Website: www.chalkfoot.org.uk
e-mail: info@chalkfoot.org.uk
Fax: 01843 280088   Tel: 01843 280077

CHATS PALACE ARTS CENTRE
42-44 Brooksby's Walk, Hackney, London E9 6DF
Fax: 020-8985 6878   Tel: 020-8533 0227

CHEEKY MAGGOT THEATRE
Website: www.cheekymaggot.allhere.com
e-mail: cmtheatreinto@aol.com

CHERUB COMPANY LONDON The
Office: 9 Park Hill, London W5 2JS
email: mgcherub@yahoo.com
Fax: 020-8248 0318   Tel: 020-8723 4358

CHICKEN SHED THEATRE
Chase Side, Southgate, London N14 4PE
Website: www.chickenshed.org.uk
e-mail: info@chickenshed.org.uk
Minicom: 020-8350 0676   Tel: 020-8351 6161

CLEAN BREAK THEATRE COMPANY
(Theatre Education, New Writing)
2 Patshull Road, London NW5 2LB
Website: www.cleanbreak.org.uk
e-mail: general@cleanbreak.org.uk
Fax: 020-7482 8611   Tel: 020-7482 8600

CLOSE FOR COMFORT THEATRE COMPANY
34 Boleyn Walk, Leatherhead, Surrey KT22 7HU
Website: www.hometown.aol.com/close4comf
e-mail: close4comf@aol.com   Tel: 01372 378613

COLLUSION THEATRE COMPANY
Millworks, Field Road, Busby, Glasgow G76 8SE
Website: www.collusiontheatre.co.uk
e-mail: admin@collusiontheatre.co.uk
Fax: 0141-644 4163   Tel: 0141-644 0163

COMPLETE WORKS THEATRE COMPANY Ltd The
12 Willowford, Bancroft Park, Milton Keynes
Buckinghamshire MK13 0RH
Website: www.tcw.org.uk   e-mail: info@tcw.org.uk
Fax: 01908 320263   Tel: 01908 316256

CORNELIUS & JONES ORIGINAL PRODUCTIONS
49 Carters Close, Sherington, Newport Pagnell
Buckinghamshire MK16 9NW
Website: www.corneliusjones.com
e-mail: admin@corneliusjones.com
Fax: 01908 616779   Tel: 01908 612593

CRAGRATS THEATRE
The Mill, Dunford Road, Holmfirth, Huddersfield HD9 2AR
Website: www.cragrats.com
e-mail: theatre@cragrats.com
Fax: 01484 686212   Tel: 01484 686451

CUT-CLOTH THEATRE
41 Beresford Road, Highbury
London N5 2HR   Tel: 020-7503 4393

DRAMA ZONE
Dramazone, Arundel Town Hall, Arundel
West Sussex BN18 9AP
Website: www.dramazone.net
e-mail: admin@dramazone.net   Tel/Fax: 01963 889821

ELAN WALES
(European Live Arts Network)
17 Douglas Buildings, Royal Stuart Lane, Cardiff CF10 5EL
Website: www.elanw.demon.co.uk
e-mail: info@elan-wales.fsnet.co.uk   Tel/Fax: 029-2019 0077

EUROPEAN THEATRE COMPANY The
39 Oxford Avenue, London SW20 8LS
Website: www.europeantheatre.co.uk
e-mail: admin@europeantheatre.co.uk
Fax: 020-8544 1999   Tel: 020-8544 1994

FAMILY CURIOSO THEATRE COMPANY
38 Ferme Park Road, London N4 4ED
Website: www.familycurioso.co.uk
e-mail: mail@familycurioso.co.uk   Tel: 020-8340 3053

FOREST FORGE THEATRE COMPANY
The Theatre Centre, Endeavour Park
Crow Arch Lane, Ringwood, Hampshire BH24 1SF
e-mail: theatre@forestforge.demon.co.uk
Fax: 01425 471158   Tel: 01425 470188

FOURSIGHT THEATRE Ltd
Newhampton Arts Centre
Dunkley Street, Wolverhampton WV1 4AN
Website: www.foursight.theatre.boltblue.net
e-mail: foursight.theatre@boltblue.com
Fax: 01902 428413   Tel: 01902 714257

FRANTIC THEATRE COMPANY
32 Woodlane, Falmouth TR11 4RF
Website: www.frantictheatre.com
e-mail: info@frantictheatre.com   Tel/Fax: 01326 312985

GALLEON THEATRE COMPANY Ltd
Greenwich Playhouse, Greenwich BR Station Forecourt
189 Greenwich High Road, London SE10 8JA
Website: www.galleontheatre.co.uk
Fax: 020-8310 7276   Tel: 020-8858 9256

GRANGE ARTS CENTRE
Rochdale Road, Oldham, Greater Manchester OL9 6EA
e-mail: joanne.draper@oldham.ac.uk
Fax: 0161-785 4263   Tel: 0161-785 4239

GREASEPAINT ANONYMOUS
4 Gallus Close, Winchmore Hill, London N21 1JR
e-mail: info@greasepaintanonymous.co.uk
Fax: 020-8882 9189   Tel: 020-8886 2263

HALL FOR CORNWALL
(Community & Education) (Contact Anna Coombs)
Back Quay, Truro, Cornwall TR1 2LL
Website: www.hallforcornwall.co.uk
e-mail: anna@hallforcornwall.org.uk
Fax: 01872 260246   Tel: 01872 321964

HIJINX THEATRE
(Adults with Learning Disabilities, Community)
Bay Chambers, West Bute Street, Cardiff Bay CF10 5BB
Website: www.hijinx.org.uk
e-mail: info@hijinx.org.uk
Fax: 029-2030 0332   Tel: 029-2030 0331

HISTORIA THEATRE COMPANY
8 Cloudesley Square, London N1 0HT
Website: www.historiatheatre.com
e-mail: kateprice@lineone.net
Fax: 020-7278 4733   Tel: 020-7837 8008

ICON THEATRE
66 Borthwick Road, London E15 1UE
e-mail: sally@icontheatre.org.uk   Tel: 020-8534 0618

IMAGE MUSICAL THEATRE
23 Sedgeford Road, Shepherd's Bush, London W12 0NA
Website: www.imagemusicaltheatre.co.uk
e-mail: brian.thresh@btconnect.com
Fax: 020-8749 9294   Tel: 020-8743 9380

IMMEDIATE THEATRE
Unit C2/62 Beechwood Road, London E8 3DY
e-mail: immediatejo@aol.com
Fax: 020-7683 0247   Tel: 020-7683 0233

INOCENTE ART & FILM Ltd
(Film, Multimedia, Music Videos & two Rock 'n' Roll
Musicals)
5 Denmans Lane, Haywards Heath, Sussex RH16 2LA
e-mail: tarascas@btinternet.com   Mobile: 07973 518132

ISOSCELES
7 Amity Grove, Raynes Park, London SW20 0LQ
Website: www.isosceles.freeserve.co.uk
e-mail: patanddave@isosceles.freeserve.co.uk
     Tel: 020-8946 3905

JET THEATRE
11 Clovelly Road, London W5 5HF
Website: www.jettheatre.co.uk
e-mail: jettheatre@aol.com   Tel: 020-8579 1029

KOMEDIA
44-47 Gardner Street, Brighton BN1 1UN
Website: www.komedia.co.uk
e-mail: info@komedia.co.uk
Fax: 01273 647102   Tel: 01273 647101

LADDER TO THE MOON ENTERTAINMENT
Unit 105, Battersea Business Centre
99-109 Lavender Hill, London SW11 5QL
e-mail: enquiries@laddertothemoon.co.uk
     Tel: 020-7228 9700

LATCHMERE THEATRE
(Chris Fisher)
Unit 5A, Imex Business Centre
Ingate Place, London SW8 3NS
e-mail: latchmere.theatre@zen.co.uk
Fax: 020-7978 2631   Tel: 020-7978 2620

LIVE THEATRE
(New Writing)
7-8 Trinity Chare, Quayside, Newcastle upon Tyne NE1 3DF
Website: www.live.org.uk
e-mail: info@live.org.uk
Fax: 0191-232 2224   Tel: 0191-261 2694

LONDON ACTORS THEATRE COMPANY
Unit 5A, Imex Business Centre, Ingate Pl, London SW8 3NS
e-mail: latchmere.theatre@zen.co.uk
Fax: 020-7978 2631   Tel: 020-7978 2620

LONDON BUBBLE THEATRE COMPANY Ltd
5 Elephant Lane, London SE16 4JD
Website: www.londonbubble.org.uk
e-mail: admin@londonbubble.org.uk
Fax: 020-7231 2366   Tel: 020-7237 4434

LSW JUNIOR INTER-ACT
181A Faunce House, Doddington Grove, London SE17 3TB
Website: www.londonshakespeare.org.uk
e-mail: londonswo@hotmail.com　　Tel/Fax: 020-7793 9755

LSW PRISON PROJECT
181A Faunce House
Doddington Grove, Kennington, London SE17 3TB
Website: www.londonshakespeare.org.uk
e-mail: londonswo@hotmail.com　　Tel/Fax: 020-7793 9755

LSW SENIOR RE-ACTION
181A Faunce House, Doddington Grove, London SE17 3TB
Website: www.londonshakespeare.org.uk
e-mail: londonswo@hotmail.com　　Tel/Fax: 020-7793 9755

LUNG HAS THEATRE COMPANY
Central Hall, West Tollcross, Edinburgh EH3 9BP
e-mail: info@lunghas.co.uk
Fax: 0131-229 8965　　　　　　Tel: 0131-228 8998

M6 THEATRE COMPANY
Hamer CP School, Albert Royds Street, Rochdale OL16 2SU
Website: www.m6theatre.co.uk
e-mail: info@m6theatre.co.uk
Fax: 01706 712601　　　　　　Tel: 01706 355898

MADDERMARKET THEATRE
(Resident Community Theatre Company & Small-Scale
Producing & Receiving House)
St John's Alley, Norwich NR2 1DR
Website: www.maddermarket.co.uk
e-mail: mmtheatre@btconnect.com
Fax: 01603 661357　　　　　　Tel: 01603 626560

MAN MELA THEATRE COMPANY
(Admin Contact: Caroline Goffin)
PO Box 24987, London SE23 3XS
Website: www.man-mela.dircon.co.uk
e-mail: man-mela@dircon.co.uk
Mobile: 07973 349101　　　　Mobile: 07966 215090

MANCHESTER ACTORS COMPANY
PO Box 54, Manchester M60 7AB
Website: www.manactco.org.uk
e-mail: stephenboyes@amserve.net　　Tel: 0161-227 8702

MAYA PRODUCTIONS Ltd
156 Richmond Road, London E8 3HN
Website: www.mayaproductions.co.uk
e-mail: mayachris@aol.com　　Tel/Fax: 020-7923 0675

MIKRON THEATRE COMPANY Ltd
Marsden Mechanics, Peel Street
Marsden, Huddersfield HD7 6BW
Website: www.mikron.org.uk
e-mail: admin@mikron.org.uk　　Tel: 01484 843701

MONTAGE THEATRE ARTS
(Artistic Director Judy Gordon)
441 New Cross Gate, London SE14 6TA
Website: www.montagetheatre.com
e-mail: info@montagetheatre.com　　Tel: 020-8692 7007

MOVING THEATRE
16 Laughton Lodge, Laughton
Nr Lewes, East Sussex BN8 6BY
Website: www.movingtheatre.com
e-mail: info@movingtheatre.com
Fax: 01323 815736　　　　　　Tel: 01323 815726

NATURAL THEATRE COMPANY
(Street Theatre & Touring)
Widcombe Institute, Widcombe Hill, Bath BA2 6AA
Website: www.naturaltheatre.co.uk
e-mail: info@naturaltheatre.co.uk
Fax: 01225 442555　　　　　　Tel: 01225 469131

NET CURTAINS THEATRE COMPANY
The Bath House, 96 Dean Street, London W1D 3TD
e-mail: claire@netcurtains.org　　Tel: 07968 564687

NETI-NETI THEATRE COMPANY
Whitefield School, Claremont Road
London NW2 1TR　　　　　　Tel/Fax: 020-8458 3251

NETTLEFOLD The
West Norwood Library Centre
1 Norwood High Street, London SE27 9JX
Fax: 020-7926 8071　　　　　　Tel: 020-7926 8070

NEW COMPANY
24 Lidfield Road, London N16 9LX
Website: www.newcompany.org.uk
e-mail: info@newcompany.org.uk　　Tel: 020-7923 7431

NEW PECKHAM VARIETIES@MAGIC EYE THEATRE
Havil Street, London SE5 7SD
Website: www.npvarts.co.uk
e-mail: npv-arts@easynet.co.uk　　Tel: 020-7708 5401

NEW PERSPECTIVES THEATRE COMPANY
(Touring & Community Theatre Projects)
The Old Library, Leeming Street, Mansfield
Nottinghamshire NG18 1NG
Website: www.newperspectives.co.uk
e-mail: info@newperspectives.co.uk　　Tel: 01623 635225

NORTHERN STAGE THEATRICAL PRODUCTIONS Ltd
Barras Bridge, Haymarket, Newcastle upon Tyne NE1 7RH
Website: www.northernstage.com
e-mail: info@northernstage.com
Fax: 0191-261 8093　　　　　　Tel: 0871 7000124

NTC TOURING THEATRE COMPANY
(Touring Regionally & Nationally)
The Playhouse, Bondgate Without, Alnwick
Northumberland NE66 1PQ
Website: www.ntc-touringtheatre.co.uk
e-mail: admin@ntc-touringtheatre.co.uk
Fax: 01665 605837　　　　　　Tel: 01665 602586

NUFFIELD THEATRE
(Touring & Projects)
University Road, Southampton SO17 1TR
Website: www.nuffieldtheatre.co.uk
e-mail: abi.linnartz@nuffieldtheatre.co.uk
Fax: 023-8031 5511　　　　　　Tel: 023-8034 4515

OLD TYME PLAYERS THEATRE COMPANY
(Musicals, Revues - Locally Based)
140 Manor Road, New Milton, Hampshire BH25 5ED
Website: www.oldetymeplayers.co.uk
e-mail: oldetymeplayers@tiscali.co.uk　　Tel: 01425 612830

ONATTI THEATRE COMPANY
9 Field Close, Warwick, Warwickshire CV34 4QD
Website: www.onatti.co.uk
e-mail: info@onatti.co.uk
Fax: 0870 1643629　　　　　　Tel: 01926 495220

OPEN STAGE PRODUCTIONS
49 Springfield Road, Moseley
Birmingham B13 9NN　　　　　Tel/Fax: 0121-777 9086

OXFORDSHIRE TOURING THEATRE COMPANY
The Annexe, SS Mary & John School
Meadow Lane, Oxford OX4 1TJ
Website: www.ottc.org.uk
e-mail: info@ottc.oxfordshire.co.uk
Fax: 01865 247266　　　　　　Tel: 01865 249444

PANDEMONIUM TOURING PARTNERSHIP
228 Railway Street
Cardiff CF24 2NJ　　　　　　Tel: 029-2047 2060

PASCAL THEATRE COMPANY
35 Flaxman Court, Flaxman Terrace
Bloomsbury, London WC1H 9AR
Website: www.pascal-theatre.com
e-mail: pascaltheatreco@aol.com
Fax: 020-7419 9798   Tel: 020-7383 0920

PAUL'S THEATRE COMPANY
Fairkytes Arts Centre
51 Billet Lane, Hornchurch, Essex RM11 1AX
e-mail: paul@the-theatreschool.fsnt.co.uk
Fax: 01708 475286   Tel: 01708 447123

PEOPLE'S THEATRE COMPANY The
12E High Street, Egham, Surrey TW20 9EA
Website: www.ptc.org.uk
e-mail: admin@ptc.org.uk   Tel: 01784 470439

PERFORMANCE PROJECT The
32 Kenbrook House, Leighton Road
London NW5 2QN   Tel: 020-7482 1850

PHANTOM CAPTAIN The
618B Finchley Road, London NW11 7RR
Website: www.phantomcaptain.netfirms.com
e-mail: lambhom@tiscali.co.uk   Tel/Fax: 020-8455 4564

PILOT THEATRE COMPANY
York Theatre Royal, St Leonards Place, York YO1 7HD
Website: www.pilot-theatre.com
e-mail: info@pilot-theatre.com
Fax: 01904 656378   Tel: 01904 635755

PLAYTIME THEATRE COMPANY
18 Bennells Avenue, Whitstable, Kent CT5 2HP
Website: www.playtime.dircon.co.uk
e-mail: playtime@dircon.co.uk
Fax: 01227 266648   Tel: 01227 266272

PRIME PRODUCTIONS
54 Hermiston Village, Currie EH14 4AQ
Website: www.primeproductions.co.uk
e-mail: mheller@primeproductions.fsnet.co.uk
     Tel/Fax: 0131-449 4055

PROTEUS THEATRE COMPANY
Queen Mary's College, Cliddesden Road, Basingstoke
Hampshire RG21 3HF
Website: www.proteustheatre.com
e-mail: info@proteustheatre.com   Tel: 01256 354541

PURSUED BY A BEAR PRODUCTIONS
4A Nelson Road, London SE10 9JB
Website: www.pbab.org
e-mail: pbab@pbab.org   Tel/Fax: 020-8480 9514

Q20 THEATRE COMPANY
19 Wellington Crescent, Shipley, West Yorkshire BD18 3PH
e-mail: info@q20theatre.co.uk   Tel: 0845 1260632

QUEST THEATRE COMPANY
(Artistic Director David Craik)
3C Mecklenburgh Street, Bloomsbury
London WC1N 2AH   Tel/Fax: 020-7713 0342

QUICKSILVER THEATRE
The Glasshouse, 4 Enfield Road, London N1 5AZ
Website: www.quicksilvertheatre.org
e-mail: talktous@quicksilvertheatre.org
Fax: 020-7254 3119   Tel: 020-7241 2942

RED LADDER THEATRE COMPANY Ltd
3 St Peter's Buildings, York Street, Leeds LS9 8AJ
Website: www.redladder.co.uk
e-mail: wendy@redladder.co.uk
Fax: 0113-245 5351   Tel: 0113-245 5311

RIDING LIGHTS THEATRE COMPANY
Friargate Theatre, Lower Friargate, York YO1 9SL
Website: www.ridinglights.org
e-mail: info@rltc.org
Fax: 01904 651532   Tel: 01904 655317

ROSE THEATRE COMPANY The
10 Riverside Forest Row
East Sussex RH18 5HB
e-mail: dan.skinner@btinternet.com   Tel: 01342 825639

SALTMINE THEATRE COMPANY
St James House, Trinity Road
Dudley, West Midlands DY1 1JB
Website: www.saltmine.org
e-mail: stc@saltmine.org   Tel: 01384 454807

SKINNING THE CAT, CIRCUS OF THE SKY
163 Washington Street, Girlington, Bradford BD8 9QP
Website: www.skinningthecat.com
e-mail: skats@globalnet.co.uk   Tel: 01535 645041

SNAP THEATRE COMPANY
29 Raynham Road
Bishops Stortford, Herts CM23 5PE
Website: www.snaptheatre.co.uk
e-mail: info@snaptheatre.co.uk
Fax: 01279 506694   Tel: 01279 461607

SPANNER IN THE WORKS
155 Station Road, Sidcup, Kent DA15 7AA
Website: www.spannerintheworks.org.uk
e-mail: info@spannerintheworks.org.uk   Tel: 020-8304 7660

SPARE TYRE THEATRE COMPANY
(Community Drama & Music Projects)
Hampstead Town Hall
213 Haverstock Hill, London NW3 4QP
Website: www.sparetyretheatrecompany.co.uk
e-mail: sttc@sparetyretheatrecompany.co.uk
     Tel/Fax: 020-7419 7007

SPECTACLE THEATRE
Coleg Morgannwg, Rhondda Campus
Llwynypia, Tonypandy CF40 2TQ
Website: www.spectacletheatre.co.uk
e-mail: info@spectacletheatre.co.uk
Fax: 01443 423080   Tel: 01443 430700

SPRINGBOARD THEATRE COMPANY
20 Lansdowne Road, London N10 2AU
e-mail: clive50@nsdf.org.uk   Tel: 020-8883 4586

STABLES GALLERY & ARTS CENTRE The
The Hayloft, Gladstone Park
Dollis Hill Lane, London NW2 6HT
e-mail: stablesgallery@msn.com   Tel: 020-8452 8655

TAG THEATRE COMPANY
18 Albion Street, Glasgow G1 1LH
Website: www.tag-theatre.co.uk
e-mail: info@tag-theatre.co.uk
Fax: 0141-552 0666   Tel: 0141-552 4949

TARA ARTS GROUP
(Gatinder Verma)
356 Garratt Lane, London SW18 4ES
Website: www.tara-arts.com
Fax: 020-8870 9540   Tel: 020-8333 4457

THEATR NA N'OG
Unit 3, Milland Road Industrial Estate, Neath SA11 1NJ
Website: www.theatr-nanog.co.uk
e-mail: cwmni@theatr-nanog.co.uk
Fax: 01639 647941   Tel: 01639 641771

THEATR POWYS
The Drama Centre
Tremont Road
Llandrindod Wells, Powys LD1 5EB
Website: www.theatrpowys.co.uk
e-mail: theatr.powys@powys.gov.uk
Fax: 01597 824381
Tel: 01597 824444

THEATRE BABEL
11 Sandyford Place
Glasgow G3 7NB
Website: www.theatrebabel.co.uk
e-mail: admin@theatrebabel.co.uk
Fax: 0141-249 9900
Tel: 0141-226 8806

THEATRE EXPRESS
(Write)
Spindle Cottage
Allens Farm
Digby Fen, Billinghay, Lincoln LN4 4DT
e-mail: perform@theatre-express.com

THEATRE IN EDUCATION TOURS (TIE TOURS)
1 The Sycamores, Celtic Way
Bleadon, Somerset BS24 0NF
Website: www.tietours.com
e-mail: tie@tietours.com
Tel: 01934 812977

THEATRE OF LITERATURE The
(Dramatised Readings)
51 The Cut
London SE1 8LF
e-mail: info@calderpublications.com
Fax: 020-7928 5930
Tel: 020-7633 0599

THEATRE RE:PUBLIC
1 Mellor Road
Leicester LE3 6HN
e-mail: theatrerepublic@hotmail.com
Tel: 0116-233 8432

THEATRE WORKSHOP
34 Hamilton Place
Edinburgh EH3 5AX
Website: www.theatre-workshop.com
Fax: 0131-220 0112
Tel: 0131-225 7942

THIRD PARTY PRODUCTIONS Ltd
87 St Thomas' Road
Hastings, East Sussex TN34 3LD
Website: www.thirdparty.demon.co.uk
e-mail: agleave@thirdparty.demon.co.uk
Tel: 01424 719320

TIME OF OUR LIVES MUSIC THEATRE Ltd
(Formerly Gilt & Gaslight Music Theatre Ltd)
5 Monkhams Drive
Woodford Green, Essex IG8 0LG
Website: www.toolmusictheatre.co.uk
e-mail: dympna@toolmusictheatre.co.uk
Tel/Fax: 020-8491 6695

TOBACCO FACTORY
Raleigh Road, Southville, Bristol BS3 1TF
Website: www.tobaccofactory.com
e-mail: admin@tobaccofactory.com
Fax: 0117-902 0162
Tel: 0117-902 0345

TRICYCLE THEATRE
269 Kilburn High Road
London NW6 7JR
Website: www.tricycle.co.uk
e-mail: admin@tricycle.co.uk
Fax: 020-7328 0795
Tel: 020-7372 6611

WAREHOUSE THEATRE COMPANY
Dingwall Road
Croydon CR0 2NF
Website: www.warehousetheatre.co.uk
e-mail: info@warehousetheatre.co.uk
Fax: 020-8688 6699
Tel: 020-8681 1257

WIGAN PIER THEATRE COMPANY
The 'Way We Were' Museum
Wigan Pier, Trencherfield Mill
Wigan, Lancashire WN3 3JQ
Website: www.wiganpier.net
e-mail: s.aitken@wlct.org
Tel: 01942 709305

WINCHESTER HAT FAIR, FESTIVAL OF STREET THEATRE
5A Jewry Street
Winchester, Hampshire SO23 8RZ
Website: www.hatfair.co.uk
e-mail: info@hatfair.co.uk
Fax: 01962 868957
Tel: 01962 849841

WOMEN & THEATRE BIRMINGHAM Ltd
220 Moseley Road
Highgate, Birmingham B12 0DG
e-mail: info@womenandtheatre.co.uk
Fax: 0121-446 4280
Tel: 0121-440 4203

Y TOURING THEATRE COMPANY
8-10 Lennox Road
Finsbury Park, London N4 3JQ
Website: www.ytouring.org.uk
e-mail: d.jackson@ytouring.org.uk
Fax: 020-7272 8413
Tel: 020-7272 5755

YELLOW EARTH THEATRE
Diorama Arts Centre
34 Osnaburgh Street
London NW1 3ND
Website: www.yellowearth.org
e-mail: admin@yellowearth.org
Fax: 020-7209 2327
Tel: 020-7209 2326

YORICK INTERNATIONALIST THEATRE ENSEMBLE
(Yorick Theatre & Film)
4 Duval Court, 36 Bedfordbury
Covent Garden, London WC2N 4DQ
e-mail: yorickx@hotmail.com
Tel/Fax: 020-7836 7637

YORKSHIRE WOMEN'S THEATRE COMPANY
(Touring Theatre in Health Education)
Host Media Centre
21 Savile Mount, Leeds LS7 3HZ
e-mail: admin@ywtheatre.com
Tel: 0113-200 7200

YOUNG VIC THEATRE COMPANY
Kennington Park, 2nd Floor
Chester House, 1-3 Brixton Road
London SW9 6DE
Website: www.youngvic.org
e-mail: info@youngvic.org
Fax: 020-7820 3355
Tel: 020-7820 3350

ZIP THEATRE
Newhampton Arts Centre
Dunkley Street
Wolverhampton WV1 4AN
Website: www.ziptheatre.co.uk
e-mail: cathy@ziptheatre.co.uk
Fax: 01902 572251
Tel: 01902 572250

6:15 THEATRE COMPANY
22 Brookfield Mansions, Highgate West Hill, London N6 6AS
Website: www.six15.dircon.co.uk
e-mail: six15@dircon.co.uk
Fax: 020-8340 5696   Tel: 020-8342 8239

ACTION TRANSPORT THEATRE COMPANY
Whitby Hall, Stanney Lane
Ellesmere Port, Cheshire CH65 9AE
Website: www.actiontransporttheatre.co.uk
e-mail: info@actiontransporttheatre.co.uk
                                        Tel: 0151-357 2120

ACTIONWORK
1 The Sycamores, Celtic Way, Bleadon, Somerset BS24 0NF
Website: www.actionwork.com
e-mail: admin@actionwork.com   Tel: 01934 815163

ASHCROFT YOUTH THEATRE
Ashcroft Academy of Dramatic Art
Malcolm Primary School
Malcolm Road, Penge, London SE20 8RH
Website: www.ashcroftacademy.co.uk
e-mail: geri.ashcroftacademy@tiscali.co.uk
Mobile: 07799 791586   Tel: 020-8693 8088

BARKING DOG THEATRE COMPANY
18 Hayley Bell Gardens, Bishop's Stortford, Herts CM23 3HB
Website: www.barkingdog.co.uk
e-mail: pat@barkingdog.co.uk
Fax: 01279 465386   Tel: 01279 465550

BECK THEATRE
Grange Road, Hayes, Middx UB3 2UE   Tel: 020-8561 7506

BIG WOODEN HORSE THEATRE FOR YOUNG PEOPLE
30 Northfield Road, West Ealing, London W13 9SY
Website: www.bigwoodenhorse.com
e-mail: info@bigwoodenhorse.com   Tel: 020-8567 8431

BIRMINGHAM STAGE COMPANY The
Suite 228 The Linen Hall, 162 Regent Street
London W1B 5TG
Website: www.birminghamstage.net
e-mail: info@birminghamstage.net
Fax: 020-7437 3395   Tel: 020-7437 3391

BITESIZE THEATRE COMPANY
8 Green Meadows, New Broughton, Wrexham LL11 6SG
Website: www.bitesizetheatre.co.uk
Fax: 01978 358315   Tel: 01978 358320

BLAH BLAH BLAH THEATRE COMPANY The
East Leeds Family Learning Centre
Brooklands View, Leeds LS14 6SA
Website: www.blahs.co.uk
e-mail: admin@blahs.co.uk
Fax: 0113-224 3685   Tel: 0113-224 3171

BLUE HAT PRODUCTIONS
43 Radwinter Road, Saffron Walden, Essex CB11 3HU
Website: www.sillybillybluehat.com
e-mail: ksweeney@ntlworld.com
Mobile: 07811 175351   Tel: 01799 502569

BLUNDERBUS THEATRE COMPANY Ltd
1st Floor, The Brook Theatre
Old Town Hall, Chatham, Kent ME4 4SE
Website: www.blunderbus.co.uk
e-mail: admin@blunderbus.co.uk
Fax: 01634 818138   Tel: 01634 818136

BOOSTER CUSHION THEATRE COMPANY
1st Floor, Building B, Chocolate Factory, Clarendon Road
London N22 6XJ
Website: www.boostercushion.com
e-mail: boostercushion@hotmail.com
Fax: 020-8365 8686   Tel: 01727 873874

BORDERLINE THEATRE COMPANY
(Producer: Eddie Jackson)
North Harbour Street, Ayr KA8 8AA
Website: www.borderlinetheartre.co.uk
e-mail: enquiries@borderlinetheatre.co.uk
Fax: 01292 263825   Tel: 01292 281010

CAUGHT IN THE ACT
The Brix, Brixton Hill, London SW2 1JF
Website: www.caughtintheact.co.uk
e-mail: cita@caughtintheact.co.uk   Tel/Fax: 020-7733 2950

CHALKFOOT THEATRE ARTS
(Artistic Director: Philip Dart)
Central Studios, 36 Park Place, Margate, Kent CT9 1LE
Website: www.chalkfoot.org.uk
e-mail: info@chalkfoot.org.uk   Tel: 01843 280077

CHICKEN SHED THEATRE
(Artistic Director: Mary Ward MBE)
Chase Side, Southgate, London N14 4PE
Website: www.chickenshed.org.uk
e-mail: info@chickenshed.org.uk
Minicom: 020-8350 0676   Tel: 020-8351 6161

CIRCUS MANIACS YOUTH CIRCUS
(International Award-Winning Youth Circus Company)
Office 8A, The Kingswood Foundation, Britannia Road
Kingswood, Bristol BS15 8DB
e-mail: youthcircus@circusmaniacs.com
Mobile: 07977 247287   Tel/Fax: 0117-947 7042

CLWYD THEATRE CYMRU THEATRE FOR YOUNG PEOPLE
(Contact - Education Administator)
Mold, Flintshire CH7 1YA
Website: www.clywd-theatr-cymru.co.uk
e-mail: education@clwyd-theatr-cymru.co.uk
Fax: 01352 701558   Tel: 01352 701575

COMPLETE WORKS THEATRE COMPANY Ltd The
(Artistic Director: Phil Evans)
12 Willowford, Bancroft Park, Milton Keynes
Buckinghamshire MK13 0RH
Website: www.tcw.org.uk   e-mail: info@tcw.org.uk
Fax: 01908 320263   Tel: 01908 316256

CRAGRATS Ltd
The Mill, Dunford Road, Holmfirth, Huddersfield HD9 2AR
Website: www.cragrats.com
e-mail: katehobson@cragrats.com
Fax: 01484 686212   Tel: 01484 686451

CTC THEATRE
Arts Centre, Vane Terrace
Darlington, County Durham DL3 7AX
Website: www.ctctheatre.org.uk
e-mail: ctc@ctctheatre.org.uk
Fax: 01325 369404   Tel: 01325 352004

DANCE FOR EVERYONE Ltd
30 Sevington Road, London NW4 3RX
Website: www.dfe.org.uk
e-mail: orders@dfe.org.uk   Tel: 020-8202 7863

DAYLIGHT THEATRE
66 Middle Street, Stroud
Glos GL5 1EA   Tel: 01453 763808

Twisting Yarn Theatre
Theatre and Theatre-in-Education
The Alhambra Theatre, Morley Street, Bradford BD7 1AJ
Tel: 01274 437490   Fax: 01274 437571
E-mail: twisting-yarn@bradford.gov.uk   Website: www.bradford-theatres.co.uk

DONNA MARIA COMPANY
16 Bell Meadow, Dulwich, London SE19 1HP
Website: www.donna-marias-world.co.uk
e-mail: info@donna-marias-world.co.uk   Tel: 020-8670 7814

DRAGON DRAMA
(Theatre Company, Tuition, Workshops, Parties)
1B Station Road, Hampton Wick, Kingston, Surrey KT1 4HG
Website: www.dragondrama.co.uk
e-mail: info@dragondrama.co.uk   Tel/Fax: 020-8943 1504

EUROPA CLOWN THEATRE SHOW
36 St Lukes Road, Tunbridge Wells, Kent TN4 9JH
Website: www.clownseuropa.co.uk   Tel: 01892 537964

EUROPEAN THEATRE COMPANY The
39 Oxford Avenue, London SW20 8LS
Website: www.europeantheatre.co.uk
e-mail: admin@europeantheatre.co.uk
Fax: 020-8544 1999   Tel: 020-8544 1994

FUTURES THEATRE COMPANY
The Deptford Albany, Douglas Way, London SE8 4AG
Website: www.futurestheatrecompany.co.uk
e-mail: info@futurestheatrecompany.co.uk
Fax: 020-8694 0289   Tel: 020-8694 8655

GAZEBO TIE COMPANY Ltd
Unit 37 Imex House, Imex Business Park
Upper Villiers Street, Wolverhampton WV2 4XE
Website: www.gazebotie.co.uk   e-mail: gazebotie@tiscali.co.uk
Fax: 01902 313229   Tel: 01902 313009

GREENWICH & LEWISHAM'S YOUNG PEOPLES THEATRE (GYPT)
Building 18, Royal Arsenal West, Woolwich, London SE18 6ST
Website: www.gypt.co.uk
e-mail: postbox@gypt.co.uk
Fax: 020-8317 8595   Tel: 020-8854 1316

GROUP 64 YOUTH THEATRE
Putney Arts Theatre, Ravenna Road, London SW15 6AW
Website: www.putneyartstheatre.org.uk
Fax: 020-8788 6940   Tel: 020-8788 6943

GWENT TIE COMPANY
The Drama Centre Pen-y-pound
Abergavenny, Monmouthshire NP7 5UD
Website: www.gwenttie.co.uk
e-mail: gwenttie@aol.com
Fax: 01873 853910   Tel: 01873 853167

HACKNEY YOUNG PEOPLE'S YOUTH THEATRE
Hoxton Hall Theatre & Arts Centre, 130 Hoxton Street
London N1 6SH
Website: www.hoxtonhall.co.uk
e-mail: admin@hoxtonhall.co.uk
Fax: 020-7729 3815   Tel: 020-7684 0060

HALF MOON YOUNG PEOPLE'S THEATRE
43 White Horse Road, London E1 0ND
Website: www.halfmoon.org.uk
e-mail: admin@halfmoon.org.uk
Fax: 020-7709 8914   Tel: 020-7265 8138

IMAGE MUSICAL THEATRE
23 Sedgeford Road, Shepherd's Bush, London W12 0NA
Website: www.imagemusicaltheatre.co.uk
e-mail: brian.thresh@btconnect.com
Fax: 020-8749 9294   Tel: 020-8743 9380

IMPACT ON LEARNING
Impact Universal, Hopebank House, Woodhead Road
Honley, Huddersfield HD6 9PF
Website: www.impactonlearning.com
e-mail: lisa.nordan@impactonlearning.com
Fax: 01484 660088   Tel: 01484 660077

INTERPLAY THEATRE
Armley Ridge Road, Leeds LS12 3LE
Website: www.interplaytheatre.org
e-mail: info@interplaytheatre.org   Tel: 0113-263 8556

KINETIC THEATRE COMPANY Ltd
Suite H, The Jubilee Centre
Lombard Road, Wimbledon, London SW19 3TZ
Website: www.kinetictheatre.co.uk
e-mail: sarah@kinetictheatre.co.uk
Fax: 020-8286 2645   Tel: 020-8286 2613

KOMEDIA
44-47 Gardner Street, Brighton BN1 1UN
Website: www.komedia.co.uk   e-mail: info@komedia.co.uk
Fax: 01273 647102   Tel: 01273 647101

LANGUAGE ALIVE!
The Play House, Longmore Street, Birmingham B12 9ED
Website: www.theplayhouse.org.uk
e-mail: info@theplayhouse.org.uk
Fax: 0121-464 5713   Tel: 0121-464 5712

LEIGHTON BUZZARD YOUTH THEATRE
1 Clifford Avenue, Bletchley, Milton Keynes MK2 2LT
Website: www.musicalandy.co.uk
e-mail: info@musicalandy.co.uk
Mobile: 07736 520930   Tel: 01908 374223

LITTLE ACTORS THEATRE COMPANY
12 Hardy Close, Surrey Quays, London SE16 6RT
e-mail: littleactorstheatrecompany@hotmail.com
Fax: 0870 1645895   Tel: 020-7231 6083

M6 THEATRE COMPANY
Hamer CP School, Albert Royds Street, Rochdale OL16 2SU
Website: www.m6theatre.co.uk   e-mail: info@m6theatre.co.uk
Fax: 01706 712601   Tel: 01706 355898

MAGIC CARPET THEATRE
18 Church Street, Sutton-on-Hull HU7 4TS
Website: www.magiccarpettheatre.com
e-mail: admin@magiccarpettheatre.com
Fax: 01482 787362   Tel: 01482 709939

MERSEYSIDE YOUNG PEOPLE'S THEATRE COMPANY
13 Hope Street, Liverpool L1 9BH
e-mail: mail@mypt.uk.com   Tel/Fax: 0151-708 0877

MUZIKANSKY YOUTH & COMMUNITY
The Forum, Fonthill, The Common
Tunbridge Wells, Kent TN4 9NQ
Website: www.mzky.co.uk
e-mail: admin@mzky.co.uk   Tel/Fax: 01892 542260

NATIONAL ASSOCIATION OF YOUTH THEATRES (NAYT)
Arts Centre, Vane Terrace
Darlington, County Durham DL3 7AX
Website: www.nayt.org.uk
e-mail: naytuk@btconnect.com
Fax: 01325 363313   Tel: 01325 363330

NATIONAL STUDENT THEATRE COMPANY
20 Lansdowne Road, London N10 2AU
Website: www.studentdrama.org.uk/nstc
e-mail: clive50@nsdf.org.uk
Fax: 020-8883 7142   Tel: 020-8883 4586

NATIONAL TRUST THEATRE The
(TMA Member)
Sutton House, 2 & 4 Homerton High Street
Hackney, London E9 6JQ
Website: www.nationaltrust.org.uk/learning
e-mail: theatre@nationaltrust.org.uk
Fax: 020-8985 2343   Tel: 020-8986 0242

NATIONAL YOUTH THEATRE OF GREAT BRITAIN
443-445 Holloway Road, London N7 6LW
Website: www.nyt.org.uk
e-mail: info@nyt.org.uk
Fax: 020-7281 8246   Tel: 020-7281 3863

NETTLEFOLD The
The Nettlefold, West Norwood Library Centre
1 Norwood High Street, London SE27 9JX
Fax: 020-7926 8071   Tel: 020-7926 8070

OILY CART
Smallwood School Annexe
Smallwood Road, London SW17 0TW
Website: www.oilycart.org.uk   e-mail: oilies@oilycart.org.uk
Fax: 020-8672 0792   Tel: 020-8672 6329

ONATTI THEATRE COMPANY
(Artistic Director: Andrew Bardwell)
9 Field Close, Warwick, Warwickshire CV34 4QD
Website: www.onatti.co.uk
e-mail: info@onatti.co.uk
Fax: 0870 1643629   Tel: 01926 495220

PANDEMONIUM TOURING PARTNERSHIP
228 Railway St, Cardiff CF24 2NJ   Tel: 029-2047 2060

PARASOL THEATRE FOR CHILDREN
(Artistic Director: Richard Gill)
Garden House, 4 Sunnyside, Wimbledon, London SW19 4SL
Website: www.parasoltheatre.co.uk
e-mail: parasoltheatre@waitrose.com
Fax: 020-8946 0228   Tel: 020-8946 9478

PAUL'S THEATRE COMPANY
Fairkytes Arts Centre
51 Billet Lane, Hornchurch, Essex RM11 1AX
Website: www.paulstheatreschool.co.uk
e-mail: info@paulstheatreschool.co.uk
Fax: 01708 475286   Tel: 01708 447123

PIED PIPER COMPANY (TIE)
(In association with The Yvonne Arnaud Theatre Guildford)
1 Lilian Place, Coxcombe Lane
Chiddingfold, Surrey GU8 4QA
e-mail: twpiedpiper@aol.com   Tel/Fax: 01428 684022

PLAYTIME THEATRE COMPANY
18 Bennells Avenue, Whitstable, Kent CT5 2HP
Website: www.playtime.dircon.co.uk
e-mail: playtime@dircon.co.uk
Fax: 01227 266648   Tel: 01227 266272

POLKA THEATRE
240 The Broadway, Wimbledon SW19 1SB
Website: www.polkatheatre.com
e-mail: admin@polkatheatre.com
Fax: 020-8545 8365   Tel: 020-8545 8320

Q20 THEATRE COMPANY
19 Wellington Crescent, Shipley
West Yorkshire BD18 3PH
e-mail: info@q20theatre.co.uk   Tel: 0845 1260632

QUAKER YOUTH THEATRE
Ground Floor, 1 The Lodge
1046 Bristol Road, Birmingham B29 6LJ
Website: www.leaveners.org
e-mail: qyt@leaveners.org
Fax: 0121-414 0090   Tel: 0121-414 0099

QUANTUM THEATRE FOR SCIENCE
(Artistic Directors: Michael Whitmore, Jessica Selous)
The Old Button Factory
1-11 Bannockburn Road, Plumstead, London SE18 1ET
Website: www.quantumtheatre.co.uk
e-mail: office@quantumtheatre.co.uk Tel: 020-8317 9000

QUERCUS THEATRE COMPANY
(Director: Therese Kitchin)
33 Broadlands Avenue
Shepperton, Middlesex TW17 9DJ
Website: www.quercustheatrecompany.org.uk
e-mail: quercus@quercustheatrecompany.org.uk
                                    Tel: 01932 252182

QUICKSILVER THEATRE COMPANY
(National Touring - New Writing for the under 12's)
4 Enfield Road, London N1 5AZ
Website: www.quicksilvertheatre.org.uk
e-mail: talktous@quicksilvertheatre.org
Fax: 020-7254 3119   Tel: 020-7241 2942

REDROOFS THEATRE COMPANY
The Novello Theatre, Sunninghill, Nr Ascot
Berkshire SL5 9NE   Tel: 01344 620881

ROUNDABOUT THEATRE IN EDUCATION
Nottingham Playhouse, Wellington Circus, Notts NG1 5AF
e-mail: roundabout@nottinghamplayhouse.co.uk
Fax: 0115-953 9055   Tel: 0115-947 4361

ROYAL & DERNGATE THEATRES
19-21 Guildhall Road, Northampton NN1 1DP
e-mail: education@ntt.org   Tel: 01604 627566

ROYAL COURT YOUNG WRITERS PROGRAMME
(Playwriting Projects for Young People aged 13-25)
The Site, Royal Court Theatre, Sloane Sq, London SW1W 8AS
Website: www.royalcourttheatre.com
e-mail: ywp@royalcourttheatre.com
Fax: 020-7565 5001   Tel: 020-7565 5050

SCOTTISH YOUTH THEATRE
3rd Floor, Forsyth House, 111 Union Street, Glasgow G1 3TA
Website: www.scottishyouththeatre.org
e-mail: info@scottishyouththeatre.org
Fax: 0141-221 9123   Tel: 0141-221 5127

SEAGULL THEATRE OF THE GORGE Ltd
(Theatre in Education)
(Artistic Directors: Margo Cooper & Sian Murray)
16 Victoria Road, Much Wenlock
Salop TF13 6AL   Tel/Fax: 01952 727803

SEAHORSE THEATRE COMPANY The
Ealing House, 33 Hanger Lane, London W5 3HJ
e-mail: verona.chard@vampevents.com Tel: 020-8997 3355

SHAKESPEARE 4 KIDZ THEATRE COMPANY The
42 Station Road East, Oxted, Surrey RH8 0PG
Website: www.shakespeare4kidz.com
e-mail: office@shakepeare4kidz.com
Fax: 01883 730384   Tel: 01883 723444

SHARED EXPERIENCE YOUTH THEATRE
The Soho Laundry
9 Dufours Place, London W1F 7SJ
e-mail: admin@sharedexperience.org.uk
Fax: 020-7287 8763   Tel: 020-7434 9248

SHEFFIELD THEATRES
(Education Administator: Sue Burley, Education Director:
Karen Simpson)
55 Norfolk Street, Sheffield S1 1DA
Website: www.sheffieldtheatres.co.uk/education
Fax: 0114-249 6003   Tel: 0114-249 5999

SNAP THEATRE COMPANY
29 Raynham Road, Bishop's Stortford, Herts CM23 5PE
Website: www.snaptheatre.co.uk
e-mail: info@snaptheatre.co.uk
Fax: 01279 506694   Tel: 01279 461607

SPECTACLE THEATRE
Coleg Morgannwg, Rhondda Campus
Llwynypia, Tonypandy CF40 2TQ
Website: www.spectacletheatre.co.uk
e-mail: info@spectacletheatre.co.uk
Fax: 01443 423080   Tel: 01443 430700

STORYTELLERS THEATRE COMPANY The
Bridge Farm, 249 Hawes Side Lane, Blackpool FY4 4AA
Website: www.pendleproductions.co.uk
e-mail: admin@pendleproductions.co.uk
                                    Tel/Fax: 01253 839375

TEAM PLAYERS THEATRE COMPANY
Lingfield Countryside Centre, Mount Pleasant Way
Coulby Newham, Middlesbrough TS8 0XF
Fax: 01642 577121   Tel: 01642 592648

THEATR IOLO Ltd
The Old School Building
Cefn Road, Mynachdy, Cardiff CF14 3HS
Website: www.theatriolo.com
e-mail: admin@theatriolo.com
Fax: 029-2052 2225   Tel: 029-2061 3782

THEATRE CENTRE
(National Touring & New Writing for Young Audiences)
Units 7 & 8, Toynbee Workshops
3 Gunthorpe Street, London E1 7RQ
Website: www.theatre-centre.co.uk
e-mail: admin@theatre-centre.co.uk
Fax: 020-7377 1376   Tel: 020-7377 0379

THEATRE IN EDUCATION TOURS (TIE TOURS)
1 The Sycamores, Celtic Way, Bleadon, Somerset BS24 0NF
Website: www.tietours.com
e-mail: tie@tietours.com   Tel: 01934 812977

THEATRE WORKSHOP Ltd
18 Weston Lane, Crewe, Cheshire CW2 5AN
Website: www.theatreworkshop.co.uk
e-mail: tw4kids@globalnet.co.uk
Fax: 07020 982098   Tel: 07020 962096

TICKLISH ALLSORTS SHOW
Cremyll, Marshmead Close
Clarendon, Salisbury, Wiltshire SP5 3DD
Website: www.ticklishallsorts.co.uk
e-mail: garynunn@lineone.net   Tel/Fax: 01722 711800

TIEBREAK THEATRE COMPANY
42-58 St George's Street
Norwich NR3 1AB
Website: www.tiebreak-theatre.com
e-mail: info@tiebreak-theatre.com
Fax: 01603 666096   Tel: 01603 665899

TRICYCLE THEATRE
(Education Director: Gillian Christie)
269 Kilburn High Road, London NW6 7JR
Website: www.tricycle.co.uk
e-mail: education@tricycle.co.uk   Tel: 020-7372 6611

TWISTING YARN THEATRE
Alhambra Theatre
Morley Street, Bradford BD7 1AJ
Website: www.bradford-theatres.co.uk
e-mail: twisting-yarn@bradford.gov.uk
Fax: 01274 437571   Tel: 01274 437490

UNICORN
St Mark's Studios, Chillingworth Road, London N7 8QJ
Website: www.unicorntheatre.com
e-mail: admin@unicorntheatre.com
Fax: 020-7700 3870   Tel: 020-7700 0702

WEST YORKSHIRE PLAYHOUSE TOURING PRODUCTIONS
West Yorkshire Playhouse
Playhouse Square, Quarry Hill, Leeds LS2 7UP
e-mail: gail.mcintyre@wyp.org.uk   Tel: 0113-213 7225

WHIRLIGIG THEATRE
(National Touring Company)
14 Belvedere Drive, Wimbledon SW19 7BY
e-mail: whirligig.theatre@virgin.net
Fax: 020-8879 7648   Tel: 020-8947 1732

THEATRE - ENGLISH SPEAKING IN EUROPE

■ **AUSTRIA**
   VIENNA
Vienna's English Theatre
(See website for casting requirements)
VIENNA, UK Representative: VM Theatre Productions Ltd
16 The Street, Ash, Kent CT3 2HJ
Website: www.englishtheatre.at   Tel/Fax: 01304 813330
Casting: Vanessa Mallatratt

■ **DENMARK**
   COPENHAGEN
The English Theatre of Copenhagen
London Toast Theatre
Kochsvej 18, 1812 Fred C. Copenhagen Denmark
Website: www.londontoast.dk
e-mail: mail@londontoast.dk   Tel: + 45 33 22 8686
Artistic Director: Vivienne McKee
Administrator: Soren Hall

■ **FRANCE**
   PARIS
ACT Company
51 rue Hoche, 92240 Malakoff, France
Website: www.actheatre.com
e-mail: andrew.wilson@wanadoo.fr
Fax: + 33 1 46 56 23 18   Tel: + 33 1 46 56 20 50
Artistic Director: Andrew Wilson
Administrator: Anne Wilson

■ **GERMANY**
   FRANKFURT
The English Theatre Frankfurt
P & S Productions
Top Flat, 51 Norroy Rd, London SW15 1PQ
Fax: 020-8788 8521   Tel: 020-8780 9115
e-mail: timsawens@msn.com

■ **GERMANY**
   HAMBURG
The English Theatre of Hamburg
Lerchenfeld 14, 22081 Hamburg, Germany
Website: www.englishtheatre.de
Fax: + 49 40 229 5040   Tel: + 49 40 227 7089
Contact: Robert Rumpf, Clifford Dean

■ **GERMAN**
   TOURING GERMANY
White Horse Theatre
Boerdenstrasse 17, 59494 Soest-Muellingsen, Germany
e-mail: theatre@whitehorse.de
Fax: + 49 29 21 339336   Tel: + 49 29 21 339339
Contact: Peter Griffith, Michael Dray

■ **HUNGARY**
   BUDAPEST
Merlin International Theatre
Gerloczy Utca 4, 1052 Budapest, Hungary
e-mail: angol@merlinszinhaz.hu
Fax: + 36 1 2660904   Tel: + 36 1 3179338
Contact: László Magács

■ **ICELAND**
   REYKJAVIK
Light Nights - The Summer Theatre
The Travelling Theatre
Baldursgata 37, IS-101 Reykjavik, Iceland
Fax: + 354 551 5015   Tel: + 354 551 9181
Artistic Director: Kristine G Magnus

■ **SWEDEN**
   STOCKHOLM
The English Theatre Company Ltd
(TMA Member)
Nybrogatan 35, 114 39 Stockholm, Sweden
Website: www.englishtheatre.se
e-mail: etc.ltd@telia.com
Fax: + 46 8 660 1159   Tel: + 46 8 662 4133
Artistic Director: Christer Berg

■ **UNITED KINGDOM**
   WARWICK
Onatti Theatre Company
9 Field Close
Warwick, Warwickshire CV34 4QD
Website: www.onatti.co.uk   e-mail: info@onatti.co.uk
Fax: 0870 1643629   Tel: 01926 495220
Artistic Director: Andrew Bardwell

■ **UNITED KINGDOM**
   OXFORD
Theatre From Oxford (Touring Europe & Beyond)
69-71 Oxford Street
Woodstock, Oxford OX20 1TJ
Contact: Robert Southam (Write)

ADELPHI
Strand, London WC2E 7NN
Manager: --------------------
Stage Door: 020-7836 1166
Box Office: 0870 4030303

ALBERY
85 St Martin's Lane, London WC2N 4AU
Manager: 020-7438 9700
Stage Door: 020-7438 9700
Box Office: 020-7438 9705

ALDWYCH
Aldwych, London WC2B 4DF
Manager: 020-7836 5537
Stage Door: 020-7836 5537
Box Office: 0870 4000805
Website: www.aldwychtheatre.com

ALMEIDA
Almeida Street, London N1 1TA
Manager: 020-7288 4900
Stage Door: --------------------
Box Office: 020-7359 4404

APOLLO
Shaftesbury Avenue, London W1D 7EZ
Manager: 020-7850 8701
Stage Door: 020-7850 8700
Box Office: 0870 8901101

APOLLO VICTORIA
17 Wilton Road, London SW1V 1LG
Manager   020-7834 6318
Stage Door: 020-7834 7231
Box Office: 0870 4000650
Website: www.ticketmaster.co.uk

ARTS THEATRE
6-7 Great Newport Street, London WC2H 7JB
Manager: 020-7836 2132
Stage Door: 020-7836 2132
Box Office: 020-7836 3334
Website: www.artstheatre.com
e-mail: foh@artstheatre.com

BARBICAN
Barbican, London EC2Y 8DS
Manager: 020-7638 4141
Stage Door: 020-7628 3351
Box Office: 020-7638 8891
Website: www.barbican.org.uk

CAMBRIDGE
Earlham Street, Seven Dials
Covent Garden, London WC2 9HU
Manager: 020-7850 8711
Stage Door: 020-7850 8710
Box Office: 0870 8901102

CARLING APOLLO HAMMERSMITH
Queen Caroline Street, London W6 9QH
Manager: 020-8563 3800
Stage Door: --------------------
Box Office: 0870 6063400

COLISEUM (English National Opera)
St Martin's Lane, London WC2N 4ES
Manager: 020-7836 0111
Stage Door: 020-7836 1416
Box Office: 020-7632 8300

COMEDY
Panton Street, London SW1Y 4DN
Manager: 020-7321 5310
Stage Door: 020-7321 5300
Box Office: 020-7369 1731

CRITERION
Piccadilly, London SW1Y 4XA
Manager: 020-7839 8811
Stage Door: 020-7839 8811
Box Office: 020-7839 4489

DOMINION
268-269 Tottenham Court Road, London W1T 7AQ
Manager: --------------------
Stage Door: 020-7927 0900
Box Office: 0870 1690116
Website: www.london-dominion.co.uk

DONMAR WAREHOUSE
41 Earlham Street, London WC2H 9LX
Admin: 020-7845 5800
Stage Door: 020-7438 9200
Box Office: 0870 060 6624
Website: www.donmarwarehouse.com
e-mail: office@donmarwarehouse.com

DUCHESS
Catherine Street, London WC2B 5LA
Manager: 020-7850 8721
Stage Door: 020-7850 8720
Box Office: 020-7850 8725

DUKE OF YORK'S
St Martin's Lane, London WC2N 4BG
Manager: 020-7836 4615
Stage Door: 020-7836 4615
Box Office: 020-7369 1791

FORTUNE
Russell Street, Covent Garden, London WC2B 5HH
Manager: 020-7010 7900
Stage Door: 020-7010 7900
Box Office: 020-7369 1737

GARRICK
Charing Cross Road, London WC2H 0HH
Manager: 020-7850 8731
Stage Door: 020-7850 8730
Box Office: 020-7494 5085

GIELGUD
Shaftesbury Avenue, London W1D 6AR
Manager: 020-7850 8741
Stage Door: 020-7850 8740
Box Office: 0870 8901105

HACKNEY EMPIRE
291 Mare Street, London E8 1EJ
Manager: 020-8510 4500
Stage Door: 020-8510 4515
Box Office: 020-8985 2424
Website: www.hackneyempire.co.uk
e-mail: info@hackneyempire.co.uk

HAMPSTEAD THEATRE
Eton Avenue, Swiss Cottage, London NW3 3EU
Manager:	020-7449 4200
Stage Door:	----------------------
Box Office:	020-7722 9301
Website:	www.hampsteadtheatre.com
e-mail:	info@hampsteadtheatre.com

HER MAJESTY'S
Haymarket, London SW1Y 4QL
Manager:	020-7850 8750
Stage Door:	020-7850 8750
Box Office:	0870 8901106

LYCEUM
21 Wellington Street, London WC2E 7RQ
Manager:	020-7420 8191
Stage Door:	020-7420 8100
Box Office:	020-7420 8114

LYRIC
Shaftesbury Avenue, London W1D 7ES
Manager:	020-7850 8761
Stage Door:	020-7850 8760
Box Office:	0870 8901107

LYRIC THEATRE HAMMERSMITH
King Street, London W6 0QL
Manager:	020-8741 0824
Stage Door:	020-8741 0824
Box Office:	08700 500511
Website:	www.lyric.co.uk
e-mail:	enquiries@lyric.co.uk

NATIONAL
South Bank, London SE1 9PX
Admin:	020-7452 3333
Stage Door:	020-7452 3333
Box Office:	020-7452 3000
Website:	www.nt-online.org

NEW AMBASSADORS
West Street, London WC2H 9ND
Manager:	020-7395 5400
Stage Door:	020-7395 5400
Box Office:	020-7369 1761
Website:	www.newambassadors.com
e-mail:	newambassadors@theambassadors.com

NEW LONDON
Drury Lane, London WC2B 5PW
Manager:	020-7242 9802
Stage Door:	020-7242 9802
Box Office:	0870 8900141

OLD VIC The
Waterloo Road, London SE1 8NB
Manager:	020-7928 2651
Stage Door:	020-7928 2651
Box Office:	0870 0606628
Website:	www.oldvictheatre.com
e-mail:	info@oldvictheatre.com

OPEN AIR THEATRE
Inner Circle, Regent's Park, London NW1 4NR
Manager:	020-7935 5756
Stage Door:	020-7935 5756
Box Office:	08700 601811

PALACE
Shaftesbury Avenue, London W1D 5AY
Manager:	020-7434 0088
Stage Door:	020-7434 0088
Box Office:	0870 8955579
Website:	www.rutheatres.com
e-mail:	info@rutheatres.com

PALLADIUM
Argyll Street, London W1F 7TF
Manager:	020-7850 8777
Stage Door:	020-7850 8770
Box Office:	0870 8901108

PEACOCK
(See SADLER'S WELLS IN THE WEST END)

PHOENIX
Charing Cross Road, London WC2H 0JP
Manager:	--------------------
Stage Door:	020-7438 9600
Box Office:	020-7438 9605

PICCADILLY
Denman Street, London W1D 7DY
Manager:	020-7478 8812
Stage Door:	020-7478 8800
Box Office:	020-7478 8805

PLAYHOUSE
Northumberland Avenue, London WC2N 5DE
Manager:	020-7839 4292
Stage Door:	020-7839 4292
Box Office:	020-7839 4401

PRINCE EDWARD
Old Compton Street, London W1D 4HS
Manager:	020-7437 2024
Stage Door:	020-7439 3041
Box Office:	0870 8509191
Website:	www.delfont-mackintosh.com

PRINCE OF WALES
Coventry Street, London W1D 6AS
Manager:	020-7766 2101
Stage Door:	020-7766 2100
Box Office:	020-7766 2104

QUEEN'S
51 Shaftesbury Avenue, London W1D 6BA
Manager:	020-7292 1351
Stage Door:	020-7292 1350
Box Office:	0870 8901110

ROYAL COURT
Sloane Square
London SW1W 8AS
Manager: 020-7565 5050
Stage Door: 020-7565 5050
Box Office: 020-7565 5000
Website: www.royalcourttheatre.com
e-mail: info@royalcourttheatre.com

ROYAL OPERA HOUSE
Covent Garden
London WC2E 9DD
Manager: 020-7240 1200
Stage Door: --------------------
Box Office: 020-7304 4000

SADLER'S WELLS
Rosebery Avenue, London EC1R 4TN
Manager: --------------------
Stage Door: 020-7863 8198
Box Office: 0870 7377737
Website: www.sadlerswells.com
e-mail: info@sadlerswells.com

SADLER'S WELLS IN THE WEST END
Peacock Theatre, Portugal Street
Kingsway, London WC2A 2HT
Manager: 020-7863 8204
Stage Door: 020-7863 8268
Box Office: 0870 7370337

SAVOY
Strand, London WC2R 0ET
Manager: 020-7240 1649
Stage Door: 020-7836 8117
Box Office: 0870 1648787

SHAFTESBURY
210 Shaftesbury Avenue
London WC2H 8DP
Manager: 020-7379 3345
Stage Door: 020-7379 3345
Box Office: 020-7379 5399
e-mail: jwilliams@toc.dltentertainment.co.uk

SHAKESPEARE'S GLOBE
21 New Globe Walk, Bankside, London SE1 9DT
Manager: 020-7902 1400
Stage Door: 020-7902 1400
Box Office: 020-7401 9919
Website: www.shakespeares-globe.org
e-mail: info@shakespearesglobe.com

SOHO THEATRE
21 Dean Street, London W1D 3NE
Manager: 020-7287 5060
Stage Door: --------------------
Box Office: 0870 4296883
Website: www.sohotheatre.com
e-mail: mail@sohotheatre.com

ST MARTIN'S
West Street, London WC2H 9NZ
Manager: 020-7497 0578
Stage Door: 020-7836 1086
Box Office: 020-7836 1443

STRAND
Aldwych, London WC2B 5LD
Manager: 020-7836 4144
Stage Door: 020-7836 4144
Box Office: 0870 8509170

THEATRE ROYAL
(Haymarket), London SW1Y 4HT
Manager: 020-7930 8890
Stage Door: 020-7930 8890
Box Office: 0870 9013356

THEATRE ROYAL DRURY LANE
Catherine Street, London WC2B 5JF
Manager: 020-7850-8793
Stage Door: 020-7850 8790
Box Office: 0870 8901109

TRAFALGAR STUDIOS AT THE WHITEHALL
14 Whitehall, London SW1A 2DY
Manager: 020-7321 5400
Stage Door: 020-7321 5400
Box Office: 020-7321 5405
e-mail: whitehall@theambassadors.com

UCL BLOOMSBURY
15 Gordon Street, London WC1H 0AH
Manager: 020-7679 2777
Stage Door: 020-7679 2922
Box Office: 020-7388 8822
Website: www.thebloomsbury.com
e-mail: blooms.theatre@ucl.ac.uk

VAUDEVILLE
404 Strand, London WC2R 0NH
Manager: 020-7836 1820
Stage Door: 020-7836 3191
Box Office: 020-7836 9987

VICTORIA PALACE
Victoria Street, London SW1E 5EA
Manager: 020-7828 0600
Stage Door: 020-7834 2781
Box Office: 0870 1658787

WYNDHAM'S
Charing Cross Road, London WC2H 0DA
Manager: 020-7438 9700
Stage Door: 020-7438 9700
Box Office: 020-7438 9755

YOUNG VIC
Kennington Park, 2nd Floor, Chester House
1-3 Brixton Road, London SW9 6DE
Manager: 020-7820 3350
Box Office: 020-7928 6363
Website: www.youngvic.org
e-mail: info@youngvic.org

ALBANY The
Douglas Way, Deptford, London SE8 4AG
Fax: 020-8469 2253   Tel: 020-8692 4446

ARCOLA THEATRE
(Artistic Director - Mehmet Ergen)
27 Arcola Street, Dalston
(Off Stoke Newington Road), London E8 2DJ
e-mail: info@arcolatheatre.com
Fax: 020-7503 1645
BO: 020-7503 1646   Admin: 020-7503 1645
Route: Victoria Line to Highbury & Islington, then North
London Line to Dalston Kingsland (Main Line) - 5 min walk.
Buses: 38 from West End, 149 from London Bridge or 30, 67,
76, 243

ARTSDEPOT
5 Nether Street, North Finchley, London N12 0GA
e-mail: info@artsdepot.co.uk
BO: 020-8449 0048

ASHCROFT THEATRE
Fairfield Halls, Park Lane, Croydon CR9 1DG
Website: www.fairfield.co.uk
e-mail: dbarr@fairfield.co.uk
BO: 020-8688 9291   Admin & SD: 020-8681 0821
Route: Victoria (Main Line) to East Croydon then 5 min
walk

BAC
Lavender Hill, London SW11 5TN
Website: www.bac.org.uk
e-mail: mailbox@bac.org.uk
Fax: 020-7978 5207
BO: 020-7223 2223   Admin: 020-7223 6557
Route: Victoria or Waterloo (Main Line) to Clapham
Junction then 5 min walk or Northern Line to Clapham
Common then 20 min walk

BARONS COURT THEATRE
'The Curtain's Up'
28A Comeragh Road
West Kensington, London W14 9RH
Fax: 020-7603 8935   Admin/BO: 020-8932 4747
Route: West Kensington or Barons Court tube

BATES Tristan THEATRE
(Theatre Manager - Suli Majithia)
The Actors Centre, 1A Tower Street
London WC2H 9NP
e-mail: act@actorscentre.co.uk
Fax: 020-7240 3896
BO: 020-7240 6283   Admin: 020-7240 3940 ext 213

BECK THEATRE
Grange Road, Hayes
Middlesex UB3 2UE
BO: 020-8561 8371   Admin: 020-8651 7506
Route: Metropolitan Line to Uxbridge then buses 207 or
607 (10 min) to Theatre or Paddington (Main Line) to Hayes
Harlington then buses 90, H98 or 195 (10 min)

BEDLAM THEATRE
11B Bristo Place
Edinburgh EH1 1EZ
Website: www.bedlamfringe.co.uk
e-mail: admin@bedlamfringe.co.uk
BO: 0131-225 9893   Admin/Fax: 0131-225 9873

BELLAIRS PLAYHOUSE
Millmead Terrace, Guildford GU2 4YT
e-mail: enquiries@conservatoire.org
BO: 01483 565787 (12-4 pm)   Admin: 01483 560701

BRENTWOOD THEATRE
(Theatre Administrator - Mark P Reed)
15 Shenfield Road, Brentwood, Essex CM15 8AG
Website: www.brentwood-theatre.org
Stage Door: 01277 226658
BO: 01277 200305   Admin/Fax: 01277 230833
Route: Liverpool Street (Main Line) to Brentwood, then 15
min walk

BRIDEWELL THEATRE The
Bride Lane, (Off Fleet Street), London EC4Y 8EQ
Website: www.bridewelltheatre.co.uk
e-mail: admin@bridewelltheatre.co.uk
Fax: 020-7583 5289
BO: 020-7936 3456   Admin: 020-7353 0259
Route: Blackfriars, St Paul's: City Thameslink. Fifteen
different bus routes

BUSH THEATRE
(Artistic Director - Mike Bradwell)
Shepherd's Bush Green, London W12 8QD
BO: 020-7610 4224
Production: 020-8743 5050   Admin: 020-7602 3703
Route: Central Line to Shepherd's Bush or Hammersmith &
City Line to Goldhawk Road or buses 49, 72*, 94*, 95, 207*,
220*, 237*, 260, 283, 295* or 607   * mobility bus

CAMDEN PEOPLE'S THEATRE
(Artistic Director - Chris Goode)
58-60 Hampstead Road, London NW1 2PY
Website: www.cpt.dircon.co.uk
e-mail: cpt@dircon.co.uk
Fax: 020-7813 3889   Tel: 020-7419 4841
Route: Victoria or Northern Line to Warren Street,
Metropolitan or Circle Line to Euston Square (2 min walk
either way)

CANAL CAFE THEATRE The
(Artistic Director - Emma Taylor)
The Bridge House, Delamere Terrace
Little Venice, London W2 6ND
Website: www.newsrevue.com
e-mail: mail@canalcafetheatre.com
Fax: 020-7266 1717
BO: 020-7289 6054   Admin: 020-7289 6056

CAPITAL ARTS THEATRE COMPANY
Capital Arts, Wyllyotts Centre
Darkes Lane, Potters Bar, Herts EN6 2HN
e-mail: capitalartstheatre@o2.co.uk
Mobile: 07885 232414   Tel/Fax: 020-8449 2342

CHANTICLEER THEATRE
(Webber Douglas Academy)
30 Clareville Street, London SW7 5AP
e-mail: webberdouglas@btconnect.com
Fax: 020-7373 5639   Tel: 020-7370 4154
Route: Piccadilly, District or Circle Line to Gloucester Road,
turn right, walk 300 yards then turn left into Clareville
Street

CHATS PALACE ARTS CENTRE
(Nick Reed)
42-44 Brooksby's Walk, Hackney, London E9 6DF
e-mail: chatspalace@hotmail.com
Fax: 020-8985 6878   Tel: 020-8533 0227

CHELSEA THEATRE
World's End Place, King's Road, London SW10 0DR
e-mail: admin@chelseatheatre.org.uk
Fax: 020-7352 2024   Tel: 020-7352 1967
Route: District or Circle Line to Sloane Square then short
bus ride 11 or 22 down King's Road

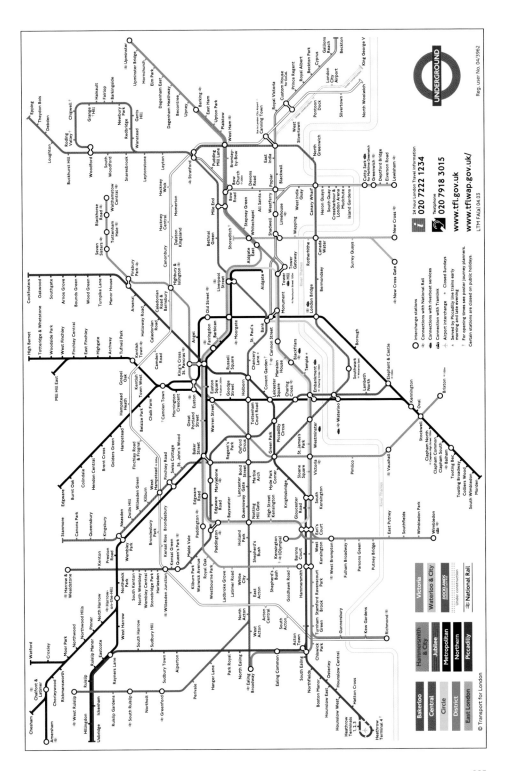

CHICKEN SHED THEATRE
(Artistic Director - Mary Ward MBE)
Chase Side, Southgate, London N14 4PE
Website: www.chickenshed.org.uk
e-mail: info@chickenshed.org.uk
Fax: 020-8292 0202   Minicom: 020-8350 0676
BO: 020-8292 9222   Admin: 020-8351 6161
Route: Piccadilly Line to Oakwood, turn left outside tube &
walk 8 min down Bramley Road or take 307 bus. Buses 298,
299, 699 or N19. Car parking available & easy access
parking by reservation

CHRIST'S HOSPITAL THEATRE
(Director - Jeff Mayhew)
Horsham, West Sussex RH13 7LW
e-mail: jm@christs-hospital.org.uk
BO: 01403 247434   Admin: 01403 247435

CLUB FOR ACTS & ACTORS The
(Concert Artistes Association)
(Bill Pertwee, Barbara Daniels)
20 Bedford St, London WC2E 9HP   Admin: 020-7836 3172
Route: Piccadilly or Northern Line to Leicester Square then
few mins walk

COCHRANE THEATRE
(Deidre Malynn)
Southampton Row, London WC1B 4AP
e-mail: info@cochranetheatre.co.uk
BO: 020-7269 1606   Admin: 020-7269 1600
Route: Central or Piccadilly Line to Holborn then 3 min
walk

COCKPIT THEATRE
Gateforth Street, London NW8 8EH
e-mail: admin@cockpittheatre.org.uk
Fax: 020-7258 2921
BO: 020-7258 2925   Admin: 020-7258 2920
Route: Tube to Marylebone/Edgware Road then short walk
or bus 139 to Lisson Grove & 6, 8 or 16 to Edgware Road

CORBETT THEATRE
(East 15 Acting School)
Rectory Lane, Loughton, Essex IG10 3RY
Website: www.east15.ac.uk
e-mail: east15@essex.ac.uk
Fax: 020-8508 7521   BO & Admin: 020-8508 5983
Route: Central Line (Epping Branch) to Debden then 6 min
walk

COURTYARD THEATRE The
(Artistic Director - June Abbott, General Manager - Tim Gill)
10 York Way, King's Cross, London N1 9AA
Website: www.thecourtyard.org.uk
e-mail: info@thecourtyard.org.uk
BO: 020-7833 0876   Admin/Fax: 020-7833 0870
Route: Side of King's Cross Station

CROYDON CLOCKTOWER
(Arts Programme Manager - Jonathan Kennedy)
Katharine Street, Croydon CR9 1ET
Website: www.croydon.gov.uk
e-mail: jonathan.kennedy@croydon.gov.uk
Fax: 020-8253 1003
BO: 020-8253 1030   Tel: 020-8253 1037

CUSTARD FACTORY
Gibb Street, Digbeth, Birmingham B9 4AA
Website: www.custardfactory.com
e-mail: post@custardfactory.com
Fax: 0121-604 8888   Tel: 0121-693 7777

DARTFORD ORCHARD THEATRE
Home Gardens, Dartford, Kent DA1 1ED
Website: www.orchardtheatre.co.uk
Fax: 01322 227122
BO: 01322 220000   Admin: 01322 220099
Route: Charing Cross (Main Line) to Dartford

DENCH Judi THEATRE
(See MOUNTVIEW THEATRE)

DIORAMA ARTS CENTRE
(Hire Venue)
34 Osnaburgh Street, London NW1 3ND
Website: www.diorama-arts.org.uk
e-mail: admin@diorama-arts.org.uk
Fax: 020-7813 3116   Admin: 020-7916 5467
Route: Circle & District Line to Great Portland Street then 1
min walk, or Victoria/Northern line to Warren Street then 5
min walk

DRILL HALL The
16 Chenies Street, London WC1E 7EX
Website: www.drillhall.co.uk
e-mail: admin@drillhall.co.uk
Fax: 020-7307 5062
BO: 020-7307 5060   Admin: 020-7307 5061
Route: Northern Line to Goodge Street then 1 min walk

EDINBURGH FESTIVAL FRINGE
180 High Street, Edinburgh EH1 1QS
Website: www.edfringe.com
e-mail: admin@edfringe.com
Fax: 0131-226 0016   Tel: 0131-226 0026

EDINBURGH UNIVERSITY THEATRE COMPANY
(See BEDLAM THEATRE)

EMBASSY THEATRE & STUDIOS
(Central School of Speech & Drama)
64 Eton Avenue, Swiss Cottage, London NW3 3HY
Website: www.cssd.ac.uk
e-mail: enquiries@cssd.ac.uk   Tel: 020-7722 8183
Route: Jubilee Line to Swiss Cottage then 1 min walk

ETCETERA THEATRE CLUB
(Directors - Zena Barrie and Michelle Flower)
Oxford Arms, 265 Camden High Street, London NW1 7BU
Website: www.etceteratheatre.com
e-mail: etc@etceteratheatre.com
Fax: 020-7482 0378   Admin/BO: 020-7482 4857

FINBOROUGH THEATRE
(Artistic Director - Neil McPherson)
The Finborough, 118 Finborough Road, London SW10 9ED
Website: www.finboroughtheatre.co.uk
e-mail: admin@finboroughtheatre.co.uk
Fax: 020-7835 1853
BO: 020-7373 3842   Admin: 020-7244 7439
Route: District or Piccadilly Line to Earls Court then 5 min
walk. Buses 74, 328, C1, C3, 74 then 3 min walk

GATE THEATRE
(Artistic Director - Thea Sharrock)
Above Prince Albert Pub
11 Pembridge Road, London W11 3HQ
Website: www.gatetheatre.co.uk
e-mail: gate@gatetheatre.co.uk
Fax: 020-7221 6055
BO: 020-7229 0706   Admin: 020-7229 5387
Route: Central, Circle or District Line to Notting Hill Gate
then 1 min walk

GREENWICH PLAYHOUSE
(Alice de Sousa)
Greenwich BR Station Forecourt
189 Greenwich High Road, London SE10 8JA
Website: www.galleontheatre.co.uk
e-mail: alice@galleontheatre.co.uk
Fax: 020-8310 7276   Tel: 020-8858 9256
Route: Main Line from Charing Cross, Waterloo East or
London Bridge, DLR to Greenwich

GREENWICH THEATRE
(Executive Director - Hilary Strong)
Crooms Hill, Greenwich, London SE10 8ES
Website: www.greenwichtheatre.org.uk
e-mail: info@greenwichtheatre.org.uk
Fax: 020-8858 8042
BO: 020-8858 7755   Admin: 020-8858 4447
Route: Jubilee Line (change Canary Wharf) then DLR to
Greenwich Cutty Sark, 3 min walk or Charing Cross (Main
Line) to Greenwich, 5 min walk

GUILDHALL SCHOOL OF MUSIC & DRAMA
Silk Street
Barbican, London EC2Y 8DT
e-mail: info@gsmd.ac.uk
Fax: 020-7256 9438   Tel: 020-7628 2571
Route: Hammersmith & City, Circle or Metropolitan line to
Barbican or Moorgate (also served by Northern line) then 5
min walk

HACKNEY EMPIRE THEATRE
291 Mare Street, Hackney, London E8 1EJ
BO: 020-8985 2424   Press/Admin: 020-8510 4500

HEN & CHICKENS THEATRE
Unrestricted View, Above Hen & Chickens Theatre Bar
109 St Paul's Road, Islington, London N1 2NA
Website: www.henandchickens.com
e-mail: james@henandchickens.com   Tel: 020-7704 2001
Route: Victoria Line or Main Line to Highbury & Islington
directly opposite station

ICA THEATRE
(No CV's, Venue only)
The Mall, London SW1Y 5AH
Website: www.ica.org.uk
Fax: 020-7873 0051
BO: 020-7930 3647   Admin: 020-7930 0493
Route: Nearest stations Piccadilly & Charing Cross

INVENTION ARTS
Lower Borough Walls, Bath BA1 1QR
e-mail: info@inventionarts.org   Tel: 01225 421700

JACKSONS LANE THEATRE
269A Archway Road, London N6 5AA
Website: www.jacksonslane.org.uk
e-mail: mail@jacksonslane.org.uk   Tel: 020-8340 5226

JERMYN STREET THEATRE
(Administrator - Penny Horner)
16B Jermyn Street, London SW1Y 6ST
Website: www.jermynstreettheatre.co.uk
Fax: 020-7287 3232
BO: 020-7287 2875   Admin: 020-7434 1443

KING'S HEAD THEATRE
(Artistic Director - Dan Crawford)
115 Upper Street, Islington, London N1 1QN
Website: www.kingsheadtheatre.org
BO: 020-7226 1916   Admin: 020-7226 8561
Route: Northern Line to Angel then 5 min walk. Approx
halfway between Angel and Highbury & Islington tube
stations

KING'S LYNN CORN EXCHANGE
Tuesday Market Place, King's Lynn, Norfolk PE30 1JW
Website: www.kingslynncornexchange.co.uk
e-mail: entertainment_admin@west-norfolk.gov.uk
Fax: 01553 762141
BO: 01553 764864   Admin: 01553 765565

KOMEDIA
(Artistic Directors: Theatre & Comedy - David Lavender.
Music, Cabaret & Children's Theatre - Marina Kobler)
44-47 Gardner Street, Brighton BN1 1UN
Website: www.komedia.co.uk
e-mail: info@komedia.co.uk
Fax: 01273 647102
BO: 01273 647100   Tel: 01273 647101

LANDMARK ARTS CENTRE
Ferry Road, Teddington Lock, Middlesex TW11 9NN
Website: www.landmarkartscentre.org
e-mail: landmarkinfo@aol.com
Fax: 020-8977 4830   Tel: 020-8977 7558

LANDOR THEATRE The
(Artistic Director - Robert McWhir)
70 Landor Road, London SW9 9PH
Website: www.landortheatre.co.uk
e-mail: info@landortheatre.co.uk   Admin/BO: 020-7737 7276
Route: Northern Line Clapham North then 2 min walk

LEIGHTON BUZZARD THEATRE
Lake Street, Leighton Buzzard
Bedfordshire LU7 1RX
Website: www.leightonbuzzardtheatre.co.uk
                                     Tel: 01525 850290

LILIAN BAYLIS THEATRE
(Information: Sadler's Wells Theatre)
Rosebery Avenue, London EC1R 4TN
Website: www.sadlerswells.com
e-mail: info@sadlerswells.com
BO: 0870 7377737   SD: 020-7863 8198

LIVE THEATRE
27 Broad Chare, Quayside
Newcastle upon Tyne NE1 3DQ
Website: www.live.org.uk
e-mail: info@live.org.uk
Fax: 0191-232 2224
BO: 0191-232 1232   Admin: 0191-261 2694

MACOWAN THEATRE
(LAMDA)
1-2 Logan Place, London W8 6QN
Website: www.lamda.org.uk
Fax: 020-7370 1980   Tel: 020-8834 0500
Route: District or Piccadilly Line to Earl's Court then 6 min
walk

MADDERMARKET THEATRE
(Artistic Director - Clare Goddard, General Manager -
Michael Lyas)
St John's Alley, Norwich NR2 1DR
Website: www.maddermarket.co.uk
e-mail: mmtheatre@btconnect.com
Fax: 01603 661357
BO: 01603 620917   Admin: 01603 626560

MAN IN THE MOON THEATRE
e-mail: manmoon@netcomuk.co.uk
Fax: 020-7351 1873   Admin: 07801 932321

MENIER CHOCOLATE FACTORY
Menier Chocolate Factory
51-53 Southwark Street
London SE1 1RU
Website: www.menierchocolatefactory.com
e-mail: office@menierchocolatefactory.com
Fax: 020-7378 1713   Tel: 020-7378 1712

MILLFIELD ARTS CENTRE
Silver Street, London N18 1PJ
Website: www.millfieldtheatre.co.uk
e-mail: info@millfieldtheatre.co.uk
Fax: 020-8807 3892
BO: 020-8807 6680   Admin: 020-8803 5283
Route: Liverpool Street (Main Line) to Silver Street or tube
to Turnpike Lane then bus 144, 15 min to Cambridge
Roundabout

MOUNTVIEW THEATRE
104 Crouch Hill, London N8 9EA   BO: 020-8829 0035
Route: Piccadilly or Victoria Line to Finsbury Park then W7
bus to Dickenson Road (5 min)

MYERS STUDIO THEATRE The
(Venues Manager - Trevor Mitchell)
The Epsom Playhouse
Ashley Avenue, Epsom, Surrey KT18 5AL
Website: www.epsomplayhouse.co.uk
e-mail: tmitchell@epsom-ewell.gov.uk
Fax: 01372 726228   Tel: 01372 742226
BO: 01372 742555

NETHERBOW SCOTTISH STORYTELLING CENTRE The
(Donald Smith)
43-45 High Street, Edinburgh EH1 1SR
Website: www.scotttishstorytellingcentre.co.uk
                                  Tel: 0131-556 9579

NETTLEFOLD The
West Norwood Library Centre, 1 Norwood High Street,
London SE27 9JX
Fax: 020-7926 8071   Admin/BO: 020-7926 8070
Route: Victoria, West Croydon or London Bridge (Main Line)
to West Norwood then 2 min walk, or tube to Brixton then
buses 2, 196, 322, 432, or buses 68, 468

NEW END THEATRE
27 New End, Hampstead, London NW3 1JD
Website: www.newendtheatre.co.uk
Fax: 020-7472 5808
BO: 08700 332733   Admin: 020-7472 5803
Route: Northern Line to Hampstead then 2 min walk off
Heath Street

NEW PLAYERS THEATRE The
(Formerly The Players Theatre)
The Arches, Villiers Street
London WC2N 6NL   BO: 08700 332626

NEW WIMBLEDON THEATRE & STUDIO
The Broadway, Wimbledon, London SW19 1QG
Website: www.newwimbledontheatre.co.uk
Fax: 020-8543 6637   BO: 0870 0606646
Admin: 020-8545 7900
Route: Main Line or District Line to Wimbledon, then 3 min
walk. Buses 57, 93, 155

NORTHBROOK THEATRE The
(Theatre co-ordinator - Conor McGivern)
Littlehampton Road, Goring-by-Sea
Worthing, West Sussex BN12 6NU
Website: www.northbrooktheatre.co.uk
e-mail: box.office@nbcol.ac.uk
Fax: 01903 606316
BO: 01903 606162   Marketing & Publicity: 01903 606230

NORWICH PUPPET THEATRE
St James, Whitefriars, Norwich NR3 1TN
Website: www.puppettheatre.co.uk
e-mail: info@puppettheatre.co.uk
Fax: 01603 617578
BO: 01603 629921   Admin: 01603 615564

NOVELLO THEATRE The
(Redroofs Theatre Company)
2 High Street, Sunninghill
Nr Ascot, Berkshire   Tel: 01344 620881
Route: Waterloo (Main Line) to Ascot then 1 mile from
station

OLD RED LION THEATRE PUB
(Artistic Director - Melanie Tait)
418 St John Street, Islington, London EC1V 4NJ
BO: 020-7837 7816   Admin/Fax: 020-7833 3053
Route: Northern Line to Angel then 1 min walk

ORANGE TREE
(Artistic Director - Sam Walters)
1 Clarence Street, Richmond TW9 2SA
e-mail: admin@orange-tree.demon.co.uk
Fax: 020-8332 0369
BO: 020-8940 3633   Admin: 020-8940 0141
Route: District Line, Waterloo (Main Line) or North London
Line then virtually opposite station

OVAL HOUSE THEATRE
52-54 Kennington Oval, London SE11 5SW
Website: www.ovalhouse.com
e-mail: info@ovalhouse.com
Fax: 020-7820 0990
BO: 020-7582 7680   Admin: 020-7582 0080
Route: Northern Line to Oval then 1 min walk, Victoria Line
& Main Line to Vauxhall then 10 min walk

PAVILION THEATRE
Marine Road, Dun Laoghaire, County Dublin, Eire
Website: www.paviliontheatre.ie
e-mail: info@paviliontheatre.ie
Fax: 353 1 663 6328   Tel: 353 1 231 2929

PENTAMETERS
Three Horseshoes, 28 Heath Street
London NW3 6TE   BO/Admin: 020-7435 3648
Route: Northern Line to Hampstead then 1 min walk

PLACE The
(Main London Venue for Contemporary Dance)
17 Duke's Road, London WC1H 9PY
Website: www.theplace.org.uk
e-mail: theatre@theplace.org.uk
BO: 020-7387 0031   Admin: 020-7380 1268
Route: Northern or Victoria Line to Euston or King's Cross
then 5 min walk (Opposite rear of St Pancras Church)

PLEASANCE LONDON
Carpenters Mews, North Road
(Off Caledonian Road), London N7 9EF
Website: www.pleasance.co.uk
e-mail: info@pleasance.co.uk
Fax: 020-7700 7366
BO: 020-7609 1800   Admin: 020-7619 6868
Route: Piccadilly Line to Caledonian Road, turn left, walk
50 yds, turn left into North Road, 2 min walk. Buses 10, 17,
91, 259, N91

POLISH THEATRE
(Polish Social & Cultural Association Ltd)
238-246 King Street, London W6 0RF
BO: 020-8741 0398   Admin: 020-8741 1940
Route: District Line to Ravenscourt Park, or District,
Piccadilly or Metropolitan Lines to Hammersmith then 7
min walk. Buses 27, 267, 190, 391, H91

POLKA THEATRE
240 The Broadway, Wimbledon SW19 1SB
Website: www.polkatheatre.com
e-mail: info@polkatheatre.com
Fax: 020-8545 8365
BO: 020-8543 4888   Admin: 020-8545 8320
Route: Waterloo (Main Line) or District Line to Wimbledon
then 10 min walk. Northern Line to South Wimbledon then
10 min walk

PRINCESS THEATRE HUNSTANTON
The Green, Hunstanton, Norfolk PE36 5AH
Fax: 01485 534463
BO: 01485 532252   Admin: 01485 535937

PUTNEY ARTS THEATRE
Ravenna Road, Putney SW15 6AW
Website: www.putneyartstheatre.org.uk
e-mail: mail@putneyartstheatre.org.uk
Fax: 020-8788 6940   Tel: 020-8788 6943

QUEEN'S THEATRE
(Artistic Director - Bob Carlton)
Billet Lane, Hornchurch, Essex RM11 1QT
Website: www.queens-theatre.co.uk
e-mail: info@queens-theatre.co.uk
Fax: 01708 462363   SD/Admin: 01708 462362
BO: 01708 443333
Route: District Line to Hornchurch, Main Line to
Romford/Gidea Park. 15 miles from West End take A13,
A1306 then A125 or A12 then A127

QUESTORS THEATRE EALING The
12 Mattock Lane, London W5 5BQ
Website: www.questors.org.uk
e-mail: enquiries@questors.org.uk
Fax: 020-8567 8736
BO: 020-8567 5184   Admin: 020-8567 0011
Route: Central or District Line to Ealing Broadway then 5
min walk

RED HEDGEHOG The
(Artistic Director - Clare Fischer)
257 Archway Road
Highgate, London N6 5BS
BO: 020-8348 5050   Admin: 020-8348 8485
Route: 50 Yards on left from Highgate Tube

RICHMOND THEATRE
The Green, Richmond, Surrey TW9 1QJ
Website: www.richmondtheatre.net
e-mail: richmondstagedoor@theambassadors.com
Fax: 020-8948 3601
BO: 020-8940 0088   Admin & SD: 020-8940 0220
Route: 20 minutes from Waterloo (South West Trains) or
District Line or Silverlink to Richmond then 2 min walk

RIDWARE THEATRE
(Alan & Margaret Williams)
Wheelwright's House, Pipe Ridware
Rugeley, Staffs WS15 3QL
e-mail: alan@christmas-time.com   Tel: 01889 504 380

RIVERSIDE STUDIOS
Crisp Road, London W6 9RL
Website: www.riversidestudios.co.uk
e-mail: info@riversidestudios.co.uk
BO: 020-8237 1111   Admin: 020-8237 1000
Route: District, Piccadilly or Hammersmith & City Line to
Hammersmith Broadway then 5 min walk. Buses 9, 11, 27,
73, 91, 220, 283, 295

ROSEMARY BRANCH THEATRE
2 Shepperton Road, London N1 3DT
Website: www.rosemarybranch.co.uk
e-mail: cecilia@rosemarybranch.co.uk   Tel: 020-7704 6665

SEVENOAKS PLAYHOUSE
London Road, Sevenoaks, Kent TN13 1ZZ
Website: www.sevenoaksplayhouse.co.uk
BO: 01732 450175   Admin: 01732 451548
Route: Charing Cross (Main Line) to Sevenoaks then 15 min
up the hill from station

SHAW THEATRE The
The Novotel Hotel, 100-110 Euston Road, London NW1 2AJ
Fax: 020-7794 4044
BO: 08700 332626   Admin: 020-7794 7088

SOHO THEATRE & WRITERS' CENTRE
21 Dean Street, London W1D 3NE
Website: www.sohotheatre.com
Fax: 020-7287 5061
BO: 0870 4296883   Admin: 020-7287 5060
Route: Tube to Tottenham Court Road then second left up
Oxford Street

SOUTH HILL PARK ARTS CENTRE
Bracknell, Berkshire RG12 7PA
Website: www.southhillpark.org.uk
e-mail: admin@southhillpark.org.uk
BO: 01344 484123   Admin & SD: 01344 484858
Route: Waterloo (Main Line) to Bracknell then 10 min bus
ride or taxi rank at station

SOUTH LONDON THEATRE
(Bell Theatre & Prompt Corner)
2A Norwood High Street, London SE27 9NS
Website: www.southlondontheatre.co.uk
e-mail: southlondontheatre@yahoo.co.uk
    Tel: 020-8670 3474
Route: Victoria or London Bridge (Main Line) to West
Norwood then 2 min walk, or Victoria Line to Brixton then
buses 2, 68, 196, 322

SOUTHWARK PLAYHOUSE
(Artistic Director - Gareth Machin, Chief Executive - Juliet
Alderdice, Education Director - Tom Wilson)
5 Playhouse Court
62 Southwark Bridge Road, London SE1 0AT
Website: www.southwarkplayhouse.co.uk
e-mail: admin@southwarkplayhouse.co.uk
BO: 020-7620 3494   Admin: 020-7652 2224
Route: Northern Line to Borough or Jubilee Line/Main Line
to London Bridge. Buses 133, 35, 344, 40, P3

THEATRE 503
503 Battersea Park Road, London SW11 3BW
Website: www.theatre503.com
e-mail: mail@theatre503.com
BO: 020-7978 7040   Admin/Fax: 020-7978 7041
Route: Victoria or Waterloo (Main Line) to Clapham
Junction then 10 min walk or buses 44, 219, 319, 344, 345 or
tube to South Kensington then buses 49 or 345 or tube to
Sloane Square then bus 319

THEATRE OF ALL POSSIBILITIES
(Artistic Director - Kathlin Gray)
24 Old Gloucester Street, London WC1N 3AL
Website: www.allpossibilities.org
e-mail: engage@allpossibilities.org   Tel: 020-7242 9831

THEATRE ROYAL STRATFORD EAST
(Artistic Director - Kerry Michael)
Gerry Raffles Square, London E15 1BN
Website: www.stratfordeast.com
e-mail: theatreroyal@stratfordeast.com
Fax: 020-8534 8381
BO: 020-8534 0310   Admin: 020-8534 7374
Route: Central or Jubilee Line to Stratford then 2 min walk

THEATRO TECHNIS
(Artistic Director - George Eugeniou)
26 Crowndale Road, London NW1
Website: www.theatrotechnis.com
e-mail: info@theatrotechnis.com   BO & Admin: 020-7387 6617
Route: Northern Line to Mornington Crescent then 3 min
walk

TRICYCLE THEATRE
(Artistic Director - Nicolas Kent, General Manager - Mary
Lauder)
269 Kilburn High Road, London NW6 7JR
Website: www.tricycle.co.uk
e-mail: admin@tricycle.co.uk
Fax: 020-7328 0795
BO: 020-7328 1000   Admin: 020-7372 6611
Route: Jubilee Line to Kilburn then 5 min walk or buses 16,
189, 32 pass the door, 98, 31, 206, 316 pass nearby

TRON THEATRE
(Director - Neil Murray)
63 Trongate, Glasgow G1 5HB
Website: www.tron.co.uk
e-mail: admin@tron.co.uk
Fax: 0141-552 6657
BO: 0141-552 4267   Admin: 0141-552 3748

UCL BLOOMSBURY THEATRE
15 Gordon Street, Bloomsbury, London WC1H 0AH
Website: www.thebloomsbury.com
e-mail: blooms.theatre@ucl.ac.uk
BO: 020-7388 8822   Admin: 020-7679 2777
Route: Tube to Euston, Euston Square or Warren Street

UNION THEATRE The
(Artistic Director - Sasha Regan, Resident Director - Ben De
Wynter) (All Casting Enquiries - Paul Flynn)
204 Union Street
Southwark, London SE1 0LX
Website: www.uniontheatre.freeserve.co.uk
e-mail: sasha@uniontheatre.com   Tel/Fax: 020-7261 9876
Route: Jubilee Line to Southwark then 2 min walk

UPSTAIRS AT THE GATEHOUSE
(Ovation Theatres Ltd)
The Gatehouse Pub
Corner of Hampstead Lane/North Road, London N6 4BD
Website: www.upstairsatthegatehouse.com
e-mail: events@ovationproductions.com
BO: 020-8340 3488   Admin: 020-8340 3477
Route: Northern Line to Highgate then 10 min walk. Buses
143, 210, 214, 271

VENUE The
5 Leicester Place, London WC2H 7BP   Tel: 0870 8993335

WAREHOUSE THEATRE
(Artistic Director - Ted Craig)
Dingwall Road
Croydon CR0 2NF
Website: www.warehousetheatre.co.uk
e-mail: info@warehousetheatre.co.uk
Fax: 020-8688 6699
BO: 020-8680 4060   Admin: 020-8681 1257
Adjacent to East Croydon (Main Line). Direct from Victoria
(15 mins), Clapham Junction (10 mins) or by Thameslink
from West Hampstead, Kentish Town, Kings Cross,
Blackfriars & London Bridge

WATERMANS
40 High Street
Brentford TW8 0DS
Website: www.watermans.org.uk
e-mail: info@watermans.org.uk
Fax: 020-8232 1030
BO: 020-8232 1010   Admin: 020-8232 1020
Route: Buses: 237, 267, 65, N9. Tube: Gunnersbury or South
Ealing Main Line: Kew Bridge then 5 min walk, Gunnersbury
then 10 min walk, or Brentford

WESTRIDGE (OPEN CENTRE)
(Drawing Room Recitals)
Star Lane, Highclere
Nr Newbury
Berkshire RG20 9PJ   Tel: 01635 253322

WHITE BEAR THEATRE
(Favours New Writing)
138 Kennington Park Road
London SE11 4DJ
e-mail: mkwbear@hotmail.com   Admin/BO: 020-7793 9193

WILTONS MUSIC HALL
Graces Alley
Off Ensign Street, London E1 8JB
Fax: 020-7702 1414   Tel: 020-7702 9555
Route Tube: Under 10 minutes walk from Aldgate East (exit
for Leman Street)/Tower Hill. DLR: Shadwell & Tower
Gateway. Car: Look out for the yellow AA signs to Wiltons
Music Hall from the Highway, Aldgate & Tower Hill.

WIMBLEDON STUDIO THEATRE
(See NEW WIMBLEDON THEATRE & STUDIO)

WYCOMBE SWAN
St Mary Street
High Wycombe
Buckinghamshire HP11 2XE
Website: www.wycombeswan.co.uk
e-mail: enquiries@wycombeswan.co.uk
BO: 01494 512000   Admin: 01494 514444

ABERDEEN

His Majesty's Theatre
Rosemount Viaduct, Aberdeen AB25 1GL
Box Office: 01224 641122
Stage Door: 01224 638677
Admin: 01224 637788
Website: www.hmtheatre.com
e-mail: info@hmtheatre.com

ABERYSTWYTH

Aberystwyth Arts Centre
University of Wales, Aberystwyth SY23 3DE
Box Office: 01970 623232
Stage Door: 01970 624239
Admin: 01970 622882
Website: www.aber.ac.uk/artscentre
e-mail: lla@aber.ac.uk

ASHTON-UNDER-LYNE

Tameside Hippodrome
Oldham Road, Ashton-under-Lyne OL6 7SE
Box Office: 0161-308 3223
Stage Door: -------------------
Admin: 0161-330 2095

AYR

Gaiety Theatre
Carrick Street, Ayr KA7 1NU
Box Office: 01292 611222
Stage Door: 01292 617414
Admin: 01292 617400

BACUP

Royal Court Theatre
Rochdale Road, Bacup OL13 9NR
Box Office: 01706 874080
Stage Door: -------------------
Admin: -------------------

BASINGSTOKE

Haymarket Theatre
Wote Street, Basingstoke RG21 7NW
Box Office: 0870 7701088
Stage Door: 0870 7701029
Admin: 0870 7701029
Website: www.haymarket.org.uk
e-mail: info@haymarket.org.uk

BATH

Theatre Royal
Sawclose, Bath BA1 1ET
Box Office: 01225 448844
Stage Door: 01225 448815
Admin: 01225 448815
Website: www.theatreroyal.org.uk
e-mail: forename.surname@theatreroyal.org.uk

BELFAST

Grand Opera House
Great Victoria Street, Belfast BT2 7HR
Box Office: 028-9024 1919
Stage Door: 028-9024 0411
Admin: 028-9024 0411
Website: www.goh.co.uk
e-mail: info@goh.co.uk

BILLINGHAM

Forum Theatre
Town Centre, Billingham TS23 2LJ
Box Office: 01642 552663
Stage Door: -------------------
Admin: 01642 551389

BIRMINGHAM

Alexandra Theatre
Station Street, Birmingham B5 4DS
Box Office: 0870 6077533
Stage Door: 0121-230 9102
Admin: 0121-643 5536
Website: www.ticketmaster.co.uk

BIRMINGHAM

Hippodrome
Hurst Street, Birmingham B5 4TB
Box Office: 0870 7301234
Stage Door: -------------------
Admin: 0870 7305555

BLACKPOOL

Grand Theatre
33 Church Street, Blackpool FY1 1HT
Box Office: 01253 290190
Stage Door: 01253 743218
Admin: 01253 290111
Website: www.blackpoolgrand.co.uk
e-mail: geninfo@blackpoolgrand.co.uk

BLACKPOOL

Opera House
Church Street, Blackpool FY1 1HW
Box Office: 01253 292029
Stage Door: 01253 625252 ext 148
Admin: 01253 625252

BOURNEMOUTH

Pavilion Theatre
Westover Road, Bournemouth BH1 2BU
Box Office: 0870 1113000
Stage Door: 01202 451863
Admin: 01202 456400

BRADFORD

Alhambra Theatre
Morley Street, Bradford BD7 1AJ
Box Office: 01274 432000
Stage Door: 01274 432375
Admin: 01274 432375
Website: www.bradford-theatres.co.uk
e-mail: administration@ces.bradford.gov.uk

BRADFORD

Theatre in the Mill
University of Bradford, Shearbridge Road, Bradford BD7 1DP
Box Office: 01274 233200
Stage Door: -------------------
Admin: 01274 233185
Website: www.bradford.ac.uk/theatre
e-mail: theatre@bradford.ac.uk

BRIGHTON

The Dome, Corn Exchange & Pavilion Theatres
29 New Road, Brighton BN1 1UG
Box Office: 01273 709709
Stage Door: 01273 261550
Admin: 01273 700747
e-mail: info@brighton-dome.org.uk

BRIGHTON

Theatre Royal
New Road, Brighton BN1 1SD
Box Office: 01273 328488
Stage Door: 01273 764400
Admin: 01273 764400
e-mail: brightontheatremanager@theambassadors.com

BRISTOL

Hippodrome
St Augustines Parade, Bristol BS1 4UZ
Box Office: 0870 6077500
Stage Door: 0117-302 3251
Admin: 0117-302 3310
Website: www.getlive.co.uk/bristol

BROXBOURNE (Herts)

Broxbourne Civic Hall
High Street, Hoddesdon, Herts EN11 8BE
Box Office: 01992 441946
Stage Door: -------------------
Admin: 01992 441931
Website: www.broxbourne.gov.uk
e-mail: civic.leisure@broxbourne.gov.uk

BURY ST EDMUNDS

Theatre Royal
Westgate Street, Bury St Edmunds IP33 1QR
Box Office: 01284 769505
Stage Door: 01284 755127
Admin: 01284 755127
Website: www.theatreroyal.org
e-mail: admin@theatreroyal.org

BUXTON

Buxton Opera House
Water Street, Buxton SK17 6XN
Box Office: 0845 1272190
Stage Door: 01298 71382
Admin: 01298 72050
Website: www.buxton-opera.co.uk
e-mail: admin@buxtonopera.co.uk

CAMBERLEY

The Camberley Theatre
Knoll Road, Camberley, Surrey GU15 3SY
Box Office: 01276 707600
Stage Door: -------------------
Admin: 01276 707612
Website: www.camberleytheatre.biz
e-mail: camberleytheatre@surreyheath.gov.uk

CAMBRIDGE

Cambridge Arts Theatre
6 St Edward's Passage, Cambridge CB2 3PJ
Box Office: 01223 503333
Stage Door: 01223 578933
Admin: 01223 578933
Website: www.cambridgeartstheatre.com
e-mail: info@cambridgeartstheatre.com

CAMBRIDGE

Mumford Theatre
Anglia Polytechnic University, East Road, Cambridge CB1 1PT
Box Office: 01223 352932
Stage Door: 01223 417748
Admin: 01223 417748
e-mail: mumford@apu.ac.uk

CANTERBURY

Gulbenkian Theatre
University of Kent, Canterbury CT2 7NB
Box Office: 01227 769075
Stage Door: -------------------
Admin: 01227 827861
Website: www.kent.ac.uk/gulbenkian
e-mail: gulbenkian@kent.ac.uk

CANTERBURY

The Marlowe Theatre
The Friars, Canterbury CT1 2AS
Box Office: 01227 787787
Stage Door: 01227 763262
Admin: 01227 763262
Website: www.marlowetheatre.com
e-mail: mark.everett@canterbury.gov.uk

CARDIFF

New Theatre
Park Place, Cardiff CF10 3LN
Box Office: 029-2087 8889
Stage Door: 029-2087 8900
Admin: 029-2087 8787

CHELTENHAM

Everyman Theatre
Regent Street, Cheltenham GL50 1HQ
Box Office: 01242 572573
Stage Door: 01242 512515
Admin: 01242 512515
Website: www.everymantheatre.org.uk
e-mail: admin@everymantheatre.org.uk

CHESTER

Gateway Theatre
Hamilton Place, Chester, Cheshire CH1 2BH
Stage Door: -------------------
Box Office: 01244 340392
Admin: 01244 318603
Website: www.chestergateway.co.uk
e-mail: jasminehendry@gateway-theatre.org

CHICHESTER

Festival Theatre
Oaklands Park, Chichester PO19 6AP
Box Office: 01243 781312
Stage Door: 01243 784437
Admin: 01243 784437
Website: www.cft.org.uk
e-mail: admin@cft.org.uk

CRAWLEY

The Hawth
Hawth Avenue, Crawley, West Sussex RH10 6YZ
Box Office: 01293 553636
Stage Door: -------------------
Admin: 01293 552941
Website: www.hawth.co.uk
e-mail: info@hawth.co.uk

CREWE

Lyceum Theatre
Heath Street, Crewe CW1 2DA
Box Office: 01270 537333
Stage Door: 01270 537336
Admin: 01270 537243

DARLINGTON

Civic Theatre
Parkgate, Darlington DL1 1RR
Box Office: 01325 486555
Stage Door: 01325 467743
Admin: 01325 387775
Website: www.darlingtonarts.co.uk

DUBLIN

Gaiety Theatre
South King Street, Dublin 2
Box Office: 00 353 1 6771717
Stage Door: 00 353 1 6795622
Admin: 00 353 1 6795622

DUBLIN

Gate Theatre
1 Cavendish Row, Dublin 1
Box Office: 00 353 1 8744045
Stage Door: --------------------
Admin: 00 353 1 8744368
Website: www.gate-theatre.ie
e-mail: info@gate-theatre.ie

DUBLIN

Olympia Theatre
72 Dame Street, Dublin 2
Box Office: 00 353 1 6793323
Stage Door: 00 353 1 6771400
Admin: 00 353 1 6725883
Website: www.mcd.ie
e-mail: info@olympia.ie

EASTBOURNE

Congress Theatre
Admin: Winter Garden, Compton Street, Eastbourne BN21 4BP
Box Office: 01323 412000
Stage Door: 01323 410048
Admin: 01323 415500
Website: www.eastbournetheatres.co.uk
e-mail: theatres@eastbourne.gov.uk

EASTBOURNE

Devonshire Park Theatre
Admin: Winter Garden, Compton Street, Eastbourne BN21 4BP
Box Office: 01323 412000
Stage Door: 01323 410074
Admin: 01323 415500
Website: www.eastbournetheatres.co.uk
e-mail: theatres@eastbourne.gov.uk

EDINBURGH

King's Theatre
2 Leven Street, Edinburgh EH3 9LQ
Box Office: 0131-529 6000
Stage Door: 0131-229 3416
Admin: 0131-662 1112
Website: www.eft.co.uk
e-mail: empire@eft.co.uk

EDINBURGH

Playhouse Theatre
18-22 Greenside Place, Edinburgh EH1 3AA
Box Office: 0870 6063424
Stage Door: 0131-524 3324
Admin: 0131-524 3333
Website: www.cclive.co.uk

GLASGOW

King's Theatre
297 Bath Street, Glasgow G2 4JN
Box Office: 0141-240 1111
Stage Door: 0141-240 1300
Admin: 0141-240 1300

GLASGOW

Theatre Royal
282 Hope Street, Glasgow G2 3QA
Box Office: 0141-332 9000
Stage Door: 0141-332 3321
Admin: 0141-332 3321
Website: www.theatreroyalglasgow.com

GRAYS THURROCK

Thameside Theatre
Orsett Road, Grays Thurrock RM17 5DX
Box Office: 01375 383961
Stage Door: --------------------
Admin: 01375 382555
Website: www.thurrock.gov.uk/theatre
e-mail: mallinson@thurrock.gov.uk

HARLOW

The Playhouse
Playhouse Square
Harlow CM20 1LS
Box Office: 01279 431945
Stage Door: --------------------
Admin: 01279 446760
Website: www.playhouseharlow.com
e-mail: philip.dale@harlow.gov.uk

HARROGATE

Harrogate International Centre
Kings Road, Harrogate HG1 5LA
Box Office: 01423 537230
Stage Door: --------------------
Admin: 01423 500500

HASTINGS

White Rock Theatre
White Rock, Hastings TN34 1JX
Box Office: 01424 462288
Stage Door: --------------------
Admin: 01424 462280

HAYES (Middlesex)

Beck Theatre
Grange Road, Hayes, Middlesex UB3 2UE
Box Office: 020-8561 8371
Stage Door: --------------------
Admin: 020-8561 7506

HIGH WYCOMBE

Wycombe Swan
St Mary Street
High Wycombe HP11 2XE
Box Office: 01494 512000
Stage Door: 01494 514444
Admin: 01494 514444
Website: www.wycombeswan.co.uk
e-mail: enquiries@wycombeswan.co.uk

HUDDERSFIELD

Cragrats Ltd
The Mill, Dunford Road, Holmfirth, Huddersfield HD9 2AR
Box Office:	------------------
Stage Door:	------------------
Admin:	01484 686451
Website:	www.cragrats.com
e-mail:	jill@cragrats.com

HUDDERSFIELD

Lawrence Batley Theatre
Queen Street, Huddersfield HD1 2SP
Box Office:	01484 430528
Stage Door:	------------------
Admin:	01484 425282
e-mail:	theatre@lbt-uk.org

HULL

Hull New Theatre
Kingston Square, Hull HU1 3HF
Box Office:	01482 226655
Stage Door:	01482 318300
Admin:	01482 613818
e-mail:	theatre.management@hullcc.gov.uk

HULL

Hull Truck Theatre
Spring Street, Hull HU2 8RW
Box Office:	01482 323638
Stage Door:	------------------
Admin:	01482 224800
Website:	www.hulltruck.co.uk
e-mail:	admin@hulltruck.co.uk

ILFORD

Kenneth More Theatre
Oakfield Road, Ilford IG1 1BT
Box Office:	020-8553 4466
Stage Door:	020-8553 4465
Admin:	020-8553 4464
Website:	www.kenneth-more-theatre.co.uk
e-mail:	kmtheatre@aol.com

IPSWICH

Sir John Mills Theatre (Hire Only)
Gatacre Road, Ipswich IP1 2LQ
Box Office:	01473 211498
Stage Door:	------------------
Admin:	01473 218202
Website:	www.easternangles.co.uk
e-mail:	admin@easternangles.co.uk

JERSEY

Opera House
Gloucester Street, St Helier, Jersey JE2 3QR
Box Office:	01534 511115
Stage Door:	------------------
Admin:	01534 511100
e-mail:	ian@jerseyoperahouse.co.uk

KIRKCALDY

Adam Smith Theatre
Bennochy Road, Kirkcaldy KY1 1ET
Box Office:	01592 412929
Stage Door:	------------------
Admin:	01592 412567

LEATHERHEAD

The Leatherhead Theatre
Church Street, Leatherhead, Surrey KT22 8DN
Box Office:	01372 365141
Stage Door:	------------------
Admin:	01372 365130
Website:	www.the-theatre.org

LEEDS

City Varieties Music Hall
Swan Street, Leeds LS1 6LW
Box Office:	0113-243 0808
Stage Door:	------------------
Admin:	0113-391 7777
Website:	www.cityvarieties.co.uk
e-mail:	info@cityvarieties.co.uk

LEEDS

Grand Theatre & Opera House
46 New Briggate, Leeds LS1 6NZ
Box Office:	0113-222 6222
Stage Door:	0113-245 6014
Admin:	0113-245 6014

LICHFIELD

The Lichfield Garrick
Castle Dyke, Lichfield WS13 6HR
Box Office:	01543 412121
Stage Door:	------------------
Admin:	01543 412110

LINCOLN

Theatre Royal
Clasketgate, Lincoln LN2 1JJ
Box Office:	01522 525555
Stage Door:	01522 523303
Admin:	01522 523303
Website:	www.theatreroyallincoln.com
e-mail:	theatre.royal@dial.pipex.com

LIVERPOOL

Empire Theatre
Lime Street, Liverpool L1 1JE
Box Office:	0870 6063536
Stage Door:	0151-708 3200
Admin:	0151-708 3200

LIVERPOOL

Neptune Theatre
Hanover Street, Liverpool L1 3DY
Box Office:	0151-709 7844
Stage Door:	0151-709 7844
Admin:	0151-709 7844
Website:	www.neptunetheatre.co.uk
e-mail:	neptune.theatre@liverpool.gov.uk

MALVERN

Malvern Theatres (Festival & Forum Theatres)
Grange Road, Malvern WR14 3HB
Box Office:	01684 892277
Stage Door:	------------------
Admin:	01684 569256
Website:	www.malvern-theatres.co.uk
e-mail:	post@malvern-theatres.co.uk

MANCHESTER
Carling Apollo
Stockport Road
Ardwick Green, Manchester M12 6AP
Box Office: 0870 4018000
Stage Door: 0161-273 2416
Admin: 0161-273 6921
Website: www.getlive.co.uk

MANCHESTER
Opera House
Quay Street, Manchester M3 3HP
Box Office: 0870 4019000
Stage Door: 0161-828 1700
Admin: 0161-828 1700

MANCHESTER
Palace Theatre
Oxford Street, Manchester M1 6FT
Box Office: 0870 4013000
Stage Door: 0161-245 6600
Admin: 0161-245 6600

MARGATE
Theatre Royal
Addington Street, Margate, Kent CT9 1PW
Box Office: 01843 293877
Stage Door: 01843 293397
Admin: 01843 293397

MILTON KEYNES
Milton Keynes Theatre
500 Marlborough Gate
Central Milton Keynes MK9 3NZ
Box Office: 01908 606090
Stage Door: 01908 547500
Admin: 01908 547500

NEWARK
Palace Theatre
Appletongate, Newark NG24 1JY
Box Office: 01636 655755
Stage Door: -------------------
Admin: 01636 655750
Website: www.palacenewark.com
e-mail: david.piper@nsdc.info

NEWCASTLE UPON TYNE
Northern Stage
Barras Bridge, Haymarket
Newcastle upon Tyne NE1 7RH
Box Office: 0871 7000124
Stage Door: -------------------
Admin: 0871 7000125
Website: www.northernstage.com
e-mail: info@northernstage.com

NEWCASTLE UPON TYNE
Theatre Royal
Grey Street, Newcastle upon Tyne NE1 6BR
Box Office: 0870 9055060
Stage Door: 0191-244 2500
Admin: 0191-232 0997

NORTHAMPTON
Royal & Derngate Theatres
19-21 Guildhall Road, Northampton NN1 1DP
Box Office: 01604 624811
Stage Door: 01604 626289
Admin: 01604 626222
Website: www.royalandderngate.com
e-mail: postbox@ntt.org.uk

NORWICH
Theatre Royal
Theatre Street, Norwich NR2 1RL
Box Office: 01603 630000
Stage Door: 01603 598500
Admin: 01603 598500
Website: www.theatreroyalnorwich.co.uk

NOTTINGHAM
Theatre Royal & Royal Concert Hall
Theatre Square, Nottingham NG1 5ND
Box Office: 0115-989 5555
Stage Door: 0115-989 5500
Admin: 0115-989 5500
Website: www.royalcentre-nottingham.co.uk
e-mail: enquiry@royalcentre-nottingham.co.uk

OXFORD
New Theatre
George Street, Oxford OX1 2AG
Box Office: 0870 6063500
Stage Door: 01865 320760
Admin: 01865 320761
Website: www.cclive.co.uk

OXFORD
The Oxford Playhouse
Beaumont Street, Oxford OX1 2LW
Box Office: 01865 305305
Stage Door: 01865 305301
Admin: 01865 305300
Website: www.oxfordplayhouse.com
e-mail: admin@oxfordplayhouse.com

PAIGNTON
Palace Theatre
Palace Avenue, Paignton TQ3 3HF
Box Office: 01803 665800
Stage Door: -------------------
Admin: 01803 558367
Website: www.torbay.gov.uk/palacetheatre
e-mail: palace.theatre@torbay.gov.uk

PLYMOUTH
Athenaeum
Derry's Cross, Plymouth PL1 2SW
Box Office: 01752 266104
Stage Door: -------------------
Admin: 01752 266079

POOLE
Lighthouse, Poole's Centre for The Arts
Kingland Road, Poole BH15 1UG
Box Office: 01202 685222
Stage Door: -------------------
Admin: 01202 665334

READING

The Hexagon
Queen's Walk, Reading RG1 7UA
Box Office: 0118-960 6060
Stage Door: 0118-939 0018
Admin: 0118-939 0390

RICHMOND (N Yorks)

Georgian Theatre Royal
Victoria Road, Richmond, North Yorkshire DL10 4DW
Box Office: 01748 825252
Stage Door: -------------------
Admin: 01748 823710
Website: www.georgiantheatreroyal.co.uk

RICHMOND (Surrey)

Richmond Theatre
The Green, Richmond, Surrey TW9 1QJ
Box Office: 020-8940 0088
Stage Door: 020-8940 0220
Admin: 020-8940 0220
Website: www.richmondtheatre.net

SHEFFIELD

Sheffield Theatres - Crucible, Lyceum & Crucible Studio
55 Norfolk Street, Sheffield S1 1DA
Box Office: 0114-249 6000
Stage Door: 0114-249 5999
Admin: 0114-249 5999
Website: www.sheffieldtheatres.co.uk

SOUTHAMPTON

The Mayflower
Commercial Road, Southampton SO15 1GE
Stage Door: -----------------------
Box Office: 023-8071 1811
Admin: 023-8071 1800
Website: www.the-mayflower.com
e-mail: info@mayflower.org.uk

SOUTHEND

Southend Theatres
(Cliffs Pavilion, Palace & Dixon Theatres)
Cliffs Pavilion, Station Road
Westcliff-on-Sea, Essex, SS0 7RA
Box Office: 01702 351135
Stage Door: -------------------
Admin: 01702 390657
Website: www.thecliffspavilion.co.uk
e-mail: info@cliffspavilion.demon.co.uk

ST ALBANS

Abbey Theatre
Holywell Hill, St Albans AL1 2DL
Box Office: 01727 857861
Stage Door: -------------------
Admin: 01727 847472
Website: www.abbeytheatre.org.uk
e-mail: manager@abbeytheatre.org.uk

ST ALBANS

Alban Arena
Civic Centre, St Albans AL1 3LD
Box Office: 01727 844488
Stage Door: -------------------
Admin: 01727 861078
Website: www.alban-arena.co.uk
e-mail: info@alban-arena.co.uk

ST HELENS

Theatre Royal
Corporation Street, St Helens WA10 1LQ
Box Office: 01744 756000
Stage Door: -------------------
Admin: 01744 756333

STAFFORD

Stafford Gatehouse Theatre
Eastgate Street, Stafford ST16 2LT
Box Office: 01785 254653
Stage Door: -------------------
Admin: 01785 253595
e-mail: gatehouse@staffordbc.gov.uk

STEVENAGE

Gordon Craig Theatre
Arts & Leisure Centre, Lytton Way, Stevenage SG1 1LZ
Box Office: 08700 131030
Stage Door: 01438 242629
Admin: 01438 242642
Website: www.stevenage-leisure.co.uk
e-mail: gordoncraig@stevenage-leisure.co.uk

STRATFORD-UPON-AVON

Royal Shakespeare Theatre
Waterside, Stratford-upon-Avon CV37 6BB
Box Office: 0870 6091110
Stage Door: 01789 296655
Admin: 01789 296655
Website: www.rsc.org.uk
e-mail: info@rsc.org.uk

STRATFORD-UPON-AVON

The Other Place
Southern Lane, Stratford-upon-Avon CV37 6BH
Box Office: 0870 6091110
Stage Door: 01789 296655
Admin: 01789 296655

SUNDERLAND

Empire Theatre
High Street West, Sunderland SR1 3EX
Box Office: 0870 6021130
Stage Door: 0191-510 0545
Admin: 0191-510 0545

SWANAGE

Mowlem Theatre
Shore Road, Swanage BH19 1DD
Box Office: 01929 422239
Stage Door: -------------------
Admin: 01929 422229

TAMWORTH

Assembly Rooms
Corporation Street, Tamworth B79 7BX
Box Office: 01827 709618
Stage Door: -------------------
Admin: 01827 709620

TEWKESBURY

The Roses
Sun Street, Tewkesbury GL20 5NX
Box Office: 01684 295074
Stage Door: -------------------
Admin: 01684 290734
e-mail: admin@rosestheatre.org

TORQUAY

Babbacombe Theatre
Babbacombe Downs, Torquay TQ1 3LU
Box Office: 01803 328385
Stage Door: 01803 328385
Admin: 01803 322233
Website: www.babbacombe-theatre.com
e-mail: mail@matpro-show.biz

TORQUAY

Princess Theatre
Torbay Road, Torquay TQ2 5EZ
Box Office: 0870 2414120
Stage Door: 01803 290068
Admin: 01803 290288
Website: www.ticketmaster.co.uk
e-mail: princess@clearchannel.co.uk

TRURO

Hall For Cornwall
Back Quay, Truro, Cornwall TR1 2LL
Box Office: 01872 262466
Stage Door: 01872 262465
Admin: 01872 262465
Website: www.hallforcornwall.co.uk
e-mail: admin@hallforcornwall..org.uk

WATFORD

Palace Theatre
Clarendon Road, Watford WD17 1JZ
Box Office: 01923 225671
Stage Door: -------------------
Admin: 01923 235455
Website: www.watfordtheatre.co.uk
e-mail: enquiries@watfordtheatre.co.uk

WESTCLIFF-ON-SEA

Palace & Dixon Theatres
London Road, Westcliff-on-Sea, Essex SS0 9LA
Stage Door: 01702 390657
Admin: See SOUTHEND Cliffs Pavilion
Admin: 01702 390657
Website: www.thecliffspavilion.co.uk
e-mail: info@cliffspavilion.demon.co.uk

WINCHESTER

Theatre Royal
21-23 Jewry Street, Winchester SO23 8SB
Box Office: 01962 840440
Stage Door: -------------------
Admin: 01962 844600
e-mail: marketing@theatre-royal-winchester.co.uk

WOLVERHAMPTON

Grand Theatre
Lichfield Street, Wolverhampton WV1 1DE
Box Office: 01902 429212
Stage Door: 01902 573320
Admin: 01902 573300
Website: www.grandtheatre.co.uk
e-mail: marketing@grandtheatre.co.uk

WORCESTER

Swan Theatre
The Moors, Worcester WR1 3EF
Box Office: 01905 611427
Stage Door: -------------------
Admin: 01905 726969
Website: www.huntingdonarts.com
e-mail: chris@huntingdonarts.com

WORTHING

Connaught Theatre
Union Place, Worthing BN11 1LG
Box Office: 01903 206206
Stage Door: -------------------
Admin: 01903 231799

YEOVIL

Octagon Theatre
Hendford, Yeovil BA20 1UX
Box Office: 01935 422884
Stage Door: 01935 845926
Admin: 01935 845900
Website: www.octagon-theatre.co.uk
e-mail: octagontheatre@southsomerset.gov.uk

YORK

Grand Opera House
Cumberland Street, York YO1 9SW
Box Office: 0870 6063595
Stage Door: -------------------
Admin: 01904 678700

AUTHENTIC PUNCH & JUDY
Puppets, Booths & Presentations (John Styles)
42 Christchurch Road
Sidcup, Kent DA15 7HQ
Website: www.johnstylesentertainer.co.uk
Tel/Fax: 020-8300 3579

BROOKER David
(Punch & Judy)
75 Northcote Road, New Malden
Surrey KT3 3HF   Tel: 020-8949 5035

BUCKLEY Simon
(Freelance Puppeteer/Presenter)
c/o Talent Artists Ltd
59 Sydner Road, London N16 7UF
Website: www.simonbuckley.co.uk
e-mail: puppet.buckley@virgin.net   Tel: 020-7923 1119

COMPLETE WORKS THEATRE COMPANY Ltd The
12 Willowford
Bancroft Park, Milton Keynes
Buckinghamshire MK13 0RH
Website: www.tcw.org.uk
e-mail: info@tcw.org.uk
Fax: 01908 320263   Tel: 01908 316256

CORNELIUS & JONES
49 Carters Close, Sherington, Newport Pagnell,
Buckinghamshire MK16 9NW
Website: www.corneliusjones.com
e-mail: admin@corneliusjones.com
Fax: 01908 616779   Tel: 01908 612593

DYNAMIC NEW ANIMATION
19 Royal Close, Manor Road, London N16 5SE
Website: www.dynamicnewanimation.co.uk
e-mail: dna@dynamicnewanimation.co.uk
Mobile: 07976 946003

GRIFFITHS Marc
(Ventriloquist & Motivational Speaker)
The Mega Centre, Bernard Road
Sheffield S2 5BQ   Tel: 0114-284 6007

INDIGO MOON THEATRE
35 Waltham Court
Beverley, East Yorkshire HU17 9JF
Website: www.indigomoontheatre.com
e-mail: info@indigomoontheatre.com
Tel/Fax: 01482 867646

JACOLLY PUPPET THEATRE
Kirkella Road
Yelverton, West Devon PL20 6BB
Website: www.jacolly-puppets.co.uk
e-mail: theatre@jacolly-puppets.co.uk   Tel: 01822 852346

LITTLE ANGEL THEATRE
14 Dagmar Passage
Cross Street, London N1 2DN
Website: www.littleangeltheatre.com
e-mail: info@littleangeltheatre.com
Fax: 020-7359 7565   Tel: 020-7226 1787

MAJOR MUSTARD'S TRAVELLING SHOW
1 Carless Avenue
Harborne, Birmingham B17 9EG
e-mail: majormustard@brum.com
Fax: 0121-427 2358   Tel: 0121-426 4329

NORWICH PUPPET THEATRE
St James
Whitefriars, Norwich NR3 1TN
Website: www.puppettheatre.co.uk
e-mail: info@puppettheatre.co.uk
Fax: 01603 617578   Tel: 01603 615564

PARASOL PUPPET THEATRE
Garden House
4 Sunnyside
Wimbledon SW19 4SL
Website: www.parasoltheatre.co.uk
e-mail: parasoltheatre@waitrose.com
Fax: 020-8946 0228   Tel: 020-8946 9478

PEKKO'S PUPPETS
92 Stanley Avenue
Greenford
Middlesex UB6 8NP   Tel: 020-8575 2311

PICCOLO PUPPET COMPANY
Maythorne Higher Park Road
Braunton
North Devon EX33 2LF
e-mail: angiepassmore@onetel.net.uk   Tel: 01271 815984

PLAYBOARD PUPPETS
94 Ockendon Road
London N1 3NW
e-mail: thebuttonmoon@aol.com
Fax: 020-7704 1081   Tel: 020-7226 5911

POM POM PUPPETS
9 Fulham Park Gardens
London SW6 4JX
Website: www.pompompuppets.co.uk
Mobile: 07974 175247   Tel: 020-7736 6532

PROFESSOR PATTEN'S PUNCH & JUDY
(Puppetry & Magic)
14 The Crest
Goffs Oak, Herts EN7 5NP
Website: www.dennispatten.co.uk   Tel: 01707 873262

PUNCH & JUDY
(Des Turner, President Punch & Judy Fellowship)
Richmond House
2 Benington Road
Aston, Herts SG2 7DX
Website: www.punchandjudy.org.uk
e-mail: desturner@aol.com   Tel: 01438 880376

THEATR BYPEDAU SBLOT (Splott Puppet Theatre)
22 Starling Road, St Athan
Vale of Glamorgan CF62 4NJ
e-mail: splottpuppets@aol.com   Tel: 01446 790634

TICKLISH ALLSORTS SHOW
Cremyll, Marshmead Close
Clarendon
Salisbury, Wiltshire SP5 3DD
Website: www.ticklishallsorts.co.uk
e-mail: garynunn@lineone.net   Tel/Fax: 01722 711800

TOPPER Chris PUPPETS
(Puppets Created & Performed)
75 Barrows Green Lane
Widnes, Cheshire WA8 3JH
Website: www.christopperpuppets.com   Tel: 0151-424 8692

ALDEBURGH
Summer Theatre (July & August) The Jubilee Hall
Crabbe Street, Aldeburgh IP15 5BW
BO: 01728 453007/454022   Admin: (Oct-May) 020-7724 5432
Admin: (June-Sept) 01502 723077
Website: www.southworldtheatre.org

BASINGSTOKE
Haymarket Theatre Company
Wote Street, Basingstoke RG21 7NW
Fax: 01256 357130
BO: 0870 7701088   Admin: 0870 7701029
Website: www.haymarket.org.uk
e-mail: info@haymarket.org.uk
Theatre Director:
Chief Executive: Zoe Curnow

BELFAST
Lyric Theatre
55 Ridgeway Street, Belfast BT9 5FB
Fax: 028-9038 1395
BO: 028-9038 1081   Admin: 028-9038 5685
Website: www.lyrictheatre.co.uk
e-mail: info@lyrictheatre.co.uk
Artistic Director: Paula McFetridge
Production Manager: Marianne Crosslé
General Manager: Mike Blair

BIRMINGHAM
Birmingham Stage Company
The Old Rep Theatre, Station Street, Birmingham B5 4DY
BO: 0121-236 5622   Admin: 0121-643 9050
Website: www.birminghamstage.co.uk
e-mail: info@birminghamstage.net
Actor/Manager: Neal Foster
Administrator: Philip Compton

London Office:
Suite 228 The Linen Hall
162 Regent Street, London W1B 5TG
Fax: 020-7437 3395   Admin: 020-7437 3391

BIRMINGHAM
Repertory Theatre
Centenary Square, Broad Street, Birmingham B1 2EP
Tel: 0121-245 2000
BO: 0121-236 4455   Press Office: 0121-245 2075
e-mail: info@birmingham-rep.co.uk
Artistic Director: Jonathan Church
Executive Director: Stuart Rogers

BOLTON
Octagon Theatre
Howell Croft South, Bolton BL1 1SB
Fax: 01204 556502
BO: 01204 520661   Admin: 01204 529407
Artistic Director: Mark Babych
Executive Director: John Blackmore
Operations Manager: Lesley Etherington

BRISTOL
Theatre Royal and New Vic Studio
(3/4 Weekly) Eves 7.30pm Thurs & Sat Mats 2.00pm
(Bristol Old Vic), King Street, Bristol BS1 4ED
Fax: 0117-949 3996
BO: 0117-987 7877   Tel: 0117-949 3993
Website: www.bristol-old-vic.co.uk
e-mail: admin@bristol-old-vic.co.uk
Artistic Directors: David Farr, Simon Reade
Administrative Director: Rebecca Morland

BROMLEY
Churchill Theatre
High Street
Bromley, Kent BR1 1HA
Fax: 020-8290 6968
BO: 0870 0606620   Tel: 020-8464 7131
Website: www.churchilltheatre.co.uk
Chief Executive: Derek Nicholls
Administrator: Christopher Glover
Production Manager: Digby Robinson
Financial Controller: Liz Gentry

CARDIFF
Sherman Theatre & Sherman Studio
Senghennydd Road CF24 4YE
Fax: 029-2064 6902
BO: 029-2064 6900   Tel: 029-2064 6901
Director: Phil Clark
General Manager: Margaret Jones

CHELMSFORD
Civic Theatre
(2 Weekly) (Nov-Feb)
Fairfield Road, Chelmsford, Essex CM1 1JG
Admin: 01245 268998   Tel: 020-8349 0802 (London)
Artistic Director: John Newman (Newpalm Prods)

CHICHESTER
Chichester Festival Theatre
(May-Oct & Touring) Eves 7.30pm Thurs & Sat Mats 2.30pm
Oaklands Park, Chichester, West Sussex PO19 6AP
Fax: 01243 787288
BO: 01243 781312   SD & Admin: 01243 784437
Website: www.cft.org.uk
e-mail: admin@cft.org.uk
Theatre Manager: Janet Burton
Artistic Directors: Martin Duncan, Ruth Mackenzie,
Steven Pimlott

CHICHESTER
Minerva Theatre at Chichester Festival Theatre
(June-Oct) Eves 7.45pm Weds & Sat Mats 2.15pm
Oaklands Park, Chichester, West Sussex PO19 6AP
Fax: 01243 787288
BO: 01243 781312   SD & Admin: 01243 784437
Website: www.cft.org.uk
e-mail: admin@cft.org.uk
Theatre Manager: Janet Burton
Artistic Director: Ruth Mackenzie

COLCHESTER
Mercury Theatre
(3-4 Weekly) Thurs & Sat Mats 2.30pm
Balkerne Gate, Colchester, Essex CO1 1PT
Fax: 01206 769607
BO: 01206 573948   Admin: 01206 577006
Website: www.mercurytheatre.co.uk
e-mail: info@mercurytheatre.co.uk
Chief Executive: Dee Evans

COVENTRY
Belgrade Theatre & Belgrade Studio
Belgrade Square, Coventry, West Midlands CV1 1GS
BO: 024-7655 3055   Admin: 024-7625 6431
Website: www.belgrade.co.uk
e-mail: admin@belgrade.co.uk
Theatre Director & Chief Executive: Hamish Glen
Special Projects Producer Freelance: Jane Hytch
Executive Director: Joanna Reid
Director of Marketing: Antony Flint

DERBY

Derby Playhouse
(4 Weekly)
Theatre Walk, Eagle Centre, Derby DE1 2NF
Fax: 01332 547200
BO: 01332 363275
SD: 01332 363271　　　　Admin: 01332 363271
Website: www.derbyplayhouse.co.uk
e-mail: admin@derbyplayhouse.co.uk
Creative Producer: Stephen Edwards
Chief Executive: Karen Hebden

DUBLIN

Abbey Theatre & Peacock Theatre
The National Theatre Society Limited
26 Lower Abbey Street, Dublin 1, Eire
Fax: 00 353 1 872 9177
BO: 00 353 1 878 7222　　　　Admin: 00 353 1 887 2200
Website: www.abbeytheatre.ie
e-mail: mail@abbeytheatre.ie
General Manager: Brian Jackson

DUNDEE

Dundee Repertory Theatre
Tay Square, Dundee DD1 1PB
Fax: 01382 228609
BO: 01382 223530　　　　Admin: 01382 227684
Website: www.dundeereptheatre.co.uk
Artistic Directors: James Brining, Dominic Hill
Executive Director: Lorna Duguid

EDINBURGH

Royal Lyceum Theatre Company
30B Grindlay Street, Edinburgh EH3 9AX
Fax: 0131-228 3955
BO: 0131-248 4848　　　　SD & Admin: 0131-248 4800
Website: www.lyceum.org.uk
e-mail: info@lyceum.org.uk
Artistic Director: Mark Thomson

EDINBURGH

Traverse Theatre
(New Writing, Own Productions & Visiting Companies)
Cambridge Street, Edinburgh EH1 2ED
Fax: 0131-229 8443
BO: 0131-228 1404　　　　Admin: 0131-228 3223
Website: www.traverse.co.uk
e-mail: admin@traverse.co.uk
Artistic Director: Philip Howard
Administrative Director: Mike Griffiths

EXETER

Northcott Theatre
(3/4 Weekly)
Stocker Road, Exeter, Devon EX4 4QB
Fax: 01392 223996
BO: 01392 493493　　　　Admin: 01392 223999
Website: www.northcott-theatre.co.uk
Artistic Director: Ben Crocker
Executive Director: Shea Connolly

EYE THEATRE

Eye Theatre
(4 Weekly) Sat 4.00pm
Broad Street, Eye, Suffolk IP23 7AF
Fax: 01379 871142　　　　Tel: 01379 870519
e-mail: tomscott@eyetheatre.freeserve.co.uk
Artistic Director: Tom Scott
Associate Director: Janeena Sims

FRINTON

Frinton Summer Theatre
(July-Sept)
Connaught Productions
WI Hall, Fourth Avenue, Frinton-on-Sea, Essex CO13 9EB
BO: 01255 674443 (July-Sept Only)
Producer and Artistic Director: Edward Max

GLASGOW

Citizens Theatre
Gorbals, Glasgow G5 9DS
Fax: 0141-429 7374
BO: 0141-429 0022　　　　Admin: 0141-429 5561
Website: www.citz.co.uk
e-mail: info@citz.co.uk
Artistic Director: Jeremy Raison
General Manager: Anna Stapleton

GUILDFORD

Yvonne Arnaud Theatre
Millbrook, Guildford, Surrey GU1 3UX
Fax: 01483 564071
BO: 01483 440000　　　　Admin: 01483 440077
Website: www.yvonne-arnaud.co.uk
e-mail: yat@yvonne-arnaud.co.uk
Director: James Barber

HARROGATE

Harrogate Theatre
(3-4 weekly) 2.30pm Sat
Oxford Street, Harrogate HG1 1QF
Fax: 01423 563205
BO: 01423 502116　　　　Admin: 01423 502710
e-mail: christianname.surname@harrogatetheatre.co.uk
Artistic Director: Hannah Chissick
Chief Executive: David Bown

IPSWICH

The New Wolsey Theatre
Civic Drive, Ipswich, Suffolk IP1 2AS
Admin Fax: 01473 295910
BO: 01473 295900　　　　Admin: 01473 295911
Website: www.wolseytheatre.co.uk
e-mail: info@wolseytheatre.co.uk
Artistic Director: Peter Rowe
Chief Executive: Sarah Holmes

KESWICK

Theatre by the Lake
Lakeside, Keswick, Cumbria CA12 5DJ
Fax: 017687 74698
BO: 017687 74411　　　　Admin: 017687 72282
Website: www.theatrebythelake.com
e-mail: enquiries@theatrebythelake.com
Artistic Director: Ian Forrest

LANCASTER

The Dukes
Moor Lane, Lancaster, Lancashire LA1 1QE
Fax: 01524 598519
BO: 01524 598500　　　　Admin: 01524 598505
Website: www.dukes-lancaster.org
e-mail: info@dukes-lancaster.org
Artistic Director: Ian Hastings
Chief Executive: Amanda Belcham

LEEDS

The West Yorkshire Playhouse
Inc Schools Company
Playhouse Square, Quarry Hill, Leeds LS2 7UP
Fax: 0113-213 7250
BO: 0113-213 7700　　　　Admin: 0113-213 7800
Website: www.wyp.org.uk
Artistic Director (Chief Executive): Ian Brown
Executive Director: Dan Bates
Casting: see Website for Casting Submissions
Producer: Henrietta Duckworth

LEICESTER
Leicester Haymarket Theatre & Studio
Belgrave Gate, Leicester LE1 3YQ
Fax: 0116-251 3310
BO: 0870 3303131   Admin: 0116-253 0021
Website: www.leicesterhaymarkettheatre.co.uk
e-mail: enquiry@lhtheatre.co.uk
Artistic Director: Paul Kerryson, Kully Thiarai
Chief Executive: Mandy Stewart

LIVERPOOL
Everyman & Playhouse Theatres
Everyman: 13 Hope Street, Liverpool L1 9BH
Playhouse: Williamson Square, Liverpool L1 1EL
Fax: 0151-709 0398
BO: 0151-709 4776   Admin: 0151-708 0338
Website: www.everymanplayhouse.com
e-mail: reception@everymanplayhouse.com
Artistic Director: Gemma Bodinetz
Executive Director: Deborah Aydon

MANCHESTER
Contact Theatre Company
Oxford Road, Manchester M15 6JA
Fax: 0161-274 0640
BO: 0161-274 0600   Admin: 0161-274 3434
Website: www.contact-theatre.org
e-mail: info@contact-theatre.org.uk
Chief Executive/Artistic Director: John Edward McGrath

MANCHESTER
Library Theatre Company
St Peter's Square, Manchester M2 5PD
Fax: 0161-228 6481
BO: 0161-236 7110   Admin: 0161-234 1913
Website: www.librarytheatre.com
e-mail: ltc@libraries.manchester.gov.uk
Artistic Director: Chris Honer
General Manager: Adrian J. P. Morgan

MANCHESTER
Royal Exchange Theatre
St Ann's Square, Manchester M2 7DH
Fax: 0161-832 0881
BO: 0161-833 9833   SD & Admin: 0161-833 9333
Website: www.royalexchange.co.uk
Artistic Directors: Braham Murray, Gregory Hersov
Executive Director: Patricia Weller
Associate Artistic Directors: Sarah Frankcom,
Jacob Murray
General Manager: Richard Morgan
Casting Director: Jerry Knight-Smith

MILFORD HAVEN
Torch Theatre
St Peter's Road, Milford Haven, Pembrokeshire SA73 2BU
Fax: 01646 698919
BO: 01646 695267   Admin: 01646 694192
Website: www.torchtheatre.org.uk
e-mail: info@torchtheatre.co.uk
Artistic Director: Peter Doran

MOLD
Clwyd Theatr Cymru
(Repertoire, 4 Weekly, also touring)
Mold, Flintshire, North Wales CH7 1YA
Fax: 01352 701558
BO: 0845 3303565   Admin: 01352 756331
Website: www.clwyd-theatr-cymru.co.uk
e-mail: drama@celtic.co.uk

MUSSELBURGH
The Brunton Theatre
(Annual programme of theatre, dance, music, comedy & children's work)
Ladywell Way, Musselburgh EH21 6AA
Fax: 0131-665 3665
BO: 0131-665 2240   Admin: 0131-665 9900
General Manager: Lesley Smith

NEWBURY
Watermill Theatre
(4-7 Weekly) (Feb-Jan)
Bagnor, Nr Newbury, Berkshire RG20 8AE
Fax: 01635 523726
BO: 01635 46044   Admin: 01635 45834
SD: 01635 44532
Website: www.watermill.org.uk
e-mail: admin@watermill.org.uk
Artistic Director: Jill Fraser
General Manager: Clare Lindsay

NEWCASTLE-UNDER-LYME
New Vic Theatre
(3-4 Weekly)
Theatre in the Round, Etruria Road
Newcastle-under-Lyme, Staffordshire ST5 0JG
Fax: 01782 712885
BO: 01782 717962   Tel: 01782 717954
Website: www.newvictheatre.org.uk
e-mail: casting@newvictheatre.org.uk
Artistic Director: Gwenda Hughes
General Manager: Nick Jones

NEWCASTLE UPON TYNE
Northern Stage (Theatrical Productions) Ltd
Barras Bridge, Haymarket NE1 7RH
Fax: 0191-261 8093
BO: 0871 7000125   Admin: 0871 7000124
Website: www.northernstage.com
e-mail: info@northernstage.com
Artistic Director: Alan Lyddiard
Executive Director: Caroline Routh

NORTHAMPTON
Royal & Derngate Theatres
Guildhall Road, Northampton, Northamptonshire NN1 1DP
TIE: 01604 627566
BO: 01604 624811   Admin: 01604 626222
Chief Executive: Donna Mundy
Artistic Director: Rupert Goold
Associate Director: Simon Godwin

NOTTINGHAM
Nottingham Playhouse
(3/4 Weekly)
(Nottingham Theatre Trust Ltd), Wellington Circus
Nottingham NG1 5AF
Fax: 0115-947 5759
BO: 0115-941 9419   Admin: 0115-947 4361
Chief Executive: Stephanie Sirr
Artistic Director: Giles Croft
Roundabout TIE Director: Andrew Breakwell

OLDHAM
Coliseum Theatre
(3-4 Weekly)
Fairbottom Street, Oldham, Lancashire OL1 3SW
Fax: 0161-624 5318
BO: 0161-624 2829   Admin: 0161-624 1731
Website: www.coliseum.org.uk
e-mail: mail@coliseum.org.uk
Chief Executive: Kevin Shaw

PERTH
Perth Repertory Theatre
(2-3 Weekly)
185 High Street, Perth PH1 5UW
Fax: 01738 624576
BO: 01738 621031
SD: 01738 621435   Admin: 01738 472700
Website: www.perththeatre.co.uk
e-mail: info@perththeatre.co.uk
Artistic Director: Ken Alexander
General Manager: Paul Hackett
Chief Executive: Jane Spiers

PETERBOROUGH
Key Theatre
(Touring & Occasional Seasonal)
Embankment Road, Peterborough, Cambridgeshire PE1 1EF
Fax: 01733 567025
BO: 01733 552439   Admin: 01733 552437
e-mail: keytheatre@freenetname.co.uk

PITLOCHRY
Pitlochry Festival Theatre
Pitlochry, Perthshire PH16 5DR
Fax: 01796 484616
BO: 01796 484626   Admin: 01796 484600
Website: www.pitlochry.org.uk
e-mail: admin@pitlochry.org.uk
Chief Executive: Nikki Axford
Artistic Director: John Durnin

PLYMOUTH
Theatre Royal & Drum Theatre
Royal Parade, Plymouth, Devon PL1 2TR
Fax: 01752 671179   Admin: 01752 668282
e-mail: s.stokes@theatreroyal.com
Artistic Director: Simon Stokes
Chief Executive: Adrian Vinken

SALISBURY
Playhouse & Salberg Studio
(3-4 Weekly)
Malthouse Lane, Salisbury, Wiltshire SP2 7RA
Fax: 01722 421991
BO: 01722 320333   Admin: 01722 320117
Website: www.salisburyplayhouse.com
e-mail: info@salisburyplayhouse.com
Artistic Director: Joanna Read

SCARBOROUGH
Stephen Joseph Theatre
(Repertoire/Repertory)
Westborough, Scarborough, North Yorkshire YO11 1JW
Fax: 01723 360506
BO: 01723 370541
SD: 01723 507047   Admin: 01723 370540
e-mail: enquiries@sjt.uk.com
Artistic Director: Alan Ayckbourn
Executive Director: Stephen Wood

SHEFFIELD
Crucible, Studio & Lyceum Theatres
55 Norfolk Street, Sheffield S1 1DA
Fax: 0114-249 6003
BO: 0114-249 6000   Admin: 0114-249 5999
Website: www.sheffieldtheatres.co.uk
e-mail: initial.surname@sheffieldtheatres.co.uk
Associate Directors: Michael Grandage & Anna Mackmin
Chief Executive: Angela Galvin

SIDMOUTH
Manor Pavilion
(Weekly) (July-Sept)
Manor Road, Sidmouth, Devon EX10 8RP
BO: 01395 579977 (Season Only)
Tel: 020-7636 4343 Charles Vance

SONNING THEATRE
The Mill at Sonning Theatre
(5-6 Weekly)
Sonning Eye, Reading RG4 6TY
SD: 0118-969 5201
BO: 0118-969 8000   Admin: 0118-969 6039
Artistic Director: Sally Hughes
Assistant Administrator: Ann Seymour

SOUTHAMPTON
Nuffield Theatre
(Sept-July, Sunday Night Concerts, Occasional Tours)
University Road, Southampton SO17 1TR
Fax: 023-8031 5511
BO: 023-8067 1771   Admin: 023-8031 5500
Website: www.nuffieldtheatre.co.uk
Artistic Director: Patrick Sandford
Administrative Director: Kate Anderson

SOUTHWOLD
Summer Theatre
(July-Sept)
St Edmund's Hall, Cumberland Road, Southwold IP18 6JP
Admin: (Oct-May) 020-7724 5432
Admin: (June-Sept) 01502 723077
Website: www.southwoldtheatre.org
e-mail: jill@southwoldtheatre.org

ST ANDREWS
Byre Theatre
Abbey Street, St Andrews KY16 9LA
Fax: 01334 475370
BO: 01334 475000   Admin: 01334 476288
Website: www.byretheatre.com
e-mail: enquiries@byretheatre.com
Artistic Director: Stephen Wrentmore
Managing Director: Tom Gardner

STRATFORD-UPON-AVON
Swan Theatre & Royal Shakespeare Theatre
Waterside, Stratford-upon-Avon CV37 6BB
Fax: 01789 294810
BO: 01789 6091110   Admin: 01789 296655
Website: www.rsc.org.uk
e-mail: info@rsc.org.uk

WATFORD
Palace Theatre
(3-4 Weekly) Weds 2.30pm, Sat 3pm
Clarendon Road, Watford, Herts WD17 1JZ
Fax: 01923 819664
BO: 01923 225671   Admin: 01923 235455
Website: www.watfordtheatre.co.uk
e-mail: enquiries@watfordtheatre.co.uk
Artistic Director: Lawrence Till
Administrative Director: Mary Caws
Casting: Andrea Bath

WINDSOR
Theatre Royal
(2-3 Weekly) (Thurs 2.30pm Sat 4.45pm)
Thames Street, Windsor, Berkshire SL4 1PS
Fax: 01753 831673
BO: 01753 853888   Admin/SD: 01753 863444
Website: www.theatreroyalwindsor.co.uk
e-mail: info@theatreroyalwindsor.co.uk
Executive Director: Mark Piper

WOKING
New Victoria Theatre, The Ambassadors
Peacocks Centre, Woking GU21 6GQ
SD: 01483 545855
BO: 01483 545900   Admin: 01483 545800
Website: www.theambassadors.com/woking
e-mail: boxoffice@theambassadors.com

YORK
Theatre Royal
St Leonard's Place, York YO1 7HD
Fax: 01904 550164
BO: 01904 623568   Admin: 01904 658162
Website: www.yorktheatreroyal.co.uk
e-mail: admin@yorktheatreroyal.co.uk
Artistic Director: Damian Cruden
Chief Executive: Ludo Keston

ACTION CARS Ltd
(Steven Royffe)
Units 3 & 4 Rosslyn Crescent, Harrow, Middlesex HA1 2RZ
e-mail: info@actioncars.co.uk
Fax: 020-8861 4876   Tel: 020-8863 6889

ANCHOR MARINE FILM & TELEVISION
(Boat Location, Charter, Marine Co-ordinators)
Spike Mead Farm, Poles Lane
Lowfield Heath, West Sussex RH11 0PX
e-mail: amsfilms@aol.com
Fax: 01293 551558   Tel: 01293 538188

ANGLO PACIFIC INTERNATIONAL Plc
(Freight Forwarders to the Performing Arts)
Unit 1 Bush Industrial Estate
Standard Road, North Acton, London NW10 6DF
Website: www.anglopacific.co.uk
e-mail: info@anglopacific.co.uk
Fax: 020-8965 4954   Tel: 020-8965 1234

AUTOMOTIVE ACTION TRACKING DIVISION
(Supplier)
2 Sheffield House, Park Road, Hampton Hill, Middlesex TW12 1HA
Website: www.cameratrackingvehicle.com
Mobile: 07974 919589   Tel: 020-8977 6186

AZTEC OF BRISTOL
20 Walnut Lane, Kingswood
Bristol BS15 4JG   Tel/Fax: 0117-940 7712

BIANCHI AVIATION FILM SERVICES
(Historic & Other Aircraft)
Wycombe Air Park, Booker
Nr Marlow, Buckinghamshire SL7 3DP
Website: www.bianchiaviation.com
e-mail: info@bianchiaviation.com
Fax: 01494 461236   Tel: 01494 449810

BLUEBELL RAILWAY Plc
(Steam Locomotives, Pullman Coaches, Period Stations.
Much Film Experience)
Sheffield Park Station, East Sussex TN22 3QL
Website: www.bluebell-railway.co.uk
Fax: 01825 720804   Tel: 01825 720800

BRUNEL'S THEATRICAL SERVICES
Unit 4, Crown Industrial Estate
Crown Road, Warmley, Bristol BS30 8JB
Fax: 0117-907 7856   Tel: 0117-907 7855

BURLINGTON SERVICES
(Online database of period vehicles)
PO Box 7484, Epping, Essex, CM16 7WB
Website: www.classicstars.co.uk
e-mail: contact@classicstars.co.uk   Tel: 01992 575720

CARLINE & CREW TRANSPORTATION
(Celebrity Services)
12A Bridge Industrial Estate
Balcombe Road, West Sussex RH6 9HU
Website: www.carlineprivatehire.co.uk
e-mail: carlinehire@btconnect.com
Fax: 01293 400508   Tel: 01293 400505

CLASSIC CAR AGENCY The
(Film, Promotional, Advertising, Publicity)
PO Box 427, Dorking, Surrey RH5 6WP
Website: www.theclassiccaragency.com
e-mail: theclassiccaragency@btopenworld.com
Mobile: 07788 977655   Tel: 01306 731052

CLASSIC CAR HIRE
(Rolls Royce Phantoms, Bentleys, a Lagonda &
Daimlers for hire 1920-70)
Unit 2 Hampton Court Estate
Summer Road, Thames Ditton KT7 0RG
Website: www.classic-weddings@supanet.com
e-mail: classic-wedding@supemet.com   Tel: 020-8398 8304

Vehicles & Transport

[CONTACTS 2005]

CLASSIC OMNIBUS
(Vintage Open-Top Buses & Coaches)
44 Welson Road, Folkestone, Kent CT20 2NP
Website: www.opentopbus.co.uk
Fax: 01303 241245   Tel: 01303 248999

DEVEREUX K. W. & SONS
(Removals)
Daimler Drive, Cowpen Industrial Estate
Billingham, Cleveland TS23 4JD
e-mail: mike.bell@kdevereux.co.uk
Fax: 01642 566664   Tel: 01642 560854

EST Ltd
(Trucking - Every Size & Country)
Marshgate Sidings, Marshgate Lane, London E15 2PB
Website: www.yourockweroll.com
e-mail: info@edwin-shirley-trucking.co.uk
Fax: 020-8522 1002   Tel: 020-8522 1000

FELLOWES Mark TRANSPORT SERVICES
(Transport/Storage)
59 Sherbrooke Road, London SW6 7QL
Website: www.fellowesproductions.com
Mobile: 07850 332818   Tel: 020-7386 7005

FRANKIE'S YANKEES
(Classic 1950s American Cars, Memorabilia & New
Superstretch Limos)
283 Old Birmingham Road
Bromsgrove B60 1HQ   Tel: 0121-445 5522

HOME JAMES CHAUFFEUR SERVICE
Victoria Cottage, Birmingham Road, Sutton Coldfield WS14 0PA
Website: www.homejamescars.com
e-mail: julie.homejames@virgin.net   Tel: 0121-323 4717

IMPACT
(Private & Contract Hire of Coaches)
1 Leighton Road, Ealing, London W13 9EL
Website: www.impactgroup.co.uk
Fax: 020-8840 4880   Tel: 020-8579 9922

JASON'S LADY ROSE
(Up-market Cruising Canal Wideboat, Daily Scheduled Trips
to Camden Lock)
Opposite. 60 Blomfield Road, Little Venice, London W9 2PD
Website: www.jasons.co.uk
e-mail: enquiries@jasons.co.uk
Fax: 020-7266 4332   Tel: 020-7286 3428

KEIGHLEY & WORTH VALLEY LIGHT RAILWAY Ltd
(Engines, Stations, Carriages, Props & Crew)
The Railway Station, Haworth
Keighley, West Yorkshire BD22 8NJ
Website: www.kwvr.co.uk
e-mail: kwvr@hotmail.com
Fax: 01535 647317   Tel: 01535 645214

LUCKING G. H. & SONS
(Transporters/Storage/Stage Hands)
NTS House, Headley Road East, Woodley
Reading, Berkshire RG5 4SZ
Website: www.luckings.co.uk
e-mail: enquiries@luckings.co.uk
Fax: 0118 969 6881   Tel: 0118 969 7878

M V DIXIE QUEEN
Thames Luxury Charters
5 The Mews, 6 Putney Common, London SW15 1HL
Website: www.thamesluxurycharters.co.uk
e-mail: sales@thamesluxurycharters.co.uk
Fax: 020-8788 0072   Tel: 020-8780 1562

MAINSTREAM LEISURE GROUP
(Riverboat/Canal Boat Hire)
5 The Mews, 6 Putney Common, London SW15 1HL
Website: www.mainstreamleisure.co.uk
Fax: 020-8788 0073   Tel: 020-8788 2669

McNEILL Brian
(Vintage Truck & Coaches)
Hawk Mount, Kebcote, Todmorden, Lancashire OL14 8SB
Website: www.rollingpast.com
e-mail: autotrams@uk2.net
Fax: 01706 812292   Tel: 01706 812291

MOTORHOUSE HIRE Ltd
(Period Vehicles 1900-80) (Michael Geary)
Weston Underwood, Olney, Buckinghamshire MK46 5LD
e-mail: michael@motorhouseltd.co.uk
Fax: 01234 240393   Tel: 020-7495 1618

NATIONAL MOTOR MUSEUM
John Montagu Building
Beaulieu, Nr Brockenhurst, Hampshire SO42 7ZN
Website: www.beaulieu.co.uk
e-mail: info@beaulieu.co.uk
Fax: 01590 612624   Tel: 01590 612345

NINE-NINE CARS Ltd
Hyde Meadow Farm, Hyde Lane
Hemel Hempstead HP3 8SA
e-mail: david@nineninecars.com   Tel: 01923 266373

PICKFORDS REMOVALS Ltd
Heritage House
345 Southbury Road, Enfield, Middlesex EN1 1UP
Website: www.pickfords.com
Fax: 020-8219 8001   Tel: 020-8219 8000

PLUS FILM Ltd
(All Periods Vehicle Hire)
1 Mill House Cottages
Winchester Road, Bishop's Waltham SO32 1AH
e-mail: stephen@plusfilms7.freeserve.co.uk
                                        Tel/Fax: 01489 895559

PROSCOOT
1-3 Leeke Street
London WC1X 9HZ
Website: www.proscoot.co.uk
Fax: 020-7833 4613   Tel: 020-7833 4607

RADCLIFFE'S TRANSPORT
(see LUCKING G. H. & SONS)

STOKE BRUERNE BOAT COMPANY Ltd
(Passenger & Commercial Boats)
29 Main Road, Shutlanger
Northamptonshire NN12 7RU
Website: www.stokebruerneboats.co.uk
Fax: 01604 864098   Tel: 01604 862107

THAMES LUXURY CHARTERS Ltd
5 The Mews, 6 Putney Common
London SW15 1HL
Website: www.thamesluxurycharters.co.uk
e-mail: sales@thamesluxurycharters.co.uk
Fax: 020-8788 0072   Tel: 020-8780 1562

TOWN TYRE SERVICES Ltd
(Tug Boat for Hire/Sale)
Valley Way, Swansea Enterprise Park
Llansamcet, Swansea SA6 8QP   Tel: 01792 773431

VINTAGE CARRIAGES TRUST
(Owners of the Museum of Rail Travel at Ingrow Railway
Centre)
Keighley, West Yorkshire BD22 8NJ
Website: www.vintagecarriagestrust.org
e-mail: admin@vintagecarriagestrust.org
Fax: 01535 610796   Tel: 01535 680425

WOFFORD INTERNATIONAL HORSE TRANSPORT Ltd
Abnalls Farm
Cross-in-Hand Lane
Lichfield, Staffordshire WS13 8DZ
Website: www.wofford.co.uk
Fax: 01543 417226   Tel: 01543 417225

ACCOMMODATION

Quinton Hotel	225
Somerset Apartments	222
www.showdigs.co.uk	223

ACCOUNTANTS

Harvey Berger	24
Brebner, Allen, Trapp	67
Breckman & Company	152
Mark Carr & Co	146
Count and See Limited	151
Gordon Leighton	149
David Summers & Co	7
Alexis Widdowson (D168 Ltd)	147

AGENTS

2 Kidz Actors	98
10 Twenty Two Casting	104
A-List Models & Entertainers Agency	10
Act One Agency	98
Activate	87
ADF Management	12
Juliet Adams Model & Talent Castings Agency	94
AKA	6
Allsorts	40
Amanda Andrews Agency	95
Angel Faces Management	32
Sharron Ashcroft Management Ltd	11
Avenue Artistes Ltd	100
Biz Management	97
BizzyKidz Agency	90
Bodens Studio & Agency	12, 86
Agency at Bodywork Company	20
Boss Model Management	13
Bromley Casting	101
Byron's Management	24, 88
Carteurs Theatrical Agency	92
Celex Casting Ltd	100
Coast 2 Coast Personalities Ltd	105
CS Management	92
D & B Management	89
Dancers	52
David Artistes Management Agency Ltd	102
Debut Models Ltd	93
Derek's Hands Agency	60
Direct Line Personal Management	24
John Doe Associates	101
Double Act	25
Elliott Agency	104
Ethnics Artiste Agency	44

Et-Nik-A, Prime Management & Castings Ltd	26
Euro Kids & Adults International Casting & Model Agency	86, 101
Expressions Casting Agency	89
Faces Casting Agency	106
Features	34
Anna Fiorentini Theatre & Film School & Agency	91
Michael Garrett Associates	29
Go For It	97
GP Associates	99
Graystons	95
Jo Gurnett Personal Management Ltd	19
Michael Hall Theatre School & Casting Agency	96
Harrispearson Management Ltd	17
Hobson's	31
Icon Actors Management	71
I-mage Hospitality & Castings	32
Jaffrey Kent Management Ltd	44
Jigsaw Arts Management	91
K Entertainments Ltd	48
Kiddiewinks Agency	96
KastKidz	92
Kelly's Kind	61
K.M.C. Agencies	73
Kreate Productions	10
L'Brooke Personal Management	68
Sasha Leslie Management	88
Life Image	66
Linton Management	97
Markham & Marsden	55
Billy Marsh Drama Ltd	54
Nemesis	103
Nidges	103
Northern Lights Management	46
Northern Professionals	102
Nyland Management	76
Oriental Casting Agency Ltd	11
Orr Management Agency	10
Jackie Palmer Agency	87
P.C. Theatrical & Model Agency	68
Performers Directory & Agency	80
Personal Appearances	15
PLA	30
Rascals Model Agency	95
Regency Agency	60
Roi-Bell Casting Co.	98
Rudeye Agency	40
Scallywags Agency	94
Scream Management	90, 104
Shining Management Ltd	120
Singers/Dancers Inc	82

Elisabeth Smith	89
Sportsmodels.com	84
Stagecoach Agency	93
Star Management	111
Success	56
Mark Summers Management	30
T.G.R. Direct	38
Thames Valley Theatrical Agency	92
Thornton Agency	42
Toner Casting Ltd	101
Tots 2 Teens	99
Truly Scrumptious	86
Tommy Tucker Agency	72
Tuesdays Child	93
Urban Talent	79
The Vallé Academy Theatrical Agency	99
Vibes UK Ltd	76
Voiceovers.co.uk	120
Voice Squad/Foreign Legion	121
Willow Personal Management	82
Edward Wyman Agency	85
Zen Directories	105

ANIMALS

Animal Ambassadors	123
Mabel's Place	122

CASTING SERVICES

Hannah Birkett Casting	132
Cyber~Artists	131

CONSULTANTS

AgentFile	52
Flames Martial Arts Academy	151
Foreign Versions	116
Daniel Hussey	150
Melanie Jones Associates	65, 265
Richard Jordan Productions Ltd	305
Q2Q Productions	301
Speak Good English Well (Neville Wortman)	147
Stage Presence	309
UK Theatre Availability Ltd	148
Voice Squad/Foreign Legion	121
VSI/Voice Script International Ltd	201

COSTUMIERS/WARDROBE SERVICES

Cosprop	153
Costume Construction	155
Gamba Theatrical Footwear Ltd	159
Kim Mask	154
Gav Nicola Theatrical Shoes	156
Allan Scott Costumes	158

DENTISTS & DENTAL SERVICES

Dr Richard Casson	157, 231
Smile Solutions	232
Smile Studio	228

ENTERTAINERS/ACTORS/CHOREOGRAPHERS

Séva Dhalivaal	106
Peter Durrent	274
Paul Harris	163

HAIR & MAKE UP

Burlingtons	73
Sophia Mason	156
New id	7, 231
Rosie's Make-Up Box	153

HEALTH & WELLBEING

Dr Philippe Chout	229
Hypnosis Works	230
Elspeth Reid Coaching	228

ORGANISATIONS

The Actors' Benevolent Fund	241
The Actors Centre	239
The Actors' Charitable Trust	235
The Agents' Association	42
British Academy of Film and Television Arts London	213
The British Academy of Film and Television Arts Los Angeles	213
Conference of Drama Schools	165
Co-operative Personal Management Association	70
Council for Dance Education & Training	163
Dance UK	162
The Directors Guild of Great Britain	237
North American Actors Association	64
UK Film Council	209

PHOTOGRAPHERS

1st Class Photography	142
Active Photography	5
Actorsheadshots.co.uk	110
Actor's 'One Stop' Shop	35
Rafe Allen	63
Stuart Allen	134
Artshot.co.uk	113
Simon Annand	77
Ric Bacon	38
Chris Baker	47

Sophie Baker	23
Coral Blake	143
Marcus Brierley	54
Sheila Burnett	21
Richenda Carey	53
Robert Carpenter Turner	83
Scott Michael Carroll	9
Casting-image.com	34
Charlie Carter	137
Linda Chapman	7
Carlos Ciccheli	74
Mark Cook	6
Melanie Cox	22
John Clark	27
Kim Cunningham	14
Dance Scene Photographic	164
Debal	4
Stephanie de Leng	53
Angus Deuchar	139
Harry Dillon	112
Jonathan Dockar-Drysdale	23
Mary Dunkin	30
Debbie Dye	8
Mike Eddowes	49
Owen Evans	26
Anne Eyre	31
David Fernandes	79
John Fletcher	143
Julian Fletcher	50
James Gill	69
Natasha Greenberg	71
Nick Gregan	43
Claire Grogan	16, 133
Chris Hall	5
Magnus Hastings	39
Daniel Harwood-Stamper	17
Jamie Hughes	81
Remy Hunter	57
Paris Jefferson	62
Olyden Johnson	10
Luke Kelly	20
Neil Kendall	78
Simon King	141
Carole Latimer	45
Steve Lawton	25
LB Photography	135
John Mackle	40
M.A.D. Photography	18
Chris Marshall	83
Murray Martin	39
Casey Moore	34

Ruth Mullholland	136
My CV Online	8
Fatimah Namdar	55
New id	7, 231
Claire Newman-Williams	69
Louise O'Shea	70
Adam Parker	113
George Passmore	63
Passport Photo Service	66
Michael Pollard	28
PR Photography	9
David Price	46
Tony Russell	50
Howard Sayer	32
Catherine Shakespeare Lane	19
Milind Shirké	9
Peter Simpkin	13
Richard H. Smith	48
Paul Spencer Clamp	61
Lucy Smith	65
Rosie Still	33
Deborah Stone	54
Anthony Straeger	56
Studio 64	Inside Back Cover
Caroline Summers	36
Take the Pose Photography	22
TM Photography	51
John Twinning	14
Steve Ullathorne	85
Katie Vandyck	19
Robin Watson	45
Will C	58, 59
Laura Woolnough	6
Robert Workman	15

PROPERTIES & TRADES

3-D Creations	255
AFX UK Ltd (incorp Kirby's Flying Ballets)	254
Bapty Ltd	246
Beat About The Bush	257
Benson's Jumparound Activity Centres	247
Flint Hire & Supply Ltd	251
Flying by Foy	250
Freedale Press	253
Greenprops	246, 257
London Business Equipment	255
Magical Mart (John Styles)	259
Moderneon London Ltd	253
Nostalgia Amusements	249
Pro Blood	157
RR Design	259
Rent-a-Sword	247
Jane Rumble	249

PUBLICATIONS & PUBLISHERS

Samuel French Ltd	107
Presenting for TV & Video	111
Production & Casting Report	132, 293
Script Breakdown Services	77, 141
Spotlight Presenters	112, 267
The Spotlight	263
The Stage	261

REHEARSAL/AUDITION ROOMS/CASTING SUITES

Alford House	277
Brixton St Vincent's	278
Clapham Community Project	279
Central Casting Facilities	281
The Drill Hall	277
The Factory Dance Centre	274
The Garden Studios	285
Holy Innocents	280
Jerwood Space	279
Lyric Theatre Hammersmith	280
Cameron Mackintosh Rehearsal Studio	276
The Maria Assumpta Centre	281
Menier Chocolate Factory	284
Neal's Yard Meeting Rooms	283
Oval House Theatre	276
PHA Casting Studio	282
Putney Arts Theatre	280
Qd Casting Studio	282
The Questors Theatre	282
RADA	283
Saam House	284
The Spotlight Rooms	142, 275, 287
Space@clarence	276
St Mary Abbot's Hall	278
Take Five Studio	78, 137, 201, 285
The UCL Bloomsbury	278

REPRO COMPANIES & PHOTOGRAPHIC RETOUCHING

Dark Side	75
Denbry Repros Ltd	Outside Back Cover
Image Photographic	37
Monolab	8
Moorfields	44
Profile Prints	41
Visualeyes Imaging Services	Inside Front Cover

SCRIPT SERVICES

Scripts by Argyle	107

SHOWREELS, VOICE TAPES, CV's, LABELS, etc

A1 Vox	114, 273
Actorsilluminated.com	48
Actor's 'One Stop' Shop	35
Bright Lights Studio	114
Contacts Label Service	50, 134, 204
Dbug Multimedia	203
Interactive Showreels	5
Minamon Productions	50
Otherwise Studios	121
Reel Breaks	218
Replay Ltd	203
Bernard Shaw	117
Silver-Tongued Productions	115
Theshowreel.com	119
Showreels 1	15
Stanton Media	140
Take Five Studio	78, 137, 201, 285
To Be or Not to Be	178
Voice-Master	115, 192
Voice Over Demos	121
VTS International Ltd	118
W6 Studio	203

THEATRES

Hall for Cornwall	337
Twisting Yarn Theatre	317

TRAINING (Private Coaches)

Actors Space	174
Eirene Beck	176
Eileen Benskin	170
Brighton Stagers	176
Tim Charrington	182
Mel Churcher	184
Valerie Colgan	138
Sharrone Comber	194
Tess Dignan	180
Victoria Fairbrother	189
Gordon Faith	167
Carole Ann Ford	171
Dee Forrest	188
Paul Gregory	183
Philip Grout	195
Stefan Gryff	172
Alexandre Harrington	167
Paul Harris	163
Jessica Higgs	182
Linda James	170
Louise Kerr	190
Gloria Lytton	168

Anna & Michael McCallion   181
Martin McKellan   186
William Oversby   186
Philip Rosch   175
Sally Tremaine   186
John Tucker   184
Moray Urquhart   192
Charles Verrall   188
Voice in Action   190
Holly Wilson   194

TRAINING (Schools, Companies & Workshops)

Act Up   174
ALRA   169
ArtsEd London   173
Artts International   219
Brighton Film School   218
Centre Stage School of Performing Arts   171
The City Lit   177
Court Theatre Training Company   180
Cygnet Training Theatre   175
Debut Theatre School   171
Drama Studio London   177
East 15 Acting School   181
Expressions Academy of Performing Arts   171
GSA Conservatoire   183
Hertfordshire Theatre School   168
Jigsaw Performing Arts Schools   172
London Academy of
   Radio, Film, TV   84, 98, 106, 110, 116, 139
London Centre for Theatre Studies/
   The Actors Company   179
The David Morris School of Performing Arts   178
Mountview Academy of Theatre Arts   185
Oxford School of Drama   187
Ridgeway Studios Performing Arts College   168
Rose Bruford College   191
Royal Welsh College of Music & Drama   193
Stagecoach Theatre Arts Schools   187
Vox Training   189
Jack Waltzer   195

TRANSPORT

Thames Luxury Charters Ltd   220

WIG SUPPLIERS

Derek Easton   158
Wig Specialities Ltd   159

A

A1 Vox	114, 273
A-List Models & Entertainers Agency	10
Act One Agency	98
Act Up	174
Activate	87
Active Photography	5
The Actors' Benevolent Fund	241
The Actors Centre	239
The Actors' Charitable Trust	235
Actor's 'One Stop' Shop	35
Actors Space	174
Actorsheadshots.co.uk	110
Actorsilluminated.com	48
Actor's 'One Stop' Shop	35
Juliet Adams Model & Castings Talent Agency	94
ADF Management	12
AFX UK Ltd (incorp Kirby's Flying Ballets)	254
AgentFile	52
The Agents' Association	42
AKA	6
Alford House	277
Rafe Allen	63
Stuart Allen	134
Allsorts	40
ALRA	169
Amanda Andrews Agency	95
Angel Faces Management	32
Animal Ambassadors	123
Simon Annand	77
ArtsEd London	173
Artshot.co.uk	113
Artts International	219
Sharron Ashcroft Management Ltd	11
Avenue Artistes Ltd	100

B

Ric Bacon	38
Chris Baker	47
Sophie Baker	23
Bapty Ltd	246
Beat About The Bush	257
Eirene Beck	176
Eileen Benskin	170
Benson's Jumparound Activity Centres	247
Harvey Berger	24
Hannah Birkett Casting	132

Biz Management	97
BizzyKidz Agency	90
Coral Blake	143
Bodens Studio & Agency	12, 86
Agency at Bodywork Company	20
Boss Model Management	13
Brebner, Allen, Trapp	67
Breckman & Company	152
Marcus Brierley	54
Bright Lights Studio	114
Brighton Film School	218
Brighton Stagers	176
British Academy of Film and Television Arts London	213
The British Academy of Film and Television Arts Los Angeles	213
Brixton St Vincent's	278
Bromley Casting	101
Burlingtons	73
Sheila Burnett	21
Byron's Management	24, 88

C

Richenda Carey	53
Robert Carpenter Turner	83
Mark Carr & Co	146
Scott Michael Carroll	9
Charlie Carter	137
Carteurs Theatrical Agency	92
Dr Richard Casson	157, 231
Casting-image.com	34
Celex Casting Ltd	100
Central Casting Facilities	281
Centre Stage School of Performing Arts	171
Linda Chapman	7
Tim Charrington	182
Dr Philippe Chout	229
Mel Churcher	184
Carlos Ciccheli	74
The City Lit	177
Clapham Community Project	279
John Clark	27
Coast 2 Coast Personalities Ltd	105
Valerie Colgan	138
Sharrone Comber	194
Conference of Drama Schools	165
Contacts Label Service	50, 134, 204
Mark Cook	6
Co-operative Personal Management Association	70

Cosprop	153
Costume Construction	155
Council for Dance Education & Training	163
Court Theatre Training Company	180
Count and See Limited	151
Melanie Cox	22
CS Management	92
Kim Cunningham	14
Cyber~Artists	131
Cygnet Training Theatre	175

D

D & B Management	89
Dance Scene Photographic	164
Dance UK	162
Dancers	52
Dark Side	75
David Artistes Management Agency Ltd	102
Dbug Multimedia	203
Debal	4
Debut Models Ltd	93
Debut Theatre School	171
Stephanie de Leng	53
Denbry Repros Ltd	Outside Back Cover
Derek's Hands Agency	60
Angus Deuchar	139
Séva Dhalivaal	106
Tess Dignan	180
Harry Dillon	112
Direct Line Personal Management	24
The Directors Guild of Great Britain	237
Jonathan Dockar-Drysdale	23
John Doe Associates	101
Double Act	25
Drama Studio London	177
The Drill Hall	277
Mary Dunkin	30
Peter Durrent	274
Debbie Dye	8

E

East 15 Acting School	181
Derek Easton	158
Mike Eddowes	49
Elliott Agency	104
Ethnics Artiste Agency	44
Et-Nik-A, Prime Management & Castings Ltd	26

Euro Kids & Adults International Casting & Model Agency	86, 101
Owen Evans	26
Expressions Academy of Performing Arts	171
Expressions Casting Agency	89
Anne Eyre	31

F

1st Class Photography	142
Faces Casting Agency	106
The Factory Dance Centre	274
Victoria Fairbrother	189
Gordon Faith	167
Features	34
David Fernandes	79
Anna Fiorentini Theatre & Film School & Agency	91
Flames Martial Arts Academy	151
John Fletcher	143
Julian Fletcher	50
Flint Hire & Supply Ltd	251
Flying by Foy	250
Carole Ann Ford	171
Foreign Versions	116
Dee Forrest	188
Freedale Press	253
Samuel French Ltd	107

G

Gamba Theatrical Footwear Ltd	159
The Garden Studios	285
Michael Garrett Associates	29
Gav Nicola Theatrical Shoes	156
James Gill	69
Go For It	97
Gordon Leighton	149
GP Associates	99
Graystons	95
Natasha Greenberg	71
Greenprops	246, 257
Nick Gregan	43
Paul Gregory	183
Claire Grogan	16, 133
Philip Grout	195
Stefan Gryff	172
GSA Conservatoire	183
Jo Gurnett Personal Management Ltd	19

H

Hall for Cornwall	337
Chris Hall	5
Michael Hall Theatre School and Casting Agency	96
Alexandre Harrington	167
Paul Harris	152
Harrispearson Management Ltd	17
Daniel Harwood-Stamper	17
Magnus Hastings	39
Hertfordshire Theatre School	168
Jessica Higgs	182
Hobson's	31
Holy Innocents	280
Jamie Hughes	81
Remy Hunter	57
Daniel Hussey	150
Hypnosis Works	230

I

Icon Actors Management	71
I-mage Hospitality & Castings	32
Image Photographic	37
Interactive Showreels	5

J

Jaffrey Kent Management Ltd	44
Linda James	170
Paris Jefferson	62
Jerwood Space	279
Jigsaw Arts Management	91
Jigsaw Performing Arts Schools	172
Olyden Johnson	10
Melanie Jones Associates	65, 265
Richard Jordan Productions Ltd	305

K

K Entertainments Ltd	48
KastKidz	92
Luke Kelly	20
Kelly's Kind	61
Neil Kendall	78
Louise Kerr	190
Kiddiewinks Agency	96
Simon King	141

K.M.C. Agencies	73
Kreate Productions	10

L

Carole Latimer	45
Steve Lawton	25
LB Photography	135
L'Brooke Personal Management	68
Sasha Leslie Management	88
Life Image	66
Linton Management	97
London Academy of Radio, Film, TV	84, 98, 106, 110, 116, 139
London Centre for Theatre Studies/ The Actors Company	179
London Business Equipment	255
Lyric Theatre Hammersmith	280
Gloria Lytton	168

M

Mabel's Place	122
Cameron Mackintosh Rehearsal Studio	276
John Mackle	40
M.A.D. Photography	18
Magical Mart (John Styles)	259
The Maria Assumpta Centre	281
Markham & Marsden	55
Billy Marsh Drama Ltd	54
Chris Marshall	83
Murray Martin	39
Kim Mask	154
Sophia Mason	156
Anna & Michael McCallion	181
Martin McKellan	186
Menier Chocolate Factory	284
Minamon Productions	50
Moderneon London Ltd	253
Monolab	8
Casey Moore	34
Moorfields	44
The David Morris School of Performing Arts	178
Mountview Academy of Theatre Arts	185
Ruth Mullholland	136
My CV Online	8

N

Fatimah Namdar	55

Neal's Yard Meeting Rooms — 283
Nemesis — 103
New id — 7, 231
Claire Newman-Williams — 69
Nidges — 103
North American Actors Association — 64
Northern Lights Management — 46
Northern Professionals — 102
Nostalgia Amusements — 249
Nyland Management — 76

O

Louise O'Shea — 70
Oriental Casting Agency Ltd — 11
Orr Management Agency — 10
Otherwise Studios — 121
Oval House Theatre — 276
William Oversby — 186
Oxford School of Drama — 187

P

Jackie Palmer Agency — 87
Adam Parker — 113
George Passmore — 63
Passport Photo Service — 66
P.C. Theatrical & Model Agency — 68
Performers Directory & Agency — 80
Personal Appearances — 15
PHA Casting Studio — 282
PLA — 30
Michael Pollard — 28
PR Photography — 9
Presenting for TV & Video — 111
David Price — 46
Pro Blood — 157
Profile Prints — 41
Production & Casting Report — 132, 293
Putney Arts Theatre — 280

Q

Q2Q Productions — 301
Qd Casting Studio — 282
The Questors Theatre — 282
Quinton Hotel — 225

R

RADA — 283
Rascals Model Agency — 95
Reel Breaks — 218
Regency Agency — 60
Elspeth Reid Coaching — 228
Rent-a-Sword — 247
Replay Ltd — 203
Ridgeway Studios Performing Arts College — 168
Roi-Bell Casting Co. — 98
Philip Rosch — 175
Rose Bruford College — 191
Rosie's Make-Up Box — 153
Royal Welsh College of Music & Drama — 193
RR Design — 259
Rudeye Agency — 40
Jane Rumble — 249
Tony Russell — 50

S

Saam House — 284
Howard Sayer — 32
Scallywags Agency — 94
Allan Scott Costumes — 158
Scream Management — 90, 104
Script Breakdown Services — 77, 141
Scripts by Argyle — 107
Catherine Shakespeare Lane — 19
Bernard Shaw — 117
Shining Management Ltd — 120
Milind Shirké — 9
Theshowreel.com — 119
Showreels 1 — 15
Silver-Tongued Productions — 115
Peter Simpkin — 13
Singers/Dancers Inc — 82
Smile Solutions — 232
Smile Studio — 228
Elisabeth Smith — 89
Lucy Smith — 65
Richard H. Smith — 48
Somerset Apartments — 222
Space@clarence — 276
Speak Good English Well (Neville Wortman) — 147
Paul Spencer Clamp — 61
Sportsmodels.com — 84
The Spotlight — 263

Spotlight Presenters   112, 267
The Spotlight Rooms   142, 275
St Mary Abbot's Hall   278
The Stage   261
Stage Presence   309
Stagecoach Theatre Arts Schools   187
Stagecoach Agency   93
Stanton Media   140
Star Management   111
Rosie Still   33
Deborah Stone   54
Anthony Straeger   56
Studio 64   Inside Back Cover
Success   56
Caroline Summers   36
David Summers & Co   7
Mark Summers Management   30

T

2 Kidz Actors   98
3-D Creations   255
10 Twenty Two Casting   104
Take Five Studio   78, 137, 201, 285
Take the Pose Photography   22
T.G.R. Direct   38
Thames Luxury Charters Ltd   220
Thames Valley Theatrical Agency   92
Thornton Agency   42
TM Photography   51
To Be or Not to Be   178
Toner Casting Ltd   101
Tots 2 Teens   99
Sally Tremaine   186
Truly Scrumptious   86
Tommy Tucker Agency   72
John Tucker   184
Tuesdays Child   93
John Twinning   14
Twisting Yarn Theatre   317

U

The UCL Bloomsbury   278
UK Film Council   209
UK Theatre Availability Ltd   148
Steve Ullathorne   85
Urban Talent   79
Moray Urquhart   192

V

The Vallé Academy Theatrical Agency   99
Katie Vandyck   19
Charles Verrall   188
Vibes UK Ltd   76
Visualeyes Imaging Services   Inside Front Cover
Voice in Action   190
Voice-Master   115, 192
Voice Over Demos   121
Voiceovers.co.uk   120
Voice Squad/Foreign Legion   121
Vox Training   189
VSI/Voice Script International Ltd   201
VTS International Ltd   118

W

W6 Studio   203
Jack Waltzer   195
Robin Watson   45
Alexis Widdowson (D168 Ltd)   147
Wig Specialities Ltd   159
Will C   58, 59
Willow Personal Management   82
Holly Wilson   194
Laura Woolnough   6
Robert Workman   15
www.showdigs.co.uk   223
Edward Wyman Agency   85

Z

Zen Directories   105